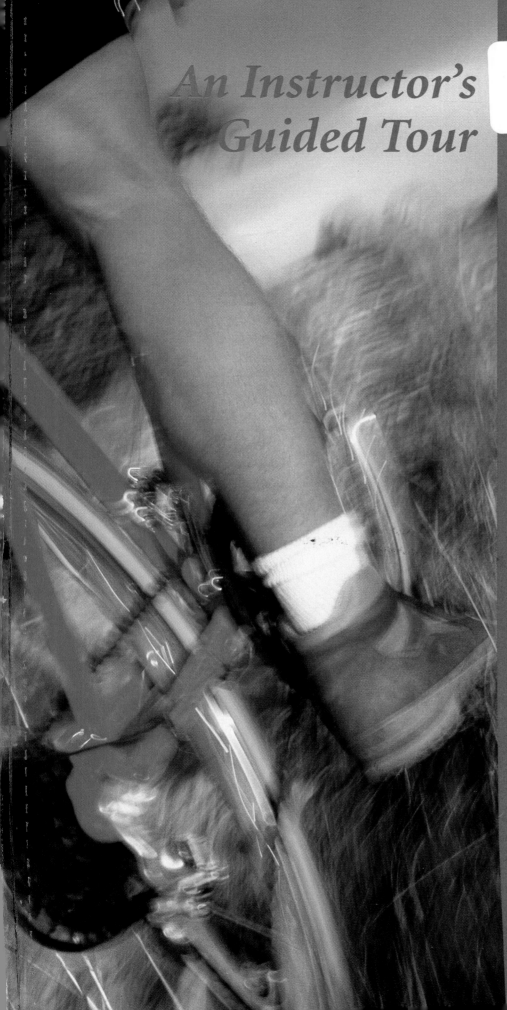

An Instructor's Guided Tour

WELL

Core Concepts and Labs in Physical Fitness and Wellness

THIRD EDITION

Thomas D. Fahey

Paul M. Insel

Walton T. Roth

Please take a few minutes for this guided tour of the third edition of *Fit and Well.* You'll find examples of the book's outstanding features, writing, and pedagogy, as well as information about the comprehensive teaching package that accompanies the book.

Building on the success of the previous two editions, the third edition of *Fit and Well* continues to provide students with the knowledge, tools, and motivation they need to take charge of their wellness-related behavior. New features and refinements make *Fit and Well* an excellent choice for any fitness or wellness course. For a complete description of features and changes, refer to the preface.

You already know that a lifestyle based on good choices and healthy behaviors maximizes quality of life. Let *Fit and Well* help you share that message with your students.

Accurate, Up-to-Date, Reliable

Fit and Well provides balanced, accurate, up-to-date coverage of all critical areas of wellness, including physical fitness (cardiorespiratory endurance, muscular strength and endurance, flexibility, body composition), nutrition, weight management, stress, cardiovascular disease, cancer, substance abuse, sexually transmitted diseases, and injury prevention. It also gives students the practical tools they need to take charge of their wellness-related behavior and adopt a healthier lifestyle.

SEDENTARY ACTIVITIES
Do infrequently
Watching television
Surfing the Internet
Talking on the telephone

STRENGTH TRAINING
2–3 days per week
(all major muscle groups)
Biceps curls, push-ups, abdominal curls, bench press, calf raises

FLEXIBILITY TRAINING
2 or more days per week (all major joints)
Calf stretch, side lunge, step stretch, hurdler stretch

CARDIORESPIRATORY ENDURANCE EXERCISE
3–5 days per week (20–60 minutes)
Walking, jogging, bicycling, swimming, aerobic dancing, in-line skating, cross-country skiing, dancing, basketball

MODERATE-INTENSITY PHYSICAL ACTIVITY
Most days—preferably every day (about 30 minutes)
Walking to the store or bank
Washing windows or your car
Climbing stairs
Working in your yard
Walking your dog
Cleaning your room

Figure 2-3 Physical activity pyramid. Similar to the Food Guide Pyramid, this physical activity pyramid is designed to help people become more active. If you are currently sedentary, begin at the bottom of the pyramid and gradually increase the amount of moderate-intensity physical activity in your life. If you are already moderately active, begin a formal exercise program that includes cardiorespiratory endurance exercise, flexibility training, and strength training to help you develop all the health-related components of fitness.

NEW!

For the third edition, all chapters have been carefully revised and updated. New topics and key issues addressed in the third edition include the following:

- The Surgeon General's report on physical activity *(Chapter 2 and throughout the text)*
- New American College of Sports Medicine (ACSM) recommendations for exercise *(Chapters 2–7)*
- New Dietary Reference Intakes for vitamins and minerals, including recommendations for supplements *(Chapter 8)*
- Energy (ATP) production for exercise *(Chapter 3)*
- Binge drinking on college campuses *(Chapter 13)*
- Stress-management techniques *(Chapter 10)*
- Exercise and dietary recommendations for special population groups *(Chapters 7 and 8)*

- Prescription drugs for weight loss *(Chapter 9)*
- Spiritual wellness *(Chapters 1 and 15)*
- Dietary fats and health *(Chapters 8, 11, and 12)*
- Eating disorders *(Chapter 9)*
- Addictive behavior *(Chapter 13)*
- HIV treatment and testing *(Chapter 14)*
- Safe use of air bags *(Appendix A)*

For a complete list of changes to the third edition, contact your local Mayfield sales representative or call the Marketing and Sales Department at 800-433-1279. You may also e-mail Mayfield at calpoppy@mayfieldpub.com.

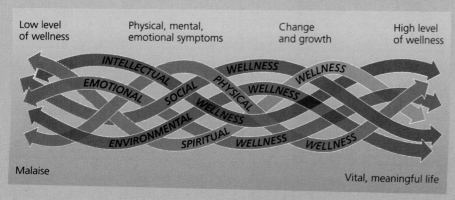

Low level of wellness — Physical, mental, emotional symptoms — Change and growth — High level of wellness

INTELLECTUAL WELLNESS
EMOTIONAL WELLNESS
SOCIAL PHYSICAL WELLNESS
ENVIRONMENTAL WELLNESS
SPIRITUAL WELLNESS

Malaise

Vital, meaningful life

Figure 1-1 The wellness continuum. Wellness is composed of six interrelated dimensions, all of which must be developed in order to achieve overall wellness.

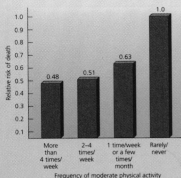

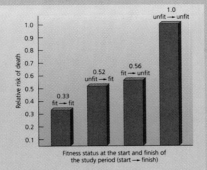

(a) Physical activity level and mortality

(b) The effects of changes in fitness status on mortality rates

VITAL STATISTICS

Figure 1-3 Physical activity, physical fitness, and mortality. Many long-term research studies have clearly shown the benefits of regular physical activity. (a) A study that followed more than 40,000 postmenopausal women for 7 years found a strong relationship between physical activity and relative risk of death: the more frequent the activity, the lower the relative risk of death. (b) A study of more than 9500 men that tracked changes in fitness level for periods of 1–18 years found that fitness level was closely tied to risk of death: The lowest death rate was seen in men who were physically fit at the start and end of the study period; the highest death rate was in men who were unfit throughout the study. Men who improved from unfit to fit during the study experienced a 44% reduction in mortality risk relative to men who remained unfit. SOURCES: Kushi, L.H., et al. 1997. Physical activity and mortality in postmenopausal women. *Journal of the American Medical Association* 277(16): 1287–1292. Blair, S. N., et al. 1995. Changes in physical fitness and all-cause mortality: A prospective study of healthy and unhealthy men. *Journal of the American Medical Association* 272(14) 1093–1098.

VITAL STATISTICS

TABLE 1-2	Actual Causes of Death in the United States	
Cause		Approximate Number of Deaths per Year
Tobacco		400,000
Diet and activity habits		300,000
Alcohol		100,000
Microbial agents		90,000
Toxic agents		60,000
Secondhand tobacco smoke		50,000
Motor vehicle crashes		40,000
Firearms		35,000
Sexual behavior		30,000
Illegal drug use		20,000

SOURCES: American Heart Association. National Center for Health Statistics. 1997. Births and deaths: United States, 1996. *Monthly Vital Statistics Report* 46(1S2): 5. McGinnis, J. M., and W. H. Foege. 1993. Actual causes of death in the United States. *Journal of the American Medical Association* 270(18): 2207–2212.x

VITAL STATISTICS

Figures and tables marked with the Vital Statistics label display important facts and figures in an accessible format.

---

limiting sugar, salt, alcohol, and smoked and nitrate-cured foods.

- A vegetarian diet requires special planning to meet all nutrient requirements; grains, legumes, and a variety of fruits and vegetables are central.
- Careful planning can help people of all ages, activity levels, and medical conditions meet special dietary challenges.

FOR MORE INFORMATION

For reliable nutrition advice, talk to a faculty member in the nutrition department on your campus, a registered dietitian (R.D.), or your physician. Many large communities have a telephone service called Dial a Dietitian. By calling this number, you can receive free nutrition information from an R.D.

Experts on quackery suggest that you steer clear of anyone who puts forth any of the following false statements:

- Most diseases are caused primarily by faulty nutrition.
- Large doses of vitamins are effective against many diseases.
- Hair analysis can be used to determine a person's nutritional state.
- A computer-scored nutritional deficiency test is a basis for prescribing vitamins.

Any practitioner—licensed or not—who sells vitamins in his or her office should be thoroughly scrutinized.

Books

Duyff, R. L. 1998. *The American Dietetic Association's Complete Food and Nutrition Guide.* Minneapolis, Minn.: Chronimed Publishing. *An excellent review of current nutrition information and issues.*

Coleman, E. 1997. *Eating for Endurance.* Rev. ed. Palo Alto, Calif.: Bull Publishing. *A concise, easy-to-understand guide to sports nutrition.*

Editors of Vegetarian Times Magazine. 1995. *Vegetarian Times Complete Cookbook.* New York: Macmillan. *Contains introductory chapters on the health benefits of vegetarianism and on meal planning, along with over 600 recipes.*

Finn, S. C. 1997. *The American Dietetic Association Guide to Women's Nutrition for Healthy Living.* New York: Perigee Books. *A complete guide to eating right for lifelong health.*

Nutrition and Your Health: Dietary Guidelines for Americans. 1995. U.S. Department of Health and Human Services and U.S. Department of Agriculture. Home and Garden Bulletin No. 232. *A 42-page booklet that describes the Guidelines and provides helpful tips for implementing them.*

Newsletters

Environmental Nutrition: P.O. Box 420235, Palm Coast, FL 32142; 800-829-5384.

Nutrition Action Health Letter: 1875 Connecticut Ave., N.W., Suite 300, Washington DC 20009; 202-332-9110 (http://www.cspinet.org).

Tufts University Health & Nutrition Letter: P.O. Box 57857, Boulder, CO 80322; 800-274-7581.

Organizations, Hotlines, and Web Sites

American Dietetic Association. Provides a wide variety of nutrition-related educational materials.
  800-366-1655 (For general nutrition information and referrals to registered dietitians.)
  900-CALL-AN-RD (For customized answers to nutrition questions.)
  http://www.eatright.org

Ask the Dietitian. Questions and answers on many topics relating to nutrition.
  http://www.dietitian.com

CyberDiet Nutritional Profile. Calculates calorie and nutrient needs based on your current or target body weight and creates a personalized nutrient profile.
  http://www.CyberDiet.com/profile/profile.html

FDA Center for Food Safety and Applied Nutrition. Offers information about topics such as food labeling, food additives, and foodborne illness.
  http://vm.cfsan.fda.gov

Meals Online. Includes over 10,000 healthful recipes.
  http://www.meals.com

National Osteoporosis Foundation. Provides up-to-date information on the causes, prevention, detection, and treatment of osteoporosis.
  202-223-2226
  http://www.nof.org

Tufts University Nutrition Navigator. Provides descriptions and ratings for many nutrition-related Web pages.
  http://www.navigator.tufts.edu

USDA Food and Nutrition Information Center. Provides a variety of materials relating to the Dietary Guidelines, food labels, and many other topics; Web site includes extensive links.
  301-504-5719
  http://www.nal.usda.gov/fnic

USDA Meat and Poultry Hotline. Information from USDA experts on topics such as the proper handling, preparation, storage, and cooking of food.
  800-535-4555

Vegetarian Resource Group. Information and links for vegetarians and people interested in learning more about vegetarian diets.
  http://www.vrg.org

You can obtain nutrient breakdowns of individual food items from the following sites:

Nutribase
  http://www.nutribase.com
Nutrition Analysis Tool, University of Illinois, Urbana/Champaign
  http://www.ag.uiuc.edu/~food-lab/nat
USDA Food and Nutrition Information Center
  http://www.nal.usda.gov/fnic/foodcomp
See also the resources listed in Chapters 9, 11, and 12.

SELECTED BIBLIOGRAPHY

The American Dietetic Association. 1996. Position Statement: Nutrition Education for the Public. *Journal of the American Dietetic Association* 96(11): 1183–1187.

The American Dietetic Association and the Canadian Dietetic Association. 1997. *Position Statement: Nutrition for Physical*

NEW!

FOR MORE INFORMATION

For the third edition, For More Information sections have been expanded to include descriptions of books, newsletters, organizations, hotlines, and Web sites that students can turn to for additional advice and information.

Behavior Change Workbook

This workbook is designed to take you step by step through the process of behavior change. The first eight activities in the workbook will help you develop a successful plan—beginning with choosing a target behavior and moving through the program planning steps described in Chapter 1, including the completion and signing of a behavior change contract. The final seven activities will help you work through common obstacles to behavior change and maximize your program's chances of success.

Part 1   Developing a Plan for Behavior Change and Completing a Contract

1. Choosing a Target Behavior
2. Gathering Information About Your Target Behavior
3. Monitoring Your Current Patterns of Behavior
4. Setting Goals
5. Examining Your Attitudes About Your Target Behavior
6. Choosing Rewards
7. Breaking Behavior Chains
8. Completing a Contract for Behavior Change

Part 2   Overcoming Obstacles to Behavior Change

9. Building Motivation and Commitment
10. Managing Your Time Successfully
11. Developing Realistic Self-Talk
12. Involving the People Around You
13. Dealing with Feelings
14. Overcoming Peer Pressure: Communicating Assertively
15. Maintaining Your Program over Time

ACTIVITY 1   CHOOSING A TARGET BEHAVIOR

Use your knowledge of yourself and the results of Lab 1-1 (Lifestyle Evaluation) to identify five behaviors that you could change to improve your level of wellness. Examples of target behaviors include smoking cigarettes, not exercising regularly, eating candy bars every night, not getting enough sleep, getting drunk frequently on weekends, and not wearing a safety belt when driving or riding in a car. List your five behaviors below.

1. _____
2. _____
3. _____
4. _____
5. _____

For successful behavior change, it's best to focus on one behavior at a time. Review your list of behaviors and select one to start with. Choose a behavior that is important to you and that you are strongly motivated to change. If this will be your first attempt at behavior change, start with a simple change, such as wearing your bicycle helmet regularly, before tackling a more difficult change, such as quitting smoking. Circle the behavior on your list that you've chosen to start with; this will be your target behavior throughout this workbook.

Behavior Change Workbook   W-1

NEW!

BUILT-IN BEHAVIOR CHANGE WORKBOOK

The new built-in Behavior Change Workbook is designed to complement the step-by-step lifestyle management model presented in Chapter 1. Based on the behavior change activities that appeared in the second edition, the workbook takes students through each of the steps of behavior change—from choosing a target behavior to completing a contract. It also helps students overcome common obstacles to behavior change, including poor time management, negative self-talk, and peer pressure. The workbook is printed on easy-to-use perforated pages at the end of the text.

Additional behavior change tools available with *Fit and Well* include the Daily Fitness Log and the Nutrition and Weight Management Journal. These two booklets, described later in the tour, are shrink-wrapped with the text at no additional cost to students.

SAMPLE PROGRAMS FOR POPULAR ACTIVITIES

Sample programs based on four different types of cardiorespiratory activities—walking/jogging/running, bicycling, swimming, and in-line skating—are presented below. Each sample program includes regular cardiorespiratory endurance exercise, resistance training, and stretching. To choose a sample program, first compare your fitness goals with the benefits of the different types of endurance exercise featured in the sample programs (see Table 7-1). Identify the programs that meet your fitness needs. Next, read through the descriptions of the programs you're considering and decide which will work best for you based on your present routine, the potential for enjoyment, and adaptability to your lifestyle. If you choose one of these programs, complete the personal fitness program plan in Lab 7-1, just as if you had created a program from scratch.

No program will bring about enormous changes in your fitness level in the first few weeks. Give your program a good chance. Follow the specifics of the program for 3–4 weeks. Then if the exercise program doesn't seem suitable, make adjustments to adapt it to your particular needs. But retain the basic elements of the program that make it effective for developing fitness.

General Guidelines

The following guidelines can help make the activity programs more effective for you.

- *Intensity.* To work effectively for cardiorespiratory endurance training or to improve body composition, you must raise your heart rate into its target zone. Monitor your pulse, or use rates of perceived exertion to monitor your intensity.
  If you've been sedentary, begin very slowly. Give your

muscles a chance to adjust to their increased workload. It's probably best to keep your heart rate below target until your body has had time to adjust to new demands. At first you may not need to work very hard to keep your heart rate in its target zone, but as your cardiorespiratory endurance improves, you will probably need to increase intensity.

- *Duration and frequency.* To experience training effects, you should exercise for 20–60 minutes at least three times per week.
- *Interval training.* Some of the sample programs involve continuous activity. Others rely on interval training, which calls for alternating a relief interval with exercise (walking after jogging, for example, or coasting after biking uphill). Interval training is an effective way to achieve progressive overload. When your heart rate gets too high, slow down to lower your pulse rate until you're at the low end of your target zone. Interval training can also prolong the total time you spend in exercise and delay the onset of fatigue.
- *Warm-up and cool-down.* Begin each exercise session with a 10-minute warm-up. Begin your activity at a slow pace, and work up gradually to your target heart rate. Always slow down gradually at the end of your exercise session to bring your system back to its normal state. It's a good idea to do stretching exercises to increase your flexibility after cardiorespiratory exercise or strength training because your muscles will be warm and ready to stretch.
- *Record keeping.* After each exercise session, record your daily distance or time on a progress chart like the one shown in Lab 7-2.

WALKING/JOGGING/RUNNING SAMPLE PROGRAM

Walking, jogging, and running are the most popular forms of training for people who want to improve cardiorespiratory endurance; they also improve body composition and muscular endurance of the legs. It's not always easy to distinguish among these three endurance activities. For clarity and consistency, we'll consider walking to be any on-foot exercise of less than 5 miles per hour, jogging any pace between 5 and 7.5 miles per hour, and running any pace faster than that. Table 1 divides walking, jogging, and running into nine categories, with rates of speed (in both miles per hour and minutes per mile) and calorie costs for each. The faster your pace or the longer you exercise, the more calories you burn. The greater the number of calories burned, the higher the potential training effects of these activities.

Equipment and Technique

These activities require no special skills, expensive equipment, or unusual facilities. Comfortable clothing, well-fitted walking or running shoes, and a stopwatch or ordinary watch with a second hand are all you need.

Developing Cardiorespiratory Endurance

The four variations of the basic walking/jogging/running sam-

ple program that follow are designed to help you regulate the intensity, duration, and frequency of your program. Use the following guidelines to choose the variation that is right for you.

- *Variation 1: Walking (Starting).* Choose this program if you have medical restrictions, are recovering from illness or surgery, tire easily after short walks, are obese, or have a sedentary lifestyle, and if you want to prepare for the advanced walking program to improve cardiorespiratory endurance, body composition, and muscular endurance.
- *Variation 2: Advanced Walking.* Choose this program if you already can walk comfortably for 30 minutes and if you want to develop and maintain cardiorespiratory fitness, a lean body, and muscular endurance.
- *Variation 3: Preparing for a Jogging Program.* Choose this program if you already can walk comfortably for 30 minutes and if you want to prepare for the jogging/running program to improve cardiorespiratory endurance, body composition, and muscular endurance.
- *Variation 4: Jogging/Running.* Choose this program if you already can jog comfortably without muscular discomfort, if you already can jog for 15 minutes without stopping or 30 minutes with brief walking intervals within your target

170   Chapter 7   Putting Together a Complete Fitness Program

SAMPLE FITNESS PROGRAMS

For further guidance in adopting a fit and well lifestyle, Chapter 7 concludes with seven complete sample fitness programs built around four popular cardiorespiratory endurance activities: walking/ jogging/ running, bicycling, swimming, and—new to the third edition—in-line skating. Each sample program explains how to start a fitness program, how to adjust intensity, duration, and frequency as fitness improves, and how to combine strength training and stretching with cardiorespiratory endurance exercise.

LABORATORY ACTIVITIES

To help students apply the principles of fitness, wellness, and behavior change to their own lives, *Fit and Well* includes 28 laboratory activities. These hands-on activities give students the opportunity to assess their current level of wellness, to create plans for changing their behavior to reach wellness, and to monitor their progress. The labs have a user-friendly format and are located on perforated pages at the ends of the chapters. A complete list of all the laboratory activities can be found on page xvi in the table of contents.

Many of the labs are also found on the Lab Activities and Fitness Log Software. In addition, the Instructor's Resource Binder includes more than 70 additional lab activities, formatted for easy duplication and use. The software and additional lab activities are described later in the tour.

Name _____ **Section** _____ **Date** _____

LAB 5-1 *Assessing Your Current Level of Flexibility*

Part I. Sit-and-Reach Test

Equipment

A flexibility box or measuring device (see photograph). If you make your own measuring device, use two pieces of wood 12 inches high attached at right angles to each other. Use a ruler or yardstick to measure the extent of reach. With the low numbers of the ruler toward the person being tested, set the 6-inch mark of the ruler at the footline of the box. (Individuals who cannot reach as far as the footline will have scores below 6 inches; those who can reach past their feet will have scores above 6 inches.)

Preparation

Warm up your muscles with some low-intensity activity such as walking or easy jogging.

Instructions

1. Remove your shoes, and sit facing the flexibility box with your knees fully extended and your feet about 4 inches apart. Your feet should be flat against the box.
2. Reach as far forward as you can, with palms down and one hand placed on top of the other. Hold the position of maximum reach for 1–2 seconds. Keep your knees locked at all times.
3. Repeat the stretch two times. Your score is the most distant point reached with the fingertips of both hands on the third trial, measured to the nearest quarter of an inch.

The sit-and-reach test.

Footline of your box: _____ in.   Score of third trial: _____ in.

Rating Your Flexibility

Find your score in the table below to determine your flexibility rating.

Rating: _____

Ratings for Sit-and-Reach Test

Men
Age: 15–19
20–29
30–39
40–49
50–59
60 and

Women
Age: 15–19
20–29
30–39
40–49
50–59
60 and

*Footline is set
SOURCE: Publi
Canadian Socie

Name _____ **Section** _____ **Date** _____

LAB 10-2 *Stress-Management Techniques*

Part I. Lifestyle Stress Management

For each of the areas listed in the table below, describe your current lifestyle as it relates to stress management. For example, do you have enough social support? How are your exercise and nutrition habits? Is time management a problem for you? For each area, list two ways that you could change your current habits to help you manage your stress. Sample strategies might include calling a friend before a challenging class, taking a short walk before lunch, and buying and using a date book to track your time.

	Current lifestyle	Lifestyle change #1	Lifestyle change #2
Social support system			
Exercise habits			
Nutrition habits			
Time-management techniques			
Self-talk patterns			
Sleep habits			

Part II. Relaxation Techniques

Choose two relaxation techniques described in this chapter (progressive relaxation, visualizati tation, yoga, t'ai chi ch'uan). If a taped recording is available for progressive relaxation or visu can be performed by your entire class as a group.

List the techniques you tried.

1. _____
2. _____

Lab 10-2   Stress-M

Name _____ **Section** _____ **Date** _____

LAB 7-1 *A Personal Fitness Program Plan and Contract*

A. I, _____ (name), am contracting with myself to follow a physical fitness program to work toward the following goals:

Specific or short-term goals

1. _____
2. _____
3. _____
4. _____

General or long-term goals

1. _____
2. _____
3. _____
4. _____

B. My program plan is as follows:

Activities	Components (Check ✓)					Intensity*	Duration	Frequency (Check ✓)						
	CRE	MS	ME	F	BC			M	Tu	W	Th	F	Sa	Su

*Conduct activities for achieving CRE goals at your target heart rate or RPE value.

C. My program will begin on _____ (date). My program includes the following schedule of mini-goals. For each step in my program, I will give myself the reward listed.

(mini-goal 1)	(date)	(reward)
(mini-goal 2)	(date)	(reward)
(mini-goal 3)	(date)	(reward)
(mini-goal 4)	(date)	(reward)
(mini-goal 5)	(date)	(reward)

Lab 7-1   A Personal Fitness Program Plan and Contract   **179**

Building Lifelong Skills

TACTICS AND TIPS BOXES

Tactics and Tips boxes present the practical advice students need to apply information from the text to their own lives.

CRITICAL CONSUMER BOXES

Critical Consumer boxes help students develop and apply critical thinking skills so that they can make sound choices related to wellness.

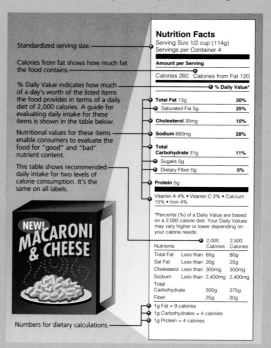

DIMENSIONS OF DIVERSITY *Gender Differences in Muscular Strength*

Men are generally stronger than women because they typically have larger bodies overall and larger muscles. But when strength is expressed per unit of cross-sectional area of muscle tissue, men are only 1–2% stronger than women in the upper body and about equal to women in the lower body. (Men have a larger proportion of muscle tissue in the upper body, so it's easier for them to build upper-body strength than it is for women.) Individual muscle fibers are larger in men, but the metabolism of cells within those fibers is the same in both sexes.

Two factors that help explain these disparities between the sexes are androgen levels and the speed of nervous control of muscle. Androgens are naturally occurring male hormones that are responsible for the development of secondary sex characteristics (facial hair, deep voice, and so forth). Androgens also promote the growth of muscle tissue. Androgen levels are about 6–10 times higher in men than in women, so men tend to have larger muscles. Also, because the male nervous system can activate muscles faster, men tend to have more power.

Some women are concerned that they will develop large muscles from weight training. Most studies show that women do not develop big muscles, but the evidence of top women body builders suggests that they can. Some of these women may have taken drugs to increase their muscle size, but many muscular women have not. Evidence suggests, though, that it is difficult for women to gain a large amount of muscle without training intensely over many years.

The bottom line is that both men and women can increase strength through weight training. Women may not be able to lift as much weight as men, but pound for pound of muscle, they have nearly the same capacity to gain strength as men. The lifetime wellness benefits of strength training are available to everyone.

SOURCE: Fahey, T. D. 1997. *Weight Training for Men and Women*, 3d ed. Mountain View, Calif.: Mayfield.

DIMENSIONS OF DIVERSITY BOXES

Dimensions of Diversity boxes enable students to identify and overcome special challenges they face because of who they are, either as individuals or as members of groups. Wellness-related differences among people can be related to biological and cultural influences, such as gender, age, socioeconomic status, and ethnicity. Dimensions of Diversity boxes describe areas where individual and group differences are important for wellness, and they help students respond appropriately.

WELLNESS CONNECTION *Spiritual Wellness*

Spiritual wellness means different things to different people. For many, it involves developing a set of guiding beliefs, principles, or values that give meaning and purpose to life. It helps people achieve a sense of wholeness within themselves and in their relationships with others. Spiritual wellness influences people on an individual level, as well as on a community level, where it can bond people together through compassion, love, forgiveness, and self-sacrifice. For some, spirituality includes a belief in a higher power. Regardless of how it is defined, the development of spiritual wellness is critical for overall health and well-being. Its development is closely tied to the other components of wellness, particularly psychological health.

There are many paths of spiritual wellness. One of the most common in our society is organized religion. Some people object to the notion that organized religion can contribute to wellness, asserting that it reinforces people's tendency to deny real difficulties and to accept what can and should be changed. However, many elements of religious belief and practice can promote psychological health.

Organized religion usually involves its members in a community where social and material support is available. Religious organizations offer a social network to those who might otherwise be isolated. The major religions provide paths for transforming the self in ways that can lead to greater happiness and serenity and reduce feelings of anxiety and hopelessness. In Christianity, salvation follows turning away from the selfish

ego to God's sovereignty and grace, where a joy is found that frees the believer from anxious self-concern and despair. Islam is the word for a kind of self-surrender leading to peace with God. Buddhism teaches how to detach oneself from selfish desire, leading to compassion for the suffering of others and freedom from fear-engendering illusions. Judaism emphasizes the social and ethical redemption the Jewish community can experience if it follows the laws of God. Religions teach specific techniques for achieving these transformations of the self: prayer, both in groups and in private; meditation; the performance of rituals and ceremonies symbolizing religious truths; and good works and service to others.

Spiritual wellness does not require participation in organized religion. Many people find meaning and purpose in other ways. By spending time in nature or working on environmental issues, people can experience continuity with the natural world.

Spiritual wellness can come through helping others in one's community or by promoting human rights, peace and harmony among people, and opportunities for human development on a global level. Other people develop spiritual wellness through art or through their personal relationships.

Particularly in the second half of life, people seem to have an urge to view their activities and consciousness from a transcendent perspective. At every age, however, people seem to feel better if they have beliefs about the ultimate purpose of life

WELLNESS CONNECTION BOXES

Wellness Connection boxes focus on total wellness by exploring the close connection between people's feelings and states of mind and their physical health. They show how developing one dimension of wellness leads to changes in other dimensions.

See pp. xv–xvi in the table of contents for a complete list of the boxes.

Clear and Accessible

BENCH PRESS

Muscles developed: Pectoralis major, anterior deltoids, triceps

Instructions: Lie on the bench so the tops of the handles are aligned with the tops of your armpits. Place your feet flat on the floor; if they don't reach, place them on the bench. **(a)** Grasp the handles with your palms facing away from you. **(b)** Push the bars until your arms are fully extended. Return to the starting position.

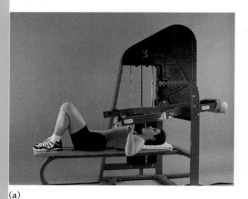

(a)

(b)

ILLUSTRATED EXERCISE PROGRAMS

To ensure that students exercise safely and effectively, *Fit and Well* includes full-color photographs showing proper technique for exercises and stretches that develop muscular strength and endurance, flexibility, and low-back health.

COMMON QUESTIONS ANSWERED

How long must I weight train before I begin to see changes in my body? You will increase strength very rapidly during the early stages of a weight training program, primarily the result of muscle learning (the increased ability of the nervous system to recruit muscle fibers to exert force). Actual changes in muscle size usually begin after about 6–8 weeks of training.

I am concerned about my body composition. Will I gain weight if I do resistance exercises? Your weight probably will not change significantly as a result of a recreational-type weight training program: 1 set of 8–12 repetitions of 8–10 exercises. You will tend to increase muscle mass and lose body fat, so your weight will stay about the same. (Men will tend to build larger muscles than women because of the tissue-building effects of male hormones.) Increased muscle mass will help you control body fat. Muscle increases your metabolism, which means you burn up more calories every day. If you combine resistance exercises with endurance exercises, you will be on your way to developing a healthier body composition. Concentrate on fat loss rather than weight loss.

Do I need more protein in my diet when I train with weights? No. While there is some evidence that power athletes involved in heavy training have a higher-than-normal protein requirement, there is no reason for most people to consume extra protein. Most Americans take in more protein than they need, so even if there is an increased protein need during heavy training, it is probably supplied by the average diet. (See Chapter 8 for more on dietary needs of athletes.)

Are there any supplements or drugs that will help me make larger and more rapid increases in strength and endurance? No nutritional supplement or drug will change a weak, untrained person into a strong, fit person. Those changes require regular training that stresses the muscles, heart, lungs, and metabolism and causes the body to adapt. Supplements or drugs that are promoted as instant or quick "cures" usually don't work and are either dangerous or expensive, or both. **Anabolic steroids**—the drugs most often taken in an effort to build strength and power—have dangerous side effects, described in Table 4-4. You are better off staying with proven principles of nutrition and a steady, progressive fitness program.

What causes muscle soreness the day or two following a weight training workout? The muscle pain you feel a day or two after a heavy weight training workout is caused by injury to the muscle fibers and surrounding connective tissue. Contrary to popular belief, delayed-onset muscle soreness is not caused by lactic acid buildup. Scientists believe that injury to muscle fibers causes the release of excess calcium into muscles. The calcium causes the release of substances called **proteases**, which break down part of the muscle tissue and cause pain. After a bout of intense exercise that causes muscle injury and delayed-onset muscle soreness, the muscles produce protective proteins that prevent soreness during future workouts. If you don't work out regularly, you lose these protective proteins and become susceptible to muscle soreness again.

Will strength training improve my sports performance? Strength developed in the weight room does not automatically increase your power in sports such as skiing, tennis, or cycling. Hitting a forehand in tennis or making a turn on skis is highly specific and requires precise coordination between your nervous system and muscles. In skilled people, movements become reflex—you don't think about them when you do them. Increasing strength can disturb this coordination. Only by simultaneously practicing a sport and improving fitness can you expect to become more powerful in the skill. Practice helps you integrate your new strength with your skills, which makes you more powerful. Consequently, you can hit the ball harder in tennis or make more graceful turns on the ski slopes. (Refer to Chapter 2 for more on the concept of specificity of physical training.)

Will I improve faster if I train every day? No. Your muscles need time to recover between training sessions. Doing resistance exercises every day will cause you to become overtrained, which will increase your chance of injury and impede your progress. If you find that your strength training program has reached a plateau, try one of these strategies:

- Train less frequently. If you are currently training the same muscle groups three or more times per week, you may not be allowing your muscles to fully recover from intense workouts.
- Change exercises. Using different exercises for a particular muscle group may stimulate further strength development.
- Vary the load and number of repetitions. Try increasing or decreasing the loads you are using and changing the number of repetitions accordingly.
- Vary the number of sets. If you have been performing 1 set of each exercise, add sets.
- If you are training alone, find a motivated training partner. A partner can encourage you and assist you with difficult lifts, forcing you to work harder.

If I stop weight training, will my muscles turn to fat? No. Fat and muscle are two different kinds of tissue, and one cannot turn into the other. Muscles that aren't used become smaller (atrophy), and body fat may increase if caloric intake exceeds calories burned. Although the result of inactivity may be smaller muscles and more fat, the change is caused by two separate processes.

anabolic steroids Synthetic male hormones taken to enhance athletic performance and body composition.
proteases Enzymes that break down proteins.

TERMS

COMMON QUESTIONS ANSWERED

Sections labeled Common Questions Answered address practical concerns of special interest to students.

RUNNING GLOSSARY

Important terms appear in boldface type in the text and are defined in a running glossary on the same page.

COLORFUL, INFORMATIVE ILLUSTRATIONS

Innovative graphics and illustrations add visual appeal to the text and help students understand important concepts.

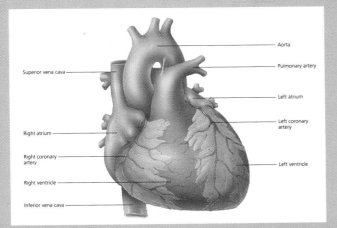

Figure 11-4 Blood supply to the heart. Blood is supplied to the heart from the right and left coronary arteries, which branch off the aorta. If a coronary artery becomes blocked by plaque buildup and a blood clot, a heart attack occurs; part of the heart muscle may die due to lack of oxygen.

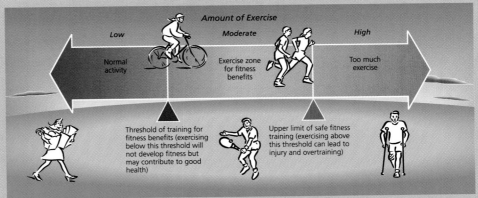

Figure 2-2 Amount of exercise for improving physical fitness.

A CLOSER LOOK — *Preventive Medicine for Healthy Adults*

While many people associate medical care solely with an illness or injury, preventive medicine can help healthy people stay healthy. Good preventive care includes:

1. Counseling and support to develop healthy habits and reduce health risks.
2. Selective screening tests based on your age, gender, and medical or family history (see the chart below).
3. Appropriate immunizations and use of medications to prevent disease.

The prevention recommendations below are based on scientific research. They apply to generally healthy adults. If you have ongoing health problems, if certain diseases run in your family, or if you have other special health needs or risks, your prevention plan may be somewhat different. Your health care providers can help you design a personalized plan for staying healthy based on your individual needs. And remember, don't rely just on medical exams, tests, and treatments to protect your health. Developing and maintaining a wellness lifestyle is the cornerstone of disease prevention and health promotion.

SOURCES: U.S. Preventive Services Task Force. 1996. *Guide to Clinical Preventive Services: Report of the U.S. Preventive Services Task Force,* 2d ed. Baltimore: Williams & Wilkins.

Screening Tests for Men

Prostate cancer: Routine screening is not recommended.

Screening Tests for Men and Women

Cholesterol: Every 5 years for men 35–65 and women 45–85.

Hypertension: Routine blood pressure measurement if below 130/85, annually if above.

HIV infection and other STDs: Routine screening for pregnant women, for people with multiple sex partners, or for members of high-risk groups.

Colorectal cancer: Screening with an annual fecal occult blood testing or sigmoidoscopy is recommended for people over 50 every 3–5 years.

Tuberculosis: Recommended for members of high-risk groups only.

Screening Tests for Women

Mammography: Routine screening for women ages 50–69 every 1–2 years.

Pap smear: Routine screening every 3 years for women.

Iron-deficiency anemia: Recommended for pregnant women and high-risk infants.

The recommendations of the U.S. Preventive Services Task Force differ from those of the American Heart Association, American Cancer Society, and other organizations. See Chapters 11 and 12 for other sets of testing guidelines, and check with your physician about which tests are best for you.

DYNAMIC BOX PROGRAM

Fit and Well has five different types of boxes, all aimed at highlighting areas of particular interest and importance to students. The five box types are Tactics and Tips, Critical Consumer, Dimensions of Diversity, Wellness Connection—all described earlier—and A Closer Look.

Valuable Resources

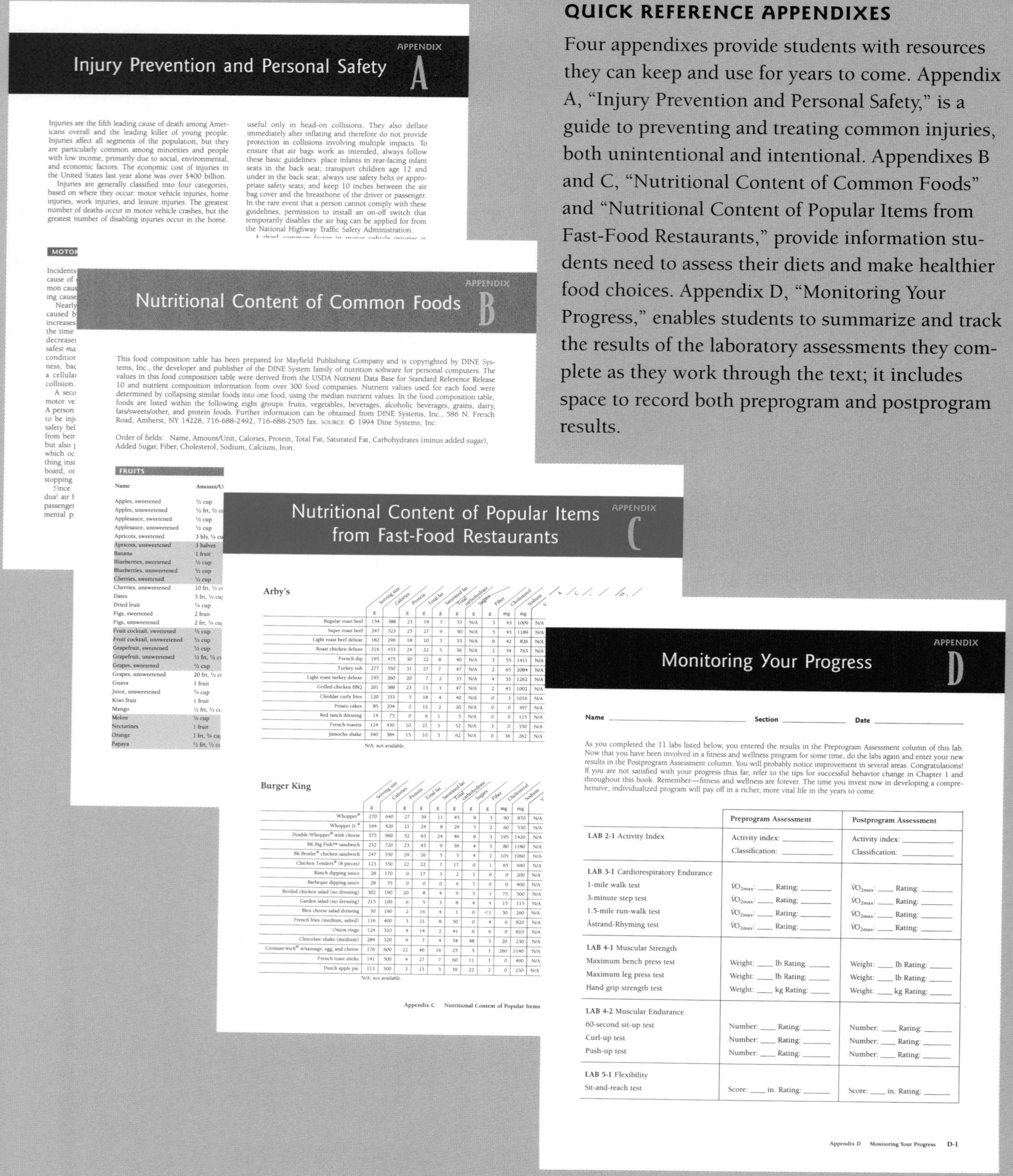

Injury Prevention and Personal Safety

APPENDIX A

Injuries are the fifth leading cause of death among Americans overall and the leading killer of young people. Injuries affect all segments of the population, but they are particularly common among minorities and people with low income, primarily due to social, environmental, and economic factors. The economic cost of injuries in the United States last year alone was over $400 billion.

Injuries are generally classified into four categories, based on where they occur: motor vehicle injuries, home injuries, work injuries, and leisure injuries. The greatest number of deaths occur in motor vehicle crashes, but the greatest number of disabling injuries occur in the home.

useful only in head-on collisions. They also deflate immediately after inflating and therefore do not provide protection in collisions involving multiple impacts. To ensure that air bags work as intended, always follow these basic guidelines: place infants in rear-facing infant seats in the back seat; transport children age 12 and under in the back seat; always use safety belts or appropriate safety seats; and keep 10 inches between the air bag cover and the breastbone of the driver or passenger. In the rare event that a person cannot comply with these guidelines, permission to install an on-off switch that temporarily disables the air bag can be applied for from the National Highway Traffic Safety Administration.

Nutritional Content of Common Foods

APPENDIX B

This food composition table has been prepared for Mayfield Publishing Company and is copyrighted by DINE Systems, Inc., the developer and publisher of the DINE System family of nutrition software for personal computers. The values in this food composition table were derived from the USDA Nutrient Data Base for Standard Reference Release 10 and nutrient composition information from over 300 food companies. Nutrient values used for each food were determined by collapsing similar foods into one food, using the median nutrient values. In the food composition table, foods are listed within the following eight groups: fruits, vegetables, beverages, alcoholic beverages, grains, dairy, fats/sweets/other, and protein foods. Further information can be obtained from DINE Systems, Inc., 586 N. French Road, Amherst, NY 14228, 716-688-2492, 716-688-2505 fax. SOURCE: © 1994 Dine Systems, Inc.

Order of fields: Name, Amount/Unit, Calories, Protein, Total Fat, Saturated Fat, Carbohydrates (minus added sugar), Added Sugar, Fiber, Cholesterol, Sodium, Calcium, Iron.

FRUITS

Name	Amount/U...
Apples, sweetened	½ cup
Apples, unsweetened	½ frt, ½ c...
Applesauce, sweetened	½ cup
Applesauce, unsweetened	½ cup
Apricots, sweetened	3 hlv, ¼ cu...
Apricots, unsweetened	3 halves
Banana	1 fruit
Blueberries, sweetened	½ cup
Blueberries, unsweetened	½ cup
Cherries, sweetened	½ cup
Cherries, unsweetened	10 frt, ¼ cu...
Dates	5 frt, ¼ cup
Dried fruit	¼ cup
Figs, sweetened	2 fruit
Figs, unsweetened	2 frt, ⅓ cup
Fruit cocktail, sweetened	½ cup
Fruit cocktail, unsweetened	½ cup
Grapefruit, sweetened	½ cup
Grapefruit, unsweetened	½ frt, ⅓ cu...
Grapes, sweetened	½ cup
Grapes, unsweetened	20 frt, ½ cu...
Guava	1 fruit
Juice, unsweetened	¾ cup
Kiwi fruit	1 fruit
Mango	½ frt, ½ cu...
Melon	½ cup
Nectarines	1 fruit
Orange	1 frt, ¾ cup
Papaya	½ frt, ½ cu...

Nutritional Content of Popular Items from Fast-Food Restaurants

APPENDIX C

Arby's

	Serving size (g)	Calories	Protein (g)	Total fat (g)	Saturated fat (g)	Total carbohydrate (g)	Sugars (g)	Fiber (g)	Cholesterol (mg)	Sodium (mg)
Regular roast beef	154	388	23	19	7	33	N/A	3	43	1009
Super roast beef	247	523	25	27	9	50	N/A	5	43	1189
Light roast beef deluxe	182	296	18	10	3	33	N/A	6	42	826
Roast chicken deluxe	216	433	24	22	5	36	N/A	2	34	763
French dip	195	475	30	22	8	40	N/A	3	55	1411
Turkey sub	277	550	31	27	7	47	N/A	2	65	2084
Light roast turkey deluxe	195	260	20	7	2	33	N/A	4	33	1262
Grilled chicken BBQ	201	388	23	13	3	47	N/A	2	43	1002
Cheddar curly fries	120	333	5	18	4	40	N/A	0	3	1016
Potato cakes	85	204	2	12	2	20	N/A	0	0	397
Red ranch dressing	14	75	0	6	1	5	N/A	0	0	115
French-toastix	124	430	10	21	5	52	N/A	3	0	563
Jamocha shake	340	384	15	10	3	62	N/A	0	36	262

N/A: not available.

Burger King

	Serving size (g)	Calories	Protein (g)	Total fat (g)	Saturated fat (g)	Total carbohydrate (g)	Sugars (g)	Fiber (g)	Cholesterol (mg)	Sodium (mg)
Whopper®	270	640	27	39	11	45	8	3	90	870
Whopper Jr.®	164	420	21	24	8	29	5	2	60	530
Double Whopper® with cheese	375	960	52	63	24	46	8	3	195	1420
BK Big Fish™ sandwich	252	720	23	43	9	59	4	3	80	1180
BK Broiler® chicken sandwich	247	530	29	26	5	5	4	2	105	1060
Chicken Tenders® (8 pieces)	123	350	22	22	7	17	0	1	65	940
Ranch dipping sauce	28	170	0	17	3	2	1	0	0	200
Barbeque dipping sauce	28	35	0	0	0	9	7	0	0	400
Broiled chicken salad (no dressing)	302	190	20	8	4	9	5	3	75	500
Garden salad (no dressing)	215	100	6	5	3	8	4	4	15	115
Bleu cheese salad dressing	30	160	2	16	4	1	0	<1	30	260
French fries (medium, salted)	116	400	5	21	8	50	0	4	0	820
Onion rings	124	310	4	14	2	41	6	6	0	810
Chocolate shake (medium)	284	320	9	7	4	54	48	3	20	230
Croissan'wich® w/sausage, egg, and cheese	176	600	22	46	16	25	3	1	260	1140
French toast sticks	141	500	4	27	7	60	11	1	0	490
Dutch apple pie	113	300	3	15	3	39	22	2	0	230

N/A: not available.

Appendix C Nutritional Content of Popular Items

Monitoring Your Progress

APPENDIX D

Name _____ Section _____ Date _____

As you completed the 11 labs listed below, you entered the results in the Preprogram Assessment column of this lab. Now that you have been involved in a fitness and wellness program for some time, do the labs again and enter your new results in the Postprogram Assessment column. You will probably notice improvement in several areas. Congratulations! If you are not satisfied with your progress thus far, refer to the tips for successful behavior change in Chapter 1 and throughout this book. Remember—fitness and wellness are forever. The time you invest now in developing a comprehensive, individualized program will pay off in a richer, more vital life in the years to come.

	Preprogram Assessment	Postprogram Assessment
LAB 2-1 Activity Index	Activity index: _____ Classification: _____	Activity index: _____ Classification: _____
LAB 3-1 Cardiorespiratory Endurance 1-mile walk test 3-minute step test 1.5-mile run-walk test Åstrand-Rhyming test	$\dot{V}O_{2max}$: ___ Rating: ___ $\dot{V}O_{2max}$: ___ Rating: ___ $\dot{V}O_{2max}$: ___ Rating: ___ $\dot{V}O_{2max}$: ___ Rating: ___	$\dot{V}O_{2max}$: ___ Rating: ___ $\dot{V}O_{2max}$: ___ Rating: ___ $\dot{V}O_{2max}$: ___ Rating: ___ $\dot{V}O_{2max}$: ___ Rating: ___
LAB 4-1 Muscular Strength Maximum bench press test Maximum leg press test Hand grip strength test	Weight: ___ lb Rating: ___ Weight: ___ lb Rating: ___ Weight: ___ kg Rating: ___	Weight: ___ lb Rating: ___ Weight: ___ lb Rating: ___ Weight: ___ kg Rating: ___
LAB 4-2 Muscular Endurance 60-second sit-up test Curl-up test Push-up test	Number: ___ Rating: ___ Number: ___ Rating: ___ Number: ___ Rating: ___	Number: ___ Rating: ___ Number: ___ Rating: ___ Number: ___ Rating: ___
LAB 5-1 Flexibility Sit-and-reach test	Score: ___ in. Rating: ___	Score: ___ in. Rating: ___

Appendix D Monitoring Your Progress   D-1

QUICK REFERENCE APPENDIXES

Four appendixes provide students with resources they can keep and use for years to come. Appendix A, "Injury Prevention and Personal Safety," is a guide to preventing and treating common injuries, both unintentional and intentional. Appendixes B and C, "Nutritional Content of Common Foods" and "Nutritional Content of Popular Items from Fast-Food Restaurants," provide information students need to assess their diets and make healthier food choices. Appendix D, "Monitoring Your Progress," enables students to summarize and track the results of the laboratory assessments they complete as they work through the text; it includes space to record both preprogram and postprogram results.

Flexible Formats to Fit Your Course

Fit and Well, Third Edition, is available in three different formats to fit a variety of courses.

FULL VERSION

ALTERNATE EDITION

CUSTOM FITNESS EDITION

1. Introduction to Wellness, Fitness, and Lifestyle Management
2. Basic Principles of Physical Fitness
3. Cardiorespiratory Endurance
4. Muscular Strength and Endurance
5. Flexibility
6. Body Composition
7. Putting Together a Complete Fitness Program
8. Nutrition
9. Weight Management
10. Stress
11. Cardiovascular Health
12. Cancer
13. Substance Use and Abuse
14. Sexually Transmitted Diseases
15. Wellness for Life

Appendix A Injury Prevention and Personal Safety
Appendix B Nutritional Content of Common Foods
Appendix C Nutritional Content of Popular Items from Fast-Food Restaurants
Appendix D Monitoring Your Progress
Behavior Change Workbook

Fit and Well. The full version of *Fit and Well* is an excellent choice for courses that cover a wide range of fitness and wellness topics, including cancer, substance abuse, and STDs (ISBN 0-7674-0535-8).

Fit and Well: Alternate Edition. The Alternate Edition is designed for courses that focus on the basics of fitness and wellness. It includes the first eleven chapters of the full version of *Fit and Well*, along with all four appendixes and the Behavior Change Workbook (ISBN 0-7674-0537-4).

Fit and Well: Custom Fitness Edition. The Custom Fitness Edition is for courses that focus on the fundamentals of physical fitness. It includes the first seven chapters of the full version of *Fit and Well*, along with Appendixes B and D (ISBN 0-7674-0833-0).

The complete package of teaching tools and all the student supplements are available with all versions of *Fit and Well*.

Comprehensive Teaching Package

Available with the third edition of *Fit and Well* is a comprehensive teaching and learning package that will help both you and your students succeed.

INSTRUCTOR'S RESOURCE BINDER

The Instructor's Resource Binder contains a variety of helpful teaching materials in an easy-to-use format—a comprehensive Instructor's Resource Guide, an Internet handbook, an extensive set of examination questions, additional laboratory activities, and transparency masters and handouts. The elements of the binder are also available as separate bound volumes.

The **Instructor's Resource Guide** provides a variety of supplementary materials to help you direct and facilitate students' learning. For the third edition, the Guide was prepared by Meredith Busby, University of North Carolina, Chapel Hill.

- **Learning objectives** identify the major concepts in each chapter. They can be used to plan lectures and to guide students in their review of the text.

- **Extended chapter outlines** provide a detailed summary of the chapter in an easy-to-use outline form.

- **Additional resources** include current films and videos suitable for classroom use, books and journal articles, software programs and CD-ROMs, and community resources.

- **Internet resources** provide descriptions and addresses of useful sites on the World Wide Web. The listings include sites not described in the text; they can be used for student research projects and other activities.

- **Descriptions of lab activities in the text, additional lab activities in the binder, transparency acetates, and transparency masters and handouts** provide information to aid you in creating lectures and assignments.

NEW!

The **Internet Handbook** includes a brief introduction to the Internet, a complete directory of all the sites listed in the text and Instructor's Resource Guide, guidelines for evaluating information from the Internet, and 11 reproducible worksheets with student Internet activities.

The **Examination Questions** have been completely revised and updated for the third edition by John D. Emmett, Eastern Illinois University. The test bank contains over 1000 true/false, multiple-choice, and essay questions. The answer key lists the page number in the text where each answer is found.

The **Additional Laboratory Activities** supplement the labs that are included in the text. Expanded for the third edition, the more than 70 labs include activities such as blood pressure measurement, bioelectrical impedance analysis, isometric and Universal Gym program development, serving size assessment, progressive muscle relaxation and imagery, and dietary analysis for the prevention of heart disease and cancer.

Powerful Presentation Tools

Also included in the Instructor's Resource Binder are more than 100 **Transparency Masters and Handouts.** The transparency masters include tables, graphs, and key points from the text; additional illustrations not found in the text are also included. The hand-outs provide additional information on topics of interest as well as resources for behavior change programs. Many of the transparency masters and handouts are new to the third edition of *Fit and Well*.

TRANSPARENCY ACETATES

Fifty transparency acetates, half in color, are available as a lecture resource. The acetates do not duplicate the transparency masters in the Instructor's Resource Guide.

NEW!
IMAGE BANK AND POWERPOINT®
PRESENTATION CD-ROM

New to the third edition, the CD-ROM includes both an image bank and a set of PowerPoint slides. The **image bank** contains more than 80 graphs, drawings, and other images from the third edition of *Fit and Well*. These electronic transparencies can be used with LCD overhead projectors, printed out as

color transparencies, and imported into PowerPoint and other presentation software. The **PowerPoint slides**, prepared by Christopher M. Janelle at the University of Florida, are lecture outlines in slide format that can be customized to fit any lecture. Used together or separately, the image bank and PowerPoint slides provide a complete package of presentation resources for both IBM-compatible and Macintosh computers. The CD-ROM also includes material from the Instructor's Resource Guide in editable format as well as versions of selected transparency acetates and masters suitable for use with presentation software.

NEW!
MAYFIELD *FIT AND WELL* WEB SITE

A new, fully interactive Web site has been created for the third edition. The **Mayfield *Fit and Well* Web site** (http://www.mayfieldpub.com/fahey) includes up-to-date links to current Internet resources, student study questions that provide immediate feedback to students and instructors, a customized syllabus builder for instructors to design their own course outlines, and more. If you have students who are new to the Internet, see the description of our free Internet Guide later in the tour.

NEW!
STUDENTS ON HEALTH AND WELLNESS: CUSTOM VIDEO TO ACCOMPANY *FIT AND WELL*

Filmed at college campuses across the country, this unique video features students discussing how wellness-related issues and choices affect their daily lives. The 8- to 10-minute segments focus on key aspects of wellness—exercise, nutrition, stress, intimate relationships, alcohol and tobacco use, sexually transmitted diseases, and personal safety. Each video segment is designed to stimulate critical thinking and class discussion. The accompanying Instructor's Video Guide provides summaries of each segment and discussion questions.

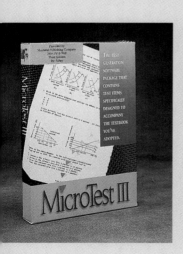

COMPUTERIZED TEST BANK

MicroTest III, developed by Chariot Software Group, allows you to design tests using the test questions included with *Fit and Well* and/or to incorporate your own questions. MicroTest is available in both Windows and Macintosh formats. MicroTest Pro, a software package that offers secure Web-based testing, is also available.

DINE HEALTHY NUTRITIONAL ANALYSIS SOFTWARE

DINE Healthy software provides an easy way for students to evaluate the nutritional value of their current diet. It also includes an exercise section that allows students to track their energy expenditure. DINE Healthy can be networked or site-licensed for qualifying adopters.

ADDITIONAL VIDEOS, SOFTWARE, AND OTHER MULTIMEDIA

Videos and other multimedia—including nutrition, fitness, and health risk appraisal software—are available to qualified adopters. The Mayfield video library includes tapes on topics such as fitness, nutrition, stress, alcohol use, AIDS, and violence.

NEW!
NUTRITION AND WEIGHT MANAGEMENT JOURNAL

Packaged with each copy of the text at no additional cost to students.

New to the third edition, the **Nutrition and Weight Management Journal** guides students in assessing their current diet and making appropriate changes. It provides many valuable tools, including the Food Guide Pyramid, serving size recommendations, the Dietary Guidelines for Americans, a sample food label, and information about the nutritional content of popular items from fast-food restaurants.

DAILY FITNESS LOG

Packaged with each copy of the text at no additional cost to students.

The **Daily Fitness Log** is an easy-to-use booklet that includes forms for planning and tracking a fitness program for up to 40 weeks. Logs for both an overall fitness program and a weight training program are included.

NEW!
LAB ACTIVITIES AND FITNESS LOG SOFTWARE

Available for an additional $3 when shrink-wrapped with the text; it can also be networked or site-licensed free for users of the text.

The Lab Activities and Fitness Log Software presents completely revised laboratory activities and new fitness logs in an electronic format. The lab activities component of the software calculates and prints out the results of selected self-assessment and fitness tests; it also includes information about behavior change and a behavior change contract that students can complete. The fitness log component includes a general log for tracking an overall program for up to 40 weeks. Students can print out their logs and can also graph their progress. The software is available in both Windows and Macintosh formats.

NEW!
MAYFIELD'S QUICK VIEW GUIDE TO THE INTERNET FOR STUDENTS OF HEALTH AND PHYSICAL EDUCATION

Available at no additional cost to students when shrink-wrapped with the text.

This invaluable guide provides step-by-step instructions on how to access the Internet and how to find and use information about fitness and wellness. It includes extensive lists of Internet resources for both students and instructors. The Quick View Guide also shows students how to evaluate the credibility of online information sources, communicate via e-mail, use listservs and newsgroups, find jobs through the Internet, and even create a Web page.

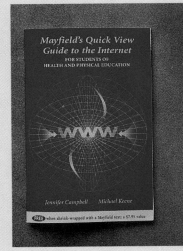

Quality, dependability, flexibility, accuracy, currency

Our goal is to provide you with the most complete teaching package available. If you have any questions concerning the text or teaching package, please call your local Mayfield sales representative or our Marketing and Sales Department at 800-433-1279. You may also e-mail us at calpoppy@mayfieldpub.com.

ORDERING INFORMATION

To use *Fit and Well*, Third Edition, in your course, give your bookstore the appropriate ISBN(s):

Text[*] . . . . .ISBN 0-7674-0535-8

Mayfield Value Packs:

Text[*] plus Internet Guide . . . . .Package ISBN 0-7674-0857-8

Text[*] plus Lab Activities and Fitness Log Software (Win 95) . . . . .Package ISBN 0-7674-0851-9

Text[*] plus Lab Activities and Fitness Log Software (Win 3.1) . . . . .Package ISBN 0-7674-0853-5

Text[*] plus Lab Activities and Fitness Log Software (Mac) . . . . .Package ISBN 0-7674-0855-1

[*] Each copy of the text is packaged with the Daily Fitness Log and the Nutrition and Weight Management Journal.

Note: The ISBNs listed above are for the full version of *Fit and Well*. For ordering information on the Alternate Edition or the Custom Fitness Edition, contact your local sales representative or the Mayfield office.

Fit & Well

Core Concepts and Labs in Physical Fitness and Wellness

THIRD EDITION

Thomas D. Fahey
California State University, Chico

Paul M. Insel
Stanford University

Walton T. Roth
Stanford University

Mayfield Publishing Company
Mountain View, California
London • Toronto

Library of Congress Cataloging-in-Publication Data
Fahey, Thomas D. (Thomas Davin)
    Fit and well : core concepts and labs in physical fitness and wellness / Thomas D. Fahey, Paul M. Insel, Walton T. Roth.—3rd ed.
        p.   cm.
    Includes bibliographical references and index.
    ISBN 0-7674-0535-8
    1. Physical fitness. 2. Health. I. Insel, Paul M. II. Roth, Walton T. III. Title.
GV481.F26   1998
613.7'043—DC21   98-21016
                                                                    CIP

Manufactured in the United States of America
10   9   8   7   6   5   4   3   2   1

Mayfield Publishing Company
1280 Villa Street
Mountain View, CA 94041

Sponsoring editor, Michele Sordi; *developmental editors,* Kirstan Price, Susan Shook, Megan Rundel, and Kathleen Engelberg; *production editor,* Julianna Scott Fein; *manuscript editor,* Margaret Moore; *art director, text designer,* Jeanne M. Schreiber; *cover designer,* Laurie Anderson; *cover photo,* © Philip and Karen Smith/Tony Stone Images; *art manager,* Robin Mouat; *illustrators,* Joan Carol, Kristin Mount, Judy and John Waller, and Susan Seed; *photo researcher,* Brian Pecko; *manufacturing manager,* Randy Hurst. The text was set in 10.5/12 Berkeley Book by GTS Graphics, Inc., and printed on acid-free 45# Chromatone by Banta Book Group.

The Internet addresses listed in the text were accurate at the time of publication. The inclusion of a Web site does not indicate an endorsement by the authors or Mayfield Publishing Company, and Mayfield does not guarantee the accuracy of the information presented at these sites.

Photo Credits

Title Page © David Madison
Chapter 1 p. 1, © J. Nordell/The Image Works; p. 3, © Myrleen Ferguson Cate/PhotoEdit; p. 12, © Mary Kate Denny/PhotoEdit
Chapter 2 p. 19, © Charles Gupton/Stock Boston; p. 22, © Steven Ferry/P & F Communications; p. 24, © Michael Newman/PhotoEdit; p. 30, © Michael Newman/PhotoEdit
Chapter 3 p. 39, © Michael Newman/PhotoEdit; p. 45, © Alán Gallegos/AG Photograph; p. 50, Courtesy Shirlee Stevens; p. 56, © Bob Daemmrich/The Image Works; p. 64, Courtesy Shirlee Stevens
Chapter 4 p. 69, © David Madison; p. 73, 74, 79, Courtesy Neil A. Tanner; p. 84, 85T, Courtesy Shirlee Stevens; p. 85B, Courtesy Neil A. Tanner; p. 86T, Courtesy Shirlee Stevens; p. 86B, 87, 88, 89T, Courtesy Neil A. Tanner; p. 89B, Courtesy Shirlee Stevens; p. 90T, Courtesy Neil A. Tanner; p. 90B, 91, 92T, Courtesy Shirlee Stevens; p. 92B, Courtesy Neil A. Tanner; p. 93, Courtesy Shirlee Stevens; p. 94T, Courtesy Neil A. Tanner; p. 94B, Courtesy Shirlee Stevens; p. 99, 100, Photos furnished by Universal Gym Equipment, Inc., Cedar Rapids, Iowa; p. 101, 103, 104, 106, Courtesy Neil A. Tanner
Chapter 5 p. 109, © J. Sohm/The Image Works; p. 114, 115, 116T, 116M, Courtesy Shirlee Stevens; p. 116B, 117T, Courtesy Neil A. Tanner; p. 117M, 117B, 118, Courtesy Shirlee Stevens; p. 119, 123T, Courtesy Neil A. Tanner; p. 123B, 124, 125T, 125M, Courtesy Shirlee Stevens; p. 125B, Courtesy Neil A. Tanner; p. 129, Courtesy Shirlee Stevens; p. 130, Courtesy Neil A. Tanner
Chapter 6 p. 137, © Mark Richards/PhotoEdit; p. 144, Courtesy Shirlee Stevens; p. 145, © Frank Siteman/Stock Boston; p. 150, Courtesy Shirlee Stevens
Chapter 7 p. 157, © Alán Gallegos/AG Photograph; p. 158, © Bonnie Kamin; p. 167, © Melanie Carr/Zephyr Images
Chapter 8 p. 183, © Alán Gallegos/AG Photograph; p. 191, © Bonnie Kamin; p. 209, © David Young-Wolff/PhotoEdit
Chapter 9 p. 227, © Bob Daemmrich/Stock Boston; p. 232, © Lawrence Migdale/Stock Boston; p. 234, © Ben Barnhart/Offshoot Stock; p. 238, © Bill Davila/Retna, Ltd.
Chapter 10 p. 253, © Bob Daemmrich/The Image Works; p. 257, © Michael Grecco/Stock Boston; p. 260, © John Nordell/The Image Works; p. 262, © Dorothy Littell Grecco/The Image Works
Chapter 11 p. 273, © NIH/Custom Medical Stock Photo; p. 277, © Joel Gordon; p. 281, © Christopher Brown/Stock Boston; p. 284, © Lawrence Migdale/Stock Boston
Chapter 12 p. 291, © AMC/Custom Medical Stock Photo; p. 293, © Matthew Neal McVay/Stock Boston; p. 297, © Joel Gordon; p. 303, © Richard Lord/The Image Works
Chapter 13 p. 311, © Alán Gallegos/AG Photograph; p. 313, © Amanda Merullo/Stock Boston; p. 318, © David Young-Wolff/PhotoEdit; p. 326, © Michael Newman/PhotoEdit
Chapter 14 p. 337, © Mark C. Burnett/Stock Boston; p. 340, © Mark Richards/PhotoEdit; p. 347, © Mary Kate Denny/PhotoEdit; p. 350, © Joel Gordon
Chapter 15 p. 357, © John Cleare/Offshoot Stock; p. 360, © Jennifer Bishop/Actuality, Inc.; p. 364, © Charles Harbutt/Actuality, Inc.; p. 369, © Susan Van Etten/PhotoEdit

Preface

For today's fitness-conscious student, *Fit and Well* combines the best of two worlds. In the area of physical fitness, *Fit and Well* offers expert knowledge based on the latest findings in exercise physiology and sports medicine, along with tools for self-assessment and guidelines for becoming fit. In the area of wellness, it offers accurate, current information on today's most important health-related topics and issues, again with self-tests and guidelines for achieving wellness. To create this book, we have drawn on our combined expertise and experience in exercise physiology, athletic training, personal health, scientific research, and teaching.

OUR AIMS

Our aims in writing this book can be stated simply:

- To show students that becoming fit and well greatly improves the quality of their lives
- To show students how they can become fit and well
- To motivate students to make healthy choices and to provide them with tools for change

The first of these aims means helping students see how their lives can be enhanced by a fit and well lifestyle. This book offers convincing evidence of a simple truth: To look and feel our best, to protect ourselves from degenerative diseases, and to enjoy the highest quality of life, we need to place fitness and wellness among our top priorities. *Fit and Well* makes clear both the imprudence of our modern, sedentary lifestyle and the benefits of a wellness lifestyle.

Our second aim is to give students the tools and information they need to become fit and well. This book provides students with everything they need to create their own personal fitness programs, including instructions for fitness tests, explanations of the components of fitness and guidelines for developing them, descriptions and illustrations of exercises, sample programs, and more. In addition, *Fit and Well* provides accurate, up-to-date, scientifically based information about other key topics in wellness, including nutrition, weight management, stress, cardiovascular health, cancer, drugs, alcohol, STDs, and a multitude of others.

In providing this material, we have pooled our efforts. Thomas Fahey has contributed his knowledge as an exercise physiologist, teacher, and author of numerous exercise science textbooks. Paul M. Insel and Walton T. Roth have contributed their knowledge of current topics in health as the authors of the leading personal health textbook, *Core Concepts in Health*.

Because we know this expert knowledge can be overwhelming, we have balanced the coverage of complex topics with student-friendly features designed to make the book accessible. Written in a straightforward, easy-to-read style and presented in a colorful, open format, *Fit and Well* invites the student to read, learn, and remember. Boxes, labs, tables, figures, artwork, photographs, and other features add interest to the text and highlight areas of special importance.

Our third aim is to involve students in taking responsibility for their health. *Fit and Well* makes use of interactive features to get students thinking about their own levels of physical fitness and wellness. We offer students assessment tools and laboratory activities to evaluate themselves in terms of each component of physical fitness and each major wellness area, ranging from cardiorespiratory endurance and muscular strength to heart disease, cancer, and STDs.

We also show students how they can make difficult lifestyle changes by using the principles of behavior change. Chapter 1 contains a step-by-step description of this simple but powerful tool for change. The chapter not only explains the five-step process but also offers a wealth of tips for ensuring success. Behavior management aids, including personal contracts, behavior checklists, and self-tests, appear throughout the book. *Fit and Well*'s combined emphasis on self-assessment, self-development in each area of wellness, and behavior change ensures that students not only are inspired to become fit and well but also have the tools to do so.

When students use these tools to make significant lifestyle changes, they begin to realize that they are in charge of their health—and their lives. From this realization comes a sense of competence and personal power. Perhaps our overriding aim in writing *Fit and Well* is to convey the fact that virtually everyone has the ability to understand, monitor, and make changes in his or her own level of fitness and wellness. By making healthy choices from an early age, individuals can minimize the amount of professional medical care they will ever require. Our hope is that *Fit and Well* will help people make this exciting discovery—that they have the power to shape their own futures.

CONTENT AND ORGANIZATION OF THE THIRD EDITION

The basic content of *Fit and Well* remains unchanged in the third edition. Chapter 1 provides an introduction to fitness and wellness and explains the principles of behavior change. Chapters 2–7 focus on the various areas of physical fitness. Chapter 2 provides an overview, discussing the five components of fitness, the principles of physical training, and the factors involved in designing a well-rounded, personalized exercise program. Chapter 3 provides basic information on how the cardiorespiratory system functions, how the body produces energy for exercise, and how to create a successful cardiorespiratory fitness program. Chapters 4, 5, and 6 look at muscular strength and endurance, flexibility, and body composition, respectively. Chapter 7 "puts it all together," describing the nature of a complete fitness program that develops all the components of fitness. This chapter also includes several sample exercise programs for developing overall fitness.

Chapters 8, 9, and 10 treat three important areas of wellness promotion: nutrition, weight management, and stress management, respectively. It is in these areas that individuals have some of the greatest opportunities for positive change. Chapters 11 and 12 focus on two of the most important reasons for making lifestyle changes: cardiovascular disease and cancer. Students learn the basic mechanisms of these diseases, how they are related to lifestyle, and what individuals can do to prevent them. Chapters 13 and 14 focus on other important wellness issues—addictive behaviors, including the use and abuse of tobacco, alcohol, and other drugs (Chapter 13) and sexually transmitted diseases (Chapter 14). Finally, Chapter 15 looks at four additional wellness topics: intimate relationships, aging, using the health care system, and environmental health.

For the third edition, each chapter was carefully reviewed, revised, and updated. The latest information from scientific and wellness-related research is incorporated in the text, and newly emerging topics are discussed. The following list gives a sample of some of the new and updated material included in the third edition of *Fit and Well*:

- The Surgeon General's report on physical activity and health

- Exercise recommendations from the American College of Sports Medicine
- The 1998 Dietary Reference Intakes for vitamins and minerals, including recommendations for supplements
- Energy (ATP) production for exercise
- Binge drinking on college campuses
- Stress-management techniques
- Exercise and dietary recommendations for special population groups and people with special health concerns
- Prescription drugs for weight loss
- Spiritual wellness
- Dietary fats and health
- Eating disorders
- Addictive behavior
- HIV treatment and testing
- Safe use of air bags

Research in the areas of health and wellness is ongoing, with new discoveries advances, trends, and theories reported nearly every week. For this reason, no wellness book can claim to have the final word on every topic. Yet within these limits, *Fit and Well* does present the latest available information and scientific thinking on important wellness topics. Taken together, the chapters of the book provide students with a complete, up-to-date guide to maximizing their well-being, now and through their entire lives.

FEATURES OF THE THIRD EDITION

This edition of *Fit and Well* builds on the features that attracted and held our readers' interest in previous editions. These features are designed to help students increase their understanding of the key concepts of wellness and to make better use of the book.

Laboratory Activities

To help students apply the principles of fitness and wellness to their own lives, *Fit and Well* includes **laboratory activities** for classroom use. These hands-on activities give students the opportunity to assess their current level of fitness and wellness, to create plans for changing their lifestyle to reach wellness, and to monitor their progress. They can assess their level of cardiorespiratory endurance, for example, or their daily energy balance; they can design a program to improve muscular strength or meet weight-loss goals; they can explore their risk of developing cardiovascular disease or cancer; and they can examine their attitudes and behaviors in relation to alcohol use and STDs. Labs are found at the end of each chapter; they are perforated for easy use.

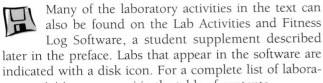 Many of the laboratory activities in the text can also be found on the Lab Activities and Fitness Log Software, a student supplement described later in the preface. Labs that appear in the software are indicated with a disk icon. For a complete list of laboratory activities, see p. xvi in the table of contents.

Illustrated Exercise Sections

To ensure that students understand how to perform important exercises and stretches, *Fit and Well* includes three separate **illustrated exercise sections,** one in Chapter 4 and two in Chapter 5. The section in Chapter 4 covers a total of 22 exercises for developing muscular strength and endurance, as performed both with free weights and on Nautilus equipment. One section in Chapter 5 presents 12 stretches for flexibility, and the other presents 11 exercises to stretch and strengthen the lower back. Each exercise is illustrated with one or more full-color photographs showing proper technique.

Sample Programs

To help students get started, Chapter 7 offers seven complete **sample programs** designed to develop overall fitness. The programs are built around four popular cardiorespiratory endurance activities: walking/jogging/running, bicycling, swimming, and—new to the third edition—in-line skating. They also include weight training and stretching exercises. Each one includes detailed information and guidelines on equipment and technique; target intensity, duration, and frequency; calorie cost of the activity; record keeping; and adjustments to make as fitness improves. The chapter also includes general guidelines for putting together a personal fitness program—setting goals; selecting activities; setting targets for intensity, duration, and frequency; making and maintaining a commitment; and recording and assessing progress.

Boxes

Boxes are used in *Fit and Well* to explore a wide range of current topics in greater detail than is possible in the text itself. Boxes fall into five different categories, each marked with a special icon and label.

 Tactics and Tips boxes distill from the text the practical advice students need to apply information to their own lives. By referring to these boxes, students can easily find information about such topics as becoming more active, rehabilitating athletic injuries, exercising in hot weather, proper weight training technique, reducing fat in the diet, helping a

friend who has an eating disorder, breathing techniques for stress reduction, responsible drinking behavior, preventing STDs, and many others.

 Critical Consumer boxes are designed to help students develop and apply critical thinking skills, thereby enabling them to make sound choices related to health and well-being. Critical Consumer boxes provide specific guidelines for choosing fitness centers, exercise footwear and equipment, and health insurance; for evaluating health news and commercial weight-loss programs; and for using food labels to make informed dietary choices.

 A Closer Look boxes highlight current topics and issues of particular interest to students. These boxes focus on such topics as benefits of physical activity, exercise machines versus free weights, diabetes, risk factors for low-back pain, health implications of obesity, preventive medicine, osteoporosis, and many others.

 Dimensions of Diversity boxes focus on the important theme of diversity. Most wellness issues are universal; we all need to exercise and eat well, for example. However, certain differences among people—based on gender, socioeconomic status, ethnicity, age, and other factors—do have important implications for wellness. Dimensions of Diversity boxes give students the opportunity to identify special wellness concerns that affect them because of who they are, as individuals or as members of a group. Topics of Dimensions of Diversity boxes include fitness for people with disabilities, gender differences in cardiorespiratory endurance, ethnic foods, and the relationship between poverty and cancer risk.

Wellness Connection boxes highlight important links among the different dimensions of wellness—physical, emotional, social/interpersonal, intellectual, spiritual, and environmental—and emphasize that all the dimensions must be developed in order for an individual to achieve optimal health and well-being. Included in Wellness Connection boxes are topics such as how exercise improves mood and mental functioning, how support group participation improves the survival of cancer patients, and how spiritual wellness affects overall health and well-being.

Vital Statistics

Vital Statistics tables and figures highlight important facts and figures in an accessible format. From tables and figures marked with the Vital Statistics label, students learn about such matters as the leading causes of death for

Americans and the factors that play a part in each one; the relationship between level of physical fitness and mortality; the most popular fitness activities; populations of special concern for obesity; incidence of cancer by site and gender; routes of HIV infection; and a wealth of other information. For students who learn best when material is displayed graphically or numerically, Vital Statistics tables and figures offer a way to grasp information quickly and directly.

Common Questions Answered

Sections called **Common Questions Answered** appear at the ends of Chapters 2–14. In these student-friendly sections, the answers to the most-often-asked questions are presented in easy-to-understand terms. Included are such questions as, Are there any stretching exercises I shouldn't do? Do I need more protein in my diet when I train with weights? If I stop weight training, will my muscles turn to fat? Does drinking benefit health? How can I safely gain weight? and, Who should have an HIV test?

Quick-Reference Appendixes

Included at the end of the book are four appendixes containing vital information in an easy-to-use format. **Appendix A, Injury Prevention and Personal Safety,** is a reference guide to preventing and treating common injuries, whether at home, at work, at play, or on the road. It includes such information as how to treat poisoning, choking, and burns; how to prevent injuries from falls, fires, and motor vehicle crashes; how to be safe when walking, jogging, and biking; and how to protect oneself from assault and rape, including acquaintance rape. It also provides information on giving emergency care when someone else's life is in danger. A chart shows proper technique for administering the Heimlich maneuver and performing rescue breathing.

Appendix B, Nutritional Content of Common Foods, allows students to assess their daily diet in terms of 11 nutrient categories, including protein, fat, saturated fat, fiber, added sugar, cholesterol, and sodium. Keyed to the software available with the text, this guide puts vital nutritional information at students' fingertips.

Appendix C, Nutritional Content of Popular Items from Fast-Food Restaurants, provides a breakdown of the nutritional content of the most commonly ordered menu items at eight popular fast-food restaurants. Especially useful are the facts about calories, fat, and sodium in different items and about the proportion of fat calories to total calories.

Appendix D, Monitoring Your Progress, is a log that enables students to record and summarize the results of the assessment tests they complete as part of the laboratory activities. With space for preprogram and postprogram assessment results, the log provides an easy way to track the progress of a behavior change program.

Built-In Behavior Change Workbook

The new built-in Behavior Change Workbook complements the lifestyle management model presented in Chapter 1. Based on the behavior change activities that appeared in the second edition, the workbook contains 15 separate activities. It guides students in developing a successful program by walking them through each of the steps of behavior change—from choosing a target behavior to completing and signing a contract. It also includes activities to help students overcome common obstacles to behavior change.

LEARNING AIDS

Several specific learning aids have been incorporated in *Fit and Well.* At the beginning of each chapter, under the heading **Looking Ahead,** five or six questions preview the main points of the chapter for the student and serve as learning objectives. Within each chapter, important terms appear in boldface type and are defined on the same page of text in a **running glossary,** helping students handle new vocabulary.

Chapter summaries offer students a concise review and a way to make sure they have grasped the most important concepts in the chapter. Also found at the end of chapters are **selected bibliographies** and sections called **For More Information.** These sections list books, journal articles, newsletters, organizations, hotlines, and Web sites that may be of interest to students, as well as further resources that can often be found on campus or in the community.

TEACHING TOOLS

Available with the third edition of *Fit and Well* is a comprehensive package of supplementary materials designed to enhance teaching and learning. Included in the package are the following items:

- Instructor's Resource Binder
- Transparency acetates
- Image Bank and PowerPoint® Presentation CD-ROM
- Students on Health and Wellness: Custom Video to Accompany *Fit and Well*
- Computerized test bank
- Nutritional analysis software
- Mayfield *Fit and Well* Web site

- Nutrition and Weight Management Journal
- Daily Fitness Log
- Lab Activities and Fitness Log Software
- Internet guide

The **Instructor's Resource Binder** contains a variety of helpful teaching materials in an easy-to-use form:

- The **Instructor's Resource Guide,** prepared for the third edition by Meredith Busby at the University of North Carolina, Chapel Hill, includes learning objectives; extended chapter outlines; lists of additional resources, including books and articles, videos, software, Internet sites, and other multimedia tools; and descriptions of the labs and transparencies.

- The new **Internet Handbook** includes a brief introduction to the Internet, a complete directory of all the sites listed in the text and Instructor's Resource Guide, guidelines for evaluating information from the Internet, and student Internet activities.

- The **Examination Questions,** completely revised and updated for the third edition by John D. Emmett, Eastern Illinois University, include over 1000 true/false, multiple choice, and essay questions.

- Over 70 **Additional Laboratory Activities,** formatted for easy duplication and distribution, supplement the labs that are included in the text.

- Over 100 **Transparency Masters and Handouts** are provided as additional lecture resources.

The set of **transparency acetates** includes 50 acetates, half of which are in color. The transparencies provide material suitable for lecture and demonstration purposes and complement the transparency masters in the Instructor's Resource Binder.

New to the third edition, the **Image Bank and Power-Point® Presentation CD-ROM** includes an image bank of over 80 images from the third edition that can be displayed, printed, or imported into presentation software. The PowerPoint slides, prepared by Christopher M. Janelle at the University of Florida, can be customized to fit any lecture. The CD-ROM also includes material from the Instructor's Resource Guide in editable format as well as versions of selected transparency acetates and masters suitable for use with presentation software. It is compatible with both IBM and Macintosh computers.

Also new to the third edition is **Students on Health and Wellness: Custom Video to Accompany *Fit and Well*.** Filmed with students at college campuses across the country, this unique video is designed to stimulate critical thinking and class discussion. The 8- to 10-minute segments focus on key wellness concerns—fitness, nutrition, stress, intimate relationships, alcohol, tobacco, STDs, and personal safety. The accompanying Instructor's

Video Guide provides summaries of each segment and discussion questions.

The **computerized test bank** (Microtest III from Chariot Software Group) allows instructors to design tests using the questions from the test item file and/or their own questions. It is available for Macintosh and Windows. **DINE Healthy software** provides an easy way for students to evaluate the nutritional value of their current diet; it also includes an exercise section that allows students to track their energy expenditures. **Other videos, software, and multimedia,** on topics such as weight training, body composition, healthy diets, and heart disease prevention, are also available.

Also new to the third edition is the **Mayfield *Fit and Well* Web site** (http://www.mayfieldpub.com/fahey). The site includes up-to-date links to useful Internet resources, student study questions that provide immediate feedback, a customized syllabus builder for instructors, and more.

Several practical items for students can be shrink-wrapped with the textbook:

- The **Nutrition and Weight Management Journal,** new to the third edition of *Fit and Well,* guides students in assessing their current diet and making appropriate changes.

- The **Daily Fitness Log** is a 48-page booklet that contains logs for students to plan and track the progress of their general fitness and weight training programs for up to 40 weeks.

- The **Lab Activities and Fitness Log Software** presents lab activities and fitness logs in an electronic format (Macintosh or Windows). The software calculates and prints out the results of selected self-assessments and fitness tests; it also includes information about behavior change and a behavior change contract. Students can print out their logs and graph the progress of their fitness program. A disk icon indicates which lab activities from the text are also found on the software; see p. xvi in the table of contents for a complete list.

- Also new to the third edition is *Mayfield's Quick View Guide to the Internet for Students of Health and Physical Education,* by Jennifer Campbell and Michael Keene at the University of Tennessee, Knoxville. It provides step-by-step instructions on how to access the Internet; how to find, evaluate, and use information about wellness; how to communicate via e-mail and chat rooms; how to use listservs and newsgroups; and many other topics.

If you have any questions concerning the book or teaching package, please call your local Mayfield sales representative or the Marketing and Sales Department at 800-433-1279. You may also e-mail Mayfield at calpoppy@mayfieldpub.com.

A NOTE OF THANKS

Many people have contributed to the production of *Fit and Well*. The book has benefited from their thoughtful commentaries, expert knowledge, and helpful suggestions. We are deeply grateful for their participation in the project.

Academic reviewers of the first edition:

Liz Applegate, University of California, Davis
E. Harold Blackwell, Lamar University
Laura L. Borsdorf, Ursinus College
Vicki Boye, Concordia College
William J. Considine, Springfield College
Arlene Crosman, Linn-Benton Community College
Robert Cross, Salisbury State University
Jean F. Dudney, San Antonio College
Eunice Goldgrabe, Concordia College
Susan J. Hibbs, Bloomsburg University of Pennsylvania
William Hottinger, Wake Forest University
Kenneth W. Kambis, College of William and Mary
Russell R. Pate, University of South Carolina
Charles J. Pelitera, Canisius College
Margaret A. Peterson, Central Oregon Community College
Jacalyn J. Robert, Texas Tech University
Rob Schurrer, Black Hills State University
Eugenia S. Scott, Butler University
Charles R. Seager, Miami-Dade Community College
J. L. Sexton, Fort Hays State University
Jack Stovall, Salisbury State University
Karen Teresa Sullivan, Marymount University
Glenn R. West, Transylvania University
Anthony Zaloga, Frostburg State University

Academic reviewers of the second edition:

Viviane L. Avant, University of North Carolina-Charlotte
Elaine H. Blair, Indiana University of Pennsylvania
Susan Brown, Johnson County Community College
Arlene Crosman, Linn-Benton Community College
Todd Crowder, U.S. Military Academy
Michael A. Dupper, University of Mississippi
Richard J. Fopeano, Rowan College of New Jersey
Mike Johnson, Berea College
Patricia A. Miller, Anderson University
Roland J. Schick, Tyler Junior College
Rob Schurrer, Black Hills State University
Mark G. Urtel, Indiana University-Purdue University-Indianapolis
Ann Ward, University of Wisconsin-Madison
Christopher J. Womack, Longwood College

Academic reviewers of the third edition text:

Phil Bogle, Eastern Michigan University
Anita D'Angelo, Florida Atlantic University
Carol A. Giroud, Monmouth University
Joyce Huner, Macomb Community College
Shahla Kahn, Kennesaw State University

Jeanne M. Mathias, Binghamton University
Steve Sansone, Chemeketa Community College
Susan T. Saylor, Shelton State Community College

Academic reviewers of the third edition teaching tools:

Mary Jo Adams, Illinois State University
Barbara Coleman, Northern Michigan University
Robert Femat, El Paso Community College
Dorothy P. Haugen, Bethel College
Elizabeth Fell Kelly, Monroe Community College
Christine M. Miskec, Mankato State University
Rob Schurrer, Black Hills State University
Lois M. Smith, University of Maryland, Eastern Shore

Special fitness consultants:

Warren D. Franke, Iowa State University
David C. Nieman, Appalachian State University
Michael Pollock, University of Florida

Technology focus group participants:

Ken Allen, University of Wisconsin, Oshkosh
Lisa Farley, Butler University
Barbara Greenburg, Butler University
Bill Johnson, Stephen F. Austin State University
Rita Nugent, University of Evansville
Patricia Dotson Pettit, Nebraska Wesleyan University
Carol Plugge, Lamar University
Steve Sedbrook, Fort Hays State University
Marilyn Strawbridge, Butler University

We are also grateful to the staff of Mayfield Publishing Company and the *Fit and Well* book team, without whose efforts the book could not have been published. Special thanks to Michele Sordi, sponsoring editor; Kirstan Price, Susan Shook, Megan Rundel, and Kate Engelberg, developmental editors; Julianna Scott Fein, production editor; Jeanne M. Schreiber, art director; Robin Mouat, art manager; Marty Granahan, permissions editor; Brian Pecko, photo researcher; Randy Hurst, manufacturing manager; Heather Collins, production assistant; Michelle Rodgerson, marketing manager; and Jay Bauer, product manager.

Thomas D. Fahey
Paul M. Insel
Walton T. Roth

Brief Contents

CHAPTER 1   *Introduction to Wellness, Fitness, and Lifestyle Management*   1

CHAPTER 2   *Basic Principles of Physical Fitness*   19

CHAPTER 3   *Cardiorespiratory Endurance*   39

CHAPTER 4   *Muscular Strength and Endurance*   69

CHAPTER 5   *Flexibility*   109

CHAPTER 6   *Body Composition*   137

CHAPTER 7   *Putting Together a Complete Fitness Program*   157

CHAPTER 8   *Nutrition*   183

CHAPTER 9   *Weight Management*   227

CHAPTER 10   *Stress*   253

CHAPTER 11   *Cardiovascular Health*   273

CHAPTER 12   *Cancer*   291

CHAPTER 13   *Substance Use and Abuse*   311

CHAPTER 14   *Sexually Transmitted Diseases*   337

CHAPTER 15   *Wellness for Life*   357

APPENDIX A   *Injury Prevention and Personal Safety*   A-1

APPENDIX B   *Nutritional Content of Common Foods*   B-1

APPENDIX C   *Nutritional Content of Popular Items from Fast-Food Restaurants*   C-1

APPENDIX D   *Monitoring Your Progress*   D-1

Behavior Change Workbook   W-1

Index   I-1

Contents

Preface   iii

CHAPTER 1

Introduction to Wellness, Fitness, and Lifestyle Management   1

WELLNESS: THE NEW HEALTH GOAL   2

The Dimensions of Wellness   2
New Opportunities, New Responsibilities   3
Behaviors That Contribute to Wellness   4
The Role of Other Factors in Wellness   7
National Wellness Goals   7

REACHING WELLNESS THROUGH LIFESTYLE MANAGEMENT   8

Getting Serious About Your Health   9
What Does It Take to Change?   9
Choosing a Target Behavior   10
Developing a Behavior Change Plan   10
Putting Your Plan into Action   12
Staying with It   13
Getting Outside Help   14
Being Fit and Well for Life   14

Summary   15
For More Information   15
Selected Bibliography   16
◆ **Lab 1-1 Lifestyle Evaluation**   17

CHAPTER 2

Basic Principles of Physical Fitness   19

PHYSICAL ACTIVITY AND EXERCISE FOR HEALTH AND FITNESS   20

Physical Activity on a Continuum   20
How Much Physical Activity Is Enough?   22

HEALTH-RELATED COMPONENTS OF PHYSICAL FITNESS   23

Cardiorespiratory Endurance   23
Muscular Strength   24
Muscular Endurance   24
Flexibility   24
Body Composition   24

PRINCIPLES OF PHYSICAL TRAINING   25

Specificity   25
Progressive Overload   25
Reversibility   26
Individual Differences   26

DESIGNING YOUR OWN EXERCISE PROGRAM   27

Assessment   27
Setting Goals   27
Choosing Activities for a Balanced Program   28
Guidelines for Training   30

Summary   31
Common Questions Answered   32
For More Information   32
Selected Bibliography   34
◆ **Lab 2-1 Calculating Your Activity Index**   35
◆ **Lab 2-2 Safety of Exercise Participation: PAR-Q**   37

CHAPTER 3

Cardiorespiratory Endurance   39

BASIC PHYSIOLOGY OF CARDIORESPIRATORY ENDURANCE EXERCISE   40

The Cardiorespiratory System   40
Energy Production   42
Exercise and the Three Energy Systems   43

BENEFITS OF CARDIORESPIRATORY ENDURANCE EXERCISE   44

Improved Cardiorespiratory Functioning   44
Improved Cellular Metabolism   45
Reduced Risk of Chronic Disease   45
Better Control of Body Fat   46
Improved Immune Function   47
Improved Psychological and Emotional Well-Being   47

ASSESSING CARDIORESPIRATORY FITNESS   47

Four Assessment Tests   48
Monitoring Your Heart Rate   49
Interpreting Your Score   49

DEVELOPING A CARDIORESPIRATORY ENDURANCE PROGRAM 50

Setting Goals 50
Choosing Sports and Activities 51
Determining Frequency of Training 51
Determining Intensity of Training 51
Determining Duration of Training 53
Warming Up and Cooling Down 53
Maintaining Cardiorespiratory Fitness 53

EXERCISE INJURIES 53

When to Call a Physician 54
Managing Minor Exercise Injuries 54
Preventing Injuries 54

Summary 56

For More Information 56

Common Questions Answered 57

Selected Bibliography 60

◆ **Lab 3-1 Assessing Your Current Level of Cardiorespiratory Endurance 61**

◆ **Lab 3-2 Developing an Exercise Program for Cardiorespiratory Endurance 67**

CHAPTER 4

Muscular Strength and Endurance 69

BENEFITS OF MUSCULAR STRENGTH AND ENDURANCE 70

Improved Performance of Physical Activities 70
Injury Prevention 70
Improved Body Composition 70
Enhanced Self-Image 70
Improved Muscle and Bone Health with Aging 70

ASSESSING MUSCULAR STRENGTH AND ENDURANCE 71

FUNDAMENTALS OF WEIGHT TRAINING 71

Physiological Effects of Weight Training 72
Types of Weight Training Exercises 73

CREATING A SUCCESSFUL WEIGHT TRAINING PROGRAM 75

Choosing Equipment: Weight Machines Versus Free Weights 75
Selecting Exercises 75
Resistance 76
Repetitions and Sets 76
The Warm-Up and Cool-Down 77
Frequency of Exercise 77
Making Progress 77
More Advanced Strength Training Programs 78
Weight Training Safety 78
Weight Training Exercises 81

Common Questions Answered 95

Summary 97

For More Information 97

Selected Bibliography 97

◆ **Lab 4-1 Assessing Your Current Level of Muscular Strength 99**

◆ **Lab 4-2 Assessing Your Current Level of Muscular Endurance 103**

◆ **Lab 4-3 Designing and Monitoring a Weight Training Program 107**

CHAPTER 5

Flexibility 109

BENEFITS OF FLEXIBILITY AND STRETCHING EXERCISES 110

Joint Health 110
Low-Back Pain and Injuries 110
Additional Potential Benefits 111
Flexibility and Lifetime Wellness 111

WHAT DETERMINES FLEXIBILITY? 111

Joint Structure 111
Muscle Elasticity and Length 111
Nervous System Activity 112

ASSESSING FLEXIBILITY 112

CREATING A SUCCESSFUL PROGRAM TO DEVELOP FLEXIBILITY 112

Types of Stretching Techniques 112
Passive and Active Stretching 113
Intensity and Duration 114
Frequency 114
Exercises to Improve Flexibility 114

PREVENTING AND MANAGING LOW-BACK PAIN 119

Function and Structure of the Spine 119
Causes of Back Pain 121
Preventing Low-Back Pain 121

Common Questions Answered 126

Summary 126

For More Information 128

Selected Bibliography 128

◆ **Lab 5-1 Assessing Your Current Level of Flexibility 129**

◆ **Lab 5-2 Creating a Personalized Program for Developing Flexibility 135**

CHAPTER 6

Body Composition 137

WHAT IS BODY COMPOSITION, AND WHY IS IT IMPORTANT? 138

Health 139
Performance of Physical Activities 141

Self-Image   141
Wellness for Life   142

ASSESSING BODY COMPOSITION   142

Body Mass Index   142
Skinfold Measurements   144
Other Methods of Measuring Body Composition   144
Assessing Body Fat Distribution   146

DETERMINING RECOMMENDED BODY WEIGHT   146

Common Questions Answered   146

Summary   147

For More Information   147

Selected Bibliography   148

◆ **Lab 6-1 Assessing Body Composition   149**

◆ **Lab 6-2 Determining Desirable Body Weight   155**

CHAPTER 7

Putting Together a Complete Fitness Program   157

DEVELOPING A PERSONAL FITNESS PLAN   158

1. Set Goals   158
2. Select Activities   158
3. Set a Target Intensity, Duration, and Frequency for Each Activity   162
4. Set Up a System of Mini-Goals and Rewards   163
5. Include Lifestyle Physical Activity in Your Program   163
6. Develop Tools for Monitoring Your Progress   163
7. Make a Commitment   164

PUTTING YOUR PLAN INTO ACTION   164

EXERCISE GUIDELINES FOR PEOPLE WITH SPECIAL HEALTH CONCERNS   167

Arthritis   167
Asthma   167
Diabetes   167
Heart Disease and Hypertension   168
Obesity   168
Osteoporosis   168

Common Questions Answered   168

Summary   169

For More Information   169

Selected Bibliography   169

SAMPLE PROGRAMS FOR POPULAR ACTIVITIES   170

Walking/Jogging/Running Sample Program   170
Bicycling Sample Program   173
Swimming Sample Program   175
In-Line Skating Sample Program   177

◆ **Lab 7-1 A Personal Fitness Program Plan and Contract   179**

◆ **Lab 7-2 Monitoring Your Program Progress   181**

CHAPTER 8

Nutrition   183

COMPONENTS OF A HEALTHY DIET   184

Proteins   184
Fats   186
Carbohydrates   190
Vitamins   192
Minerals   194
Water   194
Other Substances in Food   197

NUTRITIONAL GUIDELINES   197

Recommended Dietary Allowances (RDAs) and Dietary Reference Intakes (DRIs)   198
The Food Guide Pyramid   201
Dietary Guidelines for Americans   205
Reading Food Labels   206
The Vegetarian Alternative   206
Dietary Challenges for Special Population Groups   208

A PERSONAL PLAN: APPLYING NUTRITIONAL PRINCIPLES   210

Assessing and Changing Your Diet   211
Staying Committed to a Healthy Diet   212

Common Questions Answered   212

Summary   214

For More Information   215

Selected Bibliography   215

◆ **Lab 8-1 Your Daily Diet Versus the Food Guide Pyramid   217**

◆ **Lab 8-2 Dietary Analysis   221**

◆ **Lab 8-3 Informed Food Choices   225**

CHAPTER 9

Weight Management   227

HEALTH IMPLICATIONS OF OVERWEIGHT AND OBESITY   228

FACTORS THAT CONTRIBUTE TO A WEIGHT PROBLEM   228

Genetic Factors Versus Environmental Factors   228
Metabolism and Energy Balance   229
Other Explanations for Overweight   230

WEIGHT MANAGEMENT AND LIFESTYLE   230

Diet and Eating Habits   231
Physical Activity and Exercise   233
Thoughts and Emotions   234
Coping Strategies   235

STRATEGIES FOR LOSING WEIGHT   235

Do-It-Yourself Approaches   235
Getting Help   236
Hazards and Rewards in the Search for the "Perfect"
Body   237

EATING DISORDERS   238

Anorexia Nervosa   238
Bulimia Nervosa   239
Binge-Eating Disorder   239
Treating Eating Disorders   239

**CREATING AN INDIVIDUAL WEIGHT-MANAGEMENT
PLAN   240**

Assess Your Motivation and Commitment   240
Set Reasonable Goals   240
Assess Your Current Energy Balance   240
Increase Your Level of Physical Activity   240
Make Changes in Your Diet and Eating Habits   241
Put Your Plan into Action   241

Common Questions Answered   242

Summary   243

For More Information   243

Selected Bibliography   244

◆ **Lab 9-1 Calculating Daily Energy Balance   245**

◆ **Lab 9-2 Identifying Weight-Loss Goals and Ways
to Meet Them   249**

◆ **Lab 9-3 Eating Disorder Checklist   251**

CHAPTER 10

Stress   253

WHAT IS STRESS?   254

Physical Responses to Stressors   254
Emotional and Behavioral Responses to Stressors   256
The Stress Experience as a Whole   256

STRESS AND DISEASE   257

The General Adaptation Syndrome   257
Psychoneuroimmunology   258
Links Between Stress and Specific Conditions   258

COMMON SOURCES OF STRESS   258

Major Life Changes   258
Daily Hassles   259
College Stressors   259
Job-Related Stressors   259
Interpersonal and Social Stressors   260
Other Stressors   260

MANAGING STRESS   260

Social Support   260
Exercise   260
Nutrition   261

Time Management   261
Cognitive Techniques   262
Clear Communication   263
Relaxation Techniques   263

GETTING HELP   265

Summary   266

For More Information   266

Common Questions Answered   267

Selected Bibliography   268

◆ **Lab 10-1 Identifying Your Stressors   269**

◆ **Lab 10-2 Stress-Management Techniques   271**

CHAPTER 11

Cardiovascular Health   273

RISK FACTORS FOR CARDIOVASCULAR DISEASE   274

Major Risk Factors That Can Be Changed   274
Contributing Risk Factors That Can Be Changed   276
Major Risk Factors That Can't Be Changed   277
Possible Risk Factors Currently Being Studied   278

MAJOR FORMS OF CARDIOVASCULAR DISEASE   279

Hypertension   279
Atherosclerosis   280
Heart Disease and Heart Attacks   281
Stroke   282
Congestive Heart Failure   283

**PROTECTING YOURSELF AGAINST CARDIOVASCULAR
DISEASE   283**

Eat Heart-Healthy   283
Exercise Regularly   284
Avoid Tobacco   284
Know and Manage Your Blood Pressure   285
Know and Manage Your Cholesterol Levels   285
Develop Ways to Handle Stress and Anger and Manage
Medical Conditions   285

Common Questions Answered   285

Summary   286

For More Information   286

Selected Bibliography   288

◆ **Lab 11-1 Cardiovascular Health   289**

CHAPTER 12

Cancer   291

WHAT IS CANCER?   292

Benign Versus Malignant Tumors   292
How Cancer Spreads: Metastasis   292

COMMON CANCERS   **292**

Lung Cancer   292
Colon and Rectal Cancer   294
Breast Cancer   294
Prostate Cancer   296
Cancers of the Female Reproductive Tract   296
Skin Cancer   297
Oral Cancer   298
Testicular Cancer   298
Other Cancers   298

THE CAUSES OF CANCER   **300**

The Role of DNA   300
Dietary Factors in Cancer   302
Inactivity   304
Carcinogens in the Environment   304
Microorganisms   304

PREVENTING CANCER   **305**

Common Questions Answered   *306*

Summary   *307*

For More Information   *307*

Selected Bibliography   *307*

◆ **Lab 12-1 Risk Factors for Cancer**   **309**

CHAPTER 13

Substance Use and Abuse   *311*

ADDICTIVE BEHAVIOR   **312**

What Is Addiction?   312
The Development of Addiction   312
Examples of Addictive Behaviors   313

PSYCHOACTIVE DRUGS   **313**

Drug Use, Abuse, and Dependence   314
Who Uses (and Abuses) Drugs?   316
Treatment for Drug Abuse   316
Preventing Drug Abuse   317
The Role of Drugs in Your Life   317

ALCOHOL   **317**

Chemistry and Metabolism   318
Immediate Effects of Alcohol   318
Effects of Chronic Use of Alcohol   318
Alcohol Abuse   320
Binge Drinking   320
Alcoholism   321
Drinking and Responsibility   322

TOBACCO   **322**

Nicotine Addiction   322
Health Hazards of Tobacco   323
Environmental Tobacco Smoke   324
Smoking and Pregnancy   326

Action Against Tobacco   327
Giving Up Tobacco   327

Common Questions Answered   *328*

Summary   *330*

For More Information   *330*

Selected Bibliography   *331*

◆ **Lab 13-1 Is Alcohol a Problem in Your Life?**   **333**

◆ **Lab 13-2 For Smokers Only: Why Do You Smoke?**   **335**

CHAPTER 14

Sexually Transmitted Diseases   *337*

HIV INFECTION AND AIDS   **338**

What Is HIV Infection?   338
Transmitting the Virus   338
Symptoms and Diagnosis   340
Treatment   342
Prevention   343

CHLAMYDIA   **343**

Symptoms   343
Diagnosis and Treatment   344

GONORRHEA   **344**

Symptoms   345
Diagnosis and Treatment   346

PELVIC INFLAMMATORY DISEASE   **346**

Symptoms   346
Diagnosis and Treatment   346

GENITAL WARTS   **346**

Symptoms   346
Diagnosis and Treatment   346

GENITAL HERPES   **347**

Symptoms   347
Diagnosis and Treatment   348

HEPATITIS B   **349**

Symptoms   349
Diagnosis and Treatment   349

SYPHILIS   **349**

Symptoms   349
Diagnosis and Treatment   350

OTHER STDS   **350**

WHAT YOU CAN DO   **350**

Education   350
Prevention   351
Diagnosis and Treatment   351

Common Questions Answered   *351*

Summary 352

For More Information 352

Selected Bibliography 354

◆ Lab 14-1 Behaviors and Attitudes Related to STDs 355

CHAPTER 15

Wellness for Life 357

DEVELOPING SUCCESSFUL INTERPERSONAL RELATIONSHIPS 358

Forming Relationships 358
Communication 359
Marriage 361
Successful Relationships, Successful Families 362

MEETING THE CHALLENGES OF AGING 362

What Happens as You Age? 362
Life-Enhancing Measures 362

USING THE HEALTH CARE SYSTEM INTELLIGENTLY 364

Managing Medical Problems 365
Getting the Most Out of Medical Care 365

ENVIRONMENTAL HEALTH 367

Population Growth 368
Pollution 369
What Can You Do? 370

FIT AND WELL FOR LIFE 370

Summary 371

For More Information 371

Selected Bibliography 372

◆ Lab 15-1 Wellness Profile 373

APPENDIX A *Injury Prevention and Personal Safety* A-1

APPENDIX B *Nutritional Content of Common Foods* B-1

APPENDIX C *Nutritional Content of Popular Items from Fast-Food Restaurants* C-1

APPENDIX D *Monitoring Your Progress* D-1

BEHAVIOR CHANGE WORKBOOK W-1

Index I-1

BOXES

TACTICS AND TIPS

Maximizing Your Chances of Success 14

Becoming More Active 23
Rehabilitation Following a Minor Athletic Injury 55
Exercising in Hot Weather 58
Safe Weight Training 79
Safe Stretching 114
Avoiding Low-Back Pain 122
Stretches to Avoid 127
Dodging Common Exercise Pitfalls 166
Setting Goals for Fat, Protein, and Carbohydrate Intake 189
Keeping the Nutrient Value in Food 194
Judging Serving Sizes 203
Reducing the Fat in Your Diet 206
Eating Strategies for College Students 210
Guidelines for Healthier Meat Choices 214
Avoiding Hidden Calories 231
A Lifestyle for Weight Management 235
If Someone You Know Has an Eating Disorder . . . 240
Strategies for Managing Your Weight 241
Overcoming Insomnia 259
Realistic Self-Talk 263
Breathing for Relaxation 266
What to Do in the Event of a Heart Attack 283
A Heart-Healthy Lifestyle 283
Breast Self-Examination 295
Protecting Your Skin from the Sun 299
Testicle Self-Examination 300
Incorporating More Cancer-Fighters into Your Diet 302
What to Do Instead of Drugs 317
Protecting Yourself on the Road 321
Drinking Behavior and Responsibility 323
Avoiding Environmental Tobacco Smoke 327
Preventing HIV Infection and Other STDs 343
Male Condoms 348
Being a Good Friend 359
Guidelines for Effective Communication 361
What You Can Do for the Environment 370

CRITICAL CONSUMER

Choosing a Fitness Center 33
Choosing Equipment for Fitness and Sport 59
Choosing Exercise Footwear 164
Using Food Labels 207
How to Evaluate Commercial Weight-Loss Programs 237
Evaluating Health News 287
Choosing How to Quit 328
Getting an HIV Test 353
Managing with Managed Care 368

DIMENSIONS OF DIVERSITY

Wellness Issues for Diverse Populations 7
Fitness and Disability 26
Gender Differences in Cardiorespiratory Endurance 51
Gender Differences in Muscular Strength 71
Ethnic Foods 211

Stress-Management Techniques from Around the World 264
African Americans and CVD 279
Can Poverty Cause Cancer? 301
Women and Alcohol 322
HIV Infection Around the World 341
Multicultural Wisdom About Aging 363

WELLNESS CONNECTION
A Runner's Rationale 21
Exercise and the Mind 47
Exercise and Body Image 141
Building Social Support 261
Religion and Wellness 278
Support Groups and Cancer Survival 296
Spiritual Wellness 363
Nature and the Human Spirit 369

A CLOSER LOOK
Benefits of Regular Physical Activity 6
Ten Warning Signs of Wellness 15
Benefits of Cardiorespiratory Endurance Exercise 48
Activities and Sports for Developing Cardiorespiratory Endurance 52
Exercise Machines Versus Free Weights 75
A Sample Weight Training Program for General Fitness 77
Risk Factors for Low-Back Pain 121
Negative Health Consequences of Obesity 139
Diabetes 140
Osteoporosis 196
Strategies of Successful Weight Managers 233
The Benefits of Quitting Smoking 325
Preventive Medicine for Healthy Adults 367

BEHAVIOR CHANGE WORKBOOK ACTIVITIES

PART 1   DEVELOPING A PLAN FOR BEHAVIOR CHANGE AND COMPLETING A CONTRACT
1. Choosing a Target Behavior W-1
2. Gathering Information About Your Target Behavior W-2
3. Monitoring Your Current Patterns of Behavior W-2
4. Setting Goals W-4
5. Examining Your Attitudes About Your Target Behavior W-4
6. Choosing Rewards W-5
7. Breaking Behavior Chains W-5
8. Completing a Contract for Behavior Change W-8

PART 2   OVERCOMING OBSTACLES TO BEHAVIOR CHANGE
9. Building Motivation and Commitment W-10
10. Managing Your Time Successfully W-11
11. Developing Realistic Self-Talk W-12
12. Involving the People Around You W-13
13. Dealing with Feelings W-14
14. Overcoming Peer Pressure: Communicating Assertively W-15
15. Maintaining Your Program over Time W-16

LABORATORY ACTIVITIES

Lab 1-1 Lifestyle Evaluation 17
Lab 2-1 Calculating Your Activity Index 35
Lab 2-2 Safety of Exercise Participation: PAR-Q 37
Lab 3-1 Assessing Your Current Level of Cardiorespiratory Endurance 61
Lab 3-2 Developing an Exercise Program for Cardiorespiratory Endurance 67
Lab 4-1 Assessing Your Current Level of Muscular Strength 99
Lab 4-2 Assessing Your Current Level of Muscular Endurance 103
Lab 4-3 Designing and Monitoring a Weight Training Program 107
Lab 5-1 Assessing Your Current Level of Flexibility 129
Lab 5-2 Creating a Personalized Program for Developing Flexibility 135
Lab 6-1 Assessing Body Composition 149
Lab 6-2 Determining Desirable Body Weight 155
Lab 7-1 A Personal Fitness Program Plan and Contract 179
Lab 7-2 Monitoring Your Program Progress 181
Lab 8-1 Your Daily Diet Versus the Food Guide Pyramid 217
Lab 8-2 Dietary Analysis 221
Lab 8-3 Informed Food Choices 225
Lab 9-1 Calculating Daily Energy Balance 245
Lab 9-2 Identifying Weight-Loss Goals and Ways to Meet Them 249
Lab 9-3 Eating Disorder Checklist 251
Lab 10-1 Identifying Your Stressors 269
Lab 10-2 Stress-Management Techniques 271
Lab 11-1 Cardiovascular Health 289
Lab 12-1 Risk Factors for Cancer 308
Lab 13-1 Is Alcohol a Problem in Your Life? 333
Lab 13-2 For Smokers Only: Why Do You Smoke? 335
Lab 14-1 Behaviors and Attitudes Related to STDs 355
Lab 15-1 Wellness Profile 373

▣ Indicates a laboratory activity that is also found on the Lab Activities and Fitness Log Software.

Introduction to Wellness, Fitness, and Lifestyle Management

LOOKING AHEAD

After reading this chapter, you should be able to answer these questions about fitness, wellness, and behavior change:

- What is wellness?

- What are the major health problems in the United States today, and what are their principal causes?

- What behaviors are part of a fit and well lifestyle?

- What is physical fitness, and why is it important to wellness?

- What are the components of a behavior change program?

A first-year college student resolves to meet the challenge of making new friends. A long-sedentary senior starts riding her bike to school every day instead of taking the bus. A busy graduate student volunteers to plant trees in a blighted inner-city neighborhood. What do these people have in common? Each is striving for optimal health and well-being. Not satisfied to be merely free of major illness, these individuals want more. They want to live life actively, energetically, and fully, in a state of optimal personal, interpersonal, and environmental well-being. They have taken charge of their health and are on the path to wellness.

WELLNESS: THE NEW HEALTH GOAL

Wellness is an expanded idea of health. Many people think of health as being just the absence of physical disease. But wellness transcends this concept of health, as when individuals with serious illnesses or disabilities rise above their physical or mental limitations to live rich, meaningful, vital lives. Some aspects of health are determined by your genes, your age, and other factors that may be beyond your control. But true wellness is largely determined by the decisions you make about how to live your life. In this book, we will use the terms "health" and "wellness" interchangeably to mean the ability to live life fully—with vitality and meaning.

The Dimensions of Wellness

No matter what your age or health status, you can optimize your health in each of the following six interrelated dimensions. Wellness in any dimension is not a static goal but a dynamic process of change and growth (Figure 1-1).

Physical Wellness Optimal physical health requires eating well, exercising, avoiding harmful habits, making responsible decisions about sex, learning about and recognizing the symptoms of disease, getting regular medical and dental checkups, and taking steps to prevent injuries at home, on the road, and on the job. The habits you develop and the decisions you make today will largely determine not only how many years you will live, but the quality of your life during those years.

Emotional Wellness Optimism, trust, self-esteem, self-acceptance, self-confidence, self-control, satisfying relationships, and an ability to share feelings are just some of the qualities and aspects of emotional wellness. Maintaining emotional wellness requires monitoring and exploring your thoughts and feelings, identifying obstacles to emotional well-being, and finding solutions to emotional problems, with the help of a therapist if necessary.

Intellectual Wellness The hallmarks of intellectual health include an openness to new ideas, a capacity to question and think critically, and the motivation to master new skills, as well as a sense of humor, creativity, and curiosity. An active mind is essential to overall wellness; it detects problems, finds solutions, and directs behavior. People who enjoy intellectual wellness never stop learning. They seek out and relish new experiences and challenges.

Spiritual Wellness To enjoy spiritual health is to possess a set of guiding beliefs, principles, or values that give meaning and purpose to your life, especially during difficult times. Spiritual wellness involves the capacity for love, compassion, forgiveness, altruism, joy, and fulfillment. It is an antidote to cynicism, anger, fear, anxiety, self-absorption, and pessimism. Spirituality transcends the individual and can be a common bond among people. Organized religions help many people develop spiritual health. Many others find meaning and purpose in their lives on their own—through nature, art, meditation, political action, or good works.

Interpersonal and Social Wellness Satisfying relationships are basic to both physical and emotional health. We need to have mutually loving, supportive people in our lives. Developing interpersonal wellness means learning good communication skills, developing the capacity for intimacy, and cultivating a support network of caring friends and/or family members. Social wellness requires participating in and contributing to your community, country, and world.

Environmental, or Planetary, Wellness Increasingly, personal health depends on the health of the planet—from the safety of the food supply to the degree of violence in a society. Other examples of environmental threats to health are ultraviolet radiation in sunlight, air and water pollution, lead in old house paint, and second-hand tobacco smoke in indoor air. Wellness requires learning about and protecting yourself against such hazards—and doing what you can to reduce or eliminate them, either on your own or with others.

The six dimensions of wellness interact continuously, influencing and being influenced by one another. Making a change in one dimension often affects some or all of the others. For example, regular exercise (developing the

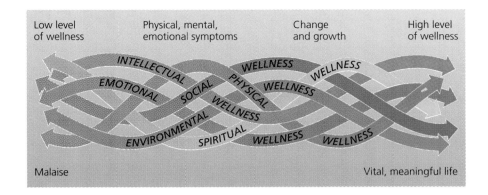

Figure 1-1   The wellness continuum.
Wellness is composed of six interrelated dimensions, all of which must be developed in order to achieve overall wellness.

physical dimension of wellness) can increase feelings of well-being and self-esteem (emotional wellness), which in turn can increase feelings of confidence in social interactions and achievements at work or school (interpersonal and social wellness). Maintaining good health is a dynamic process, and increasing your level of wellness in one area of life often influences many others. Some of the key links among different dimensions of wellness are highlighted in this text in boxes labeled Wellness Connection.

New Opportunities, New Responsibilities

Wellness is a relatively recent concept. A century ago, people considered themselves lucky just to survive to adulthood. A child born in 1890, for example, could expect to live only about 40 years. Many people died as a result of common **infectious diseases** and poor environmental conditions (unrefrigerated food, poor sanitation, air and water pollution). However, over the past 100 years, the average life expectancy has nearly doubled, thanks largely to the development of vaccines and antibiotics to prevent and fight infectious diseases and to public health campaigns to improve environmental conditions.

But a different set of diseases has emerged as our major health threat—**chronic diseases** such as cardiovascular disease (CVD), cancer, hypertension (high blood pressure), diabetes, osteoporosis, and cirrhosis of the liver. Of these diseases, the most widespread and devastating are heart disease, cancer, and stroke, the three leading causes of death for Americans today (Table 1-1). Treating these and other chronic, degenerative diseases is enormously expensive and extremely difficult. The best treatment for these diseases is prevention—people having a greater awareness about health and about taking care of their bodies.

The good news is that people do have some control over whether they develop CVD, cancer, and other chronic diseases. People make choices every day that either increase or decrease their risks for these diseases—choices involving things such as exercise, diet, and smoking and drinking habits. When researchers look at the actual behavioral and environmental causes of death in

A lifetime of healthy choices makes it possible for this man to live life actively, energetically, and fully. To enjoy health and vigor later in life, people have to cultivate wellness while they are young.

the United States, it becomes clear that individuals can profoundly influence their own health risks (Table 1-2). This knowledge has led to the realization that wellness cannot be prescribed; physicians and other health care professionals can do little more than provide information, advice, and encouragement—the rest is up to each of us.

TABLE 1-1 | *Leading Causes of Death in the United States*

Rank	Cause of Death	Number of Deaths	Percent of Total Deaths	Female/Male Ratio*	Lifestyle Factors
1	Heart disease	733,834	31.6	50/50	D I S A
2	Cancer	544,278	23.4	48/52	D I S A
3	Stroke	160,431	6.9	61/39	D I S
4	Chronic obstructive lung diseases	106,146	4.6	48/52	S
5	Unintentional injuries	93,874	4.0	34/66	S A
	Motor vehicle–related	(43,449)	(1.9)	(33/67)	
	All others	(50,425)	(2.2)	(35/65)	
6	Pneumonia and influenza	82,579	3.6	54/46	S
7	Diabetes mellitus	61,559	2.7	56/44	D I
8	HIV infection	32,655	1.4	7/93	
9	Suicide	30,862	1.3	19/81	A
10	Chronic liver disease and cirrhosis	25,135	1.1	34/66	A
	All causes	2,322,421			

Key: D Cause of death in which diet plays a part
 I Cause of death in which an inactive lifestyle plays a part
 S Cause of death in which smoking plays a part
 A Cause of death in which excessive alcohol consumption plays a part

*Ratio of females to males who died of each cause. For example, an equal number of women and men died of heart disease, but only about half as many women as men died of motor-vehicle-related injuries.

SOURCES: National Center for Health Statistics. 1997. Births and deaths: United States, 1996. *Monthly Vital Statistics Report* 46(1S2): 5. National Center for Health Statistics. 1997. Report of final mortality statistics, 1995. *Monthly Vital Statistics Report* 45(11): 23–25.

TABLE 1-2 | *Actual Causes of Death in the United States*

Cause	Approximate Number of Deaths per Year
Tobacco	400,000
Diet and activity habits	300,000
Alcohol	100,000
Microbial agents	90,000
Toxic agents	60,000
Secondhand tobacco smoke	50,000
Motor vehicle crashes	40,000
Firearms	35,000
Sexual behavior	30,000
Illegal drug use	20,000

SOURCES: American Heart Association. National Center for Health Statistics. 1997. Births and deaths: United States, 1996. *Monthly Vital Statistics Report* 46(1S2): 5. McGinnis, J. M., and W. H. Foege. 1993. Actual causes of death in the United States. *Journal of the American Medical Association* 270(18): 2207–2212.

This chapter provides an overview of a lifestyle that promotes wellness and describes a method that can help you make lasting changes in your life to promote good health. The chapters that follow provide more detailed information about fitness, nutrition, and other components of a wellness lifestyle. The book as a whole is designed to be used in a very real way, to help you take charge of your behavior and improve the quality of your life—to become fit and well.

Behaviors That Contribute to Wellness

A lifestyle based on good choices and healthy behaviors maximizes the quality of life. It helps people avoid disease, remain strong and fit, and maintain their physical and mental health as long as they live (Figure 1-2). The most important behaviors and habits are described in the following sections.

Be Physically Active Perhaps the single most important choice individuals can make to promote wellness is to be physically active. Unfortunately, a sedentary lifestyle is common among Americans today: More than 60% of Americans are not regularly physically active, and 25% are not active at all. The human body is designed to work best when it is active. It readily adapts to nearly any level of activity and exertion; in fact, **physical fitness** is defined as the ability of the body to adapt to the demands and stresses of physical effort. The more we ask of our bodies—our muscles, bones, heart, lungs—the stronger and more fit they become. However, the reverse is also

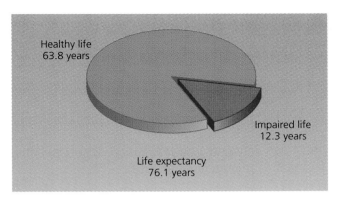

VITAL STATISTICS

Figure 1-2 Quantity of life versus quality of life. Due to improved medical and environmental practices, the average life expectancy of Americans increased greatly during the twentieth century. But quality of life is also an important consideration, and the typical American currently maintains good health for only about 85% of his or her life. Developing and maintaining a healthy lifestyle can both increase longevity and decrease the number of years of unhealthy life. SOURCES: U.S. Department of Health and Human Services. 1997. *Healthy People 2000 Review, 1997.* Hyattsville, Md.: Public Health Service, DHHS Publication No. (PHS) 98-1256. National Center for Health Statistics. 1997. Births and deaths: United States, 1996. *Monthly Vital Statistics Report* 46(1S2): 31.

true: The less we ask of them, the less they can do. When our bodies are not kept active, they begin to deteriorate. Bones lose their density, joints stiffen, muscles become weak, and cellular energy systems begin to degenerate. To be truly well, human beings must be active.

The benefits of physical activity are both physical and mental, immediate and long term (see the box "Benefits of Regular Physical Activity"). In the short term, being physically fit makes it easier to do everyday tasks, such as lifting; it provides reserve strength for emergencies; and it helps people look and feel good. In the long term, being physically fit confers protection against chronic diseases and lowers the risk of dying prematurely (Figure 1-3). Physically active individuals are less likely to develop or die from heart disease, respiratory disease, high blood pressure, cancer, diabetes, and osteoporosis. Their cardiorespiratory systems tend to resemble those of people 10 or more years younger than themselves. As they get older, they may be able to avoid weight gain, muscle and bone loss, fatigue, and other problems associated with aging. With healthy hearts, strong muscles, lean bodies, and a repertoire of physical skills they can call on for recreation and enjoyment, fit people can maintain their physical and mental well-being throughout their lives.

Choose a Healthy Diet In addition to being sedentary, many Americans have a diet that is too high in calories, fat, and added sugars and too low in fiber and complex carbohydrates. This diet is linked to a number of chronic diseases, including heart disease, stroke, and certain kinds of cancer. A healthy diet promotes wellness in both the short and long term. It provides necessary nutrients and sufficient energy without also providing too much of the dietary substances linked to diseases.

Maintain a Healthy Body Weight Overweight and obesity are associated with a number of disabling and potentially fatal conditions and diseases, including heart disease, cancer, and diabetes. Healthy body weight is an important part of wellness—but short-term dieting is not part of a fit and well lifestyle. Maintaining a healthy body weight requires a lifelong commitment to regular exercise, a healthy diet, and effective stress management.

Manage Stress Effectively Many people cope with stress by eating, drinking, or smoking too much. Others don't deal with it at all. In the short term, inappropriate stress management can lead to fatigue, sleep disturbances, and other unpleasant symptoms. Over longer periods of time, poor management of stress can lead to less efficient functioning of the immune system and increased susceptibility to disease. There *are* effective ways to handle stress, and learning to incorporate them into daily life is an important part of a fit and well lifestyle.

Avoid Use of Tobacco and Other Drugs and Use Alcohol Wisely, If at All Tobacco use is associated with 6 of the top 10 causes of death in the United States; it kills more Americans each year than any other behavioral or environmental factor (see Table 1-2). A hundred years ago, before cigarette smoking was widespread, lung cancer was considered a rare disease. Today, with nearly 25% of the American population smoking, lung cancer is the most common cause of cancer death among both men and women and one of the leading causes of death overall.

Excess alcohol consumption is linked to 5 of the top 10 causes of death. It is an especially important factor in death and disability among young people through its association with **unintentional injuries** (such as car crashes and drownings) and violence. Illegal drug use is responsible for an additional 20,000 deaths each year in the United States.

Protect Yourself from Disease and Injury The most effective way of dealing with disease and injury is to prevent them. Many of the lifestyle strategies discussed here—being physically active, managing body weight, and so on—help protect you against chronic illnesses. In addition, specific steps can be taken to avoid infectious diseases, particularly those that are sexually transmitted.

physical fitness The ability of the body to respond or adapt to the demands and stress of physical effort. **TERMS**

unintentional injury An injury that occurs without harm being intended.

Benefits of Regular Physical Activity

Regular physical activity improves physical and mental health in the following ways:

- Reduces the risk of dying prematurely from all causes
- Reduces the risk of dying from heart disease
- Reduces the risk of developing diabetes
- Reduces the risk of developing high blood pressure
- Helps reduce blood pressure in people who already have high blood pressure
- Reduces the risk of developing colon cancer
- Reduces feelings of depression and anxiety
- Helps control weight, develop lean muscle, and reduce body fat

- Helps build and maintain healthy bones, muscles, and joints
- Helps older adults become stronger and better able to move about without falling
- Promotes psychological well-being

(The changes and benefits that occur in response to physical activity are discussed in Chapters 2–6.)

SOURCE: U.S. Department of Health and Human Services. 1996. *Physical Activity and Health: A Report of the Surgeon General.* Department of Health and Human Services, Centers for Disease Control and Prevention, National Center for Chronic Disease Prevention and Health Promotion.

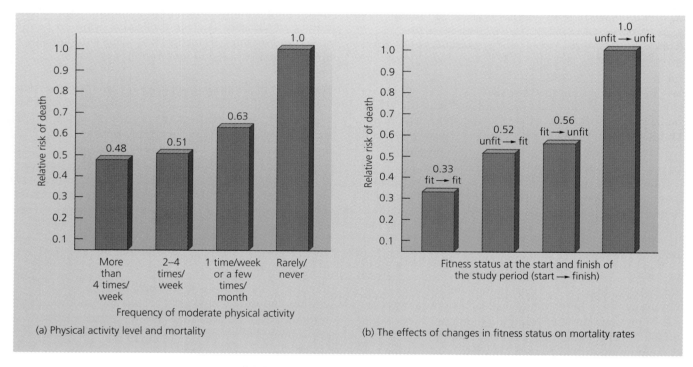

(a) Physical activity level and mortality

(b) The effects of changes in fitness status on mortality rates

VITAL STATISTICS

Figure 1-3   Physical activity, physical fitness, and mortality.   Many long-term research studies have clearly shown the benefits of regular physical activity. (a) A study that followed more than 40,000 postmenopausal women for 7 years found a strong relationship between physical activity and relative risk of death: the more frequent the activity, the lower the relative risk of death. (b) A study of more than 9500 men that tracked changes in fitness level for periods of 1–18 years found that fitness level was closely tied to risk of death: The lowest death rate was seen in men who were physically fit at the start and end of the study period; the highest death rate was in men who were unfit throughout the study. Men who improved from unfit to fit during the study experienced a 44% reduction in mortality risk relative to men who remained unfit.   SOURCES: Kushi, L. H., et al. 1997. Physical activity and mortality in postmenopausal women. *Journal of the American Medical Association* 277(16): 1287–1292. Blair, S. N., et al. 1995. Changes in physical fitness and all-cause mortality: A prospective study of healthy and unhealthy men. *Journal of the American Medical Association* 273(14):1093–1098

When it comes to striving for wellness, most differences among people are insignificant. We all need to exercise, eat well, and manage stress. We need to know how to protect ourselves from heart disease, cancer, sexually transmitted diseases, and injuries.

But some of our differences—differences among us both as individuals and as members of groups—do have implications for wellness. Some of us, for example, have grown up eating foods that increase our risk of obesity or heart disease. Some of us have inherited predispositions for certain health problems, such as osteoporosis or high cholesterol levels. These health-related differences among individuals and groups can be biological—determined genetically—or cultural—acquired as patterns of behavior through daily interactions with our family, community, and society. Many health conditions are a function of biology and culture combined.

When we talk about wellness issues as they relate to diverse populations, we face two related dangers. The first is the danger of stereotyping, of talking about people as groups rather than as individuals. The second is that of overgeneralizing, of ignoring the extensive biological and cultural diversity that exists among people who may be grouped together because of their gender, socioeconomic status, or ethnicity. Every person is an individual with her or his own unique genetic endowment as well as unique experiences in life. However, many of these influences are shared with others of similar genetic and cultural backgrounds. Information about group similarities relating to wellness issues can be useful; for example, it can alert people to areas that may be of special concern for them and their families.

Wellness-related differences among groups can be identified and described along several different dimensions, including the following:

- *Gender.* Men and women have different life expectancies and different incidences of many diseases, including heart disease, cancer, and osteoporosis. They also differ in body composition and certain aspects of physical performance.

- *Socioeconomic status.* People with low income levels have higher rates of many conditions and diseases, including overweight, alcohol and drug abuse, heart disease, and HIV infection.

- *Ethnicity.* A genetic predisposition for a particular health problem can be linked to ethnicity as a result of each ethnic group's relatively distinct history. Diabetes is more prevalent among individuals of Native American or Latino heritage, for example, and African Americans have higher rates of hypertension. Ethnic groups may also vary in other ways that relate to wellness: traditional diets; patterns of family and interpersonal relationships; and attitudes toward using tobacco, alcohol, and other drugs, to name just a few.

These are just some of the "dimensions of diversity"—differences among people and groups that are associated with different wellness concerns. Other factors, too, such as age, educational attainment, and disability, can present challenges as an individual strives for wellness. In this book, topics and issues relating to wellness that affect different American populations are given special consideration in boxes labeled Dimensions of Diversity. All of these discussions are designed to deepen our understanding of the concepts of wellness and vitality in the context of ever-growing diversity.

These diseases are preventable through responsible sexual behavior, another component of a fit and well lifestyle.

Unintentional injuries are the leading cause of death for people age 45 and under, but they, too, can be prevented. Learning and adopting safe, responsible behaviors is also part of a fit and well lifestyle.

Other important behaviors in a fit and well lifestyle include developing meaningful relationships, planning ahead for successful aging, becoming knowledgable about the health care system, and acting responsibly in relation to the environment. Lab 1-1 will help you evaluate your behaviors as they relate to wellness.

The Role of Other Factors in Wellness

Of course, behavior isn't the only factor involved in good health. Heredity, the environment, and access to adequate health care are other important influences. These factors can interact in ways that raise or lower the quality of a person's life and the risk of developing particular diseases. For example, a sedentary lifestyle combined with a ge-

netic predisposition for diabetes can greatly increase a person's risk for developing the disease. If this person also lacks adequate health care, he or she is much more likely to suffer dangerous complications from diabetes and have a lower quality of life. (For a discussion of how different factors affect people as members of groups, see the box "Wellness Issues for Diverse Populations.")

But in many cases, behavior can tip the balance toward health even if heredity or environment is a negative factor. Breast cancer, for example, can run in families, but it also may be associated with overweight and a sedentary lifestyle. A woman with a family history of breast cancer is less likely to die from the disease if she controls her weight, exercises, performs regular breast self-exams, and consults with her physician about mammograms. By taking appropriate action, this woman can influence the effects of heredity on her health.

National Wellness Goals

You may think of health and wellness as personal concerns, goals that you strive for on your own for your own

TABLE 1-3 *Selected* Healthy People 2000 *Objectives*

Objective	Estimate of Current Status	Goal
Increase the proportion of people age 6 and over who engage regularly, preferably daily, in light to moderate physical activity for at least 30 minutes per day.	24% (5 times/week) 17% (7 times/week)	30% 30%
Increase the consumption of fruits and vegetables.	4 servings/day	5 servings/day
Reduce the prevalence of overweight among people age 20 and over.	35%	20%
Reduce the proportion of people age 18 and over who experience adverse health effects from stress each year.	39.2%	Less than 35%
Reduce the prevalence of cigarette smoking among people age 18 and over.	26%	15%
Reduce the proportion of college students engaging in recent occasions of heavy drinking of alcoholic beverages.	40%	32%
Increase the proportion of sexually active, unmarried people who used a condom at last sexual intercourse.	25%	50%
Increase the use of helmets by bicyclists.	17.6%	50%

SOURCES: U.S. Department of Health and Human Services. 1990. *Healthy People 2000: National Health Promotion and Disease Prevention Objectives.* Washington, D.C.: U.S. Government Printing Office, DHHS Pub. (PHS) 91-50212. National Center for Health Statistics. 1997. *Healthy People 2000 Review, 1997.* Hyattsville, Md.: Public Health Service, DHHS Pub. (PHS) 98-1256.

benefit. But the U.S. government also has a vital interest in the health of all Americans. A healthy population is the nation's greatest resource, the source of its vigor and wealth. Poor health, in contrast, drains the nation's resources and raises national health care costs. As the embodiment of our society's values, the federal government also has a humane interest in people's health.

The U.S. government's national Healthy People initiative seeks to prevent unnecessary disease and disability and to achieve a better quality of life for all Americans. Healthy People reports, published first in 1980 and revised every decade, include national health goals based on 10-year agendas. Each report includes both broad goals—such as increasing the span of healthy life for all Americans and reducing health disparities among special populations within our society—and specific, measurable targets in many different priority areas that relate to wellness (physical activity, nutrition, and so on). Healthy People targets serve as the basis for national monitoring and tracking of health status, health risks, and use of preventive services. They encompass individual actions as well as larger-scale changes in environmental and medical services.

Examples of individual health promotion objectives from *Healthy People 2000,* as well as estimates of how we are tracking toward the goals, appear in Table 1-3. (For information on the Healthy People initiative and the development of *Healthy People 2010* objectives, contact the Healthy People office or Web sites listed in the For More Information section at the end of the chapter.) As you can see, the objectives are tied closely to the wellness lifestyle described in this chapter. The principal topics covered in this book parallel the priority concerns of the Healthy People initiative, and the approach of *Fit and Well* is based on the initiative's premise that personal responsibility is a key to achieving wellness.

REACHING WELLNESS THROUGH LIFESTYLE MANAGEMENT

The picture drawn here of a fit and well lifestyle may seem complex and out of reach to you right now. Many people fall into a lifestyle that puts them at risk. Some aren't aware of the damage they're doing, others don't want to or know how to change, and still others want to change but can't get started. These are all real problems, but they aren't insurmountable. If they were, there would be no ex-smokers, recovering alcoholics, or people who have successfully lost excess body weight. People can and do make difficult changes in their lives.

Taking big steps toward wellness may at first seem like too much work, but as you make progress, it gets easier. At first you'll be rewarded with a greater sense of control over your life, a feeling of empowerment, higher self-esteem, and more joy. These benefits will encourage you to make further improvements. Over time, you'll come to know what wellness feels like—more energy; greater vitality; deeper feelings of curiosity, interest, and enjoyment; and a higher quality of life.

This section introduces the general process of behavior change and highlights the decisions and challenges you'll face at each stage. For additional help and advice, work through the activities in the Behavior Change Workbook at the end of the text.

Getting Serious About Your Health

Before you can start changing a wellness-related behavior, you have to know that the behavior is problematic and that you *can* change it. To make good decisions, you need information about relevant topics and issues. You also need knowledge about yourself—how you relate to the wellness lifestyle described in this chapter and what strengths you can draw on to change your behavior and improve your health. While knowledge is a necessary ingredient, it isn't usually enough to make you act. Millions of smokers stick to their habit, for example, even though they know it's bad for their health.

Many people start to consider changing a behavior when they get help from others. An observation from a friend, family member, or physician can help you see yourself as others do and may get you thinking about your behavior in a new way. For example, Jason has been getting a lot of stomachaches lately. His girlfriend, Anna, notices other changes as well and suggests that the stress of classes plus a part-time job and serving as president of the school radio station might be causing some of Jason's problems. Jason never thought much about trying to control the stressors in his life, but with encouragement from Anna he starts noticing what events trigger stress for him.

Landmark events can also get you thinking about behavior change. A birthday, the birth of a child, or the death of someone close to you can be a powerful motivator for thinking seriously about behaviors that affect wellness. New information can also help you get started. As you read this text, you may find yourself reevaluating some of your wellness-related behaviors. This could be a great opportunity to make healthful changes that will stay with you for the rest of your life.

What Does It Take to Change?

As we all know, change doesn't just happen because we want it to. Some people are able to change and grow fairly easily, whereas others get stuck in problem behaviors for years. What are the secrets of moving toward wellness?

Motivation Once you recognize that you have an unhealthy behavior, you may consider changing it. But before you can change, you need strong motivation to do so. Although some people are motivated by long-term goals, such as avoiding a disease that may hit them in 20 or 30 years, most are more likely to be moved to action by shorter-term, more personal goals. Looking better, being more popular, doing better in school, getting a good job, improving at a sport, and increasing self-esteem are common sources of motivation.

You can strengthen your motivation by raising your consciousness about your problem behavior. This will enable you to focus on the negatives of the behavior and imagine the consequences if you don't make a change. At the same time, you can visualize the positive results of changing your behavior. Ask yourself: What do I want for myself, now and in the future?

For example, Ruby has never worried much about her smoking because the problems associated with it seem so far away. But lately she's noticed her performance on the volleyball team isn't as good as it used to be. Over the summer she visited her aunt, who has chronic emphysema from smoking and can barely leave her bed. Ruby knows she wants to have children and a career as a teacher someday, and seeing her aunt makes her wonder if her smoking habit could make it difficult for her to reach these goals. She starts to wonder whether her smoking habit is worth the short- and long-term sacrifices.

Social pressures can also increase the motivation to make changes. In Ruby's case, anti-smoking ordinances make it impossible for her to smoke in her dorm and in many public places. The inconvenience of finding a place to smoke—and pressure from her roommate, who doesn't like the smoky smell of Ruby's clothes in their room—add to Ruby's motivation to quit.

Locus of Control When you start thinking about changing a health behavior, a big factor in your eventual success is whether or not you believe you can change. Who do you believe is controlling your life? Is it your parents, friends, or school? Is it "fate"? Or is it you?

Locus of control refers to the figurative "place" a person designates as the source of responsibility for the events in his or her life. People who believe they are in control of their own lives are said to have an internal locus of control. Those who believe that factors beyond their control—heredity, friends and family, the environment, fate, luck, or other outside forces—are more important in determining the events of their lives are said to have an external locus of control. Most people are not purely "internalizers" or "externalizers"; their locus of control changes in response to the situation.

For lifestyle management, an internal locus of control is an advantage because it reinforces motivation and commitment. An external locus of control can sabotage efforts to change behavior. For example, if you believe you are destined to die of breast cancer because your mother died from the disease, you may view monthly breast self-exams and regular checkups as a waste of time. In contrast, an internal locus of control is an advantage. If you believe you can take action to reduce your hereditary risk of

locus of control The figurative "place" where a person locates the source of responsibility for the events in his or her life. **TERMS**

breast cancer, you will be motivated to follow guidelines for early detection of the disease.

People who tend to have an external locus of control can learn to view the events in their lives differently. Examine your attitudes carefully. If you find yourself attributing too much influence to outside forces, gather more information about your wellness-related behaviors. List all the ways that making lifestyle changes will improve your health. If you believe you'll succeed, and if you recognize and accept that you are in charge of your life, you're on your way to wellness.

Choosing a Target Behavior

The worst thing you can do is try to change everything at once—quit smoking, give up high-fat foods, eat a good breakfast, start jogging, plan your study time better, avoid drugs, get enough sleep. Overdoing it leads to burnout. Concentrate on one behavior that you want to change, your **target behavior,** and work on it systematically. Start with something simple, like substituting olive oil for butter in your diet or low-fat milk for whole milk. Or concentrate on getting to sleep by 10:00 P.M. Working on even one behavior change will make high demands on your energy.

Developing a Behavior Change Plan

Once you are committed to making a change, it's time to put together a plan of action. Your key to success is a well-thought-out plan that sets goals, anticipates problems, and includes rewards.

1. Monitor Your Behavior and Gather Data   Begin by keeping careful records of the behavior you wish to change (your target behavior) and the circumstances surrounding it. Keep these records in a health journal, a notebook in which you write the details of your behavior along with observations and comments. Note exactly what the activity was, when and where it happened, what you were doing, and what your feelings were at the time. In a journal for a weight-loss plan, for example, you would typically record how much food you ate, the time of day, the situation, the location, your feelings, and how hungry you were (Figure 1-4). If your goal is to start an exercise program, use your journal to track your daily activities to determine how best to make time for your workouts. Keep your journal for a week or two to get some solid information about the behavior you want to change.

2. Analyze the Data and Identify Patterns   After you have collected data on the behavior, analyze the data to identify patterns. When are you most likely to overeat? What events trigger your appetite? Perhaps you are especially hungry at midmorning or when you put off eating dinner until 9:00. Perhaps you overindulge in food and drink when you go to a particular restaurant or when you're with certain friends. Note the connections between your feelings and such external cues as time of day, location, situation, and the actions of others around you. Do you always think of having a cigarette when you read the newspaper? Do you always bite your fingernails when you're studying?

3. Set Specific Goals   It's a good idea to break your ultimate goal down into a few small steps. Your plan will seem less overwhelming and more manageable, increasing the chances that you'll stick to it. You'll also build in more opportunities to reward yourself (discussed in step 4), as well as milestones you can use to measure your progress.

If you plan to lose 30 pounds, for example, you'll find it easier to take off 10 pounds at a time. If you want to start an exercise program, begin by taking 10- to 15-minute walks a few times per week. Then gradually increase the amount of exercise you do. Take easier steps first and work up to harder steps.

4. Devise a Strategy or Plan of Action   As you write in your health journal, you gather a lot of information about your target behavior—the times it typically occurs; the situations in which it usually happens; the ways sight, smell, mood, situation, and accessibility trigger it. You can probably trace the chain of events that leads to the behavior and perhaps also identify points along the way where making a different choice would mean changing the behavior.

MODIFY YOUR ENVIRONMENT   You can be more effective in changing behavior if you control the environmental cues that provoke it. This might mean not having cigarettes or certain foods or drinks in the house, not going to parties where you're tempted to overindulge, or not spending time with particular people, at least for a while. If you always get a candy bar at a certain vending machine, change your route so you don't pass by it. If you always end up taking a coffee break and chatting with friends when you go to the library to study, choose a different place to study, such as your room.

It's also helpful to control other behaviors or habits that are linked to the target behavior. You may give in to an urge to eat when you have a beer (alcohol increases the appetite) or watch TV. Try substituting other activities for habits that are linked with your target behavior, such as exercising to music instead of plopping down in front of the TV. Or, if possible, put an exercise bicycle in front of the set and burn calories while watching your favorite show.

TERMS   **target behavior** An isolated behavior selected as the basis for a behavior change program.

| Date November 5 | | | | | | | Day M (TU) W TH F SA SU | | | | |

Time of day	M/S	Food eaten	Cals.	H	Where did you eat?	What else were you doing?	How did someone else influence you?	What made you want to eat what you did?	Emotions and feelings?	Thoughts and concerns?
7:30	M	1 C Crispix cereal 1/2 C skim milk coffee, black 1 C orange juice	110 40 — 120	3	dorm cafeteria	reading newspaper	eating w/ friends, but I ate what I usually eat	I always eat cereal in the morning	a little keyed up & worried	thinking about quiz in class today
10:30	S	1 apple	90	1	library	studying	alone	felt tired & wanted to wake up	tired	worried about next class
12:30	M	1 C chili 1 roll 1 pat butter 1 orange 2 oatmeal cookies 1 soda	290 120 35 60 120 150	2	cafeteria terrace	talking	eating w/ friends; we decided to eat at the cafeteria	wanted to be part of group	excited and happy	interested in hearing everyone's plans for the weekend

M/S = Meal or snack   H = Hunger rating (0–3)

Figure 1-4   Sample health journal entries.

You can change the cues in your environment so they trigger the new behavior you want instead of the old one. Tape a picture of a cyclist speeding down a hill on your TV screen. Leave your exercise shoes in plain view. Put a chart of your progress in a special place at home to make your goals highly visible and inspire you to keep going. When you're trying to change a strong habit, small cues can play an important part in keeping you on track.

REWARD YOURSELF   A second powerful way to affect your target behavior is to set up a reward system that will reinforce your efforts. Most people find it difficult to change longstanding habits for rewards they can't see right away. Giving yourself instant, real rewards for good behavior will help you stick with a plan to change your behavior.

Carefully plan your reward payoffs and what they will be. In most cases, rewards should be collected when you reach specific objectives or subgoals in your plan. For example, you might treat yourself to a movie after a week of avoiding extra snacks. Don't forget to reward yourself for good behavior that is consistent and persistent—if you simply stick with your program week after week. Decide on a reward after you reach a certain goal or mark off the sixth week or month of a valiant effort. Write it down in your health journal and remember it as you follow your plan—especially when the going gets rough.

Make a list of your activities and favorite events to use as rewards. They should be special, inexpensive, and preferably unrelated to food or alcohol. You might treat yourself to a concert, a ball game, a new CD, a long-distance phone call to a friend, a day off from studying for a long hike in the woods—whatever is rewarding to you.

INVOLVE THE PEOPLE AROUND YOU   Rewards and support can also come from family and friends. Tell them about your plan, and ask for their help. Encourage them to be active, interested participants. Ask them to support you when you set aside time to go running or avoid second helpings at Thanksgiving dinner. You may have to remind them not to do things that make you "break training" and not to be hurt if you have to refuse something when they forget. Getting encouragement, support, and praise from important people in your life can powerfully reinforce the new behavior you're trying to adopt.

5. Make a Personal Contract   Once you have set your goals and developed a plan of action, make your plan into a personal contract. A serious personal contract—one that commits your word—can result in a higher chance of follow-through than a casual, offhand promise. Your contract can help prevent procrastination by specifying the important dates and can also serve as a reminder of your personal commitment to change.

Your contract should include a statement of your goal and your commitment to reaching it. Include details of your plan: the date you'll begin, the steps you'll use to measure your progress, the concrete strategies you've

Many actions and behaviors are shaped by cues in the environment. For these softball players, easy access to a vending machine selling fruit, rather than candy, makes it more likely that they will choose a healthy snack.

developed for promoting change, and the date you expect to reach your final goal. Have someone—preferably someone who will be actively helping you with your program—sign your contract as a witness.

A Sample Behavior Change Plan Let's take the example of Michael, who wants to break a longstanding habit of eating candy and chips every afternoon and evening. Michael begins by keeping track of his snacking in a journal. He discovers that he always buys candy or a bag of chips at the snack bar on campus between two of his afternoon classes. In the evenings, he eats several candy bars or a large bag of chips while he studies at home.

Next, Michael sets specific goals. He sets a start date and decides to break his plan into two parts. He will begin by cutting out his afternoon snack of candy or chips. Once he successfully reaches this goal, he'll concentrate on his evening snacking. He decides to allow 3 weeks for each half of his behavior change plan.

Michael decides to make several changes in his behavior to help control his urges to buy and eat candy and chips. He plans to bring a healthy snack, such as an apple or orange, to eat between his afternoon classes. He decides to avoid going near the snack bar; instead, he'll spend his between-classes break taking a walk around campus or reading in the student union. To help break his evening habit, he decides to study at the library instead of at home; when he's at home, he'll try studying in a different room. He also plans to stock the refrigerator with healthy snacks. Finally, Michael decides on some rewards he'll give himself when he meets his goals, choosing things he likes that aren't too expensive.

After Michael has thought through his plan to stop snacking on candy and chips, he's ready to create and sign a behavior change contract. He decides to enlist one of his housemates as a witness to his contract; he also asks his housemate to check on his progress and offer encouragement (Figure 1-5). Once Michael has signed his contract, he's ready to take action.

Putting Your Plan into Action

The starting date has arrived, and you are ready to put your plan into action. This stage requires commitment, the resolve to stick with the plan no matter what temptations you encounter. Remember all the reasons you have to make the change—and remember that *you* are the boss.

Use all your strategies to make your plan work. Substitute behaviors are often very important—go for a walk after class instead of eating a bag of chips. Make sure your environment is change-friendly by keeping cues that trigger the problem behavior to a minimum.

Social support can make a big difference as you take action. Try to find a buddy who wants to make the same changes you do. You can support and encourage each other, as well as exchange information and motivation. For example, an exercise buddy can provide companionship and encouragement for times when you might be tempted to skip that morning jog. Or you and a friend can watch to be sure that you both have only one alcoholic beverage at a party.

Let the people around you know about your plan, and enlist their support in specific ways. Perhaps you know people who have reached the goal you are striving for; they could be role models or mentors for you. Talk to them about what strategies worked for them.

Use your health journal to keep track of how well you are doing in achieving your ultimate goal. Record your daily activities and any relevant details, such as how far you walked or how many calories you ate. Each week, chart your progress on a graph and see how it compares to the subgoals on your contract. You may want to track more than one behavior, such as the time you spend exercising each week and your weight.

If you aren't making progress, analyze your plan to see what might be causing the problem. Possible barriers to success are listed in the section "Staying with It," along with suggestions for addressing them. Once you've identified the problem, revise your plan. Refer to the box

My Personal Contract for Giving Up Snacking on Candy and Chips

I agree to stop snacking on candy and chips twice every day. I will begin my program on <u>10/4</u> and plan to reach my final goal by <u>11/15</u>. I have divided my program into two parts, with two separate goals. For each step in my program, I will give myself the reward listed.

1. I will stop having candy or chips for an afternoon snack on <u>10/4</u>.
(Reward: <u>new CD</u>)
2. I will stop having candy or chips for an evening snack on <u>10/25</u>.
(Reward: <u>Concert</u>)

My plan for stopping my snacking includes the following strategies:
1. <u>Avoid snack bar by taking a walk or reading at student union.</u>
2. <u>Eating healthy snacks instead of candy and chips.</u>
3. <u>Studying at the library instead of at home.</u>

I understand that it is important for me to make a strong personal effort to make this change in my behavior. I sign this contract as an indication of my personal commitment to reach my goal.

Michael Cook   9/28

Witness: *Katie Lim*   9/28

Figure 1-5 A sample behavior change contract.

"Maximizing Your Chances of Success" for additional suggestions.

Be sure to reward yourself for your successes by treating yourself as specified in your contract. And don't forget to give yourself a pat on the back—congratulate yourself, notice how much better you look or feel, and feel good about how far you've come and how you've gained control of your behavior.

Staying with It

As you continue with your program, don't be surprised when you run up against obstacles; they're inevitable. In fact, it's a good idea to expect problems and give yourself time to step back, see how you're doing, and make some changes before going on. If your program is grinding to a halt, identify what is blocking your progress. It may come from one of these sources.

Social Influences Take a hard look at the reactions of the people you're counting on, and see if they're really supporting you. If they come up short, connect and network with others who will be more supportive.

A related trap is trying to get your friends or family members to change *their* behaviors. The decision to make a major behavior change is something people come to only after intensive self-examination. You may be able to influence someone by tactfully providing facts or support, but that's all. Focus on yourself. If you succeed, you may become a role model for others.

Levels of Motivation and Commitment You won't make real progress until an inner drive leads you to the stage of change at which you are ready to make a personal commitment to the goal. If commitment is your problem, you may need to wait until the behavior you're dealing with makes your life more unhappy or unhealthy; then your desire to change it will be stronger. Or you may find that changing your goal will inspire you to keep going. If you really want to change but your motivation comes and goes, look at your support system and at your own level of confidence. Building these up may be the key to pushing past a barrier. For more ideas, refer to Activity 9 in the Behavior Change Workbook at the end of the text.

Choice of Techniques and Level of Effort If your plan is not working as well as you thought it would, make changes where you're having the most trouble. If you've lagged on your running schedule, for example, maybe it's because you don't like running. An aerobics class might suit you better. There are many ways to move toward your goal. Or you may not be trying hard enough. You do have to push toward your goal. If it were easy, you wouldn't need to have a plan.

Stress Barrier If you've hit a wall in your program, look at the sources of stress in your life. If the stress is temporary, such as catching a cold or having a term paper due, you may want to wait until it passes before strengthening your efforts. If the stress is ongoing, find healthy ways to manage it, such as taking a half-hour walk after lunch. You

- *Make your efforts cost-effective and time-effective.* Be sure your new behavior has a real and lasting value for you personally. Be realistic about the amount of time and energy you can put into it. Choose a strategy or approach that works for you. For example, many activities—from walking to bicycle racing—lead to physical fitness; for long-term success, you need to choose one that you enjoy and that fits smoothly into your schedule.

- *Find a buddy.* A buddy can provide support, encouragement, and motivation. The fear of letting your buddy down makes it less likely that you'll take a day off, and in a crisis, your buddy can help overcome an urge to slip (and vice versa). If you can't find a buddy who shares your goal from among your friends, family members, and classmates, try joining a group such as Weight Watchers for a ready-made set of buddies.

- *Prepare for problem situations.* If you know in advance that you're going to be in a situation that will trigger your target behavior, rehearse what you'll do. If you don't want to drink too much at a party, decide on your drink limit ahead of time, and switch to a soft drink when you reach your limit.

- *Expect success.* Change your ideas about yourself as you change your behavior. Drop your old self-image and start thinking of yourself in a new way—as a jogger, a non-smoker, a person in control.

- *Realize that lasting change takes time.* Major life changes involve giving up a familiar and comfortable part of your life in exchange for something new and unknown. They happen one day at a time, with lots of ups and downs.

- *Forgive and forget.* If you slip—miss a workout or eat a bag of candy—focus on discovering what triggered the slip and how to deal with it next time. Don't waste time blaming yourself. Keeping up your self-esteem will help you stay with your plan; negative feelings will get in your way.

---

may even want to make stress management your highest priority for behavior change (see Chapter 10).

Procrastinating, Rationalizing, and Blaming

Try to detect the games you might be playing with yourself so that you can stop them. If you're procrastinating ("It's Friday already; I might as well wait until Monday to begin"), break your plan down into still smaller steps that you can accomplish one day at a time. If you're rationalizing or making excuses ("I wanted to go swimming today, but I wouldn't have had time to wash my hair afterward"), remember that when you "win" by deceiving yourself, it's not much of a victory. If you're wasting time blaming yourself or others ("Everyone in that class talks so much that I don't get a chance to speak"), recognize that blaming is a way of taking your focus off the real problem and denying responsibility for your actions. Try refocusing by taking a positive attitude and renewing your determination to succeed.

Getting Outside Help

Outside help is often needed for changing behavior that may be too deeply rooted for a self-management approach. Alcohol and other drug addictions, excessive overeating, and other conditions or behaviors that put you at a serious health risk fall into this category; so do behaviors that interfere with your ability to function. Many communities have programs to help with these problems—Weight Watchers, Alcoholics Anonymous, Smoke Enders, and Coke Enders, for example.

On campus, you may find courses in physical fitness, stress management, and weight control. The student health center or campus counseling center may also be a source of assistance. Many communities offer a wide vari-

ety of low-cost services through adult education, school programs, health departments, and private agencies. Consult the yellow pages, your local health department, or the United Way; the latter often sponsors local referral services. Whatever you do, don't be stopped by a problem when you can tap into resources to help you solve it.

Being Fit and Well for Life

Your first attempts at making behavior changes may never go beyond the project stage. Those that do may not all succeed. But as you experience some success, you'll start to have more positive feelings about yourself. You may discover physical activities you enjoy; you may encounter new situations and meet new people. Perhaps you'll surprise yourself by accomplishing things you didn't think were possible—breaking a nicotine habit, competing in a race, climbing a mountain, developing a lean, muscular body. Most of all, you'll discover the feeling of empowerment that comes from taking charge of your health (see the box "Ten Warning Signs of Wellness").

Once you've started, don't stop. Assume that health improvement is forever. Take on the easier problems first, and then use what you learn to tackle more difficult problems later. Periodically review what you've accomplished to make sure you don't fall into old habits. And keep informed about the latest health news and trends. Research is constantly providing new information that directly affects daily choices and habits.

This book will introduce you to the main components of a fit and well lifestyle, show you how to assess your current health status, and help you put together a program that will lead to wellness. You can't control every aspect of your health—there are too many unknowns in life for that to be possible. But you can create a lifestyle that

Ten Warning Signs of Wellness

1. The persistent presence of a support network.
2. Chronic positive expectations; the tendency to frame events in a constructive light.
3. Episodic outbreaks of joyful, happy experiences.
4. A sense of spiritual involvement.
5. A tendency to adapt to changing conditions.
6. Rapid response and recovery of stress response systems to repeated challenges.
7. An increased appetite for physical activity.
8. A tendency to identify and communicate feelings.
9. Repeated episodes of gratitude and generosity.
10. A persistent sense of humor.

SOURCE: Ten warning signs of good health. 1996. *Mind/Body Health Newsletter* 5(1). Reprinted by permission.

minimizes your health risks and maximizes your enjoyment of life and well-being. You can take charge of your health in a dramatic and meaningful way. *Fit and Well* will show you how.

SUMMARY

- Wellness is the ability to live life fully, with vitality and meaning. Wellness is dynamic and multi-dimensional; it incorporates physical, emotional, intellectual, spiritual, interpersonal and social, and environmental dimensions.
- As chronic diseases have become the leading causes of death in the United States, people have recognized that they have greater control over, and greater responsibility for, their health than ever before.
- Behaviors that promote wellness include being physically active; choosing a healthy diet; maintaining a healthy body weight; managing stress effectively; avoiding use of tobacco and other drugs and using alcohol wisely, if at all; and protecting oneself from disease and injury.
- Although heredity, environment, and health care all play roles in wellness and disease, behavior can mitigate their effects.
- Knowledge about topics in wellness and about yourself is necessary to begin making changes in behavior. Observations by others and landmark events can help get people started on change.
- Strong motivation to change and an internal locus of control are keys to successful behavior change. It is best to concentrate on one target behavior at a time.
- A specific plan for change can be developed by (1) monitoring behavior by keeping a journal, (2) analyzing the recorded data, (3) setting specific goals, (4) devising strategies for modifying the environment, rewarding yourself, and involving others, and (5) making a personal contract.
- To start and maintain a behavior change program you need commitment, a well-developed and manageable plan, social support, and a system of rewards. It is also important to monitor the progress of your program, revising it as necessary.
- Obstacles sometimes come in the form of unsupportive people, a low level of motivation or commitment, inappropriate techniques, too much stress, and procrastinating, rationalizing, and blaming. Taking advantage of outside resources can help.

FOR MORE INFORMATION

Books

Hunt, P., and M. Hillsdon. 1996. *Changing Eating and Exercise Behaviour.* London: Blackwell Science. *A guide to using behavior modification techniques to change eating and exercise habits.*

Prochaska, J. O., J. C. Norcross, and C. C. DiClemente. 1994. *Changing for Good: The Revolutionary Program That Explains the Six Stages of Change and Teaches You How to Free Yourself from Bad Habits.* New York: Morrow. *Outlines the authors' model of behavior change and offers suggestions and advice for each stage of change.*

Sobel, D. S., and R. Ornstein. 1996. *The Healthy Mind, Healthy Body Handbook.* Los Altos, Calif.: DR$_x$. *Presents concrete strategies for changing behavior, staying well, managing common health problems, and becoming a better health consumer.*

Newsletters

Consumer Reports on Health, P.O. Box 56360, Boulder, CO 80323.

Harvard Health Letter, P.O. Box 420300, Palm Coast, FL 32142 (http://www.countway.harvard.edu/publications/Health_Publications).

Harvard Men's Health Watch, P.O. Box 420099, Palm Coast, FL 32142.

Harvard Women's Health Watch, P.O. Box 420234, Palm Coast, FL 32142.

Healthline, 830 Menlo Ave., Suite 100, Menlo Park, CA 94025 (http://www.healthline.com).

HealthNews, P.O. Box 52924, Boulder, CO 80322 (http://www.onhealth.com).

Mayo Clinic Health Letter, P.O. Box 53889, Boulder, CO 80322.

Mind/Body Health, P.O. Box 381069, Boston, MA 02238.

University of California at Berkeley Wellness Letter, P.O. Box 420148, Palm Coast, FL 32142 (http://magazines.enews.com/magazines/ucbwl).

Organizations, Hotlines, and Web Sites

The Internet addresses (also called uniform resource locators, or URLs) listed here were accurate at the time of publication. However, Internet information changes rapidly. If a site has moved and there is no link to the new URL, you can use a search engine to locate the new site.

Centers for Disease Control and Prevention. Through phone, fax, and the Internet, the CDC provides a wide variety of information, including materials on HIV infection, national health statistics, and governmental nutrition recommendations.

404-332-4555 (CDC Infoline)

http://www.cdc.gov

CNN/Health. Provides recent news on a wide variety of health topics.

http://www.cnn.com/HEALTH

Go Ask Alice. Sponsored by the health education and wellness program at Columbia University Health Service, this Web site provides a searchable, interactive service in which professional and peer educators answer student questions about stress, sexuality, fitness, and many other health-related topics.

http://www.goaskalice.columbia.edu

Healthfinder. A gateway to online publications, Web sites, support and self-help groups, and agencies and organizations that produce reliable health information.

http://www.healthfinder.gov

Healthy People 2000/Healthy People 2010. Provide information on Healthy People objectives and priority areas.

202-205-8583

http://odphp.osophs.dhhs.gov/pubs/hp2000

http://web.health.gov/healthypeople

Mayo Health O@sis. Sponsored by the Mayo Clinic, the site provides daily news and articles on a wide range of health topics.

http://www.mayohealth.org

National Health Information Center (NHIC). An organization that helps put consumers and health professionals in touch with the organizations that are best able to provide answers to health-related questions. Provides information on over 100 organizations and an extensive list of toll-free numbers.

800-336-4797

http://nhic-nt.health.org

National Women's Health Information Center. Provides information and answers to frequently asked questions.

800-994-WOMAN

http://www.4woman.org

University of Wisconsin, Stevens Point Wellness Links. Includes links to the top 100 wellness sites; organized by topic.

http://wellness.uwsp.edu/College_Health

Yahoo/Health. A Web site and search engine that includes a directory of hundreds of health-related Web sites, covering a wide range of topics.

http://www.yahoo.com/health

Your Health Daily. Provides health and fitness information from the *New York Times.*

http://nytsyn.com/med

SELECTED BIBLIOGRAPHY

American Cancer Society. 1998. *Cancer Facts and Figures—1998.* Atlanta: American Cancer Society.

American Heart Association. 1998. *1998 Heart and Stroke Statistical Update* (retrieved January 25, 1998; http://www.americanheart.org/scientific/HSstats98/index.html).

Blair, S. N., et al. 1996. Influences of cardiorespiratory fitness and other precursors on cardiovascular disease and all-cause mortality in men and women. *Journal of the American Medical Association* 276(3): 205–210.

Booth, F. W., and B. S. Tseng. 1995. America needs to exercise for health. *Medicine and Science in Sports and Exercise* 27:462–465.

Douglas, K. A., et al. 1997. Results from the 1995 National College Health Risk Behavior Survey. *Journal of American College Health* 46(2): 55–56.

Fuller, P. R., et al. 1998. Effects of a personalized system of skill acquisition and an educational program in the treatment of obesity. *Addictive Behavior* 23(1): 97–100.

Grace, T. W. 1997. Health problems of college students. *Journal of American College Health* 45(6): 243–250.

Hunink, M. G. M., et al. 1997. The recent decline in mortality from coronary heart disease, 1980–1990. *Journal of the American Medical Association* 277(7): 535–542.

Koff, E., and C. L. Bauman. 1997. Effects of wellness, fitness, and sport skills programs on body image and lifestyle behaviors. *Perceptual and Motor Skills* 84(2): 555–562.

Lee, I. M., C. C. Hsieh, and R. S. Paffenbarger. 1995. Exercise intensity and longevity in men. The Harvard Alumni Health Study. *Journal of the American Medical Association* 273(15): 1179–1184.

Narayan, K. M., et al. 1998. Randomized clinical trial of lifestyle interventions in Pima Indians: A pilot study. *Diabetic Medicine* 15(1): 66–72.

National Center for Health Statistics. 1997. *Healthy People 2000 Review 1997.* Hyattsville, Md.: Public Health Service, DHHS Pub. (PHS) 98-1256.

Ni, M. C., B. M. Margetts, and V. M. Speller. 1997. Applying the stages-of-change model to dietary change. *Nutrition Reviews* 55(1 Pt. 1): 10–16.

Nieman, D. C. 1999. *Exercise Testing and Prescription: A Health-Related Approach,* 4th ed. Mountain View, Calif.: Mayfield.

Parsons, J. T., A. W. Siegel, and J. H. Cousins. 1997. Late adolescent risk-taking: Effects of perceived benefits and perceived risks on behavioral intentions and behavioral changes. *Journal of Adolescence* 20(4): 381–392.

Reif, C. J., and A. B. Elster. 1998. Adolescent preventive services. *Primary Care* 25(1): 1–21.

U.S. Bureau of the Census. 1997. *Resident Population of the United States: Estimates by Sex, Race, and Hispanic Origin, with Median Age* (retrieved April 9, 1997; http://www.census.gov/population/estimates/nation/intfile3-1.txt).

U.S. Department of Health and Human Services. 1997. *Health, United States, 1996–97.* Washington, D.C.: U.S. Government Printing Office, DHHS Pub. (PHS) 96-1232.

U.S. Department of Health and Human Services. 1996. *Healthy People 2000 Midcourse Review and 1995 Revisions.* Washington, D.C.: U.S. Government Printing Office, DHHS Pub. (PHS).

LAB 1-1 *Lifestyle Evaluation*

The following brief test will give you some idea about how your current lifestyle compares to the lifestyle recommended for wellness. For each question, choose the answer that best describes your behavior; then add up your score *for each section.*

Exercise/Fitness

		Almost Always	Sometimes	Never
1.	I engage in moderate exercise, such as brisk walking or swimming, for 20–60 minutes, three to five times a week.	4	1	0
2.	I do exercises to develop muscular strength and endurance at least twice a week.	2	1	0
3.	I spend some of my leisure time participating in individual, family, or team activities, such as gardening, bowling, or softball.	2	1	0
4.	I maintain a healthy body weight, avoiding overweight and underweight.	2	1	0

Exercise/Fitness Score: _____

Nutrition

		Almost Always	Sometimes	Never
1.	I eat a variety of foods each day, including five or more servings of fruits and/or vegetables.	3	1	0
2.	I limit the amount of fat and saturated fat in my diet.	3	1	0
3.	I avoid skipping meals.	2	1	0
4.	I limit the amount of salt and sugar I eat.	2	1	0

Nutrition Score: _____

Tobacco Use

If you never use tobacco, enter a score of 10 for this section and go to the next section.

		Almost Always	Sometimes	Never
1.	I avoid using tobacco.	2	1	0
2.	I smoke only low-tar-and-nicotine cigarettes, or I smoke a pipe or cigars, or I use smokeless tobacco.	2	1	0

Tobacco Use Score: _____

Alcohol and Drugs

		Almost Always	Sometimes	Never
1.	I avoid alcohol, or I drink no more than 1 (women) or 2 (men) drinks a day.	4	1	0
2.	I avoid using alcohol or other drugs as a way of handling stressful situations or the problems in my life.	2	1	0
3.	I am careful not to drink alcohol when taking medications (such as cold or allergy medications) or when pregnant.	2	1	0
4.	I read and follow the label directions when using prescribed and over-the-counter drugs.	2	1	0

Alcohol and Drugs Score: _____

Emotional Health

1. I enjoy being a student, and I have a job or do other work that I enjoy.   2   1   0
2. I find it easy to relax and express my feelings freely.   2   1   0
3. I manage stress well.   2   1   0
4. I have close friends, relatives, or others whom I can talk to about personal matters and call on for help when needed.   2   1   0
5. I participate in group activities (such as community or church organizations) or hobbies that I enjoy.   2   1   0

Emotional Health Score: _____

Safety

1. I wear a safety belt while riding in a car.   2   1   0
2. I avoid driving while under the influence of alcohol or other drugs.   2   1   0
3. I obey traffic rules and the speed limit when driving.   2   1   0
4. I read and follow instructions on the labels of potentially harmful products or substances, such as household cleaners, poisons, and electrical appliances.   2   1   0
5. I avoid smoking in bed.   2   1   0

Safety Score: _____

Disease Prevention

1. I know the warning signs of cancer, heart attack, and stroke.   2   1   0
2. I avoid overexposure to the sun and use sunscreen.   2   1   0
3. I get recommended medical screening tests (such as blood pressure checks and Pap tests), immunizations, and booster shots.   2   1   0
4. I practice monthly breast/testicle self-exams.   2   1   0
5. I am not sexually active *or* I have sex with only one mutually faithful, uninfected partner *or* I always engage in "safer sex" (using condoms), *and* I do not share needles to inject drugs.   2   1   0

Disease Prevention Score: _____

What Your Scores Mean

Scores of 9 and 10   Excellent! Your answers show that you are aware of the importance of this area to your health. More important, you are putting your knowledge to work for you by practicing good health habits. As long as you continue to do so, this area should not pose a serious health risk. It's likely that you are setting an example for your family and friends to follow. Because you got a very high test score on this part of the test, you may want to consider other areas where your scores indicate room for improvement.

Scores of 6 to 8   Your health practices in this area are good, but there is room for improvement. Look again at the items you answered with a "Sometimes" or "Never." What changes can you make to improve your score? Even a small change can often help you achieve better health.

Scores of 3 to 5   Your health risks are showing! Would you like more information about the risks you're facing and about why it's important for you to change these behaviors? Perhaps you need help in deciding how to successfully make the changes you desire. In either case, help is available.

Scores of 0 to 2   Obviously, you were concerned enough about your health to take the test, but your answers show that you may be taking serious and unnecessary risks with your health. Perhaps you are not aware of the risks and what to do about them. You can easily get the information and help you need to improve, if you wish. The next step is up to you.

The behaviors covered in this test are recommended for most Americans, but some may not apply to people with certain chronic diseases or disabilities or to pregnant women, who may require special advice from their physician.

SOURCE: Adapted from *Healthstyle: A Self-Test,* developed by the U.S. Public Health Service.

Basic Principles of Physical Fitness

2

LOOKING AHEAD

After reading this chapter, you should be able to answer these questions about physical fitness:

- How much exercise is recommended for developing health and fitness?

- What are the components of physical fitness, and how does each one affect wellness?

- What is the goal of physical training, and what are the basic principles of training?

- What principles are involved in designing a well-rounded exercise program? What kinds of activities should be included?

- What steps can be taken to make an exercise program safe, effective, and successful?

Any list of the benefits of physical activity is impressive. A physically active lifestyle helps you generate more energy, control your weight, manage stress, and boost your immune system. It provides psychological and emotional benefits, contributing to your sense of competence and well-being. It offers protection against heart disease, diabetes, high blood pressure, osteoporosis, cancer, and even premature death. Exercise increases your physical capacity so that you are better able to meet the challenges of daily life with energy and vigor. Although people vary greatly in the levels of physical fitness and performance they can ultimately achieve, the benefits of regular physical activity are available to everyone. (For more on the benefits of exercise, see the box "A Runner's Rationale.")

This chapter provides an overview of physical fitness. It explains how lifestyle physical activity and more formal exercise programs contribute to wellness. It describes the components of fitness, the basic principles of physical training, and the essential elements of a well-rounded exercise program. Chapters 3–6 provide an in-depth look at each of the elements of a fitness program; Chapter 7 will help you put all these elements together into a complete, personalized program.

PHYSICAL ACTIVITY AND EXERCISE FOR HEALTH AND FITNESS

Despite the many benefits of an active lifestyle, levels of physical activity have declined in recent years and remain low for all populations of Americans (Table 2-1). More than 60% of U.S. adults do not engage in recommended amounts of physical activity; 25% are not active at all. In the summer of 1996, the U.S. Surgeon General published *Physical Activity and Health,* a landmark report designed to reverse these trends and get Americans moving. The report summarized current knowledge about the relationship between physical activity and health; its major findings included the following:

- People of all ages benefit from regular physical activity.

- People can obtain significant health benefits by including a moderate amount of physical activity on most, if not all, days of the week. Through a modest increase in daily activity, most Americans can improve their health and quality of life.

- Additional health benefits can be gained through greater amounts of physical activity. People who can maintain a regular regimen of more vigorous or longer-duration activity are likely to obtain even greater benefits.

Evidence is growing that simply becoming more physi-

VITAL STATISTICS

TABLE 2-1	Adults Who Regularly Engage in Physical Activity	
	Moderate Intensity[a]	High Intensity[b]
Overall	20.1%	14.4%
Sex		
Men	21.5	12.9
Women	18.9	15.8
Ethnicity		
White	20.8	15.3
Black	15.2	9.4
Hispanic (Latino)	20.1	11.9
Education		
Less than 12 years	15.6	8.2
12 years	17.8	11.5
13–15 years	22.7	14.9
16 or more years	23.5	21.9
Income		
Less than $10,000	17.6	9.0
$10,000–$19,999	18.7	10.8
$20,000–$34,999	20.3	14.2
$35,000–$49,999	20.9	16.3
$50,000 or more	23.5	20.5
Geographic region		
Northeast	20.2	13.8
North Central	18.2	13.7
South	19.0	13.8
West	24.0	16.8

[a]Adults who engage in moderate-intensity physical activity five or more times per week for at least 30 minutes per session.
[b]Adults who engage in high-intensity physical activity three or more times per week for at least 20 minutes per session.

SOURCE: U.S. Department of Health and Human Services. 1996. *Physical Activity and Health: A Report of the Surgeon General.* Atlanta, Ga.: U.S. Department of Health and Human Services.

cally active may be the single most important lifestyle change for promoting health and well-being.

Physical Activity on a Continuum

Physical activity can be defined as any movement of the body that is carried out by the muscles and requires energy to produce. Different types of physical activity can be arranged on a continuum based on the amount of energy they require. Quick, easy movements such as standing up or walking down a hallway require little energy or effort; more intense, sustained activities such as cycling 5 miles or running in a race require considerably more.

The term **exercise** is usually used to refer to a subset of physical activity—planned, structured, repetitive movement of the body designed specifically to improve or maintain physical fitness. As discussed in Chapter 1, physical

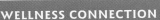

Much of the attention surrounding exercise focuses on its benefits for physical health. But for many exercisers, improved health and longevity are only part of the reason they begin and continue to train. In this selection, long-time Runner's World *columnist George Sheehan highlights the diverse and interconnected nature of the wellness benefits of exercise.*

When I lecture, I often begin with a short film on running. The opening scene is the start of the Boston Marathon. Thousands of runners stream toward the camera, while the narrator remarks that these marathoners are only the visible elite of millions of runners now surging along the world's roads and filling its parks. "The nonrunner watches," he says, "and wonders—*why?*"

The audience almost always laughs at that question. To the people in the film, running is normal; to those in my audience, running—especially marathon running—is a mystery. When the film ends and the lights go on, I ascend the stage and address the question, Why do people run?

My answer is direct: Their lives depend upon it. People begin running for any number of motives, but we stick to it for one basic reason—to find out who we really are. Running or some other form of exercise is essential in the drive to become and perpetuate the ultimate self, because finding out who we are means finding out what our limits are—and we have to *test* ourselves to do that.

I run because my life in all its aspects depends upon it. The length of my life, certainly; the hours in my day, just as surely. The person I am, my productivity, my creativity, my pursuit of happiness—all are conditioned and determined by my hours on the road.

Most non-exercisers are unaware of this global, whole-life effect of athletic training. The experts—physicians, psychologists, sociologists, teachers, even philosophers—carve out discrete territories in which they operate. They focus on certain parts of our lives, but not life in its totality—not Life with a capital *L.*

The physician tells me that my lifespan is related to my lifestyle. When I began running, my coronary risk factors practically disappeared. I stopped smoking, my weight returned to what it had been in college, and my blood pressure didn't rise as I got older. Running also added hours to my day. My physical

work capacity is far greater than it was when I was 38 years old and (presumably) in my prime. Clearly, my body benefits from fitness.

But my mind does, too. The psychologist tells me that. The negative feelings—anxiety and depression, anger and hostility—are all reduced by training. While these destructive feelings diminish, constructive ones such as self-esteem and self-confidence rise.

And the public me benefits also: The sociologist argues that my professional success is linked to the fitness I earn from running. It is no longer simply survival of the fittest, it is also success to the fittest. Fit people occupy the upper echelons in education, position, and salary.

The educator views my running and racing as a laboratory where I learn about such things as sacrifice and solitude, courage and cooperation, victory and defeat. And the philosopher reminds me that creative thinking requires the inner and outer solitude that running confers.

So it goes: Each specialist sees the role of exercise through the prism of that particular specialty. I explain this fragmentation to the audience, and then I tell them that no one piece of the puzzle is enough. Each of these experts sees only a bit of me. But I am not a cholesterol level, I am not a Rorschach profile. I am not an ergometer reading or an IQ. I am a physician, a student, a problem solver. I am also a parent, a sibling, a lover, a friend.

But none of these entirely defines me. "I absolutely deny," wrote D. H. Lawrence, "that I am a soul, or a body or an intelligence, or a nervous system or a bunch of glands, or any of the rest of the bits of me. The whole is greater than the sum of my parts. . . . I am a total living human being."

I look out over the audience and ask them, "Are you content with this total living person you are now?" American writer Lewis Mumford once remarked that today might be a fair sample of eternity. If so, who you are today would be the eternal you, the final product of your years on earth. If this were your last day, would you be satisfied?

There it is—my *why* of running, my reason for exercise—no less than the creation of the human being I become. [1986]

Runner's World, January 1995. Reprinted with the permission of the estate of George Sheehan.

---

fitness is the ability of the body to adapt to the demands of physical effort—to perform moderate-to-vigorous levels of physical activity without becoming overly tired. Levels of fitness depend on such physiological factors as the heart's ability to pump blood and the size of muscle fibers. To develop fitness, a person must perform a sufficient amount of physical activity to stress the body and cause long-term physiological changes. The precise type and amount of activity required to develop fitness will be discussed in greater detail later in the chapter. For our purposes in this section, it is important to know that only some types of physical activity—what is commonly referred to as

exercise—will develop fitness. This distinction is important for setting goals and developing a program.

Lifestyle Physical Activity for Health Promotion
The Surgeon General's report recommends that all Americans

physical activity Any movement of the body that is carried out by the skeletal muscles and that requires energy to produce.

exercise Planned, structured, repetitive movement of the body designed to improve or maintain physical fitness.

TERMS

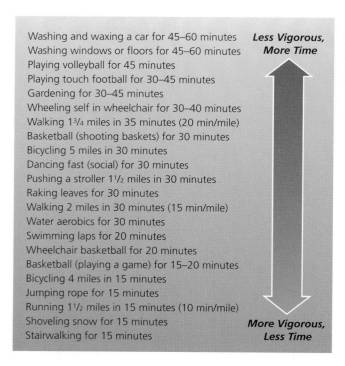

Washing and waxing a car for 45–60 minutes
Washing windows or floors for 45–60 minutes
Playing volleyball for 45 minutes
Playing touch football for 30–45 minutes
Gardening for 30–45 minutes
Wheeling self in wheelchair for 30–40 minutes
Walking 1¾ miles in 35 minutes (20 min/mile)
Basketball (shooting baskets) for 30 minutes
Bicycling 5 miles in 30 minutes
Dancing fast (social) for 30 minutes
Pushing a stroller 1½ miles in 30 minutes
Raking leaves for 30 minutes
Walking 2 miles in 30 minutes (15 min/mile)
Water aerobics for 30 minutes
Swimming laps for 20 minutes
Wheelchair basketball for 20 minutes
Basketball (playing a game) for 15–20 minutes
Bicycling 4 miles in 15 minutes
Jumping rope for 15 minutes
Running 1½ miles in 15 minutes (10 min/mile)
Shoveling snow for 15 minutes
Stairwalking for 15 minutes

Less Vigorous, More Time

More Vigorous, Less Time

Figure 2-1 Examples of moderate amounts of physical activity.
A moderate amount of physical activity is roughly equivalent to physical activity that uses approximately 150 calories of energy per day, or 1000 calories per week. Some activities can be performed at various intensities; the suggested durations correspond to expected intensity of effort.   SOURCE: U.S. Department of Health and Human Services. 1996. *Physical Activity and Health. A Report of the Surgeon General: At-A-Glance.* Washington, D.C.: U.S. Department of Health and Human Services.

include a moderate amount of physical activity on most, preferably all, days of the week. The report suggests a goal of 150 calories per day, or about 1000 calories per week, expended in physical activity. Because energy expenditure is a function of both the intensity and the duration of the activity, the same amount of activity can be obtained in longer sessions of moderately intense activities as in shorter sessions of more strenuous activities. Thus, 30 minutes of brisk walking or raking leaves is equivalent to 15 minutes of running or shoveling snow. Examples of moderate physical activities are given in Figure 2-1.

In this lifestyle approach to physical activity, the daily total of activity can be accumulated in multiple short bouts—for example, two 10-minute bicycle rides to and from class and a brisk 15-minute walk to the post office. People can choose activities that they find enjoyable and that fit into their daily routine; everyday tasks at school, work, and home can be structured to contribute to the daily activity total (see the box "Becoming More Active" for suggestions). In addition to recommending moderate-intensity physical activity, the Surgeon General's report recommends that people perform resistance training (exercising against an opposing force such as a weight) at least twice per week to build and maintain muscular strength.

The Surgeon General recommends that all Americans accumulate at least 30 minutes of moderate-intensity activity on most days of the week. Yard work is one of many household chores that can contribute to your daily total of physical activity.

By increasing lifestyle physical activity in accordance with the guidelines given in the Surgeon General's report, people can expect to significantly improve their health and well-being. If all the Americans who are now completely sedentary were to adopt a more active lifestyle, there would be enormous benefit to the public's health and to individual well-being. Such a program may not, however, increase physical fitness.

Exercise Programs to Develop Physical Fitness The Surgeon General's report also summarized the benefits of more formal exercise programs. It concluded that people can obtain even greater health benefits by increasing the duration and intensity of activity. Thus a person who engages in a structured, formal exercise program designed to measurably improve physical fitness will obtain even greater improvements in quality of life and greater reductions in disease and mortality risk. Chapters 3–7 provide specific guidelines for developing an exercise program that will develop total fitness.

How Much Physical Activity Is Enough?

The Surgeon General's report has generated controversy among researchers. Some experts feel that people get most of the health benefits of an exercise program simply by becoming more active over the course of the day. Others feel that the lifestyle approach sets too low of an activity goal; they argue that people should exercise long enough and intensely enough to improve their body's capacity for exercise—that is, to improve physical fitness. More research is needed to clarify the health effects of moderate-intensity vs. high-intensity exercise and continuous vs. intermittent exercise. However, there is probably truth in both of these positions.

Regular physical activity, regardless of intensity, makes you healthier and can help protect you from many chronic diseases. However, exercising at low intensities does little to improve physical fitness. While you get

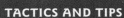
- Take the stairs instead of the elevator or escalator.
- Walk to the mailbox, post office, store, bank, or library whenever possible.
- Park your car a mile or even just a few blocks from your destination, and walk briskly.
- Do at least one chore every day that requires physical activity: wash the windows or your car, clean your room or house, mow the lawn, rake the leaves.
- Take study or work breaks to avoid sitting for more than 30 minutes at a time. Get up and walk around the library, your office, or your home or dorm; go up and down a flight of stairs.
- Stretch when you stand in line or watch TV.
- When you take public transportation, get off one stop down the line and walk to your destination.
- Go dancing instead of to a movie.
- Walk to visit a neighbor or friend rather than calling him or her on the phone. Go for a walk while you chat.
- Put your remote controls in storage; when you want to change TV or radio stations, get up and do it by hand.
- Seize every opportunity to get up and walk around. Move more and sit less.

many of the health benefits of exercise by simply being more active, you obtain even more benefits when you are physically fit. In addition to long-term health benefits, fitness also significantly contributes to quality of life. Fitness can give you freedom—freedom to move your body the way you want. Fit people have more energy and better body control. They can enjoy a more active lifestyle—cycling, hiking, skiing, and so on—than their more sedentary counterparts. Even if you don't like sports, you need physical energy and stamina in your daily life and for many nonsport leisure activities—visiting museums, playing with children, gardening, and so on.

Where does this leave you? Most experts agree that some physical activity is better than none, but that more—as long as it does not result in injury—is probably better than some. At the very least, strive to become more active and meet the goal set by the Surgeon General's report of using about 150 calories per day in physical activity—the equivalent of about 30 minutes of moderate-intensity activity such as brisk walking (see Figure 2-1). Choose to be active whenever you can—walk to class, mow the lawn, wash your car, climb the stairs, work in the garden, quit using all your remote control devices. And for even better health and well-being, participate in a structured exercise program that develops physical fitness. Any increase in physical activity will contribute to your health and well-being, now and in the future.

Next, let's take a closer look at the components of physical fitness and the basic principles of fitness training.

HEALTH-RELATED COMPONENTS OF PHYSICAL FITNESS

Physical fitness has many components, some related to general health and others related more specifically to particular sports or activities. The five components of fitness most important for health are cardiorespiratory endurance, muscular strength, muscular endurance, flexibility, and body composition (proportion of fat to fat-free weight). Health-related fitness contributes to your capacity to enjoy life, helps your body withstand physical and psychological challenges, and protects you from chronic disease.

Cardiorespiratory Endurance

Cardiorespiratory endurance is the ability to perform prolonged, large-muscle, dynamic exercise at moderate-to-high levels of intensity. It depends on such factors as the ability of the lungs to deliver oxygen from the environment to the bloodstream, the heart's capacity to pump blood, the ability of the nervous system and blood vessels to regulate blood flow, and the capability of the body's chemical systems to use oxygen and process fuels for exercise.

When levels of cardiorespiratory fitness are low, the heart has to work very hard during normal daily activities and may not be able to work hard enough to sustain high-intensity physical activity in an emergency. As cardiorespiratory fitness improves, the heart begins to function more efficiently. It doesn't have to work as hard at rest or during low levels of exercise. The heart pumps more blood per heartbeat, resting heart rate slows down, blood volume increases, blood supply to the tissues improves, the body is better able to cool itself, and resting blood pressure decreases. A healthy heart can better withstand the strains of everyday life, the stress of occasional emergencies, and the wear and tear of time. Endurance training also improves

cardiorespiratory endurance The ability of the body to perform prolonged, large-muscle, dynamic exercise at moderate-to-high levels of intensity. **TERMS**

Cardiorespiratory endurance is a key component of health-related fitness. These stationary cyclists are conditioning their hearts and lungs as well as gaining many other health benefits.

the functioning of the chemical systems, particularly in the muscles and liver, thereby enhancing the body's ability to use energy supplied by food.

Cardiorespiratory endurance is a central component of health-related fitness because the functioning of the heart and lungs is so essential to overall good health. A person can't live very long or very well without a healthy heart. Low levels of cardiorespiratory fitness are linked with heart disease, the leading cause of death in the United States.

Muscular Strength

Muscular strength is the amount of force a muscle can produce with a single maximum effort. Strong muscles are important for the smooth and easy performance of everyday activities, such as carrying groceries, lifting boxes, and climbing stairs, as well as for emergency situations. They help keep the skeleton in proper alignment, preventing back and leg pain and providing the support necessary for good posture. Muscular strength has obvious importance in recreational activities. Strong people can hit a tennis ball harder, kick a soccer ball farther, and ride a bicycle uphill more easily. Muscle tissue is an important element of overall body composition. Greater muscle mass means a higher rate of **metabolism** and faster energy use. Maintaining strength and muscle mass is vital for healthy aging. Older people tend to lose muscle cells, and many of the remaining muscle cells become nonfunctional because they lose their attachment to the nervous system. Strength training helps maintain muscle mass and function and possibly helps decrease the risk of osteoporosis in older people, which greatly enhances their quality of life and prevents life-threatening injuries.

Muscular Endurance

Muscular endurance is the ability to sustain a given level of muscle tension—that is, to hold a muscle contraction for a long period of time or to contract a muscle over and over again. Muscular endurance is important for good posture and for injury prevention. For example, if abdominal and back muscles can't hold the spine correctly, the chances of low-back pain and back injury are increased. Muscular endurance helps people cope with the physical demands of everyday life and enhances performance in sports and work. It is also important for most leisure and fitness activities.

Flexibility

Flexibility is the ability to move the joints through their full range of motion. Although range of motion isn't a significant factor in everyday activities for most people, inactivity causes the joints to become stiffer with age. Stiffness often causes older people to assume unnatural body postures that can stress joints and muscles. Stretching exercises can help ensure a healthy range of motion for all major joints.

Body Composition

Body composition refers to the relative amounts of **fat-free mass** (muscle, bone, and water) and fat in the body. Healthy body composition involves a high proportion of fat-free mass and an acceptably low level of body fat, adjusted for age and gender. A person with excessive body fat is more likely to experience a variety of health problems, including heart disease, high blood pressure, stroke, joint problems, diabetes, gallbladder disease, cancer, and back pain. The best way to lose fat is through a lifestyle that includes a sensible diet and exercise. The best way to add muscle mass is through weight training, also known as strength or resistance training.

In addition to these five health-related components of physical fitness, physical fitness for a particular sport or activity might include any or all of the following: coordination, speed, reaction time, agility, balance, and skill. Sport-specific skills are best developed through practice. The skill and coordination needed to play basketball, for example, are developed by playing basketball.

PRINCIPLES OF PHYSICAL TRAINING

The human body is very adaptable. The greater the demands made on it, the more it adjusts to meet the demands. Over time, immediate, short-term adjustments translate into long-term changes and improvements. When breathing and heart rate increase during exercise, for example, the heart gradually develops the ability to pump more blood with each beat. Then, during exercise, it doesn't have to beat as fast to meet the cells' demands for oxygen. The goal of **physical training** is to bring about these long-term changes and improvements in the body's functioning. Although people differ in the maximum levels of physical fitness and performance they can achieve through training, the wellness benefits of exercise are available to everyone (see the box "Fitness and Disability").

Particular types and amounts of exercise are most effective in developing the various components of fitness. To put together an effective exercise program, a person should first understand the basic principles of physical training. Important principles are specificity, progressive overload, reversibility, and individual differences.

Specificity

To develop a particular fitness component, exercises must be performed that are specifically designed for that component. This is the principle of **specificity**. Weight training, for example, develops muscular strength, not cardiorespiratory endurance or flexibility. Specificity also applies to the skill-related fitness components—to improve at tennis, you must practice tennis—and to the different parts of the body—to develop stronger arms, you must exercise your arms. A well-rounded exercise program includes exercises geared to each component of fitness, to different parts of the body, and to specific activities or sports.

Progressive Overload

The body adapts to the demands of exercise by improving its functioning. When the amount of exercise (also called overload or stress) is progressively increased, fitness continues to improve. This is the principle of **progressive overload.**

The amount of overload is very important. Too little exercise will have no effect on fitness (although it may improve health); too much may cause injury. For every type of exercise, there is a training threshold at which fitness benefits begin to occur, a zone within which maximum fitness benefits occur, and an upper limit of safe training (Figure 2-2). The amount of exercise needed depends on the individual's current level of fitness, his or her fitness goals, and the component being developed. A novice, for example, might experience fitness benefits from jogging a mile in 10 minutes, but this level of exercise would cause no physical adaptations in a trained distance runner. Beginners should start at the lower end of the fitness benefit zone; fitter individuals will make more rapid gains by exercising at the higher end of the fitness benefit zone.

The amount of overload needed to maintain or improve a particular level of fitness is determined in terms of three dimensions: exercise frequency (how often), intensity (how hard), and duration (how long).

Frequency Developing fitness requires regular exercise. Optimum exercise frequency, expressed in number of days per week, varies with the component being developed and the individual's fitness goals. For most people, a frequency of 3–5 days per week for cardiorespiratory endurance exercise and 2–3 days per week for resistance and flexibility training is appropriate for a general fitness program.

TERMS

muscular strength The amount of force a muscle can produce with a single maximum effort.

metabolism The sum of all the vital processes by which food energy and nutrients are made available to and used by the body.

muscular endurance The ability of a muscle or group of muscles to remain contracted or to contract repeatedly for a long period of time.

flexibility The range of motion in a joint or group of joints; flexibility is related to muscle length.

body composition The relative proportion of fat-free mass (muscle, bone, and water) and fat in the body.

fat-free mass The nonfat component of the human body, consisting of skeletal muscle, bone, and water.

physical training The performance of different types of activities that cause the body to adapt and improve its level of fitness.

specificity The training principle according to which the body adapts to the particular type and amount of stress placed on it.

progressive overload The training principle according to which increasing amounts of stress are placed on the body, causing adaptations that improve fitness.

Intensity   Fitness benefits occur when a person exercises harder than his or her normal level of activity. The appropriate exercise intensity varies with each fitness component. To develop cardiorespiratory endurance, for example, a person must raise his or her heart rate above normal; to develop muscular strength, a person must lift a heavier weight than normal; to develop flexibility, a person must stretch muscles beyond their normal length. The intensity required to develop each fitness component is discussed in detail in Chapters 3–5. In general, the intensity required to improve fitness is greater than that needed to obtain health benefits from lifestyle physical activity.

Duration   If fitness benefits are to occur, exercise sessions must last for an extended period of time. For cardiorespiratory endurance exercise, a total duration of 20–60 minutes is recommended; exercise can take place in a single session or in multiple bouts that last 10 or more minutes. The intensity of exercise affects the total duration required to obtain fitness benefits. For high-intensity exercise such as running, for example, a total duration at the low end of the range—20–30 minutes—is appropriate. For more-moderate-intensity exercise, such as walking, a longer duration—perhaps 45–60 minutes—is required. High-intensity exercise poses a greater risk of injury than lower-intensity exercise, so if you are a nonathletic adult, it's probably best to emphasize lower-to-moderate-intensity activity of longer duration.

For muscular strength, muscular endurance, and flexibility, similar amounts of time are advisable, but these exercises are more commonly organized in terms of a specific number of repetitions of particular exercises. For resistance training, for example, a recommended program includes 1 or more sets of 8–12 repetitions of 8–10 different exercises that work the major muscle groups.

Reversibility

Fitness is a reversible adaptation. The body adjusts to lower levels of physical activity the same way it adjusts to higher levels. This is the principle of **reversibility.** When a person stops exercising, up to 50% of fitness improvements are lost within 2 months. If a training schedule must be curtailed temporarily, fitness improvements are best maintained if exercise intensity is kept constant and frequency and/or duration is reduced.

Individual Differences

Anyone watching the Olympics, a professional football game, or a tennis championship match can readily see that from a physical standpoint, we are not all created

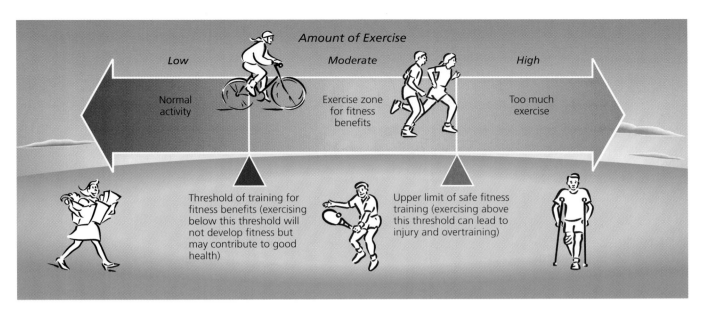

Figure 2-2 Amount of exercise for improving physical fitness.

equal. There are large individual differences in our ability to improve fitness and perform and learn sports skills. Some people are able to run longer distances, or lift more weight, or kick a soccer ball more skillfully than others will ever be able to, no matter how much they train. There are limits on the adaptability—the potential for improvement—of any human body. The body's ability to transport and use oxygen, for example, can be improved by only about 15–30% through training. An endurance athlete must therefore inherit a large metabolic capacity in order to reach competitive performance levels.

However, an individual doesn't have to be an Olympic sprinter to experience health benefits from running. Physical training improves fitness regardless of heredity. For the average person, the body's adaptability is enough to achieve all fitness goals. An improvement of 15–30% in oxygen consumption can mean the difference between lifelong health and the development of a chronic disease.

DESIGNING YOUR OWN EXERCISE PROGRAM

Physical training works best when you have a plan. The plan helps you make gradual but steady progress toward your goals in all five areas of health-related fitness. The basic idea of a workout or training session is to introduce a stress powerful enough to cause adaptation but not so severe as to cause injury.

Assessment

The first step in creating a successful fitness program is to assess your current level of physical activity and fitness for each of the five health-related fitness components. The results of the assessment tests will help you set specific fitness goals and plan your fitness program. Lab 2-1 gives you the opportunity to assess your current overall level of activity and determine if it is appropriate. Assessment tests in Chapters 3, 4, 5, and 6 will help you evaluate your cardiorespiratory endurance, muscular strength, muscular endurance, flexibility, and body composition.

Setting Goals

The ultimate goal of every health-related fitness program is the same—wellness that lasts a lifetime. Is this goal inspiring enough to motivate you to begin and stay with a program of regular exercise? Think carefully about your goals and your reasons for exercising. You may want to exercise to improve your body composition, have more energy, or lower your blood pressure; you may want to be able to run a 10K road race or ski a more advanced slope; or you may just want to feel better about yourself.

Whatever your goals, they must be important enough to you to keep you motivated. Studies have shown that exercising for yourself, rather than for the impression you think you'll make on others, is more likely to lead to long-lasting commitment. After you complete the assessment tests in Chapters 3–6, you will be able to set goals directly related to each fitness component, such as working toward a 3-mile jog or doing 20 push-ups. First, though, think carefully about your overall goals, and be clear about why you are starting a program.

reversibility   The training principle according to which fitness improvements are lost when demands on the body are lowered.   **TERMS**

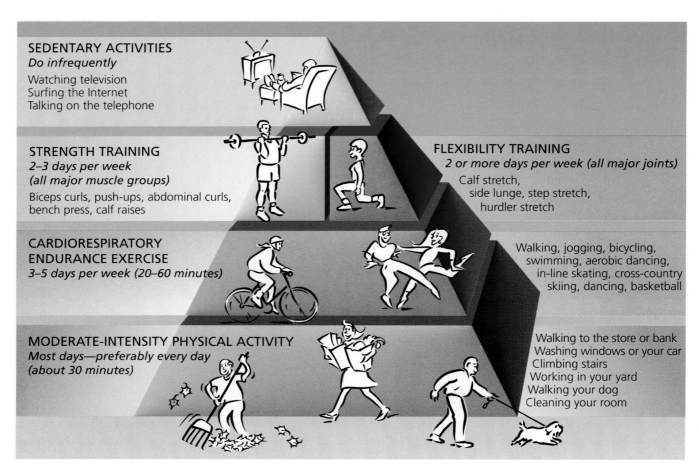

Figure 2-3 Physical activity pyramid. Similar to the Food Guide Pyramid, this physical activity pyramid is designed to help people become more active. If you are currently sedentary, begin at the bottom of the pyramid and gradually increase the amount of moderate-intensity physical activity in your life. If you are already moderately active, begin a formal exercise program that includes cardiorespiratory endurance exercise, flexibility training, and strength training to help you develop all the health-related components of fitness.

Choosing Activities for a Balanced Program

An ideal fitness program combines a physically active lifestyle with a systematic exercise program to develop and maintain physical fitness. This overall program is illustrated in the physical activity pyramid shown in Figure 2-3. If you are currently sedentary, your goal is to start at the bottom of the pyramid and gradually increase the amount of moderate-intensity physical activity in your daily life. Appropriate activities include brisk walking, climbing stairs, yard work, and washing your car. You don't have to exercise vigorously, but you should experience a moderate increase in your heart and breathing rates. As described earlier, your activity time can be broken up into small blocks over the course of a day. The time it takes to walk to the library, climb a flight of stairs five times, and clean the house can quickly add up to 30 or more minutes of moderate activity.

The next two levels of the pyramid illustrate parts of a formal exercise program. The American College of Sports

Medicine has established guidelines for creating an exercise program that will develop physical fitness (Table 2-2). A balanced program includes activities to develop all the health-related components of fitness.

• *Cardiorespiratory endurance* is developed by activities that involve continuous rhythmic movements of large muscle groups. Walking, jogging, cycling, swimming, and aerobic dance (also referred to as group exercise) are all good activities for developing endurance. Choose activities that you enjoy and that are convenient. Many popular leisure activities can develop endurance, including in-line skating, dancing, and backpacking. Start-and-stop activities such as tennis, racquetball, and soccer can also develop endurance if one's skill level is sufficient to enable periods of continuous play. Training for cardiorespiratory endurance is discussed in Chapter 3.

TABLE 2-2 — *Exercise Recommendations for Healthy Adults*

Exercise to Develop and Maintain Cardiorespiratory Endurance and Body Composition

Mode of activity	Any activity that uses large muscle groups, can be maintained continuously, and is rhythmical and aerobic in nature; for example, walking-hiking, running-jogging, cycling-bicycling, cross-country skiing, group exercise (aerobic dance), rope skipping, rowing, stairclimbing, swimming, skating, and endurance game activities.
Frequency of training	3–5 days per week.
Intensity of training	55/65–90% of maximum heart rate or 40/50–85% of maximum oxygen uptake reserve. The lower intensity values (55–64% of maximum heart rate and 40–49% of maximum oxygen uptake reserve) are most applicable to individuals who are quite unfit.*
Duration of training	20–60 total minutes of continuous or intermittent (in sessions lasting 10 or more minutes) aerobic activity. Duration is dependent on the intensity of activity; thus, lower-intensity activity should be conducted over a longer period of time (30 minutes or more). Lower-to-moderate-intensity activity of longer duration is recommended for the nonathletic adult.

Exercise to Develop and Maintain Muscular Strength and Endurance, Flexibility, and Body Composition

Resistance training	One set of 8–10 exercises that condition the major muscle groups should be performed 2–3 days per week. Most people should complete 8–12 repetitions of each exercise; for older and more frail people (approximately 50–60 years of age and above), 10–15 repetitions with a lighter weight may be more appropriate. Multiple-set regimens may provide greater benefits if time allows.
Flexibility training	Stretches for the major muscle groups should be performed a minimum of 2–3 days per week; at least four repetitions, held for 10–30 seconds, should be completed.

*Instructions for calculating target heart rate intensity for cardiorespiratory endurance exercise are presented in Chapter 3.

SOURCE: American College of Sports Medicine. 1998. Position Stand: The Recommended Quantity and Quality of Exercise for Developing and Maintaining Cardiorespiratory and Muscular Fitness, and Flexibility in Healthy Adults. *Medicine and Science in Sports and Exercise* 30(6): 975–991.

- *Muscular strength and endurance* can be developed through resistance training—training with weights or performing calisthenic exercises such as push-ups and sit-ups. Training for muscular strength and endurance is discussed in Chapter 4.

- *Flexibility* is developed by stretching the major muscle groups, regularly and with proper technique. Flexibility is discussed in Chapter 5.

- *Healthy body composition* can be developed by combining a sensible diet and a program of regular exercise. Endurance exercise is best for reducing body fat; resistance training builds muscle mass, which helps increase metabolism (the rate of energy expenditure). Body composition is discussed in Chapter 6.

There are as many different fitness programs as there are individuals. Consider the following examples:

- Maggie is a person whose life revolves around sports. She's been on softball teams and swim teams, and now she's on her college varsity soccer team. She follows a rigorous exercise regimen established by her soccer coach. Soccer practice is from four to six afternoons a week. It begins with warm-ups, drills, and practice in specific skills, and it ends with a scrimmage and then a jog around the soccer field. Games are every Saturday. Maggie likes team sports, but she also enjoys exercising alone, so she goes on long bicycle rides whenever she can fit them in. She can't imagine what it would be like not to be physically active every day.

- Maria is a busy young mother of twins. To keep in shape, she joined a health club with a weight room, exercise classes, and child care. Every Monday, Wednesday, and Friday morning, she takes the twins to the club and attends the 7:00 "wake-up" low-impact aerobics class. The instructor leads the class through warm-ups; a 20-minute aerobic workout; exercises for the arms, abdomen, buttocks, and legs; stretches; and a relaxation exercise. Maria is exhilarated and ready for the rest of the day before 9:00 A.M.

- Tom is an engineering student with a lot of studying to do and an active social life as well. For exercise, he plays tennis three times a week. He likes to head for the courts around 6:00 P.M., when most people are eating dinner. He warms up for 10 minutes by practicing his forehand and backhand against a backboard and

An important principle of exercising is to train the way you want your body to change. By working out on weight training equipment, this young man is increasing the strength and definition of specific muscles and improving the overall appearance of his body.

then plays a hard, fast game with his regular partner for 45 minutes to an hour. Afterwards, he does some stretching exercises while his muscles are still warm. Then he showers and gets ready for dinner. Twice a week he works out at the gym, with particular attention to keeping his arms strong and his shoulders limber. On Saturday nights, he goes dancing with friends.

Each of these people has worked an adequate or more-than-adequate fitness program into their busy daily routine. Chapter 7 contains guidelines to help you choose activities and put together a complete exercise program that suits your goals and preferences.

What about the tip of the activity pyramid? Although sedentary activities are often unavoidable—attending class, studying, working in an office, and so on—many people choose inactivity over activity during their leisure time. Change sedentary patterns by becoming more active whenever you can. Move more and sit less.

Guidelines for Training

The following guidelines will make your exercise program more effective and successful.

• *Train the way you want your body to change.* Stress your body such that it adapts in the desired direction.

To have a more muscular build, lift weights. To be more flexible, do stretching exercises. To improve performance in a particular sport, practice that sport or the movements used in it.

• *Train regularly.* Consistency is the key to improving fitness. Adaptations to exercise are reversible; fitness improvements are lost if too much time is allowed to pass between exercise sessions.

• *Get in shape gradually.* An exercise program can be divided into three phases: the beginning phase, during which the body adjusts to the new type and level of activity; the progress phase, during which fitness is increased; and the maintenance phase, in which the targeted level of fitness is maintained over the long term (Figure 2-4). When beginning a program, it is critical to start slowly to give your body time to adapt to the stress of exercise. As you progress, increase duration and frequency before increasing intensity. If you train too much or too intensely, you are more likely to suffer injuries or become **overtrained,** a condition characterized by lack of energy, aching muscles and joints, and decreased physical performance. Injuries and overtraining slow down an exercise program and impede motivation. The goal is not to get in shape as quickly as possible but to gradually become and remain physically fit. When you reach your desired level of fitness, maintain it by exercising regularly.

• *Warm up before exercising, and cool down afterward.* Warming up decreases the chances of injury by helping the body gradually progress from rest to activity. A warm-up should include low-intensity movements similar to those used in the activity that will follow. Stretching exercises are also often recommended. Cooling down after exercise is important for restoring circulation to its normal resting condition. Cool down by continuing to exercise but at a lower level of intensity.

• *Listen to your body.* Don't exercise if it doesn't feel right. Sometimes you need a few days of rest to recover enough to train with the intensity required for improving fitness. On the other hand, you can't train sporadically either. If you listen to your body and it always tells you to rest, you won't make any progress. You have to work to improve fitness, so try to maintain a structured —but flexible—workout program.

• *Try training with a partner.* Training partners can motivate and encourage each other through hard spots and help each other develop proper exercise techniques. Training with a partner can make exercising seem easier and more fun.

• *Train your mind.* This is one of the most difficult skills to acquire, but it is critical for achieving and maintaining fitness. Becoming fit requires commitment, discipline, and patience. These qualities come from understanding the importance of exercise and having clear

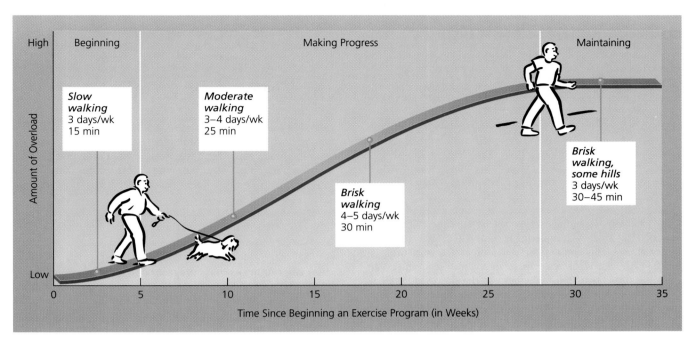

Figure 2-4 Phases of an exercise program. This figure shows how the amount of overload is increased gradually over time in a sample walking program. Regardless of the activity chosen, it is important that an exercise program begin slowly and progress gradually. Once a person achieves the desired level of fitness, she or he can maintain it by exercising at least 3 days per week.   SOURCE: Progression data from American College of Sports Medicine. 1995. *Guidelines for Exercise Testing and Prescription,* 5th ed. Baltimore, Md.: Williams and Wilkins.

and reachable goals. Use the lifestyle management techniques discussed in Chapter 1 to keep your program on track. Believe in yourself and your potential—and you *will* achieve your goals!

• *Keep your exercise program in perspective.* As important as physical fitness is, it is only part of a well-rounded life. You have to have time for work and school, family and friends, relaxation and hobbies. Some people become overinvolved in exercise and neglect other parts of their lives. They think of themselves as runners, dancers, swimmers, or triathletes rather than as people who participate in those activities. Balance and moderation are the key ingredients of a fit and well life.

SUMMARY

• Regular, moderate activity on most days of the week substantially contributes to good health. Even if you do not participate in a formal, vigorous exercise program, you can get many of the health benefits of exercise by becoming more active during the day. If you are already physically active, you will benefit even more by increasing the intensity or duration of your activity.

• The five components of physical fitness most important for health are cardiorespiratory endurance, muscular strength, muscular endurance, flexibility, and body composition.

• Physical training is the process of bringing about long-term improvements in the body's functioning through exercise. Four important principles of training are specificity, progressive overload, reversibility, and individual differences.

• Progressive overload is quantified in terms of frequency, intensity, and duration of exercise.

• Individual differences mean that people will vary in the maximum level of fitness or performance they can achieve. However, every person is capable of reaching personal fitness goals.

• Important steps in designing an exercise program include assessing your current level of fitness, setting realistic goals, and choosing activities that develop all the components of fitness.

overtraining A condition caused by training too much or too intensely, characterized by lack of energy, decreased physical performance, fatigue, depression, aching muscles and joints, and susceptibility to injury.   **TERMS**

COMMON QUESTIONS ANSWERED

Is exercise safe for me? People of any age who are not at high risk for serious health problems can safely exercise at a moderate intensity (60% or less of maximum heart rate) without a prior medical evaluation. (See Chapter 3 for a discussion of maximum heart rate.) Likewise, if you are male and under 40 or female and under 50 and in good health, exercise is probably safe for you. If you are over these ages or have health problems (especially high blood pressure, heart disease, muscle or joint problems, or obesity), see your physician before starting a vigorous exercise program. The Canadian Society for Exercise Physiology has developed a questionnaire called PAR-Q to help determine exercise safety. This questionnaire is included in Lab 2-2. Completing it should alert you to any potential problems you may have. If a physician isn't sure whether exercise is safe for you, he or she may recommend an **exercise stress test** to see whether you develop symptoms of heart disease during exercise. For most people, however, it's far safer to exercise than to remain sedentary.

You must also consider your physical safety when exercising. If you ride a bicycle or run on public streets, wear clothing that can be seen easily. Bicyclists should always wear helmets. Even though you may have the right-of-way, give cars plenty of leeway; in a collision, a car will usually sustain less damage than a bicycle or your unprotected body. Don't train in isolated areas unless you're with a friend. Exercising alone, you could easily be injured or become a crime victim. (See Appendix A for more information on personal safety.)

Where can I get help and advice about exercise? Because fitness is essential to a wellness lifestyle, you need to learn as much as you can about exercise. One of the best places to get help is an exercise class. There, expert instructors can help you learn the basics of training and answer your questions. Read articles by credible experts in fitness magazines. Because of competition among publications, these magazines include articles by leading experts in exercise science written at a layperson's level.

A qualified personal trainer can also be helpful in getting you started in an exercise program or a new form of training. Make sure this person has proper qualifications, such as a college degree in exercise physiology or physical education or ACSM certification. Don't seek out a person for advice simply because he or she looks fit.

Should I follow my exercise program if I'm sick? If you have a mild head cold or feel one coming on, it is probably OK to exercise moderately. Just begin slowly and see how you feel. However, if you have symptoms of a more serious illness—fever, swollen glands, nausea, extreme tiredness, muscle aches—wait until you have fully recovered before resuming your exercise program. Continuing to exercise while suffering from an illness more serious than a cold can compromise your recovery and may even be dangerous.

How can I fit my exercise program into my day? Good time management is an important skill in creating and maintaining an exercise program. Choose a regular time to exercise, preferably the same time every day. Don't tell yourself you'll exercise "sometime during the day" when you have free time—that free time may never come. Schedule your workout, and make it a priority. Include alternative plans in your program to account for circumstances like bad weather or vacations.

You don't have to work on all fitness components in the same exercise session. You can jog and stretch in one session and lift weights in another. The important thing is to have a regular schedule. (You'll have the chance to develop strategies for successful time management in the Behavior Change Workbook at the end of the text.)

Where can I work out? Identify accessible and pleasant places to work out. For running, find a field or park with a soft surface. For swimming, find a pool that's open at times convenient for you. For cycling, find an area with minimal traffic and air pollution. Make sure the place you exercise is safe and convenient.

If you join a health club or fitness center, choose one close to your home or place of work. You'll be less likely to go to the club if it's farther away. Choose a club with an atmosphere that fits with your personality and offers the activities you want. For guidelines, refer to the box "Choosing a Fitness Center."

- Guidelines that can make an exercise program more effective include training the way you want your body to change, training regularly, getting in shape gradually, warming up and cooling down, maintaining a structured but flexible program, training with a partner, training your mind, and keeping exercise in perspective.

TERMS **exercise stress test** A test usually administered on a treadmill or cycle ergometer that involves analysis of the changes in electrical activity in the heart from an electrocardiogram (EKG or ECG) taken during exercise. Used to determine if any heart disease is present and to assess current fitness level.

FOR MORE INFORMATION

Books

American College of Sports Medicine. 1995. *ACSM's Guidelines for Exercise Testing and Prescription,* 5th ed. Baltimore: Williams & Wilkins. *Includes the ACSM guidelines for safety of exercising, a basic discussion of exercise physiology, and information about fitness testing and prescription.*

American College of Sports Medicine. 1998. *ACSM Fitness Book,* 2d ed. Champaign, Ill.: Human Kinetics. *A brief, easy-to-use guide to creating a successful fitness program.*

Burke, E., and E. Burke. 1996. *Complete Home Fitness Handbook.* Champaign, Ill.: Human Kinetics. *A comprehensive exercise plan for people who want to exercise at home.*

If you're thinking of becoming a member of a health club or fitness center, the following guidelines will help you make a final choice.

1. Does the center provide programs that are appropriate for you and at convenient times? You may wish to consult with a physician about your specific exercise needs.

2. Ask members and former members about the operation, services, staff, and programs.

3. Visit the club at the time of day when you plan to use it. Are the classes crowded, or are there long lines for the equipment you plan to use?

4. Check the atmosphere of the club. Are personnel well trained, friendly, enthusiastic, attentive, and well informed? Do instructors have special training? Is there a fitness supervisor who has a degree in exercise science or certification from the ACSM or another recognized organization?

5. Observe the facility. Is it clean, well ventilated, and properly maintained? Is the equipment in good condition? Is there shock-absorbent flooring for aerobics workouts? Is safety information provided for using weight machines? Are dressing rooms and showers available and clean?

6. Find out about the different types of memberships and payment plans the club offers. Ask for a short-term trial membership. Don't be rushed into signing a long-term contract. Before signing any contract, ask for a few days to think it over; a reputable facility will let you consider joining without applying pressure.

7. Read the contract carefully before signing, or get a knowledgeable person to read it. Be sure you understand the provisions and agreements. Don't hesitate to ask questions.

8. Understand what happens if you wish to cancel the membership. What type of refund policy does the club have?

9. Find out if the club will suspend your membership temporarily when you're on vacation or unable to exercise for another reason.

10. Find out how long the club has been in your area. The longer the better, and if under the same management, that's another plus. Beware of new clubs offering "pre-opening" membership discounts.

11. Find out if the club belongs to the Association of Physical Fitness Centers or the International Racquet Sports Association. These trade associations have established standards to help protect consumer health, safety, and rights. You can also check with the Better Business Bureau to see if any complaints have been filed against the club.

In addition, be wary of promotion gimmicks and high-pressure sales techniques. Be alert to practices such as special reduced prices, free visits, reservation forms, and guarantees of fitness improvements or weight loss. Get all the facts before making a decision. If you feel any excessive amount of pressure, leave or at least ask for more time. Under no circumstances should you feel badgered, embarrassed, or threatened. You want to find a facility that you feel comfortable with and that meets your needs.

SOURCES: Health Clubs: The right choice for you? 1996. *Consumer Reports*, January, 27–30; Cornacchia, H. 1994. How to choose a fitness center. *Healthline*, April. Krucoff, C. 1989. Joining the club. *Washington Post Health*, 5 September, 20.

Diamond, J. 1996. *Exercises for Airplanes: (And Other Confined Spaces)*. New York: Excalibur. *A guide to exercising in airplanes and confined spaces, such as the office.*

Farquhar, J. W. 1996. *Fresh Start: The Stanford Medical School Health and Fitness Program.* San Francisco: KQED. *An excellent guide to exercising for health and prevention of disease.*

Nieman, D. C. 1999. *Exercise Testing and Prescription: A Health-Related Approach,* 4th ed. Mountain View, Calif.: Mayfield. *Comprehensive discussions of fitness testing, exercise and disease, nutrition and physical performance, and exercise prescription.*

Rippe, J. M., and M. A. Waite. 1996. *Fit over Forty: A Revolutionary Plan to Achieve Lifelong Physical and Spiritual Health and Well-Being.* New York: William Morrow. *A sensible approach to incorporating exercise into a wellness lifestyle.*

U.S. Department of Health and Human Services. 1996. *Physical Activity and Health: A Report of the Surgeon General.* Department of Health and Human Services. (Also available online: http://www.cdc.gov/nccdphp/sgr/sgr.htm) *Provides a summary of the evidence for the benefits of physical activity as well as all the recent recommendations.*

Journals

ACSM Health and Fitness Journal (401 West Michigan Street, Indianapolis, IN 46202; http://www.wwilkins.com/esources/journdex/FIT/index.html)

Physician and Sportsmedicine (4530 W. 77th Street, Minneapolis, MN 55435; many of the articles are also available online at http://www.physsportsmed.com)

Organizations, Hotlines, and Web Sites

American Alliance for Health, Physical Education, Recreation, and Dance (AAHPERD). A professional organization dedicated to promoting quality education programs to improve the health and fitness of Americans.
800-213-7193
http://www.aahperd.org

American College of Sports Medicine (ACSM). Provides brochures, publications, and audio- and videotapes on the positive effects of exercise.
317-637-9200
http://www.acsm.org/sportsmed

American Council on Exercise (ACE). Promotes exercise and fitness for all Americans; the Web site features fact sheets on many consumer topics, including choosing shoes, cross-training, steroids, and getting started on an exercise program.

800-529-8227 (Consumer Fitness Hotline)
http://www.acefitness.org

American Medical Association/Personal Trainer. Includes a fitness assessment and guidelines for creating a safe, effective program for developing the health-related components of fitness.
http://www.ama-assn.org/insight/gen_hlth/trainer

Balance Magazine. An online health and fitness magazine with practical advice for exercisers.
http://www.hyperlink.com/balance

Disabled Sports USA. Provides sports and recreation services to people with physical or mobility disorders.
301-217-0960
http://www.nas.com/~dsusa

Fitness Management Magazine's Fitness World. Includes current issues of the magazine, information about exercise books and videos, news highlights related to exercise, and answers to frequently asked questions.
http://www.fitnessworld.com

Fitness Partner Connection Jumpsite. A resource of fitness-related information on the Internet.
http://primusweb.com/fitnesspartner

Fitness-Related Web Sites. Includes many links to helpful fitness- and health-related sites.
http://www.montana.com/Stafford/fitnesslinks.html

Internet's Fitness Resource. Provides extensive links to sites about general fitness, specific activities, and fitness equipment.
http://www.netsweat.com

Melpomene Institute. Provides information about physical activity and health for women.
612-642-1951
http://www.melpomene.org

Physical Activity & Health Network. Provides resources and links on the relationship between physical activity and health.
http://www.pitt.edu/~pahnet

Worldguide Health and Fitness Forum. Provides information on anatomy, cardiorespiratory endurance exercise, strength training, nutrition, and sports medicine.
http://www.worldguide.com/Fitness/hf.html

SELECTED BIBLIOGRAPHY

American College of Sports Medicine. 1998. ACSM Position Stand: The Recommended Quantity and Quality of Exercise for Developing and Maintaining Cardiorespiratory and Muscular Fitness, and Flexibility in Healthy Adults. *Medicine and Science in Sports and Exercise* 30(6):975–991.

American College of Sports Medicine. 1995. *ACSM's Guidelines for Exercise Testing and Prescription,* 5th ed. Baltimore: Williams & Wilkins.

Brooks, G. A., T. D. Fahey, and T. P. White. 1996. *Exercise Physiology: Human Bioenergetics and Its Applications,* 2d ed. Mountain View, Calif.: Mayfield.

Coogan, P. F., et al. 1997. Physical activity in usual occupation and risk of breast cancer (United States). *Cancer Causes Control* 8:626–631.

Folsom, A. R., et al. 1997. Physical activity and incidence of coronary heart disease in middle-aged women and men.

Medicine and Science in Sports and Exercise 29:901–909.

Haapanen, N., et al. 1997. Association of leisure time physical activity with the risk of coronary heart disease, hypertension and diabetes in middle-aged men and women. *International Journal of Epidemiology* 26:739–747.

How far should you go to stay fit: The battle between tough and tame. 1997. *U.S. News & World Report,* 10 November, 95–96.

Hyperthermia and dehydration-related deaths associated with intentional rapid weight loss in three collegiate wrestlers. 1998. *Morbidity and Mortality Weekly Report* 47(6): 105–108.

Kujala, U. M., et al. 1998. Relationship of leisure-time physical activity and mortality: The Finnish twin cohort. *Journal of the American Medical Association* 279(6): 440–444.

Kushi, L. H., et al. 1997. Physical activity and mortality in post-menopausal women. *Journal of the American Medical Association* 277(16): 1287–1292.

Lee, I. M., C. C. Hsieh, and R. S. Paffenbarger. 1995. Exercise intensity and longevity in men. The Harvard Alumni Health Study. *Journal of the American Medical Association* 273(15): 1179–1184.

Lee, I. M., et al. 1997. Physical activity and risk of colon cancer: The Physicians' Health Study (United States). *Cancer Causes Control* 8:568–574.

McInnis, K. J., S. Hayakawa, and G. J. Balady. 1997. Cardiovascular screening and emergency procedures at health clubs and fitness centers. *American Journal of Cardiology* 80: 380–383.

National Center for Chronic Disease Prevention and Health Promotion, Centers for Disease Control and Prevention. 1997. Guidelines for school and community programs to promote lifelong physical activity among young people. *Journal of School Health* 67:202–219.

National Institutes of Health. 1996. *Physical Activity and Cardiovascular Health.* National Institutes of Health Consensus Development Conference Statement, December 18–20, 1995 (retrieved March 10, 1996; http://text.nlm.gov/nih/cdc/www/101.html).

Nattiv, A., J. C. Puffer, and G. A. Green. 1997. Lifestyles and health risks of collegiate athletes: A multi-center study. *Clinical Journal of Sports Medicine* 7:262–272.

Nieman, D. C. 1997. Moderate exercise boosts the immune system: Too much exercise can have the opposite effect. *ACSM's Health and Fitness Journal* 1(5): 14–19.

Pate, R. R., et al. 1995. Physical activity and public health: A recommendation from the Centers for Disease Control and Prevention and the American College of Sports Medicine. *Journal of the American Medical Association* 273(5): 402–407.

Roos, R. J. 1997. The Surgeon General's report: A prime resource for exercise advocates. *The Physician and Sportsmedicine* 25(4): 122–132.

Sacco, R. L., et al. 1998. Leisure-time physical activity and ischemic stroke risk: The Northern Manhattan Stroke Study. *Stroke* 29(2): 380–387.

U.S. Department of Health and Human Services. 1996. *Physical Activity and Health: A Report of the Surgeon General.* Atlanta, Ga.: U.S. Department of Health and Human Services, Centers for Disease Control and Prevention, National Center for Chronic Disease Prevention and Health Promotion.

Name _____   **Section** _____   **Date** _____

 LAB 2-1 *Calculating Your Activity Index*

Answer the questions below to assess your overall level of activity.

1. Frequency: How often do you exercise?

If you exercise:	Your frequency score is:
Less than 1 time a week	0
1 time a week	1
2 times a week	2
3 times a week	3
4 times a week	4
5 or more times a week	5

2. Duration: How long do you exercise?

If your total duration of exercise is:	Your duration score is:
Less than 5 minutes	0
5–14 minutes	1
15–29 minutes	2
30–44 minutes	3
45–59 minutes	4
60 minutes or more	5

3. Intensity: How hard do you exercise?

If exercise results in:	Your intensity score is:
No change in pulse from resting level	0
Little change in pulse from resting level (slow walking, bowling, yoga)	1
Slight increase in pulse and breathing (table tennis, active golf with no golf cart)	2
Moderate increase in pulse and breathing (leisurely bicycling, easy continuous swimming, rapid walking)	3
Intermittent heavy breathing and sweating (tennis singles, basketball, squash)	4
Sustained heavy breathing and sweating (jogging, cross-country skiing, rope skipping)	5

To assess your activity index, multiply your three scores:

Frequency _____ × Duration _____ × Intensity _____ = Activity index _____

To assess your activity index, refer to the following table:

If your activity index is:	Your estimated level of activity is:
Less than 15	Sedentary
15–24	Low active
25–40	Moderate active
41–60	Active
Over 60	High active

If your activity level is in one of the lower categories, review the components of your score (frequency, duration, intensity) to see how you can raise your score. Add to your current exercise program, or devise a new one.

To monitor your progress toward your goal, enter the results of this lab in the Preprogram Assessment column of Appendix D. After several weeks of an exercise program, do this lab again, and enter the results in the Postprogram Assessment column of Appendix D. How do the results compare?

SOURCE: Kusinitz, I., and M. Fine. 1995. *Your Guide to Getting Fit,* 3d ed. Mountain View, Calif.: Mayfield.

Name _____ Section _____ Date _____

 LAB 2-2 *Safety of Exercise Participation: PAR-Q*

PAR-Q & YOU

(A Questionnaire for People Aged 15 to 69)

Regular physical activity is fun and healthy, and increasingly more people are starting to become more active every day. Being more active is very safe for most people. However, some people should check with their doctor before they start becoming much more physically active.

If you are planning to become much more physically active than you are now, start by answering the seven questions in the box below. If you are between the ages of 15 and 69, the PAR-Q will tell you if you should check with your doctor before you start. If you are over 69 years of age, and you are not used to being very active, check with your doctor.

Common sense is your best guide when you answer these questions. Please read the questions carefully and answer each one honestly: check YES or NO.

YES	NO	
☐	☐	1. Has your doctor ever said that you have a heart condition <u>and</u> that you should only do physical activity recommended by a doctor?
☐	☐	2. Do you feel pain in your chest when you do physical activity?
☐	☐	3. In the past month, have you had chest pain when you were not doing physical activity?
☐	☐	4. Do you lose your balance because of dizziness or do you ever lose consciousness?
☐	☐	5. Do you have a bone or joint problem that could be made worse by a change in your physical activity?
☐	☐	6. Is your doctor currently prescribing drugs (for example, water pills) for your blood pressure or heart condition?
☐	☐	7. Do you know of <u>any other reason</u> why you should not do physical activity?

If you answered

YES to one or more questions

Talk with your doctor by phone or in person BEFORE you start becoming much more physically active or BEFORE you have a fitness appraisal. Tell your doctor about the PAR-Q and which questions you answered YES.
- You may be able to do any activity you want—as long as you start slowly and build up gradually. Or, you may need to restrict your activities to those which are safe for you. Talk with your doctor about the kinds of activities you wish to participate in and follow his/her advice.
- Find out which community programs are safe and helpful for you.

NO to all questions

If you answered NO honestly to <u>all</u> PAR-Q questions, you can be reasonably sure that you can:
- start becoming much more physically active—begin slowly and build up gradually. This is the safest and easiest way to go.
- take part in a fitness appraisal—this is an excellent way to determine your basic fitness so that you can plan the best way for you to live actively.

DELAY BECOMING MUCH MORE ACTIVE:
- if you are not feeling well because of a temporary illness such as a cold or a fever—wait until you feel better; or
- if you are or may be pregnant—talk to your doctor before you start becoming more active

Please note: If your health changes so that you then answer YES to any of the above questions, tell your fitness or health professional. Ask whether you should change your physical activity plan.

<u>Informed Use of the PAR-Q:</u> The Canadian Society for Exercise Physiology, Health Canada, and their agents assume no liability for persons who undertake physical activity, and if in doubt after completing this questionnaire, consult your doctor prior to physical activity.

You are encouraged to copy the PAR-Q but only if you use the entire form.

Note: If the PAR-Q is being given to a person before he or she participates in a physical activity program or a fitness appraisal, this section may be used for legal or administrative purposes.

I have read, understood and completed this questionnaire. Any questions I had were answered to my full satisfaction.

NAME _____

SIGNATURE _____   DATE _____

SIGNATURE OF PARENT _____   WITNESS _____
or GUARDIAN (for participants under the age of majority)

© *Canadian Society for Exercise Physiology*
  Société canadienne de physiologie de l'exercice

Supported by: Health   Santé
                  Canada   Canada

Cardiorespiratory Endurance

LOOKING AHEAD

After reading this chapter, you should be able to answer these questions about cardiorespiratory endurance:

- How does the body produce the energy it needs for exercise?

- What are the major effects and benefits of cardiorespiratory endurance exercise?

- How is cardiorespiratory endurance measured and assessed?

- How do type, intensity, duration, and frequency of exercise affect the development of cardiorespiratory endurance?

- What elements go into a successful cardiorespiratory fitness program?

- What are the best ways to prevent and treat exercise injuries?

Cardiorespiratory endurance—the ability of the body to perform prolonged, large-muscle, dynamic exercise at moderate-to-high levels of intensity—is a key health-related component of fitness. As explained in Chapter 2, a healthy cardiorespiratory system is essential to high levels of fitness and wellness.

This chapter reviews the short- and long-term effects and benefits of cardiorespiratory endurance exercise. It then describes several tests that are commonly used to assess cardiorespiratory fitness. Finally, it provides guidelines for creating your own cardiorespiratory endurance program, one that is geared to your current level of fitness and built around activities you enjoy.

BASIC PHYSIOLOGY OF CARDIORESPIRATORY ENDURANCE EXERCISE

A basic understanding of the body processes involved in cardiorespiratory endurance exercise can help you design a safe and effective fitness program. In this section, we'll take a brief look at how the cardiorespiratory system functions and how the body produces the energy it needs to respond to the challenge of physical activity.

The Cardiorespiratory System

The cardiorespiratory system picks up and transports oxygen, nutrients, and other key substances to the organs and tissues that need them; it also picks up waste products and carries them to where they can be used or expelled. The cardiorespiratory system consists of the heart, the blood vessels, and the respiratory system (Figure 3-1).

The Heart The heart is a four-chambered, fist-sized muscle located just beneath the ribs under the left breast. Its role is to pump oxygen-poor blood to the lungs and oxygenated (oxygen-rich) blood to the rest of the body. Blood actually travels through two separate circulatory systems: The right side of the heart pumps blood to the lungs in what is called **pulmonary circulation,** and the left side pumps blood through the rest of the body in **systemic circulation.**

Waste-carrying, oxygen-poor blood enters the right upper chamber, or **atrium,** of the heart through the **venae cavae,** the largest veins in the body (Figure 3-2). As the right atrium fills, it contracts and pumps blood into the right lower chamber, or **ventricle,** which, when it contracts, pumps blood through the pulmonary artery into the lungs. There, blood picks up oxygen and discards carbon dioxide. Cleaned, oxygenated blood then flows from the lungs through the pulmonary veins into the left atrium. As this chamber fills, it contracts and pumps blood into the powerful left ventricle, which pumps it

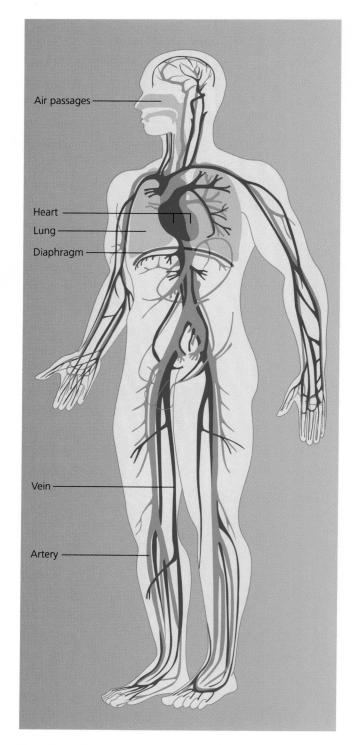

Figure 3-1 The cardiorespiratory system.

through the **aorta,** the body's largest artery, to be fed into the rest of the body's blood vessels.

The period of the heart's contraction is called **systole;** the period of relaxation is called **diastole.** During systole, the atria contract first, pumping blood into the ventricles;

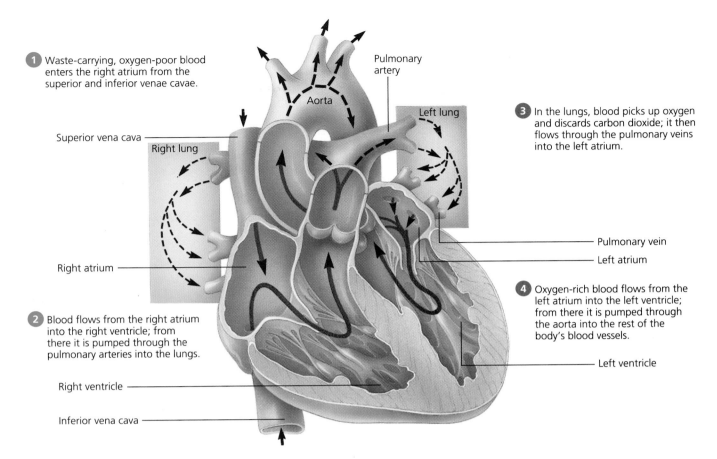

1 Waste-carrying, oxygen-poor blood enters the right atrium from the superior and inferior venae cavae.

Pulmonary artery

Aorta

Left lung

Superior vena cava

Right lung

3 In the lungs, blood picks up oxygen and discards carbon dioxide; it then flows through the pulmonary veins into the left atrium.

Right atrium

Pulmonary vein

Left atrium

2 Blood flows from the right atrium into the right ventricle; from there it is pumped through the pulmonary arteries into the lungs.

4 Oxygen-rich blood flows from the left atrium into the left ventricle; from there it is pumped through the aorta into the rest of the body's blood vessels.

Left ventricle

Right ventricle

Inferior vena cava

Figure 3-2   Circulation in the heart.

a fraction of a second later, the ventricles contract, pumping blood to the lungs and the body. During diastole, blood flows into the heart. A person weighing 150 pounds has about 5 quarts of blood, which are circulated about once every minute.

The heartbeat—the split-second sequence of contractions of the heart's four chambers—is controlled by electrical impulses. These signals originate in a bundle of specialized cells in the right atrium called the pacemaker. Unless it is speeded up or slowed down by the brain in response to such stimuli as danger or exhaustion, the heart produces electrical impulses at a steady rate.

The Blood Vessels   Blood vessels are classified by size and function. **Veins** carry blood to the heart; **arteries** carry it away from the heart. Veins have thin walls, but arteries have thick elastic walls that enable them to expand and relax with the volume of blood being pumped through them. After leaving the heart, the aorta branches into smaller and smaller vessels. The smallest arteries branch still further into **capillaries**, tiny vessels only one cell thick. The capillaries deliver oxygen and nutrient-rich blood to the tissues and receive oxygen-poor, waste-

TERMS

pulmonary circulation   The part of the circulatory system that moves blood between the heart and the lungs; controlled by the right side of the heart.

systemic circulation   The part of the circulatory system that moves blood between the heart and the rest of the body; controlled by the left side of the heart.

atria   The two upper chambers of the heart in which blood collects before passing to the ventricles; also called auricles.

venae cavae   The large veins through which blood is returned to the right atrium of the heart.

ventricles   The two lower chambers of the heart from which blood flows through arteries to the lungs and other parts of the body.

aorta   The large artery that receives blood from the left ventricle and distributes it to the body.

systole   Contraction of the heart.

diastole   Relaxation of the heart.

veins   Vessels that carry blood to the heart.

arteries   Vessels that carry blood away from the heart.

capillaries   Very small blood vessels that distribute blood to all parts of the body.

carrying blood. From the capillaries, this blood empties into small veins and then into larger veins that return it to the heart to repeat the cycle.

Blood pumped through the heart doesn't reach its cells, so the heart has its own network of arteries, veins, and capillaries. Two large vessels, the right and left coronary arteries, branch off the aorta and supply the heart muscle with oxygenated blood. Blockage of a coronary artery is a leading cause of heart attacks (see Chapter 11).

The Respiratory System   The **respiratory system** supplies oxygen to the body and carries off carbon dioxide, a waste product of body processes. Air passes in and out of the lungs as a result of pressure changes brought about by the contraction and relaxation of the diaphragm and rib muscles; the lungs expand and contract about 12–20 times a minute. As air is inhaled, it passes through the nasal passages, the throat, larynx, trachea (windpipe), and bronchi into the lungs. The lungs consist of many branching tubes that end in tiny, thin-walled air sacs called **alveoli.**

Carbon dioxide and oxygen are exchanged between alveoli and capillaries in the lungs. Carbon dioxide passes from blood cells into the alveoli, where it is carried up and out of the lungs (exhaled). Oxygen from inhaled air is passed from the alveoli into blood cells; these oxygen-rich blood cells then return to the heart and are pumped throughout the body. Oxygen is an important component of the body's energy-producing system, so the cardiorespiratory system's ability to pick up and deliver oxygen is critical for the functioning of the body—at rest and during exercise.

Energy Production

Metabolism is the sum of all the chemical processes necessary to maintain the body. Energy is required to fuel vital body functions—to build and break down tissue, contract muscles, conduct nerve impulses, regulate body temperature, and so on. The rate at which your body uses energy—its metabolic rate—depends on your level of activity. At rest, you have a low metabolic rate; if you stand up and begin to walk, your metabolic rate increases. If you jog, your metabolic rate may increase more than 800% above its resting level. Olympic-caliber distance runners can increase their metabolic rate by a whopping 2000% or more.

Energy from Food   The body converts chemical energy from food into substances that cells can use as fuel. These fuels can be used immediately or stored for later use. The body's ability to store fuel is critical, because if all the energy from food were released immediately, much of it would be wasted.

The three classes of energy-containing nutrients in food are carbohydrates, fats, and proteins. During digestion, most carbohydrates are broken down into the simple sugar **glucose.** Some glucose remains circulating in the blood ("blood sugar"), where it can be used as a quick source of fuel to produce energy. Glucose may also be converted to **glycogen** and stored in the liver, muscles, and kidneys. If glycogen stores are full and the body's immediate need for energy is met, the remaining glucose is converted to fat and stored in the body's fatty tissues. Excess energy from dietary fat is also stored as body fat. Protein in the diet is used primarily to build new tissue, but it can be broken down for energy or incorporated into fat stores. Glucose, glycogen, and fat are important fuels for the production of energy in the cells; protein is used for energy only when other fuels are lacking. (See Chapter 8 for more on the other roles of carbohydrate, fat, and protein in the body.)

ATP: The Energy "Currency" of Cells   The basic form of energy used by cells is **adenosine triphosphate,** or **ATP.** When a cell needs energy, it breaks down ATP, a process that releases energy in the only form the cell can use directly. Cells store a small amount of ATP; when they need more, they create it through chemical reactions that utilize the body's stored fuels—glucose, glycogen, and fat. When you exercise, your cells need to produce more energy. Consequently, your body mobilizes its stores of fuel to increase ATP production.

TERMS **respiratory system**   The lungs, air passages, and breathing muscles; supplies oxygen to the body and carries off carbon dioxide.

alveoli   Tiny air sacs in the lungs through whose walls gases such as oxygen and carbon dioxide diffuse in and out of blood.

glucose   A simple sugar that circulates in the blood and can be used by cells to fuel ATP production.

glycogen   A complex carbohydrate stored principally in the liver and skeletal muscles; the major fuel source during most forms of intense exercise.

adenosine triphosphate (ATP)   Energy source for cellular processes.

immediate energy system   Energy system that supplies energy to muscle cells through the breakdown of cellular stores of ATP and creatine phosphate.

nonoxidative (anaerobic) energy system   Energy system that supplies energy to muscle cells through the breakdown of muscle stores of glucose and glycogen; also called the *anaerobic system* or the *lactic acid system* because chemical reactions take place without oxygen and produce lactic acid.

anaerobic   Occurring in the absence of oxygen.

lactic acid   A metabolic acid resulting from the metabolism of glucose and glycogen; an important source of fuel for many tissues of the body, its accumulation may produce fatigue.

oxidative (aerobic) energy system   Energy system that supplies energy to cells through the breakdown of glucose, glycogen, fats, and amino acids; also called the *aerobic system* because chemical reactions require oxygen.

aerobic   Dependent on the presence of oxygen.

TABLE 3-1	Characteristics of the Body's Energy Systems		
	Energy System*		
	Immediate	Nonoxidative	Oxidative
Duration of activity for which system predominates	0–10 seconds	10 seconds–2 minutes	>2 minutes
Intensity of activity for which system predominates	High	High	Low to moderately high
Rate of ATP production	Immediate, very rapid	Rapid	Slower but prolonged
Fuel	Adenosine triphosphate (ATP), creatine phosphate (CP)	Muscle stores of glycogen and glucose	Body stores of glycogen, glucose, fat, and protein
Oxygen used?	No	No	Yes
Sample activities	Weight lifting, picking up a bag of groceries	400-meter run, running up several flights of stairs	1500-meter run, 30-minute walk, standing in line for a long time

*For most activities, all three systems contribute to energy production; the duration and intensity of the activity determine which system predominates.

SOURCE: Adapted from Brooks, G. A., T. D. Fahey, and T. P. White. 1996. *Exercise Physiology: Human Bioenergetics and Its Applications*, 2d ed. Mountain View, Calif.: Mayfield.

Exercise and the Three Energy Systems

The muscles in your body have three energy systems by which they can create ATP and fuel cellular activity. These systems utilize different fuels and chemical processes, and they perform different, specific functions during exercise (Table 3-1).

The Immediate Energy System

The **immediate energy system** provides energy rapidly but for only a short period of time. It is used to fuel activities that last for about 10 or fewer seconds—examples in sport include weight lifting and shot-putting; examples in daily life include rising from a chair or picking up a bag of groceries. The components of this energy system include existing cellular ATP stores and creatine phosphate (CP), a chemical that cells can use to make ATP. CP levels are depleted rapidly during exercise, so the maximum capacity of this energy system is reached within a few seconds. Cells must then switch to the other energy systems to restore levels of ATP and CP. (Without adequate ATP, muscles will stiffen and become unusable.)

The Nonoxidative (Anaerobic) Energy System

The **nonoxidative energy system** is used at the start of an exercise session and for high-intensity activities lasting for about 10 seconds to 2 minutes, such as the 400-meter run. During daily activities, this system may be called on to help you run to catch a bus or dash up several flights of stairs. The nonoxidative energy system creates ATP by breaking down glucose and glycogen. This system doesn't require oxygen, which is why it is sometimes referred to as the **anaerobic** system. The capacity of this system to produce energy is limited, but it can generate a great deal of ATP in a short period of time. For this reason, it is the most important energy system for very intense exercise.

There are two key limiting factors for the nonoxidative energy system. First, the body's supply of glucose and glycogen is limited. Once these are depleted, a person may experience fatigue and dizziness, and judgment may be impaired. (The brain and nervous system rely on carbohydrates as fuel and must have a continuous supply to function properly.) Second, the nonoxidative system results in the production of **lactic acid**. Although lactic acid is an important fuel for the body, it releases substances called hydrogen ions that are thought to interfere with metabolism and muscle contraction, thereby causing fatigue. During heavy exercise, such as sprinting, the body produces large amounts of lactic acid and hydrogen ions, and muscles fatigue rapidly. Fortunately, exercise training increases the body's ability to cope with these substances.

The Oxidative (Aerobic) Energy System

The **oxidative energy system** is used during any physical activity that lasts longer than about 2 minutes, such as distance running, swimming, hiking, or even standing in line for a long time. The oxidative system requires oxygen to generate ATP, which is why it is considered an **aerobic** process. The oxidative system cannot produce energy as quickly as the other two systems, but it can supply energy for much longer periods of time. It provides energy during most daily activities.

In the oxidative energy system, ATP production takes place in cellular structures called **mitochondria.** Because mitochondria can use carbohydrates (glucose and glycogen) or fats to produce ATP, the body's stores of fuel for this system are much greater than those for the other two energy systems. The actual fuel used depends on the intensity and duration of exercise and on the fitness status of the individual. Carbohydrates are favored during intense exercise, fats for lower-intensity activities. During a prolonged exercise session, carbohydrates are the predominant fuel at the start of the workout, but fat utilization increases over time. Fit individuals use a greater proportion of fat as fuel, an important adaptation because glycogen depletion is one of the limiting factors for the oxidative energy system. Thus, by being able to use more fat as fuel, a fit individual can exercise for a longer duration before glycogen is depleted and muscles become fatigued.

Oxygen is another limiting factor. The oxygen requirement of this energy system is proportional to the intensity of exercise—as intensity increases, so does oxygen consumption. There is a limit to the body's ability to increase the transport and use of oxygen; this limit is referred to as **maximal oxygen consumption,** or $\dot{V}O_{2max}$. $\dot{V}O_{2max}$ is determined partly by genetics and partly by fitness status. It depends on many factors, including the capacity of blood to carry oxygen, the rate at which oxygen is transported to the tissues, and the amount of oxygen that cells extract from the blood. $\dot{V}O_{2max}$ determines how intensely a person can perform endurance exercise and for how long, and it is considered the best overall measure of the capacity of the cardiorespiratory system. (The assessment tests described later in the chapter are designed to help you predict your $\dot{V}O_{2max}$.)

The Energy Systems in Combination Your body typically uses all three energy systems when you exercise. The intensity and duration of the activity will determine which system predominates. For example, when you play tennis, you use the immediate energy system when hitting the ball, but you replenish cellular energy stores using the nonoxidative and oxidative systems. When cycling, the oxidative system predominates. However, if you must suddenly exercise very intensely—ride up a steep hill, for example—the other systems become important because the oxidative system is unable to supply ATP fast enough to sustain high-intensity effort.

Physical Fitness and Energy Production Physically fit people can increase their metabolic rate substantially, generating the energy needed for powerful or sustained exercise. People with lower levels of fitness cannot respond to exercise in the same way. Their bodies are less capable of delivering oxygen and fuel to exercising muscles; they are also less able to cope with lactic acid and other substances produced during intense physical activity. Because of this, they fatigue more rapidly—their legs hurt and they breathe heavily walking up a flight of stairs, for example. Regular physical training can substantially improve the body's ability to produce energy and meet the challenges of increased physical activity.

For many sports, one energy system will be most important. For weight lifters, for example, it is the immediate energy system; for sprinters, the nonoxidative system; and for endurance runners, the oxidative system. In designing an exercise program, focus on the energy system most important to your goals. Because improving the functioning of the cardiorespiratory system is critical to overall wellness, endurance exercise that utilizes the oxidative energy system—activities performed at moderate to high intensities for a prolonged duration—is a key component of any health-related fitness program.

BENEFITS OF CARDIORESPIRATORY ENDURANCE EXERCISE

Cardiorespiratory endurance exercise helps the body become more efficient and better able to cope with physical challenges. It also lowers risk for many chronic diseases. Let's take a closer look at the physiological adaptations and long-term benefits of regular endurance exercise.

Improved Cardiorespiratory Functioning

At rest, a healthy cardiorespiratory system has little difficulty keeping pace with the body's need for oxygen, fuel, and waste removal. During exercise, however, the demands on the system increase dramatically as metabolic rate goes up. The principal cardiorespiratory responses to exercise include the following:

- Increased cardiac output. More blood is pumped by

TERMS **mitochondria** Intracellular structures containing enzymes used in the chemical reactions that convert the energy in food to a form the body can use.

maximal oxygen consumption, expressed as $\dot{V}O_{2max}$ The highest rate of oxygen consumption an individual is capable of during maximum physical effort, reflecting the body's ability to transport and use oxygen; measured in milliliters used per minute for each kilogram of body weight.

blood pressure The force exerted by the blood on the walls of the blood vessels; created by the pumping action of the heart. Blood pressure increases during systole and decreases during diastole.

free radicals Highly reactive compounds that can damage cells by taking electrons from key cellular components such as DNA or the cell membrane; produced by normal metabolic processes and through exposure to environmental factors, including sunlight.

the heart each minute because both heart rate and stroke volume (the amount of blood pumped with each beat) go up. Increased cardiac output speeds the delivery of oxygen and fuel and the removal of waste products.

- Increased ventilation (rate and depth of breathing).
- Increased blood flow to active skeletal muscles and to the heart; constant or slightly increased blood flow to the brain.
- Increased blood flow to the skin and increased sweating. The chemical reactions that produce energy for exercise release heat, which must be dissipated to maintain a safe body temperature.
- Decreased blood flow to the stomach, intestines, liver, and kidneys, resulting in reduced activity in the gastrointestinal tract and reduced urine output.

All of these changes help the body respond to the challenge of exercise in the short term. When performed regularly, endurance exercise also causes more permanent adaptations. It improves the functioning of the heart, the ability of the cardiorespiratory system to carry oxygen to the body's tissues, and the capacity of the cells to take up and use oxygen. These improvements reduce the effort required to carry out everyday activities and make the body better able to respond to physical challenges.

Endurance training enhances the health of the heart by maintaining or increasing its blood and oxygen supply, decreasing work and oxygen demand of the heart, and increasing the function of the heart muscle. The trained heart is more efficient and subject to less stress. It pumps more blood per beat, so heart rate is lower at rest and during exercise. The resting heart rate of a fit person is often 10–20 beats per minute lower than that of a sedentary person; this translates into as many as 10 million fewer beats in the course of one year. Improved heart efficiency results because endurance training improves heart contraction strength, increases heart cavity size (in young adults), and increases blood volume so that the heart pushes more blood into the circulation system during each of its contractions. Training also tends to reduce **blood pressure,** so the heart does not have to work as hard when it contracts.

Improved Cellular Metabolism

Regular endurance exercise also improves metabolism at the cellular level. It increases the number of capillaries in the muscles so that they can be supplied with more oxygen and fuel. It also trains the muscles to make the most of available oxygen and fuel so that they work more efficiently. Exercise increases the size and number of mitochondria in muscle cells, thereby increasing the energy capacity of the cells. Endurance training also helps in energy production by preventing glycogen depletion and increasing the muscles' ability to use lactic acid and fat as fuels.

Exercise offers both long-term health benefits and immediate pleasures. Many popular sports and activities, including rugby, develop cardiorespiratory endurance.

Fitness programs that best develop metabolic efficiency are characterized by both long-duration, moderately intense endurance exercise and brief periods of more intense effort. For example, climbing a small hill while jogging or cycling introduces the kind of intense exercise that leads to more efficient use of lactic acid and fats. (As described earlier, activities of different intensities utilize different energy systems and will cause different adaptations.)

Regular exercise may also help protect your cells from chemical damage. Many scientists believe that aging and some chronic diseases are linked to cellular damage caused by **free radicals.** Training activates antioxidant enzymes that prevent free radical damage to cell structures, thereby enhancing health. (See Chapter 8 for more on free radicals and antioxidants.) Training also improves the functional stability of cells and tissues by improving the regulation of salts and fluids in the cells. This is particularly important in the heart, where instability can lead to cardiac arrest and death.

Reduced Risk of Chronic Disease

Regular endurance exercise lowers your risk of many chronic, disabling diseases. It can also help people with those diseases improve their health.

Cardiovascular Disease A sedentary lifestyle is one of the five major risk factors for **cardiovascular disease (CVD)** (see Chapter 11). The other factors are smoking, unhealthy cholesterol levels, high blood pressure, and obesity. People who are sedentary have CVD death rates significantly higher than those of fit individuals.

Endurance exercise has a positive effect on levels of fats in the blood. High concentrations of blood fats such as cholesterol and triglycerides are linked to cardiovascular disease because they contribute to the formation of fatty deposits on the lining of arteries. If one of the coronary arteries, which supply oxygenated blood to the heart, becomes blocked by such a deposit, the result is a heart attack; blockage of a cerebral artery can cause a stroke.

Cholesterol is carried in the blood by **lipoproteins,** which are classified according to size and density. Cholesterol carried by low-density lipoproteins (LDLs) tends to stick to the walls of arteries. High-density lipoproteins (HDLs), on the other hand, pick up excess cholesterol in the bloodstream and carry it back to the liver for excretion from the body. High LDL levels and low HDL levels are associated with a high risk of CVD. High levels of HDL and low levels of LDL are associated with lower risk. More information about cholesterol and heart disease is provided in Chapter 11. For our purposes in this chapter, it is important to know only that endurance exercise influences blood fat levels in a positive way—by increasing HDL and decreasing triglycerides (and possibly LDL)—thereby reducing the risk of CVD.

Regular exercise tends to reduce high blood pressure, a contributing factor in diseases such as **coronary heart disease,** stroke, kidney failure, and blindness. It also helps prevent obesity and diabetes, both of which contribute to CVD.

Cancer Some studies have shown a relationship between increased physical activity and a reduction in a person's risk of all types of cancer, but these findings are not conclusive. There is strong evidence that exercise reduces the risk of colon cancer and promising data that it reduces the risk of cancer of the breast and reproductive organs in women. Exercise may decrease the risk of colon cancer by speeding the movement of food through the gastrointestinal tract (quickly eliminating potential carcinogens), enhancing immune function, and reducing blood fats. The protective mechanism in the case of reproductive system cancers is less clear, but physical activity during the high school and college years may be particularly important for preventing breast cancer later in life.

Diabetes Recent studies have shown that regular exercise helps prevent the development of the most common form of diabetes (see Chapter 6 for more on diabetes). Exercise burns excess sugar and makes cells more sensitive to the hormone insulin, which is involved in the regulation of blood sugar levels. Obesity is a key risk factor for diabetes, and exercise helps keep body fat at healthy levels. For people who have diabetes, physical activity is an important part of treatment.

Osteoporosis A special benefit of exercise, especially for women, is protection against osteoporosis, a disease that results in loss of bone density and poor bone strength. Weight-bearing exercise helps build bone during the teens and twenties. People with denser bones can better endure the bone loss that occurs with aging. With stronger bones and muscles and better balance, fit people are less likely to experience debilitating falls and bone fractures. (See Chapter 8 for more on osteoporosis.)

Better Control of Body Fat

Too much body fat is linked to a variety of health problems, including cardiovascular disease, cancer, and diabetes. Healthy body composition can be difficult to achieve and maintain because a diet that contains all essential nutrients can be relatively high in calories, especially for someone who is sedentary. Excess calories are stored in the body as fat. Regular exercise increases daily calorie expenditure so that a healthy diet is less likely to lead to weight gain. Endurance exercise burns calories directly and, if intense enough, continues to do so by raising resting metabolic rate for several hours following an exercise session. A higher metabolic rate means that a person can consume more calories without gaining weight.

Endurance exercise can also help maintain or increase metabolic rate by helping people maintain a high proportion of fat-free mass: The more muscle mass, the higher the metabolic rate. Strength training, discussed in Chapter 4, is even more effective at building muscle mass than endurance training. (Energy balance and the role of exercise in improving body composition are discussed in detail in Chapter 6.)

TERMS **cardiovascular disease (CVD)** Disease of the heart and blood vessels.

lipoproteins Substances in blood, classified according to size, density, and chemical composition, that transport fats.

coronary heart disease Heart disease caused by the buildup of fatty deposits on the arteries that supply oxygen to the heart; also called *coronary artery disease.*

epinephrine A hormone secreted in response to stress that stimulates the heart, makes carbohydrates available in the liver and muscles, and releases fat from fat cells.

norepinephrine A stress hormone with many of the same effects as epinephrine.

endorphins Substances resembling morphine that are secreted by the brain and that decrease pain, suppress fatigue, and produce euphoria.

neurotransmitters Brain chemicals that transmit nerve impulses.

If you've ever gone for a long, brisk walk after a hard day's work, you know how refreshing exercise can be. Exercise can improve mood, stimulate creativity, clarify thinking, relieve anxiety, and provide an outlet for anger or aggression. But why does exercise make you feel good? Does it simply take your mind off your problems? Or does it cause a physical reaction that affects your mental state?

Current research indicates that exercise triggers many physical changes in the body that can alter mood. Scientists are now trying to explain how and why exercise affects the mind. One theory has to do with the physical structure of the brain. The area of the brain responsible for the movement of muscles is near the area responsible for thought and emotion. As muscles work vigorously, the resulting stimulation in the muscle center of the brain may also stimulate the thought and emotion center, producing improvements in mood and cognitive functions.

Other researchers suggest that exercise stimulates the release of **endorphins**, chemicals in the brain that can suppress fatigue, decrease pain, and produce euphoria. The "runner's high" often experienced after running several miles may be due to an increased production of endorphins.

A third area of research focuses on changes in brain activity during and after exercise. One change is an increase in alpha brain-wave activity. Alpha waves indicate a highly relaxed state; meditation also induces alpha wave activity. A second change is an alteration in the levels of **neurotransmitters**, brain chemicals that increase alertness and reduce stress.

Higher levels of neurotransmitters may explain how exercise improves mild to moderate cases of depression. Researchers have found that cardiorespiratory endurance exercise can be as effective as psychotherapy in treating depression, and even more effective when used in conjunction with other therapies. In addition to boosting neurotransmitter activity, exercise provides a distraction from stressful stimuli, enhances self-esteem, and may provide an opportunity for positive social interactions.

Although most people don't associate exercise with mental skills, physical activity has been shown to have positive effects on cognitive functioning in both the short term and the long term. Exercise improves alertness and memory and can help you perform cognitive tasks at your peak level. Exercise may also help boost creativity. In a study of college students, those who ran regularly or took aerobic dance classes scored significantly higher on standard psychological tests of creativity than sedentary students. Over the long term, exercise can slow and possibly even reverse certain age-related declines in cognitive performance, including slowed reaction time and loss of short-term memory and nonverbal reasoning skills.

The message from all this research is that exercise is a critical factor in developing *all* the dimensions of wellness, not just physical health. Even moderate exercise like walking briskly a few times per week can significantly improve your well-being. A lifetime of physical activity can leave you with a healthier body and a sharper, happier, more creative mind.

Improved Immune Function

Exercise can have either positive or negative effects on the immune system, the physiological processes that protect us from disease. Moderate endurance exercise boosts immune function, whereas excessive training (overtraining) depresses it. Physically fit people get fewer colds and upper respiratory tract infections than people who are not fit. In addition to regular exercise, the immune system can be strengthened by eating a well-balanced diet rich in whole grains, fruits, vegetables, and low-fat dairy and meat products; managing stress; and getting 7–8 hours of sleep every night.

Improved Psychological and Emotional Well-Being

Most people who participate in regular endurance exercise experience social, psychological, and emotional benefits. Performing physical activities provides proof of skill mastery and self-control, thus enhancing self-image. Recreational sports provide an opportunity to socialize, have fun, and strive to excel.

Endurance exercise also provides protection against the effects of stress that have been linked to poor cardiorespiratory health. Psychological stress causes increased secretion of **epinephrine** and **norepinephrine**, the so-called fight-or-flight hormones, which are thought to speed the buildup of fatty deposits in the arteries. Excessive hostility and anger are also associated with the risk of heart disease. Endurance exercise decreases the secretion of hormones triggered by emotional stress. It can diffuse hostility and alleviate depression and anxiety by providing an emotional outlet and inducing feelings of relaxation (see the box "Exercise and the Mind"). Regular exercise can also relieve sleeping problems.

Refer to the box "Benefits of Cardiorespiratory Endurance Exercise" for a summary of specific physiological benefits. As cardiorespiratory fitness is developed, these benefits translate into both physical and emotional well-being and a much lower risk of chronic disease.

ASSESSING CARDIORESPIRATORY FITNESS

The body's ability to maintain a level of exertion (exercise) for an extended period of time is a direct reflection of cardiorespiratory fitness. It is determined by the body's abil-

Cardiorespiratory System

Cardiorespiratory endurance exercise tends to increase the following:

- Heart size
- Stroke volume (the amount of blood pumped per beat)
- Total blood volume
- Number of red blood cells
- Blood concentration of high-density lipoproteins (HDLs)
- Capillary density (associated with the increased ability of cells to extract oxygen from blood)
- Overall efficiency of the delivery of oxygen to the tissues ($\dot{V}O_{2max}$)
- Blood flow to active muscles during exercise

Cardiorespiratory endurance exercise tends to decrease the following:

- Resting heart rate and heart rate at different workloads
- Concentrations of epinephrine and norepinephrine during exercise
- Blood levels of triglycerides and possibly low-density lipoproteins (LDLs)
- Blood pressure
- Platelet stickiness (a factor in coronary artery disease)

Skeletal Muscles

Cardiorespiratory endurance exercise tends to increase the following:

- Amount of stored glycogen

- Number and size of mitochondria (the energy-producing parts of cells)
- Myoglobin content (aids in the delivery of oxygen to the mitochondria)
- Capacity to use fat and lactic acid as fuel

Other Benefits

Cardiorespiratory endurance exercise tends to increase or maintain the following:

- Fat-free mass
- Density and strength of bones, ligaments, and tendons
- Sensitivity to insulin (helps prevent Type 2 diabetes)
- Ability to exercise during hot weather
- Performance in sports, recreational activities, and work
- Feelings of well-being
- Self-concept

Cardiorespiratory endurance exercise tends to decrease the following:

- Total body fat
- Strain associated with stress
- Anxiety and depression
- Risk of death from coronary artery disease, colon cancer, and some types of reproductive cancers (women)

---

ity to take up, distribute, and use oxygen during physical activity. As explained earlier, the best quantitative measure of cardiorespiratory endurance is maximal oxygen consumption, expressed as $\dot{V}O_{2max}$, the amount of oxygen the body uses when a person reaches maximum ability to supply oxygen during exercise (measured in milliliters of oxygen used per minute for each kilogram of body weight). Maximal oxygen consumption can be measured precisely in an exercise physiology laboratory through analysis of the air a person inhales and exhales when exercising to a level of exhaustion (maximum intensity). This procedure can be expensive and time-consuming, making it impractical for the average person.

Four Assessment Tests

Fortunately, several simple assessment tests provide reasonably good estimates of maximal oxygen consumption (within ±10–15% of the results of a laboratory test).

Four methods are described here and presented in Lab 3-1: a 1-mile walk test, a 3-minute step test, a 1.5-mile run-walk test, and the Åstrand-Rhyming cycle ergometer test. To assess yourself, choose among these methods based on your access to equipment, your current physical condition, and your own preference. Don't take any of these tests without checking with your physician if you are ill or have any of the risk factors for exercise discussed in Chapter 2 and Lab 2-2. Table 3-2 lists the fitness prerequisites and cautions recommended for each test.

You'll get more accurate results from these tests if you avoid strenuous activity the day of the test; avoid caffeine, which can affect heart rate; and don't smoke or eat a heavy meal for up to 3 hours before the test. Record your test results in Lab 3-1, and then use the appropriate formula to calculate your maximal oxygen consumption.

The 1-Mile Walk Test   The 1-mile walk test estimates your level of cardiorespiratory fitness (maximal oxygen

TABLE 3-2 Fitness Prerequisites and Cautions for the Cardiorespiratory Endurance Assessment Tests

Note: The conditions for exercise safety given in Chapter 2 apply to all fitness assessment tests. If you answered yes to a question on the PAR-Q in Lab 2-2, see your physician before taking any assessment test. If you experience any unusual symptoms while taking a test, stop exercising, and discuss your condition with your instructor.

Test	Fitness Prerequisites/Cautions
1-mile walk test	Recommended for anyone who meets the criteria for safe exercise. Can be used by individuals who cannot perform other tests because of low fitness level or injury.
3-minute step test	If you suffer from joint problems in your ankles, knees, or hips or are significantly overweight, check with your physician before taking this test.
1.5-mile run-walk test	Recommended for people who are healthy and at least moderately active. If you have been sedentary, you should participate in a 4- to 8-week walk-run program before taking the test. Don't take this test in extremely hot or cold weather if you aren't used to exercising under those conditions.
Åstrand-Rhyming test	Recommended for people who are healthy and at least moderately active. It can be taken by people with some joint problems because body weight is supported by the cycle.

consumption) based on the amount of time it takes you to complete 1 mile of brisk walking and your exercise heart rate at the end of your walk; age, gender, and body weight are also considered. A fast time and a low heart rate indicate a high level of cardiorespiratory endurance.

The 3-Minute Step Test The rate at which the pulse returns to normal after exercise is also a good measure of cardiorespiratory capacity; heart rate remains lower and recovers faster in people who are more physically fit. For the step test, you step continually at a steady rate for 3 minutes and then monitor your heart rate during recovery.

The 1.5-Mile Run-Walk Test The 1.5-mile run-walk test is considered one of the best indirect measures of cardiorespiratory capacity. Oxygen consumption increases with speed in distance running; a fast time on this test indicates high maximal oxygen consumption.

The Åstrand-Rhyming Cycle Ergometer Test A cycle ergometer measures power output, the amount of resistance the cycle exerts against a person's pedaling. A higher power output means the cyclist is applying more pressure—that is, pedaling harder or faster. The Åstrand-Rhyming test estimates maximal oxygen consumption from the exercise heart rate reached after pedaling a cycle ergometer for 6 minutes at a constant rate and resistance. A low exercise heart rate after pedaling at a high power output indicates a high maximal oxygen consumption.

Monitoring Your Heart Rate

Each time your heart beats, it pumps blood into your arteries; this surge of blood causes a pulse that you can feel by holding your fingers against an artery. Counting your pulse to determine your exercise heart rate is a key part of most assessment tests for maximal oxygen consumption. Heart rate can also be used to monitor exercise intensity during a workout. (Intensity is described in more detail in the next section.)

The two most common sites for monitoring heart rate are the carotid artery in the neck and the radial artery in the wrist. To take your pulse, press your index and middle fingers gently on the correct site. You may have to shift position several times to find the best position to feel your pulse. Don't use your thumb to check your pulse; it has a pulse of its own that can confuse your count. Be careful not to push too hard, particularly when taking your pulse in the carotid artery (strong pressure on this artery may cause a reflex that slows the heart rate).

Heart rates are usually assessed in beats per minute (bpm). But counting your pulse for an entire minute isn't practical when you're exercising. And because heart rate slows rapidly when you stop exercising, it can give inaccurate results. It's best to do a shorter count—10 seconds—and then multiply the result by 6 to get your heart rate in beats per minute. The same procedure can be used to take someone else's pulse, as in the cycle ergometer test.

Interpreting Your Score

Once you've completed one or more of the assessment tests, use Table 3-3 to determine your level of cardiorespiratory fitness. Find the row that corresponds to your age and gender, and then find the category that contains your score for maximal oxygen consumption. For example, a 19-year-old female with a maximal oxygen consumption score of 36 ml/kg/min would be classified as

A pulse count can be used to determine exercise heart rate. The pulse can be taken at the carotid artery in the neck (left) or at the radial artery in the wrist (right).

TABLE 3-3 *Cardiorespiratory Fitness Classification*

	Maximal Oxygen Consumption (ml/kg/min)					
	Very Poor	*Poor*	*Fair*	*Good*	*Excellent*	*Superior*
Women						
Age: 18–29	Below 30.6	30.6–33.7	33.8–36.6	36.7–40.9	41.0–46.7	Above 46.7
30–39	Below 28.7	28.7–32.2	32.3–34.5	34.6–38.5	38.6–43.8	Above 43.8
40–49	Below 26.5	26.5–29.4	29.5–32.2	32.3–36.2	36.3–40.9	Above 40.9
50–59	Below 24.3	24.3–26.8	26.9–29.3	29.4–32.2	32.3–36.7	Above 36.7
60 and over	Below 22.8	22.8–24.4	24.5–27.1	27.2–31.1	31.2–37.4	Above 37.4
Men						
Age: 18–29	Below 37.1	37.1–40.9	41.0–44.1	44.2–48.1	48.2–53.9	Above 53.9
30–39	Below 35.4	35.4–38.8	38.9–42.3	42.4–46.7	46.8–52.4	Above 52.4
40–49	Below 33.0	33.0–36.7	36.8–39.8	39.9–44.0	44.1–50.3	Above 50.3
50–59	Below 30.2	30.2–33.7	33.8–36.6	36.7–40.9	41.0–47.0	Above 47.0
60 and over	Below 26.5	26.5–30.1	30.2–33.5	33.6–38.0	38.1–45.1	Above 45.1

SOURCE: Based on norms from the Cooper Institute for Aerobics Research, Dallas, Texas; used with permission.

having fair cardiorespiratory fitness. You can see from Table 3-3 that there are differences in ratings for $\dot{V}O_{2max}$ between men and women; for more on this disparity, see the box "Gender Differences in Cardiorespiratory Endurance."

You can monitor the progress of your fitness program by repeating the cardiorespiratory assessment test(s) from time to time. Because your $\dot{V}O_{2max}$ score will vary somewhat for different types of tests, always compare scores for the *same* test.

DEVELOPING A CARDIORESPIRATORY ENDURANCE PROGRAM

Cardiorespiratory endurance exercises are best for developing the type of fitness associated with good health, so they should serve as the focus of your exercise program.

To create a successful endurance exercise program, you must set realistic goals; choose suitable activities; set your starting frequency, intensity, and duration of exercise at appropriate levels; remember to warm up and cool down; and adjust your program as your fitness improves.

Setting Goals

You can use the results of cardiorespiratory fitness assessment tests to set a specific oxygen consumption goal for your cardiorespiratory endurance program. Your goal should be high enough to ensure a healthy cardiorespiratory system, but not so high that it will be impossible to achieve. Scores in the fair and good ranges for maximal oxygen consumption suggest good fitness; scores in the excellent and superior ranges indicate a high standard of physical performance. You can also set more general goals, such as lowering your risk for diabetes or being able to hike 5 miles.

Research has shown that there are significant differences in the average levels of cardiorespiratory endurance, as measured by maximal oxygen consumption, for men and women. When expressed in absolute terms, maximal oxygen consumption is about 40% higher in men. When this is adjusted for body weight, as it is in Table 3-3, the difference drops to 20%—a smaller difference, but still significant.

Several factors are believed to contribute to this difference. Males tend to be larger than females, and they have larger hearts, in both size and volume. This means that their hearts pump more blood with each beat (stroke volume), thereby delivering more oxygenated blood to working muscles. Females tend to have higher heart rates during exercise, but this higher rate does not entirely compensate for their lower stroke volume.

Men have relatively higher concentrations of hemoglobin in their blood than women. Hemoglobin is a blood protein that transports oxygen throughout the body; higher hemoglobin levels translate into a higher maximal oxygen consumption. Men have higher levels of androgens (steroid hormones), which stimulate their bodies to produce more hemoglobin. And menstrual blood loss contributes to lower hemoglobin levels among women.

Differences in body composition also affect maximal oxygen consumption. Men tend to have relatively more muscle mass, while women's bodies have a higher percentage of fat. (Body composition is discussed in greater detail in Chapter 6.) This additional muscle mass gives men more strength and power in both absolute and relative terms, and it raises maximal oxygen consumption. The relationship between maximal oxygen consumption and fat-free mass is so strong that when $\dot{V}O_{2max}$ is expressed in terms of fat-free weight instead of total body weight, the gender difference in maximal oxygen consumption drops to about 10%.

One area in which there is no difference between the sexes is in the benefits of training. Both men and women can improve their maximal oxygen consumption by up to 15–30%. Physical activity is critical for the health and wellness of everyone.

SOURCE: Adapted from Brooks, G. A., T. D. Fahey, and T. P. White. 1996. *Exercise Physiology: Human Bioenergetics and Its Applications,* 2d ed. Mountain View, Calif.: Mayfield.

Choosing Sports and Activities

As mentioned in Chapter 2, cardiorespiratory endurance exercises include activities that involve the rhythmic use of large muscle groups for an extended period of time, such as jogging, walking, cycling, aerobic dancing (group exercise), cross-country skiing, and swimming. Start-and-stop sports, such as tennis and racquetball, also qualify, as long as you have enough skill to play continuously and intensely enough to raise your heart rate to target levels. Cardiorespiratory fitness ratings of many common activities are listed in the box "Activities and Sports for Developing Cardiorespiratory Endurance."

Having fun is a strong motivator; select a physical activity that you enjoy, and it will be easier to stay with your program. Exercising with a friend can also be helpful as a motivator. Consider whether you prefer competitive or individual sports, or whether starting something new would be best. Other important considerations are access to facilities, expense, and the time required to achieve an adequate skill level and workout.

Determining Frequency of Training

To build cardiorespiratory endurance, you should exercise 3–5 days per week. Beginners should start with 3 and work up to 5 days per week. Training more than 5 days per week can lead to injury and isn't necessary for the typical person on an exercise program designed to promote wellness. Training fewer than 3 days per week

makes it difficult to improve your fitness (unless exercise intensity is very high) or to use exercise to lose weight. In addition, you risk injury because your body never gets a chance to fully adapt to regular exercise training.

Determining Intensity of Training

Intensity is the most important factor in achieving training effects. You must exercise intensely enough to stress your body so that fitness improves. Two methods of monitoring exercise intensity are described below; choose the method that works best for you. Be sure to make adjustments in your intensity levels for environmental or individual factors. For example, on a hot and humid day or on your first day back to your program after an illness, you should decrease your intensity level.

Target Heart Rate Zone One of the best ways to monitor the intensity of cardiorespiratory endurance exercise is to measure your heart rate. It isn't necessary to exercise at your maximum heart rate to improve maximal oxygen consumption. Fitness adaptations occur at lower heart rates with a much lower risk of injury.

According to the American College of Sports Medicine, your **target heart rate zone**—rates at which you should

target heart rate zone The range of heart rates that should **TERMS** be reached and maintained during cardiorespiratory endurance exercise to obtain training effects.

The potential of an activity to develop cardiorespiratory endurance depends primarily on the intensity, duration, and frequency of training. The ratings given here are general guidelines.

High Potential		**Medium Potential**	
Aerobic dance	Lacrosse	Ballet	Slide boarding
Backpacking	Outdoor fitness trails	Ballroom dancing	Surfing
Badminton (singles)	Racquetball (singles)	Baseball (pitcher and catcher)	Synchronized swimming
Basketball	Rope skipping	Canoeing and kayaking	Table tennis
Bicycling	Rowing	Cheerleading	Volleyball
Cross-country skiing	Rugby	Fencing	Water aerobics
Cross-country skiing machine	Soccer	Folk and square dancing	Water skiing
Field hockey	Squash (singles)	Football, touch	
Frisbee, ultimate	Stationary cycling	Horseback riding	**Low Potential**
Handball (singles)	Step aerobics	Judo	Archery
Hiking	Swimming	Modern dance	Bowling
Hockey, ice and roller	Tennis (singles)	Popular dancing	Golf (riding cart)
In-line skating	Treadmill	Rock climbing	Sailing
Jogging and running	Walking	Skating, ice and roller	Weight training
Karate	Water Polo	Skiing, alpine	Yoga
	Wrestling		

exercise to experience cardiorespiratory benefits—is between 65% and 90% of your maximum heart rate. To calculate your target heart rate zone, follow these steps:

1. Estimate your maximum heart rate (MHR) by subtracting your age from 220, or have it measured precisely by undergoing an exercise stress test in a physician's office, hospital, or sports medicine laboratory.

2. Multiply your MHR by 65% and 90% to calculate your target heart rate zone.

For example, a 19-year-old would calculate her target heart rate zone as follows:

$$MHR = 220 - 19 = 201$$
$$65\% \text{ training intensity} = 0.65 \times 201 = 131 \text{ bpm}$$
$$90\% \text{ training intensity} = 0.90 \times 201 = 181 \text{ bpm}$$

To gain fitness benefits, the young woman in our example would have to exercise at an intensity that raises her heart rate to between 131 and 181 bpm.

Use Lab 3-2 to determine your target heart rate zone. If you have been sedentary, start by exercising at the lower end of your target heart rate range (65% training intensity) for at least 4–6 weeks. Fast and significant gains in maximal oxygen consumption can be made by exercising closer to the top of the range, but you may increase your risk of injury and overtraining. You *can* achieve significant health benefits by exercising at the bottom of your target range, so don't feel pressured into exercising at an unnecessarily intense level. If you exercise at a lower intensity, you can increase the duration or frequency of training to obtain as much benefit to your health, as long

as you are above the 65% training threshold. (For people with a very low initial level of fitness, a lower training intensity, 55–64% of maximum heart rate, may be sufficient to achieve improvements in maximal oxygen consumption, especially at the start of an exercise program.)

By monitoring your heart rate, you will always know if you are working hard enough to improve, not hard enough, or too hard. To monitor your heart rate during exercise, count your pulse while you're still moving or immediately after you stop exercising. Count beats for 10 seconds, and then multiply that number by 6 to see if your heart rate is in your target zone. If the young woman in our example were aiming for 144 bpm, she would want a 10-second count of 24 beats.

Ratings of Perceived Exertion The second way to monitor intensity is to monitor your perceived level of exertion. Repeated pulse counting during exercise can become a nuisance if it interferes with the activity. As your exercise program progresses, you will probably become familiar with the amount of exertion required to raise your heart rate to target levels. In other words, you will know how you feel when you have exercised intensely enough. If this is the case, you can use the scale of **ratings of perceived exertion (RPE)** shown in Figure 3-3 to monitor the intensity of your exercise session without checking your pulse.

To use the RPE scale, select a rating that corresponds to your subjective perception of how hard you are exercising when you are training in your target heart rate zone. If your target zone is about 135–155 bpm, exercise in-

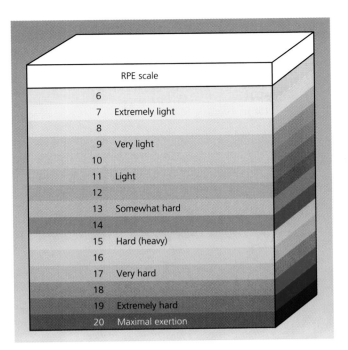

RPE scale	
6	
7	Extremely light
8	
9	Very light
10	
11	Light
12	
13	Somewhat hard
14	
15	Hard (heavy)
16	
17	Very hard
18	
19	Extremely hard
20	Maximal exertion

Figure 3-3   Ratings of perceived exertion.

tensely enough to raise your heart rate to that level, and then associate a rating—for example, "somewhat hard" or "hard" (14 or 15)—with how hard you feel you are working. To reach and maintain intensity in future workouts, exercise hard enough to reach what you feel is the same level of exertion. You should periodically check your RPE against your target heart rate zone to make sure it's correct. Research has shown RPE to be an accurate means of monitoring exercise intensity, and you may find it more convenient than pulse counting.

Determining Duration of Training

A total duration of 20–60 minutes is recommended; exercise can take place in a single session or in multiple bouts lasting 10 or more minutes. The total duration of exercise depends on its intensity. To improve cardiorespiratory endurance during a low-to-moderate-intensity activity such as walking or slow swimming, you should exercise for 45–60 minutes. For high-intensity exercise performed at the top of your target heart rate zone, a duration of 20 minutes is sufficient. Some studies have shown that 5–10 minutes of extremely intense exercise (greater than 90% of maximal oxygen consumption) improves cardiorespiratory endurance. However, training at this intensity, particularly during high-impact activities, increases the risk of injury. Also, because of the discomfort of high-intensity exercise, you are more likely to discontinue your exercise program. Longer-duration, low-to-moderate-intensity activities generally result in more gradual gains in maximal oxygen consumption. You

should start off with less-vigorous activities and only gradually increase intensity.

Warming Up and Cooling Down

It's important to warm up before every session of cardiorespiratory endurance exercise and to cool down afterward. Because the body's muscles work better when their temperature is slightly above resting level, warming up enhances performance and decreases the chance of injury. It gives the body time to redirect blood to active muscles and the heart time to adapt to increased demands. Warming up also helps spread **synovial fluid** throughout the joints, which helps protect their surfaces from injury.

As mentioned in Chapter 2, a warm-up session should include low-intensity movements similar to those in the activity that will follow. Low-intensity movements include walking slowly before beginning a brisk walk, hitting forehands and backhands before a tennis match, and running a 12-minute mile before progressing to an 8-minute one. Some experts also recommend including stretching exercises in your warm-up; however, it's best to stretch after your body temperature has been elevated by the active part of the warm-up (see Chapter 5).

Cooling down after exercise is important for returning the body to a nonexercising state. A cool-down, consisting of 5–10 minutes of reduced activity, should follow every workout to allow heart rate, breathing, and circulation to return to normal. Stretching exercises can be part of a cool-down.

The general pattern of a safe and successful workout for cardiorespiratory fitness is illustrated in Figure 3-4.

Maintaining Cardiorespiratory Fitness

Although your fitness level will probably improve quickly at the beginning of your fitness program, this rate of progress will probably slow after 4–6 weeks. The more fit you become, the harder you will have to work to improve. But there is a limit. Increasing intensity and duration indefinitely can lead to injury. Once you reach an acceptable level of fitness, maintain it by continuing to exercise at the same intensity at least 3 nonconsecutive days every week.

EXERCISE INJURIES

Even the most careful physically active person can suffer an injury. Most injuries are annoying rather than serious

ratings of perceived exertion (RPE)   A system of monitoring exercise intensity based on assigning a number to the subjective perception of target intensity.   **TERMS**

synovial fluid   Fluid found within many joints that provides lubrication and nutrition to the cells of the joint surface.

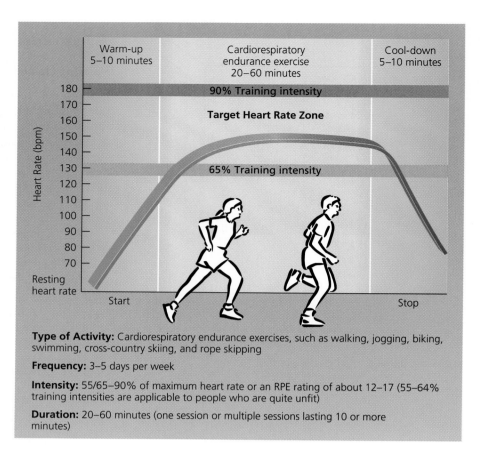

| Warm-up 5–10 minutes | Cardiorespiratory endurance exercise 20–60 minutes | Cool-down 5–10 minutes |

90% Training intensity

Target Heart Rate Zone

65% Training intensity

Heart Rate (bpm): 180, 170, 160, 150, 140, 130, 120, 110, 100, 90, 80, 70

Resting heart rate

Start   Stop

Type of Activity: Cardiorespiratory endurance exercises, such as walking, jogging, biking, swimming, cross-country skiing, and rope skipping

Frequency: 3–5 days per week

Intensity: 55/65–90% of maximum heart rate or an RPE rating of about 12–17 (55–64% training intensities are applicable to people who are quite unfit)

Duration: 20–60 minutes (one session or multiple sessions lasting 10 or more minutes)

Figure 3-4   A cardiorespiratory endurance workout.   Longer-duration exercise at lower intensities can often be as beneficial for promoting health as shorter-duration, high-intensity exercise.

or permanent. However, an injury that isn't cared for properly can escalate into a chronic problem, sometimes serious enough to permanently curtail the activity. It's important to learn how to deal with injuries so they don't derail your fitness program. Strategies for the care of common exercise injuries appear in Table 3-4; some general guidelines are given below.

When to Call a Physician

Some injuries require medical attention. Consult a physician for head and eye injuries, possible ligament injuries, broken bones, and internal disorders such as chest pain, fainting, elevated body temperature, and intolerance to hot weather. Also seek medical attention for ostensibly minor injuries that do not get better within a reasonable amount of time. You may need to modify your exercise program for a few weeks to allow an injury to heal. A knowledgeable physician can often give you important medical advice that will speed healing and get you back to your program sooner.

Managing Minor Exercise Injuries

For minor cuts and scrapes, stop the bleeding and clean the wound. Treat injuries to soft tissue (muscles and joints) immediately with rest and ice packs. Elevate the affected part of the body, and compress it with an elastic

bandage to minimize swelling. Apply ice regularly for 36–48 hours after an injury occurs or until all the swelling is gone. (Don't leave ice on one spot for more than 20 minutes.) Some experts also recommend taking an over-the-counter medication such as aspirin, ibuprofen, or naproxen to decrease inflammation.

Don't apply heat to an injury at first because heat draws blood to the area and increases swelling. After the swelling has subsided, apply either moist heat (hot towels, heat packs, warm water immersion) or dry heat (heating pads) to speed up healing.

To rehabilitate your body, follow the steps listed in the box "Rehabilitation Following a Minor Athletic Injury."

Preventing Injuries

The best method for dealing with exercise injuries is to prevent them. If you choose activities for your program carefully and follow the training guidelines described here and in Chapter 2, you should be able to avoid most types of injuries. Important guidelines for preventing athletic injuries include the following:

- Train regularly, and stay in condition.
- Gradually increase the intensity, duration, or frequency of your workouts.
- Avoid or minimize high-impact activities.
- Get proper rest between exercise sessions.

TABLE 3-4	*Care of Common Exercise Injuries*	

Injury	Symptoms	Treatment
Blister	Accumulation of fluid in one spot under the skin	Don't pop or drain it unless it interferes too much with your daily activities. If it does pop, clean the area with antiseptic and cover with a bandage. Do not remove the skin covering the blister.
Bruise (contusion)	Pain, swelling, and discoloration	R-I-C-E: rest, ice, compression, elevation.
Fractures and dislocations	Pain, swelling, tenderness, loss of function, and deformity	Seek medical attention, immobilize the affected area, and apply cold.
Joint sprain	Pain, tenderness, swelling, discoloration, and loss of function	R-I-C-E.
Muscle cramp	Painful, spasmodic muscle contractions	Gently stretch and/or massage the cramped area. Drink fluids if exercising in hot weather.
Muscle soreness or stiffness	Pain and tenderness in the affected muscle	Stretch the affected muscle gently; exercise at a low intensity; apply heat.
Muscle strain	Pain, tenderness, swelling, and loss of strength in the affected muscle	R-I-C-E; apply heat after 36–48 hours if swelling has disappeared. Stretch and strengthen the affected area.
Shin splints	Pain and tenderness on the front of the lower leg; sometimes also pain in the calf muscle	Rest; apply ice to the affected area several times a day and before exercise; wrap with tape for support.
Side stitch	Pain on the side of the abdomen	Decrease the intensity of your workout, or stop altogether; bend over in the direction of the stitch.
Tendinitis	Pain and tenderness of the affected area; loss of use	R-I-C-E; apply heat after 36–48 hours if swelling has disappeared. Stretch and strengthen the affected area.

SOURCES: Adapted from Fahey, T. D., ed. 1986. *Athletic Training Principles and Practice.* Mountain View, Calif.: Mayfield. Pryor, E., and M. G. Kraines. 1996. *Keep Moving! It's Aerobic Dance,* 3d ed. Mountain View, Calif.: Mayfield.

TACTICS AND TIPS	*Rehabilitation Following a Minor Athletic Injury*

1. Reduce the initial inflammation using the R-I-C-E principle:

   Rest: Stop using the injured area as soon as you experience pain. Avoid any activity that causes pain.

   Ice: Apply ice to the injured area to reduce swelling and alleviate pain. Apply ice immediately for 10–20 minutes, and repeat every few hours until the swelling disappears. Let the injured part return to normal temperature between icings, and do not apply ice to one area for more than 20 minutes. An easy method for applying ice is to freeze water in a paper cup, peel some of the paper away, and rub the exposed ice on the injured area. If the injured area is large, you can surround it with several bags of crushed ice or ice cubes; bags of frozen vegetables can also be used. Place a thin towel between the bag and your skin. If you use a cold gel pack, limit application time to 10 minutes.

   Compression: Wrap the injured area firmly with an elastic or compression bandage between icings. If the area starts throbbing or begins to change color, the bandage may be wrapped too tightly. Do not sleep with the wrap on.

   Elevation: Raise the injured area above heart level to decrease the blood supply and reduce swelling. Pillows,

books, or a low chair or stool can be used to raise the injured area.

2. After 36–48 hours, apply heat if the swelling has completely disappeared. Immerse the affected area in warm water or apply warm compresses, a hot water bottle, or a heating pad. As soon as it's comfortable, begin moving the affected joints slowly. If you feel pain, or if the injured area begins to swell again, reduce the amount of movement. Continue stretching and moving the affected area until you have regained normal range of motion.

3. Gradually begin exercising the injured area to build strength and endurance. Depending on the type of injury, weight training, walking, and resistance training with a partner can all be effective.

4. Gradually reintroduce the stress of an activity until you can return to full intensity. Don't progress too rapidly or you'll reinjure yourself. Before returning to full exercise participation, you should have a full range of motion in your joints, normal strength and balance among your muscles, normal coordinated patterns of movement (with no injury compensation movements, such as limping), and little or no pain.

Many exercise injuries can be handled by the individual, but serious injuries, such as broken bones and torn ligaments, require medical attention.

- Warm up thoroughly before you exercise, and cool down afterward.
- Achieve and maintain a good level of flexibility.
- Use proper body mechanics when lifting objects or executing sports skills.
- Don't exercise when you are ill or overtrained.
- Use proper equipment, particularly shoes, and choose an appropriate exercise surface. If you exercise on a grass field, soft track, or wooden floor, you are less likely to be injured than on concrete or a hard track.
- Don't return to your normal exercise program until your athletic injuries have healed.

SUMMARY

- The cardiorespiratory system consists of the heart, blood vessels, and respiratory system; it picks up and transports oxygen, nutrients, and waste products.
- Chemical energy from food is used to produce ATP and fuel cellular activities. During exercise, ATP can be produced by the immediate, nonoxidative, and oxidative energy systems; the duration and intensity of the activity determine which energy system predominates. Cardiorespiratory fitness is measured by maximal oxygen consumption ($\dot{V}O_{2max}$).
- Benefits of cardiorespiratory endurance exercise include improved cardiorespiratory functioning; improved cellular metabolism; reduced risk of

chronic diseases, including cardiovascular disease, cancer, diabetes, and osteoporosis; better control of body fat; improved immune function; and improved psychological and emotional well-being.

- Direct measurement of $\dot{V}O_{2max}$ is performed in scientific laboratories. Indirect assessment methods include the 1-mile walk test, the 3-minute step test, the 1.5-mile walk-run test, and the Åstrand-Rhyming cycle ergometer test.
- A successful endurance exercise program sets realistic goals; includes suitable activities; sets starting frequency, intensity, and duration at appropriate levels; includes warm-up and cool-down activities; and is adjusted as fitness improves.
- Intensity of training, the most important factor in achieving cardiorespiratory benefits, can be measured through target heart rate zone and ratings of perceived exertion.
- Serious injuries require medical attention. Application of the R-I-C-E principle (rest, ice, compression, elevation) is appropriate for treating many types of muscle or joint injuries.

FOR MORE INFORMATION

Refer to Chapter 2 for resources on exercise physiology and fitness testing. Additional sources of information and programs include the YMCA and campus or private sports medicine centers for fitness testing; health clubs for places to exercise and training advice; and physical education departments for activity classes.

Books

American Heart Association. 1995. *The Healthy Heart Walking Book.* Indianapolis: Macmillan General Reference. *Includes advice for getting started, building endurance, and maintaining a walking program.*

Edwards, S. 1996. *Sally Edwards' Heart Zone Training: Exercise Smart, Stay Fit and Live Longer.* Holbrook, Mass.: Adams Media. *Describes the use of heart rate and heart rate monitors for the development of fitness; upbeat and motivational.*

Katz, J. 1996. *The All-American Aquatic Handbook: Your Passport to Lifetime Fitness.* Needham Heights, Mass.: Allyn and Bacon. *A guide for people interested in swimming as their primary form of exercise.*

Kusinitz, I., and M. Fine. 1995. *Your Guide to Getting Fit,* 3d ed. Mountain View, Calif.: Mayfield. *Includes assessment tests and a step-by-step guide to developing a cardiorespiratory endurance exercise program.*

Lebow, F., and G. Averbuch, eds. 1997. *The New York Road Runners Club Complete Book of Running and Fitness.* New York: Random House. *A complete guide to running for everyone from the casual jogger to the competitive marathoner.*

Pfeiffer, R. P., and B. C. Mangus. 1998. *Concepts of Athletic Training.* Sudbury, Mass.: Jones and Bartlett. *A comprehensive look at the prevention and treatment of athletic injuries.*

Pryor, E., and M. Kraines. 1997. *Keep Moving! It's Aerobic Dance,*

COMMON QUESTIONS ANSWERED

What kind of clothing should I wear during exercise? Exercise clothing should be comfortable, let you move freely, and allow your body to cool itself. Avoid clothing that constricts normal blood flow or is made from nylon or rubberized fabrics that prevent evaporation of perspiration. Cotton is an excellent material for facilitating the evaporation of sweat. If you sweat heavily when you exercise and find that too much moisture accumulates in cotton clothing, try fabrics containing synthetic materials such as polypropylene that wick moisture away from the skin. Socks made with moisture-wicking compounds may be particularly helpful for people whose feet sweat heavily.

What kind of equipment should I buy? Once you have chosen activities to develop cardiorespiratory fitness, carefully consider what equipment you'll need. Good equipment enhances your enjoyment and decreases your risk of injury. The recent surge of interest in physical activity has been accompanied by a wave of new equipment, but some new products are either overpriced or of poor quality. See the box "Choosing Equipment for Fitness and Sport" for ways to make sound decisions about equipment.

Do I need a special diet for my endurance exercise program? No. For most people, a nutritionally balanced diet contains all the energy and nutrients needed to sustain an exercise program. Don't waste your money on unnecessary vitamins, minerals, and protein supplements. (Chapter 8 has information about putting together a healthy diet.)

Should I drink extra fluids before or during exercise? Yes. your body depends on water to carry out many chemical reactions and to regulate body temperature. Sweating during exercise depletes your body's water supply and can lead to dehydration if fluids aren't replaced. Serious dehydration can cause reduced blood volume, increased heart rate, elevated body temperature, muscle cramps, heat stroke, and even death. Drinking water before and during exercise is important to prevent dehydration and enhance your performance.

Thirst alone isn't a good indication of how much you need to drink because one's sense of thirst is quickly depressed by drinking even small amounts of water. As a rule of thumb, try to drink about 8 ounces of water (more in hot weather) for every 30 minutes of heavy exercise. Bring a water bottle when you exercise so you can replace your fluids while they're being depleted. Water, preferably cold, and diluted carbohydrate drinks are the best fluid replacements. (See Chapter 8 for more on diet and fluid recommendations for active people.)

What is cross-training? Cross-training is a pattern of training in which your program centers on two or more different cardiorespiratory endurance activities. Alternating activities can make your exercise program more fun, but it may slow your development of activity-specific adaptations. For example, if you alternate jogging and tennis, you will probably not develop the coordination, speed, and upper-body strength associated with tennis as quickly as if you just played tennis.

However, if you are quickly bored with a single activity, you'll be more likely to stick with your exercise program if you alternate activities to make it more interesting. Alternating activities may also reduce your risk of some types of injuries.

Is it all right to participate in cardiorespiratory endurance exercise while menstruating? Yes. There is no evidence that exercise during menstruation is unhealthy or that it has negative effects on performance. If you have headaches, backaches, and abdominal pain during menstruation, you may not feel like exercising; for some women, exercise helps relieve these symptoms. Listen to your body, and exercise at whatever intensity is comfortable for you.

Is endurance exercise safe during pregnancy? For most women, there is no reason not to exercise during pregnancy. In the absence of either medical or obstetric complications, pregnant women can continue with an established exercise program and can obtain all the benefits of regular exercise. However, although maternal fitness and a sense of well-being may be enhanced by exercise, no level of exercise during pregnancy has been conclusively demonstrated to be beneficial in improving the outcome of pregnancy.

Consult your physician before continuing or beginning an exercise program. If you were exercising before your pregnancy, you can probably continue with your regular program and modify it as necessary. If you weren't exercising before pregnancy, begin slowly. Throughout pregnancy you should listen to your body and adjust your exercise program to keep it comfortable. Follow the general pattern for cardiorespiratory endurance exercise described in this chapter. Be sure to warm up, cool down, and drink plenty of fluids. General guidelines for exercise during pregnancy from the American College of Obstetricians and Gynecologists are summarized below.

- Exercise regularly (at least three times per week) rather than intermittently.

- Avoid exercise in a supine position—lying on your back—after the first trimester. Research indicates that this position restricts blood flow to the uterus. Also avoid prolonged periods of motionless standing.

- Modify the intensity of your exercise according to how you feel. Stop exercising if you feel fatigued, and don't exercise to exhaustion. You may find that non-weight-bearing exercises such as cycling and swimming are more comfortable than weight-bearing activities in the later months of pregnancy; they also minimize the risk of injury.

- Take care when performing any activity in which balance is important or in which losing balance would prove dangerous. Pregnancy shifts your center of gravity. Also avoid any type of exercise that has the potential for even mild abdominal trauma.

- Eat an adequate diet.

(continued)

- Avoid heat stress, particularly during the first trimester, by drinking an adequate amount of fluids, wearing appropriate clothing, and avoiding exercise in hot and humid weather.

- Resume prepregnancy exercise routines gradually. Many of the changes of pregnancy persist 4–6 weeks postpartum.

- If you experience any unusual symptoms, stop exercising, and consult your physician.

Is it safe to exercise in hot weather? Prolonged, vigorous exercise can be dangerous in hot and humid weather. Heat from exercise is released in the form of sweat, which cools the skin and the blood circulating near the body surface as it evaporates. The hotter the weather, the more water the body loses through sweat; the more humid the weather, the less efficient the sweating mechanism is at lowering body temperature. If you lose too much water or if your body temperature rises too high, you may suffer from a heat disorder such as heat exhaustion or heat stroke. Use caution when exercising if the temperature is above 80°F or if humidity is above 60%. To exercise safely, watch for the signals of heat disorder, regardless of the weather, and follow the tips given in the box "Exercising in Hot Weather."

Is it safe to exercise in cold weather? If you dress warmly in layers and don't stay out in very cold temperatures for too long, exercise can be safe even in subfreezing temperatures. Take both the temperature and the wind-chill factor into account when choosing clothing. Dress in layers so you can subtract them as you warm up and add them if you get cold. A substantial amount of heat loss comes from the head and neck, so keep these areas covered. In subfreezing temperatures, protect the areas of your body most susceptible to frostbite—fingers, toes, ears, nose, and cheeks—with warm socks, mittens or gloves, and a cap, hood, or ski mask. Wear clothing that "breathes" and will wick moisture away from your skin to avoid being overheated by trapped perspiration. Warm up thoroughly, and drink plenty of fluids.

Is it safe to exercise in a smoggy city? Do not exercise outdoors during a smog alert or if air quality is very poor (symptoms of poor air quality include eye and throat irritation and respiratory discomfort). If you have any type of cardiorespiratory difficulty, avoid exertion outdoors when air quality is poor. You can avoid smog and air pollution by exercising in parks, near water (riverbanks, lakeshores, and ocean beaches), or in residential areas with less traffic (areas with stop-and-go traffic will have lower air quality than areas where traffic moves quickly). Air quality is usually better in the early morning and late evening.

TACTICS AND TIPS *Exercising in Hot Weather*

- Use caution when exercising in extreme heat or humidity (over 80°F and/or 60% humidity).

- Expose yourself gradually to exercise in hot and humid environments; work up slowly to your usual levels of intensity and duration. Use target heart rate to monitor exercise intensity in the heat.

- Exercise in the early morning or evening, when temperatures are lowest.

- Drink a glass or two of fluids before you begin exercising, and drink 4–8 ounces of fluid every 10–15 minutes during exercise (more frequently during high-intensity activities).

- Wear clothing that "breathes," allowing air to circulate and cool the body. Wearing white or light colors will help by reflecting, rather than absorbing, heat. A hat can help keep direct sun off your face. Do not wear rubber, plastic, or other nonporous clothing.

- Rest frequently in the shade.

- Keep a record of your morning body weight to track whether weight lost through sweating is restored.

- Slow down or stop if you begin to feel uncomfortable. Watch for the signs of heat disorders listed below; if they occur, act appropriately.

Problem	Symptoms	Treatment
Heat cramps	Muscle cramps, usually in the muscles most used during exercise.	Stop exercising, drink fluids, and stretch cramped muscles.
Heat exhaustion	Paleness; headache; nausea; fainting; dizziness; profuse sweating; weakness; cold, clammy skin; and a rapid, weak pulse.	Cool the body: Stop exercising, get out of the heat, remove excess clothing, drink cold fluids, and apply cool and/or damp towels to the body.
Heat stroke	Hot, flushed skin (skin may be dry or sweaty); rapid pulse; high body temperature; dizziness; confusion or disorientation; vomiting; diarrhea; unconsciousness.	Get immediate medical attention, and try to lower body temperature: Get out of the heat, remove excess clothing, drink cold fluids, and apply cool and/or damp towels or immerse the body in cold water.

Your choice of exercise equipment often affects your enjoyment, your risk of injury, and the likelihood of your continued participation. Nothing will ruin the joy of an activity more than ill-fitting or defective equipment. Following a few simple principles of equipment selection will greatly enhance your sport and exercise experiences.

Price

Try to purchase the best equipment you can afford. If you shop around, you can often find merchandise of good quality at a discount. Bargains are often available through mail-order companies and discount stores. Look in the back of sports specialty magazines for good prices on items such as tennis rackets, running shoes, and windsurf boards.

Good-quality used equipment can often be purchased at a fraction of the retail price. Used sporting goods shops have become very popular throughout the United States and Canada. Sporting goods are also often listed in newspaper classified ads.

Quality

While price and quality generally go hand in hand, you can often buy good-quality equipment at less than premium prices. Before you invest in a new piece of equipment, investigate it. Ask coaches and instructors if the results are worth the price. Most magazines devoted to individual sports and activities review new equipment. The January 1998 issue of *Consumer Reports* rated several types of home exercise equipment. Don't buy without doing some research. It's also a good idea to buy equipment with a money-back guarantee or a free trial period; if the equipment doesn't meet your expectations, you can return it.

Fit

Equipment that fits properly will enhance your enjoyment and prevent injury. Shoes that pinch your feet will make running unbearable. The wrong size grip on a tennis racket can lead to an elbow injury. When shopping for exercise equipment, take your time and get the help you need to ensure a proper fit.

Intended Use

Many people purchase expensive home exercise equipment, only to have it sit in a corner gathering dust. Before buying an expensive home treadmill, stationary cycle, or stair-climber, try it for several weeks at a local health club or gym. Ask yourself how often you'll actually use the equipment. If you honestly will use it regularly, go ahead and buy a home treadmill or stationary cycle. If you will use a piece of equipment only occasionally, you are better off using one at a gym. Also make sure you have space to use and store it at home. If you really decide you want to own one, buy it for your home.

Also consider how intense your workouts will be. If you intend to push your equipment to the limit, buy a model that can handle the stress. There's nothing more frustrating than a tennis racket that breaks the first time you use it, or a treadmill belt that slips when you try to run fast. While heavy-duty equipment tends to cost more, it may be worth the extra money. But take care not to pay extra for features you don't need.

Your Skill Level

Some equipment is designed for people with superior levels of strength, fitness, and skill. Buying "advanced" equipment can actually diminish your enjoyment of an activity. For example, slalom skis designed for a racer would be extremely difficult for a beginning skier to turn. Shoes designed for competitive marathon runners may have less padding to protect the legs and feet from injury, making them inappropriate for a recreational runner (see Chapter 7 for more on choosing footwear). Buy equipment that is appropriate for your current skill level.

Safety

Don't skimp on safety equipment. For popular sports like in-line skating, failing to buy a helmet and appropriate pads can lead to a serious injury. Check your safety equipment frequently to ensure that it's in good working condition. For example, ski bindings that work perfectly one season may not release properly after sitting in your garage for a year.

3d ed. Mountain View, Calif.: Mayfield. *The fitness principles and techniques every aerobic dancer should know.*

Sharkey, B. J. 1996. *Fitness and Health.* Champaign, Ill.: Human Kinetics. *An excellent guide to fitness and health for people serious about their exercise program.*

Sloane, E. A. 1995. *Sloane's Complete Book of Bicycling,* 5th ed. New York: Simon & Schuster. *A comprehensive guide for beginning and expert cyclists that includes information on equipment selection and maintenance and cycling health and safety.*

YMCA of the USA and T. W. Hanlon. 1995. *Fit for Two: The official YMCA Prenatal Exercise Guide.* Champaign, Ill.: Human Kinetics. *A practical guide to safe exercise during pregnancy.*

Organizations and Web Sites

Aerobics and Fitness Association of America/Your Body. Provides information on exercise, including how to choose an instructor, class, or facility; how to begin a walking program; and how to maintain an exercise program while traveling.
http://www.afaa.com/your_body/yourbody.html

American Heart Association. Provides information on cardiovascular health and disease, including the role of exercise in maintaining heart health and exercise tips for people of all ages.
800-AHA-USA1
http://www.americanheart.org

Dr. Pribut's Running Injuries Page. Provides information about running and many types of running injuries.
http://www.clark.net/pub/pribut/spsport.html

Exploratorium's Science of Cycling. Describes different types of bikes and how muscles work to power a cycle.
http://www.exploratorium.edu/cycling

Franklin Institute Science Museum/The Heart: An Online Exploration. An online museum exhibit with information on the structure and function of the heart, blood vessels, and respiratory system.

http://www.fi.edu/biosci/heart.html

Physician and Sportsmedicine. Provides many articles with easy-to-understand advice about exercise injuries.

http://www.physsportsmed.com

Runner's World Online. Contains a wide variety of information about running, including tips for beginning runners, advice about training, and a shoe buyer's guide.

http://www.runnersworld.com

Yahoo/Recreation. Contains links to many sites with practical advice on many sports and activities.

http://www.yahoo.com/recreation/sports

See also the listings in Chapter 2.

SELECTED BIBLIOGRAPHY

Alessio, H. M., and E. R. Blasi. 1997. Physical activity as a natural antioxidant booster and its effect on a healthy life span. *Research Quarterly in Exercise and Sport* 68(4): 292–302.

American College of Sports Medicine. 1998. ACSM Postition Stand: The Recommended Quantity and Quality of Exercise for Developing and Maintaining Cardiorespiratory and Muscular Fitness, Flexibility in Healthy Adults. *Medicine and Science in Sports and Exercise* 30(6): 975–991.

American College of Sports Medicine. 1995. *Guidelines for Exercise Testing and Prescription,* 5th ed. Baltimore: Williams & Wilkins.

American College of Sports Medicine. 1997. *ACSM's Health/Fitness Facility Standards and Guidelines,* 2d ed. Champaign, Ill.: Human Kinetics.

Araujo, D. 1997. Expecting questions about exercise and pregnancy? *Physician and Sportsmedicine* 25(4): 84–93.

Åstrand, P. O., U. Bergh, and A. Kilbom. 1997. A 33-yr follow-up of peak oxygen uptake and related variables of former physical education students. *Journal of Applied Physiology* 82: 1844–1852.

Borg, G. A. V. 1982. Psychophysical bases of perceived exertion. *Medicine and Science in Sports and Exercise* 14:377–381.

Brooks, G. A., T. D. Fahey, and T. P. White. 1996. *Exercise Physiology: Human Bioenergetics and Its Applications,* 2d ed. Mountain View, Calif.: Mayfield.

Brown, M. D., et al. 1997. Improvement of insulin sensitivity by short-term exercise training in hypertensive African American women. *Hypertension* 30(6): 1549–1553.

Centers for Disease Control and Prevention. 1998. Heat-related mortality—United States, 1997. *Morbidity and Mortality Weekly Report* 47(23):473–476.

Charlton, G. A., and M. H. Crawford. 1997. Physiologic consequences of training. *Cardiology Clinics* 15:345–354.

Chesler, R. M., et al. 1997. Cardiovascular response to sudden strenuous exercise: An exercise echocardiographic study. *Medicine and Science in Sports and Exercise* 29:1299–1303.

Crouse, S. F., et al. 1997. Effects of training and a single session of exercise on lipids and apolipoproteins in hypercholesterolemic men. *Journal of Applied Physiology* 83:2019–2028.

Evans, W. J., and D. Cyr-Campbell. 1997. Nutrition, exercise, and healthy aging. *Journal of the American Dietetics Association* 97:632–638.

Exercise during pregnancy and the postpartum period. ACOG Technical Bulletin Number 189. 1994. *International Journal of Gynaecology and Obstetrics* 45(1): 65–70.

Gibbons, R. J., et al. 1997. ACC/AHA Guidelines for Exercise Testing. A report of the American College of Cardiology/American Heart Association Task Force on Practice Guidelines (Committee on Exercise Testing). *Journal of the American College of Cardiology* 30:260–311.

Hakim, A. A., et al. 1998. Effects of walking on mortality among nonsmoking retired men. *New England Journal of Medicine* 338(2): 94–99.

Ivy, J. L. 1997. Role of exercise training in the prevention and treatment of insulin resistance and non-insulin-dependent diabetes mellitus. *Sports Medicine* 24:321–336.

Jennings, G. L. 1997. Exercise and blood pressure: Walk, run or swim? *Journal of Hypertension* 15:567–569.

Kelley, G. 1998. Aerobic exercise and lumbar spine bone mineral density in postmenopausal women: A meta-analysis. *Journal of the American Geriatrics Society* 46(2): 143–152.

Mackinnon, L. T., L. Hubinger, and F. Lepre. 1997. Effects of physical activity and diet on lipoprotein(a). *Medicine and Science in Sports and Exercise* 29:1429–1436.

Mengelkoch, L. J., et al. 1997. Effects of age, physical training, and physical fitness on coronary heart disease risk factors in older track athletes at twenty-year follow-up. *Journal of the American Geriatrics Society* 45(12): 1446–1453.

Nicoloff, G., and T. L. Schwenk. 1995. Using exercise to ward off depression. *Physician and Sportsmedicine* 23(9): 44–58.

Radegran, G., and B. Saltin. 1998. Muscle blood flow at onset of dynamic exercise in humans. *American Journal of Physiology* 274(1 Pt 2): H314–H322.

Roitman, J. 1998. *ACSM's Resource Manual for Guidelines for Exercise Testing and Prescription.* 3d ed. Baltimore: Williams and Wilkens.

Sandor, R. P. 1997. Heat illness: On-site diagnosis and cooling. *Physician and Sportsmedicine* 25(6): 35–41.

Shaping Up. 1998. *Consumer Reports,* January.

Shephard, R. J., and P. N. Shek. 1995. Cancer, immune function, and physical activity. *Canadian Journal of Applied Physiology* 20:1–25.

Sipila, S., et al. 1997. Effects of strength and endurance training on muscle fibre characteristics in elderly women. *Clinical Physiology* 17:459–474.

Stamford, B. 1997. Choosing and using exercise equipment. *Physician and Sportsmedicine* 25(1): 107–109.

Tsintzas, K., and C. Williams. 1998. Human muscle glycogen metabolism during exercise. Effect of carbohydrate supplementation. *Sports Medicine* 25(1): 7–23.

Turley, K. R., and J. H. Wilmore. 1997. Cardiovascular responses to treadmill and cycle ergometer exercise in children and adults. *Journal of Applied Physiology* 83:948–957.

Utter, A., et al. 1997. Effect of carbohydrate substrate availability on ratings of perceived exertion during prolonged running. *International Journal of Sports Nutrition* 7(4): 274–285.

Van Boxtel, M. P. J., et al. 1997. Aerobic capacity and cognitive performance in a cross-sectional aging study. *Medicine and Science in Sports and Exercise* 29(10): 1357–1365.

Weltan, S. M., et al. 1998. Preexercise muscle glycogen content affects metabolism during exercise despite maintenance of hyperglycemia. *American Journal of Physiology* 274(1 Pt 1): E83–E88.

LAB 3-1 *Assessing Your Current Level of Cardiorespiratory Endurance*

Before taking any of the cardiorespiratory endurance assessment tests, refer to the fitness prerequisites and cautions given in Table 3-2. For best results, don't exercise strenuously or consume caffeine the day of the test, and don't smoke or eat a heavy meal within about 3 hours of the test.

The 1-Mile Walk Test

Equipment

1. A track or course that provides a measurement of 1 mile
2. A stopwatch, clock, or watch with a second hand
3. A weight scale

Preparation

Measure your body weight (in pounds) before taking the test.

Body weight: _____ lb

Instructions

1. Warm up before taking the test. Do some walking, easy jogging, or calisthenics and some stretching exercises.
2. Cover the 1-mile course as quickly as possible. Walk at a pace that is brisk but comfortable. You must raise your heart rate above 120 bpm.
3. As soon as you complete the distance, note your time and take your pulse for 10 seconds.

    Walking time: _____ min _____ sec

    10-second pulse count: _____ beats

4. Cool down after the test by walking slowly for several minutes.

Determining Maximal Oxygen Consumption

1. Convert your 10-second pulse count into a value for exercise heart rate by multiplying it by 6.

    Exercise heart rate: _____ × 6 = _____ bpm

                                    _{10-sec pulse count}

2. Convert your walking time from minutes and seconds to a decimal figure. For example, a time of 14 minutes and 45 seconds would be 14 + (45/60), or 14.75 minutes.

    Walking time: _____ min + (_____ sec ÷ 60 sec/min) = _____ min

3. Insert values for your age, gender, weight, walking time, and exercise heart rate in the following equation, where

    W = your weight (in pounds)

    A = your age (in years)

    G = your gender (male = 1; female = 0)

    T = your time to complete the 1-mile course (in minutes)

    H = your exercise heart rate (in beats per minute)

    $\dot{V}O_{2max} = 132.853 - (0.0769 \times W) - (0.3877 \times A) + (6.315 \times G) - (3.2649 \times T) - (0.1565 \times H)$

LABORATORY ACTIVITIES

For example, a 20-year-old, 190-pound male with a time of 14.75 minutes and an exercise heart rate of 152 bpm would calculate maximal oxygen consumption as follows:

$$\dot{V}O_{2max} = 132.853 - (0.0769 \times 190) - (0.3877 \times 20) + (6.315 \times 1) - (3.2649 \times 14.75) - (0.1565 \times 152)$$
$$= 45 \text{ ml/kg/min}$$

$$\dot{V}O_{2max} = 132.853 - (0.0769 \times \underline{\qquad}) - (0.3877 \times \underline{\qquad}) + (6.315 \times \underline{\qquad})$$
$$\underset{\text{weight (lb)}}{} \qquad \underset{\text{age (years)}}{} \qquad \underset{\text{gender}}{}$$
$$- (3.2649 \times \underline{\qquad}) - (0.1565 \times \underline{\qquad}) = \underline{\qquad} \textbf{ ml/kg/min}$$
$$\underset{\text{walking time (min)}}{} \qquad \underset{\text{exercise heart rate (bpm)}}{}$$

4. Copy this value for $\dot{V}O_{2max}$ into the appropriate place in the chart on the final page of this lab.

The 3-Minute Step Test

Equipment

1. A step, bench, or bleacher step that is 16.25 inches from ground level
2. A stopwatch, clock, or watch with a second hand
3. A metronome

Preparation

Practice stepping up and down from the step before you begin the test. Each step has four beats: up-up-down-down. Males should perform the test with the metronome set for a rate of 96 beats per minute, or 24 steps per minute. Females should set the metronome at 88 beats per minute, or 22 steps per minute.

Instructions

1. Warm up before taking the test. Do some walking, easy jogging, and stretching exercises.
2. Set the metronome at the proper rate. Your instructor or a partner can call out starting and stopping times; otherwise, have a clock or watch within easy viewing during the test.
3. Begin the test, and continue to step at the correct pace for 3 minutes.
4. Stop after 3 minutes. Remain standing, and count your pulse for the 15-second period from 5 to 20 seconds into recovery.

   15-second pulse count: _____ beats

5. Cool down after the test by walking slowly for several minutes.

Determining Maximal Oxygen Consumption

1. Convert your 15-second pulse count to a value for recovery heart rate by multiplying by 4.

   Recovery heart rate: $\underline{\qquad}$ × 4 = $\underline{\qquad}$ bpm
   $\underset{\text{15-sec pulse count}}{}$

2. Insert your recovery heart rate in the equation below, where

   H = recovery heart rate (in beats per minute)
   Males: $\dot{V}O_{2max} = 111.33 - (0.42 \times H)$
   Females: $\dot{V}O_{2max} = 65.81 - (0.1847 \times H)$

   For example, a man with a recovery heart rate of 162 bpm would calculate maximal oxygen consumption as follows:

   $$\dot{V}O_{2max} = 111.33 - (0.42 \times 162) = 43 \text{ ml/kg/min}$$

   Males: $\dot{V}O_{2max} = 111.33 - (0.42 \times \underline{\qquad}) = \underline{\qquad} \textbf{ ml/kg/min}$
   $\underset{\text{recovery heart rate (bpm)}}{}$
   Females: $\dot{V}O_{2max} = 65.81 - (0.1847 \times \underline{\qquad}) = \underline{\qquad} \textbf{ ml/kg/min}$
   $\underset{\text{recovery heart rate (bpm)}}{}$

3. Copy this value for $\dot{V}O_{2max}$ into the appropriate place in the chart on the final page of this lab.

The 1.5-Mile Run-Walk Test

Equipment

1. A running track or course that is flat and provides exact measurements of up to 1.5 miles
2. A stopwatch, clock, or watch with a second hand

Preparation

You may want to practice pacing yourself prior to taking the test to avoid going too fast at the start and becoming prematurely fatigued. Allow yourself a day or two to recover from your practice run before taking the test.

Instructions

1. Warm up before taking the test. Do some walking, easy jogging, and stretching exercises.
2. Try to cover the distance as fast as possible, at a pace that is comfortable for you. If possible, monitor your own time, or have someone call out your time at various intervals of the test to determine whether your pace is correct.
3. Record the amount of time, in minutes and seconds, it takes for you to complete the 1.5-mile distance.

   Running-walking time: _____ min _____ sec

4. Cool down after the test by walking or jogging slowly for about 5 minutes.

Determining Maximal Oxygen Consumption

1. Convert your running time from minutes and seconds to a decimal figure. For example, a time of 14 minutes and 25 seconds would be 14 + (25/60), or 14.4 minutes.

   Running-walking time: _____ min + (_____ sec ÷ 60 sec/min) = _____ min

2. Insert your running time in the equation below, where

   T = running time (in minutes)

   $\dot{V}O_{2max} = (483 \div T) + 3.5$

   For example, a person who completes 1.5 miles in 14.4 minutes would calculate maximal oxygen consumption as follows:

   $\dot{V}O_{2max} = (483 \div 14.4) + 3.5 = 37$ ml/kg/min

   $\dot{V}O_{2max} = (483 \div \underset{\text{run-walk time (min)}}{\underline{\hspace{1.5cm}}}) + 3.5 = \underline{\hspace{1.5cm}}$ **ml/kg/min**

3. Copy this value for $\dot{V}O_{2max}$ into the appropriate place in the chart on the final page of this lab.

The Åstrand-Rhyming Cycle Ergometer Test

Equipment

1. Cycle ergometer that allows for regulation of power output in kilopounds per meter (kpm)
2. A stopwatch, clock, or watch with a second hand
3. Weight scale
4. Metronome or meter on cycle ergometer to measure pedal revolutions
5. Partner to monitor heart rate

Preparation

Weigh yourself before taking the test. Adjust the seat height of the cycle so that your knees are almost completely extended as your foot goes through the bottom of the pedaling cycle. Practice pedaling the cycle ergometer at the speed of 50 pedal revolutions per minute. Each revolution includes a downstroke with each foot, so set your metronome at 100 beats per minute.

Body weight: _____ lb

Instructions

1. Warm up before taking the test. Do some walking, easy jogging, and stretching exercises. A few minutes' practice on the cycle ergometer can also be part of your warm-up.

2. Set up the metronome to monitor your pace. If you aren't using a metronome, have a partner call out times at regular intervals.

3. Set the power output between 300 and 1200 kpm. If you are small or have been sedentary, a setting of 300–600 kpm is appropriate. If you are larger or fitter, try a setting of 600–900 kpm. Find a setting high enough to raise your heart rate to between 125 and 170 bpm, but not so high that you can't continue pedaling for 6 minutes.

   Note: If your heart rate goes above 170 or you experience any unusual symptoms, stop pedaling, rest for 15–20 minutes, and then repeat the test at a lower workload.

4. Ride the cycle ergometer for 6 minutes at a rate of 50 pedal revolutions per minute. Your partner should monitor your heart rate by counting your pulse for the last 10 seconds of each minute of your ride (see the photograph). Your heart rate should rise to a level in the target range (125–170 bpm) and then level off, staying relatively constant during the last few minutes of your ride. If your exercise heart rate stays below 125 bpm, rest for 15–20 minutes, and then repeat the test at a higher workload. If your heart rate gets too high or if it continues to rise throughout your ride (not leveling off in the last few minutes), rest for 15–20 minutes, and repeat the test at a lower workload.

During the cycle ergometer test, a partner monitors heart rate for the last 10 seconds of every minute.

5. If your heart rate levels off within the target range (125–170 bpm), your partner should make a final count during the last 10 seconds of the sixth minute of your ride.

   10-second pulse count: _____ beats

   Power output: _____ kpm

6. Cool down after the test by pedaling, walking, or jogging slowly for several minutes.

Determining Maximal Oxygen Consumption

1. Calculate your exercise heart rate by multiplying your final 10-second count by 6.

   Exercise heart rate: $\underset{\text{10-sec pulse count}}{\underline{\hspace{2cm}}}$ × 6 = _____ bpm

2. On the nomogram on p. 65, connect the point that represents your exercise heart rate with the point that represents the power output you used (on the scale for your sex). Read your total oxygen uptake score (in liters) at the point where the line you've drawn crosses the maximal oxygen consumption line.

   Maximal oxygen consumption (from nomogram): _____ l/min

3. Adjust your maximal oxygen consumption score for your age by multiplying it by the appropriate age-correction factor in the table below.

Age	15	20	25	30	35	40	45	50	55	60	65
Factor	1.10	1.05	1.0	0.94	0.87	0.83	0.78	0.75	0.71	0.68	0.65

   $\dot{V}O_{2max}$ corrected for age: $\underset{\dot{V}O_{2max}}{\underline{\hspace{2cm}}}$ l/min × $\underset{\text{age-correction factor}}{\underline{\hspace{2cm}}}$ = _____ l/min

4. Convert your score to one for maximal oxygen consumption (in milliliters of oxygen per minute per kilogram of body weight).

   a. Convert your weight from pounds to kilograms by dividing it by 2.2.

   b. Multiply your $\dot{V}O_{2max}$ by 1000 (to convert from liters to milliliters).

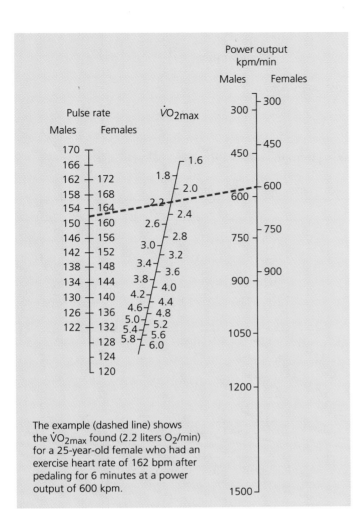

Power output
kpm/min

Males   Females

Pulse rate $\dot{V}O_{2max}$

Males   Females

The example (dashed line) shows
the $\dot{V}O_{2max}$ found (2.2 liters O_2/min)
for a 25-year-old female who had an
exercise heart rate of 162 bpm after
pedaling for 6 minutes at a power
output of 600 kpm.

Nomogram for use with the Åstrand-
Rhyming cycle ergometer test.

c.   Divide this number by your weight (in kilograms).

For example, a 135-pound, 25-year-old female whose 10-second count was 27 at a workload
of 600 kpm would calculate maximal oxygen consumption as follows:

1.   27 beats × 6 = 162 bpm

2.   Connecting 600 kpm and 162 bpm on the nomogram gives a $\dot{V}O_{2max}$ value of 2.2 l/min

3.   The age-adjustment factor for a 25-year-old is 1.00.
     2.2 l/min × 1.00 = 2.2 l/min

4.   To convert 135 pounds to kilograms:
     135 lb ÷ 2.2 lb/kg = 61.4 kg

     To convert liters to milliliters:

     2.2 l/min × 1000 ml/l = 2200 ml/min

     To adjust for weight:

     2200 ml/min ÷ 61.4 kg = 35.8 ml/kg/min

Convert body weight to kg: _____ lb ÷ 2.2 lb/kg = _____ kg

Convert from liters to milliliters: _____ l/min × 1000 ml/l = _____ ml/min
                                    age-corrected $\dot{V}O_{2max}$

Adjust for weight:

$$\dot{V}O_{2max} = \underline{\hspace{2cm}}_{\dot{V}O_{2max}} \text{ ml/min} \div \underline{\hspace{2cm}}_{\text{body weight}} \text{ kg} = \underline{\hspace{2cm}} \textbf{ml/kg/min}$$

5. Copy this value for $\dot{V}O_{2max}$ into the appropriate place in the chart below.

Rating Your Cardiovascular Fitness

Record your $\dot{V}O_{2max}$ score(s) and the corresponding fitness rating from the table in the chart below.

	Maximal Oxygen Consumption (ml/kg/min)					
Women	*Very Poor*	*Poor*	*Fair*	*Good*	*Excellent*	*Superior*
Age: 18–29	Below 30.6	30.6–33.7	33.8–36.6	36.7–40.9	41.0–46.7	Above 46.7
30–39	Below 28.7	28.7–32.2	32.3–34.5	34.6–38.5	38.6–43.8	Above 43.8
40–49	Below 26.5	26.5–29.4	29.5–32.2	32.3–36.2	36.3–40.9	Above 40.9
50–59	Below 24.3	24.3–26.8	26.9–29.3	29.4–32.2	32.3–36.7	Above 36.7
60 and over	Below 22.8	22.8–24.4	24.5–27.1	27.2–31.1	31.2–37.4	Above 37.4
Men						
Age: 18–29	Below 37.1	37.1–40.9	41.0–44.1	44.2–48.1	48.2–53.9	Above 53.9
30–39	Below 35.4	35.4–38.8	38.9–42.3	42.4–46.7	46.8–52.4	Above 52.4
40–49	Below 33.0	33.0–36.7	36.8–39.8	39.9–44.0	44.1–50.3	Above 50.3
50–59	Below 30.2	30.2–33.7	33.8–36.6	36.7–40.9	41.0–47.0	Above 47.0
60 and over	Below 26.5	26.5–30.1	30.2–33.5	33.6–38.0	38.1–45.1	Above 45.1

SOURCE: Based on norms from the Cooper Institute for Aerobics Research, Dallas, Texas; used with permission.

	$\dot{V}O_{2max}$	Cardiovascular Fitness Rating
1-mile walk test		
3-minute step test		
1.5-mile run-walk test		
Åstrand-Rhyming cycle ergometer test		

Is your rating as high as you want it to be? If not, what is your goal for $\dot{V}O_{2max}$? _____

_____

_____

To monitor your progress toward your goal, enter the results of this lab in the Preprogram Assessment column of Appendix D. After several weeks of a cardiorespiratory endurance exercise program, complete this lab again, and enter the results in the Postprogram Assessment column of Appendix D. How do the results compare? (For accuracy, it's best to compare $\dot{V}O_{2max}$ scores for the same test.)

SOURCES: Kline, G. M., et al. 1987. Estimation of $\dot{V}O_{2max}$ from a one-mile track walk, gender, age, and body weight. *Medicine and Science in Sports and Exercise* 19(3): 253–259. McArdle, W. D., F. I. Katch, and V. L. Katch. 1991. *Exercise Physiology: Energy, Nutrition, and Human Performance*. Philadelphia: Lea and Febiger, pp. 225–226. Brooks, G. A., and T. D. Fahey. 1987. *Fundamentals of Human Performance*. New York: Macmillan. Åstrand, P. O., and I. Rhyming. 1954. A nomogram for calculation of aerobic capacity (physical fitness) from pulse rate during submaximal work. *Journal of Applied Physiology* 7:218–221. Used with permission.

Name _____ **Section** _____ **Date** _____

 LAB 3-2 *Developing an Exercise Program for Cardiorespiratory Endurance*

1. *Goals.* Determine goals for your cardiorespiratory endurance exercise program, and record them below. Goals can be specific or general, short or long term.

   _____

   _____

   _____

   _____

2. *Activities.* Refer to the box "Activities and Sports for Developing Cardiorespiratory Endurance" (p. 52) and choose one or more activities for your program. Fill in the activity name and general intensity rating sections on the program plan below.

3. *Duration.* Fill in an appropriate duration for each activity (20–60 minutes).

4. *Intensity.* Determine your exercise intensity, and fill in below.

   a. Calculate your target heart rate range.

   Maximum heart rate: 220 − _____ = _____ bpm

age (years)

   65% training intensity = _____ bpm × 0.65 = _____ bpm

maximum heart rate

   90% training intensity = _____ bpm × 0.90 = _____ bpm

maximum heart rate

   Target heart rate range = _____ to _____ bpm
   (Note: If you are very unfit, use 55% of maximum heart rate as the lower end of your target heart rate range.)

   b. If you prefer, determine an RPE value that corresponds to your target heart rate range (see pp. 52–53 and Figure 3-3).

5. *Frequency.* Fill in how often you plan to participate in each activity.

Program Plan

Activity	General Intensity Rating (L, M, H)	Duration (min)	Intensity (bpm or RPE)	Frequency (check ✓)						
				M	T	W	Th	F	Sa	Su

6. *Monitoring your program.* Complete a log like the one on the next page to monitor your program and track your progress. Fill in the duration of exercise for each workout. To monitor your progress more closely, you can also track another variable, such as distance. For example, if your cardiorespiratory endurance program includes walking and swimming, you can keep track of miles walked and yards swum in addition to the duration of each exercise session.

Activity/Date															
1	Duration														
2	Duration														
3	Duration														
4	Duration														
5	Duration														

Activity/Date															
1	Duration														
2	Duration														
3	Duration														
4	Duration														
5	Duration														

Activity/Date															
1	Duration														
2	Duration														
3	Duration														
4	Duration														
5	Duration														

Muscular Strength and Endurance

LOOKING AHEAD

After reading this chapter, you should be able to answer these questions about muscular strength and endurance:

- What are muscular strength and endurance, and how do they relate to wellness?

- How can muscular strength and endurance be assessed?

- How do weight training exercises affect muscles?

- What type, frequency, and number of weight training exercises make up a successful program?

- What are the most important strategies for avoiding injuries in a weight training program?

- How are common weight training exercises performed using weight machines and free weights?

Exercise experts have long emphasized the importance of cardiovascular fitness. Other physical fitness factors, such as muscle strength and flexibility, were mentioned almost as an afterthought. As more was learned about how the body responds to exercise, however, it became obvious that these other factors are vital to health, wellness, and overall quality of life. Muscles make up over 40% of your body mass. You depend on them for movement, and, because of their mass, they are the site of a large portion of the energy reactions (metabolism) that take place in your body. Strong, well-developed muscles help you perform daily activities with greater ease, protect you from injury, and enhance your well-being in other ways.

This chapter explains the benefits of strength training and describes methods of assessing muscular strength and endurance. It then explains the basics of weight training and provides guidelines for setting up your own weight training program.

BENEFITS OF MUSCULAR STRENGTH AND ENDURANCE

Enhanced muscular strength and endurance can lead to improvements in the areas of performance, injury prevention, body composition, self-image, and lifetime muscle and bone health.

Improved Performance of Physical Activities

A person with a moderate-to-high level of muscular strength and endurance can perform everyday tasks—such as climbing stairs and carrying books or groceries—with ease. Muscular strength and endurance are also important in recreational activities: People with poor muscle strength tire more easily and are less effective in activities like hiking, skiing, and playing tennis. Increased strength can enhance your enjoyment of recreational sports by making it possible to achieve high levels of performance and to handle advanced techniques.

TERMS
tendon A tough band of fibrous tissue that connects a muscle to a bone or other body part and transmits the force exerted by the muscle.

ligament A tough band of tissue that connects the ends of bones to other bones or supports organs in place.

testosterone The principal male hormone, responsible for the development of secondary sex characteristics and important in the increase of muscle size.

repetition maximum (RM) The maximum amount of resistance that can be moved a specified number of times; 1 RM is the maximum weight that can be lifted once.

repetitions The number of times an exercise is performed during one set.

Injury Prevention

Increased muscle strength provides protection against injury because it helps people maintain good posture and appropriate body mechanics when carrying out everyday activities like walking, lifting, and carrying. Strong muscles in the abdomen, hips, low back, and legs support the back in proper alignment and help prevent low-back pain, which afflicts over 85% of all Americans at some time in their lives. (Prevention of low-back pain is discussed in Chapter 5.) Training for muscular strength also makes the **tendons, ligaments,** and joint surfaces stronger and less susceptible to injury.

Improved Body Composition

As Chapter 2 explained, healthy body composition means that the body has a high proportion of fat-free mass (primarily composed of muscle) and a relatively small proportion of fat. Strength training improves body composition by increasing muscle mass, thereby tipping the body composition ratio toward fat-free mass and away from fat. Building muscle mass through strength training also helps with losing fat because metabolic rate is directly proportional to muscle mass: The more muscle mass, the higher the metabolic rate. A high metabolic rate means that a nutritionally sound diet will not lead to an increase in body fat.

Enhanced Self-Image

Weight training leads to an enhanced self-image by providing stronger, firmer-looking muscles and a toned, healthy-looking body. Men tend to build larger, stronger, more shapely muscles. Women tend to lose inches, increase strength, and develop greater muscle definition. The larger muscles in men combine with high levels of the hormone **testosterone,** the principal androgen, for a strong tissue-building effect; see the box "Gender Differences in Muscular Strength."

Because weight training provides measurable objectives (pounds lifted, repetitions accomplished), a person can easily recognize improved performance, leading to greater self-confidence. It's especially satisfying to work on improving one's personal record.

Improved Muscle and Bone Health with Aging

Research has shown that good muscle strength helps people live healthier lives. A lifelong program of regular strength training prevents muscle and nerve degeneration that can compromise the quality of life and increase the risk of hip fractures and other potentially life-threatening injuries. After age 30, people begin to lose muscle mass. At first they may notice that they can't play sports as well as they could in high school. After more years of inactivity and strength loss, people may have trouble performing even the simple movements of daily life—getting out of a bathtub or automobile, walking up a flight of stairs, or

Men are generally stronger than women because they typically have larger bodies overall and larger muscles. But when strength is expressed per unit of cross-sectional area of muscle tissue, men are only 1–2% stronger than women in the upper body and about equal to women in the lower body. (Men have a larger proportion of muscle tissue in the upper body, so it's easier for them to build upper-body strength than it is for women.) Individual muscle fibers are larger in men, but the metabolism of cells within those fibers is the same in both sexes.

Two factors that help explain these disparities between the sexes are androgen levels and the speed of nervous control of muscle. Androgens are naturally occurring male hormones that are responsible for the development of secondary sex characteristics (facial hair, deep voice, and so forth). Androgens also promote the growth of muscle tissue. Androgen levels are about 6–10 times higher in men than in women, so men tend to have larger muscles. Also, because the male nervous system can activate muscles faster, men tend to have more power.

Some women are concerned that they will develop large muscles from weight training. Most studies show that women do not develop big muscles, but the evidence of top women body builders suggests that they can. Some of these women may have taken drugs to increase their muscle size, but many muscular women have not. Evidence suggests, though, that it is difficult for women to gain a large amount of muscle without training intensely over many years.

The bottom line is that both men and women can increase strength through weight training. Women may not be able to lift as much weight as men, but pound for pound of muscle, they have nearly the same capacity to gain strength as men. The lifetime wellness benefits of strength training are available to everyone.

SOURCE: Fahey, T. D. 1997. *Weight Training for Men and Women*, 3d ed. Mountain View, Calif.: Mayfield.

doing yard work. Poor strength makes it much more likely that a person will be injured during the course of everyday activities.

As a person ages, motor nerves can become disconnected from the portion of muscle they control. Muscle physiologists estimate that by age 70, 15% of the motor nerves in most people are no longer connected to muscle tissue. Aging and inactivity also cause muscles to become slower and therefore less able to perform quick, powerful movements. Strength training helps maintain motor nerve connections and the quickness of muscles.

Osteoporosis is common in people over age 55, particularly postmenopausal women. Osteoporosis leads to fractures that can be life-threatening. Hormonal changes from aging account for much of the bone loss that occurs, but lack of bone stress due to inactivity and a poor diet are contributing factors. Recent research indicates that strength training can lessen bone loss even if it is taken up later in life. Increased muscle strength can also help prevent falls, which are a major cause of injury in people with osteoporosis. (Strategies for preventing osteoporosis are described in Chapter 8.)

ASSESSING MUSCULAR STRENGTH AND ENDURANCE

Muscular strength and muscular endurance are distinct but related components of fitness. Muscular strength, the maximum amount of force a muscle can produce in a single effort, is usually assessed by measuring the maximum amount of weight a person can lift one time. This single maximal movement is referred to as one **repetition maximum (RM)**. You can assess the strength of your major

muscle groups by taking the one-repetition maximum tests for the bench press and the leg press. Refer to Lab 4-1 for guidelines on taking these tests. Instructions for assessing grip strength using a dynamometer are also included in Lab 4-1. For more accurate results, avoid any strenuous weight training for 48 hours beforehand.

Muscular endurance is the ability of a muscle to exert a submaximal force repeatedly or continuously over time. This ability depends on muscular strength because a certain amount of strength is required for any muscle movement. Muscular endurance is usually assessed by counting the maximum number of **repetitions** of a muscular contraction a person can do (such as in push-ups) or the maximum amount of time a person can hold a muscular contraction (such as in the flexed-arm hang). You can test the muscular endurance of major muscle groups in your body by taking the 60-second sit-up test or the curl-up test and the push-up test. Refer to Lab 4-1 for complete instructions on taking these assessment tests.

Record your results and your fitness rating from the assessment tests in Lab 4-1. If the results show that improvement is needed, a weight training program will enable you to make rapid gains in muscular strength and endurance.

FUNDAMENTALS OF WEIGHT TRAINING

Weight training develops muscular strength and endurance in the same way that endurance exercise develops cardiovascular fitness: When the muscles are stressed by a greater load than they are used to, they adapt and improve their function. The type of adaptation that occurs depends on the type of stress applied.

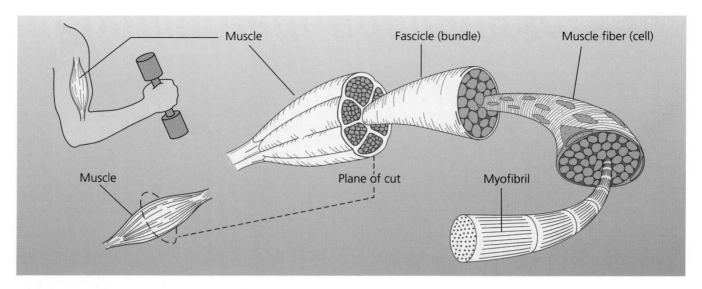

Figure 4-1 Components of skeletal muscle tissue.

Physiological Effects of Weight Training

Muscles move the body and enable it to exert force because they move the skeleton. When a muscle contracts (shortens), it moves a bone by pulling on the tendon that attaches the muscle to the bone. Muscles consist of individual muscle cells, or **muscle fibers,** connected in bundles (Figure 4-1). A single muscle is made up of many bundles of muscle fibers and is covered by layers of connective tissue that hold the fibers together. Muscle fibers, in turn, are made up of smaller units called **myofibrils.** (When your muscles are given the signal to contract, pro-

tein filaments within the myofibrils slide across one another, causing the muscle fiber to shorten.) Weight training causes the size of individual muscle fibers to increase by increasing the number of myofibrils. Larger muscle fibers mean a larger and stronger muscle. The development of large muscle fibers is called **hypertrophy.**

Muscle fibers are classified as fast-twitch or slow-twitch fibers according to their strength, speed of contraction, and energy source. **Slow-twitch fibers** are relatively fatigue-resistant, but they don't contract as rapidly or strongly as fast-twitch fibers. The principal energy system that fuels slow-twitch fibers is aerobic. **Fast-twitch fibers** contract more rapidly and forcefully than slow-twitch fibers but fatigue more quickly. Although oxygen is important in the energy system that fuels fast-twitch fibers, they rely more on anaerobic metabolism than do slow-twitch fibers (see Chapter 3 for a discussion of energy systems).

Most muscles contain a mixture of slow-twitch and fast-twitch fibers. The type of fiber that acts depends on the type of work required. Endurance activities like jogging tend to use slow-twitch fibers, whereas strength and **power** activities like sprinting use fast-twitch fibers. Weight training can increase the size and strength of both fast-twitch and slow-twitch fibers, although fast-twitch fibers are preferentially increased.

To exert force, the body recruits one or more motor units to contract. A **motor unit** is made up of a nerve connected to a number of muscle fibers. When a motor nerve calls upon its fibers to contract, all the fibers contract to their maximum capacity. The number of motor units recruited depends on the amount of strength required: When a person picks up a small weight, he or she uses fewer motor units than when picking up a large weight. Training with weights improves the body's ability to

TERMS **muscle fiber** A single muscle cell, usually classified according to strength, speed of contraction, and energy source.

myofibrils Protein structures that make up muscle fibers.

hypertrophy An increase in the size of a muscle fiber, usually stimulated by muscular overload.

slow-twitch fibers Red muscle fibers that are fatigue-resistant but have a slow contraction speed and a lower capacity for tension; usually recruited for endurance activities.

fast-twitch fibers White muscle fibers that contract rapidly and forcefully but fatigue quickly; usually recruited for actions requiring strength and power.

power The ability to exert force rapidly.

motor unit A motor nerve (one that initiates movement) connected to one or more muscle fibers.

isometric The application of force without movement; also called static.

isotonic The application of force resulting in movement; also called dynamic.

concentric muscle contraction An isotonic contraction in which the muscle gets shorter as it contracts.

eccentric muscle contraction An isotonic contraction in which the muscle lengthens as it contracts.

TABLE 4-1	*Physiological Changes and Benefits from Weight Training*
Change	**Benefits**
Increased muscle mass*	Increased muscular strength Improved body composition Higher rate of metabolism Toned, healthy-looking muscles
Increased utilization of motor units during muscle contractions	Increased muscular strength and power
Improved coordination of motor units	Increased muscular strength and power
Increased strength of tendons, ligaments, and bones	Lower risk of injury to these tissues
Increased storage of fuel in muscles	Increased resistance to muscle fatigue
Increased size of fast-twitch muscle fibers (from a high-resistance program)	Increased muscular strength and power
Increased size of slow-twitch muscle fibers (from a high-repetition program)	Increased muscular endurance
Increased blood supply to muscles (from a high-repetition program)	Increased delivery of oxygen and nutrients Increased elimination of wastes

*Due to genetic and hormonal differences, men will build more muscle mass than women.

recruit motor units—a phenomenon called muscle learning—which increases strength even before muscle size increases.

In summary, weight training increases muscle strength because it increases the size of muscle fibers and improves the body's ability to call upon motor units to exert force. The physiological changes and benefits that result from weight training are summarized in Table 4-1.

Types of Weight Training Exercises

Weight training exercises are generally classified as isometric or isotonic. Each involves a different way of using and strengthening muscles.

Isometric Exercise   Also called static exercise, **isometric** exercise involves applying force without movement. To perform an isometric exercise, a person can use an immovable object like a wall to provide resistance, or the individual can just tighten a muscle while remaining still (for example, tightening the abdominal muscles while sitting at a desk). In isometrics, the muscle contracts, but there is no movement.

Isometric exercises aren't as widely used as isotonic exercises because they don't develop strength throughout a joint's entire range of motion. However, isometric exercises are useful in strengthening muscles after an injury or surgery, when movement of the affected joint could delay healing. Isometrics are also used to overcome weak points in an individual's range of motion. Isometrically strengthening a muscle at its weakest point will allow more weight to be lifted with that muscle during isotonic exercise. For maximum strength gains, hold the isometric contraction maximally for 6 seconds; do 5–10 repetitions.

This isometric exercise for the arms and upper back involves locking the hands together and attempting to pull them apart. Isometric contractions involve force without movement.

Isotonic Exercise   **Isotonic** (or dynamic) exercise involves applying force with movement. Isotonic exercises are the most popular type of exercises for increasing muscle strength and seem to be most valuable for developing strength that can be transferred to other forms of physical activity. They can be performed with weight machines, free weights, or a person's own body weight (as in sit-ups or push-ups).

There are two kinds of isotonic muscle contractions: concentric and eccentric. A **concentric muscle contraction** occurs when the muscle applies force as it shortens. An **eccentric muscle contraction** occurs when the muscle applies force as it lengthens. For example, in an arm curl, the biceps muscle works concentrically as the weight is raised toward the shoulder and eccentrically as the weight is lowered.

Left: A concentric contraction: The biceps muscle shortens as the arm lifts a weight toward the shoulder. **Right:** An eccentric contraction: The biceps muscle lengthens as the arm lowers a weight toward the thigh.

Two of the most common isotonic exercise techniques are constant resistance exercise and variable resistance exercise. Constant resistance exercise uses a constant load (weight) throughout a joint's entire range of motion. Training with free weights is a form of constant resistance exercise. A problem with this technique is that, because of differences in leverage, there are points in a joint's range of motion where the muscle controlling the movement is stronger and points where it is weaker. The amount of weight a person can lift is limited by the weakest point in the range. In variable resistance exercise, the load is changed to provide maximum load throughout the entire range of motion. This form of exercise uses machines that place more stress on muscles at the end of the range of motion, where a person has better leverage and is capable of exerting more force. The Nautilus pullover machine is an example of a variable resistance exercise machine.

Four other kinds of isotonic techniques, used mainly by athletes for training and rehabilitation, are eccentric loading, plyometrics, speed loading, and isokinetics.

- **Eccentric loading** involves placing a load on a muscle as it lengthens. The muscle contracts eccentrically in order to control the weight. Eccentric loading is practiced during most types of resistance training. For example, you are performing an eccentric movement as you lower the weight to your chest during a bench press in preparation for the active movement.

- **Plyometrics** is the sudden eccentric loading and stretching of muscles followed by a forceful concentric contraction. An example would be jumping from a bench to the ground and then jumping back onto the bench. This type of exercise is used to develop explosive strength.

- **Speed loading** involves moving a weight as rapidly as possible in an attempt to approach the speeds used in movements like throwing a softball or sprinting. In the bench press, for example, speed loading might involve doing 5 repetitions as fast as possible using a weight that is half the maximum load you can lift. You can gauge your progress by timing how fast you can perform the repetitions.

- **Isokinetic** exercise involves exerting force at a constant speed against an equal force exerted by a special strength training machine. The isokinetic machine provides variable resistance at different points in the joint's range of motion, matching the effort applied by the individual, while keeping the speed of the movement constant. In other words, the force exerted by the individual at any point in the range of motion is resisted by an equal force from the isokinetic machine. Isokinetic exercises are excellent for building strength and endurance, but the equipment is expensive and less commonly available than other kinds of weight machines.

Exercise Machines

Advantages

- Safe
- Convenient
- Don't require spotters
- Don't require lifter to balance bar
- Provide variable resistance
- Require less skill
- Make it easy to move from one exercise to the next
- Allow easy isolation of individual muscle groups
- Support back (on many machines)

Disadvantages

- Limited availability
- Inappropriate for performing dynamic movements
- Allow a limited number of exercises

Free Weights

Advantages

- Allow dynamic movements
- Allow the user to develop control of the weights
- Allow a greater variety of exercises
- Widely available
- Truer to real-life situations; strength transfers to daily activities

Disadvantages

- Not as safe
- Require spotters
- Require more skill
- Cause more blisters and calluses

Comparing the Different Types of Exercise   Isometric exercises require no equipment, so they can be done virtually anywhere. They build strength rapidly and are useful for rehabilitating injured joints. On the other hand, they have to be performed at several different angles for each joint to improve strength throughout the joint's entire range of motion. Isotonic exercises can be performed without equipment (calisthenics) or with equipment (weight lifting). They are excellent for building strength and endurance, and they tend to build strength through a joint's full range of motion.

Most people develop muscular strength and endurance using isotonic exercises. Ultimately, the type of exercise a person chooses depends on individual goals, preferences, and access to equipment.

CREATING A SUCCESSFUL WEIGHT TRAINING PROGRAM

To get the most out of your weight training program, you must design it to achieve maximum fitness benefits with a low risk of injury. Before you begin, seriously consider the type and amount of training that's right for you.

Choosing Equipment: Weight Machines Versus Free Weights

Your muscles will get stronger if you make them work against a resistance. Resistance can be provided by free weights, by your own body weight, or by sophisticated exercise machines. Weight machines are preferred by

many people because they are safe, convenient, and easy to use. You just set the resistance (usually by placing a pin in the weight stack), sit down at the machine, and start working. Machines make it easy to isolate and work specific muscles. You don't need a **spotter,** someone who stands by to assist when free weights are used, and you don't have to worry about dropping a weight on yourself.

Free weights require more care, balance, and coordination to use, but they strengthen your body in ways that are more adaptable to real life. Free weights are more popular with athletes for developing explosive strength for sports.

Unless you are training seriously for a sport that requires a great deal of strength, training on machines is probably safer, more convenient, and just as effective as training with free weights. However, you can increase strength either way; which to use is a matter of personal preference. The box "Exercise Machines Versus Free Weights" can help you make a decision.

Selecting Exercises

A complete weight training program works all the major muscle groups. It usually takes about 8–10 different exercises to get a complete workout. For overall fitness, you need to include exercises for your neck, upper back, shoulders, arms, chest, abdomen, lower back, thighs, buttocks, and calves. If you are also training for a particular sport, include exercises to strengthen the muscles important for optimal performance *and* the muscles most likely to be injured. A program of weight training exercises for general fitness is presented later in this chapter.

It is important to balance exercises between **agonist** and **antagonist** muscle groups. (When a muscle contracts, it is known as the agonist; the opposing muscle, which must relax and stretch to allow contraction by the agonist, is known as the antagonist.) If you do an exercise that moves a joint in one direction, also select an exercise that works the joint in the opposite direction. For example, if you do knee extensions to develop the muscles on the front of your thighs, also do leg curls to develop the antagonistic muscles on the back of your thighs.

The order of exercises can also be important. Do exercises for large muscle groups or for more than one joint before you do exercises that use small muscle groups or single joints. This allows for more effective overload of the larger, more powerful muscle groups. Small muscle groups fatigue more easily than larger ones, and small muscle fatigue limits your capacity to overload larger muscle groups. For example, lateral raises, which work the shoulder muscles, should be performed after bench presses, which work the chest and arms in addition to the shoulders. If you fatigue your shoulder muscles by doing lateral raises first, you won't be able to lift as much weight and effectively fatigue all the key muscle groups used during the bench press.

Resistance

The amount of weight (resistance) you lift in weight training exercises is equivalent to intensity in cardiorespiratory endurance training. It determines the way your body will adapt to weight training and how quickly these adaptations will occur. Choose weights based on your current level of muscular fitness and your fitness goals. To build strength rapidly, you should lift weights as heavy as 80% of your maximum capacity (1 RM). If you're more interested in building endurance, choose a lighter weight, perhaps 40–60% of 1 RM. For example, if your maximum capacity for the leg press is 160 pounds, you might lift 130 pounds to build strength and 80 pounds to build endurance. For a general fitness program to develop both strength and endurance, choose a weight in the middle of this range, perhaps 70% of 1 RM.

Because it can be tedious and time-consuming to continually reassess your maximum capacity for each exercise, you might find it easier to choose a weight based on the number of repetitions of an exercise you can perform with a given resistance.

Repetitions and Sets

In order to improve fitness, you must do enough repetitions of each exercise to fatigue your muscles. The number of repetitions needed to cause fatigue depends on the amount of resistance: the heavier the weight, the fewer repetitions to reach fatigue. In general, a heavy

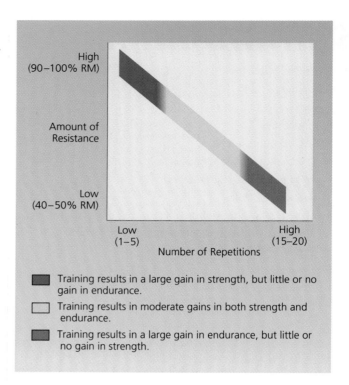

Figure 4-2 **Training for strength versus training for endurance.**

weight and a low number of repetitions (1–5) build strength, whereas a light weight and a high number of repetitions (15–20) build endurance (Figure 4-2). For a general fitness program to build both strength and endurance, try to do about 8–12 repetitions of each exercise; a few exercises, such as abdominal crunches and calf raises, may require more. Choose a weight heavy enough to fatigue your muscles but light enough for you to complete the repetitions with good form. Due to an increased risk of injury, it is recommended that older and more frail people (approximately 50–60 years of age and above) perform more repetitions (10–15) using a lighter weight.

In weight training, a **set** refers to a group of repetitions of an exercise followed by a rest period. Surprisingly, exercise scientists have not identified the optimal number of sets for increasing strength. For developing strength and endurance for general fitness, a single set of each exercise is sufficient, provided you use enough resistance to fatigue your muscles. (You should just barely be able to complete the 8–12 repetitions for each exercise.) Doing more than 1 set of each exercise may increase strength development, and most serious weight trainers do at least 3 sets of each exercise (see below for additional guidelines for more advanced programs).

If you perform more than 1 set of an exercise, you need to rest long enough between sets to allow your muscles to work at a high enough intensity to increase fitness. The length of the rest interval depends on the amount of resistance. In a program to develop a combination of strength

TERMS **set** A group of repetitions followed by a rest period.

A Sample Weight Training Program for General Fitness

Guidelines

Type of activity: 8–10 weight training exercises that focus on major muscle groups

Frequency: 2–3 days per week

Resistance: Weights heavy enough to cause muscle fatigue when performed for the selected number of repetitions

Repetitions: 8–12 of each exercise (10–15 with a lower weight for people over age 50–60)

Sets: 1 (Doing more than 1 set per exercise may result in faster and greater strength gains.)

Sample Program

1. Warm-up (5–10 minutes)
2. Weight training exercises (see table at right)
3. Cool-down (5–10 minutes)

Exercise	Resistance (lb)	Repetitions	Sets
Bench press	60	10	1
Overhead press	40	10	1
Lat pulls	40	10	1
Lateral raises	5	10	1
Biceps curls	25	10	1
Squats	30	10	1
Toe raises	25	15	1
Abdominal curls	—	30	1
Spine extensions	—	10	1
Neck flexion	—	10	1

and endurance for wellness, a rest period of 1–3 minutes between sets is appropriate; if you are lifting heavier loads to build maximum strength, rest 3–5 minutes between sets. You can save time in your workouts if you alternate sets of different exercises. Each muscle group can rest between sets while you work on other muscles.

The Warm-Up and Cool-Down

As with cardiorespiratory endurance exercise, you should warm up before every weight training session and cool down afterward. You should do both a general warm-up—several minutes of walking or easy jogging—and a warm-up for the weight training exercises you plan to perform. For example, if you plan to do 1 or more sets of 10 repetitions of bench presses with 125 pounds, you might do 1 set of 10 repetitions with 50 pounds as a warm-up. Do similar warm-up exercises for each exercise in your program.

To cool down after weight training, relax for 5–10 minutes after your workout. Including a period of post-exercise stretching may help prevent muscle soreness; warmed-up muscles and joints make this a particularly good time to work on flexibility.

Frequency of Exercise

For general fitness, the American College of Sports Medicine recommends a frequency of 2–3 days per week for weight training. Allow your muscles at least 1 day of rest between workouts; if you train too often, your muscles won't be able to work at a high enough intensity to improve their fitness, and soreness and injury are more likely to result. If you enjoy weight training and would

like to train more often, try working different muscle groups on alternate days. For example, work your arms and upper body one day, work your lower body the next day, and then return to upper-body exercises on the third day. Refer to the box "A Sample Weight Training Program for General Fitness" for suggestions on beginning a program.

Making Progress

The first few weeks of weight training should be devoted to learning the exercises. You need to learn the movements, and your nervous system needs to practice communicating with your muscles so you can develop strength effectively. To start, choose a weight that you can move easily through 8–12 repetitions, and do only 1 set of each exercise. Gradually add weight and (if you want) sets to your program over the first few weeks until you are doing 1–3 sets of 8–12 repetitions of each exercise.

As you progress, add weight when you can do more than 12 repetitions of an exercise. If adding weight means you can do only 7 or 8 repetitions, stay with that weight until you can again complete 12 repetitions per set. If you can do only 4–6 repetitions after adding weight, you've added too much and should take some off.

You can expect to improve rapidly during the first 6–10 weeks of training: a 10–30% increase in the amount of weight lifted. Gains will then come more slowly. Your rate of improvement will depend on how hard you work and how your body responds to resistance training. There will be individual differences in the rate of improvement. Factors such as age, motivation, and heredity will affect your progress.

Your ultimate goal depends on you. After you have achieved the level of strength and muscularity that you

Scott Peterson

Exercise/Date		9/14	9/16	9/18	9/21	9/23	9/25	9/28	9/30	10/2	10/5	10/7	10/9	10/12	10/14	10/16							
Bench press	Wt.	70	70	70	75	75	75	80	80	80	90	90	95	105	105	105							
	Sets	1	1	1	1	1	1	1	1	1	1	1	1	1	1	1							
	Reps.	10	10	12	10	12	12	10	9	12	12	12	12	8	7	8							
Overhead press	Wt.	40	40	40	55	55	60	60	60	70	70	75	75	75	80	85							
	Sets	1	1	1	1	1	1	1	1	1	1	1	1	1	1	1							
	Reps.	10	10	12	10	12	10	10	12	10	12	8	11	12	12	8							
Lat pulls	Wt.	50	50	50	60	60	60	60	60	60	70	70	70	80	80	80							
	Sets	1	1	1	1	1	1	1	1	1	1	1	1	1	1	1							
	Reps.	10	10	12	8	8	10	8	11	12	10	10	12	8	8	8							
Lateral raises	Wt.	5	5	5	7.5	7.5	7.5	7.5	7.5	7.5	7.5	7.5	7.5	10	10	10							
	Sets	1	1	1	1	1	1	1	1	1	1	1	1	1	1	1							
	Reps.	10	10	10	7	8	7	10	8	8	11	12	12	7	7	8							
Biceps curls	Wt.	35	35	35	40	40	40	45	45	45	50	50	50	50	50	50							
	Sets	1	1	1	1	1	1	1	1	1	1	1	1	1	1	1							
	Reps.	10	10	10	10	12	12	10	12	12	10	8	8	10	10	10							
Squats	Wt.	–	–	–	45	45	85	85	105	115	125	135	135	145	145	145							
	Sets	1	1	1	1	1	1	1	1	1	1	1	1	1	1	1							
	Reps.	10	10	10	12	15	10	12	12	15	12	10	12	9	8	9							
Toe raises	Wt.	–	–	–	45	45	85	85	105	115	125	135	135	145	145	145							
	Sets	1	1	1	1	1	1	1	1	1	1	1	1	1	1	1							
	Reps.	15	15	15	15	15	15	15	15	15	15	15	15	15	15	15							
Abdominal curls	Wt.	–	–	–	–	–	–	–	–	–	–	–	–	–	–	–							
	Sets	1	1	1	1	1	1	1	1	1	1	1	1	1	1	1							
	Reps.	20	20	20	20	20	20	25	25	25	30	30	30	30	30	30							
Spine extensions	Wt.	–	–	–	–	–	–	–	–	–	–	–	–	–	–	–							
	Sets	1	1	1	1	1	1	1	1	1	1	1	1	1	1	1							
	Reps.	5	5	5	8	8	8	10	10	10	10	10	10	10	10	10							
Neck flexion	Wt.	–	–	–	–	–	–	–	–	–	–	–	–	–	–	–							
	Sets	1	1	1	1	1	1	1	1	1	1	1	1	1	1	1							
	Reps.	5	5	5	10	10	10	10	10	10	10	10	10	10	10	10							

Figure 4-3   A sample workout card.

want, you can maintain your gains by training 2–3 days per week. You can monitor the progress of your program by recording the amount of resistance and the number of repetitions and sets you perform on a workout card like the one shown in Figure 4-3.

More Advanced Strength Training Programs

The weight training program described in this section— 1 set of 8–12 repetitions of 8–10 exercises, performed 2–3 days per week—is sufficient to develop and maintain muscular strength and endurance for general fitness. If you have a different goal, you may need to adjust your program accordingly. As described above, performing more sets of a smaller number of repetitions with a heavier load will cause greater increases in strength. A program designed to build strength might include 3–5 sets of 4–6 repetitions each; the load used should be heavy enough to cause fatigue with the smaller number of repetitions. Be sure to rest long enough after a set to allow your muscles to recover and to work intensely during the next set.

Experienced weight trainers often engage in some form of cycle training, in which the exercises, number of sets and repetitions, and intensity are varied within a workout and/or between workouts. For example, you might do a particular exercise more intensely during some sets or on some days than others; you might also vary the exercises you perform for particular muscle groups. For information on these more advanced training techniques, consult your instructor, your coach, or the trainer at your school's weight room or the local gym; several of the books listed in the For More Information section at the end of the chapter also provide information on program design. If you decide to adopt a more advanced training regimen, start off slowly to give your body a chance to adjust and to minimize the risk of injury.

Weight Training Safety

Injuries do happen in weight training. Maximum physical effort, elaborate machinery, rapid movements, and heavy weights can combine to make the weight room a dangerous place if proper precautions aren't taken. To help ensure that your workouts are safe and productive, follow the guidelines in the box "Safe Weight Training" and the suggestions given below.

Use Proper Lifting Technique   Every exercise has a proper technique that is important for obtaining maximum benefits and preventing injury. Your instructor or weight room attendant can help explain the specific tech-

- Lift weights from a stabilized body position.
- Be aware of what's going on around you. Stay away from other people when they're doing exercises. If you bump into someone, you could cause an injury.
- Don't use defective equipment. Report any equipment malfunctions immediately.
- Protect your back by maintaining control of your spine (protect your spine from dangerous positions). Observe proper lifting techniques, and use a weight-lifting belt when doing heavy lifts.
- Don't hold your breath while doing weight training exercises.
- Always warm up before training, and cool down afterward.
- Don't exercise if you're ill, injured, or overtrained.

(a)   **(b)**

Spotters should be present when a person trains with free weights. **(a)** If two spotters are used, one spotter should stand at each end of the barbell. **(b)** If one spotter is present, he or she should stand behind the lifter.

niques for performing different exercises and using different weight machines. Perform exercises smoothly and with good form. Lift or push the weight forcefully during the active phase of the lift and then lower it slowly with control. Perform all lifts through the full range of motion.

Use Spotters and Collars with Free Weights   Spotters are necessary when an exercise has potential for danger: A weight that is out of control or falls can cause a serious injury. A spotter can assist you if you cannot complete a lift or if the weight tilts. A spotter can also help you move a weight into position before a lift and provide help or additional resistance during a lift. Spotting requires practice and coordination between the lifter and spotter(s).

Collars are devices that secure weights to a barbell or dumbbell. Although people lift weights without collars, doing so is dangerous. It is easy to lose your balance or to raise one side of the weight faster than the other. Without collars, the weights on one side of the bar will slip off, and the weights on the opposite side will crash to the floor.

Proper lifting technique for free weights also includes the following:

- Keep weights as close to your body as possible.
- Do most of your lifting with your legs. Keep your hips and buttocks tucked in.
- When you pick a weight up from the ground, keep your back straight and your head level or up. Don't bend at the waist with straight legs.
- Don't twist your body while lifting.

- Lift weights smoothly and slowly; don't jerk them. Control the weight through the entire range of motion.
- Don't bounce weights against your body during an exercise.
- Never hold your breath when you lift. Exhale when exerting the greatest force, and inhale when moving the weight into position for the active phase of the lift. (Holding your breath causes a decrease in blood returning to the heart and can make you become dizzy and faint.)
- Rest between sets if you perform more than one set of each exercise. Fatigue hampers your ability to obtain maximum benefits from your program and is a prime cause of injury.
- When lifting barbells and dumbbells, wrap your thumbs around the bar when gripping it. You can easily drop the weight when using a "thumbless" grip.
- Gloves are not mandatory but may prevent calluses on your hands.
- When doing standing lifts, maintain a good posture so that you protect your back.
- Don't lift beyond the limits of your strength.

Use Common Sense When Exercising on Weight Machines   Although notable for their safety, weight

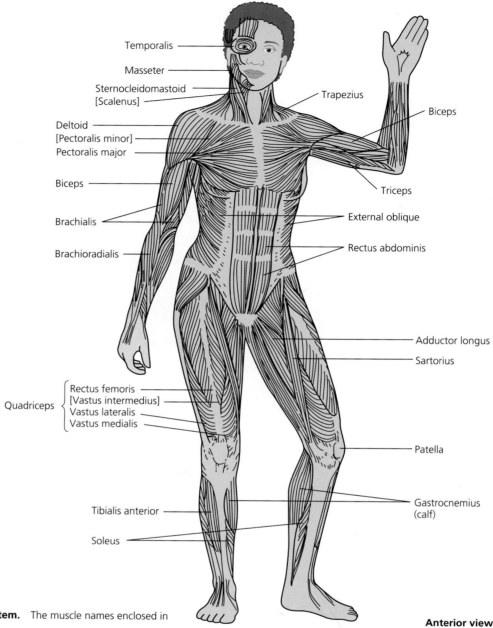

Temporalis

Masseter

Sternocleidomastoid
[Scalenus]

Trapezius

Deltoid
[Pectoralis minor]

Pectoralis major

Biceps

Biceps

Triceps

Brachialis

External oblique

Brachioradialis

Rectus abdominis

Adductor longus

Sartorius

Rectus femoris
[Vastus intermedius]
Vastus lateralis
Vastus medialis

Quadriceps

Patella

Gastrocnemius
(calf)

Tibialis anterior

Soleus

Anterior view

Figure 4-4   The muscular system.   The muscle names enclosed in brackets refer to deep muscles.

machines are not completely danger-free. The following strategies can help prevent injuries.

- Keep away from moving weight stacks. Pay attention when you're changing weights. Someone may jump on the machine ahead of you and begin an exercise while your fingers are close to the weight stack.

- Stay away from moving parts of the machine that could pinch your skin.

- Adjust each machine for your body so that you don't have to work in an awkward position. Lock everything in place before you begin.

- Beware of broken bolts, frayed cables, broken chains, or loose cushions that can give way and cause serious injury. If you notice a broken or frayed part, tell an instructor immediately.

- Make sure the machines are clean. Dirty vinyl is a breeding ground for germs that can cause skin diseases. Carry a towel around with you and place it on the machine where you will sit or lie down.

- Be aware of what's happening around you. Talking between exercises is a great way to relax and have fun, but inattention can lead to injury.

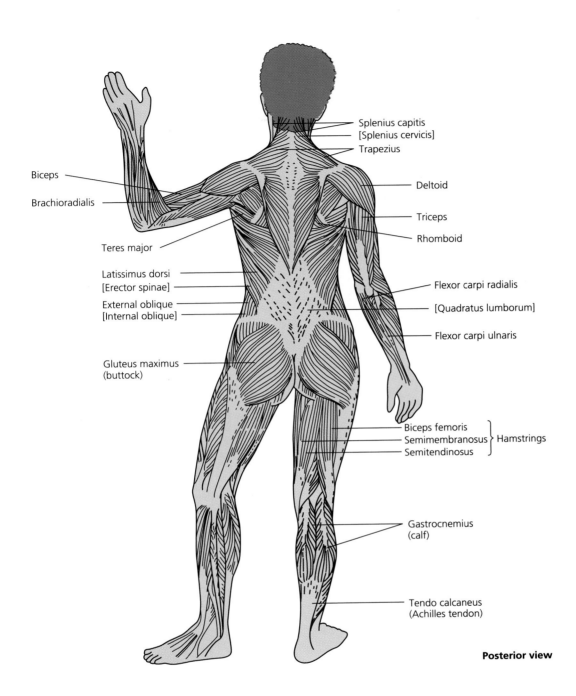

Splenius capitis
[Splenius cervicis]
Trapezius
Biceps
Brachioradialis
Deltoid
Triceps
Rhomboid
Teres major
Latissimus dorsi
[Erector spinae]
External oblique
[Internal oblique]
Flexor carpi radialis
[Quadratus lumborum]
Flexor carpi ulnaris
Gluteus maximus
(buttock)
Biceps femoris
Semimembranosus } Hamstrings
Semitendinosus
Gastrocnemius
(calf)
Tendo calcaneus
(Achilles tendon)

Posterior view

Be Alert for Injuries Report any obvious muscle or joint injuries to your instructor or physician, and stop exercising the affected area. Training with an injured joint or muscle can lead to a more serious injury. Make sure you get the necessary first aid. Even minor injuries heal faster if you use the R-I-C-E principle of treating injuries described in Chapter 3.

Consult a physician if you're having any unusual symptoms during exercise or if you're uncertain whether weight training is a proper activity for you. Conditions such as heart disease and high blood pressure can be aggravated during weight training. Symptoms such as headaches, dizziness, labored breathing, numbness, vision disturbances, and chest, neck, or arm pains should be reported immediately.

Weight Training Exercises

A general book on fitness and wellness cannot include a detailed description of all weight training exercises. Here we present a basic program for developing muscular strength and endurance for general fitness using free weights and Nautilus weight machines. Instructions for each exercise are accompanied by photographs and a listing of the muscles being trained. (Figure 4-4 is a diagram

TABLE 4-2 *Weight Training Exercises for Machines and Free Weights*

Body Part	Nautilus	Universal Gym	Free Weights
Neck	4-way neck	Neck conditioning station	Neck harness Manual exercises
Trapezius ("Traps")	Overhead press Lateral raise Reverse pullover Compound row Shoulder shrug Rowing back	Shoulder press Shoulder shrug Upright row Bent-over row Rip-up Front raise Pull-up	Overhead press Lateral raise Shoulder shrug Power clean Upright row
Deltoids	Lateral raise Overhead press Reverse pullover Double chest 10° chest 50° chest Seated dip Bench press Compound row Rotary shoulder	Bench press Shoulder shrug Shoulder press Upright row Rip-up Front raise Pull-up	Raise Bench press Shoulder press Upright row Pull-up
Biceps	Biceps curl Lat pull	Biceps curl Lat pull	Biceps curl Lat pull Pull-up
Triceps	Triceps extension Seated dip Triceps exten. (lat machine) Bench press Overhead press	French curl Dip Triceps exten. (lat machine) Bench press Seated press	French curl Dip Triceps exten. (lat machine) Bench press Military press
Latissimus dorsi ("Lats")	Pullover Behind neck Torso arm Lat pull Seated dip Compound row	Pull-up Lat pull Bent-over row Pull-over Dip	Pull-up Pull-over Dip Bent-over row Lat pull
Abdominals	Abdominal Rotary torso	Hip flexor Leg raise Crunch Sit-up Side-bend	Hip flexor Leg raise Crunch Sit-up Side-bend Isometric tightener
Lower back	Lower back	Back extension Back leg raise	Back extension Good-morning
Thigh and buttocks	Leg press Leg extension Leg curl Hip adductor Hip abductor	Leg press Leg curl Leg extension Adductor kick Abductor kick Back hip extension	Squat Leg press Leg extension Leg curl Power clean Snatch Dead lift
Calf	Seated calf Heel raise: multiexercise	Calf press	Heel raise

TABLE 4-3 · Weight Training for Sports and Activities

Emphasize these muscle groups when training for the following sports and activities. Although it is important to condition all major muscle groups, specific activities require extra conditioning in specific muscles.

Activity or Sport	Neck	Shoulders	Chest	Arms	Forearms	Upper Back	Lower Back	Abdominals	Thighs	Hamstrings	Calves
Badminton		✓	✓	✓	✓	✓			✓	✓	✓
Basketball		✓	✓	✓		✓	✓	✓	✓	✓	✓
Billiards		✓		✓	✓	✓	✓				
Canoeing		✓	✓	✓	✓	✓	✓	✓			
Cycling		✓		✓	✓	✓	✓	✓	✓	✓	✓
Dancing							✓	✓	✓	✓	✓
Field hockey		✓	✓	✓	✓	✓	✓	✓	✓	✓	✓
Fishing				✓	✓				✓	✓	✓
Football	✓	✓	✓	✓	✓	✓	✓	✓	✓	✓	✓
Golf		✓		✓	✓	✓	✓	✓	✓	✓	✓
Gymnastics	✓	✓	✓	✓	✓	✓	✓	✓	✓	✓	✓
Jogging		✓		✓		✓	✓	✓	✓	✓	✓
Rock climbing		✓	✓	✓	✓	✓	✓	✓	✓	✓	✓
Scuba diving				✓		✓	✓	✓	✓	✓	
Skating, in-line		✓				✓	✓	✓	✓	✓	✓
Skiing, cross-country		✓		✓	✓	✓	✓	✓	✓	✓	✓
Skiing, downhill		✓		✓		✓	✓	✓	✓	✓	✓
Squash		✓	✓	✓	✓	✓	✓	✓	✓	✓	
Swimming		✓	✓	✓	✓	✓	✓	✓	✓	✓	
Table tennis		✓		✓	✓				✓	✓	✓
Tennis		✓	✓	✓	✓	✓	✓	✓	✓	✓	✓
Triathlon		✓	✓	✓	✓	✓	✓	✓	✓	✓	✓
Volleyball		✓	✓	✓	✓	✓	✓	✓	✓	✓	✓
Water skiing	✓	✓		✓	✓	✓	✓	✓	✓	✓	✓
Wrestling	✓	✓	✓	✓	✓	✓	✓	✓	✓	✓	✓

of the muscular system.) Table 4-2 lists alternative and additional exercises that can be performed on Nautilus or Universal machines or with free weights. If you are interested in learning how to do these exercises, ask your instructor or coach for assistance.

If you want to develop strength for a particular activity, your program should contain exercises for general fitness, exercises for the muscle groups most important for the activity, and exercises for muscle groups most often injured.

To create a weight training program for your favorite sport or activity, choose from among the exercises listed in Table 4-3, as well as from those listed in Table 4-2. Regardless of the goals of your program or the type of equipment you use, your program should be structured so that you obtain maximum results without risking injury. You should train at least 2 days per week, and each exercise session should contain a warm-up, 1 or more sets of 8–12 repetitions of 8–10 exercises, and a period of rest.

WEIGHT TRAINING EXERCISES
Free Weights

EXERCISE 1

BENCH PRESS

Muscles developed: Pectoralis major, triceps, deltoids

Instruction: (a) Lying on a bench on your back with your feet on the floor, grasp the bar with palms upward and hands shoulder-width apart. (b) Lower the bar to your chest. Then return it to the starting position. The bar should follow an elliptical path, during which the weight moves from a low point at the chest to a high point over the chin. If your back arches too much, try doing this exercise with your feet on the bench.

(a)   **(b)**

EXERCISE 2

SHOULDER PRESS (Overhead or Military Press)

Muscles developed: Deltoids, triceps, trapezius

Instructions: This exercise can be done standing or seated, with dumbbells or barbells. The shoulder press begins with the weight at your chest, preferably on a rack. (a) Grasp the weight with your palms facing away from you. (b) Push the weight overhead until your arms are extended. Then return to the starting position (weight at chest). Be careful not to arch your back excessively.

If you are a more advanced weight trainer, you can "clean" the weight to your chest (lift it from the floor to your chest). The clean should be attempted only after instruction from a knowledgeable coach; otherwise, it can lead to injury.

(a)   **(b)**

Although a spotter does not appear in these demonstration photographs, spotters should be used for most exercises with free weights.

LAT PULL

Muscles developed: Latissimus dorsi, biceps

Instructions: Begin in a seated or kneeling position, depending on the type of lat machine and the manufacturer's instructions. **(a)** Grasp the bar of the machine with arms fully extended. **(b)** Slowly pull the weight down until it reaches the back of your neck. Slowly return to the starting position.

(a) (b)

LATERAL RAISE

Muscles developed: Deltoids

Instructions: **(a)** Stand with feet shoulder-width apart and a dumbbell in each hand. Hold the dumbbells parallel to each other. **(b)** With elbows slightly bent, slowly lift both weights until they reach shoulder level. Keep your wrists in a neutral position, in line with your forearms. Return to the starting position.

(a) (b)

BICEPS CURL

Muscles developed: Biceps, brachialis

Instructions: (a) From a standing position, grasp the bar with your palms upward and your hands shoulder-width apart. (b) Keeping your upper body rigid, flex (bend) your elbows until the bar reaches a level slightly below the collarbone. Return the bar to the starting position.

(a)　　　　　　　　(b)

SQUAT

Muscles developed: Quadriceps, gluteus maximus, hamstrings, gastrocnemius

Instructions: Stand with feet shoulder-width apart and toes pointed slightly outward. (a) Rest the bar on the back of your shoulders, holding it there with hands facing forward. (b) Keeping your head up and lower back straight, squat down until your thighs are almost parallel with the floor. Drive upward toward the starting position, keeping your back in a fixed position throughout the exercise.

(a)　　　　　　　　(b)

Although a spotter does not appear in these demonstration photographs, spotters should be used for most exercises with free weights.

TOE RAISE

Muscles developed: Gastrocnemius, soleus

Instructions: Stand with feet shoulder-width apart and toes pointed straight ahead. **(a)** Rest the bar on the back of your shoulders, holding it there with hands facing forward. **(b)** Press down with your toes while lifting your heels. Return to the starting position.

(a)   (b)

CURL-UP OR CRUNCH

Muscles developed: Rectus abdominis, obliques

Instructions: **(a)** Lie on your back on the floor with your arms folded across your chest and your feet on the floor or on a bench. **(b)** Curl your trunk up and forward by raising your head and shoulders from the ground. Lower to the starting position.

(a)   (b)

SPINE EXTENSIONS (Isometric Exercises)

Muscles developed: Erector spinae, gluteus maximus, hamstrings, deltoids

Instructions: Begin on all fours with your knees below your hips and your hands below your shoulders.

Unilateral spine extension: (a) Extend your right leg to the rear, and reach forward with your right arm. Keep your neck neutral and your raised arm and leg in line with your torso. Don't arch your back or let your hip or shoulder sag. Hold this position for 10–30 seconds. Repeat with your left leg and left arm.

Bilateral spine extension: (b) Extend your left leg to the rear, and reach forward with your right arm. Keep your neck neutral and your raised leg in line with your torso. Don't arch your back or let your hip or shoulder sag. Hold this position for 10–30 seconds. Repeat with your right leg and left arm.

You can make this exercise more difficult by attaching weights to your ankles and wrists.

(a)

(b)

NECK FLEXION AND LATERAL FLEXION (Isometric Exercises)

Muscles developed: Sternocleidomastoids, scaleni

Instructions:

Neck Flexion: (a) Place your hand on your forehead with fingertips pointed up. Using the muscles at the back of your neck, press your head forward and resist the pressure with the palm of your hand.

Lateral flexion: (b) Place your hand on the right side of your face, fingertips pointed up. Using the muscles on the left side of your neck, press your head to the right and resist the pressure with the palm of your hand. Repeat on the left side.

(a)

(b)

Nautilus Weight Machines

BENCH PRESS

Muscles developed: Pectoralis major, anterior deltoids, triceps

Instructions: Lie on the bench so the tops of the handles are aligned with the tops of your armpits. Place your feet flat on the floor; if they don't reach, place them on the bench. **(a)** Grasp the handles with your palms facing away from you. **(b)** Push the bars until your arms are fully extended. Return to the starting position.

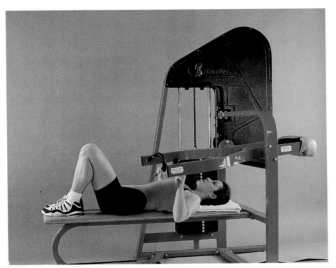

(a)

(b)

OVERHEAD PRESS (Shoulder Press)

Muscles developed: Deltoids, trapezius, triceps

Instructions: Adjust the seat so the two bars are slightly above your shoulders. **(a)** Sit down, facing away from the machine, and grasp the bars with your palms facing inward. **(b)** Press the weight upward until your arms are extended. Return to the starting position.

(a)

(b)

PULLOVER

Muscles developed: Latissimus dorsi, pectoralis major and minor, triceps, abdominals

Instructions: Adjust the seat so your shoulders are aligned with the cams. Push down on the foot pads with your feet to bring the bar forward until you can place your elbows on the pads. Rest your hands lightly on the bar. If possible, place your feet flat on the floor. **(a)** To get into the starting position, let your arms go backward as far as possible. **(b)** Pull your elbows forward until the bar almost touches your abdomen. Return to the starting position.

(a)   (b)

LATERAL RAISE

Muscles developed: Deltoids, trapezius

Instructions: **(a)** Adjust the seat so the pads rest just above your elbows when your upper arms are at your sides, your elbows are bent, and your forearms are parallel to the floor. **(b)** Lightly grasp the handles and push outward and up with your arms until the pads are shoulder height. Lead with your elbows rather than trying to lift the bars with your hands. Return to the starting position.

(a)   (b)

MULTITRICEPS

Muscles developed: Triceps

Instructions: Adjust the seat so your elbows are slightly lower than your shoulders when you sit down. **(a)** Place your elbows on the support cushions and your forearms on the bar pads. **(b)** Extend your elbows as much as possible. Return to the starting position.

(a) (b)

LEG PRESS

Muscles developed: Gluteus maximus, quadriceps, hamstrings

Instructions: **(a)** Adjust the seat so your knees are bent at a 90-degree angle. **(b)** Sit with your hands on the side handles, your feet on the pedals, and your legs fully extended. **(c)** From this position, bend your right leg 90 degrees, and then forcefully extend it. Repeat with your left leg. Alternate between right and left legs.

(a) (b) (c)

LEG EXTENSION (Knee Extension)

Muscles developed: Quadriceps

Instructions: **(a)** Sit on the seat with your shins under the knee-extension pads. **(b)** Extend your knees until they are straight. Return to the starting position.

Knee extensions cause kneecap pain in some people. If you have kneecap pain during this exercise, check with an orthopedic specialist before repeating it.

(a)

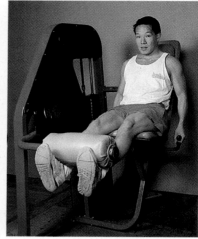

(b)

PRONE LEG CURL (Knee Flexion)

Muscles developed: Hamstrings

Instructions: **(a)** Lie on your stomach, resting the pads of the machine just below your calf muscles and with your knees just off the edge of the bench. **(b)** Flex your knees until they approach your buttocks. Return to the starting position.

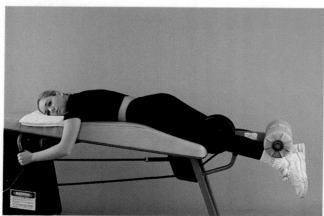

(a)

(b)

TOE RAISE

Muscles developed: Gastrocnemius, soleus

Instructions: (a) Stand with your head between the pads and one pad on each shoulder. **(b)** Press down with your toes while lifting your heels. Return to the starting position. Changing the direction your feet are pointing (straight ahead, inward, and outward) will work different portions of your calf muscles.

(a)   (b)

ABDOMINAL CURL

Muscles developed: Rectus abdominis, internal and external obliques

Instructions: (a) Adjust the seat so the machine rotates at the level of your navel, the pad rests on your upper chest, and your feet can rest comfortably on the floor. **(b)** Move your trunk forward as far as possible. Return to the starting position.

 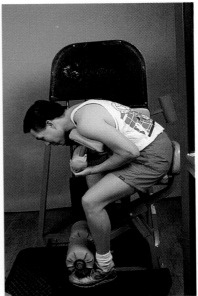

(a)   (b)

LOW-BACK MACHINE (Back Extensions)

Muscles developed: Erector spinae, quadratus lumborum

Instructions: (a) Sit on the seat with your upper legs under the thigh-support pads, your back on the back roller pad, and your feet on the platform. **(b)** Extend backward until your back is straight. Return to the starting position. Try to keep your spine rigid during the exercise.

(a)   (b)

FOUR-WAY NECK MACHINE

Muscles developed: Sternocleidomastoids, scaleni (flexion and lateral flexion); splenius capitis, splenius cervicis, trapezius (extension)

Instructions:

Flexion: (a) Adjust the seat so the front of your forehead rests in the center of the two pads. Bend your head forward as far as possible, using your neck muscles, and then return to the starting position.

Lateral flexion: (b) Adjust the seat so the side of your head rests in the center of the two pads. Bend your head sideways toward your shoulder as far as possible, and then return to the starting position. Perform the exercise for both the right and left sides of your head.

Extension: (c) Adjust the seat so the back of your head rests in the center of the two pads. Bend your head backward as far as possible, and then return to the starting position.

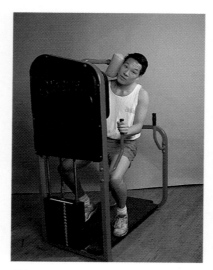

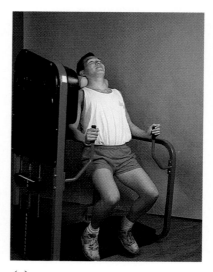

(a)   (b)   (c)

COMMON QUESTIONS ANSWERED

How long must I weight train before I begin to see changes in my body? You will increase strength very rapidly during the early stages of a weight training program, primarily the result of muscle learning (the increased ability of the nervous system to recruit muscle fibers to exert force). Actual changes in muscle size usually begin after about 6–8 weeks of training.

I am concerned about my body composition. Will I gain weight if I do resistance exercises? Your weight probably will not change significantly as a result of a recreational-type weight training program: 1 set of 8–12 repetitions of 8–10 exercises. You will tend to increase muscle mass and lose body fat, so your weight will stay about the same. (Men will tend to build larger muscles than women because of the tissue-building effects of male hormones.) Increased muscle mass will help you control body fat. Muscle increases your metabolism, which means you burn up more calories every day. If you combine resistance exercises with endurance exercises, you will be on your way to developing a healthier body composition. Concentrate on fat loss rather than weight loss.

Do I need more protein in my diet when I train with weights? No. While there is some evidence that power athletes involved in heavy training have a higher-than-normal protein requirement, there is no reason for most people to consume extra protein. Most Americans take in more protein than they need, so even if there is an increased protein need during heavy training, it is probably supplied by the average diet. (See Chapter 8 for more on dietary needs of athletes.)

Are there any supplements or drugs that will help me make larger and more rapid increases in strength and endurance? No nutritional supplement or drug will change a weak, untrained person into a strong, fit person. Those changes require regular training that stresses the muscles, heart, lungs, and metabolism and causes the body to adapt. Supplements or drugs that are promoted as instant or quick "cures" usually don't work and are either dangerous or expensive, or both. **Anabolic steroids**—the drugs most often taken in an effort to build strength and power—have dangerous side effects, described in Table 4-4. You are better off staying with proven principles of nutrition and a steady, progressive fitness program.

What causes muscle soreness the day or two following a weight training workout? The muscle pain you feel a day or two after a heavy weight training workout is caused by injury to the muscle fibers and surrounding connective tissue. Contrary to popular belief, delayed-onset muscle soreness is not caused by lactic acid buildup. Scientists believe that injury to muscle fibers causes the release of excess calcium into muscles. The calcium causes the release of substances called **proteases**, which break down part of the muscle tissue and

cause pain. After a bout of intense exercise that causes muscle injury and delayed-onset muscle soreness, the muscles produce protective proteins that prevent soreness during future workouts. If you don't work out regularly, you lose these protective proteins and become susceptible to muscle soreness again.

Will strength training improve my sports performance? Strength developed in the weight room does not automatically increase your power in sports such as skiing, tennis, or cycling. Hitting a forehand in tennis or making a turn on skis is highly specific and requires precise coordination between your nervous system and muscles. In skilled people, movements become reflex—you don't think about them when you do them. Increasing strength can disturb this coordination. Only by simultaneously practicing a sport and improving fitness can you expect to become more powerful in the skill. Practice helps you integrate your new strength with your skills, which makes you more powerful. Consequently, you can hit the ball harder in tennis or make more graceful turns on the ski slopes. (Refer to Chapter 2 for more on the concept of specificity of physical training.)

Will I improve faster if I train every day? No. Your muscles need time to recover between training sessions. Doing resistance exercises every day will cause you to become overtrained, which will increase your chance of injury and impede your progress. If you find that your strength training program has reached a plateau, try one of these strategies:

- Train less frequently. If you are currently training the same muscle groups three or more times per week, you may not be allowing your muscles to fully recover from intense workouts.

- Change exercises. Using different exercises for a particular muscle group may stimulate further strength development.

- Vary the load and number of repetitions. Try increasing or decreasing the loads you are using and changing the number of repetitions accordingly.

- Vary the number of sets. If you have been performing 1 set of each exercise, add sets.

- If you are training alone, find a motivated training partner. A partner can encourage you and assist you with difficult lifts, forcing you to work harder.

If I stop weight training, will my muscles turn to fat? No. Fat and muscle are two different kinds of tissue, and one cannot turn into the other. Muscles that aren't used become smaller (atrophy), and body fat may increase if caloric intake exceeds calories burned. Although the result of inactivity may be smaller muscles and more fat, the change is caused by two separate processes.

TABLE 4-4 Performance Aids Marketed to Weight Trainers

Substance	Supposed Effects	Actual Effects	Selected Potential Side Effects
Adrenal steroids: DHEA, androstenedione	Increased testosterone, muscle mass, and strength; decreased body fat	Increased testosterone, strength, and fat-free mass and decreased fat in older subjects (more studies needed in younger people)	Gonadal suppression, prostate hypertrophy, breast development in males, masculinization in women and children. Long-term effects unknown
Amino acids	Increased muscle mass	No effects if dietary protein intake is adequate	Minimal side effects; unbalanced amino acid intake can cause problems with protein metabolism
Anabolic steroids	Increased muscle mass, strength, power, psychological aggressiveness, and endurance	Increased strength, power, fat-free mass, and aggression; no effects on endurance	Minor to severe: gonadal suppression, liver disease, acne, breast development in males, masculinization in women and children, heart disease, cancer. Steroids are controlled substances[a]
Chromium picolinate	Increased muscle mass; decreased body fat	Well-controlled studies show no significant effect on fat-free mass or body fat	Moderate doses (50–200 μg) appear safe; higher doses may cause DNA damage and other serious effects. Long-term effects unknown
Creatine monohydrate	Increased muscle creatine phosphate, muscle mass, and capacity for high-intensity exercise	Increased muscle mass and performance in some types of high-intensity exercise	Minimal side effects; some reports of muscle cramping. Long-term effects unknown
Ephedrine	Decreased body fat; increased training intensity due to stimulant effect	Decreased appetite, particularly when taken with caffeine; no evidence for increased training intensity	Abnormal heart rhythms, nervousness, headache, and gastrointestinal distress. Not recommended
Ginseng	Decreased effects of physical and emotional stress; increased oxygen consumption	Most well-controlled studies show no effect on performance	No serious side effects; high doses can cause high blood pressure, nervousness, and insomnia
Growth hormone	Increased muscle mass, strength, and power; decreased body fat	Increased muscle mass and strength	Diabetes, acromegaly (disease characterized by increased growth of bones in hands and face), enlarged heart and other organs. An extremely expensive controlled substance[a]
HMB (beta-hydroxy-beta-methylbutyrate)	Increased strength and muscle mass; decreased body fat	Some studies show increased fat-free mass and decreased fat; more research needed	No reported side effects. Long-term effects unknown
"Metabolic optimizer" meals for athletes	Increased muscle mass; energy supply; decreased body fat	No proven effects beyond that of balanced meals	No reported side effects; extremely expensive
Plant sterols	Increased muscle mass and strength; enhanced release of growth hormone and testosterone	No evidence of beneficial effects on body composition or performance	No known side effects; can cause allergic reactions in some people
Protein	Increased muscle mass	No effects if dietary protein intake is adequate	Can be dangerous for people with liver or kidney disease

[a]Possession of a controlled substance is illegal without a prescription, and physicians are not allowed to prescribe them for the improvement of athletic performance. In addition, the use of anabolic steroids, growth hormone, or any of several other substances listed on this table is banned for athletic competition.

SOURCES: Williams, M. H. 1998. *The Ergogenics Edge: Pushing the Limits of Sports Performance.* Champaign, Ill.: Human Kinetics. Armsey, T. D., and G. A. Green. 1997. Nutrition supplements: Science vs. hype. *The Physician and Sportsmedicine* 25(4). Brooks, G. A., T. D. Fahey, and T. P. White. 1996. *Exercise Physiology: Human Bioenergetics and Its Applications,* 2d ed. Mountain View, Calif.: Mayfield.

SUMMARY

- Improvements in muscular strength and endurance lead to enhanced physical performance, protection against injury, improved body composition, better self-image, and improved muscle and bone health with aging.

- Muscular strength can be assessed by determining the amount of weight that can be lifted in one repetition of an exercise; muscular endurance can be assessed by determining the number of repetitions of a particular exercise that can be performed.

- Hypertrophy, increased muscle fiber size, occurs when weight training causes the number of myofibrils to increase; total muscle size thereby increases. Strength also increases through muscle learning.

- Isometric exercises (contraction without movement) are most useful when a person is recovering from an injury or surgery or needs to overcome weak points in a range of motion.

- Isotonic exercises involve contraction that results in movement. The two most common types are constant resistance (free weights) and variable resistance (weight machines).

- Free weights and weight machines are basically equally effective in producing fitness, although machines tend to be safer.

- Lifting heavy weights for only a few repetitions helps develop strength. Lifting lighter weights for more repetitions helps develop muscular endurance.

- A weight training program for general fitness includes at least 1 set of 8–12 repetitions (enough to cause fatigue) of 8–10 exercises, along with warm-up and cool-down periods; the program should be carried out 2–3 times a week.

- Safety guidelines for weight training include using proper technique, using spotters and collars when necessary, using common sense and remaining alert, and taking care of injuries.

FOR MORE INFORMATION

Information on and programs in weight training are available through physical education and athletics departments, private health clubs, and weight-lifting clubs.

Books

Fahey, T. D. 1997. *Basic Weight Training for Men and Women,* 3d ed. Mountain View, Calif.: Mayfield. *A practical guide to developing training programs using free weights tailored to individual needs.*

Fleck, S. J., and W. J. Kraemer. 1997. *Designing Resistance Training Programs.* Champaign, Ill.: Human Kinetics. *A book aimed* at personal trainers or serious weight trainers who want a thorough discussion of program design methods for weight training.

Ward, P. E., and R. D. Ward. 1997. *The Encyclopedia of Weight Training.* Los Angeles: Q P T Publishing. *An authoritative guide to weight training for athletes and body builders written by two of America's top strength coaches.*

Westcott, W. 1996. *Building Strength and Stamina: New Nautilus Training for Total Fitness.* Champaign, Ill.: Human Kinetics. *An updated guide to training using Nautilus machines.*

Williams, M. H. 1998. *The Ergogenics Edge: Pushing the Limits of Sports Performance.* Champaign, Ill.: Human Kinetics. *Written by one of the top sports nutrition researchers in the world, this is an excellent book on the scientific basis of substances and techniques used to improve athletic performance.*

Organizations and Web Sites

Biomechanics World Wide. A resource site with links to many other sites relating to biomechanics; topics include muscle mechanics and sports techniques.

http://www.per.ualberta.ca/biomechanics

Human Anatomy On-line. Provides text, illustrations, and animation about the muscular system, nerve-muscle connections, muscular contraction, and other topics.

http://www.innerbody.com/indexbody.html

National Strength and Conditioning Association. Provides education and certification for professionals in strength and conditioning.

402-476-6669

http://www.nsca-cc.org

Nicholas Institute of Sports Medicine and Athletic Trauma. Includes information on exercise physiology, physical therapy, sports medicine, and training.

http://www.nismat.org

University of California, San Diego/Muscle Physiology Home Page. Provides an introduction to muscle physiology, including information about types of muscle fibers and energy cycles.

http://muscle.ucsd.edu

University of Michigan/Muscles in Action. Interactive descriptions of muscle movements.

http://www.med.umich.edu/lrc/Hypermuscle/Hyper.html

See also the listings in Chapter 2.

SELECTED BIBLIOGRAPHY

American College of Sports Medicine. 1995. *Guidelines for Exercise Testing and Prescription,* 5th ed. Baltimore: Williams & Wilkins.

American College of Sports Medicine. 1998. Position Stand: The Recommended Quantity and Quality of Exercise for Developing and Maintaining Cardiorespiratory and Muscular Fitness, and Flexibility in Healthy Adults. *Medicine and Science in Sports and Exercise* 30(6): 975–991.

Ashe, J. 1997. Force and the motor cortex. *Behavioral Brain Research* 86:1–15.

Bohannon, R. W. 1997. Hand-held dynamometry: Factors influencing reliability and validity. *Clinical Rehabilitation* 11:263–264.

Brooks, G. A., T. D. Fahey, and T. P. White. 1996. *Exercise Physiology: Human Bioenergetics and Its Applications,* 2d ed.

Mountain View, Calif.: Mayfield.

Burr, D. B. 1997. Muscle strength, bone mass, and age-related bone loss. *Journal of Bone Mineral Research* 12:1547–1551.

Chandler, J. M., et al. 1998. Is lower extremity strength gain associated with improvement in physical performance and disability in frail, community-dwelling elders? *Archives of Physical Medicine and Rehabilitation* 79(1): 24–30.

Chilibeck, P. D., et al. 1998. A comparison of strength and muscle mass increases during resistance training in young women. *European Journal of Applied Physiology* 77(1–2): 170–175.

Delecluse, C. 1997. Influence of strength training on sprint running performance. Current findings and implications for training. *Sports Medicine* 24:147–156.

Feigenbaum, M. S., and M. L. Pollock. 1997. Strength training: Rationale for current guidelines for adult fitness programs. *The Physician and Sportsmedicine* 25(2): 44–49.

Geliebter, A., et al. 1997. Effects of strength or aerobic training on body composition, resting metabolic rate, and peak oxygen consumption in obese dieting subjects. *American Journal of Clinical Nutrition* 66:557–563.

Harris, T. 1997. Muscle mass and strength: Relation to function in population studies. *Journal of Nutrition* 127:1004S–1006S.

Klinge, K., et al. 1997. The effect of strength and flexibility training on skeletal muscle electromyographic activity, stiffness, and viscoelastic stress relaxation response. *American Journal of Sports Medicine* 25:710–716.

Lindle, R. S., et al. 1997. Age and gender comparisons of muscle strength in 654 women and men aged 20–93 yr. *Journal of Applied Physiology* 83:1581–1587.

Longhurst, J. C., and C. L. Stebbins. 1997. The power athlete. *Cardiology Clinics* 15:413–429.

Mayhew, J. L., et al. 1997. Changes in upper body power following heavy-resistance strength training in college men. *International Journal of Sports Medicine* 18:516–520.

Pincivero, D. M., S. M. Lephart, and R. G. Karunakara. 1997. Effects of rest interval on isokinetic strength and functional performance after short-term high intensity training. *British Journal of Sports Medicine* 31:229–234.

Ploutz-Snyder, L. L., P. A. Tesch, and G. A. Dudley. 1998. Increased vulnerability to eccentric exercise-induced dysfunction and muscle injury after concentric training. *Archives of Physical Medicine and Rehabilitation* 79(1): 58–61.

Pollock, M. L., et al. 1997. Twenty-year follow-up of aerobic power and body composition of older track athletes. *Journal of Applied Physiology* 82:1508–1516.

Stanford, B. 1998. Weight training basics: Part 1: Choosing the best options. *The Physician and Sportsmedicine* 26(2).

Thompson, H. S., et al. 1997. The effects of oral contraceptives on delayed onset muscle soreness following exercise. *Contraception* 56:59–65.

Toji, J., K. Suei, and M. Kaneko. 1997. Effects of combined training loads on relations among force, velocity, and power development. *Canadian Journal of Applied Physiology* 22: 328–336.

Vandenberghe, K., et al. 1997. Long-term creatine intake is beneficial to muscle performance during resistance training. *Journal of Applied Physiology* 83:2055–2063.

Van Etten, L. M., et al. 1997. Effect of an 18-wk weight-training program on energy expenditure and physical activity. *Journal of Applied Physiology* 82:298–304.

Vincent, H. K., and K. R. Vincent. 1997. The effect of training status on the serum creatine kinase response, soreness and muscle function following resistance exercise. *International Journal of Sports Medicine* 18:431–437.

Wiemann, K., and K. Hahn. 1997. Influences of strength, stretching and circulatory exercises on flexibility parameters of the human hamstrings. *International Journal of Sports Medicine* 18:340–346.

Wu, F. C. 1997. Endocrine aspects of anabolic steroids. *Clinical Chemistry* 43:1289–1292.

Name _____ **Section** _____ **Date** _____

LAB 4-1 *Assessing Your Current Level of Muscular Strength*

For best results, don't do any strenuous weight training within 48 hours of any test.

The Maximum Bench Press Test

Equipment

1. Universal Gym Dynamic Variable Resistance machine
2. Weight scale

The ratings for this test were developed using the Universal Gym Dynamic Variable Resistance machine; results will be somewhat less accurate if the test is performed on another type of machine or with free weights.

If free weights are used, the following equipment is needed:

1. Flat bench (with or without racks)
2. Barbell
3. Assorted weight plates
4. Collars to hold weight plates in place
5. One or two spotters
6. Weight scale

Maximum bench press test.

Preparation

Try a few bench presses with a small amount of weight so you can practice your technique, warm up your muscles, and, if you use free weights, coordinate your movements with those of your spotters. Weigh yourself, and record the results.

Body weight: _____ lb

Instructions

1. Set the machine (or place weights on the barbell) for a weight that is lower than the amount you believe you can lift.
2. Lie on the bench with your feet firmly on the floor. If you are using a weight machine, grasp the handles with palms away from you; the tops of the handles should be aligned with the tops of your armpits.

   If you are using free weights, grasp the bar at shoulder width with your palms away from you. If you have one spotter, she or he should stand directly behind the bench; if you have two spotters, they should stand to the side, one at each end of the barbell. Lower the bar to your chest in preparation for the lift.
3. Push the bars or barbell until your arms are fully extended. Exhale as you lift. If you are using free weights, the bar should follow an elliptical path, during which the weight moves from a low point at the chest to a high point over the chin. Keep your feet firmly on the floor, don't arch your back, and push the weight evenly with your right and left arms. Don't bounce the weight on your chest.
4. Rest for several minutes, then repeat the lift with a heavier weight. It will probably take several attempts to determine the maximum amount of weight you can lift (1 RM).

   1 RM: _____ lb

Rating Your Bench Press Result

1. Divide your 1 RM value by your body weight.

   1 RM _____ lb ÷ body weight _____ lb = _____

2. Find this ratio in the table below to determine your bench press strength rating. Record the result here and in the chart at the end of this lab.

Bench press strength rating: _____

Strength Ratings for the Maximum Bench Press Test

	Pounds Lifted/Body Weight (lb)					
Men	*Very Poor*	*Poor*	*Fair*	*Good*	*Excellent*	*Superior*
Age: Under 20	Below 0.89	0.89–1.05	1.06–1.18	1.19–1.33	1.34–1.75	Above 1.75
20–29	Below 0.88	0.88–0.98	0.99–1.13	1.14–1.31	1.32–1.62	Above 1.62
30–39	Below 0.78	0.78–0.87	0.88–0.97	0.98–1.11	1.12–1.34	Above 1.34
40–49	Below 0.72	0.72–0.79	0.80–0.87	0.88–0.99	1.00–1.19	Above 1.19
50–59	Below 0.63	0.63–0.70	0.71–0.78	0.79–0.89	0.90–1.04	Above 1.04
60 and over	Below 0.57	0.57–0.65	0.66–0.71	0.72–0.81	0.82–0.93	Above 0.93
Women						
Age: Under 20	Below 0.53	0.53–0.57	0.58–0.64	0.65–0.76	0.77–0.87	Above 0.87
20–29	Below 0.51	0.51–0.58	0.59–0.69	0.70–0.79	0.80–1.00	Above 1.00
30–39	Below 0.47	0.47–0.52	0.53–0.59	0.60–0.69	0.70–0.81	Above 0.81
40–49	Below 0.43	0.43–0.49	0.50–0.53	0.54–0.61	0.62–0.76	Above 0.76
50–59	Below 0.39	0.39–0.43	0.44–0.47	0.48–0.54	0.55–0.67	Above 0.67
60 and over	Below 0.38	0.38–0.42	0.43–0.46	0.47–0.53	0.54–0.71	Above 0.71

SOURCE: Based on norms from the Cooper Institute for Aerobics Research, Dallas, Texas; used with permission.

The Maximum Leg Press Test

Equipment

1. Universal Gym Dynamic Variable Resistance leg press machine (If you're using a Universal Gym leg press with two sets of pedals, use the lower pedals.)
2. Weight scale

The ratings for this test were developed using the Universal Gym Dynamic Variable Resistance machine; results will be somewhat less accurate if the test is performed on another type of machine.

Preparation

Try a few leg presses with the machine set for a small amount of weight so you can practice your technique and warm up your muscles. Weigh yourself, and record the results.

Body weight: _____ lb

Maximum leg press test.

Instructions

1. Set the machine for a weight that is lower than the amount you believe you can press.
2. Adjust the seat so that your knees are bent at a 70-degree angle to start.
3. Grasp the side handlebars, and push with your legs until your knees are fully extended.
4. Rest for several minutes, then repeat the press with a higher weight setting. It will probably take several attempts to determine the maximum amount of weight you can press.

1 RM: _____ lb

Rating Your Leg Press Result

1. Divide your 1 RM value by your body weight.

   1 RM _____ lb ÷ body weight _____ lb = _____

2. Find this ratio in the table below to determine your leg press strength rating. Record the result below and in the chart at the end of this lab.

   Leg press strength rating: _____

Strength Ratings for the Maximum Leg Press Test

			Pounds Lifted/Body Weight (lb)			
Men	*Very Poor*	*Poor*	*Fair*	*Good*	*Excellent*	*Superior*
Age: Under 20	Below 1.70	1.70–1.89	1.90–2.03	2.04–2.27	2.28–2.81	Above 2.81
20–29	Below 1.63	1.63–1.82	1.83–1.96	1.97–2.12	2.13–2.39	Above 2.39
30–39	Below 1.52	1.52–1.64	1.65–1.76	1.77–1.92	1.93–2.19	Above 2.19
40–49	Below 1.44	1.44–1.56	1.57–1.67	1.68–1.81	1.82–2.01	Above 2.01
50–59	Below 1.32	1.32–1.45	1.46–1.57	1.58–1.70	1.71–1.89	Above 1.89
60 and over	Below 1.25	1.25–1.37	1.38–1.48	1.49–1.61	1.62–1.79	Above 1.79
Women						
Age: Under 20	Below 1.22	1.22–1.37	1.38–1.58	1.59–1.70	1.71–1.87	Above 1.87
20–29	Below 1.22	1.22–1.36	1.37–1.49	1.50–1.67	1.68–1.97	Above 1.97
30–39	Below 1.09	1.09–1.20	1.21–1.32	1.33–1.46	1.47–1.67	Above 1.67
40–49	Below 1.02	1.02–1.12	1.13–1.22	1.23–1.36	1.37–1.56	Above 1.56
50–59	Below 0.88	0.88–0.98	0.99–1.09	1.10–1.24	1.25–1.42	Above 1.42
60 and over	Below 0.85	0.85–0.92	0.93–1.03	1.04–1.17	1.18–1.42	Above 1.42

SOURCE: Based on norms from the Cooper Institute for Aerobics Research, Dallas, Texas; used with permission.

Hand Grip Strength Test

Equipment

Grip strength dynamometer

Preparation

If necessary, adjust the hand grip size on the dynamometer into a position that is comfortable for you; then lock the grip in place. The second joint of your fingers should fit snugly under the handle of the dynamometer.

Instructions

1. Stand with the hand to be tested first at your side, away from your body. The dynamometer should be in line with your forearm and held at the level of your thigh. Squeeze the dynamometer as hard as possible without moving your arm; exhale as you squeeze. During the test, don't let the dynamometer touch your body or any other object.

2. Perform two trials with each hand. Rest for about a minute between trials. Record the scores for each hand to the nearest kilogram.

   Hand grip strength test.

   Right hand: Trial 1: _____ kg   Trial 2: _____ kg

   Left hand: Trial 1: _____ kg   Trial 2: _____ kg

(Scores on the dynamometer should be given in kilograms. If the dynamometer you are using gives scores in pounds, convert pounds to kilograms by dividing your score by 2.2.)

Rating Your Hand Grip Strength

Your total score is the sum of the best trial for each hand.

Right hand best trial _____ kg

Left hand best trial _____ kg

Total score _____ kg

Refer to the table below for a rating of your grip strength. Record the result below and in the chart at the end of this lab.

Rating for hand grip strength: _____

Grip Strength* (kg)

Men	Needs Improvement	Fair	Good	Very Good	Excellent
Age: 15–19	Below 84	84–94	95–102	103–112	Above 112
20–29	Below 97	97–105	106–112	113–123	Above 123
30–39	Below 97	97–104	105–112	113–122	Above 122
40–49	Below 94	94–101	102–109	110–118	Above 118
50–59	Below 87	87–95	96–101	102–109	Above 109
60–69	Below 79	79–85	86–92	93–101	Above 101
Women					
Age: 15–19	Below 54	54–58	59–63	64–70	Above 70
20–29	Below 55	55–60	61–64	65–70	Above 70
30–39	Below 56	56–60	61–65	66–72	Above 72
40–49	Below 55	55–58	59–64	65–72	Above 72
50–59	Below 51	51–54	55–58	59–64	Above 64
60–69	Below 48	48–50	51–53	54–59	Above 59

*Combined right and left hand grip strength.

Source: *The Canadian Physical Activity, Fitness and Lifestyle Appraisal: CSEP's Plan for Healthy Active Living, 1996.* Reprinted by permission from the Canadian Society for Exercise Physiology.

Summary of Results

Maximum bench press test

Weight pressed: _____ lb Rating: _____

Maximum leg press test

Weight pressed: _____ lb Rating: _____

Hand grip strength test

Total score: _____ kg Rating: _____

Remember that muscular strength is specific: Your ratings may vary considerably for different parts of your body. You can use these results to guide you in planning a weight training program.

To monitor your progress toward your goal, enter the results of this lab in the Preprogram Assessment column of Appendix D. After several weeks of a weight training program, do this lab again, and enter the results in the Postprogram Assessment column of Appendix D. How do the results compare?

Name _____ **Section** _____ **Date** _____

LAB 4-2 *Assessing Your Current Level of Muscular Endurance*

For best results, don't do any strenuous weight training within 48 hours of any test. To assess endurance of the abdominal muscles, perform the sit-up test or the curl-up test. The push-up test assesses endurance of muscles in the upper body.

The 60-Second Sit-Up Test

Do not take this test if you suffer from low-back pain.

Equipment

1. Stopwatch, clock, or watch with a second hand
2. Partner to hold your ankles
3. Mat or towel to lie on (optional)

Preparation

Try a few sit-ups to get used to the proper technique and warm up your abdominal muscles.

Instructions

1. Lie flat on your back on the floor with knees bent, feet flat on the floor, and your fingers interlocked behind your neck. Your partner should hold your ankles firmly so that your feet stay on the floor as you do the sit-ups.

2. When someone signals you to begin, raise your head and chest off the floor until your elbows touch your knees or thighs, and then return to the starting position. Keep your neck neutral. Keep your breathing as normal as possible; don't hold your breath.

3. Perform as many sit-ups as you can in 60 seconds.

The 60-second sit-up test.

   Note: The norms for this test were established with subjects interlocking their fingers behind their neck; your results will be most accurate if you use this technique. However, some experts feel that sit-ups done in this position can cause injury to the neck. If this is a concern, perform the test with your hands cupped over your ears rather than behind your neck. Alternatively, complete the curl-up test described later in this lab. If you perform sit-ups with your hands behind your neck, take care not to force your neck forward, and stop if you feel any pain in your neck.

   Number of sit-ups: _____

Rating Your Muscular Endurance

Refer to the table below for a rating of your abdominal muscle endurance. Record your rating below and in the chart at the end of this lab.

Rating: _____

Ratings for the 60-Second Sit-Up Test

			Number of Sit-Ups			
Men	Very Poor	Poor	Fair	Good	Excellent	Superior
Age: Under 20	Below 36	36–40	41–46	47–50	51–61	Above 61
20–29	Below 33	33–37	38–41	42–46	47–54	Above 54
30–39	Below 30	30–34	35–38	39–42	43–50	Above 50
40–49	Below 24	24–28	29–33	34–38	39–46	Above 46
50–59	Below 19	19–23	24–27	28–34	35–42	Above 42
60 and over	Below 15	15–18	19–21	22–29	30–38	Above 38

(continued)

Women	Very Poor	Poor	Fair	Good	Excellent	Superior
Age: Under 20	Below 28	28–31	32–35	36–45	46–54	Above 54
20–29	Below 24	24–31	32–37	38–43	44–50	Above 50
30–39	Below 20	20–24	25–28	29–34	35–41	Above 41
40–49	Below 14	14–19	20–23	24–28	29–37	Above 37
50–59	Below 10	10–13	14–19	20–23	24–29	Above 29
60 and over	Below 3	3–5	6–10	11–16	17–27	Above 27

SOURCE: Based on norms from the Cooper Institute for Aerobics Research, Dallas, Texas; used with permission.

The Curl-Up Test

The curl-up test is preferred by some exercise scientists as a test of abdominal endurance. In a full sit-up, part of the lift is provided by the hip flexor muscles. Curl-ups optimize the use of the abdominal muscles without involving the hip flexors.

Equipment

1. Metronome
2. Stopwatch, clock, or watch with a second hand
3. Heavy tape
4. Ruler
5. Partner
6. Mat (optional)

Preparation

1. Set the metronome at a rate of 50 beats per minute.
2. Place a tape strip approximately 1 meter long on the floor or mat. Place another strip of tape 10 centimeters away from the first one.

Instructions

1. Start by lying on your back on the floor, arms by your sides, palms down and on the floor, elbows locked, and fingers straight. The longest fingertip of each hand should touch the edge of the near strip of tape. Your knees should be bent at about 90 degrees, with your feet 12–18 inches away from your buttocks.
2. To perform a curl-up, curl your head and upper back upward, keeping your arms straight. Slide your fingertips forward along the floor until you touch the other strip of tape, 10 centimeters from the starting position. Then curl back down so that your upper back and head touch the floor. Palms, feet, and buttocks should stay on the floor throughout the curl-up. (For this test, your partner does not hold your feet.) Maintain the 90-degree angle in your knees. Exhale during the lift phase of the curl-up.

Curl-up test: (a) starting position.

(b) Curl-up.

3. Start the metronome at the correct cadence. You will perform curl-ups at the steady, continuous rate of 25 per minute. Curl up on one beat and curl down on the next. Your partner counts the number of curl-ups you complete and makes sure that you maintain correct form.

4. Perform as many curl-ups as you can in one minute. If at any point during the test you can no longer maintain proper form and keep up with the rhythm set by the metronome, stop the test and record the number of curl-ups you performed up to that point.

Number of curl-ups: _____

Rating Your Muscular Endurance

Your score is the number of completed curl-ups. Refer to the appropriate portion of the table below for a rating of your abdominal muscular endurance. Record your rating below and in the chart at the end of this lab.

Rating: _____   .

Ratings for the Curl-Up Test

			Number of Curl-Ups		
Men	Needs Improvement	Fair	Good	Very Good	Excellent
Age: 15–19	Below 16	16–20	21–22	23–24	25
20–29	Below 13	13–20	21–22	23–24	25
30–39	Below 13	13–20	21–22	23–24	25
40–49	Below 11	11–15	16–21	22–24	25
50–59	Below 9	9–13	14–19	20–24	25
60–69	Below 4	4–9	10–15	16–24	25
Women					
Age: 15–19	Below 16	16–20	21–22	23–24	25
20–29	Below 13	13–18	19–22	23–24	25
30–39	Below 11	11–15	16–21	22–24	25
40–49	Below 6	6–12	13–20	21–24	25
50–59	Below 4	4–8	9–15	16–24	25
60–69	Below 2	2–5	6–10	11–17	18–25

SOURCE: *The Canadian Physical Activity, Fitness and Lifestyle Appraisal: CSEP's Plan for Healthy Active Living,* 1996. Reprinted by permission of the Canadian Society for Exercise Physiology.

The Push-Up Test

Equipment

Mat or towel (optional)

Preparation

In this test, you will perform either standard push-ups or modified push-ups, in which you support yourself with your knees. The Cooper Institute developed the ratings for this test with men performing push-ups and women performing modified push-ups. (Biologically, males tend to be stronger than females; the modified technique reduces the need for upper-body strength in a test of muscular endurance.) Therefore, for an accurate assessment of upper-body endurance, men should perform standard push-ups and women should perform modified push-ups.

Instructions

1. *For push-ups:* Start in the push-up position with your body supported by your hands and feet. *For modified push-ups:* Start in the modified push-up position with your body supported by your hands and knees. *For both positions,* your arms and your back should be straight and your fingers pointed forward.

(a) Push-up.

(b) Modified push-up.

2. Lower your chest to the floor with your back straight, and then return to the starting position.

3. Perform as many push-ups or modified push-ups as you can without stopping.

Number of push-ups: _____ or number of modified push-ups: _____

Rating Your Push-Up Test Result

Your score is the number of completed push-ups or modified push-ups. Refer to the appropriate portion of the table below for a rating of your upper body endurance. Record your rating below and in the chart at the end of this lab.

Rating: _____

Ratings for the Push-Up and Modified Push-Up Tests

Number of Push-Ups

Men	Very Poor	Poor	Fair	Good	Excellent	Superior
Age: 18–29	Below 22	22–28	29–36	37–46	47–61	Above 61
30–39	Below 17	17–23	24–29	30–38	39–51	Above 51
40–49	Below 11	11–17	18–23	24–29	30–39	Above 39
50–59	Below 9	9–12	13–18	19–24	25–38	Above 38
60 and over	Below 6	6–9	10–17	18–22	23–27	Above 27

Number of Modified Push-Ups

Women	Very Poor	Poor	Fair	Good	Excellent	Superior
Age: 18–29	Below 17	17–22	23–29	30–35	36–44	Above 44
30–39	Below 11	11–18	19–23	24–30	31–38	Above 38
40–49	Below 6	6–12	13–17	18–23	24–32	Above 32
50–59	Below 6	6–11	12–16	17–20	21–27	Above 27
60 and over	Below 2	2–4	5–11	12–14	15–19	Above 19

SOURCE: Based on norms from the Cooper Institute for Aerobics Research, Dallas, Texas; used with permission.

Summary of Results

60-second sit-up test

Number of sit-ups: _____ Rating: _____

Curl-up test

Number of curl-ups: _____ Rating: _____

Push-up test

Number of push-ups: _____ Rating: _____

Remember that muscular endurance is specific: Your ratings may vary considerably for different parts of your body. You can use these results to guide you in planning a weight training program.

To monitor your progress toward your goal, enter the results of this lab in the Preprogram Assessment column of Appendix D. After several weeks of a weight training program, do this lab again, and enter the results in the Postprogram Assessment column of Appendix D. How do the results compare?

Name _____   **Section** _____   **Date** _____

LAB 4-3 *Designing and Monitoring a Weight Training Program*

1. *Set goals.* List the goals of your weight training program. Goals can be general, such as developing greater muscle definition, or specific, such as increasing the power in a golf swing. If your goals involve the development of a specific muscle group, note that also.

1. _____

2. _____

3. _____

4. _____

2. *Choose exercises.* Based on your goals, choose 8–10 exercises to perform during each weight training session. If your goal is general training for wellness, use the sample program in the box "A Sample Weight Training Program for General Fitness" on p. 77. If your goals relate to a specific sport, use Table 4-3 to put together a program to develop the important muscle groups. List your exercises and the muscles they develop in the space provided in the program plan below.

3. *Choose starting weights.* Experiment with different amounts of weight until you settle on a good starting weight, one that you can lift easily for 10–12 repetitions. As you progress in your program, you can add more weight. Fill in the starting weight for each exercise on the program plan.

4. *Choose a starting number of sets and repetitions.* Include at least 1 set of 8–12 repetitions of each exercise. (As you add weight, you may have to decrease the number of repetitions slightly until your muscles adapt to the heavier load.) If your program is focusing on strength alone, your sets can contain fewer repetitions using a heavier load. If you are over approximately 50–60 years of age, your sets should contain more repetitions (10–15) using a lighter load. Fill in the starting number of sets and repetitions of each exercise on the program plan.

5. *Choose the number of training sessions per week.* Work out at least 2 days per week. Indicate the days you will train on your program plan; be sure to include days of rest to allow your body to recover.

6. *Monitor your progress.* Use the workout card on the next page to monitor program progress and keep track of exercises, weights, sets, and repetitions. (A more extensive series of weight training logs is included in the Daily Fitness Log booklet.)

Program Plan for Weight Training

Exercise	Muscle(s) Developed	Weight (lb)	Repetitions	Sets	Frequency (check ✓)						
					M	T	W	Th	F	Sa	Su

WORKOUT CARD FOR _____

Exercise/Date	Wt	Sets	Reps	Wt	Sets	Reps	Wt	Sets	Reps	Wt	Sets	Reps	Wt	Sets	Reps	Wt	Sets	Reps	Wt	Sets	Reps	Wt	Sets	Reps	Wt	Sets	Reps	Wt	Sets	Reps	Wt	Sets	Reps	Wt	Sets	Reps

Flexibility 5

LOOKING AHEAD

After reading this chapter, you should be able to answer these questions about flexibility and stretching exercises:

- What are the potential benefits of flexibility and stretching exercises?

- What determines the amount of flexibility in each joint?

- What are the different types of stretching exercises, and how do they affect muscles?

- What type, intensity, duration, and frequency of stretching exercises will develop the greatest amount of flexibility with the lowest risk of injury?

- What are some common stretching exercises for major joints?

- How can low-back pain be prevented and managed?

109

Flexibility—the ability of a joint to move through its full **range of motion**—is extremely important for general fitness and wellness. The smooth and easy performance of everyday and recreational activities is impossible if flexibility is poor. Flexibility is a highly adaptable physical fitness component. It increases in response to a regular program of stretching exercises and decreases with inactivity. Flexibility is also specific: Good flexibility in one joint doesn't necessarily mean good flexibility in another. Flexibility can be increased through stretching exercises for all major joints.

There are two basic types of flexibility: static and dynamic. Static flexibility refers to the ability to assume and maintain an extended position at one end or point in a joint's range of motion; it is what most people mean by the term *flexibility*. Dynamic flexibility, unlike static flexibility, involves movement; it is the ability to move a joint quickly through its range of motion with little resistance. For example, static shoulder flexibility would determine how far you could extend your arm across the front of your body or out to the side. Dynamic shoulder flexibility would affect your ability to pitch a softball, swing a golf club, or swim the crawl stroke. For a gymnast to perform a split on the balance beam, she must have good static flexibility in her legs and hips; in order to perform a split leap, she must have good dynamic flexibility.

Static flexibility depends on many factors, including the structure of a joint and the tightness of muscles, tendons, and ligaments that are attached to it. Dynamic flexibility is dependent on static flexibility, but it also involves such factors as strength, coordination, and resistance to movement. Dynamic flexibility can be important for both daily activities and sports. However, because static flexibility is easier to measure and better researched, most assessment tests and stretching programs—including those presented in this chapter—target static flexibility.

This chapter describes the factors that affect flexibility and the benefits of maintaining good flexibility. It provides guidelines for assessing your current level of flexibility and putting together a successful stretching program. It also examines the common problem of low-back pain.

BENEFITS OF FLEXIBILITY AND STRETCHING EXERCISES

Good flexibility provides benefits for the entire muscular and skeletal system; it may also prevent injuries and soreness and improve performance in sports and other activities.

Joint Health

Good flexibility is essential to good joint health. When the muscles and other tissues that support a joint are tight, the joint is subject to abnormal stresses that can cause joint deterioration. For example, tight thigh muscles cause excessive pressure on the kneecap, leading to pain in the knee joint. Tight shoulder muscles can compress sensitive soft tissues in the shoulder, leading to pain and disability in the joint. Poor joint flexibility can also cause abnormalities in joint lubrication, leading to deterioration of the sensitive cartilage cells lining the joint; pain and further joint injury can result.

Improved flexibility can greatly improve your quality of life, particularly as you get older. Aging decreases the natural elasticity of muscles, tendons, and joints, resulting in stiffness. The problem is compounded if you have arthritis. Flexibility exercises improve the elasticity in your tissues, making it easier to move your body. When you're flexible, everything from tying your shoes to reaching for a jar on an upper shelf becomes easier.

Low-Back Pain and Injuries

Low-back pain is sometimes related to poor spinal alignment, which puts pressure on the nerves leading out from the spinal column. Good strength and flexibility in the back, pelvis, and thighs may help prevent this type of back pain. Unfortunately, research studies have not yet clearly defined the relationship between back pain and lack of flexibility.

Poor flexibility does increase one's risk for injury. A general stretching program has been shown to be effective in reducing the frequency of injuries as well as their severity. When injuries do occur, flexibility exercises can be used in treatment: They reduce symptoms and help restore normal range of motion in affected joints.

Overstretching—stretching muscles to extreme ranges of motion—may actually decrease the stability of a joint. While some activities, such as gymnastics and ballet, re-

TERMS **range of motion** The full motion possible in a joint.

delayed-onset muscle soreness Soreness that occurs 1–2 days after exercising, probably caused by tissue damage that stimulates the release of calcium and enzymes that break down muscle fibers.

joint capsules Semielastic structures, composed primarily of connective tissue, that surround major joints.

soft tissues Tissues of the human body that include skin, fat, linings of internal organs and blood vessels, connective tissues, tendons, ligaments, muscles, and nerves.

collagen White fibers that provide structure and support in connective tissue.

elastin Yellow fibers that make connective tissue flexible.

titin A filament in muscle that helps align proteins that cause muscle contraction; titin has elastic properties and also plays a role in flexibility.

quire extreme joint movements, such flexibility is not recommended for the average person. In fact, extreme flexibility may increase risk of injury in activities such as skiing, basketball, and volleyball. Again, as with other types of exercise, moderation is the key to safe training.

Additional Potential Benefits

- *Reduction of postexercise muscle soreness.* **Delayed-onset muscle soreness,** occurring 1–2 days after exercise, is thought to be caused by damage to the muscle fibers and supporting connective tissue. Some studies (though not others) have shown that stretching after exercise decreases the degree of muscle soreness.

- *Relief of aches and pains.* Flexibility exercises help relieve pain that develops from stress or prolonged sitting. Studying or working in one place for a long time can cause your muscles to become tense. Stretching helps relieve tension, so you can go back to work refreshed and effective.

- *Improved body position and strength for sports (and life).* Good flexibility lets a person assume more efficient body positions and exert force through a greater range of motion. For example, swimmers with more flexible shoulders have stronger strokes because they can pull their arms through the water in the optimal position. Flexible joints and muscles let you move more fluidly without constraint. Some studies also suggest that flexibility training enhances strength development.

- *Maintenance of good posture.* Good flexibility also contributes to body symmetry and good posture. Bad postural habits can gradually change your body structures. Sitting in a slumped position, for example, can lead to tightness in the muscles in the front of your chest and overstretching and looseness in the upper spine, causing a rounding of the upper back. This condition, called kyphosis, is common in older people. It may be prevented by doing stretching exercises regularly.

- *Relaxation.* Flexibility exercises are a great way to relax. Studies have shown that doing flexibility exercises reduces mental tension, slows your breathing rate, and reduces blood pressure.

Flexibility and Lifetime Wellness

Part of wellness is being able to move without pain or hindrance. Flexibility exercises are an important part of this process. Sedentary people often effectively lose their mobility at an early age. Even relatively young people are often handicapped by back, shoulder, knee, and ankle pain. As they age, the pain can become debilitating, leading to injuries and a lower quality of life. Good flexibility helps keep your joints and muscles moving without pain so that you can do all the things you enjoy.

The flexibility of a joint is affected by its structure, by muscle elasticity and length, and by nervous system activity. Some factors—joint structure, for example—can't be changed. Other factors, such as the length of resting muscle fibers, can be changed through exercise; these factors should be the focus of a program to develop flexibility.

Joint Structure

The amount of flexibility in a joint is determined in part by the nature and structure of the joint. Hinge joints such as those in your fingers and knees allow only limited forward and backward movement; they lock when fully extended. Ball-and-socket joints like the hip enable movement in many different directions and have a greater range of motion. Major joints are surrounded by **joint capsules,** semielastic structures that give joints strength and stability but limit movement. Heredity also plays a part in joint structure and flexibility; for example, although everyone has a broad range of motion in the ball-and-socket hip joint, not everyone can do a split.

Muscle Elasticity and Length

Soft tissues, including skin, muscles, tendons, and ligaments, also limit the flexibility of a joint. Muscle tissue is the key to developing flexibility because it can be lengthened if it is regularly stretched. As described in Chapter 4, muscles contain proteins that create movement by causing muscles to contract. These contractile proteins can also stretch, and they are involved in the development of flexibility. However, the most important component of muscle tissue related to flexibility is the connective tissue that surrounds and envelops every part of muscle tissue, from individual muscle fibers to entire muscles. Connective tissue provides structure, elasticity, and bulk and makes up about 30% of muscle mass. Two principal types of connective tissue are **collagen,** white fibers that provide structure and support, and **elastin,** yellow fibers that are elastic and flexible. Muscles contain both collagen and elastin, closely intertwined, so muscle tissue exhibits the properties of both types of fibers. A recently discovered structural protein in muscles called **titin** also has elastic properties and contributes to flexibility.

When a muscle is stretched, the wavelike elastin fibers straighten; when the stretch is relieved, they rapidly snap back to their resting position. If gently and regularly stretched, connective tissues will lengthen and flexibility will improve (Figure 5-1). Without regular stretching, the process reverses: these tissues shorten, resulting in decreased flexibility. Regular stretching also contributes to flexibility by lengthening muscle fibers through the addition of contractile units called sarcomeres.

The stretch characteristics of connective tissue in

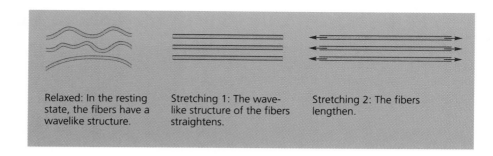

Figure 5-1   Relaxed versus stretched connective tissue in muscle.

Relaxed: In the resting state, the fibers have a wavelike structure.

Stretching 1: The wavelike structure of the fibers straightens.

Stretching 2: The fibers lengthen.

muscle are important considerations for a stretching program. The amount of stretch a muscle will tolerate is limited, and as the limits of its flexibility are reached, connective tissue becomes more brittle and may rupture if overstretched (Figure 5-2). A safe and effective program stretches muscles enough to slightly elongate the tissues but not so much that they are damaged. Research has shown that flexibility is improved best by stretching when muscles are warm (following exercise or the application of heat) and the stretch is applied gradually and conservatively. Sudden, high-stress stretching is less effective and can lead to muscle damage.

Nervous System Activity

Muscles contain **stretch receptors** that control their length. If a muscle is stretched suddenly, stretch receptors send signals to the spinal cord, which then sends a signal back to the same muscle, causing it to contract. These reflexes occur frequently in active muscles. They help the body know what the muscles are doing and allow for fine control of muscle length.

Small movements that only slightly stimulate these receptors cause small reflex actions. Rapid, powerful, and sudden movements that strongly stimulate the receptors cause large, powerful reflex muscle contractions. Stretches that involve rapid, bouncy movements are considered dangerous because they may stimulate a reflex muscle contraction during a stretch. A muscle that contracts at the same time it's being stretched can be easily injured, so slow, gradual stretches are always safest.

Strong muscle contractions produce a reflex of the opposite type—one that causes muscles to relax and keeps them from contracting too hard. This inverse stretch reflex has recently been introduced as an aid to improving flexibility: Contracting a muscle prior to stretching it causes it to relax, allowing it to stretch farther. The contraction-stretch technique for developing flexibility is called **proprioceptive neuromuscular facilitation (PNF).** More research needs to be done, however, to determine precisely the degree to which PNF techniques cause muscle relaxation and help develop flexibility.

Doing each stretching exercise several times in a row can "reset" the sensitivity of muscle stretch receptors. Stretching a muscle, relaxing, and then stretching it again cause

the stretch receptors to become slightly less sensitive, thereby enabling the muscle to stretch farther. It is not known if stretch receptor sensitivity continues to change following prolonged flexibility training, but it's likely that neural changes do occur to help increase flexibility.

ASSESSING FLEXIBILITY

Because flexibility is specific to each joint, there are no tests of general flexibility. The most commonly used flexibility test is the sit-and-reach test. This test rates the flexibility of the muscles in the lower back and hamstrings; flexibility in these muscles may be important in preventing low-back pain. To assess your flexibility and identify inflexible joints, complete Lab 5-1.

CREATING A SUCCESSFUL PROGRAM TO DEVELOP FLEXIBILITY

A successful program for developing flexibility contains safe exercises executed with the most effective techniques.

Types of Stretching Techniques

Stretching techniques vary from simply stretching the muscles during the course of normal activities to sophisticated methods based on patterns of muscle reflexes. Improper stretching techniques can do more harm than good, so it's important to understand the different types of stretching exercises and how they affect the muscles. Three common techniques are static stretches, ballistic stretches, and PNF.

Static Stretching   In **static stretching**, each muscle is gradually stretched, and the stretch is held for 10–30 seconds. (Holding the stretch longer than 30 seconds will not further improve flexibility, while stretching for less than 10 seconds will provide little benefit.) A slow stretch prompts less reaction from stretch receptors, and the muscles can safely stretch farther than usual. Static stretching is the type most often recommended by fitness

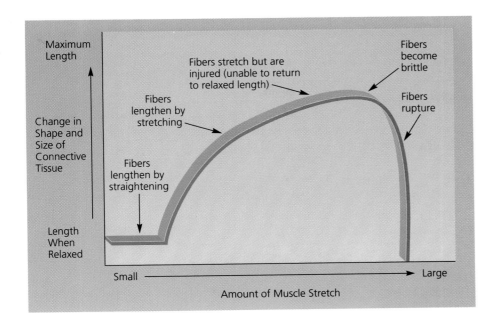

Figure 5-2   The effect of stretch on connective tissue.

experts because it's safe and effective. The key to this technique is to stretch the muscles and joints to the point where a pull is felt, but not to the point of pain.

Ballistic Stretching   The technique of **ballistic stretching** involves dynamic muscle action whereby the muscles are stretched suddenly in a bouncing movement. For example, touching the toes repeatedly in rapid succession is a ballistic stretch for the hamstrings. The problem with this technique is that the heightened activity of stretch receptors caused by the rapid stretches can continue for some time, possibly causing injuries during any physical activities that follow. For this reason, ballistic stretching is not recommended.

Proprioceptive Neuromuscular Facilitation   As mentioned earlier, PNF techniques use reflexes initiated by muscle and joint receptors to cause greater training effects. The most popular PNF stretching technique is the contract-relax stretching method, in which a muscle is contracted before it is stretched. For example, in a seated stretch of calf muscles, the first step in PNF is to contract the calf muscles: A partner can provide resistance for an isometric contraction. Following a brief period of relaxation, the next step is to stretch the calf muscles by pulling the tops of the feet toward the body. A duration of 6 seconds for the contraction and 10–30 seconds for the stretch is recommended. PNF appears to allow for more effective stretching, but it tends to cause more muscle stiffness and soreness than static stretching; furthermore, it usually requires a partner and takes more time.

Passive and Active Stretching

Stretches can be done either passively or actively.

Passive Stretching   In **passive stretching,** an outside force or resistance provided by yourself, a partner, gravity, or a weight helps your joints move through their range of motion. For example, a seated stretch of the hamstring and back muscles can be done by reaching the hands toward the feet until a "pull" is felt in those muscles. You can achieve a greater range of motion (a more intense stretch) using passive stretching. However, because the stretch is not controlled by the muscles themselves, there is a greater risk of injury. Communication between partners in passive stretching is very important so joints aren't forced outside their normal functional range of motion.

Active Stretching   In **active stretching,** a muscle is stretched by a contraction of the opposing muscle (the muscle on the opposite side of the limb). For example, an

TERMS

stretch receptors   Sense organs in skeletal muscles that initiate a nerve signal to the spinal cord in response to a stretch; a contraction follows.

proprioceptive neuromuscular facilitation (PNF)   A technique in which the inverse stretch reflex induces relaxation in a muscle prior to its being stretched, allowing for more stretch and more rapid development of joint flexibility.

static stretching   A technique in which a muscle is slowly and gently stretched and then held in the stretched position.

ballistic stretching   A technique in which muscles are stretched by the force generated as a body part is repeatedly bounced, swung, or jerked.

passive stretching   A technique in which muscles are stretched by force applied by an outside source.

active stretching   A technique in which muscles are stretched by the contraction of the opposing muscles.

- Do stretching exercises statically. Stretch to the point of mild discomfort, and hold the position for 10–30 seconds, rest for 30–60 seconds, and repeat, trying to stretch a bit farther.

- Do not stretch until the point of pain.

- Relax and breathe easily as you stretch. Try to relax the muscles being stretched.

- Perform all exercises on both sides of your body.

- Increase intensity and duration gradually over time. Improved flexibility takes many months to develop.

- Stretch when your muscles are warm. Do gentle warm-up exercises such as easy jogging or calisthenics before doing a pre-exercise stretching routine.

- There are large individual differences in joint flexibility. Don't feel you have to compete with others during stretching workouts.

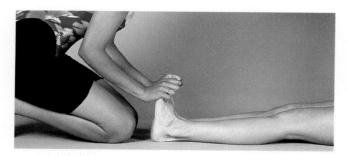 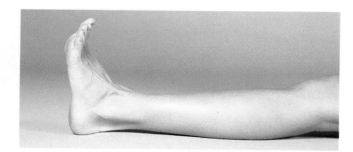

In passive stretching (left), an outside force—such as pressure exerted by another person—helps move the joint and stretch the muscles. In active stretching (right), the force to move the joint and stretch the muscles is provided by a contraction of the opposing muscles.

active seated stretch of the calf muscles occurs when a person actively contracts the muscles on the top of the shin. The contraction of this opposing muscle produces a reflex that relaxes the muscles to be stretched. The muscle can be stretched farther with a low risk of injury.

The only disadvantage of active stretching is that a person may not be able to produce enough stress (enough stretch) to increase flexibility using only the contraction of opposing muscle groups. The safest and most convenient technique is active static stretching, with an occasional passive assist. For example, you might stretch your calves both by contracting the muscles on the top of your shin and by pulling your feet toward you. This way you combine the advantages of active stretching—safety and the relaxation reflex—with those of passive stretching—greater range of motion.

Intensity and Duration

For each exercise, slowly apply stretch to your muscles to the point of slight tension or mild discomfort. Hold the stretch for 10–30 seconds. As you hold the stretch, the feeling of slight tension should slowly subside; at that point, try to stretch a bit farther. Throughout the stretch, try to relax and breathe easily. Rest for about 30–60 seconds between each stretch, and do at least 4 repetitions of each stretch. A complete flexibility workout usually takes about 20–30 minutes.

Frequency

The American College of Sports Medicine recommends that stretching exercises be performed a minimum of 2–3 days per week. Many people do flexibility training more often—3–5 days per week—for even greater benefits. It's best to stretch when your muscles are warm, so try incorporating stretching into your cool-down after cardiorespiratory endurance exercise or weight training. Stretching can also be a part of your warm-up, but it's best to increase the temperature of your muscles first by doing the active part of the warm-up (for example, walking or slow jogging).

Refer to the box "Safe Stretching" for additional tips on creating a safe and successful stretching program, and complete Lab 5-2 when you're ready to start your own program.

Exercises to Improve Flexibility

There are hundreds of exercises that can improve flexibility. Your program should include exercises that work all the major joints of the body by stretching their associated muscles. The exercises illustrated here are simple to do and pose a minimum risk of injury. Use these exercises, or substitute your favorite stretches, to create a well-rounded program for developing flexibility. Be sure to perform each stretch using the proper technique. Hold each position for 10–30 seconds, and perform at least 4 repetitions of each exercise.

FLEXIBILITY EXERCISES

EXERCISE 1

HEAD TURNS AND TILTS

Areas stretched: Neck, upper back

Instructions:

Head turns: Turn your head to the right and hold the stretch. Repeat to the left.

Head tilts: Tilt your head to the left and hold the stretch. Repeat to the right.

Variation: Place your right palm on your right cheek; try to turn your head to the right as you resist with your hand. Repeat on the left side.

EXERCISE 2

TOWEL STRETCH

Areas stretched: Triceps, shoulders, chest

Instructions: Roll up a towel and grasp it with both hands, palms down. With your arms straight, slowly lift it back over your head as far as possible. The closer together your hands are, the greater the stretch.

Variation: Repeat the stretch with your arms down and the towel behind your back. Grasp the towel with your palms forward and thumbs pointing out. Gently raise your arms behind your back.

EXERCISE 3

ACROSS-THE-BODY STRETCH

Areas stretched: Shoulders, upper back

Instructions: Keeping your back straight, cross your left arm in front of your body and grasp it with your right hand. Stretch your arm, shoulders, and back by gently pulling your arm as close to your body as possible. Repeat the stretch with your right arm.

Variation: Bend your right arm over and behind your head. Grasp your right hand with your left, and gently pull your arm until you feel the stretch. Repeat for your left arm.

UPPER-BACK STRETCH

Areas stretched: Upper back

Instructions: Stand with your feet shoulder-width apart, knees slightly bent, and pelvis tucked under. Clasp your hands in front of your body, and press your palms forward.

Variation: In the same position, wrap your arms around your body as if you were giving yourself a hug.

LATERAL STRETCH

Areas Stretched: Trunk muscles

Instructions: Stand with your feet shoulder-width apart, knees slightly bent, and pelvis tucked under. Raise one arm over your head and bend sideways from the waist. Support your trunk by placing the hand or forearm of your other arm on your thigh or hip for support. Be sure you bend directly sideways, and don't move your body below the waist. Repeat on the other side.

Variation: Perform the same exercise in a seated position.

STEP STRETCH

Areas stretched: Hip, front of thigh (quadriceps)

Instructions: Step forward and flex your forward knee, keeping your knee directly above your ankle. Stretch your other leg back so that it is parallel to the floor. Press your hips forward and down to stretch. Your arms can be at your sides, on top of your knee, or on the ground for balance. Repeat on the other side.

SIDE LUNGE

Areas stretched: Inner thigh, hip, calf

Instructions: Stand in a wide straddle with your legs turned out from your hip joints and your hands on your thighs. Lunge to one side by bending one knee and keeping the other leg straight. Keep your knee directly over your ankle; do not bend it more than 90 degrees. Repeat on the other side.

Variation: In the same position, lift the heel of the bent knee to provide additional stretch. The exercise may also be performed with your hands on the floor for balance.

SOLE STRETCH

Areas stretched: Inner thigh, hip

Instructions: Sit with the soles of your feet together. Push your knees toward the floor using your hands or forearms.

Variation: When you first begin to push your knees toward the floor, use your legs to resist the movement. Then relax and press your knees down as far as they will go.

TRUNK ROTATION

Areas stretched: Trunk, outer thigh and hip, lower back

Instructions: Sit with your right leg straight, left leg bent and crossed over the right knee, and left hand on the floor next to your left hip. Turn your trunk as far as possible to the left by pushing against your left leg with your right forearm or elbow. Keep your left foot on the floor. Repeat on the other side.

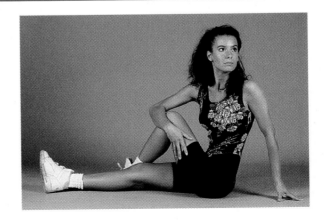

ALTERNATE LEG STRETCHER

Areas stretched: Back of the thigh (hamstring), hip, knee, ankle, buttocks

Instructions: Lie flat on your back with both legs straight. **(a)** Grasp your left leg behind the thigh, and pull in to your chest. **(b)** Hold this position, and then extend your left leg toward the ceiling. **(c)** Hold this position, and then bring your left knee back to your chest and pull your toes toward your shin with your left hand. Stretch the back of the leg by attempting to straighten your knee. Repeat for the other leg.

Variation: Perform the stretch on both legs at the same time.

(a)

(b)

(c)

MODIFIED HURDLER STRETCH
(Seated Single-Toe Touch)

Areas stretched: Back of the thigh (hamstring), lower back

Instructions: Sit with your right leg straight and your left leg tucked close to your body. Reach toward your right foot as far as possible. Repeat for the other leg.

Variation: As you stretch forward, alternately flex and point the foot of your extended leg.

LOWER LEG STRETCH

Areas stretched: Back of the lower leg (calf, soleus, Achilles tendon)

Instructions: Stand with one foot about 1–2 feet in front of the other, with both feet pointing forward. **(a)** Keeping your back leg straight, lunge forward by bending your front knee and pushing your rear heel backward. Hold this position. **(b)** Then pull your back foot in slightly, and bend your back knee. Shift your weight to your back leg. Hold. Repeat on the other side.

Variation: Place your hands on a wall and extend one foot back, pressing your heel down to stretch; or stand with the balls of your feet on a step or bench and allow your heels to drop below the level of your toes.

(a)   (b)

PREVENTING AND MANAGING LOW-BACK PAIN

Over 85% of Americans will experience back pain at some time in their lives. Low-back pain is the second most common ailment in the United States—headache tops the list—and the second most common reason for absences from work. Low-back pain is estimated to cost as much as $50 billion per year in lost productivity, medical and legal fees, and disability insurance and compensation.

Back pain can result from sudden traumatic injuries, but it is more often the long-term result of weak and inflexible muscles, poor posture, or poor body mechanics during activities like lifting and carrying. Any abnormal strain on the back can result in pain. Most cases of low-back pain clear up on their own within a few weeks, but some people have recurrences or suffer from chronic pain.

Function and Structure of the Spine

The spinal column performs many important functions in the body.

- It provides structural support for the body, especially the thorax (upper-body cavity).
- It surrounds and protects the spinal cord.
- It supports much of the body's weight and transmits it to the lower body.
- It serves as an attachment site for a large number of muscles, tendons, and ligaments.
- It allows movement of the neck and back in all directions.

The spinal column is made up of bones called **vertebrae** (Figure 5-3). The spine consists of 7 cervical verte-brae in the neck, 12 thoracic vertebrae in the upper back, and 5 lumbar vertebrae in the lower back. The 9 vertebrae at the base of the spine are fused into two sections and form the sacrum and the coccyx (tailbone). The spine has four curves: the cervical, thoracic, lumbar, and sacral curves. These curves help bring the body weight supported by the spine in line with the axis of the body.

Although the structure of vertebrae depends on their location on the spine, the different types of vertebrae do share common characteristics. Each consists of a body, an arch, and several bony processes (Figure 5-4). The vertebral body is cylindrical, with flattened surfaces where **intervertebral disks** are attached. The vertebral body is designed to carry the stress of body weight and physical activity. The vertebral arch surrounds and protects the spinal cord. The bony processes serve as joints for adjacent vertebrae and attachment sites for muscles and ligaments. **Nerve roots** from the spinal cord pass through notches in the vertebral arch.

Intervertebral disks, which absorb and disperse the stresses placed on the spine, separate vertebrae from each other. Disks are made up of a gel- and water-filled nucleus surrounded by a series of fibrous rings. The liquid

TERMS

vertebrae Bony segments composing the spinal column that provide structural support for the body and protect the spinal cord.

intervertebral disk A tough, elastic disk located between adjoining vertebrae consisting of a gel- and water-filled nucleus surrounded by fibrous rings; it serves as a shock absorber for the spinal column.

nerve root The base of one of the 31 pairs of spinal nerves that branch off the spinal cord through spaces between vertebrae.

Spinal curves

Vertebrae

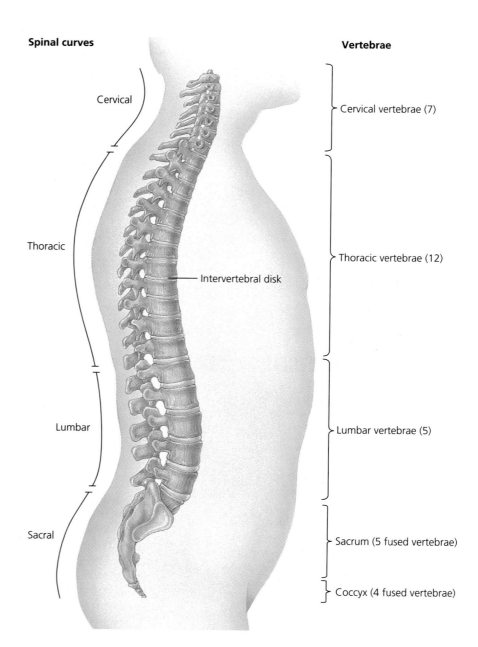

Cervical

Thoracic

Intervertebral disk

Lumbar

Sacral

Cervical vertebrae (7)

Thoracic vertebrae (12)

Lumbar vertebrae (5)

Sacrum (5 fused vertebrae)

Coccyx (4 fused vertebrae)

Figure 5-3   The spinal column.   The spine is made up of five separate regions and has four distinct curves. An intervertebral disk is located between vertebrae.

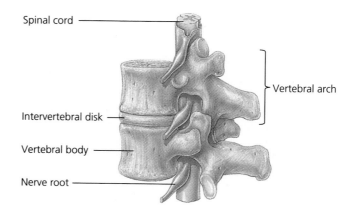

Spinal cord

Intervertebral disk

Vertebral body

Nerve root

Vertebral arch

Figure 5-4   Vertebrae and an intervertebral disk.

 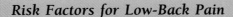

- Age greater than 34 years
- Degenerative disease (e.g., osteoporosis, arthritis)
- Family history of back pain
- History of back trauma
- Lack of physical activity
- Low job satisfaction
- Low muscular strength relative to body weight
- Low socioeconomic status
- Male sex (in some studies)
- Obesity

- Occupations or activities requiring frequent lifting, twisting, bending, or standing up
- Occupations with high concentration demands (e.g., computer programming)
- Physically hard work
- Poor posture
- Psychological depression
- Repetitive strain in forced positions over long time periods
- Smoking (linked to increased disk degeneration)
- Vibration affecting the whole body (such as experienced by truck drivers)

nucleus can change shape when it is compressed, allowing the disk to absorb shock. The intervertebral disks also help maintain the spaces between vertebrae where the spinal nerve roots are located.

Causes of Back Pain

Back pain can occur at any point along your spine; the lumbar area, because it bears the majority of your weight, is the most common site. Any movement that causes excessive stress on the spinal column can cause injury and pain. The spine is well equipped to bear body weight and the force or stress of body movements along its long axis. However, it is less capable of bearing loads at an angle to its long axis. You do not have to carry a heavy load or participate in a vigorous contact sport to injure your back. Picking a pencil up from the floor using poor body mechanics—reaching too far out in front of you or bending over with your knees straight, for example—can also result in back pain (see the box "Risk Factors for Low-Back Pain").

Underlying causes of back pain include weak or inflexible muscles in the back, hips, abdomen, and legs; excess body weight; poor posture when standing, sitting, or sleeping; and poor body mechanics when performing actions like lifting and carrying, or sports movements. Abnormal spinal loading resulting from any of these causes can have short-term or long-term direct and indirect effects on the spine. Strained muscles, tendons, or ligaments can cause pain and can, over time, lead to injuries to vertebrae or the intervertebral disks.

Stress can cause disks to break down and lose some of their ability to absorb shock. A damaged disk may bulge out between vertebrae and put pressure on a nerve root, a condition commonly referred to as a slipped disk. Painful pressure on nerves can also occur if damage to a disk narrows the space between two vertebrae. With age, you lose fluid from the disks, making them more likely to bulge and put pressure on nerve roots. Depending on the

amount of pressure on a nerve, symptoms may include numbness in the back, hip, leg, or foot; radiating pain; loss of muscle function; depressed reflexes; and muscle spasm. If the pressure is severe enough, loss of function can be permanent.

Preventing Low-Back Pain

Incorrect posture when standing, sitting, lying, and lifting is responsible for many back injuries. In general, think about moving your spine as a unit, with the force directed through its long axis. Strategies for maintaining good posture during daily activities are presented in the box "Avoiding Low-Back Pain." Follow the same guidelines for posture and movement when you engage in sports or recreational activities. Maintain control over your body movements, and warm up thoroughly before you exercise. Take special care when lifting weights as part of a strength training program. (Refer to Chapter 4 for more information on proper weight-lifting technique.)

The role of exercise in preventing and treating back pain is still being investigated. However, many experts do recommend exercise, especially for people who have already experienced an episode of low-back pain. Lifestyle physical activity such as walking is often recommended for the prevention of back pain. When walking, stand up straight, keep your head centered over your body, and swing your arms freely. Movement helps lubricate your spinal disks and increases muscle fitness in your trunk and legs. To help maintain a healthy back, you should also regularly perform exercises that stretch and strengthen the major muscle groups that affect your back. The following exercises focus on the key areas: the abdominal muscles, the muscles along your spine and sides, and the muscles of your hips and thighs. If you have back problems, check with your physician before beginning any exercise program. Perform the exercises slowly, and progress very gradually. Stop and consult your physician if any exercise causes back pain.

Changes in everyday behavior can help prevent and alleviate low-back pain.

- *Lying down.* When resting or sleeping, lie on your side with your knees and hips bent. If you lie on your back, place a pillow under your knees. Don't lie on your stomach. If your mattress isn't firm, place a plywood board under it.

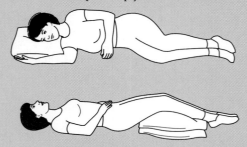

- *Sitting.* Sit with your lower back slightly rounded, knees bent, and feet flat on the floor. Alternate crossing your legs, or use a foot rest to keep your knees higher than your hips. If this position is uncomfortable or if your back flattens when you sit, try using a lumbar roll pillow behind your lower back.

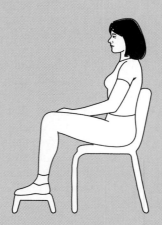

- *Lifting.* If you need to lower yourself to grasp an object, bend at the knees and hips rather than at the waist. Your feet should be about shoulder-width apart. Lift gradually, keeping your arms straight, by standing up or by pushing with your leg muscles. Keep the object close to your body. Don't twist; if you have to turn with the object, change the position of your feet.

- *Standing.* When you are standing, a straight line should run from the top of your ear through the center of your shoulder, the center of your hip, the back of your kneecap, and the front of your ankle bone. Support your weight mainly on your heels, with one or both knees slightly bent. Try to keep your lower back flat by placing one foot on a stool. Don't let your pelvis tip forward or your back arch. Shift your weight back and forth from foot to foot. Avoid prolonged standing. (To check your posture, stand in a normal way with your back to a wall. Your upper back and buttocks should touch the wall; your heels may be a few inches away. Slide one hand into the space between your lower back and the wall. It should slide in easily but should almost touch both your back and the wall. Adjust your posture as needed, and try to hold this position as you walk away from the wall.)

- *Walking.* Walk with your toes pointed straight ahead. Keep your back flat, head up, and chin in. Don't wear high-heeled shoes.

LOW-BACK EXERCISES

EXERCISE 1

WALL STRETCH

Areas stretched: Back of thigh (hamstring), calf

Instructions: Sit on the floor with one leg extended and your foot flat against a wall or other immovable object. Bend the other leg and place your foot flat on the floor next to the knee of the straight leg. Clasp your hands behind your back or rest them loosely on the floor behind you. Bend forward from your hips, keeping your lower back flat and straight. Your bent knee can be moved slightly to the side to make room for your upper body as you lean forward. Repeat with the other leg.

EXERCISE 2

STEP STRETCH (see Exercise 6 in the flexibility program)

EXERCISE 3

ALTERNATE LEG STRETCHER (see Exercise 10 in the flexibility program)

EXERCISE 4

DOUBLE KNEE-TO-CHEST

Areas stretched: Lower back, hips

Instructions: Lie on your back with both knees bent and feet flat on the floor. **(a)** With one hand on the back of each thigh, slowly pull both knees to your chest; hold the stretch. **(b)** Then straighten your knees so that both legs are extended toward the ceiling. Return to the starting position by drawing your legs back to your chest and then placing your feet on the floor.

(a)

(b)

TRUNK TWIST

Area stretched: Lower back, sides

Instructions: Lie on your side with top knee bent, lower leg straight, lower arm extended out in front of you on the floor, and upper arm at your side. Push down with your upper knee while you twist your trunk backward. Try to get your shoulders and upper body flat on the floor, turning your head as well. Return to the starting position, and then repeat on the other side.

BACK BRIDGE

Areas strengthened: Hips, buttocks

Instructions: Lie on your back with knees bent and arms extended to the side. Tuck your pelvis under, and then lift your tailbone, buttocks, and lower back from the floor. Hold this position for 5–10 seconds with your weight resting on your feet, arms, and shoulders, and then return to the starting position. Work up to 10 repetitions of the exercise.

PELVIC TILT

Areas strengthened: Abdomen, buttocks

Instructions: Lie on your back with knees bent and arms extended to the side. Tilt your pelvis under, and try to flatten your lower back against the floor. Tighten your buttock and abdominal muscles while you hold this position for 5–10 seconds. Don't hold your breath. Work up to 10 repetitions of the exercise. Pelvic tilts can also be done standing or leaning against a wall.

MODIFIED SIT-UP

Areas strengthened: Abdomen

Instructions: Lie on your back with knees bent and arms crossed on your chest. Tilt your pelvis under, flattening your back. Tuck your chin in and slowly curl up, one vertebra at a time as you lift your head first and then your shoulders. Stop when you can see your heels, and hold for 5–10 seconds before returning to the starting position. Do 10 repetitions.

Variation: Add a twist to develop other abdominal muscles. When you have curled up so that your shoulder blades are off the floor, twist your upper body so that one shoulder is higher than the other; reach past your knee with your upper arm. Hold, and then return to the starting position. Repeat on the opposite side.

PRESS-UP

Areas stretched: Lower back, abdomen

Instructions: Lie face down with your hands under your face. Slowly push yourself up until your upper body is resting on your forearms. Relax and hold for 5–10 seconds. Gradually progress to straightening your elbows while keeping your pubic bone on the floor. (Stop if this exercise produces any pain.)

WALL SQUAT (Phantom Chair)

Areas strengthened: Lower back, thighs, abdomen

Instructions: Lean against a wall and bend your knees as though you are sitting in a chair. Support your weight with your legs. Begin by holding the position for 5–10 seconds. Build up to 1 minute or more.

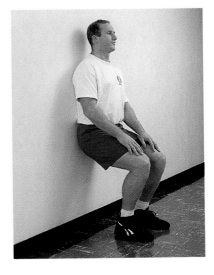

SPINE EXTENSIONS (see Exercise 9 in the free weights program in Chapter 4, p. 88)

COMMON QUESTIONS ANSWERED

Are there any stretching exercises I shouldn't do?   Yes. Avoid exercises that put excessive pressure on your joints, particularly your spine and knees. Previous injuries and poor flexibility may make certain exercises dangerous for some people. Exercises that may cause problems are described in the box "Stretches to Avoid."

Is stretching the same as warming up?   People often confuse stretching and pre-exercise warm-up. While they are complementary, they're two distinct activities. A warm-up involves light exercise that increases body temperature so that your metabolism works better when you're exercising at high intensity. Stretching increases the movement capability of your joints, so you can move more easily, with less risk of injury.

Whenever you stretch, you should ideally first spend 5–10 minutes engaged in some form of low-intensity exercise, such as walking, jogging, or low-intensity calisthenics. When your muscles are warmed, begin your stretching routine. Warmed muscles stretch better than cold ones and are less prone to injury.

How much flexibility do I need?   This question is not always easy to answer. If you're involved in a sport such as gymnastics, figure skating, or ballet, you are often required to reach extreme joint motions to achieve success. However, nonathletes do not need to reach these extreme joint positions. In fact, too much flexibility may, in some cases, increase your risk of injury. As with other types of fitness, moderation is the key. You should regularly stretch your major joints and muscle groups but not aspire to reach extreme flexibility.

Can I stretch too far?   Yes. As muscle tissue is progressively stretched, it reaches a point where it becomes damaged and may rupture. The greatest danger occurs during passive stretching when a partner is doing the stretching for you. It is critical that your stretching partner not force your joint outside its normal functional range of motion.

Does weight training limit flexibility?   Weight training, or any physical activity, will decrease flexibility if the exercises are not performed through a full range of motion. When done properly, weight training increases flexibility.

Does jogging impair flexibility?   Because of the limited range of motion used during the running stride, jogging tends to compromise flexibility. It is very important for runners to practice flexibility exercises for the hamstrings and quadriceps regularly.

SUMMARY

- Flexibility, the ability of joints to move through their full range of motion, is highly adaptable and specific to each joint.

- The benefits of flexibility include preventing abnormal stresses that lead to joint deterioration and possibly reducing the risk of injuries and low-back pain.

- Range of motion can be limited by joint structure, by limited muscle elasticity, and by stretch receptor activity.

- Developing flexibility depends on stretching the elastic tissues within muscles regularly and gently until they lengthen. Overstretching can make connective tissue brittle and lead to rupture.

- Signals sent between stretch receptors and the spinal cord can enhance flexibility because contracting a muscle stimulates a relaxation response, thereby allowing a longer muscle stretch, and because stretch receptors become less sensitive after repeated stretches, initiating fewer contractions.

- The sit-and-reach test is most often used to assess flexibility; comparisons can also be made to a chart showing normal range of motion for major joints.

- Static stretching is done slowly and held to the point of mild tension; ballistic stretching consists of bouncing stretches and can lead to injury. Proprioceptive neuromuscular facilitation uses muscle receptors in contracting and relaxing a muscle.

- Passive stretching, using an outside force in moving muscles and joints, achieves a greater range of motion (and has a higher injury risk) than active stretching, which uses opposing muscles to initiate a stretch.

- Stretches should be held for 10–30 seconds; perform at least 4 repetitions. Flexibility training should be done 2 or more days a week, preferably following activity when muscles are warm.

The safe alternatives listed here are described and illustrated on pages 115–119 as part of the complete program of safe flexibility exercises presented in this chapter.

Standing Toe Touch

Problem: Puts excessive strain on the spine

Alternatives: Alternate leg stretcher (Exercise 10), modified hurdler stretch (Exercise 11), and lower leg stretch (Exercise 12)

Full Squat

Problem: Puts excessive strain on the ankles, knees, and spine

Alternatives: Alternate leg stretcher (Exercise 10) and lower leg stretch (Exercise 12)

Standing Ankle-to-Buttocks Quadriceps Stretch

Problem: Puts excessive strain on the ligaments of the knee

Alternative: Step stretch (Exercise 6)

Prone Arch

Problem: Puts excessive strain on the spine, knees, and shoulders

Alternatives: Towel stretch (Exercise 2) and step stretch (Exercise 6)

Standing Hamstring Stretch

Problem: Puts excessive strain on the knee and lower back

Alternatives: Alternate leg stretcher (Exercise 10) and modified hurdler stretch (Exercise 11)

Yoga Plow

Problem: Puts excessive strain on the neck, shoulders, and back

Alternatives: Head turns and tilts (Exercise 1), across-the-body stretch (Exercise 3), and upper-back stretch (Exercise 4)

Hurdler Stretch

Problem: Turning out the bent leg can put excessive strain on the ligaments of the knee

Alternative: Modified hurdler stretch (Exercise 11)

- The spinal column consists of vertebrae separated by intervertebral disks. It provides structure and support for the body and protects the spinal cord.
- In addition to good posture, proper body mechanics, and regular physical activity, a program for preventing low-back pain includes exercises that stretch and strengthen major muscle groups that affect the lower back.

FOR MORE INFORMATION

Books

Alter, M. J. 1996. *Science of Flexibility,* 2d ed. Champaign, Ill.: Human Kinetics. *An extremely well researched book that discusses the scientific basis of stretching exercises and flexibility.*

Anderson, B., and J. Anderson. 1997. *Stretching at Your Computer or Desk.* Bolinas, Calif.: Shelter Publications. *Stretching routines for workplace and school settings.*

Maharam, L. 1998. *A Healthy Back: A Sports Medicine Doctor's Back-Care Program for Everybody.* New York: Henry Holt. *Lifestyle advice for preventing and eliminating back pain.*

Martins, P. 1997. *The New York City Ballet Workout: Fifty Stretches and Exercises Anyone Can Do for a Strong, Graceful, and Sculpted Body.* New York: William Morrow. *Stretching exercises with a dance orientation.*

Smith, B. 1997. *Flexibility for Sport.* Wiltshire, Eng.: Crowood Press. *Stretching workouts for people interested in various sports.*

St. George, F. 1997. *Stretching for Flexibility and Health.* Freedom, Calif.: Crossing Press. *A good basic book on stretching exercises.*

Web Sites

Back Pain Prevention. Tips for use at home, at work, and during exercise.
http://cst.lanl.gov/CST/backpain/mainback.html

FitnessLink/Stretching Exercises. Information on a safe, effective stretching program.
http://www.fitnesslink.com/exercise/stretch.htm

NIH Back Pain Fact Sheet. Provides basic information on the prevention and treatment of back pain.
http://www.ninds.nih.gov/HEALINFO/DISORDER/back%20pain/backpain.htm

Southern California Orthopedic Institute. Provides information about a variety of orthopedic problems, including back injuries; also has illustrations of spinal anatomy.
http://www.scoi.com

Stretching and Flexibility. Provides information about the physiology of stretching and different types of stretching exercises.
http://www.cs.huji.ac.il/papers/rma/stretching_toc.html

See also the listings for Chapters 2 and 4.

SELECTED BIBLIOGRAPHY

Agency for Health Care Policy and Research. 1994. *Clinical Practice Guidelines. Acute Low Back Problems in Adults.* Silver Spring, Md.: Publications Clearinghouse.

Alter, M. J. 1996. *The Science of Flexibility,* 2d ed. Champaign, Ill.: Human Kinetics.

American College of Sports Medicine. 1998. ACSM Position Stand: The Recommended Quantity and Quality of Exercises for Developing and Maintaining Cardiorespiratory and Muscular Fitness, and Flexibility in Healthy Adults. *Medicine and Science in Sports and Exercise* 30(6): 975–991.

American Medical Association. 1995. *The AMA Pocket Guide to Back Pain.* New York: Random House.

Andersson, G. B. 1997. Low back pain. *Journal of Rehabilitation Research and Development* 34:IX–X.

Bandy, W. D., J. M. Irion, and M. Briggler. 1997. The effect of time and frequency of static stretching on flexibility of the hamstring muscles. *Physical Therapy* 77:1090–1096.

Burton, A. K., and E. Erg. 1997. Back injury and work loss. Biomechanical and psychosocial influences. *Spine* 22: 2575–2580.

Callaghan, J. P., J. L. Gunning, and S. M. McGill. 1998. The relationship between lumbar spine load and muscle activity during extensor exercises. *Physical Therapy* 78(1): 8–18.

Craib, M. W., et al. 1996. The association between flexibility and running economy in sub-elite male distance runners. *Medicine and Science in Sports and Exercise* 28:737–743.

Daltroy, L. H., et al. 1997. A controlled trial of an educational program to prevent low back injuries. *New England Journal of Medicine* 337:322–328.

Dempsey, P. G., A. Burdorf, and B. S. Webster. 1997. The influence of personal variables on work-related low-back disorders and implications for future research. *Journal of Occupational and Environmental Medicine* 39:748–759.

Hurwitz, E. L., and H. Morgenstern. 1997. Correlates of back problems and back-related disability in the United States. *Journal of Clinical Epidemiology* 50:669–681.

Jackson, A. W., et al. 1998. Relations of sit-up and sit-and-reach tests to low back pain in adults. *Journal of Orthopaedic and Sports Physical Therapy* 27(1): 22–26.

Leboeuf-Yde, C., J. M. Lauritsen, and T. Lauritzen. 1997. Why has the search for causes of low back pain largely been nonconclusive? *Spine* 22:877–881.

Nieman, D. C. 1999. *Exercise Testing and Prescription: A Health-Related Approach,* 4th ed. Mountain View, Calif.: Mayfield.

Schwartz, E., R. E. Yodaiken, and R. Sokas. 1997. An educational program to prevent disabling low back pain. *New England Journal of Medicine* 337:1923–1924.

Shiple, D. O. 1997. Relieving low-back pain with exercise. *The Physician and Sportsmedicine* 25(8): 67–68.

Wiemann, K., and K. Hahn. 1997. Influences of strength, stretching and circulatory exercises on flexibility parameters of the human hamstrings. *International Journal of Sports Medicine* 18:340–346.

LAB 5-1 *Assessing Your Current Level of Flexibility*

Part I. Sit-and-Reach Test

Equipment

A flexibility box or measuring device (see photograph). If you make your own measuring device, use two pieces of wood 12 inches high attached at right angles to each other. Use a ruler or yardstick to measure the extent of reach. With the low numbers of the ruler toward the person being tested, set the 6-inch mark of the ruler at the footline of the box. (Individuals who cannot reach as far as the footline will have scores below 6 inches; those who can reach past their feet will have scores above 6 inches.)

Preparation

Warm up your muscles with some low-intensity activity such as walking or easy jogging.

Instructions

1. Remove your shoes, and sit facing the flexibility box with your knees fully extended and your feet about 4 inches apart. Your feet should be flat against the box.

2. Reach as far forward as you can, with palms down and one hand placed on top of the other. Hold the position of maximum reach for 1–2 seconds. Keep your knees locked at all times.

3. Repeat the stretch two times. Your score is the most distant point reached with the fingertips of both hands on the third trial, measured to the nearest quarter of an inch.

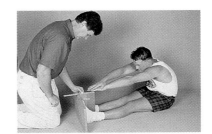

The sit-and-reach test.

Footline of your box: _____ in.   Score of third trial: _____ in.

Rating Your Flexibility

Find your score in the table below to determine your flexibility rating.

Rating: _____

Ratings for Sit-and-Reach Test

	Rating/Score (in.)*				
Men	*Very Poor*	*Poor*	*Moderate*	*High*	*Very High*
Age: 15–19	Below 5.25	5.25–6.75	7.00–8.75	9.00–10.75	Above 10.75
20–29	Below 5.50	5.50–7.00	7.25–8.75	9.00–11.00	Above 11.00
30–39	Below 4.75	4.75–6.50	6.75–8.50	8.75–10.25	Above 10.25
40–49	Below 2.75	2.75–5.00	5.25–6.75	7.00–9.25	Above 9.25
50–59	Below 2.00	2.00–5.00	5.25–6.50	6.75–9.25	Above 9.25
60 and over	Below 1.75	1.75–3.25	3.50–5.25	5.50–8.50	Above 8.50
Women					
Age: 15–19	Below 7.25	7.25–8.75	9.00–10.50	10.75–12.25	Above 12.25
20–29	Below 6.75	6.75–8.50	8.75–10.00	10.25–11.50	Above 11.50
30–39	Below 6.50	6.50–8.00	8.25–9.50	9.75–11.50	Above 11.50
40–49	Below 5.50	5.50–7.25	7.50–8.75	9.00–10.50	Above 10.50
50–59	Below 5.50	5.50–7.25	7.50–8.50	8.75–10.75	Above 10.75
60 and over	Below 4.75	4.75–6.00	6.25–7.75	8.00–9.25	Above 9.25

*Footline is set at 6 inches.

SOURCE: Published in the *Canadian Standardized Test of Fitness Operations Manual*, 3rd edition, 1986. Reprinted by permission from the Canadian Society for Exercise Physiology.

LABORATORY ACTIVITIES

Part II. Range-of-Motion Assessment

This portion of the lab can be completed by doing visual comparisons or by measuring joint range of motion with a goniometer or other instrument.

Equipment

1. A partner to do visual comparisons or to measure the range of motion of your joints. (You can also use a mirror to perform your own visual comparisons.)
2. For the measurement method, you need a goniometer, flexometer, or other instrument to measure range of motion.

Preparation

None

Instructions

A. *Visual comparison method:* On the following pages, the average range of motion is illustrated for some of the major joints. Compare the range of motion in your joints to that shown in the illustration. For each joint, note (with a check mark) whether your range of motion is average or greater or needs improvement.

B. *Measurement method:* Measure the appropriate range of motion with a goniometer, flexometer, or other instrument. Record your range of motion in degrees, and find your rating in the appropriate table. (Ratings are taken from several published sources.)

For both methods, record your scores on the following pages and on the chart on the final page of this lab.

Assessment of range of motion using a goniometer.

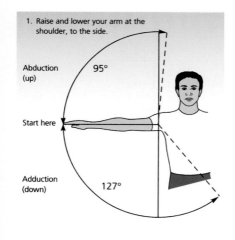

1. Raise and lower your arm at the shoulder, to the side.

Abduction (up) 95°

Start here

Adduction (down) 127°

A. Comparison Method (✓)

Abduction: Average or above _____ Needs improvement _____

Adduction: Average or above _____ Needs improvement _____

B. Measurement Method

Abduction: _____ ° Rating: _____

Adduction: _____ ° Rating: _____

Ratings

	Abduction	Adduction
Below average	<92°	<124°
Average	92°–95°	124°–127°
Above average	96°–99°	128°–130°
Excellent	>99°	>130°

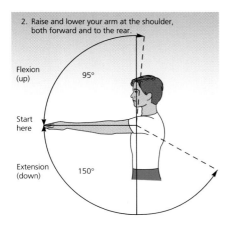

A. Comparison Method (✓)

    Flexion: Average or above _____ Needs improvement _____

    Extension: Average or above _____ Needs improvement _____

B. Measurement Method

    Flexion: _____ °   Rating: _____

    Extension: _____ °   Rating: _____

Ratings

	Flexion	*Extension*
Below average	<92°	<145°
Average	92°–95°	145°–150°
Above average	96°–99°	151°–156°
Excellent	>99°	>156°

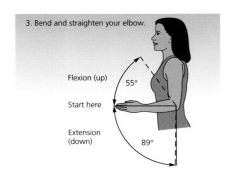

A. Comparison Method (✓)

    Flexion: Average or above _____ Needs improvement _____

    Extension: Average or above _____ Needs improvement _____

B. Measurement Method

    Flexion: _____ °   Rating: _____

    Extension: _____ °   Rating: _____

Ratings

	Flexion	*Extension*
Below average	<51°	<88°
Average	51°–55°	88°–89°
Above average	56°–60°	90°–91°
Excellent	>60°	>91°

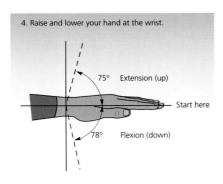

A. Comparison Method (✓)

    Extension: Average or above _____ Needs improvement _____

    Flexion: Average or above _____ Needs improvement _____

B. Measurement Method

    Extension: _____ °   Rating: _____

    Flexion: _____ °   Rating: _____

Ratings

	Extension	*Flexion*
Below average	<70°	<73°
Average	70°–75°	73°–78°
Above average	76°–81°	79°–84°
Excellent	>81°	>84°

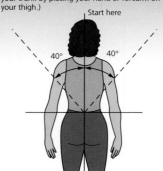

5. Bend directly sideways at your waist. (To prevent injury, keep your knees slightly bent, and support your trunk by placing your hand or forearm on your thigh.)

Start here

40° 40°

A. Comparison Method (✓)

Right lateral flexion: Average or above _____ Needs improvement _____

Left lateral flexion: Average or above _____ Needs improvement _____

B. Measurement Method:

Right lateral flexion: _____ ° Rating: _____

Left lateral flexion: _____ ° Rating: _____

Ratings

	Right or Left Lateral Flexion
Below average	<36°
Average	36°–40°
Above average	41°–45°
Excellent	>45

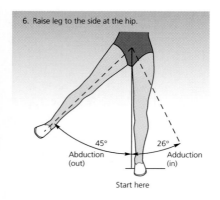

6. Raise leg to the side at the hip.

45°
Abduction (out)

26°
Adduction (in)

Start here

A. Comparison Method (✓)

Abduction: Average or above _____ Needs improvement _____

Adduction: Average or above _____ Needs improvement _____

B. Measurement Method

Abduction: _____ ° Rating: _____

Adduction: _____ ° Rating: _____

Ratings

	Abduction	*Adduction*
Below average	<40°	<23°
Average	40°–45°	23°–26°
Above average	46°–51°	27°–30°
Excellent	>51°	>30°

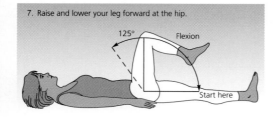

7. Raise and lower your leg forward at the hip.

125° Flexion

Start here

A. Comparison Method (✓)

Average or above _____ Needs improvement _____

B. Measurement Method

Flexion: _____ ° Rating: _____

Ratings

	Flexion
Below average	<121°
Average	121°–125°
Above average	126°–130°
Excellent	>130°

LABORATORY ACTIVITIES

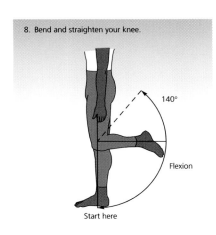

8. Bend and straighten your knee.

140°

Flexion

Start here

A. Comparison Method (✓)

Average or above _____ Needs improvement _____

B. Measurement Method

Flexion: _____ °   Rating: _____

Ratings

	Flexion
Below average	<136°
Average	136°–140°
Above average	141°–145°
Excellent	>145°

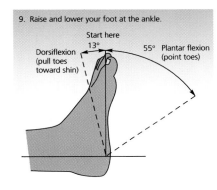

9. Raise and lower your foot at the ankle.

Start here

13°

Dorsiflexion
(pull toes
toward shin)

55°   Plantar flexion
(point toes)

A. Comparison Method (✓)

Dorsiflexion: Average or above _____ Needs improvement _____

Plantar flexion: Average or above _____ Needs improvement _____

B. Measurement Method

Dorsiflexion: _____ °   Rating: _____

Plantar flexion: _____ °   Rating: _____

Ratings

	Dorsiflexion	*Plantar flexion*
Below average	<9°	<50°
Average	9°–13°	50°–55°
Above average	14°–17°	56°–60°
Excellent	>17°	>60°

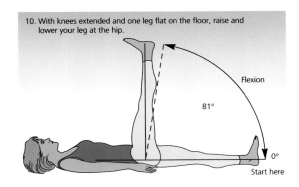

10. With knees extended and one leg flat on the floor, raise and lower your leg at the hip.

Flexion

81°

0°

Start here

A. Comparison Method (✓)

Average or above _____ Needs improvement _____

B. Measurement Method

Flexion: _____ °   Rating: _____

Ratings

	Flexion
Below average	<79°
Average	79°–81°
Above average	82°–84°
Excellent	>84°

Rating Your Flexibility

Sit-and-Reach Test

Score: _____ in.   Rating: _____

Range of Motion Assessment

Joint		Average ROM	Comparison Method (✓)		Measurement Method	
			Average or above	Needs improvement	Current range of motion (°)	Rating
Shoulder (side-to-side)	Abduction	95°				
	Adduction	127°				
Shoulder (front-to-back)	Flexion	95°				
	Extension	150°				
Elbow (up-and-down)	Flexion	55°				
	Extension	89°				
Wrist (up-and-down)	Extension	75°				
	Flexion	78°				
Low back (side-to-side)	Right flexion	40°				
	Left flexion	40°				
Hip (side-to-side)	Abduction	45°				
	Adduction	26°				
Hip (bent knee)	Flexion	125°				
Knee	Flexion	140°				
Ankle	Dorsiflexion	13°				
	Plantar flexion	55°				
Hip (straight knee)	Flexion	81°				

To monitor your progress toward your goal, enter the results of this lab in the Preprogram Assessment column of Appendix D. After following the stretching program for several weeks, do this lab again, and enter the results in the Postprogram Assessment column of Appendix D. How do the results compare?

Name _____   Section _____   Date _____

LAB 5-2 *Creating a Personalized Program for Developing Flexibility*

Complete the program plan below, and start on your flexibility program.

Exercises: The exercises contained in the program plan below are those from the general stretching program presented in Chapter 5. You can add or delete exercises depending on your needs, goals, and preferences. For any exercises you add, fill in the areas of the body affected.

Frequency: A minimum frequency of 2–3 days per week is recommended. You may want to do your stretching exercises the same days you plan to do cardiorespiratory endurance exercise or weight training, because muscles stretch better following exercise, when they are warm.

Intensity: All stretches should be done to the point of mild discomfort, not pain.

Duration: All stretches should be held for 10–30 seconds. (PNF techniques should include a 6-second contraction followed by a 10–30-second assisted stretch.)

Repetitions: All stretches should be performed at least 4 times.

Program Plan for Flexibility

Exercise	Areas Stretched	Frequency (check ✔)						
		M	T	W	Th	F	Sa	Su
Head turns and tilts	Neck, upper back							
Towel stretch	Triceps, shoulders, chest							
Across-the-body stretch	Shoulders, upper back							
Upper-back stretch	Upper back							
Lateral stretch	Trunk muscles							
Step stretch	Hip, front of thigh (quadriceps)							
Side lunge	Inner thigh, hip, calf							
Sole stretch	Inner thigh, hip							
Trunk rotation	Trunk, outer thigh and hip, lower back							
Alternate leg stretcher	Backs of the thigh (hamstring), hip, knee, ankle, buttocks							
Modified hurdler stretch	Back of the thigh (hamstring), lower back							
Lower leg stretch	Back of the lower leg (calf, soleus, Achilles tendon)							

You can monitor your program using a chart like the one on the next page.

Flexibility Program Chart

Fill in the dates you perform each stretch, the number of seconds you hold each stretch (should be 10–30), and the number of repetitions of each (should be at least 4). For an easy check on the duration of your stretches, count "one thousand one, one thousand two," and so on. You will probably find that over time you'll be able to hold each stretch longer (in addition to being able to stretch farther).

Exercise/Date																			
	Duration																		
	Reps																		
	Duration																		
	Reps																		
	Duration																		
	Reps																		
	Duration																		
	Reps																		
	Duration																		
	Reps																		
	Duration																		
	Reps																		
	Duration																		
	Reps																		
	Duration																		
	Reps																		
	Duration																		
	Reps																		
	Duration																		
	Reps																		
	Duration																		
	Reps																		
	Duration																		
	Reps																		
	Duration																		
	Reps																		
	Duration																		
	Reps																		
	Duration																		
	Reps																		
	Duration																		
	Reps																		
	Duration																		
	Reps																		
	Duration																		
	Reps																		

Body Composition

LOOKING AHEAD

After reading this chapter, you should be able to answer these questions about body composition:

- What are fat-free mass, essential fat, and nonessential fat, and what are their functions in the body?

- How does body composition affect wellness?

- How are body composition and body fat distribution measured?

- What is recommended body weight, and how is it determined?

Body composition, the body's relative amount of fat and fat-free mass, is an important component of fitness for wellness. People whose body composition is optimal tend to be healthier, to move more efficiently, and to feel better about themselves. To reach wellness, you must determine what body composition is right for you and then work to achieve and maintain it.

Although people pay lip service to the idea of exercising for health, a more immediate goal for many is to look fit and healthy. Unfortunately, many people don't succeed in their efforts to obtain a fit and healthy body because they emphasize short-term weight loss rather than the permanent changes in lifestyle that lead to fat loss and a healthy body composition. Successful management of body composition requires the coordination of many aspects of a wellness program, including proper nutrition, adequate exercise, and stress management.

This chapter focuses on defining and measuring body composition and determining recommended body weight; Chapter 9 provides specific strategies for changing your lifestyle to reach your body composition goal.

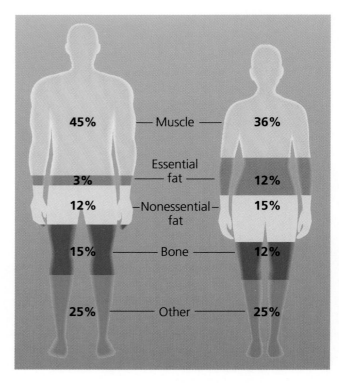

Figure 6-1   Body composition of a typical man and woman, 20–24 years old.   SOURCE: Adapted from Brooks, G. A., T. D. Fahey, and T. P. White. 1996. *Exercise Physiology: Human Bioenergetics and Its Applications,* 2d ed. Mountain View, Calif.: Mayfield.

WHAT IS BODY COMPOSITION, AND WHY IS IT IMPORTANT?

The human body can be divided into fat-free mass and body fat. Fat-free mass is composed of all the body's non-fat tissues: bone, water, muscle, connective tissue, organ tissues, and teeth. Body fat includes both essential and nonessential body fats (Figure 6-1). **Essential fat** includes lipids incorporated into the nerves, brain, heart, lungs, liver, and mammary glands. These fat deposits, crucial for normal body functioning, make up approximately 3% of total body weight in men and 12% in women. (The larger percentage in women is due to fat deposits in the breasts, uterus, and other sites specific to females.) **Nonessential (storage) fat** exists primarily within fat cells, or **adipose tissue,** often located just below the skin and around major organs. The amount of storage fat varies from individual to individual based on many factors, including gender, age, heredity, metabolism, diet, and activity level. Excess storage fat is usually the result of consuming more energy (as food) than is expended (in metabolism and physical activity).

How much body fat is too much? In the past, many people relied on height-weight tables based on insurance company mortality statistics to answer this question. Unfortunately, these tables can be highly inaccurate for some people; at best, they provide only an indirect measure of fatness. Because, as explained in Chapter 4, muscle tissue is denser and heavier than fat, a fit person can easily weigh more and an unfit person weigh less than recommended weights on a height-weight table.

The most important consideration when a person is looking at body composition is the proportion of the body's total weight that is fat—the **percent body fat.** For example, two women may both be 5 feet, 5 inches tall and weigh 130 pounds. But one woman, a runner, may have only 15% of her body mass as fat, whereas the second, sedentary woman could have 33% body fat. While neither woman is overweight by most standards, the second woman is overfat. Too much body fat (not total weight) has a negative effect on health and well-being.

Some of the most commonly used methods to assess and classify body composition are described later in the chapter. Although less accurate than standards based on body fat, some methods are based on total body weight because it is easier to measure. **Overweight** is usually defined as total body weight above the recommended range for good health (as determined by large-scale population surveys). **Obesity** is defined as a more serious degree of overweight; the cutoff point for obesity may be set in terms of percent body fat, as in Table 6-1, or in terms of some measure of total body weight.

By any measure, Americans are getting fatter. Since 1960, the number of Americans having a body composition categorized as obese has nearly doubled (from 13% to 22%), and more than 50% of American adults are now overweight. The reason for increased body fat in the pop-

Negative Health Consequences of Obesity

An obese person is at increased risk for the following:

Early death

Death from CVD, including sudden death

Hypertension

Diabetes

Gallbladder disease

Cancer of the colon, prostate, esophagus, gallbladder, ovary, endometrium, breast, and cervix

Arthritis and gout

Back pain

Complications during pregnancy

Menstrual abnormalities

Shortness of breath

Sleep apnea (intermittent cessation of breathing while sleeping)

Obesity is also associated with the following:

Increased LDL and triglyceride concentrations

Decreased HDL concentration

Impaired heart function (ventricles)

Impaired immune function

---

ulation is not totally clear, but it is related to decreased physical activity and increased caloric consumption. As discussed in Chapter 2, more than half of all Americans do not meet the minimum recommendation of 30 minutes per day of moderate physical activity. More people are working in white-collar and service professions than in jobs involving physical activity. And increased access to items such as home computers and cable television has also contributed to more sedentary lifestyles. In addition to exercising less, Americans are eating more. The Centers for Disease Control and Prevention has estimated that caloric intake has increased by 100–300 calories per day during the past decade. (For more on the causes of obesity, see Chapter 9.)

Though not as prevalent a problem, having too little body fat is also dangerous (see Table 6-1). Too much or too little body fat can have negative effects on health, performance, and self-image.

Health

Obesity is associated with a wide variety of health problems, many of which are listed in the box "Negative Health Consequences of Obesity." Obese people have an overall mortality rate almost twice that of nonobese people. They are more than five times as likely to develop diabetes (see the box "Diabetes"). In 1998, the American Heart Association classified obesity as one of the five major risk factors for heart disease. It is estimated that if all Americans had a healthy body composition, the incidence of coronary heart disease would drop by 25%.

The distribution of fat is also an important indicator of future health. People who tend to gain weight in the abdominal area ("apples") have a risk of coronary heart disease, high blood pressure, diabetes, and stroke twice as high as that of people who tend to gain weight in the hip area ("pears"). The reason for this increased risk is not

| TABLE 6-1 | Percent Body Fat Classifications |

Percent Body Fat

Males	Females	Classification
Less than 5%	Less than 8%	Excessively lean
5–11%	8–19%	Lean
12–20%	20–30%	Acceptable
21–25%	31–33%	Borderline obese
More than 25%	More than 33%	Obese

These represent approximate standards for body composition; the healthy range varies, depending on health status and risk factors for disease. For example, a man with high blood pressure and high cholesterol levels might want to reduce his percentage of body fat, even if it is within the acceptable range for the general population.

TERMS

essential fat   The fat in the body necessary for normal body functioning.

nonessential (storage) fat   Extra fat or fat reserves stored in the body.

adipose tissue   Connective tissue in which fat is stored.

percent body fat   The percentage of total body weight that is composed of fat.

overweight   Characterized by a body weight above a recommended range for good health; ranges are set through large-scale population surveys.

obese   Severely overweight, characterized by an excessive accumulation of body fat: more than 25% of body weight as fat in men, and more than 33% as fat in women. Obesity may also be defined in terms of some measure of total body weight.

Diabetes mellitus is a disease that causes a disruption of normal metabolism. The pancreas, a long, thin organ located behind the stomach, normally secretes the hormone insulin, which stimulates cells to take up glucose to produce energy. In a person with diabetes, this process is disrupted, causing a buildup of glucose in the bloodstream. Over the long term, diabetes is associated with kidney failure, nerve damage, circulation problems, retinal damage and blindness, and increased rates of heart attack, stroke, and hypertension. The rate of diabetes has increased steadily over the past 40 years, and it is currently the seventh leading cause of death in the United States.

Types of Diabetes

Approximately 16 million Americans—nearly 6% of the population—have one of two major forms of diabetes. About 5–10% of people with diabetes have the more serious form, known as Type 1 diabetes. In this type of diabetes, the pancreas produces little or no insulin, so daily doses of insulin are required. (Without insulin, a person with Type 1 can lapse into a coma.) Type 1 diabetes usually strikes before age 20.

The remaining 15 million Americans with diabetes have Type 2 diabetes. This condition can develop slowly, and about half of affected individuals are unaware of their condition. In Type 2 diabetes, the pancreas doesn't produce enough insulin, the cells don't respond to the hormone, or both. This condition is usually diagnosed in people over age 40. About one-third of people with Type 2 diabetes must inject insulin; others may take medications that increase insulin production or stimulate cells to take up glucose.

A third type of diabetes occurs in some women during pregnancy. So-called *gestational diabetes* usually disappears after pregnancy, but more than half of women who experience it eventually develop Type 2 diabetes.

The major factors involved in the development of diabetes are age, obesity, physical inactivity, a family history of diabetes, and lifestyle. Excess body fat reduces cell sensitivity to insulin, and it is a major risk factor for Type 2 diabetes. Ethnic background also plays a role. African Americans and people of Hispanic background are 55% more likely than non-Hispanic whites to develop Type 2 diabetes. Native Americans also have a higher-than-average incidence of diabetes.

Treatment

There is no cure for diabetes, but it can be successfully managed. Treatment involves keeping blood sugar levels within safe limits through diet, exercise, and, if necessary, medication. Blood sugar levels can be monitored using a home test. Recent research indicates that close monitoring and control of glucose levels can significantly reduce the rate of serious complications among people with diabetes. Nearly 90% of people with Type 2 diabetes are overweight when diagnosed, and an important step in treatment is to lose weight. Even a small amount of weight loss can be beneficial. People with diabetes should eat regular meals with an emphasis on complex carbohydrates and ample dietary fiber; a physician or dietitian can help design a healthy eating plan. Regular exercise and a healthy diet are often sufficient to control Type 2 diabetes.

Prevention

Recent studies have shown that exercise can help prevent the development of Type 2 diabetes, a benefit especially important in individuals with one or more risk factors for the disease. Exercise burns excess sugar and makes cells more sensitive to insulin. Exercise also helps keep body fat at healthy levels.

Eating a moderate diet to help control body fat is perhaps the most important dietary recommendation for the prevention of diabetes. However, there is some evidence that the composition of the diet may also be important. In a long-term study of over 65,000 nurses, a diet low in fiber and high in sugar and refined carbohydrates was found to increase risk for Type 2 diabetes. The foods most closely linked to higher diabetes risk were regular (non-diet) cola beverages, white bread, white rice, french fries, and potatoes; consumption of cereal fibers such as those found in cold breakfast cereals was associated with lower risk. (Chapter 8 includes more information on different types of carbohydrates as well as specific strategies for increasing fiber intake.)

Warning Signs and Testing

A wellness lifestyle that includes a healthy diet and regular exercise is the best strategy for preventing diabetes. If you do develop diabetes, the best way to avoid complications is to recognize the symptoms and get early diagnosis and treatment. Be alert for the following warning signs:

- Frequent urination
- Extreme hunger or thirst
- Unexplained weight loss
- Extreme fatigue
- Blurred vision
- Frequent infections, especially of the bladder, gums, skin, or vagina
- Cuts and bruises that are slow to heal
- Tingling or numbness in the hands and feet
- Generalized itching, with no rash

Type 2 diabetes is often asymptomatic in the early stages, and major health organizations now recommend routine screening for people over age 45 and anyone younger who is at high risk. (The Web site for the American Diabetes Association, listed in the For More Information section at the end of the chapter, includes an interactive diabetes risk assessment.) Screening involves a blood test to check glucose levels after either a period of fasting or the administration of a set dose of glucose. If you are concerned about your risk for diabetes, talk with your physician about being tested.

If you gaze into the mirror and wish you could change the way your body looks, consider getting some exercise—not to re-shape your contours but to firm up your self-image. According to a recent study from University College London, women who worked out on a regular basis rated their bodies as more attractive and healthy than women who didn't get much physical activity. Of course, the exercisers may have had particularly attractive bodies, but it should be noted that they were more satisfied than the sedentary women, even though they weighed an average of 11–12 pounds more, suggesting that active women are more comfortable bucking the model-thin look that has become our cultural ideal.

One reason for the findings may be that women who exercise regularly often gain a sense of mastery and competence that enhances their self-esteem and body image. In addition, exercise contributes to a more toned look, which some women prefer. Then, too, participating in sports where size and height are advantageous, like volleyball or basketball, may help tall, relatively large women appreciate their body size and shape enough to see beyond cultural stereotypes. Finally, regular exercise and a positive family environment go hand in hand; family support provides the security to accept "sporty" body shapes even if they aren't picture-perfect by society's standards.

None of this is to say that whether a woman exercises regularly is the only factor that influences the way her body looks to her. Even the sport she prefers or engages in plays a role. In the British study, female body builders, not surprisingly, rated muscular physiques more favorably than women who chose rowing as their sport. In another study in which women were randomly assigned to weight training or brisk walking, body image improved for both groups, but more so for the weight lifters. Despite these other factors, though, the research suggests that as a group, physically active women are more comfortable with their bodies than sedentary women and are particularly tolerant of shapes that deviate from the model-thin icons.

SOURCES: Adapted from "Shape Up Your Body Image." 1995. *Tufts University Diet and Nutrition Letter,* May, p. 8. Tucker, L. A., and R. Mortell. 1993. Comparison of the effects of walking and weight training programs on body image in middle-aged women: An experimental study. *American Journal of Health Promotion* 8(1): 34–42.

---

entirely clear, but it appears that fat in the abdomen is more easily mobilized and sent into the bloodstream, increasing disease-related blood fat levels. In general, men tend to gain weight in the abdominal area and women in the hip area, but women who exhibit the male pattern of fat distribution face the increased health risks associated with it. Researchers have also found ethnic differences in the relative significance of increased abdominal fat, but more studies are needed to clarify the relationship among fat distribution, ethnicity, and disease.

Body fat distribution is usually assessed by calculating the waist-to-hip ratio (the relative circumference of the waist and hips) or by simply measuring the waist. A person doesn't have to be technically overfat to have fat distribution be a risk factor, nor do all overfat people face this increased risk. However, individuals in the obese range should not be complacent about their body composition regardless of their fat distribution—all obesity has serious health consequences.

Is it possible to be too lean? Health experts have generally viewed too little body fat—less than 8% for women and 5% for men—as a threat to health and well-being. Extreme leanness has been linked with reproductive, circulatory, and immune system disorders. Extremely lean people may experience muscle wasting and fatigue; they are also more likely to suffer from a dangerous eating disorder. For women, an extremely low percentage of body fat is associated with **amenorrhea** and loss of bone mass. However, a recent study from Harvard Medical School found that among nonsmoking women who did not suffer from eating disorders, the leanest lived longer than women of "normal" weight. The authors of this study concluded that even mild to moderate overweight is associated with a substantial increase in the risk of premature death. Additional research is needed to determine all the effects of extremely low body fat levels on health.

Performance of Physical Activities

Too much body fat makes all types of physical activity more difficult because just moving the body through everyday activities means working harder and using more energy. In general, overfat people are less fit than others and don't have the muscular strength, endurance, and flexibility that make normal activity easy. Because exercise is more difficult, they do less of it, depriving themselves of an effective way to improve body composition.

Self-Image

The "fashionable" body image has changed dramatically during the past 50 years, varying from slightly plump to an almost unhealthy thinness. Today a fit and healthy-looking body, developed through a healthy lifestyle, is the goal for most people (see the box "Exercise and Body Image"). And the key to this "look" is a balance of proper nutrition and exercise—in short, a lifestyle that emphasizes wellness.

amenorrhea   Absent or infrequent menstruation, sometimes **TERMS** related to low levels of body fat and excessive quantity or intensity of exercise.

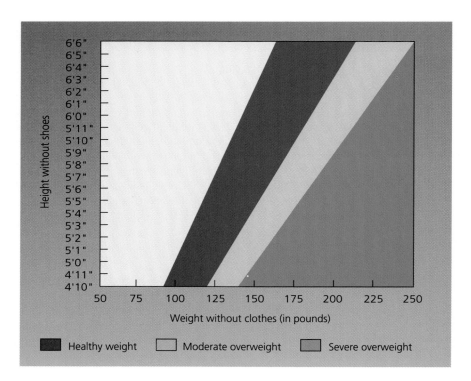

Figure 6-2 Suggested weights for adults. Weights are grouped in ranges because people of the same height may have equal amounts of body fat but different amounts of muscle and bone. The higher weights in each range apply to people with more muscle and bone, such as many men. Although weights are presented in ranges, gaining weight over time, even within the same range, is not healthy. SOURCE: Adapted from U.S. Department of Agriculture. Agricultural Research Service. Dietary Guidelines Committee. 1995. *Report of the Dietary Guidelines Advisory Committee on the Dietary Guidelines for Americans.* Springfield, Va.: National Technical Information Service, pp. 23–24.

Goals for body composition should be realistic, however; a person's ability to change body composition through diet and exercise depends not only on a wellness program, but also on heredity. Unrealistic expectations about body composition can have a negative impact on self-image and can lead to the development of eating disorders. (For more information on eating disorders, see Chapter 9.)

For most people, body fat percentage falls somewhere between ideal and a level that is significantly unhealthy. If they consistently maintain a wellness lifestyle that includes a healthy diet and regular exercise, the right body composition will naturally develop.

Wellness for Life

A healthy body composition is vital for wellness throughout life. Strong scientific evidence suggests that controlling your weight will increase your life span; reduce the risk of heart disease, cancer, diabetes, and back pain; increase your energy level; and improve your self-esteem.

TERMS **body mass index (BMI)** A measure of relative body weight correlating highly with more direct measures of body fat, calculated by dividing total body weight (in kilograms) by the square of body height (in meters).

ASSESSING BODY COMPOSITION

The morning weighing ritual on the bathroom scale can't reveal whether a fluctuation in weight is due to a change in muscle, body water, or fat and can't differentiate between overweight and overfat. A 260-pound football player may be overweight according to population height-weight standards yet actually have much less body fat than average. Likewise, a 40-year-old woman may weigh the same as she did 20 years earlier yet have a considerably different body composition. Despite these limitations, the U.S. Food and Drug Administration (FDA) and the Department of Health and Human Services have published new height and weight recommendations, shown in Figure 6-2.

There are a number of simple, inexpensive ways to estimate body composition that are superior to the bathroom scale. These methods include body mass index and skinfold measurements.

Body Mass Index

Body mass index (BMI) is a rough measure of body composition that is useful if you don't have access to sophisticated equipment. Though more accurate than height-weight tables, body mass index is also based on the concept that a person's weight should be proportional to height. The measurement is fairly accurate for people who do not have an unusual amount of muscle mass and

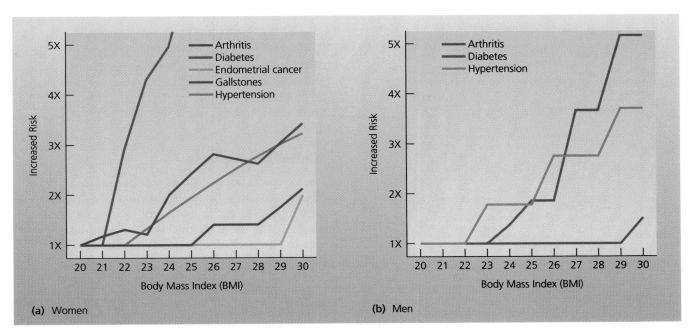

Figure 6-3 BMI and risk of health problems.   SOURCE: How's your weight? 1997. *Nutrition Action Healthletter,* December. Copyright © 1997 CSPI. Adapted from Nutrition Action Health Letter (1875 Connecticut Avenue, N. W., Suite 300, Washington D. C. 20009-5728. $24.00 for 10 issues.)

| **TABLE 6-2** | *Classification of Overweight and Obesity by BMI* |

| | | | Disease risk relative to normal weight and waist circumference[a] | |
Classification	BMI (kg/m²)	Obesity class	Men ≤ 40 in. (102 cm) Women ≤ 35 in. (88 cm)	> 40 in. (102 cm) > 35 in. (88 cm)
Underweight[b]	less than 18.5		—	—
Normal[c]	18.5–24.9		—	—
Overweight	25.0–29.9		Increased	High
Obesity	30.0–34.9	I	High	Very high
	35.0–39.9	II	Very high	Very high
Extreme obesity	40.0 and higher	III	Extremely high	Extremely high

[a]Disease risk for type 2 diabetes, hypertension, and CVD. The waist circumference cutoff points for increased risk are 40 inches (102 cm) for men and 35 inches (88 cm) for women.

[b]Research suggests that a low BMI can be healthy in some cases, as long as it is not the result of smoking, an eating disorder, or an underlying disease process.

[c]Increased waist circumference can also be a marker for increased risk even in persons of normal weight.

SOURCE: Adapted from National Heart, Lung, and Blood Institute. 1998. *Clinical Guidelines on the Identification, Evaluation, and Treatment of Overweight and Obesity in Adults: The Evidence Report.* Bethesda, Md.: National Institutes of Health.

who are not very short. BMI is calculated by dividing your body weight (expressed in kilograms) by the square of your height (expressed in meters). For example, a person who weighs 130 pounds (59 kilograms) and is 5 feet, 3 inches tall (1.6 meters) would have a BMI of 59 kg ÷ (1.6 m)², or 23 kg/m². (Refer to Lab 6-1 for instructions on how to calculate your BMI.)

The relative risk for several health problems associated with different values of BMI is shown in Figure 6-3. At high values of BMI, the risk of arthritis, diabetes, hypertension, endometrial cancer, and other disorders increases substantially. The increased risk of diabetes at even fairly low values of BMI especially among women is of particular concern.

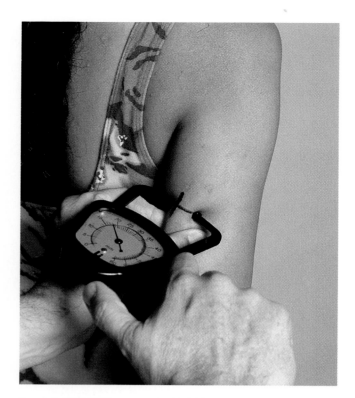

Proper technique is important in skinfold measurement. It's best to take several measurements at each site to ensure accuracy.

In June 1998, new federal guidelines for classifying overweight and obesity on the basis of BMI were released by the National Heart, Lung, and Blood Institute (NHLBI), a division of the National Institutes of Health. Under these guidelines, a person is classified as overweight if he or she has a BMI of 25 or above and obese if he or she has a BMI of 30 or above (Table 6-2). Previously, the cutoff point for defining overweight was higher; the new guidelines reflect standards used in other countries as well as by the World Health Organization. Nearly 55% of American adults have a BMI of 25 or above.

In classifying the health risks associated with overweight and obesity, the new NHLBI guidelines consider body fat distribution and other disease risk factors in addition to BMI. As described earlier, excess fat in the abdomen is of greater concern that excess fat in other areas. Methods of assessing body fat distribution are discussed later in the chapter; the NHLBI guidelines use measurement of waist circumference (see Table 6-2). At a given level of overweight, people with a large waist circumference and/or additional disease risk factors are at greater risk for health problems. For example, a man with a BMI of 27, a waist circumference above 40 inches, and high

blood pressure is at greater risk for health problems than another man who has a BMI of 27 but has a smaller waist circumference and no other risk factors. Thus, optimal BMI for good health depends on many factors; if your BMI is 25 or above, consult a physician for help in determining a healthy BMI for you. (Weight loss recommendations based on the NHLBI guidelines are discussed further in Chapter 9.)

Skinfold Measurements

Skinfold measurement is a simple, inexpensive, and practical way to assess body composition. Skinfold measurements can be used to assess body composition because equations can link the thickness of skinfolds at various sites to percent body fat calculations from more precise laboratory techniques.

Skinfolds are measured with a device called a **caliper,** which consists of a pair of spring-loaded, calibrated jaws. High-quality calipers are made of metal and have parallel jaw surfaces and constant spring tension. Inexpensive plastic calipers are also available; to ensure accuracy, plastic calipers should be spring-loaded and have metal jaws.

Refer to Lab 6-1 for the procedure for taking skinfold measurements. Taking accurate measurements with calipers requires patience, experience, and considerable practice. It's best to take several measurements at each site (or have several different people take each measurement) to help ensure accuracy. Be sure to take the measurements in the exact location called for in the procedure. Because the amount of water in your body changes during the day, skinfold measurements taken in the morning and evening often differ. If you repeat the measurements in the future to track changes in your body composition, measure skinfolds at approximately the same time of day.

Other Methods of Measuring Body Composition

Most of the many other methods for determining body composition are very sophisticated and require expensive equipment. Two methods available in many health clubs and sports medicine clinics are underwater weighing and bioelectrical impedance analysis.

Underwater Weighing Hydrostatic (underwater) weighing is considered the most accurate indirect way to measure body composition. It is the standard used for other techniques, including skinfold measurements. For this method, an individual is submerged and weighed under water. The percentages of fat and fat-free weight are calculated from body density. Muscle has a higher density and fat a lower density than water (1.1 grams per cubic centimeter for fat-free mass, 0.91 gram per cubic centimeter for fat, and 1 gram per cubic centimeter for water). Therefore, fat people tend to float and weigh less under water, and lean people tend to sink and weigh more under water.

TERMS **caliper** A pressure-sensitive measuring instrument with two jaws that can be adjusted to determine thickness.

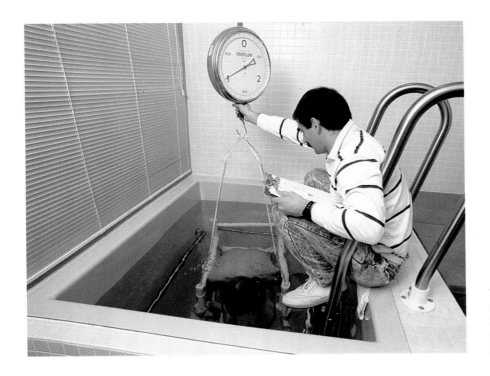

This man is having his body composition assessed in an underwater weighing tank. Muscle has a higher density than water, so people with more lean body mass weigh more under water.

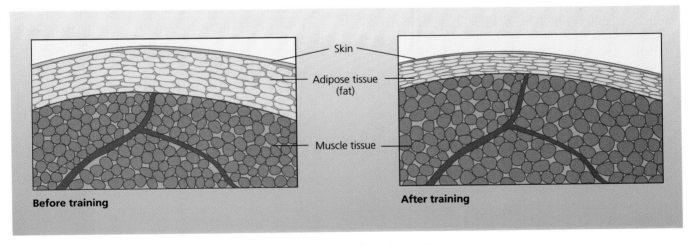

Before training

After training

Skin

Adipose tissue (fat)

Muscle tissue

Figure 6-4   Effects of exercise on body composition.   Endurance exercise and strength training reduce body fat and increase muscle mass.

Although somewhat cumbersome and expensive, this method is not beyond limited budgets. A harness and a spring-loaded scale can be connected to a diving board, and the school pool can be used as the underwater weighing tank. Most university exercise physiology departments or sports medicine laboratories will have an underwater weighing facility. If you want an accurate assessment of your body composition, find a place that does underwater weighing.

Bioelectrical Impedance Analysis (BIA)   The technique works by sending a small electrical current through the body and measuring the body's resistance to it. Fat-free tissues, where most body water is located, are good conductors of electrical current, while fat is not. Thus, the amount of resistance to electrical current is related to the amount of fat-free tissue in the body can be used to estimate percent body fat. Bioelectrical impedance analysis is fairly accurate for most people (about the same as skinfold measurements). To avoid error, it is important to follow the manufacturer's instructions carefully and to avoid overhydration or underhydration (more or less body water than normal). Because measurement varies with the type of BIA analyzer, use the same instrument to compare measurements over time.

Assessing Body Fat Distribution

Researchers have studied many different methods for determining the risk associated with body fat distribution. Two of the simplest to perform are waist circumference measurement and waist-to-hip ratio calculation. In the first method, you measure your waist circumference; in the second, you divide your waist circumference by your hip circumference. More research is needed to determine the precise degree of risk associated with specific values for these two assessments of body fat distribution. However, a total waist measurement over 40 inches (102 cm) for men and 35 inches (88 cm) for women and a waist-to-hip ratio above 0.95 for men and 0.86 for women are associated with a significantly increased risk of disease. Follow the instructions in Lab 6-1 to measure and rate your body fat distribution.

DETERMINING RECOMMENDED BODY WEIGHT

If the assessment tests indicate that fat loss would be beneficial for you, your first step is to establish a goal. Use the ratings in Table 6-1 or Table 6-2 to choose a target value for percent body fat or BMI (depending on which type of assessment you completed). Select a goal for percent body fat or BMI that is realistic for you and will ensure good health. Make sure your goal is realistic. Genetics may limit your capacity to change your body composition. Few people can expect to develop the body of a fashion model or competitive body builder. However, you can improve your body composition through a regular program of exercise and a healthy diet. If you have known risk factors for disease, such as high blood pressure or high levels of blood cholesterol, consult your physician to determine the ideal body composition for your individual risk profile.

Once you've established your goal, you can calculate a target body weight. (Though body weight is not an accurate means of assessing body composition, it's a useful method for tracking progress in a program to change body composition. If you're losing a small or moderate amount of weight and exercising, you're probably losing fat while building muscle mass.) Follow the instructions in Lab 6-2 to put the results of all the assessment tests together, get an overview of your body composition, and determine a range for recommended body weight.

Using percent body fat or BMI will generate a fairly accurate target body weight for most people. However, it's best not to stick rigidly to a recommended body weight calculated from any formula; individual genetic, cultural, and lifestyle factors are also important. Decide whether the body weight that the formulas generate for you is realistic, meets all your goals, is healthy, *and* is reasonable for you to maintain.

After selecting your overall goal, set realistic intermediate goals. For example, if you want to lose a total of 10 pounds, you might set short-term goals of losing 2 pounds during the first month of your program and 2 more pounds during the second month. To help ensure success, reevaluate your program and your goals frequently.

Track your progress toward your target body composition by checking your body weight periodically. To get a more accurate idea of your progress, especially when weight loss is large, you should directly reassess your body composition occasionally during your program: Body composition changes as weight changes. Losing a lot of weight usually includes losing some muscle mass no matter how hard a person exercises, partly because carrying less weight requires the muscular system to bear a smaller burden. (Conversely, a large gain in weight without exercise still causes some gain in muscle mass because muscles are working harder to carry the extra weight.)

See Chapter 9 for specific strategies for losing or gaining weight and improving body composition.

COMMON QUESTIONS ANSWERED

Is spot reducing effective?   No. Spot reducing refers to attempts to lose body fat in specific parts of the body by doing exercises for those parts. For example, a person might try to spot reduce in the legs by doing leg lifts. Spot-reducing exercises contribute to fat loss only to the extent that they burn calories. The only way you can reduce fat in any specific area is to create an overall negative energy balance: Take in less energy (food) than you use up through exercise and metabolism.

How does exercise affect body composition?   Cardiorespiratory endurance exercise burns calories, thereby helping create a negative energy balance. Weight training does not use many calories and therefore is of little use in creating a negative

energy balance. However, weight training increases muscle mass, which maintains a high metabolic rate (the body's energy level) and helps improve body composition. To minimize body fat and increase muscle mass, thereby improving body composition, combine cardiorespiratory endurance exercise and weight training (Figure 6-4).

How do I develop a toned, healthy-looking body?   The development of a healthy-looking body requires regular exercise, proper diet, and other good health habits. However, it helps to have heredity on your side. Some people put on or take off fat more easily than others just as some people are taller than

(continued)

others. Be realistic in your goals, and be satisfied with the improvements in body composition you can make by observing the principles of a wellness lifestyle.

Are people who have a desirable body composition physically fit? Having a healthy body composition is not necessarily associated with overall fitness. For example, many body builders have very little body fat but have poor cardiorespiratory capacity and flexibility. To be fit, you must rate high on all the components of fitness.

What is liposuction, and will it help me lose body fat? Suction lipectomy, popularly known as liposuction, has become the most popular type of elective surgery in the United States. The procedure involves removing limited amounts of fat from specific areas. Typically, no more than 2.5 kg (5.5 lb) of adipose tissue is removed at a time. The procedure is usually successful if the amount of excess fat is limited and skin elas-

ticity is good. The procedure is most effective if integrated into a program of dietary restriction and exercise. Side effects include infection, dimpling, and wavy skin contours. Although serious complications are rare, liposuction, like any surgical procedure, can lead to blood clots, shock, bleeding, impaired blood flow to vital organs, and even death. Liposuction is not an effective way to lose large amounts of fat, nor should it be a substitute for a healthy weight-management program.

What is cellulite, and how do I get rid of it? Cellulite is the name commonly given to ripply, wavy fat deposits that collect just under the skin. However, these rippling fat deposits are really the same as fat deposited anywhere else in the body. The only way to control them is to create a negative energy balance—burn up more calories than are taken in. There are no creams or lotions that will rub away surface (subcutaneous) fat deposits, and spot reducing is also ineffective. The only solution is sensible eating habits and exercise.

SUMMARY

- The human body is composed of fat-free mass (which includes bone, muscle, organ tissues, and connective tissues) and body fat (essential and nonessential).

- Having too much body fat has negative health consequences, especially in terms of cardiovascular disease. Distribution of fat is also a significant factor in health.

- A fit and healthy-looking body, with the right body composition for a particular person, develops from habits of proper nutrition and exercise.

- Measuring body weight is not an accurate way to assess body composition because it does not differentiate between muscle weight and fat weight.

- Two measurements of body composition are body mass index (formulated through weight and height measurements) and percent body fat (formulated through skinfold measurements).

- Hydrostatic weighing, the most accurate indirect measure of body composition, is based on body density; muscle has a higher density and fat a lower density than water. Bioelectrical impedance analysis estimates the amount of body water (and thereby fat-free tissue) by measuring the body's resistance to a small electrical current.

- Body fat distribution can be assessed through the waist-to-hip ratio or the total waist measurement.

- Recommended body weight can be determined by choosing a target BMI or target body fat percentage. Keep heredity in mind when setting a goal.

FOR MORE INFORMATION

Underwater weighing and bioelectrical impedance analysis are often available through campus adult fitness programs, and health clubs may also provide tests for percent body fat.

Books

American Diabetes Association. 1997. *American Diabetes Association Complete Guide to Diabetes: The Ultimate Home Diabetes Reference.* Alexandria, Va.: American Diabetes Association. *Explains the symptoms, causes, diagnosis, treatment, and self-care of diabetes.*

Brooks, G. A., T. D. Fahey, and T. P. White. 1996. *Exercise Physiology: Human Bioenergetics and Its Applications,* 2d ed. Mountain View, Calif.: Mayfield. *A basic exercise physiology textbook that describes principles of metabolism and body composition.*

Heyward, V. H., and L. M. Stolarczyk. 1996. *Applied Body Composition Assessment.* Champaign, Ill.: Human Kinetics. *Describes different methods of measuring and assessing body composition.*

Roche, A. F., S. T. Heymsfield, and T. G. Lohman. 1996. *Human Body Composition.* Champaign, Ill.: Human Kinetics. *This book discusses the theory and measurement of human body composition. Although it is mainly directed at sports scientists, people who are seriously interested in exercise might also be interested.*

Organizations and Web Sites

American Diabetes Association. Provides information, a free newsletter, and referrals to local support groups; the Web site includes an online diabetes risk assessment.

800-342-2383

http://www.diabetes.org

Healthy Body Calculator. Calculates and evaluates BMI, body weight, and waist-to-hip ratio.

http://www.dietitian.com/ibw

Shape Up America. A site devoted to promoting healthy weight management; calculates and rates BMI and looks at why BMI is an important measure of health.

http://shapeup.org

National Heart, Lung, and Blood Institute. Provides information on the latest federal obesity standards and a BMI calculator.

http://www.nhlbi.nih.gov/nhlbi/nhlbi.htm

National Institute of Diabetes and Digestive and Kidney Diseases Health Information/Nutrition and Obesity. Provides information about adult obesity: how it is defined and assessed, the risk factors associated with it, and its causes.

800-WIN-8090

http://www.niddk.nih.gov/health/nutrit/nutrit.htm

See also the listings for Chapters 2 and 9.

SELECTED BIBLIOGRAPHY

American College of Sports Medicine. 1995. *Guidelines for Exercise Testing and Prescription.* Baltimore: Williams & Wilkins.

American Heart Association. 1998. Press Release: Obesity Joins American Heart Association's List of Major Risk Factors for Heart Attack (retrieved June 2, 1998; http:www.american heart.org/whats_News/AHA_News_Releases/obesity.html).

Bender, R., C. Trautner, M. Spraul, and M. Berger. 1998. Assessment of excess mortality in obesity. *American Journal of Epidemiology* 147:42–48.

Broeder, C. E., et al. 1997. Assessing body composition before and after resistance or endurance training. *Medicine and Science in Sports and Exercise* 29(5): 705–712.

Center for Disease Control and Prevention. 1997. Trends in the prevalence and incidence of self-reported diabetes mellitus—United States, 1980–1994. *Morbidity and Mortality Weekly Report* 46(43): 1014–1018.

Chow, W. H., et al. 1998. Body mass index and risk of adenocarcinomas of the esophagus and gastric cardia. *Journal of the National Cancer Institute* 90(2): 150–155.

De Lorenzo, A., et al. 1997. Predicting body cell mass with bioimpedance by using theoretical methods: A technological review. *Journal of Applied Physiology* 82:1542–1558.

Diabetes: Weight control and exercise may keep you off the road to high blood sugar. 1998. *Mayo Clinic Health Letter Supplement,* February.

Ellis, K. J. 1997. Body composition of a young, multiethnic, male population. *American Journal of Clinical Nutrition* 66:1323–1331.

Guo, S. S., et al. 1997. Age- and maturity-related changes in body composition during adolescence into adulthood: The Fels Longitudinal Study. *International Journal of Obesity Related Metabolic Disorders* 21:1167–1175.

Han, T. S., et al. 1996. Waist circumference as a screening tool for cardiovascular risk factors: Evaluation of receiver operating characteristics (ROC). *Obesity Research* 4:533–547.

Huddy, D. C., et al. 1997. Relationship between body image and percent body fat among male and female college students enrolled in an introductory 14-week weight-training course. *Perceptual and Motor Skills* 85(3 Pt 1): 1075–1078.

Keller, C., and K. T. Thomas. 1997. Assessment of overweight and obese patients. *Nurse Pract Forum* 8:99–104.

Lemieux, S., et al. 1996. A single threshold value of waist girth identifies normal-weight and overweight subjects with excess visceral adipose tissue. *American Journal of Clinical Nutrition* 64:685–693.

Manson, J. E., et al. 1995. Body weight and mortality among women. *New England Journal of Medicine* 333(11): 677–685.

National Heart, Lung, and Blood Institute. 1998. *Clinical Guidelines on the Identification, Evaluation, and Treatment of Overweight and Obesity in Adults: The Evidence Report.* Bethesda, Md.: National Institutes of Health.

Nguyen, T. V., et al. 1998. Bone mass, lean mass, and fat mass: Same genes or same environments? *American Journal of Epidemiology* 147(1): 3–16.

Norgan, N. G. 1997. The beneficial effects of body fat and adipose tissue in humans. *International Journal of Obesity Related Metabolic Disorders* 21:738–746.

Otis, C. L., et al. 1997. American College of Sports Medicine position stand. The Female Athlete Triad. *Medicine and Science in Sports and Exercise* 29:I–IX.

Pichard, C., et al. 1997. Body composition by x-ray absorptiometry and bioelectrical impedance in female runners. *Medicine and Science in Sports and Exercise* 29(11): 1527–1534.

Salmeró, J., et al. 1997. Dietary fiber, glycemic load, and risk of non-insulin-dependent diabetes mellitus in women. *Journal of the American Medical Association* 277(6): 472–477.

Snyder, K. A., et al. 1997. The effects of long-term, moderate intensity, intermittent exercise on aerobic capacity, body composition, blood lipids, insulin and glucose in overweight females. *International Journal of Obesity Related Metabolic Disorders* 21:1180–1189.

Stevens, J., et al. 1998. The effect of age on the association between body-mass index and mortality. *New England Journal of Medicine* 338(1): 1–7.

Taylor, R. W., et al. 1998. Body mass index, waist girth, and waist-to-hip ratio as indexes of total and regional adiposity in women: Evaluation using receiver operating characteristic curves. *American Journal of Clinical Nutrition* 67:44–49.

To, W. W., M. W. Wong, and K. M. Chan. 1997. Association between body composition and menstrual dysfunction in collegiate dance students. *Journal of Obstetrics and Gynaecology Research* 23:529–535.

Wallberg-Henriksson, H., J. Rincon, and J. R. Zierath. 1998. Exercise in the management of non-insulin-dependent diabetes mellitus. *Sports Medicine* 25(1): 25–35.

Zannolli, R., and G. Morgese. 1996. Waist percentiles: A simple test for atherogenic disease? *Acta Paediatrica* 85:1368–1369.

LAB 6-1 *Assessing Body Composition*

Body Mass Index

Equipment

1. Weight scale
2. Tape measure or other means of measuring height

Preparation

None

Instructions

Measure your height and weight, and record the results. Be sure to record the unit of measurement.

Height: _____   Weight: _____

Calculating BMI

1. Convert your body weight to kilograms by dividing your weight in pounds by 2.2.

   Body weight _____ lb ÷ 2.2 lb/kg = body weight _____ kg

2. Convert your height measurement to meters by multiplying your height in inches by 0.0254.

   Height _____ in. × 0.0254 m/in. = height _____ m

3. Square your height measurement.

   Height _____ m × height _____ m = height _____ m^2

4. BMI equals body weight in kilograms divided by height in meters squared (kg/m^2).

   Body weight _____ kg ÷ height _____ m^2 = BMI _____ kg/m^2

_(from step 1)   _(from step 3)

Rating Your BMI

Refer to Table 6-2 (p. 143) for a rating of your BMI. Record the results below and in the chart on the final page of this lab.

BMI _____ kg/m^2

Classification (from Table 6-2) _____

Skinfold Measurements

Equipment

1. Skinfold calipers
2. Partner to take measurements
3. Marking pen (optional)

Preparation

None

Instructions

1. *Select and locate the correct sites for measurement.* All measurements should be taken on the right side of the body with the subject standing. Skinfolds are normally measured on the natural fold line of the skin, either vertically or at a slight angle. The skinfold measurement sites for males are chest, abdomen, and thigh; for females, triceps, suprailium, and thigh. If the person taking skinfold measurements is inexperienced, it may be helpful to mark the correct sites with a marking pen.

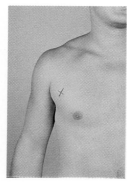 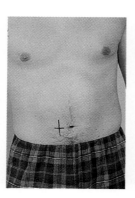 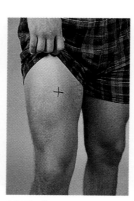  

(a) Chest   (b) Abdomen   (c) Thigh   (d) Triceps   (e) Suprailium

    (a) Chest. Pinch a diagonal fold halfway between the nipple and the shoulder crease. *(b) Abdomen.* Pinch a vertical fold about 1 inch to the right of the umbilicus (navel). *(c) Thigh.* Pinch a vertical fold midway between the top of the hipbone and the kneecap. *(d) Triceps.* Pinch a vertical skinfold on the back of the right arm midway between the shoulder and elbow. The elbow should be straight and should hang naturally. *(e) Suprailium.* Pinch a fold at the top front of the right hip-bone. The skinfold here is taken slightly diagonally according to the natural fold tendency of the skin.

2. *Measure the appropriate skinfolds.* Pinch a fold of skin between your thumb and forefinger. Pull the fold up so that no muscular tissue is included; don't pinch the skinfold too hard. Hold the calipers perpendicular to the fold, and measure the skinfold about 0.25 inch away from your fingers. Allow the tips of the calipers to close on the skinfold, and let the reading settle before marking it down. Take readings to the nearest half-millimeter. Continue to repeat the measurements until two consecutive measurements match, releasing and repinching the skinfold between each measurement. Make a note of the final measurement for each site.

    Time of day of measurements: _____

Men		*Women*	
Chest: _____ mm		Triceps: _____ mm	
Abdomen: _____ mm		Suprailium: _____ mm	
Thigh: _____ mm		Thigh: _____ mm	

Determining Percent Body Fat

Add the measurements of your three skinfolds, and then find the percent body fat that corresponds to your total in the appropriate table. For example, a 19-year-old female with measurements of 16 mm, 19 mm, and 22 mm would have a skinfold sum of 57 mm; according to the table on page 152, her percent body fat is 22.7.

Sum of three skinfolds: _____ mm

Percent body fat: _____ %

Rating Your Body Composition

Refer to the table on page 153 to rate your percent body fat. Record it below and in the chart at the end of this lab.

Rating: _____

Percent Body Fat Estimate for Men: Sum of Chest, Abdomen, and Thigh Skinfolds

Sum of Skinfolds (mm)	Age								
	Under 22	23–27	28–32	33–37	38–42	43–47	48–52	53–57	Over 57
8–10	1.3	1.8	2.3	2.9	3.4	3.9	4.5	5.0	5.5
11–13	2.2	2.8	3.3	3.9	4.4	4.9	5.5	6.0	6.5
14–16	3.2	3.8	4.3	4.8	5.4	5.9	6.4	7.0	7.5
17–19	4.2	4.7	5.3	5.8	6.3	6.9	7.4	8.0	8.5
20–22	5.1	5.7	6.2	6.8	7.3	7.9	8.4	8.9	9.5
23–25	6.1	6.6	7.2	7.7	8.3	8.8	9.4	9.9	10.5
26–28	7.0	7.6	8.1	8.7	9.2	9.8	10.3	10.9	11.4
29–31	8.0	8.5	9.1	9.6	10.2	10.7	11.3	11.8	12.4
32–34	8.9	9.4	10.0	10.5	11.1	11.6	12.2	12.8	13.3
35–37	9.8	10.4	10.9	11.5	12.0	12.6	13.1	13.7	14.3
38–40	10.7	11.3	11.8	12.4	12.9	13.5	14.1	14.6	15.2
41–43	11.6	12.2	12.7	13.3	13.8	14.4	15.0	15.5	16.1
44–46	12.5	13.1	13.6	14.2	14.7	15.3	15.9	16.4	17.0
47–49	13.4	13.9	14.5	15.1	15.6	16.2	16.8	17.3	17.9
50–52	14.3	14.8	15.4	15.9	16.5	17.1	17.6	18.2	18.8
53–55	15.1	15.7	16.2	16.8	17.4	17.9	18.5	19.1	19.7
56–58	16.0	16.5	17.1	17.7	18.2	18.8	19.4	20.0	20.5
59–61	16.9	17.4	17.9	18.5	19.1	19.7	20.2	20.8	21.4
62–64	17.6	18.2	18.8	19.4	19.9	20.5	21.1	21.7	22.2
65–67	18.5	19.0	19.6	20.2	20.8	21.3	21.9	22.5	23.1
68–70	19.3	19.9	20.4	21.0	21.6	22.2	22.7	23.3	23.9
71–73	20.1	20.7	21.2	21.8	22.4	23.0	23.6	24.1	24.7
74–76	20.9	21.5	22.0	22.6	23.2	23.8	24.4	25.0	25.5
77–79	21.7	22.2	22.8	23.4	24.0	24.6	25.2	25.8	26.3
80–82	22.4	23.0	23.6	24.2	24.8	25.4	25.9	26.5	27.1
83–85	23.2	23.8	24.4	25.0	25.5	26.1	26.7	27.3	27.9
86–88	24.0	24.5	25.1	25.7	26.3	26.9	27.5	28.1	28.7
89–91	24.7	25.3	25.9	26.5	27.1	27.6	28.2	28.8	29.4
92–94	25.4	26.0	26.6	27.2	27.8	28.4	29.0	29.6	30.2
95–97	26.1	26.7	27.3	27.9	28.5	29.1	29.7	30.3	30.9
98–100	26.9	27.4	28.0	28.6	29.2	29.8	30.4	31.0	31.6
101–103	27.5	28.1	28.7	29.3	29.9	30.5	31.1	31.7	32.3
104–106	28.2	28.8	29.4	30.0	30.6	31.2	31.8	32.4	33.0
107–109	28.9	29.5	30.1	30.7	31.3	31.9	32.5	33.1	33.7
110–112	29.6	30.2	30.8	31.4	32.0	32.6	33.2	33.8	34.4
113–115	30.2	30.8	31.4	32.0	32.6	33.2	33.8	34.5	35.1
116–118	30.9	31.5	32.1	32.7	33.3	33.9	34.5	35.1	35.7
119–121	31.5	32.1	32.7	33.3	33.9	34.5	35.1	35.7	36.4
122–124	32.1	32.7	33.3	33.9	34.5	35.1	35.8	36.4	37.0
125–127	32.7	33.3	33.9	34.5	35.1	35.8	36.4	37.0	37.6

SOURCE: Jackson, A. S., and M. L. Pollock. 1985. Practical assessment of body composition. *The Physician and Sportsmedicine* 13(5): 76–90. Reproduced by permission of McGraw-Hill, Inc.

Percent Body Fat Estimate for Women: Sum of Triceps, Suprailium, and Thigh Skinfolds

Sum of Skinfolds (mm)	Age								
	Under 22	23–27	28–32	33–37	38–42	43–47	48–52	53–57	Over 57
23–25	9.7	9.9	10.2	10.4	10.7	10.9	11.2	11.4	11.7
26–28	11.0	11.2	11.5	11.7	12.0	12.3	12.5	12.7	13.0
29–31	12.3	12.5	12.8	13.0	13.3	13.5	13.8	14.0	14.3
32–34	13.6	13.8	14.0	14.3	14.5	14.8	15.0	15.3	15.5
35–37	14.8	15.0	15.3	15.5	15.8	16.0	16.3	16.5	16.8
38–40	16.0	16.3	16.5	16.7	17.0	17.2	17.5	17.7	18.0
41–43	17.2	17.4	17.7	17.9	18.2	18.4	18.7	18.9	19.2
44–46	18.3	18.6	18.8	19.1	19.3	19.6	19.8	20.1	20.3
47–49	19.5	19.7	20.0	20.2	20.5	20.7	21.0	21.2	21.5
50–52	20.6	20.8	21.1	21.3	21.6	21.8	22.1	22.3	22.6
53–55	21.7	21.9	22.1	22.4	22.6	22.9	23.1	23.4	23.6
56–58	22.7	23.0	23.2	23.4	23.7	23.9	24.2	24.4	24.7
59–61	23.7	24.0	24.2	24.5	24.7	25.0	25.2	25.5	25.7
62–64	24.7	25.0	25.2	25.5	25.7	26.0	26.7	26.4	26.7
65–67	25.7	25.9	26.2	26.4	26.7	26.9	27.2	27.4	27.7
68–70	26.6	26.9	27.1	27.4	27.6	27.9	28.1	28.4	28.6
71–73	27.5	27.8	28.0	28.3	28.5	28.8	29.0	29.3	29.5
74–76	28.4	28.7	28.9	29.2	29.4	29.7	29.9	30.2	30.4
77–79	29.3	29.5	29.8	30.0	30.3	30.5	30.8	31.0	31.3
80–82	30.1	30.4	30.6	30.9	31.1	31.4	31.6	31.9	32.1
83–85	30.9	31.2	31.4	31.7	31.9	32.2	32.4	32.7	32.9
86–88	31.7	32.0	32.2	32.5	32.7	32.9	33.2	33.4	33.7
89–91	32.5	32.7	33.0	33.2	33.5	33.7	33.9	34.2	34.4
92–94	33.2	33.4	33.7	33.9	34.2	34.4	34.7	34.9	35.2
95–97	33.9	34.1	34.4	34.6	34.9	35.1	35.4	35.6	35.9
98–100	34.6	34.8	35.1	35.3	35.5	35.8	36.0	36.3	36.5
101–103	35.3	35.4	35.7	35.9	36.2	36.4	36.7	36.9	37.2
104–106	35.8	36.1	36.3	36.6	36.8	37.1	37.3	37.5	37.8
107–109	36.4	36.7	36.9	37.1	37.4	37.6	37.9	38.1	38.4
110–112	37.0	37.2	37.5	37.7	38.0	38.2	38.5	38.7	38.9
113–115	37.5	37.8	38.0	38.2	38.5	38.7	39.0	39.2	39.5
116–118	38.0	38.3	38.5	38.8	39.0	39.3	39.5	39.7	40.0
119–121	38.5	38.7	39.0	39.2	39.5	39.7	40.0	40.2	40.5
122–124	39.0	39.2	39.4	39.7	39.9	40.2	40.4	40.7	40.9
125–127	39.4	39.6	39.9	40.1	40.4	40.6	40.9	41.1	41.4
128–130	39.8	40.0	40.3	40.5	40.8	41.0	41.3	41.5	41.8

SOURCE: Jackson, A. S., and M. L. Pollock. 1985. Practical assessment of body composition. *The Physician and Sportsmedicine* 13(5): 76–90. Reproduced by permission of McGraw-Hill, Inc.

*Body Composition Ratings**

Percent Body Fat

Men	Very Lean	Excellent	Good	Fair	Poor	Very Poor
Age: 18–29	Below 5.3	5.3–9.4	9.5–14.1	14.2–17.4	17.5–22.4	Above 22.4
30–39	Below 9.2	9.2–13.9	14.0–17.5	17.6–20.5	20.6–24.2	Above 24.2
40–49	Below 11.5	11.5–16.3	16.4–19.6	19.7–22.5	22.6–26.1	Above 26.1
50–59	Below 13.0	13.0–17.9	18.0–21.3	21.4–24.1	24.2–27.5	Above 27.5
60 and over	Below 13.2	13.2–18.4	18.5–22.0	22.1–25.0	25.1–28.5	Above 28.5
Women						
Age: 18–29	Below 10.9	10.9–17.1	17.2–20.6	20.7–23.7	23.8–27.7	Above 27.7
30–39	Below 13.5	13.5–18.0	18.1–21.6	21.7–24.9	25.0–29.3	Above 29.3
40–49	Below 16.2	16.2–21.3	21.4–24.9	25.0–28.1	28.2–32.1	Above 32.1
50–59	Below 18.9	18.9–25.0	25.1–28.5	28.6–31.6	31.7–35.6	Above 35.6
60 and over	Below 16.9	16.9–25.1	25.2–29.3	29.4–32.5	32.6–36.6	Above 36.6

*These ratings are derived from norms based on the measurement of thousands of individuals. In evaluating your body composition, also consider the health-related recommendations for body fat given in Table 6-1 (p. 139). Obesity is defined as having more than 25% of body weight as fat for men and more than 33% of body weight as fat for women. Norms reflect the status of the population, while recommendations represent a more healthy and desirable status.

SOURCE: Based on norms from the Cooper Institute for Aerobics Research, Dallas, Texas; used with permission.

Other Methods of Assessing Percent Body Fat

Other methods of assessing percent body fat, including underwater weighing and bioelectrical impedance analysis, may be available on your campus or in your community. If you use one of these alternative methods, record the name of the method and the result below and in the chart at the end of this lab. Find your body composition rating on the table above.

Method used: _____

Percent body fat: _____ %

Rating (from table above): _____

Waist Circumference and Waist-to-Hip Ratio

Equipment

1. Tape measure
2. Partner to take measurements

Preparation

Wear clothes that will not add significantly to your measurements.

Instructions

Stand with your feet together and your arms at your sides. Raise your arms only high enough to allow for taking the measurements. Your partner should make sure the tape is horizontal around the entire circumference and pulled snugly against your skin. The tape shouldn't be pulled so tight that it causes indentations in your skin. Record measurements to the nearest millimeter or one-sixteenth of an inch.

Waist. Measure at the smallest waist circumference. If you don't have a natural waist, measure at the level of your navel.

Waist measurement: _____

Hip. Measure at the largest hip circumference.

Hip measurement: _____

Waist-to-Hip Ratio: You can use any unit of measurement (for example, inches or centimeters), as long as you're consistent. Waist-to-hip ratio equals waist measurement divided by hip measurement.

Waist-to-hip ratio: _____ ÷ _____ = _____

⠀⠀⠀⠀⠀⠀⠀⠀⠀⠀⠀⠀⠀⠀⠀⠀waist measurement⠀⠀⠀⠀⠀hip measurement

Determining Your Risk

The table below indicates values for waist circumference and waist-to-hip ratio above which the risk of health problems increases significantly. If your measurement or ratio is above either cutoff point, put a check on the appropriate line below and in the chart on the final page of this lab.

Waist circumference: _____ (✔ high risk)

Waist-to-hip ratio: _____ (✔ high risk)

Body Fat Distribution

Cutoff Points for High Risk

	Waist Circumference	Waist-to-Hip Ratio
Men	more than 40 in. (102 cm)	more than 0.95
Women	more than 35 in. (88 cm)	more than 0.86

SOURCES: National Heart, Lung, and Blood Institute. 1998. *Clinical Guidelines on the Identification, Evaluation, and Treatment of Overweight and Obesity in Adults: The Evidence Report.* Bethesda, Md.: National Institutes of Health. American College of Sports Medicine. 1995. *Guidelines for Exercise Testing and Prescription.* Baltimore, Md9.: Williams & Wilkins.

Rating Your Body Composition

Assessment	Value	Classification
BMI	_____ kg/m²	_____
Skinfold measurements or alternative method of determining percent body fat. Specify method: _____	_____ % body fat	_____
Waist circumference Waist-to-hip ratio	_____ in. or cm _____ (ratio)	_____ (✔ high risk) _____ (✔ high risk)

Enter the results of this lab in the Preprogram Assessment column of Appendix D. After several weeks of a program to improve body composition, do this lab again, and enter the results in the Postprogram Assessment column of Appendix D. How do the results compare?

![pencil and notebook icon] **LAB 6-2** *Determining Desirable Body Weight* ![disk icon]

Complete this lab if assessment tests indicate that a change in your body composition is appropriate.

Equipment

Calculator (or pencil and paper for calculations)

Preparation

Determine percent body fat and/or calculate BMI as described in Lab 6-1. Keep track of height and weight as measured for these calculations.

Height: _____

Weight: _____

Calculations for desirable body weight can be based on target values for BMI and/or percent body fat. The instructions given below contain formulas for both methods; depending on which assessments you performed in Lab 6-1, you may complete the calculations for one or both methods. Choose a target BMI from Table 6-2, and/or choose a target percent body fat from Table 6-1. For example, a 190-pound male who is 5 feet, 7 inches tall and has a BMI of 29.9 and a percent body fat of 26 might set goals of 26 for BMI and 18 for percent body fat.

Instructions

1. To calculate desirable weight from target BMI:

    a. Convert your height measurement to meters by multiplying your height in inches by 0.0254.

    b. Square your height measurement.

    c. Multiply your target BMI by your height in meters, squared, to get your target weight in kilograms.

    d. Multiply your target weight in kilograms by 2.2 to get your desirable body weight in pounds.

Example (see above)

1. Desirable weight from target BMI:

    67 in. $\times$ 0.0254 m/in. = 1.70 m

    1.70 m $\times$ 1.70 m = 2.89 m^2

    26 kg/m^2 $\times$ 2.89 m^2 = 75.1 kg

    75.1 kg $\times$ 2.2 lb/kg = 165 lb

    a. Height _____ in. $\times$ 0.0254 m/in. = height _____ m

    b. Height _____ m $\times$ height _____ m = height _____ m^2

    c. Target BMI _____ $\times$ height _____ m^2 = target weight _____ kg

    d. Target weight _____ kg $\times$ 2.2 lb/kg = desirable body weight _____ lb

2. To calculate desirable body weight from actual and target body fat percentages:

    a. To determine the fat weight in your body, multiply your current weight by percent body fat (determined through skinfold measurements and expressed as a decimal).

    b. Subtract the fat weight from your current weight to get your current fat-free weight.

    c. Subtract your target percent body fat from 1 to get target percent fat-free weight.

2. Desirable weight from actual and target body fat percentages:

    190 lb $\times$ 0.26 = 49.4 lb

    190 lb $-$ 49.4 lb = 140.6 lb

    1 $-$ 0.18 = 0.82

d. To get your desirable body weight, divide your
fat-free weight by your target percent fat-free weight.   140.6 lb ÷ 0.82 = 171 lb

Note: Weight can be expressed in either pounds or kilograms, as long as the unit of measurement is used consistently.

a. Current body weight _____ × percent body fat _____ = fat weight _____

b. Current body weight _____ − fat weight _____ = fat-free weight _____

c. 1 − target percent body fat _____ = target percent fat-free weight _____

d. Fat-free weight _____ ÷ target percent fat-free weight _____ =

   desirable body weight _____

Based on these calculations and other factors (including heredity, individual preference, and current health status), select a target weight or range of weights for yourself.

Target body weight: _____

Putting Together a Complete Fitness Program

7

LOOKING AHEAD

After reading this chapter, you should be able to answer these questions about putting together a complete personalized exercise program:

- What are the steps for putting together a successful personal fitness program?

- What strategies can help maintain a fitness program over the long term?

- How can a fitness program be tailored to accommodate special health concerns?

Understanding the physiological basis and wellness benefits of health-related physical fitness, as explained in Chapters 1–6, is the first step toward creating a well-rounded exercise program. The next challenge is to combine activities into a program that develops all the fitness components and maintains motivation.

This chapter presents a step-by-step procedure for creating and maintaining a well-rounded program. Following the chapter, you'll find sample programs based on popular activities. The structure these programs provide can be helpful if you're beginning an exercise program for the first time.

DEVELOPING A PERSONAL FITNESS PLAN

If you're ready to create a complete fitness program based around the activities you enjoy most, begin by preparing the program plan and contract in Lab 7-1. By carefully developing your plan and signing a contract, you'll increase your chances of success. The step-by-step procedure outlined here (adapted from *Your Guide to Getting Fit,* by Ivan Kusinitz and Morton Fine) will guide you through the steps of Lab 7-1 to the creation of an exercise program that's right for you. Refer to Figure 7-1 for a sample personal fitness program plan and contract.

If you'd like additional help in setting up your program, choose one of the sample programs at the end of this chapter (pp. 170–178). Sample programs are provided for walking/jogging/running, cycling, swimming, and in-line skating; they include detailed instructions for starting a program and developing and maintaining fitness.

1. Set Goals

Setting goals to reach through exercise is a crucial first step. Ask yourself, "What do I want from my fitness program?" Develop different types of goals—general and specific, long term and short term. General or long-term goals might include things like lowering your risk for chronic disease, improving posture, and having more energy. It's a good idea to also develop some specific, short-term goals based on measurable factors. Specific goals might be raising $\dot{V}O_{2max}$ by 10%, reducing the time it takes you to jog 2 miles from 22 minutes to 19 minutes, increasing the number of push-ups you can do from 15 to 25, and lowering BMI from 26 to 24. Having specific goals will allow you to track your progress and enjoy the measurable changes brought about by your fitness program. Refer to the results of the assessment tests you completed in the labs for Chapters 3–6 for help in setting specific goals.

You'll find it easier to stick with your program if you choose goals that are both important to you and realistic. Remember that heredity, your current fitness level, and other individual factors influence the amount of improve-

Weight training does little to develop cardiorespiratory endurance but is excellent for developing muscular strength and endurance. An overall fitness program includes exercises to develop all the components of physical fitness.

ment and the ultimate level of fitness you can expect to obtain through physical training. Fitness improves most quickly during the first 6 months of an exercise program. After that, gains come more slowly and usually require a higher-intensity program. So don't expect to improve indefinitely. Improve your fitness to a reasonable target level, and then train consistently to maintain it.

Think carefully about your reasons for exercising, and then fill in the goals portion of your program plan in Lab 7-1.

2. Select Activities

If you have already chosen activities and created separate program plans for different fitness components in Chapters 3, 4, and 5, you can put those plans together into a single program. It's usually best to include exercises to develop each of the health-related components of physical fitness.

- Cardiorespiratory endurance is developed by activities such as walking, cycling, and aerobic dance that involve continuous rhythmic movements of large muscle groups like those in the legs (see Chapter 3).

A. I __Tracie Kaufman__ am contracting with myself to follow a physical
   (name)
   fitness program to work toward the following goals:

   Specific or short-term goals
   1. Improving cardiorespiratory fitness by raising my $\dot{V}O_{2max}$ to 37 ml/kg/min
   2. Improving upper body muscular strength and endurance
   3. Improving body composition (from 30% to 25% body fat)
   4. Improving my tennis game (hitting 20 playable shots in a row against the ball machine)

   General or long-term goals
   1. Developing a more positive attitude about myself
   2. Reducing my risk for diabetes and heart disease
   3. Building and maintaining bone mass to reduce my risk of osteoporosis
   4. Increasing my life expectancy

B. My program plan is as follows:

| Activities | Components (Check ✓) | | | | | Intensity* | Duration | Frequency (Check ✓) | | | | | | |
	CRE	MS	ME	F	BC			M	Tu	W	Th	F	Sa	Su
Swimming	✓	✓	✓	✓	✓	140-150 bpm	35min	✓		✓		✓		
Tennis	✓	✓	✓	✓	✓	RPE = 14	90min						✓	
Weight training		✓	✓	✓	✓	see Lab 4-3	30min		✓		✓		✓	
Stretching			✓			—	25min	✓		✓		✓	✓	

   *List your target heart rate range or an RPE value if appropriate.

C. My program will begin on _Sept. 21_. My program includes the following schedule
   of mini-goals. For each step in my program, I will give myself the reward listed.

Completing 2 full weeks of program	Oct 5	movie with friends
(mini-goal 1)	(date)	(reward)
$\dot{V}O_{2max}$ of 34 ml/kg/min	Nov 2	new CD
(mini-goal 2)	(date)	(reward)
Completing 10 full weeks of program	Nov 30	new sweater
(mini-goal 3)	(date)	(reward)
Percent body fat of 28%	Dec 22	weekend away
(mini-goal 4)	(date)	(reward)
$\dot{V}O_{2max}$ of 36 ml/kg/min	Jan 18	new CD
(mini-goal 5)	(date)	(reward)

D. My program will include the addition of physical activity to my daily routine (such
   as climbing stairs or walking to class):
   1. Walking to and from campus job
   2. Taking the stairs to dorm room instead of elevator
   3. Bicycling to the library instead of driving
   4. _____
   5. _____

E. I will use the following tools to monitor my program and my progress toward
   my goals: I'll use a chart that lists the number of laps and minutes I swim and the
   charts for strength and flexibility from Labs 4-3 & 5-2.

   I sign this contract as an indication of my personal commitment to reach my goal.
   _____Tracie Kaufman_____   ____Sept 10____
   (your signature)   (date)
   I have recruited a helper who will witness my contract and _____
   swim with me three days per week
   (list any way your helper will participate in your program)
   _____Russell Walker_____   ____Sept 10____
   (witness's signature)   (date)

Figure 7-1   A sample personal fitness program plan and contract.

TABLE 7-1 A Summary of Sports and Fitness Activities

This table classifies sports and activities as high (H), moderate (M), or low (L) in terms of their ability to develop each of the five components of physical fitness: cardiorespiratory endurance (CRE), muscular strength (MS), muscular endurance (ME), flexibility (F), and body composition (BC). The skill level needed to obtain fitness benefits is noted: Low (L) means little or no skill is required to obtain fitness benefits; moderate (M) means average skill is needed to obtain fitness benefits; and high (H) means much skill is required to obtain fitness benefits. The fitness prerequisite, or conditioning needs of a beginner, is also noted: Low (L) means no fitness prerequisite is required, moderate (M) means some preconditioning is required, and high (H) means substantial fitness is required. The last two columns list the calorie cost of each activity when performed moderately and vigorously. To determine how many calories you burn, multiply the value in the appropriate column by your body weight and then by the number of minutes you exercise. Work up to using 300 or more calories per workout.

Sports and Activities	Components					Skill Level	Fitness Prerequisite	Approximate Calorie Cost (cal/lb/min)	
	CRE	MS*	ME*	F*	BC			Moderate	Vigorous
Aerobic dance	H	M	H	H	H	L	L	.046	.062
Backpacking	H	M	H	M	H	L	M	.032	.078
Badminton, skilled, singles	H	M	M	M	H	M	M	—	.071
Ballet (floor combinations)	M	M	H	H	M	M	L	—	.058
Ballroom dancing	M	L	M	L	M	M	L	.034	.049
Baseball (pitcher and catcher)	M	M	H	M	M	H	M	.039	—
Basketball, half court	H	M	H	M	H	M	M	.045	.071
Bicycling	H	M	H	M	H	M	L	.049	.071
Bowling	L	L	L	L	L	L	L	—	—
Calisthenic circuit training	H	M	H	M	H	L	L	—	.060
Canoeing and kayaking (flat water)	M	M	H	M	M	M	M	.045	—
Cheerleading	M	M	M	M	M	M	L	.033	.049
Fencing	M	M	H	H	M	M	L	.032	.078
Field hockey	H	M	H	M	H	M	M	.052	.078
Folk and square dancing	M	L	M	L	M	L	L	.039	.049
Football, touch	M	M	M	M	M	M	M	.049	.078
Frisbee, ultimate	H	M	H	M	H	M	M	.049	.078
Golf (riding cart)	L	L	L	M	L	L	L	—	—
Handball, skilled, singles	H	M	H	M	H	M	M	—	.078
Hiking	H	M	H	L	H	L	M	.051	.073
Hockey, ice and roller	H	M	H	M	H	M	M	.052	.078
Horseback riding	M	M	M	L	M	M	M	.052	.065
Interval circuit training	H	H	H	M	H	L	L	—	.062
Jogging and running	H	M	H	L	H	L	L	.060	.104

*Ratings are for the muscle groups involved.

- Muscular strength and endurance are developed by training against resistance (see Chapter 4).
- Flexibility is developed by stretching the major muscle groups (see Chapter 5).
- Healthy body composition can be developed by combining a sensible diet and a program of regular exercise, including cardiorespiratory endurance exercise to burn calories and resistance training to build muscle mass (see Chapter 6).

Table 7-1 rates many popular activities for their ability to develop each of the health-related components of fitness. Check the ratings of the activities you're considering to make sure the program you put together will develop all fitness components and help you achieve your goals. One strategy is to select one activity for each component of fitness—bicycling, weight training, and stretching, for example. Another strategy applies the principle of **cross-training**, using several different activities to develop a particular fitness component—aerobic dance, swimming, and volleyball for cardiorespiratory endurance, for example. Cross-training is discussed in the next section.

If you select activities that support your commitment rather than activities that turn exercise into a chore, the right program will be its own incentive for continuing. Consider the following factors in making your choices.

TABLE 7-1

TABLE 7-1 A Summary of Sports and Fitness Activities (continued)

Sports and Activities	Components					Skill Level	Fitness Prerequisite	Approximate Calorie Cost (cal/lb/min)	
	CRE	MS*	ME*	F*	BC			Moderate	Vigorous
Judo	M	H	H	M	M	M	L	.049	.090
Karate	H	M	H	H	H	L	M	.049	.090
Lacrosse	H	M	H	M	H	H	M	.052	.078
Modern dance (moving combinations)	M	M	H	H	M	L	L	—	.058
Orienteering	H	M	H	L	H	L	M	.049	.078
Outdoor fitness trails	H	M	H	M	H	L	L	—	.060
Popular dancing	M	L	M	M	M	M	L	—	.049
Racquetball, skilled, singles	H	M	M	M	H	M	M	.049	.078
Rock climbing	M	H	H	H	M	H	M	.033	.033
Rope skipping	H	M	H	L	H	M	M	.071	.095
Rowing	H	H	H	H	H	L	L	.032	.097
Rugby	H	M	H	M	H	M	M	.052	.097
Sailing	L	L	M	L	L	M	L	—	—
Skating, ice, roller, and in-line	M	M	H	M	M	H	M	.049	.095
Skiing, alpine	M	H	H	M	M	H	M	.039	.078
Skiing, cross-country	H	M	H	M	H	M	M	.049	.104
Soccer	H	M	H	M	H	M	M	.052	.097
Squash, skilled, singles	H	M	M	M	H	M	M	.049	.078
Stretching	L	L	L	H	L	L	L	—	—
Surfing (including swimming)	M	M	M	M	M	H	M	—	.078
Swimming	H	M	H	M	H	M	L	.032	.088
Synchronized swimming	M	M	H	H	M	H	M	.032	.052
Table tennis	M	L	M	M	M	M	L	—	.045
Tennis, skilled, singles	H	M	M	M	H	M	M	—	.071
Volleyball	M	L	M	M	M	M	M	—	.065
Walking	H	L	M	L	H	L	L	.029	.048
Water polo	H	M	H	M	H	H	M	—	.078
Water skiing	M	M	H	M	M	H	M	.039	.055
Weight training	L	H	H	H	M	L	L	—	—
Wrestling	H	H	H	H	H	H	H	.065	.094
Yoga	L	L	M	H	L	H	L	—	—

*Ratings are for the muscle groups involved.

SOURCE: Kusinitz, I., and M. Fine. 1995. *Your Guide to Getting Fit*, 3d ed. Mountain View, Calif.: Mayfield.

• *Fun and interest.* Your fitness program is much more likely to be successful if you choose activities that you enjoy doing. Start by considering any activities you currently engage in and enjoy. Often you can modify your current activities to fit your fitness program. As you consider new activities, ask yourself, "Is this activity fun?" "Will it hold my interest over time?" For new activities, it is a good idea to undertake a trial period before making a final choice. Figure 7-2 shows popular fitness activities among Americans.

• *Your current skill and fitness level.* Although many activities are appropriate for beginners, some sports and

activities require participants to have a moderate level of skill in order to obtain fitness benefits. For example, a beginning tennis player will probably not be able to sustain rallies long enough to develop cardiorespiratory endurance. Refer to the skill level column in Table 7-1 to determine the level of skill needed for full participation in the activities you're considering. If your current skill

cross-training   Alternating two or more activities to improve a single component of fitness.   TERMS

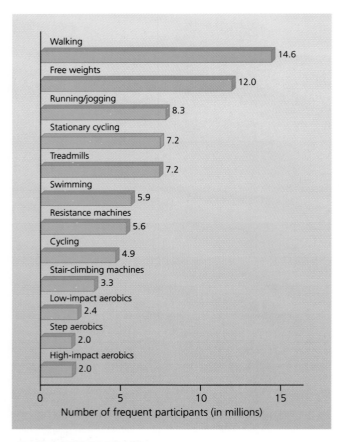

Figure 7-2 Popular fitness activities among Americans.
Frequent participants in the activities shown here are those who
engage in the activity at least 100 days per year (52 days for swimming).   DATA SOURCE: Sporting Goods Manufacturers Association. *Tracking
the Fitness Movement —1997 Edition* (http://www.sportlink.com).

level doesn't meet the requirement, you may want to
begin your program with a different activity. For example, a beginning tennis player may be better off with a
walking program while improving his or her tennis
game. To build skill for a particular activity, consider
taking a class or getting some instruction from a coach
or fellow participant.

Your current fitness level may also limit the activities
that are appropriate for your program. For example, if
you have been inactive, a walking program would be
more appropriate than a jogging program. Activities in
which participants control the intensity of effort—walking, cycling, and swimming, for example—are more
appropriate for a beginning fitness program than sports
and activities that are primarily "other paced"—soccer,
basketball, and tennis, for example. Refer to the fitness
prerequisite column of Table 7-1 to determine the minimum level of fitness required for participation in the
activities you're considering.

• *Time and convenience.* Unless exercise fits easily into
your daily schedule, you are unlikely to maintain your
program over the long term. As you consider activities,
think about whether a special location or facility is required. Can you participate in the activity close to your
residence, school, or job? Are the necessary facilities
open and available at times convenient to you? Do you
need a partner or a team to play? Can you participate in
the activity year-round, or will you need to find an alternative during the summer or winter?

• *Cost.* Some sports and activities require equipment,
fees, or some type of membership investment. If you are
on a tight budget, limit your choices to activities that are
inexpensive or free. Investigate the facilities on your
campus, which you may be able to use at little or no
cost. Many activities require no equipment beyond an
appropriate pair of shoes (see the box "Choosing Exercise Footwear" for more information). Refer back to
Chapters 2 and 3 for consumer guidelines for evaluating
exercise equipment and facilities.

• *Special health needs.* If you have special exercise
needs due to a particular health problem, choose activities that will conform to your needs and enhance your
ability to cope. If necessary, consult your physician
about how best to tailor an exercise program to your
particular needs and goals. Guidelines and safety tips for
exercisers with common chronic conditions are provided
later in the chapter.

3. Set a Target Intensity, Duration, and Frequency for Each Activity

The next step in planning your fitness program is to set a
target intensity, duration, and frequency for each activity
you've chosen (see the sample in Figure 7-1). Refer to the
calculations and plans you completed in Chapters 3, 4,
and 5.

Cardiorespiratory Endurance Exercise   For intensity,
note your target heart rate zone or RPE value. Your target
total duration should be about 20–60 minutes, depending on the intensity of the activity (shorter durations are
appropriate for high-intensity activities, longer durations
for activities of more moderate intensity). You can exercise in a single session or in multiple sessions of 10 or
more minutes. One way to check whether the total duration you've set is appropriate is to use the **calorie costs**
(calories per minute per pound of body weight) given in
Table 7-1. Your goal should be to work up to burning
about 300 calories per workout; beginners should start
with a calorie cost of about 100–150 calories per workout. You can calculate the calorie cost of your activities by
multiplying the appropriate factor from Table 7-1 by your
body weight and the duration of your workout. For example, walking at a moderate pace burns about 0.029
calorie per minute per pound of body weight. A person

Name: Tracie Kaufman																

Enter duration, distance, or other factor to track your progress.

Activity/Date	M	Tu	W	Th	F	S	S	Weekly Total	M	Tu	W	Th	F	S	S	Weekly Total
1 Swimming	800 yd		725 yd		800 yd			2325 yd	800 yd		800 yd		850 yd			2450 yd
2 Tennis				90 min				90 min						95 min		95 min
3 Weight training		✓		✓		✓				✓		✓		✓	✓	
4 Stretching	✓		✓		✓	✓			✓			✓	✓	✓	✓	
5																
6																

Figure 7-3   A sample program log.

weighing 150 pounds could begin her exercise program by walking for 30 minutes, burning about 130 calories. Once her fitness improves, she might choose to start cycling for her cardiorespiratory endurance workouts. Cycling at a moderate pace has a higher calorie cost than walking (0.049 calorie per minute per pound), and if she cycled for 40 minutes, she would burn the target 300 calories during her workout.

An appropriate frequency for cardiorespiratory endurance exercise is 3–5 times per week.

Muscular Strength and Endurance Training   As described in Chapter 4, a general fitness strength training program includes 1 or more sets of 8–12 repetitions of 8–10 exercises that work all major muscle groups. For intensity, choose a weight that is heavy enough to fatigue your muscles but not so heavy that you cannot complete the full number of repetitions with proper form. A frequency of 2–3 days per week is recommended.

Flexibility Training   Stretches should be performed for all major muscle groups. For each exercise, stretch to the point of slight tension or mild discomfort and hold the stretch for 10–30 seconds; do at least 4 repetitions of each exercise. Stretches should be performed at least 2–3 days per week, preferably when muscles are warm.

4. Set Up a System of Mini-Goals and Rewards

To keep your program on track, it is important to set up a system of goals and rewards. Break your specific goals into several steps, and set a target date for each step. For example, if one of the goals of an 18-year-old male student's program is to improve upper body strength and endurance, he could use the push-up test in Lab 4-2 to set intermediate goals. If he can currently perform 15 push-ups (for a rating of "very poor"), he might set intermedi-

ate goals of 20, 25, and 30 push-ups (for a final rating of "fair"). By allowing 4–6 weeks between mini-goals and specifying rewards, he'll be able to track his progress and reward himself as he moves toward his final goal. For more on choosing appropriate rewards, refer to p. 11 in Chapter 1 and Activity 4 in the Behavior Change Workbook at the end of the text.

5. Include Lifestyle Physical Activity in Your Program

As described in Chapter 2, daily physical activity is an important part of a fit and well lifestyle. As part of your fitness program plan, specify ways that you will be more active during your daily routine. You may find it helpful to first use your health journal to track your activities for several days. Review the records in your journal, identify routine opportunities to be more active, and add these to your program plan in Lab 7-1.

6. Develop Tools for Monitoring Your Progress

A record that tracks your daily progress will help remind you of your ongoing commitment to your program and give you a sense of accomplishment. Lab 7-2 shows you how to create a general program log and record the activity type, frequency, and durations (a sample is shown in Figure 7-3). Or if you wish, complete specific activity logs like those in Labs 3-2, 4-3, and 5-2 in addition to, or instead of, a general log. Post your log in a place where you'll see it often as a reminder and as an incentive for improvement. If you have specific, measurable goals, you

TERMS

calorie cost   The amount of energy used to perform a particular activity, usually expressed in calories per minute per pound of body weight.

Footwear is perhaps the most important item of equipment for almost any activity. Shoes protect and support your feet and improve your traction. When you jump or run, you place as much as six times more force on your feet than when you stand still. Shoes can help cushion against the stress that this additional force places on your lower legs and thus prevent injuries. Some athletic shoes are also designed to help prevent ankle rollover, another common source of injury.

Shoe Terminology

Understanding the structural features of athletic shoes can help you make sound choices.

Outsole: The bottom of the shoe that touches the ground and provides traction. The shape and composition of an outsole depend on the activity for which the shoe is designed.

Midsole: The layer of shock-absorbing material located between the insole and the outsole; typically composed of polyurethane, ethyl vinyl acetate (EVA), or another cushioning material. For improved durability, some shoe midsoles include encapsulated air or gel.

Insole: The insert or sock lining that the foot rests on inside the shoe, usually contoured to fit the foot and containing additional cushioning and arch and heel support.

Collar: The opening of the shoe where the foot goes in.

Upper: The top part of the shoe, usually made of nylon, canvas, or leather.

Toe box: The front part of the upper, which surrounds the toes.

Heel counter: The stiff cup in the back of the inside of the shoe that provides support and stability.

Notched heel: Some shoes have raised heel padding to support the Achilles tendon.

Stabilizers: Bars or strips of rubber, polyurethane, or nylon near the heel or forefoot area of some shoes; they provide additional stability.

Wedge: The thick portion of the midsole that makes the heel higher than the ball of the foot in some shoes.

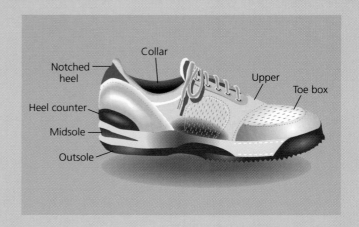

General Guidelines

When choosing athletic shoes, first consider the activity you've chosen for your exercise program. Shoes appropriate for different activities have very different characteristics. For example, running shoes typically have highly cushioned midsoles, rubber outsoles with elevated heels, and a great deal of flexibility in the forefoot. The heels of walking shoes tend to be lower, less padded, and more beveled than those designed for running. For aerobic dance, shoes must be flexible in the forefoot and have straight, nonflared heels to allow for safe and easy lateral movements. Court shoes also provide substantial support for lateral movements; they typically have outsoles made from white rubber that will not damage court surfaces.

Also consider the location and intensity of your workouts. If you plan to walk or run on trails, you should choose shoes with water-resistant, highly durable uppers and more outsole traction. If you work out intensely or have a relatively high body weight, you'll need thick, firm midsoles to avoid bottoming-out the cushioning system of your shoes.

Foot type is another important consideration. If your feet tend to roll in excessively (overpronate), you may need shoes with additional stability features on the inner side of the shoe to counteract this movement. If your feet tend to roll outward excessively (oversupinate), you may need highly flexible and cushioned shoes that promote foot motion. For aerobic dancers

---

can also graph your weekly or monthly progress toward your goal (Figure 7-4).

7. Make a Commitment

Your final step in planning your program is to make a commitment by signing a contract. Find a witness for your contract—preferably one who will be actively involved in your program. Keep your contract in a visible spot to remind you of your commitment.

Once you've developed a detailed plan and signed your contract, you are ready to begin your fitness program. Refer to the specific training suggestions provided in Chapters 2–5 for advice on beginning and maintaining your program. Some key guidelines are summarized below.

• *Start slowly and increase intensity and duration gradually.* Overzealous exercising can result in discouraging

with feet that tend to pronate or supinate, mid-cut to high-cut shoes may be more appropriate than low-cut aerobic shoes or cross-trainers (shoes designed to be worn for several different activities). Compared with men, women have narrower feet overall and narrower heels relative to the forefoot. Most women will get a better fit if they choose shoes that are specifically designed for women's feet rather than those that are down-sized versions of men's shoes.

For successful shoe shopping, keep these strategies in mind:

- Shop at an athletic shoe or specialty store that has personnel trained to fit athletic shoes and a large selection of styles and sizes.

- Shop late in the day or, ideally, following a workout. Your foot size increases over the course of the day and as a result of exercise.

- Wear socks like those you plan to wear during exercise. If you have an old pair of athletic shoes, bring them with you. The wear pattern on your old shoes can help you select a pair with extra support or cushioning in the places you need it the most.

- Ask for help. Trained salespeople know which shoes are designed for your foot type and your level of activity. They can also help fit your shoes properly.

- Don't insist on buying shoes in what you consider to be your typical shoe size. Sizes vary from shoe to shoe. In addition, foot sizes change over time, and many people have one foot that is larger or wider than the other. Try several sizes in several widths if necessary. Don't buy shoes that are too small.

- Try on both shoes, and wear them around for at least 10 minutes. Try walking on a noncarpeted surface. Approximate the movements of your activity: walk, jog, run, jump, and so on.

- Check the fit and style carefully.

    Is the toe box roomy enough? Your toes will spread out when your foot hits the ground or you push off. There should be at least one thumb's width of space from the longest toe to the end of the toe box.

    Do they have enough cushioning? Do your feet feel cushioned and supported when you bounce up and down? Try bouncing on your toes and on your heels.

    Do your heels fit snugly into the shoe? Do they stay put when you walk, or do they rise up?

    Are the arches of your feet right on top of the shoes' arch supports?

    Do the shoes feel stable when you twist and turn on the balls of your feet? Try twisting from side to side while standing on one foot.

    Do you feel any pressure points?

- If the shoe isn't comfortable in the store, don't buy it. Don't expect athletic shoes to stretch over time in order to fit your feet properly.

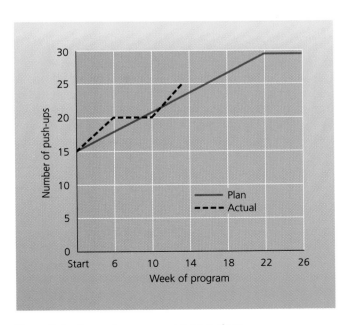

Figure 7-4   A sample program progress chart.

discomforts and injuries. Your program is meant to last a lifetime. The important first step is to break your established pattern of inactivity. Be patient and realistic. Once your body has adjusted to your starting level of exercise, slowly increase the amount of overload. Small increases are the key—achieving a large number of small improvements will eventually result in substantial gains in fitness. It's usually best to increase duration and frequency before increasing intensity.

• *Find an exercise buddy.* The social side of exercise is an important factor for many regular exercisers. Working out with a friend will make exercise more enjoyable and increase your chances of sticking with your program. Find an exercise partner who shares your goals and general fitness level.

• *Vary your program.* You can make your program more fun over the long term if you participate in a variety of different activities that you enjoy. You can also add interest by strategies such as varying the routes you take when walking, running, biking, or in-line skating;

Troublesome technique. Exercise technique is critical, even for activities that you take for granted, like walking. When increasing the pace of walking, for example, it's natural to take longer strides. But this can overstress your shins. Proper technique entails taking more rapid strides without increasing their length. If necessary, take a class or get other expert help to ensure proper technique for the activities you participate in.

A small breath of air. Novice exercisers tend to breathe rapidly and shallowly because it feels right. But with this type of breathing, oxygen does not make its way to the depths of the lungs where it's needed. This contributes to a sense of breathlessness. Instead, consciously take longer and deeper breaths.

Beginner's pluck. If you have not been active, your body is ill prepared for demanding exercise. Even so, you are likely to make rapid gains in the beginning stages of an exercise program, which can inspire you to do too much too soon. Resist the temptation. Working out like a veteran can easily lead to injury.

Veteran's overconfidence. Even if you are a seasoned exerciser, don't advance more quickly than your body will allow, and avoid overconfidence. Those who were once in shape but have quit exercising and want to start again are particularly likely to increase too rapidly—advancing, for instance, from a 2-mile run to a 6-mile run in a few weeks. Whether you are starting from scratch or restarting from a higher level, progress slowly.

Feel the burnout. Your abilities and drive may inspire you to keep adding to your exercise workload. But even small and slow increases can become too much. If you find yourself dreading exercise sessions or dragging through the day because of exhausting workouts, you may be overtraining. If so, cut back to where your workouts are comfortable again and you look forward to them. Take a few days off completely and then return at a much reduced level.

Not easing in and out. Take time to warm up and ease into exercise. Even if you walk or do other forms of mild exercise, your body needs an adjustment period. Start with a slow, comfortable walk before progressing to faster speeds. At the end of a workout, don't stop abruptly, but rather slow your pace gradually until you quit. Finish with stretching exercises.

Leave it for weekends. Many people use sports as a means of getting in shape. They push themselves on weekends in demanding sports like basketball that can stress the body to its limits. This "weekend warrior" approach is backward. Instead, get in shape first so you can enjoy sports safely. This is especially important if you do not participate regularly.

Fair-weather exercise. Regardless of your goals or the type of exercise you choose, little will be accomplished by sporadic exercise. The key to success is consistency. On occasion, you won't have time to exercise as much as you would like. On those days, it's important to do something, no matter how small. A little exercise performed daily will produce much greater results than sporadic, lengthy workouts.

Adapted from Stamford, B. 1997. Exercise adviser: Dodging common exercise pitfalls. *The Physician and Sportsmedicine* 25(7).

finding a new tennis or racquetball partner; changing your music for aerobic dance; or switching to a new volleyball or basketball court.

Varying your activities, a strategy known as cross-training, has other benefits. It can help you develop balanced, total body fitness. For example, by alternating running with swimming, you build both upper and lower body strength. Cross-training can thus prepare you for a wider range of activities and physical challenges. It can also reduce the risk of injury and overtraining because the same muscles, bones, and joints are not continuously subjected to the stresses of the same activity. Cross-training can be done either by choosing different activities on different days or by alternating activities within a single workout.

• *Expect fluctuations and lapses.* On some days, your progress will be excellent, but on others, you'll barely be able to drag yourself through your scheduled activities.

Don't let off-days or lapses discourage you or make you feel guilty. Instead, feel a renewed commitment for your fitness program. Focus on the improvements you obtain from your program and how good you feel after exercise. Reward yourself often for sticking with your program. Visualize what it will be like to reach your goals, and keep these pictures in your mind as an incentive to stick with your program.

If you notice you're slacking off, use your health journal to identify the negative thoughts and behaviors that are causing noncompliance. Devise a strategy to decrease the frequency of these negative thoughts and behaviors. Make changes in your program plan and reward system to help renew your enthusiasm and commitment to your program. Expect to make many adjustments in your program along the way.

See the box "Dodging Common Exercise Pitfalls" for additional suggestions.

EXERCISE GUIDELINES FOR PEOPLE WITH SPECIAL HEALTH CONCERNS

Regular, appropriate exercise is safe and beneficial for many people with chronic conditions or other special health concerns. For example, people with heart disease or hypertension who exercise may lower their blood pressure and improve their cholesterol levels. For people with diabetes, exercise can improve insulin sensitivity and body composition. For people with asthma, regular exercise may reduce the risk of acute attacks during exertion. For many people with special health concerns, the risks associated with *not* exercising are far greater than those associated with a moderate program of regular exercise.

The fitness recommendations for the general population presented in this text can serve as a general guideline for any exercise program. However, for people with chronic health conditions, special precautions and monitoring may be required. Anyone with special health concerns should consult a physician before beginning an exercise program. Guidelines and cautions for some common health conditions are described below.

Arthritis

- Begin an exercise program as early as possible in the course of the disease.
- Warm up thoroughly before each exercise session to loosen stiff muscles and lower the risk of injury.
- For cardiorespiratory endurance exercise, avoid high-impact activities that may damage arthritic joints; consider a swimming program or another type of exercise in a warm pool.
- Perform strength training exercises for the whole body; pay special attention to muscles that support and protect affected joints (for example, build quadriceps, hamstring, and calf strength for the knee). Start with small loads and build intensity gradually.
- Perform flexibility exercises regularly to maintain joint mobility.

Asthma

- Exercise regularly. Acute attacks are more likely if you exercise only occasionally.
- Carry medication during workouts, and avoid exercising alone.
- Warm up and cool down slowly to reduce the risk of acute attacks.
- When starting an exercise program, choose self-paced endurance activities, especially those involving **interval training** (short bouts of exercise

An individual with special health concerns can develop a safe and effective fitness program by choosing activities carefully and making appropriate modifications in the program. Swimming is an excellent activity choice for this man with asthma because breathing warm, moist air reduces the risk of asthma attacks during exercise.

followed by a rest period). Increase intensity of cardiorespiratory endurance exercise gradually.
- Cold, dry air can trigger or worsen an attack. Drink water before, during, and after a workout to moisten your airways. In cold weather, cover your mouth with a mask or scarf to warm and humidify the air your breathe. Swimming in a heated pool is an excellent activity choice for people with asthma.
- Avoid outdoor activities during pollen season or when the air is polluted. Avoid exercise in dry or dusty indoor environments.

Diabetes

- Don't begin an exercise program unless your diabetes is under control and you have checked about exercise safety with your physician. Because diabetics have an increased risk for heart disease, an exercise stress test may be recommended.
- Don't exercise alone. Wear a bracelet identifying yourself as a diabetic.
- If you are taking insulin or another medication, you may need to adjust the timing and amount of each dose. Work with your physician and check your blood sugar levels regularly so you can learn to balance your energy intake and output and your medication dosage.

interval training A training technique that alternates exercise intervals with rest intervals or intense exercise intervals with low to moderate intervals. **TERMS**

- To prevent abnormally rapid absorption of injected insulin, inject it over a muscle that won't be exercised and wait at least an hour before exercising.
- Check blood sugar levels before, during, and after exercise, and adjust your diet or insulin dosage if needed. Carry high-carbohydrate foods during a workout.
- If you have poor circulation or numbness in your extremities, check your skin regularly for blisters and abrasions, especially on your feet. Avoid high-impact activities, and wear comfortable shoes.
- For maximum benefit and minimum risk, choose low-to-moderate-intensity activities.

Heart Disease and Hypertension

- Check with your physician about exercise safety before increasing your activity level.
- Exercise at a moderate rather than a high intensity. Keep your heart rate below the level at which abnormalities appear on an exercise stress test.
- Warm-up and cool-down sessions should be gradual and last at least 10 minutes.
- Monitor your heart rate during exercise, and stop if you experience dizziness or chest pain.
- If prescribed, carry nitroglycerin with you during exercise. If you are taking beta-blockers for hypertension, use RPE rather than heart rate to monitor exercise intensity (beta-blockers reduce heart rate). Exercise at an RPE level of "somewhat hard"; your breathing should be unlabored and you should be able to talk.
- Don't hold your breath when exercising. Doing so can cause sudden, steep increases in blood pressure. Take special care during weight training; don't lift extremely heavy loads.

- Increase exercise intensity, duration, and frequency very gradually.

Obesity

- For maximum benefit and minimum risk, choose low-to-moderate-intensity activities.
- Choose non- or low-weight-bearing activities such as cycling, swimming, or walking. Low-impact activities are less likely to lead to joint problems or injuries.
- Stay alert for symptoms of heat-related problems during exercise (see Chapter 3). People who are obese are particularly vulnerable to problems with heat intolerance.
- Ease into an exercise program, and increase overload gradually. Increase duration and frequency of exercise before increasing intensity.
- Include strength training in your fitness program to build or maintain fat-free mass.

Osteoporosis

- For cardiorespiratory endurance activities, exercise at the maximum intensity that causes no significant discomfort. If possible, choose low-impact weight-bearing activities to help safely maintain bone density (see Chapter 8 for more strategies for building and maintaining bone density).
- To prevent fractures, avoid any activity or movement that stresses the back or carries a risk of falling.
- Include weight training in your exercise program to improve strength and balance and reduce the risk of falls and fractures. Avoid lifting heavy loads.

Exercise guidelines for people with other special health concerns have been discussed in other chapters: disabilities (Chapter 2), pregnancy (Chapter 3), and low-back pain (Chapter 5).

COMMON QUESTIONS ANSWERED

Should I exercise every day? Some daily exercise is beneficial, and health experts recommend that you engage in at least 30 minutes of moderate physical activity over the course of every day. However, if you train intensely every day without giving yourself a rest, you will likely get injured or become overtrained. When strength training, for example, rest at least 1 day between workouts before exercising the same muscle group. For cardiorespiratory endurance exercise, rest or exercise lightly the day after an intense or long-duration workout. Balancing the proper amount of rest and exercise will help you feel better and improve your fitness faster.

I'm just starting an exercise program; how much activity should I do at first? Be conservative. Walking is a good way

to begin almost any fitness program. At first, walk for approximately 10 minutes, and then increase the distance and pace. After several weeks, you can progress to something more vigorous. Let your body be your guide. If the intensity and duration of a workout seem easy, increase them a little the next time. The key is to be progressive; don't try to achieve physical fitness in one or two workouts. Build your fitness gradually.

I'm concerned about my safety when I go for a jog or walk. What can I do to make sure that my training sessions are safe and enjoyable? A person exercising alone in the park can be a tempting target for criminals. Don't exercise alone. You are much less likely to be a crime victim if you are training in a group or with a partner. Another alternative is to take an exercise class. Classes are fun and much more safe than exercising by yourself. If you must train alone, try to exercise where there are plenty of people. A good bet is the local high school or college track.

Make sure you're wearing proper safety equipment. If you're riding a bike, wear a helmet. If you're playing racquetball or handball, wear eye protectors. Don't go in-line skating unless you're wearing the proper pads and protective equipment. If jogging at night, wear reflective clothing that can be seen easily.

Refer to Appendix A for more information on personal safety.

SUMMARY

- Steps for putting together a complete fitness program include (1) setting realistic goals, (2) selecting activities to develop all the health-related components of fitness, (3) setting a target intensity, duration, and frequency for each activity, (4) setting up a system of mini-goals and rewards, (5) making lifestyle physical activity a part of the daily routine, (6) developing tools for monitoring progress, and (7) making a commitment.

- In selecting activities, consider fun and interest, your current skill and fitness level, time and convenience, cost, and any special health concerns.

- Keys to putting a successful plan into action are starting slowly, increasing intensity and duration gradually, finding a buddy, varying the program, and expecting fluctuations and lapses.

- Regular exercise is appropriate and highly beneficial for people with special health concerns; program modifications may be necessary to maximize safety.

FOR MORE INFORMATION

See the listings for Chapters 2–6.

SELECTED BIBLIOGRAPHY

American College of Sports Medicine. 1998. ACSM Position Stand: The Recommended Quantity and Quality of Exercise for Developing and Maintaining Cardiorespiratory and Muscular Fitness, and Flexibility in Healthy Adults. *Medicine and Science in Sports and Exercise* 30(6): 975–991.

American College of Sports Medicine and American Diabetes Association. 1997. Joint position statement: Diabetes mellitus and exercise. *Medicine and Science in Sports and Exercise* 29(12): I–VI.

Ballas, M. T., J. Tytko, and D. Cookson. 1997. Common overuse running injuries: Diagnosis and management. *American Family Physician* 77(7): 2473–2484.

Buckwalter, J. A., and N. E. Lane. 1997. Athletics and osteoarthritis. *American Journal of Sports Medicine* 25(6): 873–881.

Halbert, J. A., et al. 1997. The effectiveness of exercise training in lowering blood pressure: A meta-analysis of randomised controlled trials of 4 weeks or longer. *Journal of Human Hypertension* 11(10): 641–649.

International Inline Skating Association. *Gear Up! Guide to Inline Skating. Health Benefits* (retrieved February 11, 1998; http://www.iisa.org).

Katz, W. A. 1998. Exercise for osteoporosis. *The Physician and Sportsmedicine* 26(2).

Martin, D. R. 1997. Athletic shoes: Finding a good match. *The Physician and Sportsmedicine* 25(9): 138–144.

Morris, J. N., and A. E. Hardman. 1997. Walking to health. *Sports Medicine* 23(5): 306–332.

Nguyen, M. N., L. Potvin, and J. Otis. 1997. Regular exercise in 30- to 60-year-old men: Combining the stages-of-change model and the theory of planned behavior to identify determinants for targeting heart health interventions. *Journal of Community Health* 22:233–246.

Powell, M., and J. Svensson. 1993. *In-Line Skating*. Champaign, Ill.: Human Kinetics.

Scheiber, R. A., et al. 1996. Risk factors for injuries from in-line skating and the effectiveness of safety gear. *New England Journal of Medicine* 355(22): 1630–1635.

Stamford, B. 1996. Cross-training: Giving yourself a whole-body workout. *The Physician and Sportsmedicine* 24(9): 103.

Tan, R. A., and S. L. Spector. 1998. Exercise-induced asthma. *Sports Medicine* 25(1): 1–6.

Thompson, D. C., R. P. Rivera, and R. S. Thompson. 1996. Effectiveness of bicycle safety helmets in preventing head injuries: A case-controlled study. *Journal of the American Medical Association* 276(24): 1968–1973.

Thordarson, D. B. 1997. Running biomechanics. *Clinics in Sports Medicine* 16:239–247.

Wallberg-Henriksson, H., J. Rincon, and J. R. Zierath. 1998. Exercise in the management of non-insulin-dependent diabetes mellitus. *Sports Medicine* 25(1): 25–35.

Wallick, M. E., et al. 1995. Physiological responses to in-line skating compared to treadmill running. *Medicine and Science in Sports and Exercise* 27(2): 242–248.

Young, J. C. 1998. Exercise for clients with type 2 diabetes. *ACSM's Health and Fitness Journal* 2(3): 24–29.

Zachwieja, J. J. 1996. Exercise as treatment for obesity. *Endocrinology and Metabolism Clinics of North America* 25: 965–988.

Sample fitness programs begin on p. 170.

Sample programs based on four different types of cardiorespiratory activities—walking/jogging/running, bicycling, swimming, and in-line skating—are presented below. Each sample program includes regular cardiorespiratory endurance exercise, resistance training, and stretching. To choose a sample program, first compare your fitness goals with the benefits of the different types of endurance exercise featured in the sample programs (see Table 7-1). Identify the programs that meet your fitness needs. Next, read through the descriptions of the programs you're considering and decide which will work best for you based on your present routine, the potential for enjoyment, and adaptability to your lifestyle. If you choose one of these programs, complete the personal fitness program plan in Lab 7-1, just as if you had created a program from scratch.

No program will bring about enormous changes in your fitness level in the first few weeks. Give your program a good chance. Follow the specifics of the program for 3–4 weeks. Then if the exercise program doesn't seem suitable, make adjustments to adapt it to your particular needs. But retain the basic elements of the program that make it effective for developing fitness.

General Guidelines

The following guidelines can help make the activity programs more effective for you.

- *Intensity.* To work effectively for cardiorespiratory endurance training or to improve body composition, you must raise your heart rate into its target zone. Monitor your pulse, or use rates of perceived exertion to monitor your intensity.

    If you've been sedentary, begin very slowly. Give your muscles a chance to adjust to their increased workload. It's probably best to keep your heart rate below target until your body has had time to adjust to new demands. At first you may not need to work very hard to keep your heart rate in its target zone, but as your cardiorespiratory endurance improves, you will probably need to increase intensity.

- *Duration and frequency.* To experience training effects, you should exercise for 20–60 minutes at least three times per week.

- *Interval training.* Some of the sample programs involve continuous activity. Others rely on interval training, which calls for alternating a relief interval with exercise (walking after jogging, for example, or coasting after biking uphill). Interval training is an effective way to achieve progressive overload: When your heart rate gets too high, slow down to lower your pulse rate until you're at the low end of your target zone. Interval training can also prolong the total time you spend in exercise and delay the onset of fatigue.

- *Warm-up and cool-down.* Begin each exercise session with a 10-minute warm-up. Begin your activity at a slow pace, and work up gradually to your target heart rate. Always slow down gradually at the end of your exercise session to bring your system back to its normal state. It's a good idea to do stretching exercises to increase your flexibility after cardiorespiratory exercise or strength training because your muscles will be warm and ready to stretch.

- *Record keeping.* After each exercise session, record your daily distance or time on a progress chart like the one shown in Lab 7-2.

WALKING/JOGGING/RUNNING SAMPLE PROGRAM

Walking, jogging, and running are the most popular forms of training for people who want to improve cardiorespiratory endurance; they also improve body composition and muscular endurance of the legs. It's not always easy to distinguish among these three endurance activities. For clarity and consistency, we'll consider walking to be any on-foot exercise of less than 5 miles per hour, jogging any pace between 5 and 7.5 miles per hour, and running any pace faster than that. Table 1 divides walking, jogging, and running into nine categories, with rates of speed (in both miles per hour and minutes per mile) and calorie costs for each. The faster your pace or the longer you exercise, the more calories you burn. The greater the number of calories burned, the higher the potential training effects of these activities.

Equipment and Technique

These activities require no special skills, expensive equipment, or unusual facilities. Comfortable clothing, well-fitted walking or running shoes, and a stopwatch or ordinary watch with a second hand are all you need.

Developing Cardiorespiratory Endurance

The four variations of the basic walking/jogging/running sample program that follow are designed to help you regulate the intensity, duration, and frequency of your program. Use the following guidelines to choose the variation that is right for you.

- *Variation 1: Walking (Starting).* Choose this program if you have medical restrictions, are recovering from illness or surgery, tire easily after short walks, are obese, or have a sedentary lifestyle, and if you want to prepare for the advanced walking program to improve cardiorespiratory endurance, body composition, and muscular endurance.

- *Variation 2: Advanced Walking.* Choose this program if you already can walk comfortably for 30 minutes and if you want to develop and maintain cardiorespiratory fitness, a lean body, and muscular endurance.

- *Variation 3: Preparing for a Jogging Program.* Choose this program if you already can walk comfortably for 30 minutes and if you want to prepare for the jogging/running program to improve cardiorespiratory endurance, body composition, and muscular endurance.

- *Variation 4: Jogging/Running.* Choose this program if you already can jog comfortably without muscular discomfort, if you already can jog for 15 minutes without stopping or 30 minutes with brief walking intervals within your target

SAMPLE PROGRAM TABLE 1
Calorie Costs for Walking/Jogging/Running

This table gives the calorie costs of walking, jogging, and running for slow, moderate, and fast paces. Calculations for calorie costs are approximate and assume a level terrain. A hilly terrain would result in higher calorie cost. To get an estimate of the number of calories you burn, multiply your weight by the calories per minute per pound for the speed at which you're doing the activity (listed in the right-hand column), and then multiply that by the number of minutes you exercise.

	Speed		
Activity	Miles per Hour	Minutes: Seconds per Mile	Calories per Minute per Pound
Walking			
Slow	2.0	30:00	.020
	2.5	24:00	.023
Moderate	3.0	20:00	.026
	3.5	17:08	.029
Fast	4.0	15:00	.037
	4.5	13:20	.048
Jogging			
Slow	5.0	12:00	.060
	5.5	11:00	.074
Moderate	6.0	10:00	.081
	6.5	9:00	.088
Fast	7.0	8:35	.092
	7.5	8:00	.099
Running			
Slow	8.5	7:00	.111
Moderate	9.0	6:40	.116
Fast	10.0	6:00	.129
	11.0	5:30	.141

SOURCE: Kusinitz, I., and M. Fine. 1995. *Your Guide to Getting Fit,* 3d ed. Mountain View, Calif.: Mayfield.

heart rate range, and if you want to develop and maintain a high level of cardiorespiratory fitness, a lean body, and muscular endurance.

Variation 1: Walking (Starting)

Intensity, duration, and frequency: Walk at first for 15 minutes at a pace that keeps your heart rate below your target zone. Gradually increase to 30-minute sessions. The distance you travel will probably be 1–2 miles. At the beginning, walk every other day. You can gradually increase to daily walking if you want to burn more calories (helpful if you want to change body composition).

Calorie cost: Work up to using 90–135 calories in each session (see Table 1). To increase calorie costs to the target level, walk for a longer time or for a longer distance rather than sharply increasing speed.

At the beginning: Start at whatever level is most comfortable. Maintain a normal easy pace, and stop to rest as often as you need to. Never prolong a walk past the point of comfort. When walking with a friend (a good motivation), let a comfortable conversation be your guide to pace.

As you progress: Once your muscles have become adjusted to the exercise program, increase the duration of your sessions— but by no more than 10% each week. Increase your intensity only enough to keep your heart rate just below your target. When you're able to walk 1.5 miles in 30 minutes, using 90–135 calories per session, you should consider moving on to Variation 2 or 3. Don't be discouraged by lack of immediate progress, and don't try to speed things up by overdoing. Remember that pace and heart rate can vary with the terrain, the weather, and other factors.

Variation 2: Advanced Walking

Intensity, duration, and frequency: Start at a pace at the lower end of your target heart rate zone, and begin soon afterward to increase your pace. This might boost your heart rate into the upper levels of your target zone, which is fine for brief periods. But don't overdo the intervals of fast walking. Slow down after a short time to drop your pulse rate. Vary your pattern to allow for intervals of slow, medium, and fast walking. Walk at first for 30 minutes and gradually increase your walking time until eventually you reach 60 minutes, all the while maintaining your target heart rate. The distance you walk will probably be 2–4 miles. Walk at least every other day.

Calorie cost: Work up to using about 200–350 calories in each session (see Table 1).

At the beginning: Begin by walking somewhat faster than you did in Variation 1. Check your pulse to make sure you keep your heart rate within your target zone. Slow down when necessary to lower your heart rate when going up hills or when extending the duration of your walks.

As you progress: As your heart rate adjusts to the increased workload, gradually increase your pace and your total walking time. Gradually lengthen the periods of fast walking and shorten the relief intervals of slow walking, always maintaining target heart rate. Eventually, you will reach the fitness level you would like to maintain. And to maintain that level of fitness, continue to burn the same amount of calories in each session.

Vary your program by changing the pace and distance walked, or by walking routes with different terrains and views. Gauge your progress toward whatever calorie goal you've set by using Table 1.

Variation 3: Preparing for a Jogging Program

Intensity, duration, and frequency: Start by walking at a moderate pace (3–4 miles per hour or 15–20 minutes per mile). Staying within your target heart rate zone, begin to add brief intervals of slow jogging (5–6 miles per hour or 10–12 minutes per mile). Keep the walking intervals constant at 60 seconds or at 110 yards, but gradually increase the jogging intervals until eventually you jog 4 minutes for each minute of walking. You'll probably cover between 1.5 and 2.5 miles. Each exercise session should last 15–30 minutes. Exercise every other day. If your goals include changing body composition and you want to exercise more frequently, walk on days you're not jogging.

SAMPLE PROGRAM TABLE 2   *Walking/Jogging Progression by Time*

This table is based on a walking interval of 3.75 miles per hour, measured in seconds, and a jogging interval of 5.5 miles per hour, measured in minutes:seconds. The combination of the two intervals equals a single set. In the Number of Sets column, the higher figure represents the maximum number of sets to be completed.

	Walk Interval (sec)	Jog Interval (min:sec)	Number of Sets	Total Distance (mi)	Total Time (min:sec)
Stage 1	:60	:30	10–15	1.0–1.7	15:00–22:30
Stage 2	:60	:60	8–13	1.2–2.0	16:00–26:00
Stage 3	:60	2:00	5–19	1.3–2.3	15:00–27:00
Stage 4	:60	3:00	5–7	1.6–2.4	16:00–28:00
Stage 5	:60	4:00	3–6	1.5–2.7	15:00–30:00

SOURCE: Kusinitz, I., and M. Fine. 1995. *Your Guide to Getting Fit,* 3d ed. Mountain View, Calif.: Mayfield.

SAMPLE PROGRAM TABLE 3   *Walking/Jogging Progression by Distance*

This table is based on a walking interval of 3.75 miles per hour, measured in yards, and a jogging interval of 5.5 miles per hour, also measured in yards. The combination of the two intervals equals a singe set. (One lap around a typical track is 440 yards.)

	Walk Interval (yd)	Jog Interval (yd)	Number of Sets	Total Distance (mi)	Total Time (min:sec)
Stage 1	110	55	11–21	1.0–2.0	15:00–28:12
Stage 2	110	110	16	2.0	26:56
Stage 3	110	220	11	2.0	26:02
Stage 4	110	330	8	2.0	24:24
Stage 5	110	440	7	2.2	26:05
Stage 6	110	440	8	2.5	29:49

SOURCE: Kusinitz, I., and M. Fine. 1995. *Your Guide to Getting Fit,* 3d ed. Mountain View, Calif.: Mayfield.

Calorie cost: Work up to using 200–350 calories in each session (see Table 1).

At the beginning: Start slowly. Until your muscles adjust to jogging, you may need to exercise at less than your target heart rate. At the outset, expect to do two to four times as much walking as jogging, even more if you're relatively inexperienced. Be guided by how comfortable you feel—and by your heart rate—in setting the pace for your progress. Follow the guidelines presented in Chapter 3 for exercising in hot or cold weather. Drink enough liquids to stay adequately hydrated, particularly in hot weather. In addition, use the proper running technique described below.

- Run with your back straight and your head up. Look straight ahead, not at your feet. Shift your pelvis forward, and tuck your buttocks in.

- Hold your arms slightly away from your body. Your elbows should be bent so that your forearms are parallel to the ground. You may cup your hands, but do not clench your fists. Allow your arms to swing loosely and rhythmically with each stride.

- Your heel should hit the ground first in each stride. Then roll forward onto the ball of your foot and push off for the next stride. If you find this difficult, you can try a more flat-footed style, but don't land on the balls of your feet.

- Keep your steps short by allowing your foot to strike the ground just below your knee. Keep your knees bent at all times.

- Breathe deeply through your mouth. Try to use your abdominal muscles rather than just your chest muscles to take deep breaths.

- Stay relaxed.

As you progress: Adjust your ratio of walking to jogging to keep within your target heart rate zone as much as possible. When you have progressed to the point where most of your 30-minute session is spent jogging, consider moving on to Variation 4. To find a walking/jogging progression that suits you, refer to Tables 2 and 3 (one uses time, the other distance). Which one you choose will depend, to some extent, on where you work out. If you have access to a track or can use a measured distance with easily visible landmarks to indicate yardage covered, you may find it convenient to use distance as your organizing principle. If you'll be using parks, streets, or woods, time intervals (measured with a watch) would probably work better. The suggested progressions in Tables 2 and 3 are not meant to be rigid; they are guidelines to help you develop your own rate of progress. Let your progress be guided by your heart rate, and increase your intensity and duration only to achieve your target zone.

Variation 4: Jogging/Running

Intensity, duration, and frequency: The key is to exercise within your target heart rate zone. Most people who sustain a continuous jog/run program will find that they can stay within their target heart rate zone with a speed of 5.5–7.5 miles per hour (8–11 minutes per mile). Start by jogging steadily for 15 minutes. Gradually increase your jog/run session to a regular 30–60 minutes (or about 2.5–7 miles). Exercise at least every other day. Increasing frequency by doing other activities on alternate days will place less stress on the weight-bearing parts of your lower body than will a daily program of jogging/running.

Calorie cost: Use about 300–750 calories in each session (see Table 1).

At the beginning: The greater number of calories you burn per minute makes this program less time-consuming for altering body composition than the three other variations in the walking/jogging/running program.

As you progress: If you choose this variation, you probably already have a moderate-to-high level of cardiorespiratory fitness. To stay within your target heart rate zone, increase your distance or both pace and distance as needed. Add variety to your workouts by varying your route, intensity, and duration. Alternate short runs with long ones. If you run for 60 minutes one day, try running for 30 minutes the next session. Or try doing sets that alternate hard and easy intervals—even walking, if you feel like it. You can also try a road race now and then, but be careful not to do too much too soon.

Developing Muscular Strength and Endurance

Walking, jogging, and running provide muscular endurance workouts for your lower body; they also develop muscular strength of the lower body to a lesser degree. To develop muscular strength and endurance of the upper body, and to make greater and more rapid gains in lower-body strength, you need to include resistance training in your fitness program. Use the general wellness weight training program from Chapter 4, or tailor one to fit your personal fitness goals. If you'd like to in-crease your running speed and performance, you might want to focus your program on lower-body exercises. (Don't neglect upper-body strength, however; it is important for overall wellness.) Regardless of what strength training exercises you choose, follow the guidelines for successful training:

- Train 2–3 days per week

- Perform 1 or more sets of 8–12 repetitions of 8–10 exercises.

- Include exercises that work all the major muscle groups: neck, shoulders, chest, arms, upper and lower back, abdomen, thighs, and calves.

Depending on the amount of time you are able to set aside for exercise, you may find it more convenient to alternate between your cardiorespiratory endurance workouts and your muscular strength and endurance workouts. In other words, walk or jog one day and strength train the next day.

Developing Flexibility

To round out your fitness program, you also need to include exercises that develop flexibility. The best time for a flexibility workout is when your muscles are warm, as they are immediately following cardiorespiratory endurance exercise or strength training. Perform the stretching routine presented in Chapter 5 or one that you have created to meet your own goals and preferences. Be sure to pay special attention to the hamstrings and quadriceps, which are not worked through their complete range of motion during walking or jogging. As you put your program together, remember the basic structure of a successful flexibility program:

- Stretch at least 2–3 days per week, preferably when muscles are warm.

- Stretch all the major muscle groups.

- Stretch to the point of mild discomfort, and hold for 10–30 seconds.

- Repeat each stretch at least 4 times.

BICYCLING SAMPLE PROGRAM

Bicycling can also lead to large gains in physical fitness. For many people, cycling is a pleasant and economical alternative to driving and a convenient way to build fitness.

Equipment and Technique

Cycling has its own special array of equipment, including headgear, lighting, safety pennants, and special shoes. The bike is the most expensive item, ranging from about $100 to well over $1000. Avoid making a large investment until you're sure you'll use your bike regularly. While investigating what the marketplace has to offer, rent or borrow a bike. Consider your intended use of the bike. Most cyclists who are interested primarily in fitness are best served by a sturdy 10-speed rather than a mountain bike or sport bike. Stationary cycles are good for rainy days and areas that have harsh winters.

Clothing for bike riding shouldn't be restrictive or binding, nor should it be so loose-fitting or so long that it might get caught in the chain. Clothing worn on the upper body should be comfortable but not so loose that it catches the wind and slows you down. Always wear a helmet to help prevent injury in case of a fall or crash. Wearing glasses or goggles can protect the eyes from dirt, small objects, and irritation from wind.

To avoid saddle soreness and injury, choose a soft or padded saddle, and adjust it to a height that allows your legs to almost reach full extension while pedaling. Wear a pair of well-padded gloves if your hands tend to become numb while riding or if you begin to develop blisters or calluses. To prevent backache and neck strain, warm up thoroughly, and periodically shift the position of your hands on the handlebars and your body in the saddle. Keep your arms relaxed, and don't lock your elbows. To protect your knees from strain, pedal with your feet pointed straight ahead or very slightly inward, and don't pedal in high gear for long periods.

Bike riding requires a number of precise skills that practice makes automatic. If you've never ridden before, consider taking a course. In fact, many courses are not just for beginners.

They'll help you develop skills in braking, shifting, and handling emergencies, as well as teach you ways of caring for and repairing your bike.

The National Injury Information Clearinghouse classifies bicycle riding as the nation's most dangerous sport. Many injuries are the result of the cyclist's carelessness. For safe cycling, follow these rules:

- Always wear a helmet.
- Keep on the correct side of the road. Bicycling against traffic is usually illegal and always dangerous.
- Obey all traffic signs and signals.
- On public roads, ride in single file, except in low-traffic areas (if the law permits). Ride in a straight line; don't swerve or weave in traffic.
- Be alert; anticipate the movements of other traffic and pedestrians. Listen for approaching traffic that is out of your line of vision.
- Slow down at street crossings. Check both ways before crossing.
- Use hand signals—the same as for automobile drivers—if you intend to stop or turn. Use audible signals to warn those in your path.
- Maintain full control. Avoid anything that interferes with your vision. Don't jeopardize your ability to steer by carrying anything (including people) on the handlebars.
- Keep your bicycle in good shape. Brakes, gears, saddle, wheels, and tires should always be in good condition.
- See and be seen. Use a headlight at night, and equip your bike with rear reflectors. Use side reflectors on pedals, front and rear. Wear light-colored clothing or use reflective tape at night and bright colors or fluorescent tape by day.
- Be courteous to other road users. Anticipate the worst, and practice preventive cycling.
- Use a rear-view mirror.

Developing Cardiorespiratory Endurance

Cycling is an excellent way to develop and maintain cardiorespiratory endurance and a healthy body composition.

Intensity, duration, and frequency: If you've been inactive for a long time, begin your cycling program at a heart rate that is 10–20% below your target zone. Once you feel at home on your bike, try 1 mile at a comfortable speed, and then stop and check your heart rate. Increase your speed gradually until you can cycle at 12–15 miles per hour (4–5 minutes per mile), a speed fast enough to bring most new cyclists' heart rate into their target zone. Allow your pulse rate to be your guide: More highly fit individuals may need to ride faster to achieve their target heart rate. Cycling for at least 20 minutes three times per week will improve your fitness.

Calorie cost: Use Table 4 to determine the number of calories you burn during each outing. You can increase the number of calories burned by cycling faster or for a longer duration (it's usually better to increase distance rather than to add speed).

At the beginning: It may require several outings to get the muscles and joints of your legs and hips adjusted to this new activity. Begin each outing with a 10-minute warm-up that includes stretches for your hamstrings and your back and neck muscles. Until you become a skilled cyclist, select routes with the fewest hazards, and avoid heavy automobile traffic.

As you progress: Interval training is also effective with bicycling. Simply increase your speed for periods of 4–8 minutes or for specific distances, such as 1–2 miles. Then coast for 2–3 minutes. Alternate the speed intervals and slow intervals for a total of 20–60 minutes, depending on your level of fitness. Hilly terrain is also a form of interval training.

Developing Muscular Strength and Endurance

Bicycling develops a high level of endurance and a moderate level of strength in the muscles of the lower body. To develop muscular strength and endurance of the upper body—and to make greater and more rapid gains in lower-body strength—you need to include resistance training as part of your fitness program. Use the general wellness weight training program from Chapter 4, or tailor one to fit your personal fitness goals. If one of your goals is to increase your cycling speed and performance, be sure to include exercises for the quadriceps, hamstrings, and buttocks muscles in your strength training program. No matter which exercises you include in your program, follow the general guidelines for successful and safe training:

- Train 2–3 days per week.
- Perform 1 or more sets of 8–12 repetitions of 8–10 exercises.
- Include exercises that work all the major muscle groups: neck, shoulders, chest, arms, upper and lower back, abdomen, thighs, and calves.

Depending on your schedule, you may find it more convenient to alternate between your cardiorespiratory endurance workouts and your muscular strength and endurance workouts. In other words, cycle one day and strength train the next day.

Developing Flexibility

A complete fitness program also includes exercises that develop flexibility. The best time for a flexibility workout is when your muscles are warm, as they are immediately following a session of cardiorespiratory endurance exercise or strength training. Perform the stretching routine presented in Chapter 5, or develop one that meets your own goals and preferences. Pay special attention to the hamstrings and quadriceps, which are not worked through their complete range of motion during bike riding, and to the muscles in your lower back, shoulders, and neck. As you put your stretching program together, remember these basic guidelines:

- Stretch at least 2–3 days per week, preferably when muscles are warm.
- Stretch all the major muscle groups.
- Stretch to the point of mild discomfort, and hold for 10–30 seconds.
- Repeat each stretch at least 4 times.

This table gives the approximate calorie costs per pound of body weight for cycling from 5 to 60 minutes for distances of .50 mile up to 15 miles on a level terrain. To use the table, find on the horizontal line the time most closely approximating the number of minutes you cycle. Next, locate on the vertical column the approximate distance in miles you cover. The figure at the intersection represents an estimate of the calories used per minute per pound of body weight. Multiply this figure by your own body weight. Then multiply the product of these two figures by the number of minutes you cycle to get the total number of calories burned. For example, assuming you weigh 154 pounds and cycle 6 miles in 40 minutes, you would burn 260 calories: 154 × .042 (calories per pound, from table) = 6.5 × 40 (minutes) = 260 calories burned.

Distance (mi)	Time (min)											
	5	10	15	20	25	30	35	40	45	50	55	60
.50	.032											
1.00	.062	.032										
1.50		.042	.032									
2.00		.062	.039	.032								
3.00			.062	.042	.036	.032						
4.00				.062	.044	.039	.035	.032				
5.00				.097	.062	.045	.041	.037	.035	.032		
6.00					.088	.062	.047	.042	.039	.036	.034	.032
7.00						.081	.062	.049	.043	.040	.038	.036
8.00							.078	.062	.050	.044	.041	.039
9.00								.076	.062	.051	.045	.042
10.00								.097	.074	.062	.051	.045
11.00									.093	.073	.062	.052
12.00										.088	.072	.062
13.00											.084	.071
14.00												.081
15.00												.097

SOURCE: Kusinitz, I., and M. Fine. 1995. *Your Guide to Getting Fit*, 3d ed. Mountain View, Calif.: Mayfield.

SWIMMING SAMPLE PROGRAM

Swimming is one of the best activities for developing all-around fitness. Because water supports the body weight of the swimmer, swimming places less stress than weight-bearing activities on joints, ligaments, and tendons and tends to cause fewer injuries.

Equipment and Safety Guidelines

Aside from having access to a swimming pool, the only equipment required for a swimming program is a swimsuit and a pair of swimming goggles to protect the eyes from irritation in chlorinated pools.

Following these few simple rules can help keep you safe and healthy during your swimming sessions:

- Swim only in a pool with a qualified lifeguard on duty.
- Always walk carefully on wet surfaces.
- Dry your ears well after swimming. If you experience the symptoms of swimmer's ear (itching, discharge, or even a partial hearing loss), consult your physician. If you swim while recovering from swimmer's ear, protect your ears with a few drops of lanolin on a wad of lamb's wool.
- To avoid back pain, try not to arch your back excessively when you swim.
- Be courteous to others in the pool.

If you swim in a setting other than a pool with a lifeguard, remember the following important rules:

- Don't swim beyond your skill and endurance limits.
- Avoid being chilled by water colder than 70°F.
- Never drink alcohol before going swimming.
- Never swim alone.

Developing Cardiorespiratory Endurance

Any one or any combination of common swimming strokes—front crawl stroke, breaststroke, backstroke, butterfly stroke, sidestroke, or elementary backstroke—can help develop and maintain cardiorespiratory fitness. (Swimming may not be as helpful as walking, jogging, or cycling for body fat loss.)

Intensity, duration, and frequency: Because swimming is not a weight-bearing activity and is not done in an upright position, it elicits a lower heart rate per minute. Therefore, you need to adjust your target heart rate zone. To calculate your target heart rate for swimming, use this formula:

Maximum swimming heart rate (MSHR) = 205 − age
Target heart rate zone = 65–90% of MSHR

SAMPLE PROGRAM TABLE 5 *Calorie Costs for Swimming*

To use this table, find on the top horizontal row the distance in yards that most closely approximates the distance you swim. Next, locate on the appropriate vertical column (below the distance in yards) the time it takes you to swim the distance. Then locate in the first column on the left the approximate number of calories burned per minute per pound for the time and distance. To find the total number of calories burned, multiply your weight by the calories per minute per pound. Then multiply the product of these two numbers by the time it takes you to swim the distance (minutes:seconds). For example, assuming you weigh 130 pounds and swim 500 yards in 20 minutes, you would burn 106 calories: 130 × .041 (calories per pound, from table) = 5.33 × 20 (minutes) = 106 calories burned.

Calories per Minute per Pound	Distance (yd)					
	25	100	150	250	500	750
.033	1:15	5:00	7:30	12:30	25:00	30:30
.041	1:00	4:00	6:00	10:00	20:00	30:00
.049	0:50	3:20	5:00	8:20	18:40	25:00
.057	0:43	2:52	4:18	7:10	17:20	21:30
.065	0:37.5	2:30	3:45	6:15	10:00	
.073	0:33	2:13	3:20	5:30	8:50	
.081	0:30	2:00	3:00	5:00	8:00	
.090	0:27	1:48	2:42	4:30	7:12	
.097	0:25	1:40	2:30	4:10	6:30	

SOURCE: Kusinitz, I., and M. Fine. 1995. *Your Guide to Getting Fit*, 3d ed. Mountain View, Calif.: Mayfield.

For example, a 19-year-old would calculate her target heart rate zone for swimming as follows:

MSHR = 205 − 19 = 186 bpm

Target heart rate zone for swimming:

at 65% intensity: 0.65 × 186 = 121 bpm

at 90% intensity: 0.90 × 186 = 167 bpm

Base your duration of swimming on your intensity and target calorie costs. Swim at least three times per week.

Calorie cost: Calories burned while swimming are the result of the pace: how far you swim and how fast (see Table 5). Work up to using at least 300 calories per session.

At the beginning: If you don't have much experience swimming, invest the time and money for instruction. You'll make more rapid gains in fitness if you learn correct swimming technique. If you've been sedentary and haven't done any swimming for a long time, begin your program with 2–3 weeks, three times per week, of leisurely swimming at a pace that keeps your heart rate 10–20% below your target zone. Start swimming laps of the width of the pool if you can't swim the length. To keep your heart rate below target, take rest intervals as needed. Swim one lap, then rest 15–90 seconds as needed. Start with 10 minutes of swim/rest intervals and work up to 20 minutes. How long it takes will depend on your swimming skills and muscular fitness.

As you progress: Gradually increase the duration, or the intensity, or both duration and intensity of your swimming to raise your heart rate to a comfortable level within your target zone. Gradually increase your swimming intervals and decrease your

rest intervals as you progress. Once you can swim the length of the pool at a pace that keeps your heart rate on target, continue swim/rest intervals for 20 minutes. Your rest intervals should be 30–45 seconds. You may find it helpful to get out of the pool during your rest intervals and walk until you've lowered your heart rate. Next, swim two laps of the pool length per swim interval and continue swim/rest intervals for 30 minutes. For the 30-second rest interval, walk (or rest) until you've lowered your heart rate. Gradually increase the number of laps you swim consecutively and the total duration of your session until you reach your target calorie expenditure and fitness level. But take care not to swim at too fast a pace: It can raise your heart rate too high and limit your ability to sustain your swimming. Alternating strokes can rest your muscles and help prolong your swimming time. A variety of strokes will also let you work more muscle groups.

Developing Muscular Strength and Endurance

The swimming program outlined in this section will result in moderate gains in strength and large gains in endurance in the muscles used during the strokes you've chosen. To develop strength and endurance in all the muscles of the body, you need to include resistance training as part of your fitness program. Use the general wellness weight training program from Chapter 4, or tailor one to fit your personal fitness goals. To improve your swimming performance, include exercises that work key muscles. For example, if you swim primarily front crawl, include exercises to increase strength in your shoulders, arms, and upper back. (Training the muscles you use during swimming can also help prevent injuries.) Regardless of which strength training exercise you include in your program, follow the general guidelines for successful training:

- Train 2–3 days per week.
- Perform 1 or more sets of 8–12 repetitions of 8–10 exercises.
- Include exercises that work all the major muscle groups: neck, shoulders, chest, arms, upper and lower back, abdomen, thighs, and calves.

Depending on the amount of time you have for exercise, you might want to schedule your cardiorespiratory endurance workouts and your muscular strength and endurance workouts on alternate days. In other words, swim one day and strength train the next day.

Developing Flexibility

For a complete fitness program, you also need to include exercises that develop flexibility. The best time for a flexibility workout is when your muscles are warm, as they are immediately following cardiorespiratory endurance exercise or strength training. Perform the stretching routine presented in Chapter 5 or one you have created to meet your own goals and preferences. Be sure to pay special attention to the muscles you use during swimming, particularly the shoulders and back. As you put your program together, remember the basic structure of a successful flexibility program:

- Stretch at least 2–3 days per week, preferably when muscles are warm.
- Stretch all the major muscle groups.
- Stretch to the point of mild discomfort, and hold for 10–30 seconds.
- Repeat each stretch at least 4 times.

IN-LINE SKATING SAMPLE PROGRAM

In-line skating is currently the fastest growing sport in the United States. Skating is convenient and inexpensive (after the initial outlay for equipment); it can be done on city streets, on paved bike paths and trails, and in parks. If done intensively enough, skating can provide a cardiorespiratory endurance workout comparable to the workouts provided by jogging and cycling. Studies indicate that skating consumes about as many calories as jogging.

An advantage of skating over jogging is that skating is low impact, so it is less harmful to the knees and ankles. An advantage of skating over bicycling is that it works the hamstring muscle in the back of the thigh. Skating develops lower-body strength and endurance, working all the muscles of the leg and hip and strengthening the muscles and connective tissues surrounding the ankles, knees, and hips.

Equipment

To skate safely and enjoyably, you will need a pair of comfortable, sturdy, quality skates and adequate safety equipment. The skate consists of a hard polyurethane shell or outer boot; a padded foam liner; and a frame or chassis that holds the wheels, bearings, spacers, and brake. If you want to try out the sport before making a commitment, rent your skates and equipment from a skate shop. If you are buying, plan to spend about $110–$200 for skates that meet the basic needs of most recreational skaters. Shop for the best combination of price, quality, comfort, and service.

Essential safety equipment includes a helmet, elbow pads, knee pads, and wrist guards. (Wrist injuries are the most common in-line skating injury.) You may want to put reflective tape on your skates for those occasions when you don't get home before dark. Carry moleskin or adhesive bandages with you in case you start to develop a blister while skating. (For more on safety, see Appendix A.)

Technique

In-line skating uses many of the skills and techniques of ice skating, roller skating, and skiing, so if you have ever participated in any of those activities, you will probably take to in-line skating fairly readily. Many people begin in-line skating without instruction, but instruction will allow you to progress more quickly.

To begin, center your weight equally over both skates, bend your knees slightly so your nose, knees, and toes are all in the same line, and look straight ahead. Keep your weight forward over the balls of your feet; don't lean back.

To skate, use a stroke, glide, stroke, glide rhythm (rather than a series of quick, short strokes). Push with one leg while gliding with the other. Shift your body weight back and forth so it is always centered over the gliding skate.

To stop, use your brake, located on the back of the right skate in most skates. With knees bent and arms extended in front of your body, move the right foot forward, shift your weight to your left leg, and lift your right toe until the brake pad touches the ground and stops you. An alternative stop is the T-stop, in which you drag one skate behind the other at a 90-degree angle to the direction of your forward motion.

If you lose your balance and are about to fall, lower your center of gravity by bending at the waist and putting your hands on your knees. If you can't regain your balance, try to fall forward, directing the impact to your wrist guards and knee pads. Try not to fall backward.

Again, instruction can help you learn many moves and techniques that will make the sport safer and more enjoyable.

Developing Cardiorespiratory Endurance

Studies have shown that in-line skaters raise their heart rates and oxygen consumption comparably to joggers, bicyclers, and walkers. Skaters reached 60–75% of $\dot{V}O_{2max}$ by skating continuously (not pushing off and gliding for several seconds) at 10.6–12.5 mph for 20–30 minutes. It may be difficult for recreational skaters to safely skate this fast for this long, however, given the typical constraints of city and suburban streets. Experts suggest skating uphill as much as possible to reach the level of intensity that builds cardiorespiratory endurance. If you can reach and maintain higher speeds in parks or on paved paths, do so, but always skate safely. (If you belong to a gym or fitness club and want to do some indoor skating, Nautilus has introduced a new piece of equipment called the Skate Machine.)

Intensity, duration, and frequency: Start your early skating sessions at a pace that keeps your heart rate about 10–20% below your target zone. Skate for 5–10 minutes, and then check your heart rate. Increase your speed gradually until you can skate at about 10 miles per hour (6 minutes per mile). Use your pulse as a guide to speed, aiming for 65% of your target heart rate zone. To achieve cardiorespiratory benefits, you will have to skate at a continuous and relatively intense pace for at least 20 minutes three times a week. The more fit you are, the more intensively you will need to skate to reach your target heart rate.

Calorie cost: Use Table 6 to determine the approximate number of calories you burn during each outing. You can increase the number of calories burned by skating faster, for a longer time, or uphill.

At the beginning: If you are a beginner, practice skating in an empty schoolyard or parking lot. As you become confident with the basic techniques, you can move on to streets, parks, and paved bike trails. Maintain an easy pace, alternating stroking and gliding.

Begin each outing with a 5- to 10-minute warm-up of walking, jogging, or even slow skating. Once your muscles are warm, you can do some stretches to help loosen and warm up the primary muscles used during skating—the quadriceps, hamstrings, buttocks, hips, groin, ankles, calves, and lower back. You can also save the stretches for the end of the workout.

To launch an in-line skating fitness program, aim for slow, long-distance workouts. Start by skating for 15 minutes, and gradually increase your session to 20–30 minutes of continuous skating (or about 3.5–5 miles). Try to skate about 20 miles a week, or 5 miles a day (about 30 minutes) 4 days a week.

As you progress: After the first week or two, add about a mile a day, up to 40 miles per week (60 minutes a day). To increase intensity, add some hills, sprints (bursts of short, rapid striding), and interval training (periods of intensive exercise at your target heart rate alternating with timed rest periods when your heart rate drops below your target zone). Try to skate 30–60 minutes a day four or more times a week.

The harder and faster you skate, the more intensive your workout will be and the more your cardiorespiratory endurance and muscular strength will improve. The longer and more often you skate, the more your endurance will increase.

Developing Muscular Strength and Endurance

In-line skating develops the muscles in the entire upper leg, buttocks, and hip; lower back; and upper arms and shoulders when arms are swung vigorously. To make greater gains in lower-body strength and to develop the entire upper body, include resistance training in your overall fitness program. Use the general wellness weight training program from Chapter 4, or tailor one to fit your personal fitness goals. No matter which exercises you include in your program, follow the general guidelines for successful and safe training:

- Train 2–3 days per week.
- Perform 1 or more sets of 8–12 repetitions of 8–10 exercises.
- Include exercises that work all the major muscle groups: neck, shoulders, chest, arms, upper and lower back, thighs, and calves.

Depending on your schedule, you may find it more convenient to skate and weight train on alternate days.

Developing Flexibility

The best times for a flexibility workout are when your muscles are warm, so stretch after a short warm-up at the beginning of your skating session, or after your skating session, or after a weight training session. Use the stretching routine presented in Chapter 5, or develop one that meets your own goals and preferences. Pay particular attention to your quadriceps, hamstrings, buttocks, hips, groin, ankles, calves, and lower back. Remember these basic guidelines:

- Stretch at least 2–3 days per week, preferably when muscles are warm.
- Stretch all the major muscle groups.
- Stretch to the point of mild discomfort, and hold for 10–30 seconds.
- Repeat each stretch at least 4 times.

Name _____ Section _____ Date _____

LAB 7-1 *A Personal Fitness Program Plan and Contract*

A. I, _____, am contracting with myself to follow a physical fitness
(name)

program to work toward the following goals:

Specific or short-term goals

1. _____

2. _____

3. _____

4. _____

General or long-term goals

1. _____

2. _____

3. _____

4. _____

B. My program plan is as follows:

Activities	Components (Check ✓)					Intensity*	Duration	Frequency (Check ✓)						
	CRE	MS	ME	F	BC			M	Tu	W	Th	F	Sa	Su

*Conduct activities for achieving CRE goals at your target heart rate or RPE value.

C. My program will begin on _____. My program includes the following schedule of mini-goals. For each step
(date)

in my program, I will give myself the reward listed.

_____	_____	_____
(mini-goal 1)	(date)	(reward)
_____	_____	_____
(mini-goal 2)	(date)	(reward)
_____	_____	_____
(mini-goal 3)	(date)	(reward)
_____	_____	_____
(mini-goal 4)	(date)	(reward)
_____	_____	_____
(mini-goal 5)	(date)	(reward)

D. My program will include the addition of physical activity to my daily routine (such as climbing stairs or walking to class):

1. _____

2. _____

3. _____

4. _____

5. _____

E. I will use the following tools to monitor my program and my progress toward my goals:

_____

(list any charts, graphs, or journals you plan to use)

_____

_____

I sign this contract as an indication of my personal commitment to reach my goal.

_____   _____
(your signature)   (date)

I have recruited a helper who will witness my contract and _____

_____

(list any way your helper will participate in your program)

_____

_____   _____
(witness's signature)   (date)

LAB 7-2 *Monitoring Your Program Progress*

Track your adherence to your program and your progress by filling out a program log. Use the one below, or make one specifically designed to match your program. If you prefer detailed program logs for each of your fitness components, use the logs in Labs 3-2, 4-3, and 5-2. (A more extensive series of logs is included in the Daily Fitness Log booklet and in the Lab Activities and Fitness Log software.)

To use the log below, fill in the activities that are part of your program. Each day, note the distance and/or time for each activity. For flexibility or strength training workouts, you may prefer just to enter a check mark each time you complete a workout. At the end of each week, total your distances and/or times.

Activity/Date	M	Tu	W	Th	F	Sa	Su	Weekly Total	M	Tu	W	Th	F	Sa	Su	Weekly Total
1																
2																
3																
4																
5																
6																

Activity/Date	M	Tu	W	Th	F	Sa	Su	Weekly Total	M	Tu	W	Th	F	Sa	Su	Weekly Total
1																
2																
3																
4																
5																
6																

Activity/Date	M	Tu	W	Th	F	Sa	Su	Weekly Total	M	Tu	W	Th	F	Sa	Su	Weekly Total
1																
2																
3																
4																
5																
6																

Activity/Date	M	Tu	W	Th	F	Sa	Su	Weekly Total	M	Tu	W	Th	F	Sa	Su	Weekly Total
1																
2																
3																
4																
5																
6																

Activity/Date	M	Tu	W	Th	F	Sa	Su	Weekly Total	M	Tu	W	Th	F	Sa	Su	Weekly Total
1																
2																
3																
4																
5																
6																

Nutrition

8

LOOKING AHEAD

After reading this chapter, you should be able to answer these questions about nutrition:

- What are the different kinds of essential nutrients, and what functions do they perform in the body?

- What guidelines have been developed to help people choose a healthy diet, avoid nutritional deficiencies, and protect themselves from diet-related chronic diseases?

- What special nutritional guidelines apply to vegetarian diets?

- How can people adapt nutritional information to their own lives and circumstances?

Nutrition is a vital component of wellness. What you eat affects your energy levels, well-being, and overall health. Eating habits can also be closely linked with certain diseases, disabling conditions, and other health problems. Of particular concern is the connection between lifetime nutritional habits and the risk of the major chronic diseases, including heart disease, cancer, stroke, and diabetes. On the more positive side, however, a well-planned diet in conjunction with a fitness program can help prevent such conditions and even reverse some of them.

Creating a diet plan to support maximum fitness and protect against disease is a two-part project. First, you have to know which nutrients are necessary and in what amounts. Second, you have to translate those requirements into a diet consisting of foods you like to eat that are both available and affordable. Once you have an idea of what constitutes a healthy diet for you, you may also have to make adjustments in your current diet to bring it into line with your goals.

This chapter provides the basic principles of nutrition. It introduces the six classes of essential nutrients, explaining their role in the functioning of the body. It also provides different sets of guidelines that are available to help you design a healthy diet plan. Finally, it offers practical tools and advice to help you apply the guidelines to your own life, whether you are eating at home, at school, or in a restaurant. Diet is an area of your life in which you have almost total control. Using your knowledge and understanding of nutrition to create a healthy diet plan is a significant step toward wellness.

COMPONENTS OF A HEALTHY DIET

When you think about your diet, you probably do so in terms of the foods you like to eat—a turkey sandwich and a glass of milk, or a steak and a baked potato. What's important for your health, though, are the nutrients contained in those foods. Your body requires proteins, fats, carbohydrates, vitamins, minerals, and water—about 45 **essential nutrients.** The word *essential* in this context means that you must get these substances from food because your body is unable to manufacture them at all, or at least not fast enough to meet your physiological needs. The six classes of nutrients, along with their functions and major sources, are listed in Table 8-1.

Nutrients are released into the body by the process of **digestion,** which breaks them down into compounds that the gastrointestinal tract can absorb and the body can use (Figure 8-1). In this form, the essential nutrients provide energy, build and maintain body tissues, and regulate body functions.

Providing energy is the most immediate function of nutrients. The energy in foods is measured in **kilocalories** (abbreviated **kcalories**). One kcalorie represents the amount of heat it takes to raise the temperature of 1 kilogram of water 1°C. The average adult requires about 2000 kcalories per day to meet energy needs. Kilocalories consumed in excess of energy needs are stored as body fat. In common usage, the term *kilocalorie* is generally shortened to **calorie,** although a calorie is actually a very small energy unit—a kilocalorie contains 1000 calories. For convenience, this chapter will use the more familiar term, *calorie,* to stand for the larger energy unit.

Three of the six classes of nutrients supply energy: proteins, carbohydrates, and fats. Fats provide the most energy—9 calories per gram; protein and carbohydrates each provide 4 calories per gram. (Alcohol, although it is not an essential nutrient, also supplies energy, providing 7 calories per gram.) Experts advise against high fat consumption, in part because fats provide so many calories. Given the typical American diet, most Americans do not need the extra calories to meet energy needs.

Meeting our energy needs is only one of the functions of food. All the nutrients perform numerous other vital functions. In terms of quantity, water is the most significant nutrient: The body is approximately 60% water and can survive only a few days without it. Vitamins and minerals are needed in much smaller quantities, but they are still vital.

Practically all foods contain mixtures of nutrients, although foods are commonly classified according to their predominant nutrients. For example, spaghetti is considered a carbohydrate food although it contains small amounts of other nutrients. Let's take a closer look at the functions and sources of the six classes of nutrients.

Proteins

Protein is an important component of muscle, bone, blood, enzymes, cell membranes, and some hormones. As mentioned above, protein can also provide energy at 4 calories per gram of protein weight. Proteins are composed of **amino acids.** Twenty common amino acids are found in food; nine of these are essential to an adult diet:

TERMS **essential nutrients** Vitamins, minerals, some amino acids, linoleic and alpha-linolenic acid, carbohydrate, water, and other substances the body must obtain from food because it can't manufacture them in sufficient quantity for its physiological needs.

digestion The process of breaking down foods in the gastrointestinal tract into nutrients the body can absorb.

kilocalorie (kcalorie) The unit of fuel potential in a food. One kcalorie represents the amount of heat required to raise the temperature of 1 kilogram of water 1°C.

calorie The amount of heat required to raise the temperature of 1 gram of water 1°C; the word commonly used when kilocalorie is meant.

amino acids The components of proteins used to build muscle and other tissue.

TABLE 8-1

The Six Classes of Essential Nutrients

Nutrient	Function	Major Sources
Proteins (4 calories/gram)	Form important parts of muscles, bone, blood, enzymes, some hormones, and cell membranes; repair tissue; regulate water and acid-base balance; help in growth; supply energy	Meat, fish, poultry, eggs, milk products, legumes, nuts
Carbohydrates (4 calories/gram)	Supply energy to cells in brain, nervous system, and blood; supply energy to muscles during exercise	Grains (breads and cereals), fruits, vegetables, milk
Fats (9 calories/gram)	Supply energy; insulate, support, and cushion organs; provide medium for absorption of fat-soluble vitamins	Saturated fats primarily from animal sources, palm and coconut oils, and hydrogenated vegetable fats; unsaturated fats from grains, nuts, seeds, fish, vegetables
Vitamins	Promote (initiate or speed up) specific chemical reactions within cells	Abundant in fruits, vegetables, and grains; also found in meat and dairy products
Minerals	Help regulate body functions; aid in the growth and maintenance of body tissues; act as catalysts for the release of energy	Found in most food groups
Water	Makes up 50–70% of body weight; provides a medium for chemical reactions; transports chemicals; regulates temperature; removes waste products	Fruits, vegetables, and other liquids

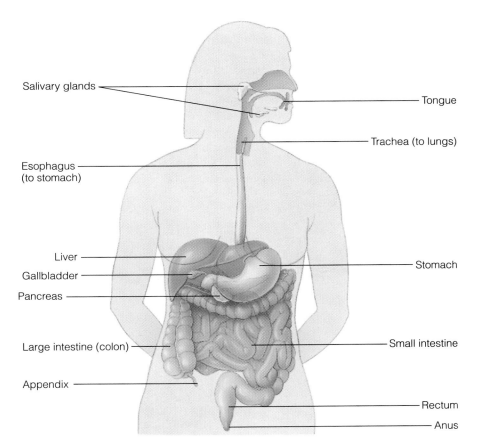

Salivary glands — Tongue

Trachea (to lungs)

Esophagus (to stomach)

Liver

Gallbladder

Pancreas

Stomach

Large intestine (colon)

Small intestine

Appendix

Rectum

Anus

Figure 8-1 The digestive system. Food is partially broken down by being chewed and mixed with saliva in the mouth. As food moves through the digestive tract, it is mixed by muscular contractions and broken down by chemicals. After traveling to the stomach via the esophagus, food is broken down further by stomach acids. Most absorption of nutrients occurs in the small intestine, aided by secretions from the pancreas, gallbladder, and intestinal lining. The large intestine reabsorbs excess water; the remaining solid wastes are collected in the rectum and excreted through the anus.

histidine, isoleucine, leucine, lysine, methionine, phenyl-alanine, threonine, tryptophan, and valine. "Essential," again, means that they are required for normal health and growth but must be provided in the diet because the body manufactures them in insufficient quantities, if at all. The other eleven amino acids can be produced by the body as long as the necessary ingredients are supplied by foods.

Foods are rated as "complete" protein sources if they supply all nine essential amino acids in adequate amounts; they are classified as "incomplete" protein sources if they supply only some. Meat, fish, poultry, eggs, milk, cheese, and other foods from animal sources provide complete proteins. Incomplete proteins come from plant sources such as beans, peas, and nuts; these are good sources of most essential amino acids but are usually low in one or two. Different vegetable proteins are low in different amino acids, so combinations can provide complete proteins. Vegetarians who eat no foods from animal sources can obtain all essential amino acids by eating a wide variety of foods each day.

The leading sources of protein in the American diet are (1) beef, steaks, and roasts; (2) hamburgers and meatloaf; (3) white bread, rolls, and crackers; (4) milk; and (5) pork. About two-thirds of the protein in the American diet comes from animal sources, which means the nation's diet is rich in amino acids. About 10–15% of the total calories in a well-balanced diet should come from protein. However, many Americans consume more than that amount every day. This excess protein is synthesized into fat for energy storage or burned for energy. For most people, extra protein in the diet is not harmful, but it does contribute fat to the diet because protein-rich foods are often fat-rich as well.

Fats

At 9 calories per gram, fats (also known as lipids) are the most concentrated source of energy. The fats stored in your body represent usable energy, help insulate your body, and support and cushion your organs. Fats in the diet help your body absorb fat-soluble vitamins and add important flavor and texture to foods. During periods of rest and light activity, fats are the major body fuel. The nervous system, brain, and red blood cells are fueled by carbohydrates, but most of the rest of the body's organs are fueled by fats. Two fats—linoleic acid and alpha-linolenic acid—are essential to the diet; they are key regulators of such body functions as the maintenance of blood pressure and the progress of a healthy pregnancy.

Types and Sources of Fats   Most of the fats in food and in your body are in the form of **triglycerides,** which are composed of a glycerine molecule (an alcohol) plus three fatty acids. A fatty acid is made up of a chain of carbon atoms with oxygen attached at the end and hydrogen atoms attached along the length of the chain. Fatty acids differ in the length of their carbon atom chains and in

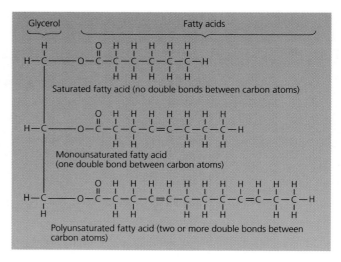

Figure 8-2 Chemical structures of saturated and unsaturated fatty acids.   This example of a triglyceride consists of a molecule of glycerol with three fatty acids attached. Fatty acids can differ in the length of their carbon chains and their degree of saturation.

their degree of saturation (the number of hydrogens attached to the chain). If every available bond from each carbon atom in a fatty acid chain is attached to a hydrogen atom, the fatty acid is said to be **saturated** (Figure 8-2). If not all the available bonds are taken up by hydrogens, the carbon atoms in the chain will form double bonds with each other. Such fatty acids are called unsaturated fats. If there is only one double bond, the fatty acid is called **monounsaturated.** If there are two or more double bonds, the fatty acid is called **polyunsaturated.** The essential fatty acids, linoleic and alpha-linolenic acids, are both polyunsaturated.

Foods fats are often composed of both saturated and unsaturated fatty acids; the dominant type of fatty acid determines the fat's characteristics. Food fats containing large amounts of saturated fatty acids are usually solid at room temperature (these are called "fats"); they are generally found in animal products. The leading sources of saturated fat in the American diet are unprocessed animal flesh (hamburger, steak, roasts), whole milk, cheese, and hot dogs and lunch meats. Food fats containing large amounts of monounsaturated and polyunsaturated fatty acids are usually from plant sources and are liquid at room temperature (these are called "oils"). Olive, canola, and peanut oils contain mostly monounsaturated fatty acids. Sunflower, corn, and safflower oils contain mostly polyunsaturated fatty acids. For the relative amounts of fatty acids in common dietary fats, see Figure 8-3.

There are notable exceptions to these generalizations. When unsaturated vegetable oils undergo the process of **hydrogenation,** a mixture of saturated and unsaturated fatty acids is produced. Hydrogenation turns many of the double bonds in unsaturated fatty acids into single bonds, increasing the degree of saturation and producing a more solid fat from a liquid oil. Hydrogenation also produces

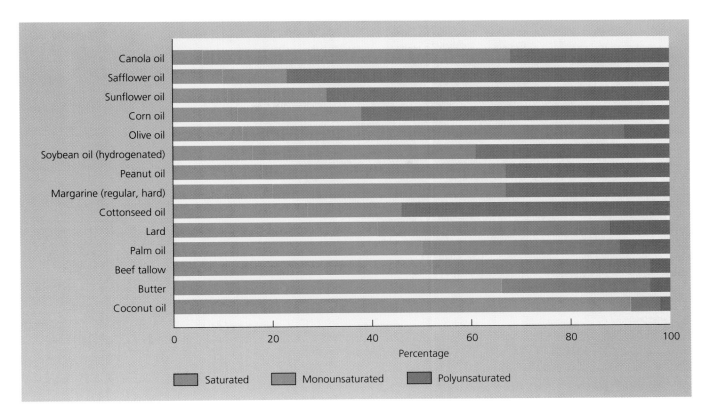

Figure 8-3   Comparisons of dietary fats.

trans fatty acids, unsaturated fatty acids with an atypical shape that affects their behavior during cooking and in the body. Food manufacturers use hydrogenation to increase the stability of an oil so it can be reused for deep frying; to improve the texture of certain foods (to make pastries and pie crusts flakier, for example); to keep oil from separating out of peanut butter; and to extend the shelf life of foods made with oil. Hydrogenation is the process used to transform a liquid oil into margarine or vegetable shortening.

Many baked and fried foods are prepared with hydrogenated vegetable oils, so they can be relatively high in saturated and trans fatty acids. Leading sources of trans fatty acids in the American diet are deep-fried fast foods such as french fries and fried chicken or fish (typically fried in vegetable shortening rather than oil); baked and snack foods such as pot pies, cakes, cookies, pastries, doughnuts, and chips; and stick margarine. In general, the more solid a hydrogenated oil is, the more saturated and trans fats it contains; for example, stick margarines typically contain more saturated and trans fatty acids than do tub or squeeze margarines. Smaller amounts of trans fats are found naturally in meat and milk.

Hydrogenated vegetable oils are not the only plant fats that contain saturated fats. Palm and coconut oils, although derived from plants, are also highly saturated. On the other hand, fish oils, derived from an animal source, are rich in polyunsaturated fats.

Recommended Fat Intake   You need only about 1 tablespoon (15 grams) of vegetable oil per day incorporated into your diet to supply the essential fats. The average American diet supplies considerably more than this amount; in fact, fats make up about 33% of our calorie intake. (This is the equivalent of about 75 grams, or 5 tablespoons, of fat per day.) Health experts recommend that we reduce our fat intake to 30%, but not less than 10%, of total daily calories, with less than 10% coming from

TERMS

triglyceride   The most common lipid found in fatty tissues; composed of a glycerol molecule and three fatty acids.

saturated fatty acid   A fatty acid that has no double bonds between carbon atoms; solid at room temperature.

monounsaturated fatty acid   A fatty acid that has one double bond between carbon atoms; liquid at room temperature.

polyunsaturated fatty acid   A fatty acid that has two or more double bonds between carbon atoms; liquid at room temperature.

hydrogenation   A process by which hydrogens are added to unsaturated fats, increasing the degree of saturation and turning liquid oils into solid fats. Hydrogenation produces a mixture of saturated fatty acids and standard and trans forms of unsaturated fatty acids.

trans fatty acid   A type of unsaturated fatty acid produced during the process of hydrogenation; trans fats have an atypical shape that changes their chemical activity.

	0–10%	10–30%	30–50%	50–75%	75–100%
Breads, cereals, rice, and pasta	Many dry cereals and breads, rice, pasta, tortillas, pretzels	Plain popcorn, hot cereals, some breads	Granola, buttered popcorn, crackers, biscuit, muffin	Croissant	
Vegetables and fruits	Most fresh, frozen, canned, and dried fruits and vegetables		French fries, onion rings	Potato chips, coconut	Avocado, olives
Milk, yogurt, and cheese	Nonfat milk, yogurt, and cottage cheese	Low-fat cottage cheese and yogurt, 1% and 2% milk, buttermilk	Whole milk, regular ice cream	Most cheeses, rich ice cream	Half and half, cream cheese, sour cream, heavy cream
Meat, poultry, fish, dry beans, eggs, nuts	Skinless turkey breast, haddock, cod, most dry beans, egg whites	Skinless white meat chicken, halibut, shrimp, clams, tuna in water, red snapper, trout, low-fat tofu	Beef top round, broiled steak, ham, skinless dark meat poultry, salmon, mackerel, swordfish	Roast beef, ground chuck; pork, lamb and veal chops; poultry with skin; tuna in oil; regular tofu; eggs	Salami, bacon, hot dogs, spare ribs, most nuts and seeds, peanut butter, egg yolks
Combination foods	Clear soup (bouillon)	Most broth-based soups; vegetarian chili	Hamburger, lasagna, chili with meat, potato salad, vegetable and cheese pizza, macaroni and cheese, enchilada	Cheeseburger; meat pizza; large meat, poultry, or cheese sandwich, taco salad	
Fats, oils, and sweets	Hard candy, chewing gum			Chocolate bar	Butter, margarine, vegetable oil, mayonnaise, salad dressing

Figure 8-4   Percent of total calories from fat for selected foods.

saturated fat. The fat content of many common foods is given in Figure 8-4; the box "Setting Goals for Fat, Protein, and Carbohydrate Intake" explains how to set a daily goal for fat consumption.

Fats and Health   Different types of fats have very different effects on health. Many studies have examined the effects of dietary fat intake on blood **cholesterol** levels and the risk of heart disease. Saturated and trans fatty acids have been found to raise blood levels of **low-density lipoprotein (LDL)**, or "bad" cholesterol, thereby increasing a person's risk of heart disease. Unsaturated fatty acids, on the other hand, lower LDL and may increase levels of **high-density lipoprotein (HDL)**, or

"good" cholesterol. Thus, to reduce the risk of heart disease, it is important to substitute unsaturated fats for saturated and trans fats. (A heart-healthy diet is described in Chapter 11.)

Most Americans consume more saturated fat (11% of total calories) than trans fat (2–4% of total calories). The best way to reduce saturated fat in your diet is to lower your intake of meat and full-fat dairy products (whole milk, cream, butter, cheese, ice cream). To lower trans fats, decrease your intake of deep-fried foods and baked goods made with hydrogenated vegetable oils; use liquid oils rather than margarine and favor tub or squeeze margarines over stick margarines. (Remember, the softer or more liquid a fat is, the less saturated and trans fat it is likely to contain.) Saturated fats are listed on the nutrition label of prepared foods. Trans fats are not, but you can check for the presence of hydrogenated oils on the ingredient list; if "partially hydrogenated" oils or fats or "vegetable shortening" appears near the top of the list, the product may be high in trans fats.

Research has indicated that certain forms of polyunsaturated fatty acids—known as **omega-3 fatty acids** and found in fish—may have a particularly positive effect on cardiovascular health. If the endmost double bond of a polyunsaturated fat occurs three carbons from the end of the fatty acid chain, an omega-3 form is produced. (The polyunsaturated fatty acid shown in Figure 8-2 is an omega-3 form.) If the endmost double bond occurs at the

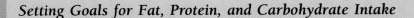

Setting Daily Goals

To meet the recommendations for nutrient intakes, start by setting some overall daily goals.

1. Determine approximately how many calories you consume each day. Depending on your activity level, daily needs range from about 2200 to 3500 calories for men and from about 1600 to 2500 for women.

2. Set percentage goals or limits for your intake of fat, protein, and carbohydrate. Those recommended for the general public are 30% or less of total daily calories from fat, 10–15% of total daily calories from protein, and 55% of total daily calories from carbohydrate. If your diet already meets these goals, you may want to set more challenging marks, such as raising your daily carbohydrate consumption to 60% of total calories.

3. Change your limits or goals from percentages to grams for easy tracking. A person who eats about 2200 calories per day could calculate her or his goals as follows:

Fat: 2200 calories per day × 30% = 660 calories of fat per day

660 calories ÷ 9 calories per gram = **73 g of fat per day**

Protein: 2200 calories per day × 15% = 330 calories of protein per day

330 calories ÷ 4 calories per gram = **83 g of protein per day**

Carbohydrate: 2200 calories per day × 55% = 1210 calories of carbohydrate per day

1210 calories ÷ 4 calories per gram = **303 g of carbohydrate per day**

(Remember, there are 9 calories per gram of fat and 4 calories per gram of protein and carbohydrate.)

Evaluating an Individual Food Item

You can do the same type of calculations to evaluate a particular food item, to determine whether it is high or low in protein, fat, or carbohydrate. For example, suppose you want to determine how high in fat peanut butter is. First, you need to know the total number of calories and grams of fat it contains. Multiply the grams of fat by 9 (because there are 9 calories in a gram of fat), and then divide that number by the total calories. For a tablespoon of peanut butter (8 grams of fat and 95 calories), you would calculate as follows: 8 × 9 = 72; 72 ÷ 95 = 0.76, or 76% of calories from fat. This means peanut butter is relatively high in fat. If your overall daily fat consumption goal is 70 grams of fat, a tablespoon of peanut butter would represent 11% of your daily target.

Of course, you can still eat high-fat foods. But it makes good sense to limit the size of your portions and to balance your intake with low-fat foods. For example, a tablespoon of peanut butter eaten on whole-wheat bread and served with a banana, carrot sticks, and a glass of nonfat milk makes a nutritious lunch—high in protein and carbohydrate, low in fat. Three tablespoons of peanut butter on high-fat crackers with potato chips, cookies, and whole milk is a less healthy combination. So while it's important to evaluate individual food items, it is more important to look at them in the context of your overall diet.

Monitoring Your Progress

Depending on your current diet and health needs, you may choose to focus on a particular goal, such as that for fat or protein. For prepared foods, food labels list the number of grams of fat, protein, and carbohydrate. The breakdown for many common foods and for popular fast-food items can be found in Appendixes B and C. Nutrition information is also posted in many grocery stores, published in inexpensive nutrition guides, and available online. By checking these resources, you can keep a running total of the grams of fat, protein, and carbohydrate you eat and determine how close you are to meeting your goals.

---

sixth carbon atom, an omega-6 form is produced. Most of the polyunsaturated fats currently consumed by Americans are omega-6 forms, primarily from corn oil and soybean oil. However, the consumption of omega-3 fatty acids in fish has been shown to reduce the tendency of blood to clot, to decrease inflammatory responses in the body, and to raise levels of HDL. It even appears to lower the risk of heart disease in some people. Because of these benefits, nutritionists now recommend that Americans increase the proportion of omega-3 polyunsaturated fats in their diet by increasing their consumption of fish to two or more times a week. Mackerel, herring, salmon, sardines, anchovies, tuna, and trout are all good sources of omega-3 fatty acids.

Dietary fat can affect health in other ways. Diets high in fat are associated with an increased risk of certain forms of cancer, especially colon cancer. A high-fat diet can also make weight management more difficult. Because fat is a concentrated source of calories (9 calories per gram versus 4 calories per gram for protein and carbohydrate), a high-fat diet is often a high-calorie diet that can lead to weight gain. In addition, there is some evidence that calories from fat are more easily converted to body fat than calories from protein or carbohydrate.

Although more research is needed on the precise effects of different types and amounts of fat on overall health, a great deal of evidence points to the fact that most people benefit from lowering their overall fat intake to recommended levels and substituting unsaturated fats for saturated and trans fats.

Carbohydrates

Carbohydrates function primarily to supply energy to body cells. Some cells, such as those in the brain and other parts of the nervous system and in the blood, use only carbohydrates for fuel. During high-intensity exercise, muscles also get most of their energy from carbohydrates. When we don't eat enough carbohydrates to satisfy the needs of the brain and red blood cells, our bodies synthesize carbohydrates from proteins. In situations of extreme deprivation, when the diet lacks sufficient amounts of both carbohydrates and proteins, the body turns to its own proteins, resulting in severe muscle wasting. This rarely occurs, however, because the body's daily carbohydrate requirement is filled by just three or four slices of bread.

Simple and Complex Carbohydrates Carbohydrates are classified into two groups: simple and complex. Simple carbohydrates contain only one or two sugar units in each molecule. A one-sugar carbohydrate is called a **monosaccharide;** a two-sugar carbohydrate, a **disaccharide.** Simple carbohydrates include sucrose (table sugar),

fructose (fruit sugar, honey), maltose (malt sugar), and lactose (milk sugar); they provide much of the sweetness in foods. Simple carbohydrates are found naturally in fruits and milk and are added to soft drinks, fruit drinks, candy, and sweet desserts. There is no evidence that any type of simple sugar is more nutritious than others.

Starches and most types of dietary fiber are complex carbohydrates; they consist of chains of many sugar molecules and are called **polysaccharides.** Starches are found in a variety of plants, especially grains (wheat, rye, rice, oats, barley, millet), **legumes,** and tubers (potatoes and yams). Most other vegetables contain a mix of starches and simple carbohydrates. Dietary fiber, discussed in the next section, is found in fruits, vegetables, and grains.

Many nutritionists also distinguish between refined (processed) and unrefined carbohydrates. The refinement of wheat flour, rice, and cereal grains transforms whole-wheat flour to white flour, brown rice to white rice, and so on. Refined carbohydrates usually retain all the calories of their unrefined counterparts, but they tend to be much lower in fiber, vitamins, and minerals. In general, unrefined carbohydrates tend to take longer to chew and digest than refined ones; they also enter the bloodstream more slowly. This slower digestive pace tends to make people feel full sooner and for a longer period, lessening the chance that they will overeat and gain weight. It also helps keep blood sugar and insulin levels low, which may decrease the risk of diabetes and heart disease. For all these reasons, unrefined carbohydrates are recommended over those that have been refined.

During digestion in the mouth and small intestine, the body breaks down starches and disaccharides into monosaccharides, such as **glucose,** for absorption into the bloodstream. Once the glucose is absorbed, cells take it up and use it for energy. The liver and muscles also take up glucose and store it in the form of a starch called **glycogen.** The muscles use glycogen as fuel during endurance events or long workouts. Carbohydrates consumed in excess of the body's energy needs are changed into fat and stored. Whenever calorie intake exceeds calorie expenditure, fat storage can lead to weight gain. This is true whether the excess calories come from carbohydrates, proteins, fat, or alcohol.

Recommended Carbohydrate Intake On average, Americans consume over 250 grams of carbohydrates per day, well above the minimum of 50–100 grams of essential carbohydrate required by the body. However, health experts recommend that Americans increase their consumption of carbohydrates—particularly complex carbohydrates—to 55% of total daily calories.

Experts also recommend that Americans alter the proportion of simple and complex carbohydrates in the diet, lowering simple carbohydrate intake from 25% to 15% or less of total daily calories. To accomplish this change, reduce your intake of foods like candy, sweet desserts, soft

TERMS **monosaccharide** A simple carbohydrate consisting of one sugar molecule.

disaccharide A simple carbohydrate consisting of two single-sugar molecules (monosaccharides) linked together.

polysaccharide A complex carbohydrate composed of many sugar molecules (monosaccharides) linked together.

legumes Vegetables such as peas and beans that are high in fiber and are also important sources of protein; examples include pinto beans, kidney beans, chickpeas, black-eyed peas, and soybeans.

glucose A simple sugar that is the body's basic fuel.

glycogen A complex carbohydrate stored principally in the liver and skeletal muscles; the major fuel source during most forms of exercise.

dietary fiber Carbohydrates and other substances in plants that are difficult or impossible for humans to digest.

soluble fiber Dietary fiber that dissolves in water or is broken down by bacteria in the large intestine. It tends to absorb cholesterol-containing compounds in the intestine.

insoluble fiber Fiber that does not dissolve in water and is not broken down by bacteria in the large intestine; it binds water and increases bulk in the stool.

Our bodies require adequate amounts of all essential nutrients—water, proteins, carbohydrates, fats, vitamins, and minerals—in order to grow and function properly. Choosing foods to satisfy these nutritional requirements is an important part of a healthy lifestyle.

drinks, and sweetened fruit drinks, which are high in simple sugars but low in other nutrients. The bulk of the simple carbohydrates in your diet should come from fruits, which are excellent sources of vitamins and minerals, and milk, which is high in protein and calcium. Instead of prepared foods high in added sugars, choose a variety of foods rich in complex, unrefined carbohydrates.

Athletes in training can especially benefit from high-carbohydrate diets (60–70% of total daily calories), which enhance the amount of carbohydrates stored in their muscles (as glycogen) and therefore provide more carbohydrate fuel for use during endurance events or long workouts. In addition, carbohydrates consumed during prolonged athletic events can help fuel muscles and extend the availability of the glycogen stored in muscles. (For more on the special nutritional needs of athletes, see pp. 209–210.)

Dietary Fiber   **Dietary fiber** consists of carbohydrate plant substances that are difficult or impossible for humans to digest. Instead, fiber passes through the intestinal tract and provides bulk for feces in the large intestine, which in turn facilitates elimination. In the large intestine, some types of fiber are broken down by bacteria into acids and gases, which explains why consuming too much fiber can lead to intestinal gas. Because humans cannot digest dietary fiber, fiber is not a source of carbohydrate in the diet; however, the consumption of dietary fiber is necessary for good health.

Nutritionists classify dietary fiber as soluble or insoluble. **Soluble fiber** slows the body's absorption of glucose and binds cholesterol-containing compounds in the intestine, lowering blood cholesterol levels and reducing the risk of cardiovascular disease. **Insoluble fiber** binds water, making the feces bulkier and softer so they pass more quickly and easily through the intestines.

Both kinds of fiber contribute to disease prevention. A diet high in soluble fiber can help people manage diabetes and high blood cholesterol levels. A diet high in insoluble fiber can help prevent a variety of health problems, including constipation, hemorrhoids, and diverticulitis (a painful condition in which abnormal pouches form and become inflamed in the wall of the large intestine). Some studies have linked high levels of insoluble fiber in the diet with a decreased incidence of colon and rectal cancer; conversely, a low-fiber diet may increase the risk of colon cancer. There is even some evidence that high levels of insoluble fiber can suppress and reverse precancerous changes that can lead to colon and rectal cancer.

All plant foods contain some dietary fiber, but fruits, legumes, oats (especially oat bran), barley, and psyllium (found in some laxatives) are particularly rich in it. Wheat (especially wheat bran), cereals, grains, and vegetables are all good sources of insoluble fiber (see Table 8-2). However, the processing of packaged foods can remove fiber, so it's important to depend on fresh fruits and vegetables and foods made from whole (unrefined) grains as sources of dietary fiber.

Although it is not yet clear precisely how much and what types of fiber are ideal, most experts believe the average American would benefit from an increase in daily fiber intake. Currently, most Americans consume about 15 grams of fiber a day, whereas the recommended daily amount is 20–35 grams of food fiber—not from supplements, which should be taken only under medical supervision. However, too much fiber—more than 40–60 grams a day—can cause health problems, such as overlarge stools or the malabsorption of important minerals. In fiber intake, as in all aspects of nutrition, balance and moderation are key principles.

To increase the amount of fiber in your diet, try the following:

TABLE 8-2	Foods High in Fiber	
Food Item	**Serving Size**	**Fiber (g)**
Fruits		
Apple, with skin	1	4.0
Apricot, with skin	3	2.0
Avocado	¼ cup	2.7
Banana	1	2.3
Cantaloupe	½	2.0
Dried fruit	¼ cup	2.4
Kiwi	1	2.1
Nectarine	1	3.3
Orange	1	3.8
Pear	1	4.8
Prunes, uncooked	5	3.9
Raisins	¼ cup	2.5
Raspberries	½ cup	3.0
Grains and Cereals*		
Bread, mixed-grain	1 slice	1.4
Bread, whole-wheat	1 slice	2.5
Oatmeal, cooked	⅔ cup	3.0
Pasta, whole-wheat, cooked	½ cup	3.0
Rice, brown, cooked	½ cup	1.8
Legumes		
Kidney beans, cooked	½ cup	4.6
Lima beans, cooked	½ cup	4.3
Pinto beans, cooked	½ cup	4.3
Tofu	½ cup	1.5
Vegetables		
Artichoke, cooked	1	4.0
Beans, green, cooked	½ cup	2.0
Beets, cooked	½ cup	2.5
Broccoli, cooked	½ cup	2.1
Brussels sprouts, cooked	½ cup	2.2
Carrot, raw	½ cup	2.2
Corn, cooked	½ cup	4.6
Eggplant, cooked	1 cup	2.0
Peas, green, cooked	½ cup	3.5
Potato, baked, with skin	1	5.0
Spinach, cooked	½ cup	3.5
Squash, winter, cooked	½ cup	3.0
Sweet potato, cooked	½ cup	4.0
Tomato, medium	1	1.8

*Many breakfast cereals contain significant amounts of dietary fiber (2–5 grams per serving). Check the labels for exact amounts.

- Choose whole-grain bread instead of white bread, brown rice instead of white rice, and whole-wheat pasta instead of regular pasta. Select high-fiber breakfast cereals. Look for breads, crackers, and cereals that list a whole grain first in the ingredient list: Whole-wheat flour, whole-grain oats, and whole-grain rice are whole grains; wheat flour is not.
- Eat whole fruits rather than drinking fruit juice. Top cereals, yogurt, and desserts with berries, apple slices, or other fruit.
- Include beans in soups and salads. Prepare salads that combine raw vegetables with pasta, rice, or beans.
- Substitute bean dip for cheese-based or sour cream—based dips or spreads. Use raw vegetables rather than chips for dipping.

Vitamins

Vitamins are organic (carbon-containing) substances required in very small amounts to promote specific chemical reactions within living cells (Table 8-3). Humans need 13 vitamins. Four are fat-soluble (A, D, E, and K), and nine are water-soluble (C and the eight B-complex vitamins: thiamin, riboflavin, niacin, vitamin B-6, folate, vitamin B-12, biotin, and pantothenic acid). Solubility affects how a vitamin is absorbed, transported, and stored in the body. The water-soluble vitamins are absorbed directly into the bloodstream, where they travel freely; excess water-soluble vitamins are detected by the kidneys and excreted in urine. Fat-soluble vitamins require a more complex digestive process; they are usually carried in the blood by special proteins and are stored in the body in fat tissues rather than excreted.

Functions of Vitamins Vitamins help chemical reactions take place. They provide no energy to the body directly but help unleash the energy stored in carbohydrates, proteins, and fats. Vitamins are critical in the production of red blood cells and the maintenance of the nervous, skeletal, and immune systems. Some vitamins also form substances that act as **antioxidants**, which help preserve healthy cells in the body. Key vitamin antioxidants include vitamin E, vitamin C, and the vitamin A derivative beta-carotene. (The actions of antioxidants will be described later in the chapter.)

Sources of Vitamins The human body does not manufacture most of the vitamins it requires and must obtain them from foods. Vitamins are abundant in fruits, vegetables, and grains. In addition, many processed foods, such as flour and breakfast cereals, are enriched with certain vitamins during the manufacturing process. On the other hand, both vitamins and minerals can be lost or destroyed during the storage and cooking of foods. For tips on

TABLE 8-3 *Facts About Vitamins*

Vitamin	Important Dietary Sources	Major Functions	Signs of Prolonged Deficiency	Toxic Effects of Megadoses
Fat-Soluble				
Vitamin A	Liver, milk, butter, cheese, and fortified margarine; carrots, spinach, and other orange and deep-green vegetables and fruits	Maintenance of vision, skin, linings of the nose, mouth, digestive and urinary tracts, immune function	Night blindness; dry, scaling skin; increased susceptibility to infection; loss of appetite; anemia; kidney stones	Headache, vomiting and diarrhea, vertigo, double vision, bone abnormalities, liver damage, miscarriage and birth defects
Vitamin D	Fortified milk and margarine, fish liver oils, butter, egg yolks (sunlight on skin also produces vitamin D)	Development and maintenance of bones and teeth, promotion of calcium absorption	Rickets (bone deformities) in children; bone softening, loss, and fractures in adults	Kidney damage, calcium deposits in soft tissues, depression, death
Vitamin E	Vegetable oils, whole grains, nuts and seeds, green leafy vegetables, asparagus, peaches	Protection and maintenance of cellular membranes	Red blood cell breakage and anemia, weakness, neurological problems, muscle cramps	Relatively nontoxic, but may cause excess bleeding or formation of blood clots
Vitamin K	Green leafy vegetables; smaller amounts widespread in other foods	Production of factors essential for blood clotting	Hemorrhaging	None observed
Water-Soluble				
Vitamin C	Peppers, broccoli, spinach, brussels sprouts, citrus fruits, strawberries, tomatoes, potatoes, cabbage, other fruits and vegetables	Maintenance and repair of connective tissue, bones, teeth, and cartilage; promotion of healing; aid in iron absorption	Scurvy, anemia, reduced resistance to infection, loosened teeth, joint pain, poor wound healing, hair loss, poor iron absorption	Urinary stones in some people, acid stomach from ingesting supplements in pill form, nausea, diarrhea, headache, fatigue
Thiamin	Whole-grain and enriched breads and cereals, organ meats, lean pork, nuts, legumes	Conversion of carbohydrates into usable forms of energy, maintenance of appetite and nervous system function	Beriberi (symptoms include muscle wasting, mental confusion, anorexia, enlarged heart, abnormal heart rhythm, nerve changes)	None reported
Riboflavin	Dairy products, enriched breads and cereals, lean meats, poultry, fish, green vegetables	Energy metabolism; maintenance of skin, mucous membranes, and nervous system structures	Cracks at corners of mouth, sore throat, skin rash, hypersensitivity to light, purple tongue	None reported
Niacin	Eggs, poultry, fish, milk, whole grains, nuts, enriched breads and cereals, meats, legumes	Conversion of carbohydrates, fats, and protein into usable forms of energy	Pellagra (symptoms include diarrhea, dermatitis, inflammation of mucous membranes, dementia)	Flushing of the skin, nausea, vomiting, diarrhea, liver dysfunction, glucose intolerance
Vitamin B-6	Eggs, poultry, fish, whole grains, nuts, soybeans, liver, kidney, pork	Protein and neurotransmitter metabolism; red blood cell synthesis	Anemia, convulsions, cracks at corners of mouth, dermatitis, nausea, confusion	Neurological abnormalities and damage
Folate	Green leafy vegetables, yeast, oranges, whole grains, legumes, liver	Amino acid metabolism, synthesis of RNA and DNA, new cell synthesis	Anemia, weakness, fatigue, irritability, shortness of breath, swollen tongue	Masking of vitamin B-12 deficiency
Vitamin B-12	Eggs, milk, meats, other animal foods	Synthesis of red and white blood cells; other metabolic reactions	Anemia, fatigue, nervous system damage, sore tongue	None reported
Biotin	Cereals, yeast, egg yolks, soy flour, liver; widespread in foods	Metabolism of fats, carbohydrates, and proteins	Rash, nausea, vomiting, weight loss, depression, fatigue, hair loss	None reported
Pantothenic acid	Animal foods, whole grains, legumes; widespread in foods	Metabolism of fats, carbohydrates, and proteins	Fatigue, numbness and tingling of hands and feet, gastrointestinal disturbances	None reported

SOURCES: Food and Nutrition Board. 1998. *Dietary Reference Intakes for Thiamin, Riboflavin, Niacin, Vitamin B$_6$, Folate, Vitamin B$_{12}$, Pantothenic Acid, and Choline.* Washington, D.C.: National Academy Press. National Research Council. 1989. *Recommended Dietary Allowances,* 10th ed. Washington, D.C.: National Academy Press. Copyright © 1989 by the National Academy of Sciences. Adapted with permission from the National Academy Press, Washington, D.C. Shils, M. E., and V. R. Young, eds. 1993. *Modern Nutrition in Health and Disease,* 8th ed. Baltimore: Williams & Wilkins.

1. *Consume or process vegetables immediately after purchasing (or harvesting).* The longer vegetables are kept before they are eaten or processed, the more vitamins are lost.

2. *Store vegetables and fruits properly.* If you can't eat fruits and vegetables immediately after purchasing (or harvesting) but plan to do so within a few days, keep them in the refrigerator. Place them in covered containers or plastic bags to minimize moisture loss. Freezing is the best method for longer-term preservation.

3. *Minimize the preparation and cooking of vegetables and other foods.* The more preparation and cooking of foods that is done before eating, the greater the nutrient loss. To reduce the losses:

   • When possible, cook vegetables, such as potatoes, in their skins.

• Don't soak and rinse rice before cooking.

• Cook in as little water as possible.

• Don't add baking soda to vegetables to enhance the green color.

• Bake, steam, broil, or microwave vegetables.

• When boiling, use tight-fitting lids to minimize evaporation of water.

• Cook vegetables as little as possible. Develop a taste for a more crunchy texture.

• Don't thaw frozen vegetables before cooking.

• Prepare lettuce salads right before eating.

---

minimizing such losses, see the box "Keeping the Nutrient Value in Food."

A few vitamins are made in certain parts of the body: The skin makes vitamin D when it is exposed to sunlight, and intestinal bacteria make biotin and vitamin K.

Vitamin Deficiencies and Excesses

If your diet lacks sufficient amounts of a particular vitamin, characteristic symptoms of deficiency develop (see Table 8-3). For example, vitamin A deficiency can cause blindness and vitamin B-6 deficiency can cause seizures. Vitamin deficiency diseases are most often seen in developing countries; they are relatively rare in the United States because vitamins are readily available from our food supply. However, intakes below recommended levels can have adverse effects on health even if they are not low enough to cause a deficiency disease. For example, low intake of folate increases a woman's chance of giving birth to a baby with a neural tube defect (a congenital malformation of the central nervous system).

Extra vitamins in the diet can be harmful, especially when taken as supplements. High doses of vitamin A are toxic and increase the risk of birth defects, for example. Vitamin B-6 can cause irreversible nerve damage when taken in large doses. Megadoses of fat-soluble vitamins are particularly dangerous because the excess will be stored in the body rather than excreted, increasing the risk of toxicity. Even when not taken in excess, relying on supplements for an adequate intake of vitamins can be a problem: There are many substances in foods other than vitamins and minerals, and some of these compounds may have important health effects. Later in the chapter we will discuss specific recommendations for vitamin intake and when a supplement is advisable. For now, keep in mind that it's best to obtain most of your vitamins from foods rather than supplements.

Minerals

Minerals are inorganic (non-carbon-containing) compounds you need in relatively small amounts to help regulate body functions, aid in the growth and maintenance of body tissues, and help release energy (Table 8-4). There are about 17 essential minerals. The major minerals, those that the body needs in amounts exceeding 100 milligrams, include calcium, phosphorus, magnesium, sodium, potassium, and chloride. The essential trace minerals, those that you need in minute amounts, include copper, fluoride, iodide, iron, selenium, and zinc.

Characteristic symptoms develop if an essential mineral is consumed in a quantity too small or too large for good health. The minerals most commonly lacking in the American diet are iron, calcium, zinc, and magnesium. Focus on good food choices for these nutrients (see Table 8-4). Lean meats are rich in iron and zinc, while low-fat or nonfat dairy products are excellent choices for calcium. Plant foods are good sources of magnesium. Iron-deficiency **anemia** is a problem in some age groups, and researchers fear poor calcium intakes are sowing the seeds for future **osteoporosis,** especially in women. See the box "Osteoporosis" to learn more.

Water

Water is the major component in both foods and the human body: You are composed of about 60% water. Your need for other nutrients, in terms of weight, is much less than your need for water. You can live up to 50 days without food, but only a few days without water.

Water is distributed all over the body, among lean and other tissues and in urine and other body fluids. Water is used in the digestion and absorption of food and is the medium in which most of the chemical reactions take place within the body. Some water-based fluids like blood

TABLE 8-4 *Facts About Selected Minerals*

Mineral	Important Dietary Sources	Major Functions	Signs of Prolonged Deficiency	Toxic Effects of Megadoses
Calcium	Milk and milk products, tofu, fortified orange juice and bread, green leafy vegetables, bones in fish	Maintenance of bones and teeth, control of nerve impulses and muscle contraction	Stunted growth in children, bone mineral loss in adults	Constipation, urinary stones, calcium deposits in soft tissues, inhibition of mineral absorption
Fluoride	Fluoride-containing drinking water, tea, marine fish eaten with bones	Maintenance of tooth (and possibly bone) structure	Higher frequency of tooth decay	Increased bone density, mottling of teeth, impaired kidney function
Iron	Meat, legumes, eggs, enriched flour, green vegetables, dried fruit, liver	Component of hemoglobin, muscle fiber, and enzymes	Iron-deficiency anemia, weakness, impaired immune function, gastrointestinal distress	Liver and kidney damage, joint pains, sterility, disruption of cardiac function, death
Iodine	Iodized salt, seafood	Essential part of thyroid hormones, regulation of body metabolism	Goiter (enlarged thyroid), cretinism (birth defect)	Depression of thyroid activity, hyperthyroidism in susceptible people
Magnesium	Widespread in foods and water (except soft water); especially found in grains, legumes, nuts, seeds, green vegetables	Transmission of nerve impulses, energy transfer, activation of many enzymes	Neurological disturbances, cardiovascular problems, kidney disorders, nausea, growth failure in children	Nausea, vomiting, diarrhea, central nervous system depression, coma; death in people with impaired kidney function
Phosphorus	Present in nearly all foods, especially milk, cereal, legumes, meat, poultry, fish	Bone growth and maintenance, energy transfer in cells	Weakness, bone loss, kidney disorders, cardiorespiratory failure	Drop in blood calcium levels, calcium deposits in soft tissues
Potassium	Meats, milk, fruits, vegetables, grains, legumes	Nerve function and body water balance	Muscular weakness, nausea, drowsiness, paralysis, confusion, disruption of cardiac rhythm	Cardiac arrest
Selenium	Seafood, meat, eggs, whole grains	Protection of cells from oxidative damage, immune response	Muscle pain and weakness, heart disorders	Hair loss, nausea and vomiting, weakness, irritability
Sodium	Salt, soy sauce, salted foods	Body water balance, acid-base balance, nerve function	Muscle weakness, loss of appetite, nausea, vomiting; sodium deficiency is rarely seen	Edema, hypertension in sensitive people
Zinc	Whole grains, meat, eggs, liver, seafood (especially oysters)	Synthesis of proteins, RNA, and DNA; wound healing; immune response; ability to taste	Growth failure, loss of appetite, impaired taste acuity, skin rash, impaired immune function, poor wound healing	Vomiting, impaired immune function, decline in blood HDL levels, impaired copper absorption

SOURCES: Food and Nutrition Board. 1997. Dietary Reference Intakes for Calcium, Phosphorus, Magnesium, Vitamin D, and Fluoride. Washington, D.C.: National Academy Press. National Research Council. 1989. *Recommended Dietary Allowances*, 10th ed. Washington, D.C.: National Academy Press. Copyright © 1989 by the National Academy of Sciences. Reprinted with permission from National Academy Press, Washington, D.C. Shils, M. E., and V. R. Young, eds. 1993. *Modern Nutrition in Health and Disease*, 8th ed. Baltimore: Williams & Wilkins.

transport substances around the body, while other fluids serve as lubricants or cushions. Water also helps regulate body temperature.

Water is contained in almost all foods, particularly in liquids, fruits, and vegetables. The foods and fluids you consume provide 80–90% of your daily water intake; the remainder is generated through metabolism. You lose water each day in urine, feces, and sweat and through

TERMS

minerals Inorganic compounds needed in relatively small amounts for regulation, growth, and maintenance of body tissues and functions.

anemia A deficiency in the oxygen-carrying material in the red blood cells.

osteoporosis A condition in which the bones become extremely thin and brittle; fractures of the wrist, spine, and hip commonly result.

Osteoporosis is a condition in which the bones become dangerously thin and fragile over time. It currently afflicts some 25 million Americans, 80% of them women, and results in 1.5 million bone fractures each year. The incidence of osteoporosis may double in the next 25 years as the population ages.

The bones in your body are continually being broken down and rebuilt in order to adapt to mechanical strain. About 20% of your body's bone mass is replaced each year. In the first few decades of life, bones become thicker and stronger as they are rebuilt. Most of your bone mass (95%) is built by age 18. After bone mass peaks between the ages of 25 and 35, the rate of bone loss exceeds the rate of replacement, and bones become less dense. In osteoporosis, this loss of density becomes so severe that bones become very fragile.

Fractures are the most serious consequences of osteoporosis; up to 25% of all people who suffer a hip fracture die within a year. Other problems associated with osteoporosis are loss of height and a stooped posture caused by vertebral fractures, severe back and hip pain, and breathing problems caused by changes in the shape of the skeleton.

Who Is at Risk?

Women are at greater risk than men for osteoporosis because they have 10–25% less bone in their skeleton. As they lose bone mass with age, women's bones become dangerously thin sooner than men's bones. More men will probably develop osteoporosis in the future as they live into their eighties and nineties. Bone loss accelerates in women during the first 5–10 years after the onset of menopause because of a drop in estrogen production. (Estrogen improves calcium absorption and reduces the amount of calcium the body excretes.)

Other risk factors for osteoporosis include a family history of osteoporosis, early menopause (before age 45), abnormal menstruation, a history of anorexia, a thin, small frame, and European or Asian background. Certain medications can also have a negative impact on bone mass, including thyroid medication and high doses of cortisonelike drugs for asthma or arthritis.

What Can You Do?

To prevent osteoporosis, the best strategy is to build as much bone as possible during your young years and then do everything you can to maintain it as you age. Up to 50% of bone loss is determined by controllable lifestyle factors.

- *Ensure an adequate intake of calcium.* Consuming an adequate amount of calcium is important throughout life to build and maintain bone mass. Americans consume an average of 400–600 mg of calcium per day, less than half of what is currently recommended. Milk, yogurt, and calcium-fortified orange juice, bread, and cereals are all good sources. Nutritionists suggest that you obtain calcium from foods first and then take supplements only if needed to make up the difference.

- *Ensure an adequate intake of vitamin D.* Vitamin D is necessary for bones to absorb calcium. It can be obtained from food (milk and fortified cereals, for example) and is manufactured by the skin when it is exposed to sunlight. Candidates for vitamin D supplements include people who don't eat many foods rich in vitamin D; those who don't expose their face, arms, and hands to the sun (without sunscreen) for 5–15 minutes each day; and people who live north of an imaginary line roughly between Boston and the Oregon-California border (the sun is weaker in northern latitudes). Many calcium supplements also contain vitamin D.

- *Exercise.* Weight-bearing aerobic activities help build and maintain bone mass throughout life, but they must be performed 5–15 minutes each day in order to have lasting effects. Strength training is also helpful: It improves bone density, muscle mass, strength, and balance, protecting against both bone loss and falls, a major cause of fractures.

- *Don't smoke.* Smoking reduces the body's estrogen levels and is linked to earlier menopause and more rapid post-menopausal bone loss.

- *Drink alcohol only in moderation.* Alcohol reduces the body's ability to absorb calcium and may interfere with estrogen's bone-protecting effects.

- *Monitor your consumption of caffeine.* The association between caffeine-containing beverages and osteoporosis isn't clear, but researchers recommend that heavy caffeine consumers take special care to include calcium-rich foods in their diet because calcium may counterbalance any caffeine-linked drop in bone mass.

- *Be moderate in your consumption of protein and sodium.* A high intake of protein and sodium has been shown to increase calcium loss in the urine and may lead to loss of calcium from the skeleton.

- *Manage depression and stress.* Some women who have depression experience significant bone loss that may increase their risk of fractures. Researchers haven't identified the mechanism, but it may be linked to increases in the stress hormone cortisol.

- *After menopause, consider hormone replacement therapy (HRT) or another drug treatment.* HRT combats bone loss as well as menopausal symptoms and heart disease. However, it is not without side effects and risks. A physician can review your risk factors and test your bone density to help you decide whether HRT is a wise choice for you. Other drug treatments include alendronate (Fosamax) and calcitonin (Miacalcin), which slow the resorption of bone by the body, and fluoride, which helps build bone in women who already have osteoporosis.

Scientists recently discovered a gene linked to bone density, so a test to identify people at high risk for osteoporosis may become available in the future. Although not helpful in treating the condition, such a test could alert those at greater risk.

evaporation in your lungs. To maintain a balance between water consumed and water lost, you need to take in about 1 milliliter of water for each calorie you burn—about 2 liters, or 8 cups, of fluid per day—more if you live in a hot climate or engage in vigorous exercise.

Thirst is one of the body's first signs of dehydration that we can actually recognize. However, by the time we are actually thirsty, our cells have been needing fluid for quite some time. A good motto to remember, especially when exercising, is: Drink *before* you're thirsty. If the thirst mechanism is faulty, as it may be during illness or vigorous exercise, hormonal mechanisms can help conserve water by reducing the output of urine. Severe dehydration causes weakness and can lead to death.

Other Substances in Food

There are many substances in food that are not essential nutrients but which may influence health.

Antioxidants When the body uses oxygen or breaks down certain fats as a normal part of metabolism, it gives rise to substances called **free radicals.** Environmental factors such as cigarette smoke, exhaust fumes, radiation, excessive sunlight, certain drugs, and stress can increase free radical production. A free radical is a chemically unstable molecule that is missing an electron; it will react with any molecule it encounters from which it can take an electron. In their search for electrons, free radicals react with fats, proteins, and DNA, damaging cell membranes and mutating genes. Because of this, free radicals have been implicated in aging, cancer, cardiovascular disease, and degenerative diseases like arthritis.

Antioxidants found in foods can help rid the body of free radicals, thereby protecting cells. Antioxidants react with free radicals and donate electrons, rendering them harmless. Some antioxidants, such as vitamin C, vitamin E, and selenium, are also essential nutrients; others, such as flavonoids, found in citrus fruits, are not. Obtaining a regular intake of these nutrients is vital for maintaining health. Many fruits and vegetables are rich in antioxidants.

Phytochemicals Antioxidants are a particular type of **phytochemical,** a substance found in plant foods that may help prevent chronic disease. Researchers have just begun to identify and study all the different compounds found in foods, and many preliminary findings are promising. For example, certain proteins found in soy foods may help lower cholesterol levels. Sulforaphane, a compound isolated from broccoli and other cruciferous vegetables, may render some carcinogenic compounds harmless. Allyl sulfides, a group of chemicals found in garlic and onions, appear to boost the activity of cancer-fighting immune cells. Further research on phytochemicals may extend the role of nutrition to the prevention and treatment of many chronic diseases.

If you want to increase your intake of phytochemicals, it is best to obtain them by eating a variety of fruits and vegetables rather than relying on supplements. Like many vitamins and minerals, isolated phytochemicals may be harmful if taken in high doses. In addition, it is likely that their health benefits are the result of chemical substances working in combination. The role of phytochemicals in disease prevention and strategies for increasing your intake of phytochemicals are discussed in Chapters 11 and 12.

NUTRITIONAL GUIDELINES

The second part of putting together a healthy food plan—after you've learned about necessary nutrients—is choosing foods that satisfy nutritional requirements and meet your personal criteria. Various tools have been created by scientific and government groups to help people design healthy diets. The **Recommended Dietary Allowances (RDAs), Dietary Reference Intakes (DRIs),** and related guidelines are standards for nutrient intake designed to prevent nutritional deficiencies and reduce the risk of chronic disease. The **Food Guide Pyramid** translates these nutrient recommendations into a balanced food group plan that includes all essential nutrients. To provide further guidance, **Dietary Guidelines for Americans** have been established to address the

TERMS

free radical An electron-seeking compound that can react with fats, proteins, and DNA, damaging cell membranes and mutating genes in its search for electrons; produced through chemical reactions in the body and by exposure to environmental factors such as sunlight and tobacco smoke.

phytochemical A naturally occurring substance found in plant foods that may help prevent and treat chronic diseases such as heart disease and cancer; *phyto* means plant.

Recommended Dietary Allowances (RDAs) Amounts of certain nutrients considered adequate to prevent deficiencies in most healthy people; will eventually be replaced by the Dietary Reference Intakes (DRIs).

Dietary Reference Intakes (DRIs) An umbrella term for four types of nutrient standards: Adequate Intake (AI), Estimated Average Requirement (EAR), and Recommended Dietary Allowance (RDA) set levels of intake considered adequate to prevent nutrient deficiencies and reduce the risk of chronic disease; Tolerable Upper Intake Level (UL) sets the maximum daily intake that is unlikely to cause health problems.

Food Guide Pyramid A food group plan that provides practical advice to ensure a balanced intake of the essential nutrients.

Dietary Guidelines for Americans General principles of good nutrition provided by the U.S. Department of Agriculture and the U.S. Department of Health and Human Services.

prevention of diet-related chronic diseases. Together, these tools make up a complete set of resources for dietary planning.

Recommended Dietary Allowances (RDAs) and Dietary Reference Intakes (DRIs)

The Food and Nutrition Board of the National Academy of Sciences establishes the RDAs, DRIs, and related guidelines. The RDAs were developed as standards to prevent nutritional deficiency diseases such as rickets, scurvy, and anemia (see Tables 8-3 and 8-4). First published in 1941, the RDAs have been updated periodically to keep pace with new research findings; the most recent version was published in 1989. RDAs include intake recommendations for individual nutrients in one of three categories: (1) the RDAs themselves, which give specific recommended intakes of nutrients that are well known and well researched; (2) the Estimated Safe and Adequate Daily Dietary Intakes (ESADDIs), which provide a range of values for nutrients about which our knowledge is still sketchy; and (3) Estimated Minimum Requirements, which provide minimum values for three minerals.

Scientific knowledge about nutrition has increased dramatically since the inception of the RDAs, and current research focuses not just on the prevention of nutrient deficiencies but also on the role of nutrients in preventing chronic diseases such as osteoporosis, cancer, and cardiovascular disease. This expanded focus is the basis for the development of a new system of recommendations, the Dietary Reference Intakes. The DRIs, which will eventually replace the RDAs, include standards for both recommended intakes and maximum safe intakes.

- Recommended nutrient intakes can be expressed as three different types of standards—Adequate Intake (AI), Estimated Average Requirement (EAR), and Recommended Dietary Allowance (RDA). The type of standard used for a particular nutrient or age group depends on the amount of scientific information available and the intended use of the standard. Regardless of the type of standard attached to a particular nutrient, the DRI represents the best available estimate of intake for optimal health.

- Maximum intake level guidelines are expressed as the Tolerable Upper Intake Level (UL), the maximum daily intake by a healthy person that is unlikely to cause health problems. Because of lack of suitable data, ULs have not been established for all nutrients. This does not mean that people can tolerate chronic intakes of these vitamins above recommended levels. Like all chemical agents, nutrients can produce adverse effects if intakes are excessive; when data are limited, extra caution may be warranted. There is no established benefit from consuming nutrients at levels above the AI or RDA.

The DRIs are being issued in stages, and they have not yet been established for all vitamins and minerals. Table 8-5 is an abridged version of the 1989 RDAs; it includes nutrients for which DRIs have not yet been set. Table 8-6 gives recommended intakes for the vitamins and minerals for which DRIs have been set. Table 8-7 lists the upper intake levels for adults; as described earlier, ULs have not been established for all nutrients.

Should You Take Supplements? The aim of the RDAs and DRIs is to guide you in meeting your nutritional needs primarily with food, rather than with vitamin and mineral supplements. This goal is important because recommendations have not yet been set for some essential nutrients. Many supplements contain only nutrients with established recommendations, so using them to meet nutrient needs can leave you deficient in other nutrients. Supplements also lack potentially beneficial phytochemicals that are found only in whole foods. Nutrition scientists generally agree that most Americans can obtain most of the vitamins and minerals they need to prevent deficiencies by consuming a varied, nutritionally balanced diet. Ongoing research is examining whether supplements of particular vitamins and minerals should be recommended for their potential disease-fighting properties, as for the antioxidant vitamins C and E.

The question of whether or not to take supplements is a serious one. Some vitamins and minerals are dangerous when ingested in excess, as shown in Tables 8-3 and 8-4. Large doses of particular nutrients can also cause health problems by affecting the absorption of other vitamins and minerals. For all these reasons, you should think carefully about whether or not to take supplements; consider consulting a physician or registered dietitian.

In 1998, the Food and Nutrition Board of the National Academy of Sciences recommended supplements of particular nutrients for the following groups:

- Women who are capable of becoming pregnant should take 400 µg per day of folic acid from fortified foods and/or supplements in addition to folate from a varied diet. Research indicates that this level of folate intake will reduce the risk of neural tube defects. (This defect occurs early in pregnancy, before most women know they are pregnant; therefore, the recommendation for folate intake applies to all women of reproductive age rather than only to pregnant women.) Since 1998, enriched breads, flours, corn meals, rice, noodles, and other grain products have been fortified with small amounts of folic acid. Folate is found naturally in leafy green vegetables, legumes, citrus fruits and juices, and most berries.

- People over age 50 should consume foods fortified with vitamin B-12, B-12 supplements, or a combination of the two in order to meet the majority of the

TABLE 8-5

TABLE 8-5 · *Recommended Dietary Allowances, Revised 1989[a,b,c] (Abridged)*

Category	Age (years) or Condition	Protein (g/kg)[d]	Vitamins Vitamin A (μg RE)[e]	Vitamin E (mg α-TE)[f]	Vitamin K (μg)	Vitamin C (mg)	Minerals Iron (mg)	Zinc (mg)	Iodine (μg)	Selenium (μg)
Infants	0.0–0.5	2.2	375	3	5	30	6	5	40	10
	0.5–1.0	1.6	375	4	10	35	10	5	50	15
Children	1–3	1.2	400	6	15	40	10	10	70	20
	4–6	1.1	500	7	20	45	10	10	90	20
	7–10	1.0	700	7	30	45	10	10	120	30
Males	11–14	1.0	1000	10	45	50	12	15	150	40
	15–18	0.9	1000	10	65	60	12	15	150	50
	19–24	0.8	1000	10	70	60	10	15	150	70
	25–50	0.8	1000	10	80	60	10	15	150	70
	51+	0.8	1000	10	80	60	10	15	150	70
Females	11–14	1.0	800	8	45	50	15	12	150	45
	15–18	0.8	800	8	55	60	15	12	150	50
	19–24	0.8	800	8	60	60	15	12	150	55
	25–50	0.8	800	8	65	60	15	12	150	55
	51+	0.8	800	8	65	60	10	12	150	55
Pregnant		+10g	800	10	65	70	30	15	175	65
Lactating	1st 6 Months	+15g	1300	12	65	95	15	19	200	75
	2nd 6 Months	+12g	1200	11	65	90	15	16	200	75

[a]This table includes RDAs for those nutrients for which DRIs had not yet been established as of June 1998. The allowances, expressed as average daily intakes over time, are intended to provide for individual variations among most normal people as they live in the United States under usual environmental stresses. Diet should be based on a variety of common foods in order to provide other nutrients for which human requirements have been less well defined.

[b]Estimated Safe and Adequate Daily Dietary Intakes (ESADDIs) for adults: 1.5–3.0 mg copper; 2.0–5.0 mg manganese; 50–200 μg chromium; 75–250 mg molybdenum. (For information on other age groups, see National Research Council. 1989. *Recommended Dietary Allowances,* 10th ed. Washington, D.C.: National Academy Press.)

[c]Estimated Minimum Requirements of healthy adults: 500 mg sodium; 750 mg chloride; 2000 mg potassium. (For information on other age groups, see *Recommended Dietary Allowances,* 10th ed.)

[d]The RDA for protein is expressed as grams of protein per kilogram of body weight. To calculate the RDA, multiply body weight in kilograms (1 kilogram = 2.2 pounds) by the appropriate number from the protein column. For example, a 19-year-old male who weighs 165 pounds would calculate his protein RDA as follows: 165 lb ÷ 2.2 kg/lb = 75 kg × 0.8 g/kg (from table) = 60 g protein per day. For pregnant or lactating women, calculate RDA based on age and then add the appropriate number of additional grams listed in the table.

[e]Retinol equivalents: 1 retinol equivalent = 1 μg retinol or 6 μg β-carotene.

[f]α-Tocopherol equivalents: 1 mg d-α tocopherol = 1 α-TE.

SOURCE: Reprinted with permission from *Recommended Dietary Allowances:* 10th Edition. Copyright © 1989 by the National Academy of Sciences. Courtesy of the National Academy Press, Washington, D.C.

DRI of 2.4 mg of B-12 daily. Up to 30% of people over 50 may have problems absorbing vitamin B-12; the consumption of supplements and fortified foods can overcome this problem and help prevent a deficiency.

Supplements may also be recommended in the following cases:

- Women with heavy menstrual flows may need extra iron to compensate for the monthly loss.
- Some vegetarians may need extra calcium, iron, zinc, and vitamin B-12.
- Newborns need a single dose of vitamin K, which must be administered under the direction of a physician.
- People who are unable to consume adequate calories may need a range of vitamins and minerals.
- People who have certain diseases or who take certain medications may need specific vitamin and mineral supplements. Such supplement decisions must be made by a physician because some vitamins and minerals counteract the actions of certain medications.

In deciding whether to take a vitamin and mineral supplement, consider whether you already regularly consume

TABLE 8-6 — Dietary Reference Intakes (DRIs): Recommended Levels for Individual Intake

Life Stage	Group	Calcium (mg/day)	Phosphorus (mg/day)	Magnesium (mg/day)	Vitamin D (μg/day)[a,b]	Fluoride (mg/day)	Thiamin (mg/day)	Riboflavin (mg/day)
Infants	0–5 months	210	100	30	5	0.01	0.2	0.3
	6–11 months	270	275	75	5	0.5	0.3	0.4
Children	1–3 years	500	460	80	5	0.7	0.5	0.5
	4–8 years	800	500	130	5	1	0.6	0.6
Males	9–13 years	1300	1250	240	5	2	0.9	0.9
	14–18 years	1300	1250	410	5	3	1.2	1.3
	19–30 years	1000	700	400	5	4	1.2	1.3
	31–50 years	1000	700	420	5	4	1.2	1.3
	51–70 years	1200	700	420	10	4	1.2	1.3
	>70 years	1200	700	420	15	4	1.2	1.3
Females	9–13 years	1300	1250	240	5	2	0.9	0.9
	14–18 years	1300	1250	360	5	3	1.0	1.0
	19–30 years	1000	700	310	5	3	1.1	1.1
	31–50 years	1000	700	320	5	3	1.1	1.1
	51–70 years	1200	700	320	10	3	1.1	1.1
	>70 years	1200	700	320	15	3	1.1	1.1
Pregnancy	≤18 years	1300	1250	400	5	3	1.4	1.4
	19–30 years	1000	700	350	5	3	1.4	1.4
	31–50 years	1000	700	360	5	3	1.4	1.4
Lactation	≤18 years	1300	1250	360	5	3	1.5	1.6
	19–30 years	1000	700	310	5	3	1.5	1.6
	31–50 years	1000	700	320	5	3	1.5	1.6

NOTE: This table includes Dietary Reference Intakes for those nutrients for which DRIs had been set through June 1998. The table includes values for the type of DRI standard—Adequate Intake (AI) or Recommended Dietary Allowance (RDA)—that has been established for that particular nutrient and life stage.

[a] As cholecalciferol. 1 μg cholecalciferol = 40 IU vitamin D.
[b] In the absence of adequate exposure to sunlight.
[c] As niacin equivalents. 1 mg of niacin = 60 mg of tryptophan.
[d] As dietary folate equivalents (DFE). 1 DFE = 1 μg food folate = 0.6 μg of folic acid (from fortified food or supplement) consumed with food = 0.5 μg of synthetic (supplemental) folic acid taken on an empty stomach.
[e] Although AIs have been set for choline, there are few data to assess whether a dietary supply of choline is needed at all stages of the life cycle, and it may be that the choline requirement can be met by endogenous synthesis at some of these stages.
[f] Since 10–30% of older people may malabsorb food-bound B-12, it is advisable for those older than 50 years to meet their RDA mainly by consuming foods fortified with B-12 or a B-12-containing supplement.
[g] In view of evidence linking folate intake with neural tube defects in the fetus, it is recommended that all women capable of becoming pregnant consume 400 μg of synthetic folic acid from fortified food and/or supplements in addition to intake of food folate from a varied diet.
[h] It is assumed that women will continue consuming 400 μg of folic acid until their pregnancy is confirmed and they enter prenatal care, which ordinarily occurs after the end of the periconceptional period—the critical time for formation of the neural tube.

SOURCES: Food and Nutrition Board. Institute of Medicine. National Academy of Sciences. 1997. *Dietary Reference Intakes for Calcium, Phosphorus, Magnesium, Vitamin D, and Fluoride.* Washington, D.C.: National Academy Press. Food and Nutrition Board. Institute of Medicine. National Academy of Sciences. 1998. *Dietary Reference Intakes for Thiamin, Riboflavin, Niacin, Vitamin B$_6$, Folate, Vitamin B$_{12}$, Pantothenic Acid, Biotin, and Choline.* Washington, D.C.: National Academy Press. Copyright © 1998 by the National Academy of Sciences. Reprinted with permission from National Academy Press, Washington, D.C.

a fortified breakfast cereal. If you do decide to take a supplement, choose a balanced formulation that contains 50–100% of the adult Daily Value for vitamins and minerals (see below). Avoid supplements containing large doses of particular nutrients.

Daily Values Because the RDAs and DRIs are far too cumbersome to use as a basis for food labels, the U.S.

Food and Drug Administration developed another set of dietary standards, the **Daily Values.** The Daily Values are based on several different sets of guidelines and include standards for fat, cholesterol, carbohydrate, dietary fiber, and selected vitamins and minerals. On food labels, they are expressed as a percentage of a 2000-calorie diet, an average daily calorie intake for Americans. Using a single set of recommendations—the Daily Values—on food la-

TABLE 8-6

Dietary Reference Intakes (DRIs) (continued)

Niacin (mg/day)[c]	Vitamin B-6 (mg/day)	Folate (µg/day)[d]	Vitamin B-12 (µg/day)	Pantothenic Acid (mg/day)	Biotin (µg/day)	Choline[e] (mg/day)
2	0.1	65	0.4	1.7	5	125
3	0.3	80	0.5	1.8	6	150
6	0.5	150	0.9	2	8	200
8	0.6	200	1.2	3	12	250
12	1.0	300	1.8	4	20	375
16	1.3	400	2.4	5	25	550
16	1.3	400	2.4	5	30	550
16	1.3	400	2.4	5	30	550
16	1.7	400	2.4[f]	5	30	550
16	1.7	400	2.4[f]	5	30	550
12	1.0	300	1.8	4	20	375
14	1.2	400[g]	2.4	5	25	400
14	1.3	400[g]	2.4	5	30	425
14	1.3	400[g]	2.4	5	30	425
14	1.5	400[g]	2.4[f]	5	30	425
14	1.5	400	2.4[f]	5	30	425
18	1.9	600[h]	2.6	6	30	450
18	1.9	600[h]	2.6	6	30	450
18	1.9	600[h]	2.6	6	30	450
17	2.0	500	2.8	7	35	550
17	2.0	500	2.8	7	35	550
17	2.0	500	2.8	7	35	550

TABLE 8-7

Tolerable Upper Intake Levels for Adults

Nutrient	Upper Intake Level
Calcium	2500 mg/day
Phosphorus	4000 mg/day
Magnesium (nonfood sources)	350 mg/day
Vitamin D	50 µg/day
Fluoride	10 mg/day
Niacin	35 mg/day
Vitamin B-6	100 mg/day
Folate	1000 µg/day
Choline	3500 mg/day

This table includes the adult Tolerable Upper Intake Level (UL) standard of the Dietary Reference Intakes (DRIs). For some nutrients, there is insufficient data on which to develop a UL. This does not mean that there is no potential for adverse effects from high intake, and when data about adverse effects are limited, extra caution may be warranted. In healthy individuals, there is no established benefit from nutrient intakes above the RDA or AI.

SOURCES: Food and Nutrition Board. Institute of Medicine. National Academy of Sciences. 1997. *Dietary Reference Intakes for Calcium, Phosphorus, Magnesium, Vitamin D, and Fluoride.* Washington, D.C.: National Academy Press. Food and Nutrition Board. Institute of Medicine. National Academy of Sciences. 1998. *Dietary Reference Intakes for Thiamin, Riboflavin, Niacin, Vitamin B6, Folate, Vitamin B12, Pantothenic Acid, Biotin, and Choline.* Washington, D.C.: National Academy Press.

bels helps make nutrition information more accessible to the consumer. Food labels are described in more detail later in the chapter.

The Food Guide Pyramid

Many of us learned about food groups in grade school. We learned that by choosing foods from each group, we could have a healthy diet. The fundamental principles of this food guide are moderation, variety, and balance—a theme echoed throughout this chapter. A diet is balanced if it contains appropriate amounts of each nutrient, and choosing foods from each of the food groups helps ensure that balance.

The latest version of the food-group plan is the U.S. Department of Agriculture's Food Guide Pyramid (Figure 8-5). It is based on a recommended number of servings from six food groups. A range of servings is given for each group. The smaller number is for people who consume about 1600 calories a day, such as many sedentary women; the larger number is for those who consume

Daily Values A simplified version of the RDAs used on food labels; also included are values for nutrients with no RDA per se.

TERMS

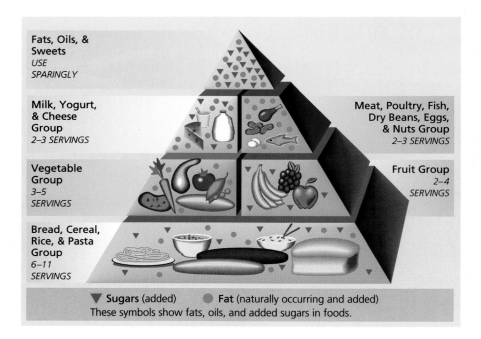

Figure 8-5 The Food Guide Pyramid: a guide to daily food choices. The Pyramid is an outline of what to eat each day—not a rigid prescription, but a general guide that lets you choose a healthful diet that's right for you. It calls for eating a variety of foods to get the nutrients you need and at the same time the right amount of calories to maintain a healthy weight. The Pyramid also focuses on fat because many Americans eat too much fat, especially saturated fat. SOURCE: U.S. Department of Agriculture, Human Nutrition Information Service. 1996. *Food Guide Pyramid.* Home and Garden Bulletin No. 252.

(Within pyramid figure:)

Fats, Oils, & Sweets
USE SPARINGLY

Milk, Yogurt, & Cheese Group
2–3 SERVINGS

Meat, Poultry, Fish, Dry Beans, Eggs, & Nuts Group
2–3 SERVINGS

Vegetable Group
3–5 SERVINGS

Fruit Group
2–4 SERVINGS

Bread, Cereal, Rice, & Pasta Group
6–11 SERVINGS

▼ Sugars (added)   ● Fat (naturally occurring and added)
These symbols show fats, oils, and added sugars in foods.

about 2800 calories a day, such as active men. Serving sizes and examples of foods are described below for each group.

It is important to choose a variety of foods within each group because different foods have different combinations of nutrients: for example, within the vegetable group, potatoes are high in vitamin C, while spinach is a rich source of vitamin A. Foods also vary in their amount of calories and nutrients, and people who do not need many calories should focus on nutrient-dense foods within each group (foods that are high in nutrients relative to the amount of calories they contain). Many foods you eat contain servings from more than one food group.

Bread, Cereals, Rice, and Pasta (6–11 Servings)
Foods from this group are usually low in fat and rich in complex carbohydrates, dietary fiber, and many vitamins and minerals, including thiamin, riboflavin, iron, niacin, folate, and zinc. Although 6–11 servings may seem like a large amount of food, many people eat several servings at a time. A single serving is the equivalent of the following:

- 1 slice of bread or half a hamburger bun, English muffin, or bagel
- 1 small roll, biscuit, or muffin
- 1 ounce of ready-to-eat cereal
- ½ cup cooked cereal, rice, or pasta
- 5–6 small or 2–3 large crackers

TERMS **cruciferous vegetables** Vegetables of the cabbage family, including cabbage, broccoli, brussels sprouts, kale, and cauliflower; the flower petals of these plants form the shape of a cross, hence the name.

If you are one of the many people who have trouble identifying an ounce of cereal or half a cup of rice, see the strategies in the box "Judging Serving Sizes." Choose foods that are typically made with little fat or sugars (bread, rice, pasta) over those that are high in fat and sugars (croissants, chips, cookies, doughnuts). For maximum nutrition, choose whole-grain breads, high-fiber cereals, whole-wheat pasta, and brown rice.

Vegetables (3–5 Servings) Vegetables are rich in carbohydrates, dietary fiber, vitamin A, vitamin C, folate, iron, magnesium, and other nutrients. They are also naturally low in fat. A serving of vegetables is equivalent to the following:

- 1 cup raw leafy vegetables
- ½ cup raw or cooked vegetables
- ½ cup tomato sauce
- ¾ cup vegetable juice
- ½ cup cooked dry beans

Dry beans (legumes) such as pinto, navy, kidney, and black beans can be counted as servings of vegetables *or* as alternatives to meat. Other good choices from this group include dark-green leafy vegetables such as spinach, chard, and collards; deep-orange and red vegetables such as carrots, winter squash, red bell peppers, and tomatoes; broccoli, cauliflower, and other **cruciferous vegetables;** peas; green beans; potatoes; and corn.

Fruits (2–4 Servings) Like vegetables, fruits are rich in carbohydrates, dietary fiber, and many vitamins, especially vitamin C. They are low in fat and sodium. The serving sizes used in the Pyramid are as follows:

Studies have shown that most people underestimate the size of their food portions, in many cases by as much as 50%. If you need to retrain your eye, try using measuring cups and spoons and an inexpensive kitchen scale when you eat at home. With a little practice, you'll learn the difference between 3 and 8 ounces of chicken or meat, and what a half-cup of rice really looks like. For quick estimates, use these equivalents:

- 1 teaspoon of margarine = the tip of your thumb.
- 1 ounce of cheese = your thumb or four dice stacked together.

- 3 ounces of chicken or meat = a deck of cards or an audio-cassette tape.
- ½ cup of rice or cooked vegetables = an ice cream scoop or one-third of a soda can.
- 2 tablespoons of peanut butter = a Ping-Pong ball.
- 1 cup of pasta = a woman's fist or a tennis ball.
- 1 medium potato = a computer mouse.

- 1 medium (apple, banana, peach, orange, pear) or 2 small (apricot, plum) whole fruit(s)
- 1 melon wedge
- ½ cup berries, cherries, or grapes
- ½ grapefruit
- ½ cup chopped, cooked, canned, or frozen fruit
- ¾ cup fruit juice (100% juice)
- ¼ cup dried fruit

Good choices from this group are citrus fruits and juices, melons, pears, apples, bananas, and berries. Choose whole fruits often—they are higher in fiber and often lower in calories than fruit juices. Fruit *juices* typically contain more nutrients than fruit *punches, ades,* and *drinks.* For canned fruits, choose those packed in their own juice rather than in syrup.

Milk, Yogurt, and Cheese (2–3 Servings)   Foods from this group are high in protein, carbohydrate, calcium, riboflavin, potassium, and zinc. To limit the fat in your diet, choose servings of low-fat or nonfat items from this group:

- 1 cup milk or yogurt
- 1½ ounces natural cheese
- 2 ounces processed cheese

Cottage cheese is lower in calcium than most other cheeses, and 1 cup of cottage cheese counts as only half a serving for this food group. Ice cream is also lower in calcium than many other dairy products (½ cup is equivalent to ⅓ serving); in addition, it is high in sugar and fat.

Meat, Poultry, Fish, Dry Beans, Eggs, and Nuts (2–3 Servings   This group of foods provides protein, niacin, iron, vitamin B-6, zinc, and thiamin, and vitamin B-12 (animal foods only). The Pyramid recommends 2–3 servings each day of foods from this group. The total amount of these servings should be the equivalent of 5–7 ounces of cooked lean meat, poultry, or fish per day. Many people misjudge what makes up a single serving for this food group:

- 2–3 ounces cooked lean meat, poultry, or fish (an average hamburger or a medium chicken breast half is about 3 ounces; 4 slices of bologna, 6 slices of hard salami, or ½ cup of drained canned tuna counts as about 2 ounces)
- The following portions of nonmeat foods are equivalent to 1 ounce of lean meat:

  ½ cup cooked dry beans (if not counted as a vegetable)

  1 egg

  2 tablespoons peanut butter

  ⅓ cup nuts

  ¼ cup seeds

  ½ cup tofu

To limit your intake of fat and saturated fat, choose lean cuts of meat and skinless poultry, and watch your serving sizes carefully. Nuts and seeds are high in fat, so eat them in moderation. Choose at least one serving of plant proteins every day.

Fats, Oils, and Sweets   The small tip of the Pyramid includes fats, oils, and sweets—foods such as salad dressings, oils, butter, margarine, gravy, mayonnaise, soft drinks, sugar, candy, jellies and jams, syrups, and sweet desserts. Foods from the tip of the Pyramid provide calories but few nutrients; they should not replace foods from the other groups. The total amount of fats, oils, and sweets you consume should be determined by your overall energy needs.

As indicated by the colored triangles and circles in the Pyramid, fats and added sugars are also found within the five major food groups (see Figure 8-5). ("Added sugars" refers to those sugars added to foods in processing or at the table, not the sugars found naturally in fruits and milk.) Foods that come from animals (the meat and milk groups) are naturally higher in fat than foods that come from plants. However, there are many lean meat and low-fat dairy choices available. Fruits, vegetables, and grain

TABLE 8-8 *Food Guide Pyramid Recommendations Compared with the Average American Diet*

	Recommended Diets at Three Calorie Levels[a]			Average American Diet	
	1600	2200	2800	Women (1600 calories)	Men (2400 calories)
Grain group (servings)	6	9	11	5.3	7.8
Vegetable group (servings)	3	4	5	3.0	4.2
Fruit group (servings)	2	3	4	1.5	1.6
Dairy group (servings)[b]	2–3	2–3	2–3	1.1	1.5
Meat group (ounces)[c]	5	6	7	4.0	6.5
Total fat (grams)[d]	53	73	93	58.0	90.8
Total added sugars (teaspoons)[d,e]	6	12	18	14.8	21.0

[a]The bottom of the recommended range of servings (1600 calories) is about right for many sedentary women and older adults. The middle range (2200 calories) is about right for most children, teenage girls, active women, and many sedentary men. The top of the range (2800 calories) is about right for teenage boys, many active men, and some very active women.
[b]Women who are pregnant or lactating, teenagers, and young adults to age 24 need 3 servings.
[c]The Pyramid recommends 2–3 servings per day, the equivalent of 5–7 ounces of cooked lean meat, poultry, or fish (see p. 203).
[d]Values for total fat and added sugars include fat and added sugars that are in food choices from the five major food groups as well as fat and added sugars from foods in the Fats, Oils, and Sweets group. The total for added sugars does not include sugars that occur naturally in foods such as fruit and milk. The recommended fat totals are based on a limit of 30% of total calories as fat.
[e]A teaspoon of sugar is equivalent to 4 grams (16 calories).

SOURCES: Shaw, A., et al. 1997. *Using the Food Guide Pyramid: A Resource for Nutrition Educators.* Center for Nutrition Policy and Promotion. U.S. Department of Agriculture (retrieved January 8, 1998; http://www.nal.usda.gov/fnic/Fpyr/guide.pdf). Cleveland, L. E., et al. 1997. *Pyramid Servings Data: Results from USDA's Continuing Survey of Food Intakes by Individuals.* Riverdale, Md.: Food Surveys Research Group. U.S. Department of Agriculture.

products are naturally low in fat, but they can be prepared in ways that make them higher-fat choices—for example, potatoes served as french fries and pasta served as fettucini alfredo. Added sugars in the food groups can be found in foods such as ice cream, sweetened yogurt, canned fruit packed in syrup, and baked goods such as cookies. Reduced-fat versions of foods such as cookies and ice cream are often *very* high in added sugars and just as high in calories as their full-fat versions.

The average American diet currently includes more fat and added sugars than recommended. The Pyramid suggests that Americans limit the fat in their diets to 30% of total calories. You will consume about half this amount if you eat the recommended number of servings from each food group, select the lowest-fat choices, and add no fat during cooking or at the table. Additional fat, up to 30% of total calories, is considered discretionary in that you can decide whether to get it from higher-fat food choices or additions to your foods.

Added sugars are less of a concern to health than fat, but consumption of large amounts of sugars adds empty calories to the diet and can make weight management more difficult. Analysis of the average diet of Americans has revealed that the number of servings from the fruit, dairy, and meat groups is below the recommended ranges, and servings from the grain and vegetable groups are near the bottom of the recommended ranges (Table 8-8). Overconsumption of fat and added sugars leaves fewer calories available for healthier food choices from the five major food groups. For example, the average daily diet among American women includes about 9 teaspoons (36 grams) of added sugars and 5 grams of fat above recommended limits. The 200 calories in these extra sugars and fats could be better used to increase the number of servings from the food groups for which women typically fall short of Pyramid recommendations.

General strategies for controlling intake of fat and added sugars include choosing lower-fat foods within each food group, eating fewer foods that are high in sugar and low in other nutrients, and limiting the amount of fats and sugars added to foods during cooking or at the table.

The Food Guide Pyramid is a general guide to what you should eat every day. By eating a balanced variety of foods from each of the six food groups and including some plant proteins, you can ensure that your daily diet is adequate in all nutrients. A diet using low-fat food choices contains only about 1600 calories but meets all known nutritional needs, except possibly for iron in some women who have heavy menstrual periods. For these women, foods fortified in iron, such as breakfast cereals, can make up the deficit.

Dietary Guidelines for Americans

To provide further guidance for choosing a healthy diet, the U.S. Department of Agriculture and the Department of Health and Human Services have issued Dietary Guidelines for Americans, most recently in December 1995. What follows is a summary of the advice provided by the Dietary Guidelines, with additional comments from other health-related organizations, including the American Heart Association, the National Cancer Institute, the National Academy of Sciences, and the Surgeon General.

Eat a Variety of Foods   To obtain the nutrients and other substances needed for good health, vary the foods you eat. Focus on the Food Guide Pyramid, choosing an appropriate number of servings from each group. Use foods from the base of the Pyramid as the foundation for your meals, and choose a variety of foods from within each group. Everyone, especially adolescent girls and women, should take special care to consume adequate calcium and iron.

Balance the Food You Eat with Physical Activity: Maintain or Improve Your Weight   Emphasize balancing food intake with regular physical activity to avoid becoming overweight. Excess body fat increases the risk of diabetes, heart disease, cancer, and other diseases. People who are overweight and have one of these problems should try to lose weight or at least not gain weight.

Those who are overweight should not try to lose more than 1/2–1 pound per week; avoid crash diets. Weight loss should be accomplished by increasing physical activity, eating less fat, and controlling portion sizes. If you are sedentary, try to become more active by accumulating 30 minutes or more of moderate physical activity on most or all days of the week. Choose low-fat, low-calorie, nutrient-dense foods—grains, vegetables, fruits, nonfat dairy products, and lean protein sources—rather than fatty foods, sugar and sweets, and alcoholic beverages.

Choose a Diet with Plenty of Grain Products, Vegetables, and Fruits   Foods from these food groups provide vitamins, minerals, complex carbohydrates, dietary fiber, and other substances important for good health. They also tend to be low in fat. Five or more servings of fruits and vegetables and six or more servings of grain products will help you reach a daily dietary fiber consumption of 20–35 grams. Emphasize complex, rather than simple, carbohydrates, and eat a variety of foods from each group. The availability of fresh fruits and vegetables varies by season and region of the country, but frozen and canned fruits and vegetables are readily available and are usually as high in nutrients. Fewer than 30% of Americans currently meet the Dietary Guidelines' goal for fruit and vegetable intake.

Choose a Diet Low in Fat, Saturated Fat, and Cholesterol   Some dietary fat is necessary for good health; good choices are monounsaturated and polyunsaturated fats found in vegetable oils, nuts, and fish. However, many Americans consume high-fat diets that increase their risk of heart disease, certain cancers, and obesity. Limit your overall intake of fat to 30% or less of daily calories, your saturated fat intake to less than one-third of your total daily fat intake (less than 10% of total daily calories), and your intake of cholesterol to 300 milligrams per day.

To control your intake of fat and saturated fat, choose lean meat, fish, poultry, and dry beans as protein sources; use nonfat or low-fat milk and milk products; and limit your consumption of high-fat foods. To reduce your intake of trans fats, avoid deep-fried fast foods and other products made with hydrogenated vegetable oils. Refer to the box "Reducing the Fat in Your Diet" for more suggestions.

Although less dangerous for heart health than saturated and trans fats, high cholesterol intake can be a problem for some people. Cholesterol is found only in animal foods. If you want to cut back on your cholesterol intake, follow the Food Guide Pyramid recommendations for consumption of animal foods; pay particular attention to serving sizes. In addition, limit your intake of foods that are particularly high in cholesterol content, including egg yolks and liver. Food labels provide the cholesterol content of prepared foods.

Choose a Diet Moderate in Sugars   Diets high in simple sugars do not cause hyperactivity or diabetes, but they do promote tooth decay. In addition, some foods that are high in sugar supply calories but few or no nutrients. For people who are very active and have high caloric needs, sugars can be an additional source of energy. However, because eating a nutritious diet and maintaining a healthy body weight are very important, most people should use sugars in moderation; people with low caloric needs should use sugars sparingly.

Moderation here means less than 15% of total calories—about 75 grams (15 teaspoons) per day from both naturally occurring simple sugars and added sugars. To reduce sugar consumption, cut back on items with added sugar, such as baked goods, candies, sweet desserts, sweetened beverages, canned fruits, and presweetened breakfast cereals.

Choose a Diet Moderate in Salt and Sodium   Sodium is an essential nutrient, but it is required only in small

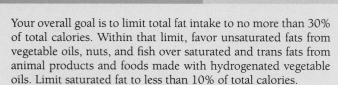
Your overall goal is to limit total fat intake to no more than 30% of total calories. Within that limit, favor unsaturated fats from vegetable oils, nuts, and fish over saturated and trans fats from animal products and foods made with hydrogenated vegetable oils. Limit saturated fat to less than 10% of total calories.

- Be moderate in your consumption of foods high in fat, especially those high in saturated and trans fat, including fast food, commercially prepared baked goods and desserts, meat, poultry, nuts and seeds, and regular dairy products (see Figure 8-4).

- When you do eat high-fat foods, limit your portion sizes, and balance your intake with foods low in fat.

- Choose lean cuts of meat, and trim any visible fat from meat before and after cooking. Remove skin from poultry before or after cooking.

- Replace whole milk with skim or low-fat milk in puddings, soups, and baked products. Substitute plain low-fat yogurt, blender-whipped cottage cheese, or buttermilk in recipes that call for sour cream.

- To reduce saturated and trans fat, use vegetable oil instead of butter or margarine. Use tub or squeeze margarine instead of stick margarine. Look for margarines that are free of trans fats.

- Season vegetables with herbs and spices rather than with sauces, butter, or margarine.

- Try lemon juice on salad, or use a yogurt-based salad dressing instead of mayonnaise or sour cream dressings.

- Steam, boil, or bake vegetables, or stir-fry them in a small amount of vegetable oil.

- Roast, bake, or broil meat, poultry, or fish so that fat drains away as the food cooks.

- Use a nonstick pan for cooking so that added fat will be unnecessary; use a vegetable spray for frying.

- Chill broths from meat or poultry until the fat becomes solid. Spoon off the fat before using the broth.

- Eat a low-fat vegetarian main dish at least once a week.

amounts—500 milligrams, or ¼ teaspoon, per day. Most Americans consume 8–12 times this amount. High sodium intake is linked to high blood pressure in some people and may also increase calcium loss, contributing to osteoporosis. It is recommended that you limit sodium intake to no more than 2400 milligrams per day, or about 1¼ teaspoons of salt per day.

Sodium is found primarily in processed and prepared foods; sodium content is provided on food labels. To lower your sodium intake, cut back on salty foods such as lunch meats, salted snack foods, canned soups, processed cheese, many tomato-based products, and many frozen dinners and baked goods. Add less salt during cooking and at the table; use lemon juice, herbs, and spices, rather than salt, to enhance the flavor of food. It usually takes only about a week or two to become accustomed to a lower-sodium diet.

If You Drink Alcoholic Beverages, Do So in Moderation   Alcoholic beverages supply calories but few or no nutrients. Current evidence suggests that moderate drinking—no more than one drink daily for women and two drinks for men—is associated with a lower risk of cardiovascular disease in some people. However, higher levels of alcohol intake are associated with an increased risk for many diseases and with higher overall mortality rates. Adults who drink alcoholic beverages should do so in moderation, with meals, and when consumption does not put themselves or others at risk.

One further recommendation geared specifically for cancer prevention is to use moderation when consuming salt-cured, smoked, and nitrate-cured foods (such as ba-

con and sausage) because these may increase the risk of colon and other gastrointestinal cancers.

Reading Food Labels

Consumers can get help in applying the principles of the Food Guide Pyramid and the Dietary Guidelines for Americans from food labels. Beginning in 1994, all processed foods regulated by either the FDA or the USDA have included standardized nutrition information on their labels (see the box "Using Food Labels"). Every food label shows serving sizes and the amount of fat, saturated fat, cholesterol, protein, dietary fiber, and sodium in each serving. To make intelligent choices about food, learn to read and understand food labels. Lab 8-3 will give you the opportunity to compare foods using the information provided on their labels.

The Vegetarian Alternative

Some people choose a diet with one essential difference from the diets we've already described: Foods of animal origin (meat, poultry, fish, eggs, milk) are eliminated or restricted. Today, about 12 million Americans follow a vegetarian diet. Most do so because they think foods of plant origin are a more natural way to nourish the body. Some do so for religious, health, ethical, or philosophical reasons. If you choose to be a vegetarian, you can be confident of meeting your nutritional needs by following a few basic rules. (Vegetarian diets for children and pregnant women warrant individual professional guidance.)

Types of Vegetarian Diets   There are a variety of vegetarian styles; the wider the variety of the diet eaten, the

Food labels are designed to help consumers make food choices based on the nutrients that are most important to good health. A food label states how much fat, saturated fat, cholesterol, protein, dietary fiber, and sodium the food contains. In addition to listing nutrient content by weight, the label puts the information in the context of a daily diet of 2000 calories that includes no more than 65 grams of fat (approximately 30% of total calories). For example, if a serving of a particular product has 13 grams of fat, the label will show that the serving represents 20% of the daily fat allowance. If your daily diet contains fewer or more than 2000 calories, you need to adjust these calculations accordingly. Refer to p. 189 for instructions on setting nutrient intake goals.

Food labels contain uniform serving sizes. This means that if you look at different brands of salad dressing, for example, you can compare calories based on the serving amount. Regulations also require that foods meet strict definitions if their packaging includes the terms "light," "low-fat," or "high-fiber" (see below). Health claims such as "good source of dietary fiber" or "low in saturated fat" on packages are signals that those products can wisely be included in your diet. Overall, the food label is an important tool to help you choose a diet that conforms to the Food Guide Pyramid and the Dietary Guidelines.

Beginning in 1999, dietary supplements will carry a similar "Supplement Facts" panel that specifies serving sizes and lists nutrients (with percent of Daily Value) and other ingredients.

Selected Nutrient Claims and What They Mean

Healthy A food that is low in fat, is low in saturated fat, has no more than 360–480 mg of sodium and 60 mg of cholesterol, *and* provides 10% or more of the Daily Value for vitamin A, vitamin C, protein, calcium, iron, or dietary fiber.

Light or lite One-third fewer calories or 50% less fat than a similar product.

Reduced or fewer At least 25% less of a nutrient than a similar product; can be applied to fat ("reduced fat"), saturated fat, cholesterol, sodium, and calories.

Extra or added 10% or more of the Daily Value per serving when compared to a similar product.

Good source 10–19% of the Daily Value for a particular nutrient.

High, rich in, or excellent source of 20% or more of the Daily Value for a particular nutrient.

Low calorie 40 calories or fewer per serving.

High fiber 5 g or more of fiber per serving.

Good source of fiber 2.5–4.9 g of fiber per serving.

Fat-free Less than 0.5 g of fat per serving.

Low-fat 3 g of fat or less per serving.

Saturated fat–free Less than 0.5 g of saturated fat and 0.5 g of trans fatty acids per serving.

Low saturated fat 1 g or less of saturated fat per serving and no more than 15% of total calories.

Cholesterol-free Less than 2 mg of cholesterol and 2 g or less of saturated fat per serving.

Low cholesterol 20 mg or less of cholesterol and 2 g or less of saturated fat per serving.

Low sodium 140 mg or less of sodium per serving.

Very low sodium 35 mg or less of sodium per serving.

Lean Cooked seafood, meat, or poultry with less than 10 g of fat, 4 g of saturated fat, and 95 mg of cholesterol per serving.

Extra lean Cooked seafood, meat, or poultry with less than 5 g of fat, 2 g of saturated fat, and 95 mg of cholesterol per serving.

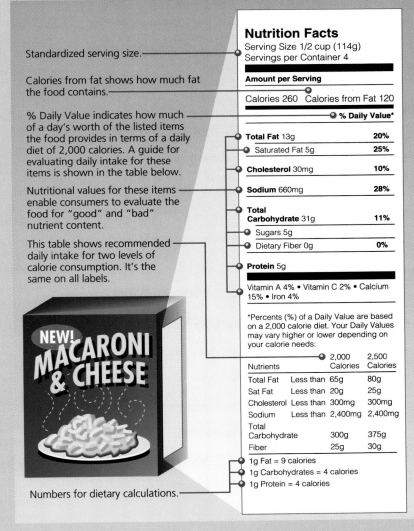

Standardized serving size.

Calories from fat shows how much fat the food contains.

% Daily Value indicates how much of a day's worth of the listed items the food provides in terms of a daily diet of 2,000 calories. A guide for evaluating daily intake for these items is shown in the table below.

Nutritional values for these items enable consumers to evaluate the food for "good" and "bad" nutrient content.

This table shows recommended daily intake for two levels of calorie consumption. It's the same on all labels.

Numbers for dietary calculations.

Nutrition Facts

Serving Size 1/2 cup (114g)
Servings per Container 4

Amount per Serving

Calories 260   Calories from Fat 120

	% Daily Value*
Total Fat 13g	**20%**
Saturated Fat 5g	**25%**
Cholesterol 30mg	**10%**
Sodium 660mg	**28%**
Total Carbohydrate 31g	**11%**
Sugars 5g	
Dietary Fiber 0g	**0%**
Protein 5g	

Vitamin A 4% • Vitamin C 2% • Calcium 15% • Iron 4%

*Percents (%) of a Daily Value are based on a 2,000 calorie diet. Your Daily Values may vary higher or lower depending on your calorie needs:

Nutrients		2,000 Calories	2,500 Calories
Total Fat	Less than	65g	80g
Sat Fat	Less than	20g	25g
Cholesterol	Less than	300mg	300mg
Sodium	Less than	2,400mg	2,400mg
Total Carbohydrate		300g	375g
Fiber		25g	30g

1g Fat = 9 calories
1g Carbohydrates = 4 calories
1g Protein = 4 calories

easier to meet nutritional needs. **Vegans** eat only plant foods. **Lacto-vegetarians** eat plant foods and dairy products. **Lacto-ovo-vegetarians** eat plant foods, dairy products, and eggs. Finally, **partial, semivegetarians,** or **pesco-vegetarians** eat plant foods, dairy products, eggs, and usually a small selection of poultry, fish, and other seafood. Including some animal protein in a diet makes planning much easier, but it is not necessary.

A Food-Group Plan for Vegetarians A food-group plan has been developed for lacto-vegetarians; it includes 6–11 servings from grains and 2–4 servings from legumes, nuts, and seeds. Add to this 3–5 servings from the vegetable group, 2–4 servings from the fruit group, and 2 or more servings from the milk, yogurt, and cheese group to complete the plan. By following this plan, lacto-vegetarians should have no problem obtaining an adequate diet. Consuming fruits with most meals is especially helpful, because any vitamin C present will improve iron absorption (the iron in plants is more difficult to absorb than the iron in animal sources).

In contrast to those who eat dairy products, vegans must do much more special diet planning to obtain all essential nutrients. A vegan must take special care to consume adequate amounts of protein, riboflavin, vitamin D, vitamin B-12, calcium, iron, and zinc; good strategies for obtaining these nutrients include the following:

- Eat proteins from a wide variety of sources, and include a couple of protein sources at each meal. A good rule of thumb is 11 servings of grains and 4 servings of legumes, nuts, and seeds. Soy milk, tofu (soybean curd), and tempeh (a cultured soy product) make important nutrient contributions to this diet plan.

- Eat green leafy vegetables, whole grains, yeast, and legumes to obtain riboflavin.

- Obtain vitamin D by spending 5–15 minutes a day out in the sun, by consuming vitamin D–fortified products like rice milk or soy milk, or by taking a supplement.

- Obtain vitamin B-12 (found only in animal foods) from a supplement or by consuming foods fortified with vitamin B-12, such as special yeast products, soy milk, and breakfast cereals.

- Consume fortified tofu, dark-green leafy vegetables, nuts, tortillas made from lime-processed corn, and fortified orange juice, bread, and soy milk to obtain calcium. Supplements may be necessary.

- Consume whole grains, fortified bread and breakfast cereals, dried fruits, dark-green leafy vegetables, nuts, and legumes to obtain iron.

- Obtain zinc from whole grains and legumes.

It takes a little planning and common sense to put together a good vegetarian diet. If you are a vegetarian or are considering becoming one, devote some extra time and thought to your diet. It's especially important that you eat as wide a variety of foods as possible to ensure that all of your nutritional needs are satisfied.

Dietary Challenges for Special Population Groups

The Food Guide Pyramid and Dietary Guidelines for Americans provide a basis that everyone can use to create a healthy diet. However, some population groups face special dietary challenges.

Women Women tend to be smaller and weigh less than men, meaning they have lower energy needs and therefore consume fewer calories. Because of this, women have more difficulty getting adequate amounts of all essential nutrients and need to focus on nutrient-dense foods. Two nutrients of special concern are calcium and iron, minerals for which many women fail to meet the RDAs. Low calcium intake may be linked to the development of osteoporosis in later life. Nonfat and low-fat dairy products and fortified cereal, bread, and orange juice are good choices. Iron is also a concern: Menstruating women have higher iron requirements than other groups, and a lack of iron in the diet can lead to iron-deficiency anemia. Studies indicate that about 10% of adolescent girls and women of childbearing age are iron deficient. Lean red meat, green leafy vegetables, and fortified breakfast cereals are good sources of iron. As discussed earlier, all women capable of becoming pregnant should consume adequate folate from fortified foods and/or supplements.

Men Men are seldom thought of as having nutritional deficiencies because they generally have high-calorie diets. However, many men have a diet that does not follow the Food Guide Pyramid but that includes more red meat and fewer fruits, vegetables, dairy products, and grains than recommended. This dietary pattern is linked to heart disease and some types of cancer. A high intake of calories can lead to weight gain in the long term if a man's activity level decreases as he ages. Men should use the Food Guide Pyramid as a basis for their overall diet and focus on increasing their consumption of fruits, vegetables, and grains to obtain vitamins, minerals, dietary fiber, and phytochemicals.

TERMS **vegan** A vegetarian who eats no animal products.

lacto-vegetarian A vegetarian who includes dairy products in the diet.

lacto-ovo-vegetarian A vegetarian who includes dairy products and eggs in the diet.

partial, semivegetarian, or **pesco-vegetarian** A person who includes plant foods, dairy products, eggs, and small amounts of poultry, fish, and seafood in the diet.

College Students   Foods that are convenient for college students are not always the healthiest choices. It is easy for students who eat in buffet-style dining halls to overeat, and the foods offered are not necessarily high in essential nutrients and low in fat. The same is true of meals at fast-food restaurants, another convenient source of quick and inexpensive meals for busy students. Although no food is entirely "bad," consuming a wide variety of foods is critical for a healthy diet. See the box "Eating Strategies for College Students" for tips on making healthy eating convenient and affordable.

Older Adults   As people age, they tend to become less active, so they require fewer calories to maintain their weight. At the same time, the absorption of nutrients tends to be lower in older adults because of age-related changes in the digestive tract. Thus, they must consume nutrient-dense foods in order to meet their nutritional requirements. As discussed earlier, foods fortified with vitamin B-12 and/or B-12 supplements are recommended for people over age 50. Because constipation is a common problem, consuming foods high in dietary fiber is another important goal.

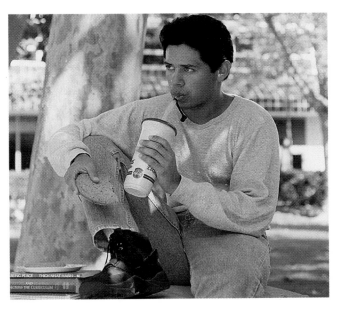

Eating on the run is a common—but not always healthy—habit among college students. After snacking on cookies, this young man should complete his day's diet with a low-fat, nutrient-dense dinner.

Athletes   Key dietary concerns for athletes are meeting their increased energy requirements and drinking enough fluids during practice and throughout the day to remain fully hydrated. Individuals engaged in vigorous training programs expend more energy (calories) than sedentary and moderately active individuals and may have energy needs ranging from 2000 to more than 6000 calories per day. For athletes, the American Dietetic Association recommends a diet with 60–65% of calories coming from carbohydrate, 10–15% from protein, and no more than 30% from fat.

Endurance athletes involved in competitive events lasting longer than 90 minutes may benefit from increasing carbohydrate intake to 65–70% of total calories. High carbohydrate intake builds and maintains muscle glycogen stores, resulting in greater endurance and delayed fatigue during competitive events. Some endurance athletes engage in "carbohydrate loading"—a practice that involves increasing carbohydrate intake in the days prior to a competition.

Athletes for whom maintaining low body weight and body fat is important—such as skaters, gymnasts, and wrestlers—should consume adequate calories and nutrients and avoid falling into unhealthy patterns of eating. The combination of low levels of body fat, high physical activity, disordered eating habits, and, in women, amenorrhea, is associated with stress fractures and other injuries and with osteoporosis. Eating disorders are discussed in Chapter 9.

Strenuous exercise can lead to rapid loss of fluids. Endurance athletes should consume at least 16 ounces (2 cups) of fluid about 2 hours before a workout, followed by another 16 ounces about 20 minutes prior to exercise. In hot and humid conditions, an additional 4–6 ounces should be consumed every 15 minutes during a workout. Athletes should consume enough fluids during activity so that their body weight remains relatively constant before and after an exercise session. For workouts lasting less than 60–90 minutes, cool water is an appropriate fluid replacement; for longer workouts or for exercise in especially hot and humid conditions, a commercial sports beverage that contains carbohydrates may be beneficial.

There is no evidence that consuming supplements containing vitamins, minerals, protein, or specific amino acids will build muscle or improve sports performance. Strength and muscle are built with exercise, not extra protein, and carbohydrates provide the fuel needed for muscle-building exercise. Strenuous physical activity does increase the need for protein and some vitamins and minerals; however, the increased energy intake of athletes more than compensates for this increased need. (Indeed, the protein intake in the average American diet is already about 50% above the RDA, representing 16% of total calories.) For athletes, the American Dietetic Association recommends a daily protein intake of 1.0–1.5 grams per kilogram of body weight, up from the RDA of 0.8 gram per kilogram. A 160-pound athlete consuming 3500 calories per day needs to obtain only 12% of total calories from protein to achieve the upper end of the protein range for athletes. A balanced high-carbohydrate,

General Guidelines

- Eat slowly, and enjoy your food.

- Eat a colorful, varied diet. The more colorful your diet is, the more varied and rich in fruits and vegetables it will be. Many Americans eat few fruits and vegetables, despite the fact that these foods are typically inexpensive, delicious, rich in nutrients, and low in fat and calories.

- Eat breakfast. You'll have more energy in the morning and be less likely to grab an unhealthy snack later on.

- Choose healthy snacks—fruits, vegetables, grains, and cereals—as often as you can.

- Combine physical activity with healthy eating. You'll look and feel better and have a much lower risk of many chronic diseases. Even a little exercise is better than none.

Eating in the Dining Hall

- Choose a meal plan that includes breakfast, and don't skip it.

- If menus are posted or distributed, decide what you want to eat before getting in line, and stick to your choices. Consider what you plan to do and eat for the rest of the day before making your choices.

- Ask for large servings of vegetables and small servings of meat and other high-fat main dishes. Build your meals around grains and vegetables.

- Choose leaner poultry, fish, or bean dishes rather than high-fat meats and fried entrees.

- Ask that gravies and sauces be served on the side; limit your intake.

- Choose broth-based or vegetable soups rather than cream soups.

- Drink nonfat milk, water, mineral water, or fruit juice rather than heavily sweetened fruit drinks or whole milk.

- Choose fruit for dessert rather than pastries, cookies, or cakes.

- Do some research about the foods and preparation methods used in your dining hall or cafeteria. Discuss any food and nutrition suggestions you have with your food service manager.

Eating in Fast-Food Restaurants

- Most fast-food chains can provide a brochure with a nutritional breakdown of the foods on the menu. Ask for it. (See also the information in Appendix C.)

- Order small single burgers with no cheese instead of double burgers with many toppings. If possible, ask for them broiled instead of fried.

- Ask for items to be prepared without mayonnaise, tartar sauce, sour cream, or other high-fat sauces. Ketchup, mustard, and fat-free mayonnaise or sour cream are better choices and are available at many fast-food restaurants.

- Choose whole-grain buns or bread for burgers and sandwiches.

- Choose chicken items made from chicken breast, not processed chicken.

- Order vegetable pizzas.

- At the salad bar, choose a lowfat dressing. Put the dressing on the side and dip your fork into it—don't pour it over your salad. Avoid heavily dressed potato and pasta salads. Don't put croutons and bacon on vegetable salads.

- If you order french fries or onion rings, get the smallest size, and/or share them with a friend.

Eating on the Run

Are you chronically short of time? The following healthy and filling items can be packed for a quick snack or meal: fresh or dried fruit, fruit juices, raw fresh vegetables, plain bagels, bread sticks, fig bars, low-fat cheese sticks or cubes, low-fat crackers or granola bars, nonfat or low-fat yogurt, pretzels, rice or corn cakes, plain popcorn, soup (if you have access to a microwave), or water.

---

moderate-protein, low-fat diet can provide all needed nutrients for athletes.

People with Special Health Concerns   Many Americans have special health concerns that affect their dietary needs. For example, women who are pregnant or breastfeeding require extra calories, vitamins, and minerals. People with diabetes benefit from a well-balanced diet that is low in simple sugars, high in complex carbohydrates, and relatively rich in monounsaturated fats. And people with high blood pressure need to control their weight and may need to limit their sodium consumption. If you have a health problem or concern that may require

a special diet, discuss your situation with a physician or registered dietitian (R.D.).

A PERSONAL PLAN: APPLYING
NUTRITIONAL PRINCIPLES

Now that you understand the basics of good nutrition, you can put together a diet that works for you. The basic principles of a healthy diet are simple—variety, balance, and moderation. But within this framework, no single diet is optimal for everyone. Many different diets can

There is no one ethnic diet that clearly surpasses all others in providing people with healthful foods. However, every diet has its advantages and disadvantages, and within each cuisine, some foods are better choices. It is in this area of personal choice that individuals can make a difference in their own health. The dietary guidelines described in this chapter can be applied to any ethnic cuisine. For additional guidance, refer to the table below, which lists some of the more and less healthful choices you can make when you eat out at various ethnic restaurants or cook ethnic meals at home.

	Choose Often	Choose Seldom
Chinese	Chinese greens Hunan or Szechuan dishes Rice, brown or white Steamed dishes Stir-fry dishes Wonton soup	Crispy duck or beef Egg rolls or fried wontons General Tso's chicken Kung pao dishes Rice, fried Sweet-and-sour dishes
Indian	Chapati (baked, tortilla-like bread) Dal (lentils) Karhi (chickpea soup) Khur (milk and rice dessert) Tandoori, chicken or fish Yogurt-based curry dishes	Bhatura, poori, or paratha (fried breads) Coconut milk–based dishes Ghee (clarified butter) Korma (rich meat dish) Pakoras (fried appetizer) Samosa (fried meat and vegetables in dough)
Italian	Cioppino (seafood stew) Minestrone soup, vegetarian Pasta with marinara sauce Pasta primavera Pasta with red or white clam sauce	Cannelloni, ravioli, or manicotti Fettucine alfredo Fried calamari Garlic bread Veal or eggplant parmigiana
Japanese	Kushiyaki (broiled foods on skewers) Nabemono (boiled dishes) Shabu-shabu (foods in boiling broth) Sushi	Agemono (deep-fried dishes) Sukiyaki Tempura (fried chicken, shrimp, or vegetables) Tonkatsu (fried pork)
Mexican	Beans and rice Burritos, bean or chicken Fajitas, chicken or vegetable Gazpacho Refried beans, nonfat or low-fat Tortillas, steamed	Chiles relleños Chimichangas, flautas, or quesadillas Enchiladas, beef or cheese Nachos or fried tortillas Refried beans made with lard Taco salad
Thai	Forest salad Larb (chicken salad with mint) Po tak (seafood soup) Yum neua (broiled beef with onions)	Fried fish, duck, or chicken Curries with coconut milk Dishes with peanut sauce Yum koon chaing (sausage with peppers)

SOURCES: The sat fat switch. 1997. *Nutrition Action Healthletter,* January/February. University of Southern Florida Student Health Service. 1997. Ethnic food (http://www.shs.usf.edu/Health/ethnic.html). The best of Asian cuisines. 1993. *University of California at Berkeley Wellness Letter,* January. Eating in ethnic restaurants. 1990. *Runner's World,* January. Reprinted by permission of *Runner's World Magazine.* Copyright © 1990 Rodek Press, Inc. All rights reserved.

meet people's nutritional requirements (see the box "Ethnic Foods"). Every individual needs to customize a food plan based on age, gender, weight, activity level, medical risk factors—and, of course, personal tastes.

Assessing and Changing Your Diet

The first step in planning a healthy diet is to examine what you currently eat. Labs 8-1 and 8-2 are designed to help you analyze your current diet and compare it to optimal dietary goals. (This analysis can be completed using either Appendix B or a nutritional analysis software program.)

Next, experiment with additions and substitutions to your current diet to bring it closer to your goals. If you are consuming too much fat, for example, try substituting fruit for a calorie-rich dessert. If you aren't getting enough iron, try adding some raisins to your cereal or garbanzo beans to your salad. If you need to plan your diet from the ground up, use the Food Guide Pyramid and the Dietary Guidelines.

To put your plan into action, use the behavioral self-management techniques and tips described in Chapter 1. If you identify several changes you want to make, focus on one at a time. You might start, for example, by substituting nonfat or low-fat milk for whole milk. When you become used to that, you can try substituting whole-wheat bread for white bread. The information on eating behavior in Lab 8-1 will help you identify and change unhealthy patterns of eating.

Staying Committed to a Healthy Diet

Beyond knowledge and information, you also need support in difficult situations. Keeping to your plan is easiest when you choose and prepare your own food at home. For meals prepared at home, advance planning is the key: mapping out meals and shopping appropriately, cooking in advance when possible, and preparing enough food for leftovers later in the week. A tight budget does not necessarily make it more difficult to eat healthy meals. It makes good health sense and good budget sense to use only small amounts of meat and to have a few meatless meals each week.

In restaurants, keeping to food plan goals becomes somewhat more difficult. Portion sizes in restaurants tend to be larger than serving sizes of the Food Guide Pyramid, but by remaining focused on your goals, you can eat only part of your meal and take the rest home for a meal later in the week. Don't hesitate to ask questions when you're eating in a restaurant. Most restaurant personnel are glad to explain how menu selections are prepared and to make small adjustments, such as serving salad dressings and sauces on the side so they can be avoided or used sparingly. To limit your fat intake, order meat or fish broiled or grilled rather than fried or sauteed, choose rice or a plain baked potato over french fries, and select a clear soup rather than a creamy one. Desserts that are irresistible can, at least, be shared.

Strategies like these can be helpful, but small changes cannot change a fundamentally high-fat, high-calorie meal into a moderate, healthful one. Often, the best advice is to bypass a steak with potatoes au gratin for a flavorful but low-fat entree. Many of the selections offered in ethnic restaurants are healthy choices (refer to the box on ethnic foods on p. 211 for suggestions).

Fast-food restaurants offer the biggest challenge to a healthy diet. Surveys show that about 70% of 18- to 24-year-olds and 64% of 25- to 34-year-olds visit a fast-food restaurant at least once a week. Fast-food meals are often high in calories, total fat, saturated fat, sodium, and sugar; they may be low in fiber and in some vitamins and minerals (see Appendix C). If you do eat at a fast-food restaurant, make sure the rest of your meals that day are low-fat meals.

Knowledge of food and nutrition is essential to the success of your program. The information provided in this chapter should give you the tools you need to design and implement a diet that promotes long-term health and well-being. If you need additional information or have questions about nutrition, be sure the source you consult is reliable.

COMMON QUESTIONS ANSWERED

Which is the healthier choice—butter or margarine? Both butter and margarine are concentrated sources of fat, containing about 11 grams of fat and 100 calories per tablespoon. However, butter is richer in saturated fat, a type of fat closely associated with elevated levels of artery-clogging LDLs ("bad" cholesterol). Each tablespoon of butter has about 8 grams of saturated fat; margarine averages only 2 grams of saturated fat per tablespoon, regardless of the type of vegetable oil it contains. In addition, butter contains cholesterol; margarine does not.

Based on this information, margarine is clearly the best choice. However, recent research has turned up a potential health problem with margarine, too. As described earlier in the chapter, the process of hydrogenation produces trans fatty acids, which also raise blood cholesterol levels. A tablespoon of stick margarine contains about 2 grams of trans fat.

So what should you choose? Because the combined total of saturated and trans fats in butter is twice that of stick margarine, most nutritionists would recommend margarine over butter. However, there are better options. Tub and squeeze margarines contain less saturated and trans fat than stick margarines, and most vegetable oils are low in saturated fat and completely free of trans fats. Consumption of unhydrogenated, unsaturated fats is associated with a decreased risk of heart disease.

The Food Guide Pyramid seems to recommend such a large number of servings. How can I possibly follow its recommendations without gaining weight? First of all, consider how many servings from each food group are appropriate for you. The suggested number of servings is given as a range, 6–11 servings of grain products, 3–5 of vegetables, and so on. The smaller number of servings is for people who consume about 1600 calories per day, such as many sedentary women. The larger number is for those who consume about 2800 calories per day, such as active men. If the smaller number of servings is appropriate for you, concentrate on choosing nutrient-dense foods—those that are rich in nutrients but relatively low in calories, such as most grains, fruits, and vegetables.

Second, compare the serving sizes of the foods you eat with those used in the Food Guide Pyramid (see pp. 201–205). Some of the Pyramid's serving sizes are smaller than what you might typically eat. For example, many people eat a cup or more of pasta or rice in a meal, which would correspond to 2 or more servings from the grain products group. You'll probably find that your current diet already includes the minimum number of servings from most of the food groups. If not, you may find that you are eating too many servings from one group and not enough from another. Try to make small changes in your eating habits and food choices to bring your diet into line with the recommendations in the Pyramid, paying particular attention to your consumption of fat and added sugars. The Food Guide Pyramid is designed to help you balance your food choices to ensure good health.

Strategies for successful weight management are described in detail in the next chapter.

Do I have to give up meat in order to lower the fat content of my diet to recommended levels? No. The keys for including beef, pork, and poultry in a healthy diet are to select lower-fat choices and to limit the size of your servings to those given in the Food Guide Pyramid. The amount of fat in meat products varies considerably; see the box "Guidelines for Healthier Meat Choices" for more information. The recommended 2- to 3-ounce serving of meat is about the size of a deck of cards—far smaller than what many Americans eat, especially when they eat out. Think of meat as a side dish rather than as the center of a meal. Try stir-frying lean strips of lean steak with vegetables or adding a small portion of extra-lean ground beef to spaghetti sauce. Limit your intake of high-fat processed meats such as sausages, salami, and cold cuts. When you eat out, try sharing a steak with a friend or taking half of it home.

How common is food poisoning? Food poisoning—or foodborne illness, as scientists call it—is very common. Tens of millions of cases occur each year; it is likely that your last case of "stomach flu" was actually a case of foodborne illness. The most common symptoms are diarrhea, abdominal cramps, vomiting, fever, and weakness. Most cases clear up in a few days, as long as people consume enough fluids to prevent dehydration. Foodborne illness poses a greater risk for young children, the elderly, and people with underlying chronic illnesses. And in cases where a particularly dangerous organism is involved, even a healthy adult can become seriously ill. Foodborne illness is believed to kill 6000–9000 Americans each year.

Bacteria and the toxins they produce cause most cases of foodborne illness; parasites and viruses are less common causes. *Salmonella* bacteria are responsible for almost 60% of all cases of foodborne illness; they are most often found in eggs, poultry, meat, milk, and inadequately refrigerated and reheated leftovers. The bacteria *Staphylococcus aureus* is responsible for 20–40% of cases. It is usually transferred to food when people handle or sneeze or cough over food; it is most common on meat, prepared salads, cream sauces, and cream-filled pastries. Illness from *Clostridium botulinum* or *Escherichia coli* is rare, but it can be deadly. Botulism results primarily from improperly canned foods; *E. coli* is spread mainly by undercooked ground beef, unpasteurized juices, and poorly washed fruits and vegetables.

Several outbreaks of illness tied to a particularly dangerous strain of *E. coli* led to the passage of new federal food inspection regulations in 1996. However, the new microbiological tests will not eliminate all contamination. The key to protecting yourself from foodborne illness is to handle, cook, and store foods in ways that prevent the bacteria from spreading and multiplying. Keep these tips in mind:

- Don't buy food in containers that leak, bulge, or are severely dented. Refrigerated foods should be cold, and frozen foods should be solid.

- Use or freeze fresh meats within 3–5 days after purchase; use or freeze fresh poultry, fish, and ground meat within 1–2 days.

- Thaw frozen food in the refrigerator or in the microwave oven, not on the kitchen counter.

- Thoroughly wash your hands with hot soapy water before and after handling food, especially raw meat, fish, poultry, or eggs.

- Make sure counters, cutting boards, dishes, and other equipment are thoroughly cleaned before and after use. If possible, use separate cutting boards for meat and for foods that will be eaten raw, such as fruits or vegetables. Wash dishcloths and kitchen towels frequently.

- Thoroughly rinse and scrub fruits and vegetables, with a brush, if possible; or peel off the skin or outer layer.

- Cook foods thoroughly, especially beef, poultry, fish, pork, and eggs. Cooking kills most microbes. When eating out, order red meat prepared "well done."

- Cook stuffing separately from poultry; or wash poultry thoroughly, stuff immediately before cooking, and then transfer the stuffing to a clean bowl immediately after cooking.

- Store foods below 40°F. Do not leave cooked or refrigerated foods, such as meats or salads, at room temperature for more than 2 hours.

- Don't eat raw animal products. Use only pasteurized milk and juice.

- According to the USDA, "when in doubt, throw it out."

For a bout of foodborne illness, drink plenty of clear fluids to prevent dehydration, and rest to speed your recovery. See a physician for a fever higher than 102°F, blood in the stool, or dehydration, especially if symptoms persist for more than 2–3 days. In cases of suspected botulism—characterized by symptoms such as double vision, paralysis, dizziness, and vomiting—consult a physician immediately

Choose Often

Any unground meats labeled "extra lean."

Beef: Eye of round, top round.

Veal: All kinds not listed in next two columns.

Pork: Tenderloin, 95% lean ham.

Lamb: Foreshank.

Chicken: Skinless breast.

Turkey: Breast, drumstick, or wing without skin.

Choose Sometimes

Any unground meats labeled "lean."

Beef: Tip or bottom round, sirloin, chuck pot roast, top loin, tenderloin, flank, T-bone, ground sirloin, extra-lean ground.

Veal: Loin, loin chop, ground.

Pork: Sirloin chop, top or center loin chop, rib chop, ham, Canadian bacon.

Lamb: Shank, leg, loin chop, sirloin.

Chicken: Skinless drumstick, thigh, or wing; breast with skin.

Turkey: Any piece with skin; thigh without skin; extra-lean ground.

Reduced-fat lunch meats or hot dogs, with 4 to 5 grams of fat per serving.

Choose Seldom

Beef: All cuts not listed in first two columns (such as brisket, rib roast, chuck blade roast, lean and regular ground).

Veal: Rib roast.

Pork: All kinds not listed in first two columns (such as spareribs, sausage, ground).

Lamb: All kinds not listed in first two columns (such as rib chop, arm, blade, shoulder, ground).

Chicken: Drumstick, thigh, or wing with skin; liver.

Turkey: Lean or regular ground.

Duck, goose.

Regular lunch meats or hot dogs, with more than 5 grams of fat per serving.

SOURCE: Beyond the Pyramid: Healthy choices for a healthy diet. 1996. *Consumer Reports on Health*, September, p. 103. Copyright © 1996 by Consumers Union of U.S., Inc., Yonkers, NY 10703-1057. Reprinted by permission from Consumer Reports on Health, September 1996.

SUMMARY

- The six classes of nutrients are carbohydrates, proteins, fats, vitamins, minerals, and water.

- The 45 nutrients essential to humans are released into the body through digestion. Nutrients in foods provide energy, measured in kilocalories (commonly called calories); build and maintain body tissues; and regulate body functions.

- Protein, an important component of body tissue, is composed of amino acids, nine of which are essential to a diet. Foods from animal sources provide complete proteins; plants provide incomplete proteins.

- Fat, the major body fuel at times of rest and light activity, also insulates the body and cushions the organs; 1 tablespoon of vegetable oil per day supplies the essential fats. Dietary fat should be limited to 30% or less of total calories.

- Limiting saturated and trans fatty acids in the diet can reduce the risk of heart disease; unsaturated fats may promote cardiovascular health.

- Carbohydrates provide energy to the brain, nervous system, and blood and to muscles during high-intensity exercise. Naturally occurring simple carbohydrates and unrefined complex carbohydrates should be favored over added sugars and refined

carbohydrates. Dietary fiber cannot be broken down by the body; it helps reduce cholesterol levels and promotes the passage of wastes through the intestines.

- The 13 essential vitamins are either water- or fat-soluble; they help unleash energy in food sources and act as antioxidants. The 17 known essential minerals regulate body functions, aid in growth and tissue maintenance, and act as catalysts to release energy. Deficiencies in vitamins and minerals can cause severe symptoms over time, but excess doses are also dangerous.

- Water, distributed in body tissues and fluids, aids in digestion and food absorption, allows chemical reactions to take place, serves as a lubricant or cushion, and helps regulate body temperature.

- Foods contain other substances, such as phytochemicals, which may not be essential nutrients but which may protect against chronic diseases.

- The Recommended Dietary Allowances, Dietary Reference Intakes, Food Guide Pyramid, and Dietary Guidelines for Americans provide standards and recommendations for getting all essential nutrients from a varied, balanced diet and for eating in ways that protect against chronic disease.

- Basic recommendations for a healthy diet include eating a variety of foods; reducing all fat, especially saturated fat; increasing complex carbohydrates; and limiting sugar, salt, alcohol, and smoked and nitrate-cured foods.

- A vegetarian diet requires special planning to meet all nutrient requirements; grains, legumes, and a variety of fruits and vegetables are central.

- Careful planning can help people of all ages, activity levels, and medical conditions meet special dietary challenges.

FOR MORE INFORMATION

For reliable nutrition advice, talk to a faculty member in the nutrition department on your campus, a registered dietitian (R.D.), or your physician. Many large communities have a telephone service called Dial a Dietitian. By calling this number, you can receive free nutrition information from an R.D.

Experts on quackery suggest that you steer clear of anyone who puts forth any of the following false statements:

- Most diseases are caused primarily by faulty nutrition.

- Large doses of vitamins are effective against many diseases.

- Hair analysis can be used to determine a person's nutritional state.

- A computer-scored nutritional deficiency test is a basis for prescribing vitamins.

Any practitioner—licensed or not—who sells vitamins in his or her office should be thoroughly scrutinized.

Books

Duyff, R. L. 1998. *The American Dietetic Association's Complete Food and Nutrition Guide.* Minneapolis, Minn.: Chronimed Publishing. *An excellent review of current nutrition information and issues.*

Coleman, E. 1997. *Eating for Endurance.* Rev. ed. Palo Alto, Calif.: Bull Publishing. *A concise, easy-to-understand guide to sports nutrition.*

Editors of Vegetarian Times Magazine. 1995. *Vegetarian Times Complete Cookbook.* New York: Macmillan. *Contains introductory chapters on the health benefits of vegetarianism and on meal planning, along with over 600 recipes.*

Finn, S. C. 1997. *The American Dietetic Association Guide to Women's Nutrition for Healthy Living.* New York: Perigee Books. *A complete guide to eating right for lifelong health.*

Nutrition and Your Health: Dietary Guidelines for Americans. 1995. U.S. Department of Health and Human Services and U.S. Department of Agriculture. Home and Garden Bulletin No. 232. *A 42-page booklet that describes the Guidelines and provides helpful tips for implementing them.*

Newsletters

Environmental Nutrition: P.O. Box 420235, Palm Coast, FL 32142; 800-829-5384.

Nutrition Action Health Letter: 1875 Connecticut Ave., N.W., Suite 300, Washington DC 20009; 202-332-9110 (http://www.cspinet.org).

Tufts University Health & Nutrition Letter: P.O. Box 57857, Boulder, CO 80322; 800-274-7581.

Organizations, Hotlines, and Web Sites

American Dietetic Association. Provides a wide variety of nutrition-related educational materials.
   800-366-1655 (For general nutrition information and referrals to registered dietitians.)
   900-CALL-AN-RD (For customized answers to nutrition questions.)
   http://www.eatright.org

Ask the Dietitian. Questions and answers on many topics relating to nutrition.
   http://www.dietitian.com

CyberDiet Nutritional Profile. Calculates calorie and nutrient needs based on your current or target body weight and creates a personalized nutrient profile.
   http://www.CyberDiet.com/profile/profile.html

FDA Center for Food Safety and Applied Nutrition. Offers information about topics such as food labeling, food additives, and foodborne illness.
   http://vm.cfsan.fda.gov

Meals Online. Includes over 10,000 healthful recipes.
   http://www.meals.com

National Osteoporosis Foundation. Provides up-to-date information on the causes, prevention, detection, and treatment of osteoporosis.
   202-223-2226
   http://www.nof.org

Tufts University Nutrition Navigator. Provides descriptions and ratings for many nutrition-related Web pages.
   http://www.navigator.tufts.edu

USDA Food and Nutrition Information Center. Provides a variety of materials relating to the Dietary Guidelines, food labels, and many other topics; Web site includes extensive links.
   301-504-5719
   http://www.nal.usda.gov/fnic

USDA Meat and Poultry Hotline. Information from USDA experts on topics such as the proper handling, preparation, storage, and cooking of food.
   800-535-4555

Vegetarian Resource Group. Information and links for vegetarians and people interested in learning more about vegetarian diets.
   http://www.vrg.org

You can obtain nutrient breakdowns of individual food items from the following sites:

Nutribase
   http://www.nutribase.com

Nutrition Analysis Tool, University of Illinois, Urbana/Champaign
   http://www.ag.uiuc.edu/~food-lab/nat

USDA Food and Nutrition Information Center
   http://www.nal.usda.gov/fnic/foodcomp

See also the resources listed in Chapters 9, 11, and 12.

SELECTED BIBLIOGRAPHY

The American Dietetic Association. 1996. Position Statement: Nutrition Education for the Public. *Journal of the American Dietetic Association* 96(11): 1183–1187.

The American Dietetic Association and the Canadian Dietetic Association. 1997. *Position Statement: Nutrition for Physical*

Fitness and Athletic Performance for Adults (retrieved September 20, 1997; http://www.eatright.org/afitperform.html).

American Society for Clinical Nutrition/American Institute of Nutrition Task Force. 1996. Position paper on *trans* fatty acids. *American Journal of Clinical Nutrition* 63:663–670.

Ascherio, A., et al. 1995. Dietary intake of marine *n-3* fatty acids, fish intake, and the risk of coronary disease among men. *New England Journal of Medicine* 332:977–982.

Bidlack, W. R. 1996. Interrelationships of food, nutrition, diet and health: The National Association of State Universities and Land Grant Colleges White Paper. *Journal of American College Nutrition* 15(5): 422–433.

Bowman, M. A., and J. G. Spangler. 1997. Osteoporosis in women. *Primary Care* 24(1): 27–36.

Burke, L. 1995. Practical issues in nutrition for athletes. *Journal of Sports Sciences* 13(Spec): S83–S80.

Clark, N. 1996. Nutrition knowledge: Answers to the top ten questions. *The Physician and Sportsmedicine* (retrieved September 20, 1997; http://www.physsportsmed.com/issues/oct_96/top_ten.htm).

Clark, N. 1997. Eating for vitamins: Do you need supplements? *The Physician and Sportsmedicine* (retrieved September 20, 1997; http://www.physsportsmed.com/issues/1997/07jul/vitamins.htm).

Coleman, E., and S. N. Steen. 1996. *The Ultimate Sports Nutrition Handbook.* Palo Alto, Calif.: Bull Publishing.

The facts about fats. 1997. *Consumer Reports on Health,* March.

Food and Nutrition Board. Institute of Medicine. National Academy of Sciences. 1998. *Dietary Reference Intakes for Thiamin, Riboflavin, Niacin, Vitamin B₆, Folate, Vitamin B₁₂, Pantothenic Acid, Biotin, and Choline.* Washington, D.C.: National Academy Press.

Georgiou, C., et al. 1996. Young adult exercisers and nonexercisers differ in food attitudes, perceived dietary changes, and food choices. *International Journal of Sport Nutrition* 6(4): 402–413.

Ghiselli, A., A. D'Amicis, and A. Giacosa. 1997. The antioxidant potential of the Mediterranean diet. *European Journal of Cancer Prevention* 6(Suppl 1): S15–S19.

Halliwell, B. 1996. Antioxidants in human health and disease. *Annual Review of Nutrition* 16:33–50.

Hu, F. B., et al. 1997. Dietary fat intake and the risk of coronary heart disease in women. *New England Journal of Medicine* 337(21): 1491–1499.

Kipp, D. E., J. D. Radel, and J. A. Hogue. 1996. The Internet and the nutritional scientist. *American Journal of Clinical Nutrition* 64(4): 659–662.

Kirwan, J. P., D. O'Gorman, and W. J. Evans. 1998. A moderate glycemic meal before endurance exercise can enhance performance. *Journal of Applied Physiology* 84(1): 53–59.

Kleiner, S. M. 1995. Nutrition on the run. *The Physician and Sportsmedicine* 23(2): 15–16.

Looker, A. C., et al. 1997. Prevalence of iron deficiency in the United States. *Journal of the American Medical Association* 277(12): 973–976.

Millen, B. E., et al. 1997. Population nutrient intake approaches dietary recommendations: 1991 to 1995 Farmingham Nutrition Studies. *Journal of the American Dietetic Association* 97(7): 742–749.

Monteleone, G. P., Jr., and D. G. Browning. 1997. Nutrition in women. Assessment and counseling. *Primary Care* 24(1): 37–51.

Muñoz, K. A., et al. 1997. Food intakes of U.S. children and adolescents compared with recommendations. *Pediatrics* 100(3 Pt 1): 323–329.

Neumark-Sztainer, D., et al. 1997. Adolescent vegetarians. A behavioral profile of a school-based population in Minnesota. *Archives of Pediatrics and Adolescent Medicine* 151(8): 833–838.

Nieman, D. C. 1999. *Exercise Testing and Prescription; A Health-Related Approach.* 4th ed. Mountain View, Calif.: Mayfield.

Schwartz, N. E., and S. T. Borra. 1997. What do consumers really think about dietary fat? *Journal of the American Dietetic Association* 97(7 Suppl): S73–S75.

Siega-Riz, A. M., T. Carson, and B. Popkin. 1998. Three squares or mostly snacks—what do teens really eat? A sociodemographic study of meal patterns. *Journal of Adolescent Health* 22(1): 29–36.

Slutsker, L., et al. 1997. *Escherichia coli* O157:H7 diarrhea in the United States: Clinical and epidemiologic features. *Annals of Internal Medicine* 126(7): 505–513.

Sundram, K., et al. 1997. Trans (elaidic) fatty acids adversely affect the lipoprotein profile relative to specific fatty acids in humans. *Journal of Nutrition* 127(3): 514S–520S.

U.S. Department of Agriculture. Center for Nutrition Policy and Promotion. 1996. *The Food Guide Pyramid.* Home and Garden Bulletin No. 252.

U.S. Food and Drug Administration. 1996. *Folic Acid Fortification.* Office of Public Affairs Fact Sheet (retrieved February 29, 1996; http://vm.cfsan.fda.gov/~dms/wh-folic.html).

Uusi-Rasi, K., et al. 1998. Associations of physical activity and calcium intake with bone mass and size in healthy women at different ages. *Journal of Bone Mineral Research* 13(1): 133–142.

Weber, J. L., et al. 1997. Multimethod training increases portion-size estimation accuracy. *Journal of the American Dietetic Association* 97(2): 176–179.

Wilson, J. W., et al. 1997. *Data Tables: Combined Results from USDA's 1994 and 1995 Continuing Survey of Food Intakes for Individuals and 1994 and 1995 Diet and Health Knowledge Survey.* ARS Food Surveys Research Group. U.S. Department of Agriculture (retrieved December 2, 1997; http://www.barc.usda.gov/bhnrc/foodsurvey/home.htm).

LAB 8-1   *Your Daily Diet Versus the Food Guide Pyramid*

Keep a record of everything you eat for 3 consecutive days. Record all foods and beverages you consume, breaking each food item into its component parts (for example, a turkey sandwich would be listed as 2 slices of bread, 3 oz of turkey, 1 tsp of mayonnaise, and so on). Complete the first two columns of the chart during the course of the day; fill in the remaining information at the end of the day using Figure 8-5 and pp. 202–203 in your text.

DAY 1

Food	Portion Size	Food Group	Number of Servings*

Daily Total

Food Group	Number of Servings
Milk, yogurt, cheese	
Meat, poultry, fish, dry beans, eggs, nuts	
Fruits	
Vegetables	
Breads, cereals, rice, pasta	

*Your portion sizes may be smaller or larger than the serving sizes given in the Food Guide Pyramid; list the actual number of Food Guide Pyramid servings contained in the foods you eat.

DAY 2

Food	Portion Size	Food Group	Number of Servings*

Daily Total

Food Group	Number of Servings
Milk, yogurt, cheese	
Meat, poultry, fish, dry beans, eggs, nuts	
Fruits	
Vegetables	
Breads, cereals, rice, pasta	

*Your portion sizes may be smaller or larger than the serving sizes given in the Food Guide Pyramid; list the actual number of Food Guide Pyramid servings contained in the foods you eat.

DAY 3

Food	Portion Size	Food Group	Number of Servings*

Daily Total

Food Group	Number of Servings
Milk, yogurt, cheese	
Meat, poultry, fish, dry beans, eggs, nuts	
Fruits	
Vegetables	
Breads, cereals, rice, pasta	

*Your portion sizes may be smaller or larger than the serving sizes given in the Food Guide Pyramid; list the actual number of Food Guide Pyramid servings contained in the foods you eat.

Next, average your serving totals for the 3 days, and enter them in the chart below. Fill in the recommended serving totals that apply to you from Figure 8-5 and Table 8-8.

Food Group	Recommended Number of Servings	Actual Number of Servings
Milk, yogurt, cheese		
Meat, poultry, fish, dry beans, eggs, nuts		
Fruits		
Vegetables		
Breads, cereals, rice, pasta		

Are there any groups for which you need to increase your consumption? Decrease your consumption? List any areas of concern below, along with ideas for changing them. Think carefully about the reasons behind your food choices. For example, if you eat doughnuts for breakfast every morning because you feel rushed, make a list of ways to save time to allow for a more healthful breakfast.

Problem: _____

Possible solutions: _____

_____

_____

_____

_____

Problem: _____

Possible solutions: _____

_____

_____

_____

_____

Problem: _____

Possible solutions: _____

_____

_____

_____

_____

To monitor your progress toward your goal, enter the results of this lab in the Preprogram Assessment column of Appendix D. After several weeks of dietary changes, do this lab again and enter the results in the Postprogram Assessment column of Appendix D. How do the results compare?

Name _____ **Section** _____ **Date** _____

 LAB 8-2 *Dietary Analysis*

You can complete this activity using either a nutrition analysis software program or the food composition data in Appendix B and the charts printed below. Information about the nutrient content of foods is also available online; see the For More Information section for recommended Web sites.

Part I. Analyze Your Diet for 3 Days

If you are using the software, follow the instructions to complete an analysis of your diet on 3 separate days; otherwise, complete the charts on the first three pages of this lab. Then go on to the second part of the lab.

Date_____	Amount	Calories	Protein (g)	Fat, total (g)	Saturated fat (g)	Carbohydrate[a] (g)	Dietary fiber (g)	Cholesterol (mg)	Sodium (mg)	Calcium (mg)	Iron (mg)
Food Day: M Tu W Th F Sa Su											
Recommended totals[b]			10–15%	≤30%	<10%	≥55%	20–35 g	≤300 mg	≤2400 mg	mg	mg
Actual totals[c]		cal	g / %	g / %	g / %	g / %	g	mg	mg	mg	mg

[a]To obtain a value for total grams of carbohydrate from Appendix B, add the values in the columns for carbohydrates ("Carbo.") and added sugars ("Sug.").
[b]Fill in the appropriate RDA or DRI values for calcium and iron from Tables 8-5 and 8-6.
[c]Total the values in each column. To calculate the percentage of total calories from protein, carbohydrate, fat, and saturated fat, use the formulas on p. 189. Protein and carbohydrate provide 4 calories per gram; fat provides 9 calories per gram. For example, if you consume a total of 270 grams of carbohydrate and 2000 calories, your percentage of total calories from carbohydrate would be (270 g × 4 cal/g) ÷ 2000 cal = 54%. Do not include data for alcoholic beverages in your calculations. Percentages may not total 100% due to rounding.

Date_____   Day: M Tu W Th F Sa Su

Food	Amount	Calories	Protein (g)	Fat, total (g)	Saturated fat (g)	Carbohydrate[a] (g)	Dietary fiber (g)	Cholesterol (mg)	Sodium (mg)	Calcium (mg)	Iron (mg)
Recommended totals[b]			10–15%	≤30%	<10%	≥55%	20–35 g	≤300 mg	≤2400 mg	mg	mg
Actual totals[c]		cal	g / %	g / %	g / %	g / %	g	mg	mg	mg	mg

Food	Amount	Calories	Protein (g)	Fat, total (g)	Saturated fat (g)	Carbohydrate[a] (g)	Dietary fiber (g)	Cholesterol (mg)	Sodium (mg)	Calcium (mg)	Iron (mg)
Recommended totals[b]			10–15%	≤30%	<10%	≥55%	20–35 g	≤300 mg	≤2400 mg	mg	mg
Actual totals[c]		cal	g / %	g / %	g / %	g / %	g	mg	mg	mg	mg

Date_____   Day: M Tu W Th F Sa Su

To monitor your progress toward your goal, enter the results of one day's dietary analysis in the Preprogram Assessment column of Appendix D. After several weeks of dietary changes, do this lab again and enter the results in the Postprogram Assessment column of Appendix D. How do the results compare?

Part II. Making Changes in Your Diet to Meet the Dietary Guidelines

(*Note:* If your daily diet follows all the recommended intakes, you don't need to complete this section.) Choose one of your daily diet records. Make changes, additions, and deletions from it until it conforms to all or most of the Dietary Guidelines. Or, if you prefer, start from scratch to create a day's diet that meets all guidelines. Use the chart below to experiment and record your final, healthy sample diet for one day.

Date_____   Day: M Tu W Th F Sa Su

Food	Amount	Calories	Protein (g)	Fat, total (g)	Saturated fat (g)	Carbohydrate[a] (g)	Dietary fiber (g)	Cholesterol (mg)	Sodium (mg)	Calcium (mg)	Iron (mg)
Recommended totals[b]			10–15%	≤30%	<10%	≥55%	20–35 g	≤300 mg	≤2400 mg	mg	mg
Actual totals[c]		cal	g	g / g	g / mg	g / mg	mg	mg			

Name _____ Section _____ Date _____

 LAB 8-3 *Informed Food Choices*

Part I. Using Food Labels

Choose three food items to evaluate. You might want to select three similar items, such as regular, low-fat, and non-fat salad dressing, or three very different items. Record the information from their food labels in the table below. How do the items you chose compare?

Food Items			
Serving size			
Total calories	cal	cal	cal
Total fat—grams	g	g	g
—% Daily Value	%	%	%
Saturated fat—grams	g	g	g
—% Daily Value	%	%	%
Cholesterol—milligrams	mg	mg	mg
—% Daily Value	%	%	%
Sodium—milligrams	mg	mg	mg
—% Daily Value	%	%	%
Carbohydrates (total)—grams	g	g	g
—% Daily Value	%	%	%
Dietary fiber—grams	g	g	g
—% Daily Value	%	%	%
Sugars—grams	g	g	g
Protein—grams	g	g	g
Vitamin A—% Daily Value	%	%	%
Vitamin C—% Daily Value	%	%	%
Calcium—% Daily Value	%	%	%
Iron—% Daily Value	%	%	%

Part II. Evaluating Fast Food

Use the information from Appendix C, Nutritional Content of Popular Items from Fast-Food Restaurants, to complete the chart on the next page for the last fast-food meal you ate. Add up your totals for the meal. Compare the values for fat, protein, carbohydrate, cholesterol, and sodium content for each food item and for the meal as a whole with the levels suggested by the Dietary Guidelines for Americans. Calculate the percent of total calories derived from fat, saturated fat, protein, and carbohydrate using the formulas given.

If you haven't recently been to one of the restaurants included in the appendix, fill in the chart for any sample meal you might eat. If some of the food items you selected don't appear in Appendix C, ask for a nutrition information brochure when you visit the restaurant, or check out online fast-food information: Arby's (http://www.arbysrestaurant.com), Burger King (http://www.burgerking.com), Domino's Pizza (http://www.dominos.com), Jack in the Box (http://www.jackinthebox.com), KFC (http://www.kfc.com), McDonald's (http://www.mcdonalds.com), Taco Bell (http://www.tacobell.com), Wendy's (http://www.wendys.com).

Food Items

	Dietary Guidelines							Total[b]
Serving size (g)		g	g	g	g	g	g	g
Calories		cal	cal	cal	cal	cal	cal	cal
Total fat—grams		g	g	g	g	g	g	g
—% calories[a]	≤30%	%	%	%	%	%	%	%
Saturated fat—grams		g	g	g	g	g	g	g
—% calories[a]	<10%	%	%	%	%	%	%	%
Protein—grams		g	g	g	g	g	g	g
—% calories[a]	15%	%	%	%	%	%	%	%
Carbohydrate—grams		g	g	g	g	g	g	g
—% calories[a]	.≥55%	%	%	%	%	%	%	%
Cholesterol[c]	100 mg	mg	mg	mg	mg	mg	mg	mg
Sodium[c]	800 mg	mg	mg	mg	mg	mg	mg	mg

[a]To calculate the percent of total calories from each food energy source (fat, carbohydrate, protein), use the following formula:

$$\frac{(\text{number of grams of energy source}) \times (\text{number of calories per gram of energy source})}{(\text{total calories in serving of food item})}$$

(*Note:* Fat and saturated fat provide 9 calories per gram; protein and carbohydrate provide 4 calories per gram.) For example, the percent of total calories from protein in a 150-calorie dish containing 10 grams of protein is

$$\frac{(10 \text{ grams of protein}) \times (4 \text{ calories per gram})}{(150 \text{ calories})} = \frac{40}{150} = 0.27, \text{ or } 27\% \text{ of total calories from protein}$$

[b]For the Total column, add up the total grams of fat, carbohydrate, and protein contained in your sample meal and calculate the percentages based on the total calories in the meal. (Percentages may not total 100% due to rounding.) For cholesterol and sodium values, add up the total number of milligrams.

[c]Recommended daily limits of cholesterol and sodium are divided by 3 here to give an approximate recommended limit for a single meal.

SOURCE: Insel, P. M., and W. T. Roth. 1998. Wellness Worksheet 48. *Core Concepts in Health.* 8th ed. Mountain View, Calif.: Mayfield.

Weight Management

9

LOOKING AHEAD

After reading this chapter, you should be able to answer these questions about weight management:

- How do overweight and obesity affect health?

- How do genetic factors and metabolic rate influence a person's weight?

- What are the components of a lifestyle that leads naturally to a healthy body weight?

- Why is dieting not a successful approach to weight loss?

- What are the most effective strategies for losing weight?

- What are the symptoms, effects, and treatments for eating disorders?

227

Controlling body weight is really a matter of controlling body fat. As explained in Chapter 6, the most important consideration for health is not total weight but body composition—the proportion of body fat to fat-free mass. Many people who are "overweight" are also overfat, and the health risks they face are due to the latter condition. Although this chapter uses the common terms *weight management* and *weight loss,* the goal of a wellness lifestyle is to achieve a healthy body composition, not to conform to rigid standards of total body weight.

Controlling body weight and body fat is not a mysterious process. The "secret" of weight management is simply balancing calories consumed with calories expended in daily activities—in other words, eating a moderate diet and exercising regularly. Unfortunately, this simple formula is not as exciting as the latest fad diet or "scientific breakthrough" that promises slimness without effort. The American public is assaulted year after year by a steady stream of diet books, dietary supplements, commercial weight-loss programs, and medical procedures for weight loss. However, dieting can undermine the development of a truly healthy lifestyle that will naturally allow a person to maintain an appropriate body weight. Dieting is not part of a wellness lifestyle. Weight management involves the adoption of healthy and sustainable eating and exercise habits that will maximize energy and well-being and reduce the risk of chronic diseases.

This chapter sorts out the factors that contribute to a weight problem, takes a closer look at weight management through lifestyle, and suggests specific strategies for permanent weight loss. This information is designed to provide all the tools necessary for integrating effective weight management into an overall wellness program.

HEALTH IMPLICATIONS OF OVERWEIGHT AND OBESITY

Excess body fat increases a person's risk of developing numerous diseases and unhealthy conditions, as discussed in Chapter 6. Obesity is one of five major controllable risk factors for heart disease; it increases risk for other forms of cardiovascular disease (CVD), hypertension, gallbladder disease, and diabetes. Obesity may also be associated with high levels of blood fats, and it is correlated with certain types of cancer, including cancer of the colon, prostate, ovary, breast, and cervix. Women who are obese are more likely to suffer from menstrual abnor-

VITAL STATISTICS

TABLE 9-1	The Prevalence of Overweight: Populations of Special Concern	
Group	Overweight and Obesity (BMI ≥25)	Obesity (BMI ≥30)
Adults (age ≥20)	54.9%	22.3%
Men	59.4	19.5
Women	50.7	25.0
Black women	66.0	36.7
Mexican American women	65.9	33.3
Men (age 50–59)	73.0	28.9
Women (age 50–59)	64.4	35.6

SOURCE: National Heart, Lung, and Blood Institute. 1998. *Clinical Guidelines on the Identification, Evaluation, and Treatment of Overweight and Obesity in Adults.* Bethesda, Md.: National Institutes of Health.

malities and complications during pregnancy; and in severely obese people of both sexes, the rates of respiratory problems and joint disease are higher than normal.

The overall health risks of obesity were illustrated in a study that followed over 120,000 women for more than 16 years. Among women who had never smoked, the slimmest—those with a body mass index (BMI) of 19 or less—had the lowest risk of death from all causes. The relative risk of death increased as BMI increased, and the risk doubled for women with a BMI over 29. Gaining pounds over the years was also shown to be hazardous: The women who reported gaining 22 or more pounds since they were 18 years old showed a sevenfold increase in their risk of coronary heart disease. The results of this study reinforce the compelling conclusion of many others: Obesity shortens lives.

Currently, about 55% of American adults are overweight and 22% are obese, making weight management one of the most serious and widespread challenges to health and wellness (Table 9-1).

FACTORS THAT CONTRIBUTE TO A WEIGHT PROBLEM

Why do some people become obese and others remain thin? A variety of factors—physical, psychological, cultural, and social—play significant roles in determining body weight. Research has linked genetic factors and metabolism, in particular, to body weight problems.

Genetic Factors Versus Environmental Factors

Both genetic and environmental factors influence the development of obesity. Genes influence body size and

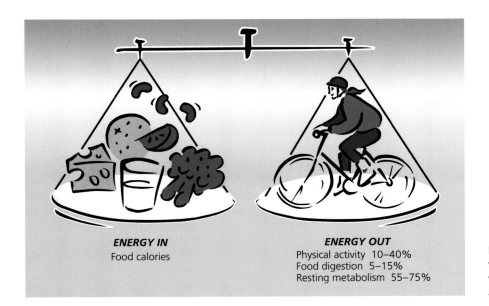

ENERGY IN
Food calories

ENERGY OUT
Physical activity 10–40%
Food digestion 5–15%
Resting metabolism 55–75%

Figure 9-1   The energy-balance equation.   In order to maintain your current weight, you must burn up as many calories as you take in as food each day.

shape, body fat distribution, and metabolic rate. Genetic factors also affect the ease with which weight is gained as a result of overeating and where on the body extra weight is added. If both parents are overweight, their children are twice as likely to be overweight as children who have only one overweight parent. In studies that compared adoptees and their biological parents, the weights of the adoptees were found to be more like those of the biological parents than those of the adoptive parents, again indicating a strong genetic link. It's estimated that 25–70% of the BMI variance among people is due to genetics and associated biological factors.

In studies of mice, scientists located a gene (named *ob*) that appears to influence appetite and the development of obesity. The gene produces a hormonelike protein called leptin that is secreted by the body's fat cells and carried to the brain. Leptin seems to let the brain know how big or small the body's fat stores are, and the brain can regulate appetite and metabolic rate accordingly. Mice with a defective or missing *ob* gene overate and gained weight. But when injected with leptin, the obese mice ate less, had higher metabolic rates, and lost weight. Even mice of normal weight lost weight when injected with leptin.

Could leptin "cure" obesity in humans? As encouraging as this finding is, obesity in humans is likely to turn out to be more complicated than a one-gene phenomenon. Many obese people have been found to have normal or higher-than-normal levels of leptin in their bloodstream; researchers hypothesize that they may have faulty leptin receptors in their brains. Other chemicals that may also be significant in controlling appetite include orexin, cortisol, gluconlike peptide-1 (GLP-1), neuropeptide Y (NPY), and peptide YY. However, additional studies will be needed before a treatment can be developed based on any of these findings.

All this research points to a genetic component in the determination of body weight. However, hereditary influences must be balanced against the contribution of environmental factors. Not all children of obese parents become obese, and normal-weight parents also have overweight children. The incidence of obesity is rising in the United States, but not in most of the rest of the world. In a study comparing men born and raised in Ireland with their biological brothers who lived in the United States, the American men were found to weigh, on average, 6% more than their Irish brothers. Environmental factors like diet and exercise are probably responsible for this difference in weight. Thus, the *tendency* to develop obesity may be inherited, but the expression of this tendency is affected by environmental influences.

The message you should take from this research is that genes are not destiny. It is true that some people have a harder time losing weight and maintaining weight loss than others. However, with increased exercise and attention to diet, even those with a genetic tendency toward obesity can maintain a healthy body weight. And regardless of genetic factors, lifestyle choices remain the cornerstone of successful weight management.

Metabolism and Energy Balance

Metabolism is the sum of all the vital processes by which food energy and nutrients are made available to and used by the body. The largest component of metabolism, **resting metabolic rate (RMR)**, is the energy required to maintain vital body functions, including respiration, heart rate, body temperature, and blood pressure, while the body is at rest. As shown in Figure 9-1, RMR accounts for 55–75% of daily energy expenditure. The energy required to digest food accounts for an additional 5–15% of daily energy expenditure. The remaining 10–40% is expended during physical activity.

Both heredity and behavior affect metabolic rate. Men, who have a higher proportion of muscle mass than women, have a higher RMR (muscle tissue is more metabolically active than fat). Also, some individuals inherit a higher or lower RMR than others. A higher RMR means that a person burns more calories while at rest and can therefore take in more calories without gaining weight.

Weight loss or gain also affects metabolic rate. When a person loses weight, both RMR and the energy required to perform physical tasks decrease. The body thus "defends" its original weight by conserving energy and making it easier to regain lost pounds. For example, a man who formerly weighed 165 pounds but who now weighs 150 pounds must eat about 15% fewer calories to maintain his new, lower weight than a man who has weighed 150 pounds throughout his adult life. The reverse occurs when weight is gained; RMR increases, pushing weight back down toward its original level. The message from this research is that although weight loss can be achieved and maintained, it requires ongoing commitment.

Exercise has a positive effect on metabolism. When people exercise, they increase their RMR—the number of calories their bodies burn at rest. They also increase their fat-free mass, which is associated with a higher metabolic rate. The exercise itself also burns calories, raising total energy expenditure. The higher the energy expenditure, the more the person can eat without gaining weight.

The two factors in the energy-balance equation illustrated in Figure 9-1 that fall under individual control are the amount of energy intake (in food) and the number of calories expended in physical activity. For these simple reasons alone, increased physical activity is a critical component of a long-term program of weight management. (To determine your own RMR, complete Lab 9-1.)

Other Explanations for Overweight

Researchers have proposed various other explanations for overweight besides heredity and metabolism. These explanations include weight cycling, binge eating, and psychological, social, and cultural factors.

Weight Cycling   It has been hypothesized that repeated dieting resulting in cycles of weight loss and weight gain ("yo-yo dieting") is harmful both to weight management and to overall health. Researchers proposed that cycling increases the body's efficiency at extracting and storing calories from food, making weight loss increasingly difficult with each successive diet. Although some studies have found support for this idea, most have not; and current thinking is that weight cycling probably does not result in increased efficiency. On balance, when the substantial health benefits of even modest weight loss are compared with the uncertain potential adverse health consequences of losing weight or weight cycling, the benefits of losing weight clearly exceed the potential risks.

The Restrained Eating Theory   According to the restrained eating theory, restrictive dieting can cause excessive hunger and feelings of deprivation, possibly leading to **binge eating.** Attempts to restrain food intake may contribute to confusion about internal hunger cues and increase susceptibility to external cues (the sight of food, for example). As hunger or fatigue increases, or if confronted with cues in the environment, a person's restraint may falter. For many restrained eaters, once they violate their self-imposed diet rules, they simply give up and overeat or even binge. This overeating is usually followed by feelings of guilt, shame, and self-blame. Binge eating may contribute to the development of obesity in some people.

Psychological, Social, and Cultural Factors   Many people have learned to use food as a means of coping with stress and negative emotions. Eating can provide a powerful distraction from difficult feelings—loneliness, anger, boredom, anxiety, shame, sadness, inadequacy. It can be used to combat low moods, low energy levels, and low self-esteem. When food and eating become the primary means of regulating emotions, binge eating or other disturbed eating patterns can develop.

Obesity is strongly associated with socioeconomic status. The prevalence of obesity goes down as income level goes up. More women are obese at lower income levels than men, but men are somewhat more obese at higher levels. These differences may reflect the greater sensitivity and concern for a slim physical appearance among upper-income women, as well as greater access to information about nutrition and to low-fat and low-calorie foods. It may also reflect the greater acceptance of obesity among certain ethnic groups, as well as different cultural values related to food choices.

In some families and cultures, food is used as a symbol of love and caring. It is an integral part of social gatherings and celebrations. In such cases, it may be difficult to change established eating patterns because they are linked to cultural and family values.

WEIGHT MANAGEMENT AND LIFESTYLE

When all the research has been assessed, it is clear that most weight problems are lifestyle problems. Looking at these problems in a historical context reveals why fad diets and other quick-fix approaches are not effective in reversing overweight.

TERMS   **binge eating**   A pattern of eating in which normal food consumption is interrupted by episodes of high consumption.

Foods that contain more calories than you might expect include the following:

- *Reduced-fat foods.* Manufacturers often replace fat with extra sugar, so many low-fat and fat-free foods have at least as many calories as their full-fat versions. Check food labels of reduced-fat foods for the appropriate serving size and total calories.

- *Regular sodas.* A 12-ounce serving of regular soda is high in added sugars and contains about 150–200 calories. Substitute plain water or, if you want something carbonated, mineral or sparkling water.

- *Alcoholic beverages.* As stated in Chapter 8, alcohol contains 7 calories per gram. A glass of wine contains about 100 calories, a beer or cocktail about 150 calories, and a wine cooler over 175 calories. Try light or nonalcoholic versions, or substitute a lower-calorie type of beverage.

- *Fruit juices, drinks, and ades.* A cup of juice contains the juice of many fruits and is therefore higher in calories than whole fruit (for example, a cup of orange juice has about 110 calories, an orange about 65 calories). Fruit drinks and ades are often low in nutrients and high in added sugar. Choose juices over drinks and ades, keep your juice servings small, and substitute whole fruits for juice often.

- *Muffins.* Many muffins are large, are high in fat, and contain more than 300–500 calories. Choose whole-grain breads, cereals, bagels, or English muffins instead.

- *Condiments.* Butter, margarine, mayonnaise, and salad dressing all contribute about 100 calories per tablespoon; jams and jellies have about 50 calories per tablespoon. Cream, sour cream, sugar, syrup, and honey are also packed with calories. Use these concentrated sources of fats and added sugars sparingly. Substitute low-fat and nonfat dairy products and dressings for the full-fat versions. Use herbs, spices, lemon juice, ketchup, mustard, or salsa to add flavor to foods.

SOURCES: Hidden calories. 1997. *Mayo Clinic Health Letter,* September. U.S. Department of Agriculture. Center for Nutrition Policy and Promotion. 1996. *The Food Guide Pyramid.* Home and Garden Bulletin No. 252.

About 100 years ago, Americans consumed a diet very different from today's diet and got much more exercise as well. Americans now eat more fat and refined sugars and fewer complex carbohydrates. And despite an increased interest in fitness, Americans today get far less exercise than their great-grandparents did. Walking, bicycling, and farm and manual labor have all declined, resulting in a decrease in daily energy expenditure of about 200 calories. This decline, coupled with dietary changes, is measurable in the number of overweight Americans: about 97 million, and rising.

Permanent weight loss is not something you start and stop. You need to adopt healthy behaviors that you can maintain throughout your life. Lifestyle factors that are critical for successful long-term weight management include diet and eating habits, physical activity and exercise, an ability to think positively and manage your emotions effectively, and the coping strategies you use to deal with the stresses and challenges in your life.

Diet and Eating Habits

In contrast to "dieting," which involves some form of food restriction, "diet" refers to your daily food choices. Everyone has a diet, but not everyone is dieting. You need to develop a diet that you enjoy and that enables you to maintain a healthy body composition.

Total Calories To maintain your current weight, the total number of calories you eat must equal the number you burn (refer to the energy-balance equation in Figure 9-1). To lose weight, you must decrease your calorie intake and/or increase the number of calories you burn. According to the Centers for Disease Control and Prevention, the average calorie intake by Americans has increased by 100–300 calories per day over the past decade (see the box "Avoiding Hidden Calories"). Levels of physical activity did not increase during this period, so the net result was a substantial increase in the number of Americans who are obese. To calculate your daily caloric needs, complete the calculations in Lab 9-1.

The best approach for weight loss is probably combining an increase in physical activity with moderate calorie restriction. Don't go on a "crash diet." You need to consume enough food to meet your need for essential nutrients. Also, to maintain weight loss, you will probably have to maintain some degree of the calorie restriction you used to lose the weight. Therefore, it is important that you adopt a level of food intake that you can live with over the long term.

Portion Sizes Overconsumption of total calories is closely tied with portion sizes. Most of us significantly underestimate the amount of food we eat. Limiting portion sizes to those recommended in the Food Guide Pyramid is critical for weight management. For many people, concentrating on portion sizes is also a much easier method of monitoring and managing total food intake than counting calories. (Refer to Chapter 8 for more on appropriate portion sizes.)

Fat Calories Although some fat is needed in the diet to provide essential nutrients, you should avoid overeating

The typical American lifestyle does not lead naturally to healthy weight management. Labor-saving devices such as lawn mowers help reinforce our sedentary habits.

fatty foods for both chronic disease prevention and weight management. There is some evidence that fat calories are more easily converted to body fat than calories from protein or carbohydrate. Limiting fat in the diet can also help you limit your total calories. As described in Chapter 8, fat should supply no more than 30% of your average total daily calories, which translates into no more than 66 grams of fat in a 2000-calorie diet each day. Foods rich in fat include oils, margarine, butter, cream, and lard, which are almost pure fat; meat and processed foods, which contain a great deal of "hidden" fat; and nuts, seeds, and avocados, which are plant sources of fats.

Some people are better fat burners than others; that is, they burn more of the fat they take in as calories and therefore have less fat to store. Low fat burners convert more dietary fat to stored body fat. This tendency to hoard fat calories may be an important part of the genetic tendency toward obesity. For low fat burners, restricting fat calories to a level even below 30% may be helpful in weight control.

As Chapter 8 made clear, moving toward a diet strong in complex carbohydrates and fresh fruits and vegetables, and away from a reliance on meat and processed foods, is an effective approach to reducing fat consumption. Watch out for processed foods labeled "fat-free" or "reduced fat." Manufacturers often add sugar to improve the taste and texture lost when fat is removed, so such foods may contain as many calories as their fattier counterparts—or even more. Limiting fat is important, but so is limiting total calories. Researchers have found that many Americans compensate for a lower-fat diet by consuming more calories overall.

Complex Carbohydrates   It has long been the fashion among dieters to cut back on bread, pasta, and potatoes to control weight. But complex carbohydrates from these sources, as well as from vegetables, legumes, and whole grains, are precisely the nutrients that can help you achieve and maintain a healthy body weight. They help provide a feeling of satiety, or fullness, that can keep you from overeating. Carbohydrates should make up about 55–65% of your total daily calories. Avoid high-fat toppings and sauces, however; try plain yogurt instead of sour cream on your baked potato and tomato-based sauces rather than cream sauces on your pasta.

Simple Sugars   Although there is no evidence to suggest that fat people consume more sugar than thin people, excess sugar can be a problem for some people. The average American consumes about 150 pounds of sugar per year. Simple sugars make up a large proportion of our "fun" foods, and, like fat, they are hidden in the convenience foods most of us rely on. Added sugars supply calories but few other nutrients. Substituting fresh fruits for sugar-rich desserts is the way to end a reliance on added sugars without giving up natural sweetness.

Protein   The typical American consumes more than an adequate amount of protein. Dietary supplements with extra protein are unnecessary for most people, and protein not needed by the body for growth and tissue repair will be stored as fat. Foods high in protein are often also high in fat, and diets high in fat and protein are linked to many serious health problems. Stick to the recommended protein intake of 10–15% of total daily calories.

Periodically, new diet books hit the market proclaiming a "scientific breakthrough" involving a high-protein, low-carbohydrate diet. Such diets usually cause an immediate and rather dramatic loss of body fluid, which may inaccurately be interpreted as fat loss. They typically involve significant calorie restriction, which is what actually causes any fat loss that does occur. A high-protein, low-carbohydrate diet does not conform to the Dietary Guidelines for Americans and is difficult to maintain. There is convincing evidence that diets rich in complex carbohydrates from grains, vegetables, and fruits lower the risk of

Studies of weight-loss programs have consistently shown that most people gain back lost weight within a fairly short period of time. But what about those people who *do* succeed in losing weight and keeping it off? Why are they successful? What can "yo-yo dieters" learn from their experiences? Researchers recently set out to answer these questions with the National Weight Control Registry (NWCR), a large-scale study of people who have dropped an average of 60 pounds and kept it off for 5 years. The average body mass index of NWCR participants fell from 35 to 24, bringing it into the healthy range (see Chapter 6). Findings from the NWCR study include the following:

- About half of the NWCR participants joined formal weight-loss programs; the remainder lost weight on their own. Fewer than 5% used any type of prescription medication.

- In order to maintain weight loss, participants made permanent changes in both their diet and their exercise habits. They incorporated the strategies they used to lose the weight into their daily routines.

- Common dietary strategies included restricting certain foods, cutting portion sizes, and monitoring calories or fat grams. (Other studies of successful weight managers have shown that increasing intake of vegetables, fruits, and

dietary fiber is also helpful.) Participants did not skip meals, and they ate out an average of three times per week.

- NWCR participants expended lots of energy in physical activity—an average of 2700 calories per week, the equivalent of walking 28 miles. This is well above the Surgeon General's minimum physical activity recommendation of 1000 calories per week. Popular activities among participants included walking, cycling, aerobic dance, and stair climbing.

- Nearly all participants reported improvements in energy level, mobility, mood, self-confidence, and physical health. They felt that the results of their lifestyle changes were well worth the effort.

People who have struggled with their weight should take heart from the NWCR. Most of the successful weight managers who participated in the study had tried unsuccessfully to lose weight in the past, and many of them had been overweight since childhood. The message from the NWCR is that weight management is possible but that it requires lifetime commitment and effort.

SOURCES: Weight loss: The secrets of success. 1998. *Harvard Women's Health Watch*, January. Klem, M. L., et al. 1997. A descriptive study of individuals successful at long-term maintenance of substantial weight loss. *American Journal of Clinical Nutrition* 66(2): 239–246.

heart disease, some types of cancer, and other chronic diseases. Most authorities recommend diets high in complex carbohydrates and moderate in protein consumption.

Eating Habits   Equally important to weight management is eating small, frequent meals—three or more a day plus snacks—on a dependable, regular schedule. Skipping meals leads to excessive hunger, feelings of deprivation, and increased vulnerability to binge eating or snacking on high-calorie, high-fat, or sugary foods. A regular pattern of eating, along with some personal "decision rules" governing food choices, is a way of thinking about and then internalizing the many details that go into a healthy, low-fat diet. Decision rules governing breakfast might be these, for example: Choose a sugar-free, high-fiber cereal with nonfat milk most of the time; no more than once a week, have a hard-boiled egg; save pancakes and waffles for special occasions.

Decreeing some foods "off limits" generally sets up a rule to be broken. The better principle is "everything in moderation." If a particular food becomes troublesome, it might be placed off limits temporarily until control over it is regained. The ultimate goal for achieving a healthy diet that ensures successful weight management is to eat in moderation; no foods need to be entirely off limits, though some should be eaten judiciously. Making the healthier choice more often than not is the essence of moderation.

Physical Activity and Exercise

Regular physical activity is another important lifestyle factor in weight management (see the box "Strategies of Successful Weight Managers). In order to achieve long-term success, you must be able to stick with your weight-management program for a lifetime. Cutting food intake in order to lose weight is a difficult strategy to maintain; increasing your physical activity is a much better approach.

Physical activity and exercise burn calories and keep the metabolism geared to using food for energy instead of storing it as fat. Moderate-intensity endurance exercise, if performed frequently for a relatively long duration, can burn a significant number of calories. Endurance training also increases the rate at which your body uses calories after your exercise session is over—burning an additional 5–180 extra calories, depending on the intensity of exercise. Resistance training builds muscle mass, and more muscle translates into a higher metabolic rate. Resistance training can also help you maintain your muscle mass during a period of weight loss, helping you avoid the significant drop in RMR associated with weight loss.

The body's fuel-use patterns vary with exercise intensity and change during recovery. During exercise, a higher proportion of energy comes from fat during low-intensity exercise (50%) compared with high-intensity exercise (40%).

Physical activity is an essential component of any effective weight-management plan. Playing basketball is just one of innumerable activities that can help you keep in shape.

Activity	Cal/lb/ min	× Body Weight	× Min	= Total Calories
Cycling (13 mph)	.071	_____	_____	_____
Digging	.062	_____	_____	_____
Driving a car	.020	_____	_____	_____
Housework	.029	_____	_____	_____
Painting a house	.034	_____	_____	_____
Shoveling snow	.052	_____	_____	_____
Sitting quietly	.009	_____	_____	_____
Sleeping and resting	.008	_____	_____	_____
Standing quietly	.012	_____	_____	_____
Typing or writing	.013	_____	_____	_____
Walking briskly (4.5 mph)	.048	_____	_____	_____

TABLE 9-2 *Calorie Costs of Selected Physical Activities**

To determine how many calories you burn when you engage in a particular activity, multiply the calorie multiplier given below by your body weight (in pounds) and then by the number of minutes you exercise.

*See Chapter 7 for the energy costs of fitness activities.

SOURCE: Adapted from Kusinitz, I., and M. Fine. 1995. *Your Guide to Getting Fit,* 3d ed. Mountain View, Calif.: Mayfield.

However, high-intensity exercise burns more calories overall, so even though a lower proportion of those calories comes from fat, high-intensity exercise tends to burn more fat than low-intensity exercise. Intense exercise also causes your body to use more fat as fuel during the recovery period. However, high-intensity exercise is not necessarily the best strategy for controlling weight. All physical activity will help you manage your weight, and most people find that a program of moderate-intensity exercise is easier to maintain over the long term.

The first step in becoming more active is to incorporate more physical activity into your daily life. Follow the recommendations in the Surgeon General's report by accumulating 30 minutes or more of moderate-intensity physical activity—walking, gardening, housework, and so on—on most, or preferably all, days of the week. Take advantage of routine opportunities to be more active. Take the stairs instead of the elevator, walk or bike instead of driving. In the long term, even a small increase in activity level can help maintain your current weight or help you lose a moderate amount of weight (Table 9-2).

Once you become more active every day, begin a formal exercise program that includes cardiorespiratory endurance exercise, resistance training, and stretching exercises. (Consult Chapter 7 for advice on creating a complete, personalized exercise program.) Regular physical activity, maintained throughout life, makes weight management easier. The sooner you establish good habits, the better. The key to success is making exercise an integral part of the lifestyle you can enjoy now and will enjoy in the future.

Thoughts and Emotions

The third component of a lifestyle for weight management is thoughts and emotions. A healthy psychological adjustment can result from *and* encourage weight control for fitness. Psychological distress, on the other hand, can discourage and undermine a healthy program. Someone who is having difficulty making a commitment to weight management may be motivated by knowing that a moderate, low-fat diet based on solid nutritional principles can yield psychological as well as physical well-being.

Research on people who have a weight problem indicates that low self-esteem and the accompanying negative emotions are a significant part of the picture. These

- Develop realistic goals for yourself and your behavior.
- Eat a moderate number of calories every day. Watch portion sizes carefully.
- Limit your intake of dietary fat and added sugars.
- Increase your intake of complex carbohydrates.
- Limit your protein intake to recommended levels.
- Eat small, frequent meals.
- Maintain a structured pattern of eating.

- Engage in moderate cardiorespiratory endurance exercise of medium to long duration as part of a program of regular exercise.
- Include weight training as part of your exercise program.
- Think positively about yourself, and praise yourself for your accomplishments.
- Develop healthy ways of dealing with stress, boredom, fatigue, and loneliness that don't involve food.

emotions, interacting with beliefs and attitudes about the "ideal self," give rise to negative **self-talk**—self-deprecating or self-blaming internal comments—that can undermine weight control and contribute to anxiety and depression. Realistic self-talk, on the other hand—internal dialogue that leads step by step toward a goal and then offers praise for success—can be an important component in sustaining the commitment to a weight-management program over time. (Chapter 10 and Activity 11 in the Behavior Change Workbook at the end of the text include strategies for developing realistic self-talk.)

Coping Strategies

The fourth component of a healthy lifestyle for weight control is appropriate strategies for handling the stresses and challenges of life. Many people use eating as a means of coping, just as many use drugs, alcohol, smoking, spending, or gambling. They might use food to alleviate loneliness, as a pickup for fatigue, as an antidote to boredom, or as a distraction from problems. Some people even overeat as a means of punishing themselves for real or imagined transgressions.

Those who recognize that they are using food in these ways can analyze their eating habits with fresh eyes. At that point, they can consciously attempt to find new coping strategies and begin to use food appropriately—to fuel life's activities, to foster growth, and to bring pleasure, *not* to manage stress. For a summary of the components of weight management through healthy lifestyle choices, see the box "A Lifestyle for Weight Management."

STRATEGIES FOR LOSING WEIGHT

In cases in which weight loss is clearly desirable, the next step is assessing the various options and the available resources for support and guidance. No single weight-reduction approach is appropriate for all people. For example, most people who are less than 20% over their healthy goal weight can safely cut back on their fat intake

and increase their exercise on their own. People who are 20–40% overweight, however, will be better served with some professional guidance and support—perhaps in a commercial weight-loss program (carefully researched to protect against dangerous or fraudulent claims) or a behavioral program supervised by a health professional. More serious degrees of overweight require a more aggressive approach under strict medical supervision.

Do-It-Yourself Approaches

People who aren't dangerously obese might find it most convenient to set up an individual program.

Doing It Alone   Research indicates that people are far more successful than was previously thought at losing weight and keeping it off. One study found that about 64% of the subjects achieved long-term success without joining a formal program or getting special help. Supporting these findings, a U.S. Public Health Service survey indicated that about 50% of the general public succeed with long-term weight management.

In developing a weight-management plan, it's important to remember that long-term success will depend on maintaining the lifestyle changes that help you lose the weight in the first place. Focus on adopting the healthy lifestyle described throughout this book. The "right" weight for you will naturally evolve, and you won't have to diet. However, if you must diet, do so in combination with exercise, and avoid very-low-calorie diets. Don't try to lose more than $\frac{1}{2}$–1 pound per week. Realize that most low-calorie diets cause a rapid loss of body water at first. When this phase passes, weight loss declines. As a result, dieters are often misled into believing that their efforts are not working. They then give up, not realizing that smaller losses later in the diet are better than the initial big losses, because later loss is mostly fat loss, whereas initial loss was primarily fluid.

self-talk   A person's internal comments and discussion; instrumental in shaping self-image.   **TERMS**

For more tips on losing weight on your own, refer to the section later in the chapter on creating an individual weight-management plan.

Using a Diet Book New diet books are published regularly, many of them making exciting but empty promises, and it can be dangerous or discouraging to rely on them too heavily. In assessing diet books, reject those that do the following:

- Advocate unbalanced meal plans—for example, those that advocate a high-carbohydrate–only diet or a low-carbohydrate, high-protein diet
- Claim to be based on a "scientific breakthrough" or a "secret"
- Use gimmicks, such as combining foods in certain ways or claiming that weight problems are due to food allergies, food sensitivities, or yeast infections
- Promise fast weight loss or limit the food selection

The most recent crop of popular diet books are those advocating high-protein regimens; these are often called 40/30/30 plans because they call for 40% of total calories from carbohydrates, 30% from protein, and 30% from fat. The American College of Sports Medicine, the American Dietetic Association, the Cooper Institute for Aerobics Research, and the Women's Sports Foundation recently released a joint statement saying that high-protein, low-carbohydrate diets are not a good weight-loss strategy, will not improve athletic performance, and can be harmful in some cases. The only reason such plans help people lose weight is that the diets they advocate provide so few calories. Remember, responsible diet books advocate a balanced, long-term approach to weight management that includes exercise and sound nutritional principles. (See the January 1998 issue of *Consumer Reports* magazine for reviews of many of the top-selling diet books.)

Using Diet Aids Diet aids are widely available without prescription, and many people are tempted to rely on them for quick-and-easy weight loss. However, the promises associated with these products are advertising gimmicks, and overreliance on them can be dangerous. Among the more common of these aids are dietary supplements for modified fasting. These supplements, in the forms of food bars and powder for shakes, provide far less than the daily nutritional and caloric requirements and should be used only under the guidance of a physician. They also teach dependence on products, not on sound, lifelong eating habits, and weight lost as a result of them is usually regained.

Diet pills are another common diet aid. The most common ingredient of diet pills sold in drugstores is phenylpropanolamine hydrochloride (PPA), which has been deemed a safe and effective mild appetite suppressant by the FDA. Nevertheless, studies on PPA's effectiveness are contradictory at best, and some reports suggest that it can cause dizziness, headaches, rapid pulse, palpitations,

sleeplessness, and hypertension. The use of PPA is approved by the FDA for periods of no more than 12 weeks.

Fiber is the second most common ingredient in diet aids sold in drugstores. However, the amount of fiber provided is usually small, and the FDA has found no data to suggest that fiber aids in weight control.

Although named for a formerly popular combination of prescription weight-loss drugs (fenfluramine and phentermine), the over-the-counter product "herbal fen-phen" does not contain either drug. Herbal fen-phen is usually a combination of ephedra (an herb containing the amphetamine-like stimulant ephedrine), caffeine, and other substances. Herbal fen-phen has not been shown to be safe or effective for weight loss.

Getting Help

Some people are helped by the support and experience of others as well as by professional guidance.

Commercial Weight-Loss Programs Some commercial weight-loss programs can be helpful for providing a food-and-exercise plan and reinforcing motivation. However, if you are considering enrolling in such a program, be sure to use your most acute consumer skills in assessing the available options (see the box "How to Evaluate Commercial Weight-Loss Programs"). Any weight-loss program should include medical supervision, counseling, nutrition education, and maintenance training.

Maintenance is an especially important feature of any program. Studies indicate that only about 10–15% of program participants maintain their weight loss—the rest gain back all or more than they had lost. One study of participants found that regular exercise was the best predictor of maintaining weight loss, while frequent television viewing was the best predictor of weight gain. This finding reinforces the idea that successful weight management requires long-term lifestyle changes.

Prescription Drugs A number of prescription drugs are designed to facilitate weight loss and treat obesity. Two drugs currently available are phentermine (Ionamin) and sibutramine (Meridia); both affect levels of serotonin, a neurotransmitter that controls appetite. Studies have generally found that these drugs produce modest weight loss—a 5–15% weight reduction. They do not eliminate the need to exercise and reduce food intake; they just help people do that by controlling appetite. Unfortunately, most people regain the weight they've lost if they stop taking the drugs.

As with all drugs, there are risks and side effects. In 1997, the FDA removed two other prescription weight-loss drugs, fenfluramine (Pondimin) and dexfenfluramine (Redux), from the market after their use was linked to potentially life-threatening heart valve problems. Such problems may not cause symptoms, so the FDA recommends that anyone who has taken either of these drugs be examined by a physician.

Clearly, prescription weight-loss drugs are not for people who want to lose a few pounds to wear a smaller size of jeans. The latest federal guidelines advise people to try lifestyle modification for at least 6 months before trying drug therapy. Prescription drugs are recommended—in conjunction with lifestyle changes—only in certain cases: for people who have been unable to lose weight with nondrug options and who have a BMI over 30 (or over 27 if two or more additional risk factors such as diabetes and high blood pressure are present).

Surgery For people who are 100% or more overweight, obesity is considered a serious medical condition, and surgical intervention may be necessary as a treatment of last resort. Surgery may involve closing off or removing parts of the stomach, thereby limiting the amount of food the stomach can hold, or connecting the stomach to the lower portion of the small intestine, causing food to be poorly digested and absorbed. Both of these procedures can have serious side effects.

Psychotherapy If concern about body weight and shape develop into an eating disorder, the help of a professional is recommended. In choosing a therapist, be sure to ask about credentials and experience. The therapist should have experience working with body image issues and eating disorders (discussed later in the chapter); a physician may be able to provide a referral.

Hazards and Rewards in the Search for the "Perfect" Body

The American focus on attaining a perfect body has prompted a flood of weight-loss programs, fad diets, health clubs, exercise equipment, appetite-reducing drugs, and books on diet, and fitness. The mass media expose us to the single "right" look relentlessly, and the beauty and fitness industries promise to help us attain it. Presumably, with the right combination of programs and products, one can attain the promised rewards of a healthier, slimmer, fitter, more aesthetically appealing body.

During adolescence, both boys and girls become sensitive about their size and physical appearance. Studies have consistently shown a high prevalence of dissatisfaction with body weight or shape among teenagers. **Body image,** the collective picture of the body as seen through the mind's eye, consists of perceptions, images, thoughts, attitudes, and emotions. A negative body image is characterized by dissatisfaction with the body in general or some part of the body in particular. This dissatisfaction can cause significant psychological distress and is associated with restrictive dieting, binge eating, and other forms of disturbed eating.

Problems related to negative body image are much more common among girls and women than boys and men: Only 30% of eighth-grade girls are content with their bodies, while 70% of their male classmates express satisfaction with their bodies. The rate of dieting among adolescent girls is twice the rate among adolescent boys. And women are 20 times more likely than men to suffer from an eating disorder.

body image The mental representation a person holds about her or his body at any given moment in time, consisting of perceptions, images, thoughts, attitudes, and emotions about the body. **TERMS**

The image of the "ideal" female body promoted by the fashion and fitness industries doesn't reflect the wide range of body shapes and sizes that are associated with good health. An overconcern with body image can contribute to low self-esteem and the development of eating disorders.

It is important to remember that the thin, toned look as a feminine ideal is just a fashion and is not shared by all American women. The African American community is much more accepting of larger, more voluptuous body shapes than white Americans have been. In many traditional African societies, full-figured women's bodies are seen as symbols of health, prosperity, and fertility. African American teenage girls have a much more positive body image than white girls. Two-thirds of black teenage girls in one survey defined beauty as "the right attitude," whereas white teenage girls were much more preoccupied with weight and body shape. African American women are also less likely to suffer from eating disorders than their Latina, Native American, or white counterparts.

For women and men of any cultural background, a sensible approach to body image is focusing on good physical and psychological health, not a number on a scale. When you see idealized standards presented by the beauty and fitness industries, realize that one of their goals is to increase your dissatisfaction with yourself so you will buy their products. Remember, your worth as a human being is not a function of how you look.

Setting unrealistic weight-loss goals in response to cultural ideals can set people up for failure and psychological distress and may predispose them to abnormal eating patterns and eating disorders. Realistic weight-loss goals are much more achievable and can have very beneficial effects. For example, for an obese person, losing as few as 10 pounds can reduce blood pressure as much as antihypertensive medication.

Obesity *is* a serious health problem, but weight management needs to take place in a positive and realistic atmosphere. The hazards of excessive dieting and overconcern about body weight need to be countered by a change in attitude about what constitutes the "perfect" body and a reasonable body weight. Weight-loss goals should take into account a person's weight history, social circumstances, metabolic profile, and psychological well-being. Eating should be viewed as an enjoyable activity that can help the body function at its best rather than as a "bad" behavior that detracts from wellness.

EATING DISORDERS

Problems with body weight and weight control are not limited to excessive body fat. A growing number of people, especially adolescent girls and young women, experience **eating disorders,** characterized by severe disturbances in eating patterns and eating-related behavior. The major eating disorders are anorexia nervosa, bulimia nervosa, and binge-eating disorder. More than 8 million Americans, most of them women, suffer from eating disorders. Many more people have abnormal eating habits and attitudes about food that, although not meeting the criteria for a full-blown eating disorder, do disrupt their lives. (To assess your eating habits, complete the eating disorder checklist in Lab 9-3.)

Although many different explanations for the development of eating disorders have been proposed, they share one central feature: a dissatisfaction with body image and body weight. Such dissatisfaction is created by distorted thinking, including perfectionistic beliefs, unreasonable demands for self-control, and excessive self-criticism. Dissatisfaction with body weight leads to dysfunctional attitudes about eating, such as fear of fat, preoccupation with food, and problematic eating behaviors.

Anorexia Nervosa

A person suffering from **anorexia nervosa** does not eat enough food to maintain a reasonable body weight. Anorexia affects 1–3 million Americans, 90% of them female. Although it can occur later, anorexia typically develops between the ages of 12 and 18. People suffering from anorexia have an intense fear of gaining weight or becoming fat. Their body image is distorted so that even when emaciated, they think they are fat. (Distorted body image is also a hallmark of *muscle dysmorphia,* a disorder experienced by some body builders in which they see themselves as out of shape despite being very muscular.) People with anorexia may engage in compulsive behaviors or rituals that help keep them from eating; they also commonly use vigorous and prolonged physical activity to reduce body weight. Although they may express a great interest in food, their own diet becomes more and more extreme. Anorexic people are typically introverted, emotionally reserved, and socially insecure. Their entire sense of self-esteem may be tied up in their evaluation of their body shape and weight.

Anorexia nervosa has been linked to a variety of medical complications, including disorders of the cardiovascular, gastrointestinal, and endocrine systems. Because of extreme weight loss, females with anorexia often stop menstruating. When body fat is virtually gone and muscles are severely wasted, the body turns to its own organs in a desperate search for protein. Death can occur from heart failure caused by electrolyte imbalances. Depression and suicide are also serious risks. As many as 18% of people with anorexia die of disease-related complications.

Bulimia Nervosa

A person suffering from **bulimia nervosa** engages in recurrent episodes of binge eating followed by **purging.** During a binge, a bulimic person may consume anywhere from 1000 to 60,000 calories within a few hours. This is followed by an attempt to get rid of the food by purging, usually by vomiting or using laxatives or diuretics. During a binge, people with bulimia feel as though they have lost control and cannot stop or limit how much they eat. Some binge and purge only occasionally, while others do so many times every day. Binges may be triggered by a major life change or other stressful event. Binge eating and purging may become a way of dealing with difficult feelings such as anger and disappointment.

The binge-purge cycle of bulimia places a tremendous strain on the body and can have serious health effects, including tooth decay, esophageal damage and chronic hoarseness, menstrual irregularities, depression, liver and kidney damage, and cardiac arrhythmia. Bulimia is often difficult to recognize because sufferers conceal their eating habits and usually maintain a normal weight, although they may experience fluctuations of 10–15 pounds. About 3% of Americans suffer from bulimia.

Binge-Eating Disorder

Binge-eating disorder is characterized by uncontrollable eating without any compensatory purging behaviors.

Common eating patterns are eating more rapidly than normal, eating until uncomfortably full, eating when not hungry, and preferring to eat alone. Uncontrolled eating is usually followed by weight gain and feelings of guilt, shame, and depression. Many people with binge-eating disorder mistakenly see rigid dieting as the only solution to their problem. However, rigid dieting usually causes feelings of deprivation and return to overeating. Compulsive overeaters rarely eat because of hunger. Instead, food is used as a means of coping with stress, conflict, and other difficult emotions. Binge eaters are almost always obese, so they face all the health risks associated with obesity. In addition, binge eaters may have higher-than-average rates of depression and anxiety. Binge-eating disorder may affect 25–50% of people who join formal weight-reduction programs.

Treating Eating Disorders

The treatment of eating disorders must address both problematic eating behaviors and the misuse of food to manage stress and emotions. Anorexia nervosa treatment first involves averting a medical crisis by restoring adequate body weight; then the psychological aspects of the disorder can be addressed. The treatment of bulimia nervosa or binge-eating disorder involves first stabilizing the eating patterns, then identifying and changing the patterns of thinking that lead to disordered eating. Treatment usually involves a combination of psychotherapy and medical management. Friends and family members often want to know what they can do to help someone with an eating disorder. For suggestions, see the box "If Someone You Know Has an Eating Disorder . . . ."

People with milder patterns of disordered eating may benefit from getting a nutrition checkup with a registered dietitian. A professional can help determine appropriate body weight and calorie intake and offer advice on how to budget calories into a balanced, healthy diet.

eating disorder A serious disturbance in eating patterns or eating-related behavior, characterized by a negative body image and concerns about body weight or body fat.

anorexia nervosa An eating disorder characterized by a refusal to maintain body weight at a minimally healthy level and an intense fear of gaining weight or becoming fat; self-starvation.

bulimia nervosa An eating disorder characterized by recurrent episodes of binge eating and purging: overeating and then using compensatory behaviors such as vomiting and excessive exercise to prevent weight gain.

purging The use of vomiting, laxatives, excessive exercise, restrictive dieting, enemas, diuretics, or diet pills to compensate for food that has been eaten and that the person fears will produce weight gain.

binge-eating disorder An eating disorder characterized by binge eating and a lack of control over eating behavior in general.

TERMS

- Educate yourself about eating disorders and their risks and about treatment resources in your community. (See the For More Information section at the end of this chapter for suggestions.)

- Write down specific ways the person's eating problem is affecting you or others in the household. Call a house meeting to talk about how others are affected by the problem and how to take action.

- Consider consulting a professional about the best way to approach the situation. Obtain information about how and where your friend can get help.

- Arrange to speak privately with the person, along with other friends or family members. Let one person lead the group and do most of the talking. Discuss specific incidents and the consequences of disordered eating.

- If you are going to speak with your friend, write down ahead of time what your concerns are and what you would like to say. Expect that the person you are concerned about will deny there is a problem, minimize it, or become angry

with you. Remain calm and nonjudgmental, and continue to express your concern.

- Avoid giving simplistic advice about eating habits. Gently encourage your friend to eat properly.

- Take time to listen to your friend, and express your support and understanding. Encourage honest communication. Emphasize your friend's good characteristics, and compliment all her or his successes.

- Help maintain the person's sense of dignity by encouraging personal responsibility and decision making. Be patient and realistic; recovery is a long process. Continue to love and support your friend.

- If the situation is an emergency—if the person has fainted or attempted suicide, for example—take immediate action. Call 911 for help.

- If you feel very upset about the situation, seek professional help. Remember, you are not to blame for another person's eating disorder.

CREATING AN INDIVIDUAL WEIGHT-MANAGEMENT PLAN

Would you like to lose weight on your own? Here are some strategies for creating a program of weight management that will last a lifetime.

Assess Your Motivation and Commitment

Before embarking on your chosen weight-management program, it's important that you take a fresh look within and assess your motivation and commitment. The point is not only to achieve success but also to guard against frustration, negative changes in self-esteem, and the sense of failure that attends broken resolves or "yo-yo dieting." Think about the reasons you want to lose weight. Self-focused reasons, such as to feel good about yourself or to have a greater sense of well-being, can often lead to success. Trying to lose weight for others or out of concern for how others view you is a poor foundation for a weight-management program. Make a list of your reasons for wanting to manage your weight, and post it in a prominent place.

Set Reasonable Goals

Choose a goal weight or body fat percentage that is both healthy and reasonable. Refer to the calculations you completed in Lab 6-2. Subdivide your long-term goal into a series of short-term goals. Be willing to renegotiate your final goal as your program moves along.

Assess Your Current Energy Balance

Your energy balance is the balance between calories consumed and calories used in physical activity. When your weight is constant, you are burning approximately the same number of calories as you are taking in. To tip your energy balance toward weight loss, you must either consume fewer calories or burn more through physical activity. To lose the recommended ½–1 pound per week, you'll need to create a negative energy balance of between 1750 and 3500 calories a week, or 250–500 calories a day. Complete Labs 9-1 and 9-2 to assess your current daily expenditure and to develop strategies for achieving a negative energy balance that will lead to gradual, moderate weight loss. (See p. 242 for guidelines for altering your energy balance to *gain* weight.)

Increase Your Level of Physical Activity

To generate a negative energy balance, it's usually best to increase your activity level rather than decrease your calorie consumption. As discussed earlier, dieting reduces RMR; exercise raises it. Further, a diet with fewer than 1600 calories per day will probably not meet the RDAs for all essential nutrients. (No diet should reduce calorie intake below 1500 for men or 1200 for women.) Increasing energy output by adopting a program of regular exercise and by incorporating more physical activity into your daily routine is a better strategy. Table 9-2 lists the calorie costs of selected physical activities; refer to Table 7-1 for the calorie costs of different types of sports and fitness activities.

You need to adopt a weight-management plan that will last a lifetime. Look through the following list of strategies, and adopt those that will be most useful for you.

- When shopping for food, make a list and stick to it. Don't shop when you're hungry. Avoid aisles that contain problem foods.
- When serving food, use a small food scale to measure out portions before putting them on your plate.
- Serve meals on small plates and in small bowls to help you eat smaller portions without feeling deprived.
- Eat three meals a day; replace impulse snacking with planned, healthy snacks. Drink plenty of water to help fill you up.
- Eat only in specifically designated spots. Remove food from other areas of your house or apartment.
- When you eat, just eat—don't do anything else, such as read or watch TV.
- Eat slowly. Pay attention to every bite and enjoy your food. Try putting your fork or spoon down between bites.
- For problem foods, try eating small amounts under controlled conditions. Go out for a scoop of ice cream, for example, rather than buying half a gallon for your freezer.
- When you eat out, choose a restaurant where you can make healthy food choices. Ask the waiter not to put bread and butter on the table before the meal; request that sauces and salad dressings be served on the side.

- If you cook a large meal for friends, send leftovers home with your guests.
- If you're eating at a friend's, eat a little and leave the rest. Don't eat to be polite; if someone offers you food you don't want, thank the person and decline firmly. To turn down dessert or second helpings, try "No thank you, I've had enough" or "It's delicious, but I'm full."
- Develop strategies for handling stress—go for a walk or use a relaxation technique. Practice positive self-talk.
- Increase your level of daily physical activity. If you have been sedentary for a long time or are seriously overweight, increase your level of physical activity slowly. Start by walking 10 minutes at a time, and work toward 30 minutes of moderate physical activity per day.
- Begin a formal exercise program that includes cardiorespiratory endurance exercise, resistance training, and stretching.
- Tell family members and friends that you're making some changes in your eating and exercise habits. Ask them to be supportive.

SOURCES: Nash, J. D. 1997. *The New Maximize Your Body Potential*. Palo Alto, Calif.: Bull Publishing. Ferguson, J. M., and C. Ferguson. 1997. *Habits Not Diets: The Secret to Lifetime Weight Control*. 3d ed. Palo Alto, Calif.: Bull Publishing. Reprinted with permission from Bull Publishing Company.

Make Changes in Your Diet and Eating Habits

If you can't generate a large enough negative calorie balance solely by increasing physical activity, you may want to supplement exercise with small cuts in your calorie intake. Don't think of this as "going on a diet"; your goal is to make small changes in your diet that you can maintain for a lifetime. Focus on cutting your fat intake and on eating a variety of nutritious foods in moderation. Don't try skipping meals, fasting, or a very-low-calorie diet. These strategies seldom work, and they can have negative effects on your ability to manage your weight and on your overall health.

Making changes in eating habits is another important strategy for succesful long-term weight management. If your program centers on conscious restriction of certain food items, you're likely to spend all your time thinking about the forbidden foods. It's better to focus on *how* you eat rather than on *what* you eat. Try adopting some of the behaviors listed in the box "Strategies for Managing Your Weight." You may find that your new eating habits make it much easier for you to achieve and maintain a healthy weight.

Put Your Plan into Action

Be systematic in your effort to change your behavior. Keeping written records of food intake and dietary changes seems to increase the likelihood of success, so devise a food journal similar to the one in Lab 8-1 or Figure 1-4. Write down what you plan to eat, in what quantity, before you eat it. Many people find that just having to record a food they know they should avoid helps stop them from eating it. Also, keep track of your daily activities and your formal exercise program so you can monitor increases in physical activity.

Other strategies for putting a successful plan into action include the following:

- Examine the environmental cues that trigger poor eating and exercise habits, and devise strategies for dealing with them. Anticipate problem situations, and plan ways to handle them more effectively. Create new cues that support healthy behaviors.
- Get others to help. Talk to friends and family members about what they can do to support your efforts. Find a buddy for your program.

- Give yourself lots of praise and rewards. Think about your accomplishments and congratulate yourself. Reward yourself often and for anything that counts toward success.

- If you do slip, get back on track immediately, and don't waste time on self-criticism. Think positively, and don't demand too much of yourself.

- Don't get discouraged. Be aware that although weight loss is bound to slow down after the first loss of body fluid, the weight loss at this slower rate is more permanent than earlier, more dramatic losses.

- Remember that weight management is a lifelong project. You need to adopt reasonable goals and strategies that you can maintain over the long term.

COMMON QUESTIONS ANSWERED

How can I safely gain weight? Although for most of us the focus of a weight-management program is losing weight, some people face the opposite challenge. Just as for losing weight, a program for weight gain should be gradual and should include both exercise and dietary changes. The foundation of a successful and healthy program for weight gain is a combination of strength training and a high-carbohydrate, high-calorie diet. Strength training is critical because it will help you add weight as muscle rather than fat.

Energy balance is also important in a program for gaining weight. You need to consume more calories than your body needs in order to gain weight, but you need to choose those extra calories wisely. Fatty, high-calorie foods may seem like an obvious choice, but consuming additional calories as fat can jeopardize your health and your weight-management program. A diet high in fat carries health risks, and your body is more likely to convert dietary fat into fat tissue than into muscle mass. A better strategy is to consume additional calories as complex carbohydrates—from grains, fruits, and vegetables. Experts recommend that a diet for weight gain should contain about 60–65% of total daily calories from carbohydrates. You do not need to be concerned with protein: Although protein requirements increase when you exercise, the protein consumption of most Americans is already well above the RDA for protein.

In order to gain primarily muscle weight instead of fat, a gradual program of weight gain is your best bet. Try these strategies for consuming extra calories:

- Don't skip any meals.

- Add two or three snacks to your daily eating routine.

- Try a sports drink or supplement that has at least 60% of calories from carbohydrates, as well as significant amounts of protein, vitamins, and minerals. (But don't use such supplements to replace meals, because they don't contain all food components.)

Can reduced-fat foods and snacks help me lose weight?
Reduced-fat foods can be a part of a weight-management program, but they must be used carefully. Consider both what the food is and how much of it you eat. A reduced-fat food contains at least 25% less fat than the "regular" version of the food. But the total amount of fat depends on the type of food. For example, a serving of regular peanut butter has 17 grams of fat; the same serving of reduced-fat peanut butter has about 12—a lower amount, but still a substantial amount of fat. In addition, reduced-fat foods often contain the same number of calories as their regular versions. Studies indicate that many of us actually take in more calories when we consume low-fat foods by rationalizing that we can eat more if we decrease our fat intake. (The prevalence of obesity has increased significantly since the introduction of artificial sweeteners.) To be part of a successful weight-management program, reduced-fat foods cannot be considered as a license to eat more.

You also need to consider nutrients. Fruits and vegetables are still likely to be lower in fat and calories and higher in vitamins and minerals than reduced-fat cookies or muffins. Nutrients may also be a concern if you eat foods made with olestra (trade name, Olean), a fat substitute approved by the FDA in 1996 for use in deep-fried foods. Although olestra does significantly lower the fat content of popular foods like potato and tortilla chips, it also binds with certain nutrients, causing them to be carried through the digestive tract without being absorbed by the body. Foods made with olestra are fortified with some of these nutrients, including vitamins A and E, but not all of them. Some scientists are concerned that consumption of significant amounts of olestra could lead to nutrient deficiencies. (In addition, olestra can cause gastrointestinal problems.)

Overall, reduced-fat desserts and snacks should be considered as occasional treats rather than as a regular part of a healthy diet.

How can I achieve a "perfect" body? The current cultural ideal of an ultrathin, ultrafit body is impossible for most people to achieve. A reasonable goal for body weight and body shape must take into account an individual's heredity, weight history, social circumstances, metabolic rate, and psychological well-being. Don't set goals based on movie stars or fashion models. Modern photographic techniques can make people look much better on film or in magazines than they look in person. Many of these people are also genetically endowed with body shapes that are impossible for most of us to emulate. The best approach is to work with what you've got. Adopting a wellness lifestyle that includes regular exercise and a healthy diet will naturally result in the best possible body shape for you. Obsessively trying to achieve unreasonable goals can lead to problems such as eating disorders, overtraining, and injuries.

SUMMARY

- Excess body weight increases the risk of numerous diseases, particularly cardiovascular disease, cancer, gallbladder disease, and diabetes.

- Although genetic factors help determine a person's weight, the influence of heredity can be overcome.

- Resting metabolic rate, the amount of energy needed to maintain body functions, is partly determined by heredity; it can be increased through exercise and an increase in muscle mass.

- Energy-balance components that an individual can control are calories taken in and calories expended in physical activity.

- Nutritional guidelines for weight control and wellness include controlling consumption of total calories, fat, sugar, and protein; monitoring portion sizes; increasing consumption of complex carbohydrates; and developing an eating schedule based on decision rules.

- Activity guidelines for weight control emphasize regular, prolonged endurance exercise and weight training.

- The sense of well-being that results from a well-balanced, low-fat diet can reinforce commitment to weight control, improve self-esteem, and lead to realistic, as opposed to negative, self-talk. Successful weight-management results in not using food as a way to cope with stress.

- In cases of extreme obesity, weight loss requires medical supervision; otherwise, people can set up individual programs, perhaps getting guidance from reliable books, or they can get help by joining a commercial weight-loss program.

- Dissatisfaction with body image and body weight can lead to physical problems and serious eating disorders, including anorexia nervosa, bulimia nervosa, and binge-eating disorder.

- A successful personal plan assesses motivation, sets reasonable and healthy goals, and emphasizes increased activity rather than decreased calories.

FOR MORE INFORMATION

Books

Cash, T. F. 1995. *What Do You See When You Look in the Mirror? Helping Yourself to a Positive Body Image.* New York: Bantam. *An 8-step self-help program for overcoming a negative body image and developing more positive perceptions of one's body.*

Fairburn, C. 1995. *Overcoming Binge Eating.* New York: Guilford Press. *A self-help manual that sets forth a cognitive-behavioral treatment for bulimia nervosa and binge-eating disorder.*

Ferguson, J. M., and C. Ferguson. 1997. *Habits Not Diets: The Secret to Lifetime Weight Control,* 3d ed. Palo Alto, Calif.: Bull Publishing. *Focuses on changing behaviors that relate to weight in order to achieve permanent weight control.*

Fraser, L. 1997. *Losing It: America's Obsession with Weight and the Industry That Feeds on It.* New York: E. P. Dutton. *An exposé on the "diet" industry in America.*

Gaesser, G. A. 1996. *Big Fat Lies.* New York: Fawcett Columbine. *Advice from an exercise physiology researcher critical of general standards for determining "healthy" body weight; his program stresses a low-fat diet and exercise over weight loss.*

Nash, J. D. 1997. *The New Maximize Your Body Potential.* Palo Alto, Calif.: Bull Publishing. *Provides in-depth coverage of nutrition, exercise, and other key aspects of weight management.*

Organizations and Web Sites

Ask the Dietitian/Overweight. Provides questions and answers on many topics related to weight control, including tips for limiting fat intake and information about eating disorders. Site is also linked to the Healthy Body Calculator™, which calculates BMI, waist-to-hip ratio, and daily nutrient and calorie goals.
  http://www.dietitian.com/overweig.html

Eating Disorders Awareness and Prevention (EDAP). Provides educational resources on eating disorders.
  206-382-3587
  http://members.aol.com/edapinc/home.html

Eating Disorders Shared Awareness (EDSA). Provides information about eating disorders, including prevention, signs and symptoms, treatment options, tips for helping a friend, and links to many resources, including online support groups.
  http://www.something-fishy.com/ed.htm

Go Ask Alice. Sponsored by Columbia University Health Service, provides answers to a wide variety of students' questions, including many about weight management, diet, and exercise.
  http://www.goaskalice.columbia.edu

National Association of Anorexia Nervosa and Associated Disorders. Provides written materials, referrals, and telephone counseling.
  847-831-3438

Natinal Heart, Lung, and Blood Institute (NHLBI). Provides information about the latest federal guidelines for the evaluation and treatment of overweight and obesity.
  http://www.nhlbi.nih.gov/nhlbi/nhlbi.htm

North American Association for the Study of Obesity (NAASO). Provides information and links about current research in obesity.
  http://www.naaso.org

National Institute of Diabetes and Digestive and Kidney Diseases (NIDDK). Health Information: Nutrition and Obesity. Provides information and referrals for problems related to obesity, weight control, and nutritional disorders.
  800-WIN-8098
  http://www.niddk.nih.gov/health/nutrit/nutrit.htm

Shape Up America! Founded by former Surgeon General C. Everett Koop, Shape Up America! provides written and online materials about safe dietary and physical fitness strategies for successful weight management. Web site includes an online BMI calculator and a physical activity IQ quiz.
  http://shapeup.org

See also the listings in Chapters 1, 6, and 8.

SELECTED BIBLIOGRAPHY

American Dietetic Association. 1996. *Position of the American Dietetic Association: Weight Management* (retrieved December 8, 1997; http://www.eatright.org/adap0197.html).

American Heart Association. 1998. *Press Release: Obesity Joins American Heart Association's List of Major Risk Factors for Heart Attack* (retrieved June 2, 1998; http://www.americanheart.org/Whats_News/AHA_News_Releases/obesity.html).

Brownell, K. D., and C. G. Fairburn, 1995. *Eating Disorders and Obesity: A Comprehensive Handbook.* New York: Guilford Press.

Carmichael, H. E., B. A. Swinburn, and M. R. Wilson. 1998. Lower fat intake as a predictor of initial and sustained weight loss in obese subjects consuming an otherwise ad libitum diet. *Journal of the American Dietetic Association* 98(1): 35–39.

Cash, T. F., and P. E. Henry. 1995. Women's body images: The results of a national survey in the U.S.A. *Sex Roles* 33:19–28.

Dietz, W. H. 1998. Childhood weight affects adult morbidity and mortality. *Journal of Nutrition* 128(2): 4118–4148.

Flynn, M. E. 1995. Fat-free food: A dieter's downfall? Studies show calories do count. *Environmental Nutrition* 18(4): 1, 6.

Foster, G. D., et al. 1996. Psychological effects of weight loss and regain: A prospective evaluation. *Journal of Consulting and Clinical Psychology* 64:752–757.

Grodstein, F., et al. 1996. Three-year follow-up of participants in a commercial weight loss program: Can you keep it off? *Archives of Internal Medicine* 156:1302–1306.

Halaas, J. L. 1995. Weight-reducing effects of the plasma protein encoded by the obese gene. *Science* 269:543–546.

Harvey-Berino, J. 1998. The efficacy of dietary fat vs. total energy restriction for weight loss. *Obesity Research* 6:202.

Kleiner, S. M. 1995. Healthy muscle gain. *The Physician and Sportsmedicine* 23(4): 21–22.

Kleiner, S. M. 1997. Fake sugars and fats: Net benefits or real risks? *The Physician and Sportsmedicine* (retrieved December 1, 1997; http://www.physsportsmed.com/issues/1997/04apr/lose.htm).

Kurtzwell, P. 1996. Taking the fat out of food. *FDA Consumer,* July/August.

Kushner, R. 1997. The treatment of obesity: A call for prudence and professionalism. *Archives of Internal Medicine* 157(6): 602–604.

Manson, J. E. 1995. Body weight and mortality among women. *New England Journal of Medicine* 333(11): 677–685.

Middleman, A. B., I. Vazquez, and R. H. Durant. 1998. Eating patterns, physical activity, and attempts to change weight among adolescents. *Journal of Adolescent Health* 22(1): 37–42.

Mussell, M. P., et al. 1995. Onset of binge eating, dieting, obesity, and mood disorders among subjects seeking treatment for binge eating disorder. *International Journal of Eating Disorders* 17:395–401.

National Heart, Lung, and Blood Institute. 1998. *Clinical Guidelines on the Identification, Evaluation, and Treatment of Overweight and Obesity in Adults: The Evidence Report.* Bethesda, Md.: National Institutes of Health.

Ogden, J., and C. Evans. 1996. The problem with weighing: Effects on mood, self-esteem and body image. *International Journal of Obesity* 20:272–277.

Parr, R. B. 1997. Exercising to lose 10 to 20 pounds. *The Physician and Sportsmedicine* 25(4).

Pelleymounter, M. A., et al. 1995. Effects of the *obese* gene product on body weight regulation in *ob/ob* mice. *Science* 269:540–543.

Pope, H. G., et al. 1997. Muscle dysmorphia: An underrecognized form of body dysmorphic disorder. *Psychosomatics* 38:548–557.

Racette, S. B., et al. 1995. Exercise enhances dietary compliance during moderate energy restriction in obese women. *American Journal of Clinical Nutrition* 62:345–349.

Thompson, J. K. (ed.). 1996. *Body Image, Eating Disorders, and Obesity.* Washington, D.C.: American Psychological Association.

U.S. Food and Drug Administration. 1997. *FDA Talk Paper: FDA Approves Sibutramine to Treat Obesity,* 24 November. FDA Press Office.

U.S. Food and Drug Administration. Center for Drug Evaluation and Research. 1997. *Questions and Answers About Withdrawal of Fenfluramine (Pondimin) and Dexfenfluramine (Redux)* (retrieved December 8, 1997; http://www.fda.gov/cder/news/fenphenqa2.htm).

U.S. Food and Drug Administration. Center for Drug Evaluation and Research. 1997. *Questions and Answers Concerning the Department of Health and Human Services (DHHS) Interim Recommendations for Patients Who Have Taken Either Fenfluramine or Dexfenfluramine* (retrieved December 8, 1997; http://www.fda.gov/cder/news/fenqa111397.htm).

Wadden, T. A., et al. 1996. Effects of weight cycling on the resting energy expenditure and body composition of obese women. *International Journal of Eating Disorders* 19:5–12.

Walsh, B. T., et al. 1997. Medication and psychotherapy in the treatment of bulimia nervosa. *American Journal of Psychiatry* 154(4): 523–531.

"Why Lost Weight Finds Its Way Back." 1995. *San Francisco Chronicle,* 9 March, A1, A13.

Wonderlich, S. A., et al. 1996. Childhood sexual abuse and bulimic behavior in a nationally representative sample. *American Journal of Public Health* 86:1082–1086.

LAB 9-1   *Calculating Daily Energy Balance*

Part I. Resting Metabolic Rate

Resting metabolic rate varies depending on age, gender, and weight. Use the equations below to calculate your approximate RMR.

World Health Organization Equations

1. Convert body weight to kilograms:

    _____ lb ÷ 2.2 lb/kg = _____ kg

2. Find the appropriate formula in the table below, and calculate your RMR. (For example, a 19-year-old male weighing 80 kg would have an RMR of approximately $(15.3 \times 80) + 679 = 1224 + 679 = 1903$ calories per day.)

	Age Range (years)	Equation to Derive RMR in cal/day
Males	10–18	$(17.5 \times wt) + 651$
	18–30	$(15.3 \times wt) + 679$
	30–60	$(11.6 \times wt) + 879$
	Over 60	$(13.5 \times wt) + 487$
Females	10–18	$(12.2 \times wt) + 746$
	18–30	$(14.7 \times wt) + 496$
	30–60	$(8.7 \times wt) + 829$
	Over 60	$(10.5 \times wt) + 596$

RMR = (_____ × _____ kg) + _____ = _____ **cal/day**
       (factor from table)   (body weight)   (factor from table)

Harris Benedict Equations

1. Convert body weight to kilograms:

    _____ lb ÷ 2.2 lb/kg = _____ kg

2. Convert height to centimeters:

    _____ in. × 2.54 cm/in. = _____ cm

3. Use the appropriate equation to calculate RMR. (For example, a 20-year-old female 160 cm tall, weighing 60 kg, would have an RMR of approximately $655 + (9.56 \times 60) + (1.85 \times 160) - (4.68 \times 20) = 1431$ calories per day.)

    Women: RMR = $655 + (9.56 \times$ weight _____ kg) + $(1.85 \times$ height _____ cm) −
        $(4.68 \times$ age _____ yr) = _____ **cal/day**

    Men: RMR = $66.5 + (13.8 \times$ weight _____ kg) + $(5 \times$ height _____ cm) −
        $(6.76 \times$ age _____ yr) = _____ **cal/day**

Approximate Resting Metabolic Rate

Average the values you obtained from these equations to determine your approximate RMR.

World Health Organization Equation: _____ cal/day

Harris Benedict Equation: _____ cal/day

Average value for RMR: _____ **cal/day**

Part II. Daily Energy Expenditures

List all of your activities for a 3-day period, and classify them according to the categories listed in the table below. (Representative values of the calorie costs of different types of activities are presented below as multiples of resting metabolic rate.) Table 7-1 provides general guidelines for how to classify the sports and fitness activities you participate in: Activities with high cardiorespiratory endurance ratings probably fall in the heavy category, those with medium CRE ratings in the moderate category, and those with low CRE ratings in the light category. Take your intensity into account when classifying fitness activities; basketball, for example, can be played at an easy pace or very intensely.

Your total daily energy expenditure can be estimated by calculating a daily activity factor based on the amount of time you engage in activities in each category of intensity. By adding up weighted activity factors and finding the average, you can calculate total daily energy requirements. Since your activity levels probably vary widely from day to day, it's more accurate to calculate energy output for several different days to come up with an average daily range of calorie output.

Activity Category	Representative Value for Activity Factor per Unit Time of Activity
Resting Sleeping, lying down	RMR × 1.0
Very light Seated and standing activities such as driving, lab work, writing, typing, cooking, playing cards or a musical instrument	RMR × 1.5
Light Walking on a level surface 2.5–3.0 mph, house cleaning, child care, carpentry, restaurant trades, and sports/activities with low fitness ratings such as golf, bowling, and sailing	RMR × 2.5
Moderate Walking 3.5–4.0 mph, gardening, carrying a load, and sports/activities with medium fitness ratings such as baseball and volleyball	RMR × 5.0
Heavy Walking with a load uphill, heavy manual labor, sports/activities with high fitness ratings such as aerobic dance and cross-country skiing	RMR × 7.0

For each day's activities, add up the total number of hours for each activity category. Then multiply the total duration for each category by the category's activity factor. Add the weighted activity factors, then divide the total weighted activity factor by 24 to get an average daily activity factor. A sample of completed calculations for one day is shown on the next page.

SAMPLE

Activity	Duration	Category
sleeping	8 hours	resting
eating in dorm	1-1/2	very light
class	5	very light
bicycling to class, lab...	1	moderate
job in library	2-1/2	very light
cleaning room/laundry	1	light
basketball	1	heavy
studying in library	4	very light

Category	Activity Factor	Duration	Weighted Activity Factor
Resting	1.0	8	8.0
Very light	1.5	13	19.5
Light	2.5	1	2.5
Moderate	5.0	1	5.0
Heavy	7.0	1	7.0
Total		24 hours	42.0
Average daily activity factor (Total of weighted factors ÷ 24)			1.75

RECORDS FOR 3 DAYS

Day 1

Activity	Duration	Category

Day 1

Category	Activity Factor	Duration	Weighted Activity Factor
Resting	1.0		
Very light	1.5		
Light	2.5		
Moderate	5.0		
Heavy	7.0		
Total		24 hours	
Average daily activity factor (Total of weighted factors ÷ 24)			

Day 2

Activity	Duration	Category

Day 2

Category	Activity Factor	Duration	Weighted Activity Factor
Resting	1.0		
Very light	1.5		
Light	2.5		
Moderate	5.0		
Heavy	7.0		
Total		24 hours	
Average daily activity factor (Total of weighted factors ÷ 24)			

Day 3

Activity	Duration	Category

Day 3

Category	Activity Factor	Duration	Weighted Activity Factor
Resting	1.0		
Very light	1.5		
Light	2.5		
Moderate	5.0		
Heavy	7.0		
Total		24 hours	
Average daily activity factor (Total of weighted factors ÷ 24)			

Day 1 average daily activity factor _____

Day 2 average daily activity factor _____

Day 3 average daily activity factor _____

Finally, use the middle or average of your three daily activity factors to calculate your average daily energy output. For RMR, use the value you calculated in the first part of this lab. (For example, a person with an average daily activity factor of 1.75 and an RMR of 1450 calories per day would have an approximate daily energy expenditure of $1.75 \times 1450 = 2540$ calories per day.)

Average of three daily activity factors _____ × RMR _____ cal/day =

approximate daily energy expenditure: _____ cal/day
(from Part I)

How does this value compare to the average number of calories you eat each day, as determined in Lab 8-2?

To monitor your progress toward your goal, enter the results of this lab in the Preprogram Assessment column of Appendix D. After several weeks of a program to increase daily energy expenditure, do this lab again and enter the results in the Postprogram Assessment column of Appendix D. How do th e results compare?

SOURCES: World Health Organization. 1985. *Energy and Protein Requirements: Report of a Joint FAO/WHO/UNO Expert Consultation*. Geneva: World Health Organization, Technical Report Series 724. National Research Council. 1989. *Recommended Dietary Allowances*, 10th ed. Washington, D.C.: National Academy Press.

LAB 9-2 *Identifying Weight-Loss Goals and Ways to Meet Them*

Negative Calorie Balance

Complete the following calculations to determine your weekly and daily negative calorie balance goals and the number of weeks to achieve your target weight.

Current weight _____ lb − target weight (from Lab 6-2) _____ lb =
    total weight to lose _____ lb

Total weight to lose _____ lb ÷ weight to lose each week _____ lb =
    time to achieve target weight _____ weeks

Weight to lose each week _____ lb × 3500 cal/lb = weekly negative calorie balance _____ cal/week

Weekly negative calorie balance _____ cal/week ÷ 7 days/week = daily negative calorie balance
    _____ cal/day

To keep your weight-loss program on schedule, you must achieve the daily negative calorie balance by either decreasing your calorie consumption (eating less) or increasing your calorie expenditure (being more active). A combination of the two strategies will probably be most successful.

Changes in Activity Level

Adding a few minutes of exercise every day is a good way of expending calories. Use the calorie costs for different activities listed in Table 7-1 and Table 9-2 to plan ways for raising your calorie expenditure level.

Activity	Duration	Calories Used
_____	_____	_____
_____	_____	_____
_____	_____	_____
_____	_____	_____
	Total calories expended:	_____

Changes in Diet

Look closely at your diet from one day, as recorded in Lab 8-2. Identify ways to cut calorie consumption by eliminating certain items or substituting lower-calorie choices. Be realistic in your cuts and substitutions; you need to develop a plan you can live with.

Food Item	Substitute Food Item	Calorie Savings
_____	_____	_____
_____	_____	_____
_____	_____	_____
_____	_____	_____
	Total calories cut:	_____

Total calories expended _____ + **total calories cut** _____ = **Total negative calorie balance** _____

Have you met your required negative energy balance? If not, revise your dietary and activity changes to meet your goal.

Common Problem Eating Behaviors

For each of the groups of statements that appear below, check those that are true for you. If you check several statements for a given pattern or problem, it will probably be a significant factor in your weight-management program. One possible strategy for dealing with each type of problem is given. For those eating problems you identify as important, add your own ideas to the strategies listed.

1. _____ I often skip meals.

   _____ I often eat a number of snacks in place of a meal.

   _____ I don't have a regular schedule of meal and snack times.

   _____ I make up for missed meals and snacks by eating more at the next meal.

   Problem: Irregular eating habits

   Possible solutions:

   • Write out a plan for each day's meals in advance. Carry it with you, and stick to it.

   • _____

   • _____

2. _____ I eat more than one sweet dessert or snack each day.

   _____ I usually snack on foods high in calories and fat (chips, cookies, ice cream).

   _____ I drink regular (not sugar-free) soft drinks.

   _____ I choose types of meat that are high in fat.

   _____ I consume more than one alcoholic beverage per day.

   Problem: Poor food choices

   Possible solutions:

   • Keep a supply of raw vegetables handy for snacks.

   • _____

   • _____

3. _____ I always eat everything on my plate.

   _____ I often go back for seconds and thirds.

   _____ I take larger helpings than most people.

   _____ I eat up leftovers instead of putting them away.

   Problem: Portion sizes too large

   Possible solutions:

   • Measure all portions with a scale or measuring cup.

   • _____

   • _____

Name _____ Section _____ Date _____

 LAB 9-3 *Eating Disorder Checklist*

For each statement, put a check in the column that best describes how often the statement is true for you.

Section One

Always 0	Very Often 0	Often 0	Some- times 1	Rarely 2	Never 3	
						1. I like eating with other people.
						2. I like my clothes to fit tightly.
						3. I enjoy eating meat.
						4. I have regular menstrual periods.
						5. I enjoy eating at restaurants.
						6. I enjoy trying new rich foods.

Section Two

Always 3	Very Often 2	Often 1	Some- times 0	Rarely 0	Never 0	
						7. I prepare foods for others, but do not eat what I cook.
						8. I become anxious prior to eating.
						9. I am terrified about being overweight.
						10. I avoid eating when I am hungry.
						11. I find myself preoccupied with food.
						12. I have gone on eating binges where I feel that I may not be able to stop.
						13. I cut my food into small pieces.
						14. I am aware of the calorie content of foods that I eat.
						15. I particularly avoid foods with a high carbohydrate content (bread, potatoes, rice, etc.).
						16. I feel bloated after meals.
						17. I feel others would prefer if I ate more.
						18. I vomit after I have eaten.
						19. I feel extremely guilty after eating.

Always 3	Very Often 2	Often 1	Some-times 0	Rarely 0	Never 0	
						20. I am preoccupied with a desire to be thinner.
						21. I exercise strenuously to burn off calories.
						22. I weigh myself several times a day.
						23. I wake up early in the morning.
						24. I eat the same foods day after day.
						25. I think about burning up calories when I exercise.
						26. Other people think I am too thin.
						27. I am preoccupied with the thought of having fat on my body.
						28. I take longer than others to eat my meals.
						29. I take laxatives.
						30. I avoid foods with sugar in them.
						31. I eat diet foods.
						32. I feel that food controls my life.
						33. I display self-control around foods.
						34. I feel that others pressure me to eat.
						35. I give too much time and thought to food.
						36. I suffer from constipation.
						37. I feel uncomfortable after eating sweets.
						38. I engage in dieting behavior.
						39. I like my stomach to be empty.
						40. I have the impulse to vomit after meals.

Total your points (use the numbers given at the top of each column for the two sections) _____

Norms	Range (0–120 points)
Eating disorder	>50 points
Borderline eating disorder	30–50 points
Normal*	<30 points

*Average score among those with normal eating habits = 15.4

SOURCE: Nieman, D. 1999. *Exercise Testing and Prescription: A Health-Related Approach,* 4th ed. Mountain View, Calif.: Mayfield.

Stress

LOOKING AHEAD

After reading this chapter, you should be able to answer these questions about stress:

- What is stress, and how does it affect health and wellness?

- How does the body respond to stress?

- How do emotional and behavioral responses to stress affect the ability to manage stress?

- What is the relationship between stress and disease, and what are some possible mechanisms of this relationship?

- What are common sources of stress?

- What are some approaches to successful stress management?

ike the term *fitness, stress* is a word many people use without really understanding its precise meaning. Stress is popularly viewed as an uncomfortable response to a negative event, which probably describes *nervous tension* more than the cluster of physical and psychological responses that actually constitute stress. In fact, stress is not limited to negative situations; it is also a response to pleasurable physical challenges and the achievement of personal goals. Whether stress is experienced as pleasant or unpleasant depends largely on the situation and the individual. Because learning effective responses to whatever induces stress can enhance psychological health and help prevent a number of serious diseases, stress management is an important component in any wellness program.

This chapter explains the physiological and psychological reactions that make up the stress response and describes how these reactions can be risks to good health. The chapter also presents ways of managing stress with a personal program or with the help of others.

TERMS

stressor Any physical or psychological event or condition that produces stress.

stress response The physiological changes associated with stress.

stress The collective physiological and emotional responses to any stimulus that disturbs an individual's homeostasis.

autonomic nervous system The branch of the peripheral nervous system that, largely without conscious thought, controls basic body processes; consists of the sympathetic and parasympathetic nervous systems.

parasympathetic division A division of the autonomic nervous system that moderates the excitatory effect of the sympathetic nervous system, slowing metabolism and restoring energy supplies.

sympathetic division A division of the autonomic nervous system that reacts to danger or other challenges by almost instantly accelerating body processes.

endocrine system The system of glands, tissues, and cells that secrete hormones into the bloodstream to influence metabolism and other body processes.

hormone A chemical messenger produced in the body and transported in the bloodstream to target cells or organs for specific regulation of their activities.

cortisol A steroid hormone secreted by the cortex (outer layer) of the adrenal gland; also called *hydrocortisone*.

epinephrine A hormone secreted by the inner core of the adrenal gland; also called *adrenaline,* the "fear hormone."

norepinephrine A hormone secreted by the inner core of the adrenal gland; also called *noradrenaline,* the "anger hormone."

endorphins Brain secretions that have pain-inhibiting effects.

fight-or-flight reaction A defense reaction that prepares an individual for conflict or escape by triggering hormonal, cardiovascular, metabolic, and other changes.

In common usage, *stress* refers to two different things: situations that trigger physical and emotional reactions *and* the reactions themselves. In this text, we'll use the more precise term **stressor** for a situation that triggers physical and emotional reactions and the term **stress response** for those reactions. A final exam, then, is a stressor; sweaty palms and a pounding heart are symptoms of the stress response. We'll use the term **stress** to describe the general physical and emotional state that accompanies the stress response. A person taking a final exam experiences stress.

Physical Responses to Stressors

Imagine a near miss: as you step off the curb, a car careens toward you. With just a fraction of a second to spare, you leap safely out of harm's way. In that split second of danger, and in the moments following it, you have experienced a predictable series of physical reactions. Your body has gone from a relaxed state to one prepared for physical action to cope with a threat to your life. Two major control systems in your body are responsible for your physical response to stressors: the nervous system and the endocrine system.

Actions of the Nervous System The nervous system consists of the brain, spinal cord, and nerves. The part of the system that is not under conscious supervision, the **autonomic nervous system,** controls your heart rate, breathing, blood pressure, and hundreds of other functions you normally take for granted. The autonomic nervous system consists of two divisions. The **parasympathetic division** is in control when you are relaxed; it aids in digesting food, storing energy, and promoting growth. In contrast, the **sympathetic division** is activated when there is an emergency, such as severe pain, anger, or fear. Sympathetic nerves act on many targets—on nearly every organ, sweat gland, blood vessel, and muscle, in fact—to enable your body to handle an emergency. In general, the sympathetic division commands your body to stop storing energy and instead to mobilize all energy resources to respond to the crisis.

Actions of the Endocrine System One important target of the sympathetic nervous system is the activation of the **endocrine system.** This system of glands, tissues, and cells helps control body functions by releasing **hormones** and other chemical messengers into the bloodstream. These chemicals act on a variety of targets throughout the body. Along with the nervous system with which it closely interacts, the endocrine system helps prepare the body to respond to a stressor.

How do both systems work together in an emergency? Let's go back to your near car collision. As the car travels

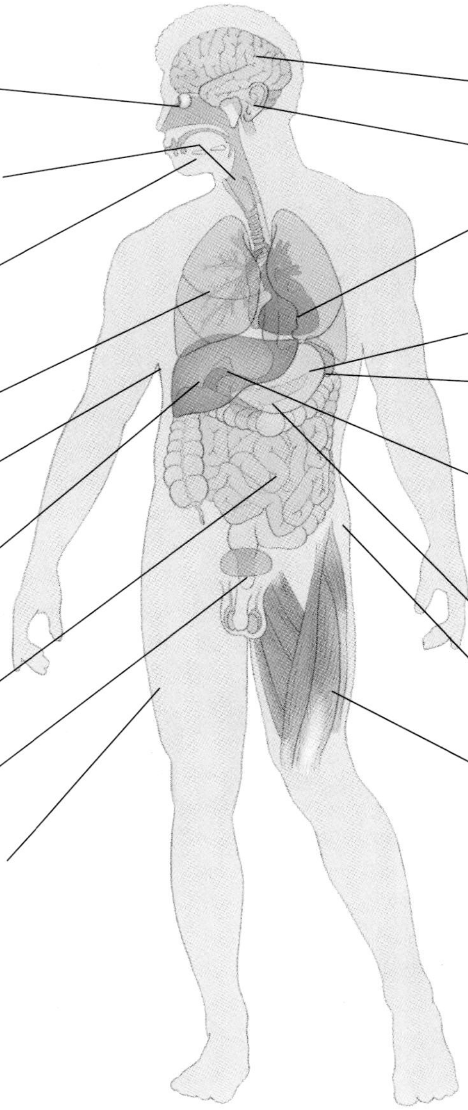

Pupils dilate to admit extra light for more sensitive vision.

Mucous membranes of nose and throat shrink, while muscles force a wider opening of passages to allow easier air flow.

Secretion of saliva and mucus decreases; digestive activities have a low priority in an emergency.

Bronchi dilate to allow more air into lungs.

Perspiration increases, especially in armpits, groin, hands, and feet, to flush out waste and cool overheating system by evaporation.

Liver releases sugar into bloodstream to provide energy for muscles and brain.

Muscles of intestines stop contracting because digestion has halted.

Bladder relaxes. Emptying of bladder contents releases excess weight, making it easier to flee.

Blood vessels in skin and viscera contract; those in skeletal muscles dilate. This increases blood pressure and delivery of blood to where it is most needed.

Endorphins are released to block any distracting pain.

Hearing becomes more acute.

Heart accelerates rate of beating, increases strength of contraction to allow more blood flow where it is needed.

Digestion, an unnecessary activity during an emergency, halts.

Spleen releases more red blood cells to meet an increased demand for oxygen and to replace any blood lost from injuries.

Adrenal glands stimulate secretion of epinephrine and norepinephrine, increasing blood sugar, blood pressure, and heart rate; also spur increase in amount of fat in blood. These changes provide an energy boost.

Pancreas decreases secretions because digestion has halted.

Fat is removed from storage and broken down to supply extra energy.

Voluntary (skeletal) muscles contract throughout the body, readying them for action.

Figure 10-1   The fight-or-flight reaction.   In response to a stressor, the autonomic nervous system and the endocrine system cause physical changes that prepare the body to deal with an emergency.

toward you, you feel only fear, but outside your awareness, things happen to prepare you to meet the danger. Chemical messages cause the release of key hormones, including **cortisol, epinephrine,** and **norepinephrine.** These hormones trigger a series of profound physiological changes (Figure 10-1):

- Hearing and vision become more acute.
- The heart rate accelerates in order to pump more oxygen through the body.
- The liver releases extra sugar into the bloodstream to provide an energy boost to the muscles and the brain.
- Perspiration increases to cool the skin.

- **Endorphins** are released to relieve pain in case of injury.

Taken together, these almost instantaneous physical changes are called the **fight-or-flight reaction.** They give you the heightened reflexes and strength you need to dodge the car or deal with other stressors. Although these physical changes may vary in intensity, the same basic set of physical reactions occurs in response to any type of stressor, positive or negative.

The Return to Homeostasis   Once a stressful situation ends, the parasympathetic division of your autonomic nervous system takes command and halts the reaction. It initiates the adjustments necessary to restore homeostasis, a state in which blood pressure, heart rate, hormone levels, and other vital functions are maintained within a narrow range of normal. Your parasympathetic nervous system calms your body down, slowing a rapid heartbeat, drying sweaty palms, and returning breathing to normal. Gradually, your body resumes its normal "housekeeping" functions, such as digestion and temperature regulation. Damage that may have been sustained during the fight-or-flight reaction is repaired. The day after you narrowly dodge the car, you wake up feeling fine. In this way, your body can grow, repair itself, and acquire reserves of energy. When the next crisis comes, you'll be ready to respond—instantly—again.

The Fight-or-Flight Reaction in Modern Life

The fight-or-flight reaction is a part of our biological heritage, and it's a survival mechanism that has served humankind well. In modern life, however, it is often absurdly inappropriate. Many of the stressors we face in everyday life do not require a physical response—for example, an exam, a mess left by a roommate, or a red traffic light. The fight-or-flight reaction prepares the body for physical action regardless of whether such action is a necessary or appropriate response to a particular stressor.

Emotional and Behavioral Responses to Stressors

The physical response to a stressor may vary in intensity from person to person and situation to situation, but we all experience a similar set of physical changes—the fight-or-flight reaction. Emotionally and behaviorally, however, individuals respond in very different ways to stressors.

Effective and Ineffective Responses

Common emotional responses to stressors include anxiety, depression, and fear. Although emotional responses are determined in part by inborn personality or temperament, we often can moderate or learn to control them. Coping techniques are discussed later in the chapter.

Behavioral responses to stressors—controlled by the somatic nervous system, which manages our conscious actions—are entirely under our control. Effective behavioral responses such as talking, laughing, exercising,

meditating, learning time-management skills, and finding a more compatible roommate can promote wellness and enable us to function at our best. Ineffective behavioral responses to stressors such as overeating and using tobacco, alcohol, or other drugs can impair wellness and even become stressors themselves.

Consider the individual variations demonstrated by two students, David and Amelia, responding to the same stressor—the first exam of the semester. David enters the exam with a feeling of dread, and, as he reads the exam questions, responds to his initial anxiety with more anxiety. The more emotionally upset he gets, the less he can remember and the more anxious he becomes. Soon he's staring into space, imagining what will happen if he fails the course. Amelia, on the other hand, takes a deep breath to relax before she reads the questions, wills herself to focus on the answers she knows, and then goes back over the exam to deal with those questions she's not sure of. She leaves the room feeling calm, relaxed, and confident that she has done well.

It's not difficult to see that avoiding destructive responses to stress and adopting effective and appropriate ones can have a direct effect on emotional and physical well-being.

Factors Influencing Emotional and Behavioral Responses to Stressors

A complex set of factors—temperament, health, life experiences, values, and coping skills—can influence an individual's response to a stressful situation. Personality, the sum of emotional and behavioral tendencies, plays a role in enabling people to cope more or less successfully with stress. People who are ultracompetitive, controlling, impatient, aggressive, and hostile (so-called Type A personalities) tend to react more explosively to stressors and have more problems coping with stress. In contrast, people with "hardy" personalities—those who view potential stressors as challenges and opportunities for growth and learning, rather than as burdens—tend to perceive fewer situations as stressful and to react more mildly to the stressors in their lives.

Past experiences can profoundly influence the evaluation of a potential stressor. Consider an individual who has had a bad experience giving a speech in the past. He or she is much more likely to perceive an upcoming speech assignment as stressful than someone who has had positive public speaking experiences. Gender and cultural background also influence our response to stressors. For example, some behavioral responses to stressors, such as crying or openly expressing anger, may be deemed more appropriate for one gender than the other.

The Stress Experience as a Whole

Physical, emotional, and behavioral responses to stressors are intimately interrelated. The more intense the emotional response, the stronger the physical response. Effec-

TERMS **homeostasis** A state of stability and consistency in an individual's physiological functioning.

somatic nervous system The branch of the peripheral nervous system that governs motor functions and sensory information; largely under our conscious control.

general adaptation syndrome (GAS) A pattern of stress responses consisting of three stages: alarm, resistance, and exhaustion.

eustress Stress resulting from a pleasant stressor.

distress Stress resulting from an unpleasant stressor.

The experience of stress depends on many factors, including the nature of the stressor. Although stress-producing events are commonly thought of as negative, exciting and fun experiences like this amusement park ride can also cause stress.

tive behavioral responses can lessen stress; ineffective ones only worsen it. Sometimes people have such intense responses to stressors or such ineffective coping techniques that they need professional help. (Lab 10-1 highlights some of the signals of excess stress.) More often, however, people can learn to handle stressors on their own.

STRESS AND DISEASE

The role of stress in health and disease is complex, and much remains to be learned about the exact mechanisms by which stress influences health. However, mounting evidence suggests that stress—interacting with a person's genetic predisposition, personality, social environment, and health-related behaviors—can increase vulnerability to numerous illnesses and ailments. Several theories have been proposed to explain the relationship between stress and disease.

The General Adaptation Syndrome

Biologist Hans Selye was one of the first scientists to develop a comprehensive theory of stress and disease. Based on his work in the 1930s and 1940s, Selye coined the term **general adaptation syndrome (GAS)** to describe what he believed is a universal and predictable response pattern to all stressors. He recognized that stressors could be pleasant, such as attending a party, or unpleasant, such as a bad grade. He called stress triggered by a pleasant stressor **eustress** and stress triggered by an unpleasant stressor **distress.** The sequence of physical responses associated with GAS is the same for both eustress and distress and occurs in three stages: alarm, resistance, and exhaustion.

Alarm The alarm stage includes the complex sequence of events brought on by the activation of the sympathetic nervous system and the endocrine system—the fight-or-flight reaction. During this stage, the body is more susceptible to disease or injury because it is geared up to deal with a crisis. A person in this phase may experience headaches, indigestion, anxiety, and disrupted sleeping and eating patterns.

Resistance Selye theorized that with continued stress, the body develops a new level of homeostasis in which it is more resistant to disease and injury than normal. During the resistance stage, a person can cope with normal life and added stress.

Exhaustion Both the mobilization of forces during the alarm reaction and the maintenance of homeostasis during the resistance stage require a considerable amount of energy. If a stressor persists, or if several stressors occur in succession, general exhaustion results. This is not the sort of exhaustion people complain of after a long, busy day. It's a life-threatening type of physiological exhaustion characterized by such symptoms as distorted perceptions and disorganized thinking.

While Selye's model of GAS is still viewed as an important contribution to modern stress theory, some of its key aspects are now discounted. For example, it is no longer believed that an increased susceptibility to disease after prolonged stress is due to a depletion of resources (Selye's exhaustion stage). Rather, the stress response itself is believed to cause illness and disease over time. In addition, the focus of research has changed to also include the emotional and behavioral responses to stressors—areas in which individuals vary significantly and where they may make positive changes to better manage stress.

Psychoneuroimmunology

One of the most fruitful areas of current research into the relationship between stress and disease is **psychoneuroimmunology (PNI)**. PNI is the study of the interactions among the nervous system, the endocrine system, and the immune system. The underlying premise of PNI is that stress, through the actions of the nervous and endocrine systems, impairs the immune system and thereby affects health.

Researchers have discovered a complex network of nerve and chemical connections between the nervous and endocrine systems and the immune system. We have already seen the profound physical effects of the hormones and other chemical messengers released during the stress response. These compounds also influence the immune system by affecting the number and efficiency of immune system cells, or lymphocytes.

The nervous, endocrine, and immune systems share other connections. Hormonelike substances called neuropeptides appear to translate emotions into physiological events. Neuropeptides are produced and received by both brain and immune cells, so that the brain and the immune system share a biochemical "language," which also happens to be the language of emotions. The biochemical changes accompanying particular emotions can strongly influence the functioning of the immune system.

Links Between Stress and Specific Conditions

Although much remains to be learned, it is clear that people who have unresolved chronic stress in their lives or who handle stressors poorly are at risk for a wide range of health problems. In the short term, the problem might just be a cold, a stiff neck, or a stomachache. Over the long term, the problems can be more severe—cardiovascular disease, high blood pressure, or impairment of the immune system.

Cardiovascular Disease   The stress response profoundly affects the cardiovascular system, and these changes have important implications for cardiovascular health, especially over the long term. During the stress response, heart rate increases and blood vessels constrict, causing blood pressure to rise. Chronic high blood pressure is a major cause of atherosclerosis, a disease in which the lining of the blood vessels becomes damaged and caked with fatty deposits. These deposits can block arteries, causing heart attacks and strokes (see Chapter 11).

Recent research suggests that certain types of emotional responses increase a person's risk of cardiovascular disease. So-called "hot reactors," people who exhibit extreme increases in heart rate and blood pressure in response to emotional stressors, may face an increased risk of cardiovascular problems.

Altered Functioning of the Immune System   Sometimes you seem to get sick when you can least afford it—during exam week, when you're going on vacation, or when you have a job interview. As described earlier regarding PNI, research suggests that this is more than mere coincidence. Some of the health problems linked to stress-related changes in immune function include vulnerability to colds and other infections, asthma and allergy attacks, susceptibility to cancer, and flare-ups of chronic diseases such as genital herpes and HIV infection.

Other Health Problems   Many other health problems may be caused or worsened by uncontrolled stress, including the following:

- Digestive problems such as stomachaches, diarrhea, constipation, irritable bowel syndrome, and ulcers
- Tension headaches and migraines
- Insomnia and fatigue (see the box "Overcoming Insomnia")
- Injuries, including on-the-job injuries caused by repetitive strain
- Menstrual irregularities, impotence, and pregnancy complications
- Psychological problems, including depression, anxiety, panic attacks, eating disorders, and post-traumatic stress disorder (PTSD), which afflicts people who have suffered or witnessed severe trauma

COMMON SOURCES OF STRESS

We are surrounded by stressors—at home, at school, on the job, and within ourselves. Being able to recognize potential sources of stress is an important step in successfully managing the stress in our lives.

Major Life Changes

Any major change in your life that requires adjustment and accommodation can be a source of stress. Early adulthood and the college years are typically associated with many significant changes, such as moving out of the family home, establishing new relationships, setting educational and career goals, and developing a sense of identity and purpose. Even changes typically thought of as positive—graduation, job promotion, marriage—can be stressful.

Researchers have hypothesized that clusters of life changes, particularly those that are perceived negatively, may be linked to health problems. (Lab 10-1 includes a

TERMS   **psychoneuroimmunology (PNI)**   The study of the interactions among the brain, the endocrine system, and the immune system.

burnout   A state of physical, mental, and emotional exhaustion.

Lack of sleep can be both a cause and an effect of excess stress. Without sufficient sleep, our mental and physical processes steadily deteriorate. We get headaches, feel irritable, are unable to concentrate, forget things, and may be more susceptible to illness. Adequate sleep, on the other hand, improves mood, fosters feelings of competence and self-worth, and supports optimal mental and emotional functioning.

At some time of life, most people have trouble falling asleep or staying asleep—a condition known as insomnia. Most people can overcome insomnia by discovering the cause of poor sleep and taking steps to remedy it. Insomnia that lasts for more than 6 months and interferes with daytime functioning requires consultation with a physician. Sleeping pills are not recommended for chronic insomnia because they can be habit-forming; they also lose their effectiveness over time.

If you're bothered by insomnia, here are some tips for getting a better night's sleep:

- Determine how much sleep you need to feel refreshed the next day, and don't sleep longer than that (but do make sure you get enough).

- Go to bed at the same time every night and, more important, get up at the same time every morning, 7 days a week. Don't nap during the day.

- Exercise every day, but not too close to bedtime. Your metabolism takes up to 6 hours to slow down after exercise.

- Avoid tobacco (nicotine is a stimulant), caffeine in the later part of the day, and alcohol before bedtime (it causes disturbed, fragmented sleep).

- Have a light snack before bedtime; you'll sleep better if you're not hungry.

- Deal with worries before bedtime. Try writing them down, along with some possible solutions, and then allow yourself to forget about them until the next day.

- Use your bed only for sleep. Don't eat, read, study, or watch television in bed.

- Relax before bedtime with a warm bath (again, not too close to bedtime—allow about 2 hours for your metabolism to slow down afterward), a book, music, or some relaxation exercises. Don't lie down in bed until you're sleepy.

- If you don't fall asleep in 15–20 minutes, or if you wake up and can't fall asleep again, get out of bed, leave the room if possible, and do something monotonous until you feel sleepy.

- Keep a perspective on your plight. Losing a night's sleep isn't the end of the world. Getting upset only makes it harder to fall asleep. Relax, and trust in your body's natural ability to drift off to sleep.

checklist of life events to help you determine if major life changes are a current source of stress in your life.) Personality and coping skills are important moderating influences, however. People with a strong support network and a stress-resistant personality are less likely to become ill in response to major life changes than people with fewer internal and external resources.

Daily Hassles

While major life changes are undoubtedly stressful, they seldom occur regularly. Researchers have proposed that minor problems—life's daily hassles—can be an even greater source of stress because they occur much more often. People who perceive hassles negatively are likely to experience a moderate stress response every time they are faced with one. Over time, this can take a significant toll on health. Studies indicate that for some people, daily hassles contribute to a general decrease in overall wellness.

College Stressors

College is a time of major life changes and abundant minor hassles. You are learning new information and skills and making major decisions about your future. You may be away from home for the first time, or you may be adding extra responsibilities to a life already filled with job and family. Some common sources of stress associated with college include academic responsibilities, social and interpersonal changes, time-related pressures, and financial concerns.

Job-Related Stressors

In recent surveys, Americans rate their jobs as one of the key sources of stress in their lives. Tight schedules and overtime leave less time to exercise, socialize, and engage in other stress-proofing activities. Worries about job performance, salary, and job security and interactions with bosses, coworkers, and customers can contribute to stress. High levels of job stress are also common for people who are left out of important decisions relating to their jobs. When workers are given the opportunity to shape how their jobs are performed, job satisfaction goes up and stress levels go down.

If job-related (or college-related) stress is severe or chronic, the result can be **burnout**, a state of physical, mental, and emotional exhaustion. Burnout occurs most often in highly motivated and driven individuals who come to feel that their work is not recognized or that they are not accomplishing their goals. People in the helping professions—teachers, social workers, caregivers, police officers, and so on—are also prone to burnout. For some

Taking exams is only one of many stressors associated with the college years. College can also be a time of major life events and numerous daily hassles.

people who suffer from burnout, a vacation or leave of absence may be appropriate. For others, a reduced work schedule, better communication with superiors, or a change in job goals may be necessary. Improving time-management skills can also help.

Interpersonal and Social Stressors

Although social support is a key buffer against stress, your interactions with others can themselves be a source of stress. Your relationships with family members and old friends may change during your college years as you develop new interests and a new course for your life. You will be meeting new people and establishing new relationships. All of these changes and experiences are potential stressors.

The community and society in which you live can also be major sources of stress. Social stressors include prejudice and discrimination. You may feel stress as you try to relate to people of other ethnic or socioeconomic groups. As a member of a particular ethnic group, you may feel pressure to assimilate into mainstream society. If English is not your first language, you face the added burden of conducting many daily activities in a language with which you may not be completely comfortable.

Other Stressors

Other stressors are found in the environment and in ourselves. Environmental stressors—external conditions or events that cause stress—include loud noises, unpleasant smells, industrial accidents, and natural disasters. Internal stressors can occur as we put pressure on ourselves to reach personal goals and evaluate our progress and performance. Physical and emotional states such as illness and exhaustion are other examples of internal stressors.

MANAGING STRESS

Stress is an inevitable part of life, and it's not going to go away. The issue is not how to avoid stress but rather how to manage it. While there are many approaches and specific techniques, in general the fundamental principles of physical and psychological fitness are themselves effective strategies for managing stress.

Social Support

People need people. Sharing fears, frustrations, and joys not only makes life richer but also seems to contribute—indirectly but significantly—to the well-being of body and mind. Research supports this conclusion: One study of college students living in overcrowded apartments, for example, found that those with a strong social support system were less distressed by their cramped quarters than were the "loners" who navigated life's challenges on their own. Other studies have shown that married people live longer than single people and have lower death rates from a wide range of conditions. And people infected with HIV remain symptom-free longer if they have a strong social support network. The crucial common denominator in all these findings is the meaningful connection with others. For more on developing and maintaining your social network, see the box "Building Social Support."

Exercise

One recent study found that taking a long walk can be effective at reducing anxiety and blood pressure. Another study showed that a brisk walk of as little as 10 minutes' duration can leave people feeling more relaxed and energetic for up to 2 hours. Regular exercise has even more

Meaningful connections with others can play a key role in stress management and overall wellness. A sense of isolation can lead to chronic stress, which in turn can increase one's susceptibility to temporary illnesses like colds and to chronic illnesses like heart disease. Although the mechanism isn't clear, social isolation can be as significant to mortality rates as factors like smoking, high blood pressure, and obesity.

There is no single best pattern of social support that works for everyone. You may need just one close friend and confidant, whereas your roommate may feel lonely without a large group of friends. To help determine whether your social network measures up, circle whether each of the following statements is true or false for you.

T F **1.** If I needed an emergency loan of $100, there is someone I could get it from.

T F **2.** There is someone who takes pride in my accomplishments.

T F **3.** I often meet or talk with family or friends.

T F **4.** Most people I know think highly of me.

T F **5.** If I needed an early morning ride to the airport, there's no one I would feel comfortable asking to take me.

T F **6.** I feel there is no one with whom I can share my most private worries and fears.

T F **7.** Most of my friends are more successful making changes in their lives than I am.

T F **8.** I would have a hard time finding someone to go with me on a day trip to the beach or country.

To calculate your score, add the number of true answers to questions 1–4 and the number of false answers to questions 5–8. If your score is 4 or more, you should have enough support to protect your health. If your score is 3 or less, you may need to reach out to strengthen your social ties. Some ways to do that include the following:

- *Foster friendships.* Keep in regular contact with your friends. Offer respect, trust, and acceptance, and provide help and support in times of need.

- *Keep your family ties strong.* Stay in touch with the family members you feel close to. Participate in family activities and celebrations.

- *Get involved with a group.* Do volunteer work, take a class, attend a lecture series, join a religious group. Choose activities that are meaningful to you and that include direct involvement with other people.

- *Build your communication skills.* The more you share your feelings with others, the closer the bonds between you will become. When others are speaking, be a considerate and attentive listener. (Chapter 15 includes more information on effective communication in intimate relationships.)

SOURCES: Social networks: The company you keep can keep you healthy. 1995. *Mayo Clinic Health Letter,* April. Ornish, D. 1991. The healing power of love. *Prevention,* February. QUIZ SOURCE: Japenga, A. 1995. A family of friends. *Health,* November/December, 94. Adapted with permission. Copyright © 1995 Health.

benefits. Researchers have found that people who exercise regularly react with milder physical stress responses before, during, and after exposure to stressors, and that their overall sense of well-being increases as well. Although even light exercise—a brisk walk, an easy bike outing—can have a beneficial effect, an integrated fitness program like the one recommended in this book can have a significant impact on stress.

One warning: For some people, exercise can become just one more stressor in a highly stressed life. People who exercise compulsively risk overtraining, a condition characterized by fatigue, irritability, depression, and diminished athletic performance. An overly strenuous exercise program can even make a person sick by compromising immune function. For the details of a safe and effective exercise program, refer to Chapter 7.

Nutrition

As discussed in Chapter 8, a healthy, balanced diet will supply the energy needed to cope with stress. Two additional nutrition tips for stress management are to limit or avoid caffeine and to avoid the high-potency vitamin compounds and amino acid supplements designated as "stress formulas." (These supplements are worthless for reducing tension or anxiety.)

Time Management

Learning to manage your time successfully can be crucial to coping with everyday stressors. Overcommitment, procrastination, and even boredom are significant stressors for many people. Along with gaining control of nutrition and exercise to maintain a healthy energy balance, time management is an important element in a wellness program. Try these strategies for improving your time-management skills:

- *Set priorities.* Divide your tasks into three groups: essential, important, and trivial. Focus on the first two. Ignore the third.

- *Schedule tasks for peak efficiency.* You've undoubtedly noticed you're most productive at certain times of the day (or night). Schedule as many of your tasks for those hours as you can, and stick to your schedule.

Exercise is a particularly effective antidote to stress. A lunchtime walk gives these coworkers a chance to both exercise and foster friendships.

- *Set realistic goals, and write them down.* Attainable goals spur you on. Impossible goals, by definition, cause frustration and failure. Fully commit yourself to achieving your goals by putting them in writing.

- *Budget enough time.* For each project you undertake, calculate how long it will take to complete. Then tack on another 10–15%, or even 25%, as a buffer.

- *Break up long-term goals into short-term ones.* Instead of waiting for or relying on large blocks of time, use short amounts of time to start a project or keep it moving.

- *Visualize the achievement of your goals.* By mentally rehearsing your performance of a task, you will be able to reach your goal more smoothly.

- *Keep track of the tasks you put off.* Analyze the reasons why you procrastinate. If the task is difficult or unpleasant, look for ways to make it easier or more fun. For example, if you find the readings for one of your classes particularly difficult, choose an especially nice setting for your reading and then reward yourself each time you complete a section or chapter.

- *Consider doing your least favorite tasks first.* Once you have the most unpleasant ones out of the way, you can work on the projects you enjoy more.

- *Consolidate tasks when possible.* For example, try walking to the store so that you run your errands and exercise in the same block of time.

- *Identify quick transitional tasks.* Keep a list of 5-minute tasks you can do while waiting or between other tasks, such as watering your plants, doing the dishes, or checking a homework assignment.

- *Delegate responsibility.* Asking for help when you have too much to do is no cop-out; it's good time management. Just don't delegate to others the jobs you know you should do yourself.

- *Say no when necessary.* If the demands made on you don't seem reasonable, say no—tactfully, but without guilt or apology.

- *Give yourself a break.* Allow time for play—free, unstructured time when you ignore the clock. Don't consider this a waste of time. Play renews you and enables you to work more efficiently.

- *Stop thinking or talking about what you're going to do, and just do it!* Sometimes the best solution for procrastination is to stop waiting for the right moment and just get started. You will probably find that things are not as bad as you feared, and your momentum will keep you going.

For more help with time management, complete Activity 10 in the Behavior Change Workbook at the end of the text.

Cognitive Techniques

Certain thought patterns and ways of thinking, including ideas, beliefs, and perceptions, can contribute to stress and have a negative impact on health. But other habits of mind, if practiced with patience and consistency, can help break unhealthy thought patterns. Below are some suggestions for changing destructive thinking.

- Modify expectations; they often restrict experience and lead to disappointment. Try to accept life as it comes.

Do your patterns of thinking make events seem worse than they truly are? Do negative beliefs about yourself become self-fulfilling prophecies? Substituting realistic self-talk for negative self-talk can help you build and maintain self-esteem and cope better with the challenges in your life. Here are some examples of common types of distorted negative self-talk, along with suggestions for more accurate and rational responses.

Cognitive Distortion	Negative Self-Talk	Realistic Self-Talk
Focusing on negatives	School is so discouraging—nothing but one hassle after another.	School is pretty challenging and has its difficulties, but there certainly are rewards. It's really a mixture of good and bad.
Expecting the worst	Why would my boss want to meet with me this afternoon if not to fire me?	I wonder why my boss wants to meet with me. I guess I'll just have to wait and see.
Overgeneralizing	(After getting a poor grade on a paper) Just as I thought—I'm incompetent at everything.	I'll start working on the next paper earlier. That way, if I run into problems, I'll have time to consult with the TA.
Minimizing	I won the speech contest, but none of the other speakers was very good. I wouldn't have done as well against stiffer competition.	It may not have been the best speech I'll ever give, but it was good enough to win the contest. I'm really improving as a speaker.
Blaming others	I wouldn't have eaten so much last night if my friends hadn't insisted on going to that restaurant.	I overdid it last night. Next time I'll make different choices.
Expecting perfection	I should have scored 100% on this test. I can't believe I missed that one problem through a careless mistake.	Too bad I missed one problem through carelessness, but overall I did very well on this test. Next time I'll be more careful.

SOURCE: Adapted from Schafer, W. 1996. *Stress Management for Wellness,* 3d ed. Copyright © 1996 by Holt, Rinehart, and Winston. Reprinted by permission of the publisher.

- Monitor your self-talk, and attempt to minimize hostile, critical, suspicious, and self-deprecating thoughts (see the box "Realistic Self-Talk").

- Live in the present; clear your mind of old debris and fears for the future in order to enjoy life as it is now.

- "Go with the flow." Accept what you can't change, forgive faults, be flexible.

- Laugh. Seek out therapeutic humor (not dark or offensive humor, which is an unconscious means of dealing with fears). Laughter can temporarily elevate the heart rate, aid digestion, relax muscles, ease pain, and trigger the release of endorphins.

Clear Communication

Clear, honest, open communication is a crucial component of healthy relationships. Poor communication can cause feelings of anger and frustration and significantly increase your levels of stress. The people who make up your social support system cannot respond to specific needs if they don't know what those needs are. See Chapter 15 for more information on effective communication.

Relaxation Techniques

According to Herbert Benson of Harvard Medical School, relaxation techniques can trigger the **relaxation response,** a physiological state characterized by a feeling of warmth and quiet mental alertness. This response is the opposite of the fight-or-flight reaction. When the relaxation response is triggered, heart rate, breathing, and metabolism slow down; blood flow to the brain and skin increases; and brain waves shift from an alert beta rhythm to a relaxed alpha rhythm.

The techniques described in this section, and in the box "Stress-Management Techniques from Around the World," are among the most popular techniques and the easiest to learn. Other techniques, such as massage, self-hypnosis, and biofeedback, require a partner or professional training or assistance. All these techniques take practice, and it may be several weeks before the benefits become noticeable in everyday life.

relaxation response A physiological state characterized by a **TERMS** feeling of warmth and quiet mental alertness.

The origins of techniques for relaxation span many continents and many centuries. Three techniques that originated outside Western culture but are growing in popularity in the United States are meditation, hatha yoga, and t'ai chi ch'uan. Although you may not choose to adopt the philosophical bases of these techniques, all of them can help you manage stress by promoting the relaxation response.

Meditation

At its most basic level, meditation, or self-reflective thought, involves quieting or emptying the mind in order to achieve deep relaxation. Some practitioners of meditation view it on a deeper level as a means of focusing concentration, increasing self-awareness, and bringing enlightenment to their lives. The origins of meditation can be traced back to the sixth century B.C. in Asia. Meditation has been integrated into the practices of several religions—Buddhism, Hinduism, Confucianism, and Taoism—but it is not a religion itself, nor does its practice require any special knowledge, belief, or background.

There are two general styles of meditation, centered around different ways of quieting the mind. In exclusive meditation, one focuses on a single word or thought, eliminating all others. In inclusive meditation, the mind is allowed to wander uncontrolled from thought to thought, but one must observe these thoughts in a detached way, without judgment or emotion. Exclusive meditation tends to be easier to learn. Several years ago, Herbert Benson developed a simple, practical technique for eliciting the relaxation response using exclusive meditation:

1. Pick a word, phrase, or object to focus on. You can choose a word or phrase that has a deep meaning for you, but any word or phrase will work. In Zen meditation, the word *mu* (literally, "absolutely nothing") is often used. Some meditators prefer to focus on their breathing.

2. Sit comfortably in a quiet place, and close your eyes if you're not focusing on an object.

3. Relax your muscles.

4. Breathe slowly and naturally. If you're using a focus word or phrase, silently repeat it each time you exhale. If you're using an object, focus on it as you breathe.

5. Keep your attitude passive. Disregard thoughts that drift in.

6. Continue for 10–20 minutes, once or twice a day.

7. After you've finished, sit quietly for a few minutes with your eyes closed, then open. Then stand up.

Allow relaxation to occur at its own pace; don't try to force it. Don't be surprised if you can't tune your mind out for more than a few seconds at a time. It's nothing to get angry about. The more you ignore the intrusions, the easier it will become. If you want to time your session, peek at a watch or clock occasionally, but don't set a jarring alarm.

The technique works best on an empty stomach, before a meal or about 2 hours after eating. Avoid times of day when you're tired, unless you want to fall asleep.

Although you'll feel refreshed even after the first session, it may take a month or more to get noticeable results. Be patient. Eventually the relaxation response will become so natural that it will occur spontaneously, or on demand, when you sit quietly for a few moments.

Progressive Relaxation   In this simple relaxation technique, you tense, then relax, the muscles of the body, one by one. Also known as deep muscle relaxation, this technique addresses the muscle tension that occurs when the body is experiencing stress. Consciously relaxing tensed muscles sends a message to other body systems to reduce the stress response.

To practice progressive relaxation, begin by inhaling as you contract your right fist. Then exhale as you release your fist. Repeat. Contract and relax your right bicep. Repeat. Do the same using your left arm. Then, working from forehead to feet, contract and relax other muscles. Repeat each contraction at least once, inhaling as you tense and exhaling as you relax. To speed up the process, tense and relax more muscles at one time—for example, both arms simultaneously. With practice you'll be able to relax quickly by simply clenching and releasing only your fists.

Visualization   Visualization, also known as using imagery, is so effective in enhancing sports performance that it has become a part of the curriculum at training camps for U.S. Olympic athletes. This same technique can be used to induce relaxation, to help change habits, or to improve performance on an exam, on stage, or on a playing field.

To practice visualization, imagine yourself floating on a cloud, sitting on a mountaintop, or lying in a meadow. Try to identify all the perceptible qualities of the environment—sight, sound, temperature, smell, and so on. Your body will respond as if your imagery were real.

An alternative is to close your eyes and imagine a deep purple light filling your body. Then change the color into a soothing gold. As the color lightens, so should your distress. Imagery can also enhance performance: Visualize yourself succeeding at a task that worries you.

Deep Breathing   Your breathing pattern is closely tied to your stress level. Deep, slow breathing is associated with relaxation. Rapid, shallow, often irregular breathing occurs during the stress response. With practice, you can learn to slow and quiet your breathing pattern, thereby

Hatha Yoga

Yoga is an ancient Sanskrit word meaning "union"; it refers specifically to the union of mind, body, and soul. The development and practice of yoga are rooted in the Hindu philosophy of spiritual enlightenment. The founders of yoga developed a system of physical postures, called *asanas,* designed to cleanse the body, unlock energy paths, and raise the level of consciousness.

Hatha yoga, the most common yoga style practiced in the United States, emphasizes physical balance and breathing control. It integrates components of flexibility, muscular strength and endurance, and muscle relaxation; it also sometimes serves as a preliminary to meditation.

A session of hatha yoga typically involves a series of *asanas,* held for a few seconds to several minutes, that stretch and relax different parts of the body. The emphasis is on breathing, stretching, and balance. There are hundreds of different *asanas,* and they must be performed correctly in order to be beneficial. For this reason, qualified instruction is recommended, particularly for beginners. Yoga classes are offered through many community recreation centers, YMCAs and YWCAs, and private clubs. Regardless of whether you accept the philosophy and symbolism of different *asanas,* the practice of yoga can induce the relaxation response as well as develop flexibility, muscular strength and endurance, and body awareness.

T'ai Chi Ch'uan

A martial art that developed in China, t'ai chi ch'uan is a system of self-defense that incorporates philosophical concepts from Taoism and Confucianism. An important part of this philosophy is *chi,* an energy force that surrounds and permeates all things. In addition to serving as a means of self-defense, the goal of t'ai chi ch'uan is to bring the body into balance and harmony with this universal energy, in order to promote health and spiritual growth. It teaches practitioners to remain calm and centered, to conserve and concentrate energy, and to harmonize with fear. T'ai chi ch'uan seeks to manipulate force by becoming part of it—"going with the flow," so to speak.

T'ai chi ch'uan is considered the gentlest of the martial arts. Instead of using quick and powerful movements, t'ai chi ch'uan consists of a series of slow, fluid, elegant movements, which reinforce the idea of moving *with* rather than *against* the stressors of everyday life. The practice of t'ai chi ch'uan promotes relaxation and concentration as well as the development of body awareness, balance, muscular strength, and flexibility. (An Emory University study found that a group of older adults who completed a t'ai chi ch'uan course reduced their risk of falling by nearly 50% compared with a control group.) It usually takes some time and practice to reap the stress-management benefits of t'ai chi ch'uan, and, as with yoga, it's best to begin with some qualified instruction.

SOURCES: Adapted from Can yoga make you fit? 1997. *UC Berkeley Wellness Letter,* May. A movement toward t'ai chi. 1997. *Harvard Health Letter,* July. Seaward, B. L. 1996. *Managing Stress: Principles and Strategies for Health and Wellbeing,* 2d ed. Boston: Jones and Bartlett. Benson, H., with W. Proctor. 1984. *Beyond the Relaxation Response.* New York: Times Books.

also quieting your mind and relaxing your body. Try one of the breathing techniques described in the box "Breathing for Relaxation" for on-the-spot tension relief, as well as for long-term stress reduction.

GETTING HELP

You can use the principles of behavioral self-management described in Chapter 1 to create a stress-management program tailored specifically to your needs. The starting point of a successful program is to listen to your body. When you learn to recognize the stress response and the emotions and thoughts that accompany it, you'll be in a position to take charge of how you handle stress. Labs 10-1 and 10-2 can guide you in identifying and finding ways to cope with stress-inducing situations.

If you have attempted to fashion a stress-management program to cope with the stressors in your life but still feel overwhelmed, you may want to seek outside help in the form of a self-help book, a peer counselor, a support group, or psychotherapy. Excellent self-help guides can be found in bookstores or in the library. Peer counseling, often available through the student health center or student affairs office, is usually staffed by volunteer students with special training that emphasizes maintaining confidentiality. Peer counselors can steer those seeking help to appropriate campus and community resources or just offer sympathetic listening.

Support groups are typically organized around a particular issue or problem; for example, all group members might be entering a new school, reentering school after a long interruption, struggling with single parenting, experiencing eating disorders, or coping with particular kinds of trauma. Simply voicing concerns that others share can relieve stress.

Psychotherapy, especially a short-term course of sessions, can also be tremendously helpful in dealing with stress-related problems. Not all therapists are right for all people, so it's a good idea to shop around for a compatible psychotherapist with reasonable fees.

Diaphragmatic Breathing

1. Lie on your back with your body relaxed.

2. Place one hand on your chest and one on your abdomen. (You will use your hands to monitor the depth and location of your breathing.)

3. Inhale slowly and deeply through your nose into your abdomen. Your abdomen should push up as far as is comfortable. Your chest should expand only a little and only in conjunction with the movement of your abdomen.

4. Exhale gently through your mouth.

5. Continue for about 5–10 minutes per session. Focus on the sound and feel of your breathing.

Breathing In Relaxation, Breathing Out Tension

1. Assume a comfortable position, lying on your back or sitting in a chair.

2. Inhale slowly and deeply into your abdomen. Imagine the inhaled, warm air flowing to all parts of your body. Say to yourself, "Breathe in relaxation."

3. Exhale from your abdomen. Imagine tension flowing out of your body. Say to yourself, "Breathe out tension."

4. Pause before you inhale.

5. Continue for 5–10 minutes or until no tension remains.

Chest Expansion

1. Sit in a comfortable chair, or stand.

2. Inhale slowly and deeply into your abdomen as you raise your arms out to the sides. Pull your shoulders and arms back and lift your chin slightly so that your chest opens up.

3. Exhale gradually as you lower your arms and chin, and return to the starting position.

4. Repeat five to ten times or until your breathing is deep and regular and your body feels relaxed and energized.

Quick Tension Release

1. Inhale into your abdomen slowly and deeply as you count slowly to 4.

2. Exhale slowly as you again count slowly to 4. As you exhale, concentrate on relaxing your face, neck, shoulders, and chest.

3. Repeat several times. With each exhalation, feel more tension leaving your body.

SOURCES: Stop stress with a deep breath. 1996. *Health,* October, 53. Breathing for health and relaxation. 1995. *Mental Medicine Update,* 4(2): 3–6. When you're stressed, catch your breath. 1995. *Mayo Clinic Health Letter,* December, 5.

SUMMARY

- Stress is the collective physiological and emotional response to any stressor. Physiological responses to stressors are the same for everyone.

- The autonomic nervous system and the endocrine system are responsible for the body's physical response to stressors. The sympathetic nervous system mobilizes the body and activates key hormones of the endocrine system, causing the fight-or-flight reaction. The parasympathetic system returns the body to homeostasis.

- Behavioral responses to stress are controlled by the somatic nervous system and fall under a person's conscious control.

- The general adaptation syndrome model and research in psychoneuroimmunology contribute to our understanding of the links between stress and disease. People who have many stressors in their lives or handle stress poorly are at risk for cardiovascular disease, impairment of the immune system, and many other problems.

- Potential sources of stress include major life changes, daily hassles, college and job-related stressors, and interpersonal and social stressors.

- Ways of managing stress include regular exercise, good nutrition, time management, support from other people, relaxation techniques, modified thought patterns, and clear communication.

- If a personal program for stress management doesn't work, peer counseling, support groups, and psychotherapy are available.

FOR MORE INFORMATION

You'll probably find courses and seminars on your campus or in your community that teach ways of dealing with stress. Some may be specifically devoted to such issues as time management, test taking, or public speaking. If you're experiencing severe symptoms of stress or if your symptoms last for several weeks, consult a physician or counselor. Most campuses provide student psychological services that are free and informal. Your student health center may also provide peer counseling.

Books

Ali, M. 1996. *What Do Lions Know About Stress?* Denville, N.J.: Life Span Press. *A provocative, often amusing look at the relationship between stress and health.*

COMMON QUESTIONS ANSWERED

Are there any relaxation techniques I can use in response to an immediate stressor? There are various strategies for dealing with stressors on the spot. In addition to the deep breathing techniques described in the chapter, try some of the following to see which ones work best for you:

- Do a full-body stretch while standing or sitting. Stretch your arms out to the sides and then reach them as far as possible over your head. Rotate your body from the waist. Bend over as far as is comfortable for you.

- Do a partial session of progressive muscle relaxation. Tense and then relax some of the muscles in your body. Focus on the muscles that are stiff or tense. Shake out your arms and legs.

- Take a short, brisk walk (3–5 minutes). Breathe deeply.

- Engage in realistic self-talk about the stressor. Mentally rehearse dealing successfully with the stressor. As an alternative, focus your mind on some other activity.

Can stress cause a person to become depressed? Although not often the sole factor in the development of depression, poor stress-management skills can contribute to depression, and depression can be a sign of excess stress. Depression is more than just having a bad day; it is a serious disorder characterized by a negative self-concept, meaning that a person feels unloved and ineffective. Poor stress-management skills can reinforce a negative self-concept by sabotaging personal relationships and academic and professional performance. In addition to a negative self-concept, severe depression can include the following:

- Pervasive feelings of sadness and hopelessness
- Loss of pleasure in usual activities
- Poor appetite and weight loss
- Insomnia, especially early morning awakening
- Restlessness or lethargy
- Thoughts of worthlessness and guilt
- An inability to concentrate
- Thoughts of suicide

Not all of these symptoms are present in everyone who is depressed, but most do experience a loss of interest or pleasure in their usual activities. In some cases, depression, like severe stress, is a clear-cut reaction to specific events, such as the loss of a loved one or failing in school or work. In other cases, no trigger event is obvious.

Suicide is a danger in cases of severe depression. Warning signs include expressing the wish to be dead; revealing contemplated suicide methods; increasing social withdrawal and isolation; and a sudden, inexplicable lightening of mood (which can indicate the person has finally decided to commit suicide). If you are severely depressed or know someone who is, expert help from a mental health professional is essential. Most communities have emergency help available, often in the form of a hotline telephone counseling service. Large colleges typically have health services and counseling centers that can provide help; professional therapists can also be located through the local telephone book.

Greenberg, J. S. 1996. *Comprehensive Stress Management.* Dubuque, Ia.: Brown and Benchmark. *An easy-to-understand guide to identifying and combatting stressors; includes a separate chapter on college stress.*

Sapadin, L., and J. Maguire. 1997. *It's About Time! The Six Styles of Procrastination and How to Overcome Them.* New York: Penguin. *Uses quizzes and case studies to trace procrastinating behavior to personality traits and early family dynamics.*

Sapolsky, R. M. 1994. *Why Zebras Don't Get Ulcers: A Guide to Stress-Related Diseases, and Coping.* New York: W. H. Freeman. *An entertaining look at the effects of stress on the body and the relationship between stress and disease.*

Smith, L. W. 1997. *Scientific American Focus: Of Mind and Body.* New York: Henry Holt. *An introduction to mind-body medicine, psychoneuroimmunology, and relaxation techniques.*

Organizations and Web Sites

American Psychological Association. Provides information on stress management and psychological disorders.
202-336-5500
http://www.apa.org

Association for Applied Psychophysiology and Biofeedback. Provides information and links about biofeedback.
800-477-8892
http://www.aapb.org

Center for Anxiety and Stress Treatment. A commercial site that includes an anxiety symptom checklist and stress-busting tips for work stress.
http://www.stressrelease.com

Duquesne University Stress Links. Provides links to sites with stress-management strategies, many designed especially for college students.
http://the-duke.duq-duke.duq.edu/special/stress.htm

The Humor Project. A clearinghouse for information and practical ideas related to humor.
518-587-8770
http://www.humorproject.com

National Institute of Mental Health (NIMH). Offers information about stress and stress management as well as other aspects of psychological health, including anxiety, depression, and eating disorders.
800-421-4211; 301-443-4536
http://www.nimh.nih.gov

Stress Free NET. A commercial Web site containing stress-related services and tools, including a directory of health and stress-management professionals.
http://www.stressfree.com

Yang Style Tai Chi. Provides an introduction to t'ai chi ch'uan, including its history and a discussion of various styles.
http://www.chebucto.ns.ca/Philosophy/Taichi

SELECTED BIBLIOGRAPHY

Andersen, B. L., et al. 1998. Stress and immune responses after surgical treatment for regional breast cancer. *Journal of the National Cancer Institute* 90(1): 30–36.

Anshel, M. 1996. Effect of chronic aerobic exercise and progressive relaxation on motor performance and affect following acute stress. *Behavioral Medicine* 21:186–196.

Arnetz, B., and C. Wilholm. 1997. Technological stress: Psychophysiological symptoms in modern offices. *Journal of Psychosomatic Research* 43(1): 35–42.

Ashton, C., Jr., et al. 1997. Self-hypnosis reduces anxiety following coronary artery bypass surgery. A prospective, randomized trial. *Journal of Cardiovascular Surgery* 38(1): 69–75.

Barnett, P. 1997. Psychological stress and the progression of carotid artery disease. *Journal of Hypertension* 15:49–55.

Birmaher, B., et al. 1994. Cellular immunity in depressed, conduct disorder, and normal adolescents: Role of adverse life events. *Journal of the American Academy of Child and Adolescent Psychiatry* 33(5): 671–678.

Brownley, K. 1996. Social support and hostility interact to influence clinic, work, and home blood pressure in black and white men and women. *Psychophysiology* 33:434–445.

Chicester, B., and P. Garfinkel. 1997. *Stress Blasters: Quick and Simple Steps to Take Control and Perform Under Pressure.* Emmaus, Pa.: Rodale Press.

Dill, P. L., and T. B. Henley. 1998. Stressors of college: A comparison of traditional and nontraditional students. *Journal of Psychology* 132(1): 25–32.

Domar, A. D., and H. Dreher. 1996. *Healing Mind, Healthy Woman: Using the Mind-Body Connection to Manage Stress and Take Control of Your Health.* New York: Henry Holt.

Flach, J., and L. Seachrist. 1994. Mind-body meld may boost immunity. *Journal of the National Cancer Institute* 86(4): 256–258.

Gillin, J. 1996. Race and sex differences in cardiovascular recovery from acute stress. *International Journal of Psychophysiology* 23:83–90.

Gramer, M. 1996. The availability of social support reduces cardiovascular reactivity to acute psychological stress. *Journal of Experimental Psychology* 43:256–278.

Hagihara, A., et al. 1997. Type A and Type B behaviors, work stressors, and social support at work. *Preventive Medicine* 26(4): 486–494.

Hansel, S. 1997. Appraisal and coping strategies in stressful situations: A comparison of individuals who binge eat and controls. *International Journal of Eating Disorders* 21:89–93.

How to get a good night's sleep. 1997. *Consumer Reports,* March.

Johansen, D. 1997. Psychological stress, cancer incidence and mortality from nonmalignant diseases. *British Journal of Cancer* 75:144–148.

Kamarck, T. W., et al. 1998. Effects of task strain, social conflict, and emotional activation on ambulatory cardiovascular activity: Daily life consequences of recurring stress in a multiethnic adult sample. *Health Psychology* 17(1): 17–29.

Kang, D. 1997. Immune responses to final exams in healthy and asthmatic adolescents. *Nurse Researcher* 46:12–19.

Krug, E. G., et al. 1998. Suicide after natural disasters. *New England Journal of Medicine* 338(6): 373–378.

Lester, D. 1996. Social stress, homicide, and suicide. *Psychological Reports* 79:922.

Pike, J. L., et al. 1997. Chronic life stress alters sympathetic, neuroendocrine, and immune responsivity to an acute psychological stressor in humans. *Psychosomatic Medicine* 59(4): 447–457.

Reinhold, B. B. 1996. *Toxic Work: How to Overcome Stress, Overload, and Burnout and Revitalize Your Career.* New York: Dutton.

Selye, H. 1976. *The Stress of Life,* rev. ed. New York: McGraw-Hill.

Spiegel, D., and R. Moore. 1997. Imagery and hypnosis in the treatment of cancer patients. *Oncology* 11(8): 1179–1189.

Strogatz, D. S., et al. 1997. Social support, stress, and blood pressure in black adults. *Epidemiology* 8(5): 482–487.

Toates, F. 1995. *Stress: Conceptual and Biological Aspects.* New York: Wiley.

Uchino, B. 1997. Cardiovascular effects of active coping behavior in mental and social stress situations during various incentive conditions. *Journal of Behavioral Medicine* 20:15–27.

Ystgaard, M. 1997. Life stress, social support, and psychological distress in late adolescence. *Social Psychiatry and Psychiatric Epidemiology* 32(5): 277–283.

LAB 10-1 *Identifying Your Stressors*

Signals of Excess Stress

To identify the sources of stress in your life, you must first be able to identify the signals of excess stress. Put a check mark next to any of the following signs you have experienced in the last month.

Emotional Signs

_____ Tendency to be irritable or aggressive
_____ Tendency to feel anxious, fearful, or edgy
_____ Hyperexcitability, impulsiveness, or emotional instability
_____ Depression
_____ Frequent feelings of boredom
_____ Inability to concentrate
_____ Fatigue

Behavioral Signs

_____ Increased use of tobacco, alcohol, or other drugs
_____ Excessive TV watching
_____ Sleep disturbances or excessive sleep
_____ Overeating or undereating
_____ Sexual problems
_____ Crying or yelling
_____ Job or school burnout

_____ Spouse or child abuse
_____ Panic attack

Physical Signs

_____ Pounding heart
_____ Trembling with nervous tics
_____ Grinding of teeth
_____ Dry mouth
_____ Excessive perspiration
_____ Gastrointestinal problems (diarrhea, constipation, indigestion, queasy stomach)
_____ Stiff neck or aching lower back
_____ Migraine or tension headaches
_____ Frequent colds or low-grade infections
_____ Cold hands and feet
_____ Allergy or asthma attacks
_____ Skin problems (e.g., hives, eczema, psoriasis)

Possible Stressful Life Changes

Listed below, in order of probable severity of effect, are 35 life events that cause stress. Put a check mark next to any item you have experienced recently or expect to experience soon. If you find you've checked several items, take time out from your daily routine to develop and cultivate your coping skills.

_____ Death of a close family member
_____ Divorce or separation from mate
_____ Detention in jail or other institution
_____ Major personal injury or illness
_____ Death of a close friend
_____ Divorce between parents
_____ Marriage
_____ Being fired from job or expelled from school
_____ Retirement
_____ Change in health of a family member
_____ Pregnancy
_____ Being a victim of crime
_____ Sexual difficulties
_____ Gaining new family members (through birth, adoption, older person moving in, etc.)
_____ New boyfriend or girlfriend
_____ Major business or academic readjustment (merger, change of job or major, failing course)
_____ Major change in financial state (a lot worse or a lot better off than before)
_____ Taking out a loan or mortgage for school or a major purchase

_____ Trouble with parents, spouse, or girlfriend or boyfriend
_____ Outstanding personal achievement
_____ Graduation
_____ First quarter/semester in college
_____ Denied admission to program or school
_____ Change in living conditions
_____ Serious argument with instructor, friend, or roommate
_____ Lower grades than expected
_____ Major change in working hours or conditions, or increased workload at school
_____ Major change in recreational, social, or church activities
_____ Major change in sleeping or eating habits
_____ Denied admission to required course
_____ Taking out a loan for a lesser purchase (e.g., a car, TV, or freezer)
_____ Chronic car trouble
_____ Change in number of family get-togethers
_____ Vacation
_____ Minor violation of the law (traffic tickets, etc.)

Weekly Stress Log

Now that you are familiar with the signals of stress, complete the weekly stress log to map patterns in your stress levels and identify sources of stress. Enter a score for each hour of each day according to the ratings listed below.

	A.M.							P.M.												Average
	6	7	8	9	10	11	12	1	2	3	4	5	6	7	8	9	10	11	12	
Monday																				
Tuesday																				
Wednesday																				
Thursday																				
Friday																				
Saturday																				
Sunday																				
Average																				

Ratings

1 = No anxiety; general feeling of well-being
2 = Mild anxiety; no interference with activity
3 = Moderate anxiety; specific signal(s) of stress present
4 = High anxiety; interference with activity
5 = Very high anxiety and panic reactions; general inability to engage in activity

To identify daily or weekly patterns in your stress level, average your stress rating for each hour and each day. For example, if your scores for 6:00 A.M. are 3, 3, 4, 3, and 4, with blanks for Saturday and Sunday, your 6:00 A.M. rating would be 17 ÷ 5, or 3.4 (moderate to high anxiety). Finally, calculate an average weekly stress score by averaging your daily average stress scores. Your weekly average will give you a sense of your overall level of stress.

Identifying Sources of Stress

External stressors: List several people, places, or events that caused you a significant amount of discomfort this week.

_____

_____

_____

Internal stressors: Make a list of any recurring thoughts or worries that produced feelings of discomfort this week.

_____

_____

_____

To monitor your progress toward your goal, enter the results of this lab in the Preprogram Assessment column of Appendix D. After several weeks of a stress-management program, do this lab again and enter the results in the Postprogram Assessment column of Appendix D. How do the results compare?

SOURCE: List of major life changes adapted with permission from Holmes, T. H., and R. H. Rahe. 1967. The social readjustment scale. *Journal of Psychosomatic Research* 11(2): 213–218. Elsevier Science, Inc.

Name _____ Section _____ Date _____

 LAB 10-2 *Stress-Management Techniques*

Part I. Lifestyle Stress Management

For each of the areas listed in the table below, describe your current lifestyle as it relates to stress management. For example, do you have enough social support? How are your exercise and nutrition habits? Is time management a problem for you? For each area, list two ways that you could change your current habits to help you manage your stress. Sample strategies might include calling a friend before a challenging class, taking a short walk before lunch, and buying and using a date book to track your time.

	Current lifestyle	Lifestyle change #1	Lifestyle change #2
Social support system			
Exercise habits			
Nutrition habits			
Time-management techniques			
Self-talk patterns			
Sleep habits			

Part II. Relaxation Techniques

Choose two relaxation techniques described in this chapter (progressive relaxation, visualization, deep breathing, meditation, yoga, t'ai chi ch'uan). If a taped recording is available for progressive relaxation or visualization, these techniques can be performed by your entire class as a group.

List the techniques you tried.

1. _____

2. _____

How did you feel before you tried these techniques?

_____

_____

_____

_____

What did you think, or how did you feel, as you performed each of the techniques you tried?

1. _____

_____

_____

2. _____

_____

_____

How did you feel after you tried these techniques?

_____

_____

_____

Cardiovascular Health

11

LOOKING AHEAD

After reading this chapter, you should be able to answer these questions about cardiovascular health and disease:

- What controllable and uncontrollable risk factors are associated with cardiovascular disease?

- What are the major forms of cardiovascular disease, and how do they develop?

- What steps can people take to keep their cardiovascular system healthy and avoid cardiovascular disease?

Cardiovascular disease (CVD) is the leading cause of death in the United States; nearly half of all Americans alive today will die from CVD. As discussed in Chapter 1, much of the incidence of CVD is attributable to the American way of life. Too many Americans eat a high-fat diet, are overweight and sedentary, smoke cigarettes, manage stress ineffectively, have uncontrolled high blood pressure or high cholesterol levels, and don't know the signs of CVD. Not all risk factors for CVD are controllable—some people have an inherited tendency toward high cholesterol levels, for example—but many are within the control of the individual.

This chapter explains the major forms of CVD, including hypertension, atherosclerosis, and stroke. It also considers the factors that put people at risk for CVD. Most important, it explains the steps individuals can take to protect their hearts and promote cardiovascular health throughout their lives.

RISK FACTORS FOR CARDIOVASCULAR DISEASE

Researchers have identified a variety of factors associated with an increased risk of developing cardiovascular disease. They are grouped into two categories: major risk factors and contributing risk factors. Some major risk factors, such as diet, exercise habits, and use of tobacco, are linked to controllable aspects of lifestyle and can therefore be changed. Others, such as age, sex, and heredity, are beyond an individual's control. (Part I of Lab 11-1 gives you the opportunity to evaluate your personal CVD risk factors.)

Major Risk Factors That Can Be Changed

The American Heart Association (AHA) has identified five major risk factors for CVD that can be changed. These are tobacco use, high blood pressure, unhealthy blood cholesterol levels, physical inactivity, and obesity.

Tobacco Use   People who smoke a pack of cigarettes a day have twice the risk of heart attack that nonsmokers have; smoking two or more packs a day triples the risk. And when smokers do have heart attacks, they are two to four times more likely than nonsmokers to die from them. Women who smoke and use oral contraceptives are up to 39 times more likely to have a heart attack and up to 22 times more likely to have a stroke than women who don't smoke and take the pill.

Smoking harms the cardiovascular system in several ways. Smoking can reduce levels of **high-density lipoproteins (HDLs)**, "good cholesterol," in the bloodstream. The psychoactive drug in tobacco, nicotine, is a central nervous system stimulant, causing increased blood pressure and heart rate. The carbon monoxide in cigarette smoke displaces oxygen in the blood, reducing the amount of oxygen available to the heart and other parts of the body. Cigarette smoking also causes the **platelets** in blood to become sticky and cluster, compromises platelet survival rate, decreases clotting time, and thickens the blood. All these effects increase a person's risk of heart attack and other forms of CVD.

You don't have to smoke to be affected. **Environmental tobacco smoke (ETS)** in high concentrations has been linked to the development of cardiovascular disease. ETS and high cholesterol levels act together to damage the cells that line artery walls. Researchers estimate that 50,000 nonsmokers die from heart attacks each year as a result of exposure to ETS.

High Blood Pressure   High blood pressure, or **hypertension,** is a risk factor for many forms of CVD but is also considered a disease itself. High blood pressure occurs when too much force or pressure is exerted against the walls of the arteries. If your blood pressure is high, your heart has to work harder to push the blood forward. Over time, a strained heart weakens and tends to enlarge, which weakens it further. Increased blood pressure also scars and hardens arteries, making them less elastic. Heart attacks, strokes, **atherosclerosis,** and kidney failure can result.

Hypertension usually has no early warning signs, so it's important to have your blood pressure tested at least once every two years—more often if you have CVD risk factors. (High blood pressure and atherosclerosis are discussed later in the chapter.)

Unhealthy Cholesterol Levels   Cholesterol is a fatty, waxlike substance that circulates through the bloodstream and is an important component of cell mem-

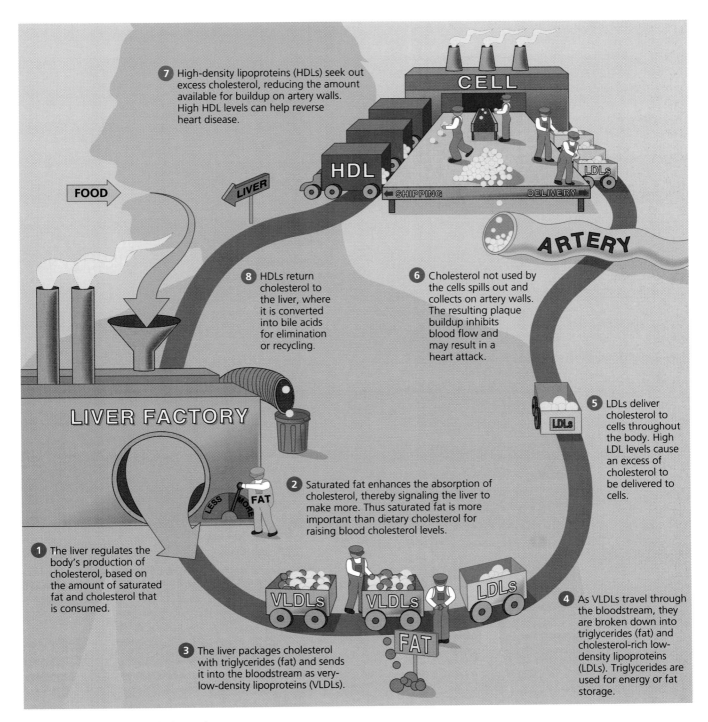

7 High-density lipoproteins (HDLs) seek out excess cholesterol, reducing the amount available for buildup on artery walls. High HDL levels can help reverse heart disease.

8 HDLs return cholesterol to the liver, where it is converted into bile acids for elimination or recycling.

6 Cholesterol not used by the cells spills out and collects on artery walls. The resulting plaque buildup inhibits blood flow and may result in a heart attack.

5 LDLs deliver cholesterol to cells throughout the body. High LDL levels cause an excess of cholesterol to be delivered to cells.

2 Saturated fat enhances the absorption of cholesterol, thereby signaling the liver to make more. Thus saturated fat is more important than dietary cholesterol for raising blood cholesterol levels.

1 The liver regulates the body's production of cholesterol, based on the amount of saturated fat and cholesterol that is consumed.

4 As VLDLs travel through the bloodstream, they are broken down into triglycerides (fat) and cholesterol-rich low-density lipoproteins (LDLs). Triglycerides are used for energy or fat storage.

3 The liver packages cholesterol with triglycerides (fat) and sends it into the bloodstream as very-low-density lipoproteins (VLDLs).

Figure 11-1   Travels with cholesterol.

branes, sex hormones, vitamin D, the fluid that coats the lungs, and the protective sheaths around nerves. Adequate cholesterol is essential for the proper functioning of the body. However, excess cholesterol can clog arteries and increase the risk of CVD (Figure 11-1).

Our bodies obtain cholesterol in two ways: from the liver, which manufactures it, and from the foods we eat.

Cholesterol levels vary depending on diet, age, sex, heredity, and other factors.

GOOD VERSUS BAD CHOLESTEROL   Cholesterol is carried in protein-lipid packages called **lipoproteins**. Lipoproteins can be thought of as shuttles that transport cholesterol to and from the liver through the circulatory system.

Low-density lipoproteins (LDLs) shuttle cholesterol from the liver to the organs and tissues that require it. LDL is known as "bad" cholesterol because if there is more than the body can use, the excess is deposited in the blood vessels. When it accumulates, it can block arteries and cause heart attacks and strokes. High-density lipoproteins (HDLs), or "good" cholesterol, shuttle unused cholesterol back to the liver for recycling.

RECOMMENDED BLOOD CHOLESTEROL LEVELS   The risk for CVD increases with increasing blood cholesterol levels. The first step in managing your cholesterol is to be tested. The National Cholesterol Education Program (NCEP) recommends testing at least once every 5 years for all adults, beginning at age 20, or at least every 3 years for people with a family history of heart disease. General cholesterol guidelines are given in Table 11-1. A total cholesterol level below 200 mg/dl (milligrams per deciliter) is considered desirable and indicates a relatively low risk of CVD; high levels, over 240 mg/dl, carry approximately double the CVD risk of desirable levels. An estimated 97 million American adults—over half the adult population—have total cholesterol levels of 200 mg/dl or higher.

Laboratory blood tests can measure your LDL and HDL levels. In general, high LDL levels and low HDL levels are associated with a high risk for CVD; low levels of LDL and high levels of HDL are associated with lower risk. HDL is especially important because a high HDL level seems to offer protection from CVD even in cases where total cholesterol is high. On the other hand, low total cholesterol may be associated with high CVD risk if HDL is also very low. For this reason, some experts use the ratio of total cholesterol to HDL to evaluate CVD risk.

IMPROVING CHOLESTEROL LEVELS   Important dietary changes that improve cholesterol levels include cutting total fat intake, substituting unsaturated for saturated and trans fats, and increasing soluble fiber intake. Decreasing your intake of saturated fat is particularly important because saturated fat promotes the production and excretion of cholesterol by the liver. You can raise your HDL levels by exercising regularly and, if you smoke, kicking the habit.

Physical Inactivity   An estimated 35–50 million Americans are so sedentary that they are at high risk for developing CVD. Exercise is thought to be the closest thing we have to a "magic bullet" against heart disease. It lowers CVD risk by helping decrease blood pressure, increase HDL levels, maintain desirable weight, improve the condition of the blood vessels, and prevent or control diabetes. One recent study found that women who accumulated at least 3 hours of brisk walking each week cut their

TABLE 11-1	*Cholesterol Guidelines*[a]	
Total blood cholesterol		
Less than 200 mg/dl	Desirable[b]	
200–239 mg/dl	Borderline high	
240 mg/dl or more	High	
LDL cholesterol		
Less than 130 mg/dl	Desirable[b]	
130–159 mg/dl	Borderline high	
160 mg/dl or more	High	
HDL cholesterol		
More than 45 mg/dl	Desirable[b]	
35–45 mg/dl	Borderline low	
Less than 35 mg/dl	Low	
Cholesterol ratio (total ÷ HDL)[c]		
4.5	Average	
3.5	Optimal	

[a]These guidelines are based on large-scale studies of middle-aged Americans; younger people should strive for somewhat lower levels. For example, for those age 19 and under, the desirable level for total blood cholesterol is below 170 mg/dl.
[b]For adults without known heart disease; for those with heart disease, an LDL level of 100 mg/dl or less is recommended.
[c]Higher ratios indicate higher risk.

SOURCES: American Heart Association. National Cholesterol Education Program.

risk of heart attack and stroke by more than half. (See Chapter 3 for more information on the physical and psychological effects of exercise.)

Obesity   In June 1998, the American Heart Association added obesity to its list of major controllable risk factors. A person whose body weight is more than 30% above the recommended level is at higher risk for heart disease and stroke, even if no other risk factors are present. Excess weight increases the strain on the heart by contributing to high blood pressure and high cholesterol. It can also lead to diabetes, another CVD risk factor (see below). As discussed in Chapter 6, distribution of body fat is also significant: Fat that collects in the torso is more dangerous than fat that collects around the hips. A sensible diet and regular exercise are the best ways to achieve and maintain a healthy body weight. For people who are obese, losing even a small amount of weight can have very beneficial effects on cardiovascular health.

Contributing Risk Factors That Can Be Changed

Various other factors that can be changed have been identified as contributing to CVD risk, including diabetes, triglyceride levels, and psychological and social factors.

TERMS **low-density lipoproteins (LDLs)**   Blood fats that transport cholesterol to organs and tissues; excess amounts result in the accumulation of deposits on artery walls.

Diabetes People with diabetes are at increased risk for CVD, partly because the disease affects the levels of cholesterol in the blood. Diabetes appears to have both a genetic component and a behavioral component. The best way to avoid diabetes is to exercise regularly and control body weight. (See Chapter 6 for more information on diabetes.)

Triglyceride Levels Like cholesterol, triglycerides are blood fats that can be obtained from the diet and manufactured by the body. Studies have shown that high triglyceride levels are a reliable predictor of heart disease, especially if associated with other risk factors, such as low HDL levels, obesity, and diabetes. Elevated triglyceride levels may be of particular concern for women and for people who smoke.

Physicians often recommend that people with other risk factors for CVD have their total triglyceride level measured. A triglyceride level below 200 mg/dl is considered normal; a level of 400 mg/dl or above is considered high. The best ways to reduce triglycerides seem to be weight loss, regular exercise, and a diet that is high in fiber and low in simple sugars and refined carbohydrates and that favors unsaturated over saturated fats. Being moderate in the use of alcohol is also important because alcohol elevates triglyceride levels.

Psychological and Social Factors Many of the psychological and social factors that influence other areas of wellness are also important risk factors for CVD.

• *Stress.* Excessive stress can strain the heart and blood vessels over time and contribute to CVD. A full-blown stress response causes blood vessels to constrict and blood pressure to rise. Blood platelets become more likely to cluster, possibly enhancing the formation of artery-clogging clots. People sometimes also adopt unhealthy habits such as smoking, overeating, or skipping meals as a means of dealing with severe stress.

• *Chronic hostility and anger.* Certain traits in the hard-driving "Type A" personality—hostility, cynicism, and anger—are associated with increased risk of heart disease. People who are prone to chronic hostility experience the stress response more intensely and frequently than more relaxed individuals. When they encounter the irritations of daily life, their blood pressure increases much more. They also seem to have trouble shutting down the stress response. Less hostile people tend to calm down much more quickly, taking the stress off their bodies—especially their hearts. (Part II of Lab 11-1 includes a hostility self-assessment and tips for managing anger.)

• *Suppressing psychological distress.* Consistently suppressing anger and other negative emotions may also be hazardous to a healthy heart. Several recent studies suggest that people who hide psychological distress—even

Before age 65, women are less susceptible to cardiovascular disease than men. Even though this woman has to cope with the same on-the-job stresses as men in her profession, she is less likely to have a heart attack in middle age than they are.

from themselves—have a higher rate of heart disease than people who experience similar distress but share it with others.

• *Depression and anxiety.* Both mild and severe depression are linked to an increased risk of fatal heart disease. Researchers have also found a strong association between anxiety disorders and an increased risk of death from heart disease, particularly sudden death from heart attack.

• *Social isolation.* People with little social support are at higher risk of dying from coronary heart disease (CHD) than people with close ties to others. A strong social support network is a major antidote to stress. Friends and family members can also promote and support healthy lifestyle behaviors (see the box "Religion and Wellness").

• *Socioeconomic status.* Low socioeconomic status and low educational attainment also increase risk for CVD. These associations are probably due to a variety of factors, including lifestyle and access to health care.

Major Risk Factors That Can't Be Changed

A number of major risk factors for CVD cannot be changed: heredity, aging, being male, and ethnicity.

Heredity The tendency to develop CVD seems to be inherited. High cholesterol levels, abnormal blood-clotting problems, diabetes, and obesity are other CVD risk factors that have genetic links. People who inherit a tendency for CVD are not destined to develop it, but they may have to work harder than other people to prevent it.

Aging The risk of heart attack increases dramatically after age 65. About 55% of all heart attack victims are age 65 or older, and almost four out of five who suffer fatal

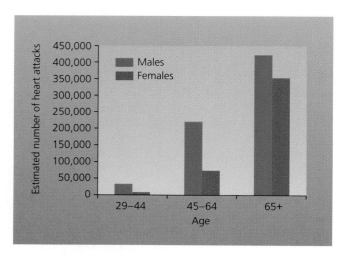

VITAL STATISTICS

Figure 11-2   Annual incidence of heart attack.   Among heart attack victims under age 65, men significantly outnumber women; after age 65, women start to catch up.   SOURCES: American Heart Association. 1998. *Heart and Stroke Statistical Update.*

heart attacks are over 65. For people over 55, the incidence of stroke more than doubles in each successive decade. However, many people in their thirties and forties, especially men, have heart attacks.

Being Male   Although CVD is the leading killer of both men and women in the United States, men face a greater risk of heart attack than women, especially earlier in life (Figure 11-2). Until age 55, men also have a greater risk

of hypertension than women. The incidence of stroke is about 19% higher for males than females. Estrogen production, which is highest during the childbearing years, may offer premenopausal women some protection against CVD.

Ethnicity   Death rates from heart disease vary among ethnic groups in the United States, with African Americans having much higher rates of hypertension, heart disease, and stroke than other groups (see the box "African Americans and CVD").

Puerto Rican Americans, Cuban Americans, and Mexican Americans are also more likely to suffer from high blood pressure and angina (a warning sign of heart disease) than non-Hispanic white Americans. These differences may be due in part to differences in education, income, and other socioeconomic factors.

Asian Americans historically have had far lower rates of CVD than white Americans. However, recent studies indicate that cholesterol levels among Asian Americans are rising, presumably because of the adoption of a high-fat American diet.

Possible Risk Factors Currently Being Studied

In recent years, several other possible risk factors for CVD have been identified. These include homocysteine, lipoprotein(a), and certain infectious agents.

Homocysteine is an amino acid circulating in the blood. High levels of homocysteine are associated with an increased risk of CVD, but researchers are not yet certain whether it is a direct cause or simply a marker for some

African American men are nearly 50% more likely to die from a heart attack than white men, and death from stroke is five times more common among African Americans than in other Americans. Hypertension is twice as common in blacks. What accounts for these higher rates of CVD among African Americans? Contributing factors can be grouped into three areas: biological/genetic factors, low income and discrimination, and lifestyle factors.

Biological/Genetic Factors

Researchers are investigating a number of genetic factors that may contribute to CVD in African Americans, including heightened sensitivities to lead and salt, which can lead to high blood pressure. Heredity may also play a role in higher cholesterol levels among blacks. And sickle-cell disease, a genetic disorder that occurs mainly in blacks, can lead to impaired blood flow and heart failure.

Low Income and Discrimination

Another factor in the high incidence of CVD among African Americans is low income. One-third live below the official poverty line. Economic deprivation usually means reduced access to adequate health care and health insurance. Associated with low income are poorer educational opportunities, which often mean less information about preventive health measures, such as diet and stress management.

Discrimination may also play a role in CVD among blacks. Research has shown that many physicians and hospitals treat the medical problems of African Americans differently than those of whites. Discrimination, along with low income and other forms of deprivation, may also increase stress, which is linked with hypertension and CVD.

Lifestyle Factors

Lifestyle factors may be the key in explaining high CVD rates among African Americans. A recent large-scale study determined that birthplace, not ethnicity, is the key indicator of CVD risk among African Americans. The study found that among New Yorkers born in the Northeast, blacks and whites have nearly identical risk for CVD. But black New Yorkers who were born in the South have a sharply higher risk, and black New Yorkers born in the Caribbean have a significantly lower risk. In fact, blacks who were born in the South and moved to New York City were twice as likely to die of heart disease as blacks or whites born in the Northeast.

Researchers speculate that some risk factors for CVD, including smoking and a high-fat diet, may be more common in the South. When combined with urban stress, these factors create a lifestyle that is far from heart-healthy. And people with low incomes, who are disproportionately African American, tend to smoke more, use more salt, and exercise less than those with higher incomes. In addition, half of African American women and one-third of African American men are significantly overweight.

Medical experts advise all Americans to have their blood pressure checked regularly, exercise, eat a healthy diet, manage stress, and avoid smoking. These preventive strategies may be particularly important for African Americans.

---

other risk factor. In laboratory studies, homocysteine appears to intensify blood clotting and damage the linings of blood vessels, both of which increase the risk of heart disease. Homocysteine levels tend to be higher among men than women and are particularly high among people who smoke; other risk factors include hypertension, high cholesterol levels, a sedentary lifestyle, and a diet deficient in vitamins B-12, B-6, and folic acid.

A specific type of LDL called lipoprotein(a), or Lp(a), has been identified as a possible independent risk factor for CHD. Lp(a) has a strong genetic component and is not influenced by diet or most cholesterol-lowering drugs. Preliminary research indicates that hormone replacement therapy and other treatments for lowering elevated LDL levels may also reduce the risk associated with high Lp(a).

Several infectious agents have also been identified as possible culprits in the development of heart disease. They are *Chlamydia pneumoniae, cytomegalovirus (CMV),* and *Helicobacter pylori,* a bacterium linked to ulcers and stomach cancer. Although the mechanism is not yet clear, it appears that some chronic infections may contribute to inflammation and the buildup of fatty deposits in arteries.

MAJOR FORMS OF CARDIOVASCULAR DISEASE

Collectively, the various forms of CVD kill more Americans than the next four leading causes of death combined. The financial burden of CVD, including the costs of medical treatments and lost productivity, exceeds $250 billion annually. Although the main forms of CVD are interrelated and have elements in common, we treat them separately here for the sake of clarity.

Hypertension

Blood pressure, the force exerted by the blood on blood vessel walls, is created by the pumping action of the heart. When the heart contracts (systole), blood pressure increases; when the heart relaxes (diastole), pressure decreases. Short periods of high blood pressure are normal, but blood pressure that is continually at an abnormally high level is known as hypertension.

Blood pressure is measured with a stethoscope and an instrument called a sphygmomanometer. It is expressed as two numbers—for example, 120 over 80—and

TABLE 11-2	Blood Pressure Classification for Healthy Adults			
Category[a]	Systolic (mm Hg)		Diastolic (mm Hg)	Recommended Follow-Up
Optimal[b]	below 120	and	below 80	Recheck in 2 years
Normal	below 130	and	below 85	Recheck in 2 years
High-normal	130–139	or	85–89	Recheck in 1 year
Hypertension[c]				
Stage 1	140–159	or	90–99	Confirm within 2 months
Stage 2	160–179	or	100–109	Physician evaluation within 1 month
Stage 3	180 and above	or	110 and above	Immediate physician evaluation

[a]When systolic and diastolic blood pressure fall into different categories, the higher category should be selected to classify an individual's blood pressure status.

[b]Optimal blood pressure with respect to cardiovascular risk is below 120/80 mm Hg; however, unusually low readings should be evaluated.
[c]Based on the average of two or more readings taken at different physician visits.

SOURCE: *The Sixth Report of the Joint National Committee on Prevention, Detection, Evaluation, and Treatment of High Blood Pressure.* 1997. Bethesda, Md.: National Heart, Lung, and Blood Institute. National Institutes of Health (NIH Publication No. 98-4080).

measured in millimeters of mercury. The first and larger number is the systolic blood pressure; the second is the diastolic blood pressure. Average blood pressure readings for young adults in good physical condition are 110–120 systolic over 70–80 diastolic. High blood pressure in adults is defined as equal to or greater than 140 over 90 (Table 11-2).

High blood pressure results from either an increased output of blood by the heart, often as a result of overweight, or because of increased resistance to blood flow in the arteries from narrowing and hardening. When a person has high blood pressure, the heart must work harder than normal to force blood through the arteries, and the arteries are under a greater strain than normal. Over time, high blood pressure causes the heart to enlarge and weaken, and the process of atherosclerosis speeds up.

High blood pressure is often called a "silent killer," because it usually has no symptoms or warning signs. In fact, it is possible to have high blood pressure for years without realizing it. Over that course of time, hypertension might be damaging vital organs (particularly the heart, brain, kidneys, and eyes) and increasing the risk of heart attack, congestive heart failure, stroke, kidney failure, and blindness. The key to avoiding the complications of hypertension is having your blood pressure measured regularly.

Hypertension cannot be cured, but it can be treated and controlled through diet, exercise, and medication. An estimated 50 million Americans, one in four adults, have hypertension; only about one-third of them have it under control. Cases of mild hypertension can frequently be treated by changes in diet alone, such as increased intake of fruits and vegetables and restricted salt intake in salt-sensitive people. Other lifestyle measures for preventing and treating hypertension include exercising regularly, maintaining a healthy weight, limiting alcohol intake, and not smoking. Treating more severe hypertension usually involves long-term drug therapy.

Atherosclerosis

Atherosclerosis is a slow, progressive hardening and narrowing of the arteries that can begin in childhood. Arteries become narrowed by deposits of fat, cholesterol, and other substances. As these deposits, called **plaques**, accumulate on artery walls, the arteries lose their elasticity and their ability to expand and contract, restricting blood flow. Once narrowed by a plaque, an artery is vulnerable to blockage by blood clots (Figure 11-3).

If the heart, brain, and/or other organs are deprived of blood, and thus the vital oxygen it carries, the effects of atherosclerosis can be deadly. **Coronary arteries,** which supply the heart with blood, are particularly susceptible to plaque buildup, a condition called **coronary heart disease (CHD)**, or coronary artery disease. The blockage of

TERMS

plaque A deposit of fatty (and other) substances on the inner wall of the arteries.

coronary arteries Two arteries branching from the aorta that provide blood to the heart muscle.

coronary heart disease (CHD) Heart disease caused by hardening of the arteries that supply oxygen to the heart muscle.

heart attack Damage to, or death of, heart muscle, sometimes resulting in a failure of the heart to deliver enough blood, carrying vital oxygen, to other organs of the body.

angina pectoris A condition in which the heart muscle does not receive enough blood, causing severe pain in the chest and often in the left arm and shoulder.

arrhythmia An irregularity in the force or rhythm of the heartbeat that often precedes a heart attack.

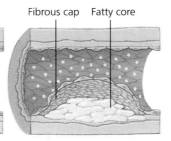

Blood lipids (cholesterol)   Artery-lining cells   Platelets   Fibrous cap   Fatty core

Figure 11-3 Stages of plaque development.

Plaque buildup begins when excess fat particles (lipids) collect beneath cells lining the artery that have been damaged by smoking, high blood pressure, or other causes.

Platelets, components of one of the body's protective mechanisms, collect at the damaged area and cause a cap of cells to form, isolating the plaque within the artery wall.

The narrowed artery is now vulnerable to blockage by clots that can form if the cap breaks and the fatty core of the plaque combines again with platelets and other clot-producing factors in the blood.

a coronary artery causes a heart attack. If a cerebral artery (leading to the brain) is blocked, the result is a stroke.

The main risk factors for atherosclerosis are cigarette smoking, physical inactivity, high levels of blood cholesterol, and high blood pressure. A 1998 study found that smoking and exposure to environmental tobacco smoke permanently accelerate the rate of plaque accumulation in the coronary arteries—50% for smokers, 25% for ex-smokers, and 20% for people regularly exposed to ETS.

Heart Disease and Heart Attacks

A **heart attack** is the end result of a long-term disease process. The heart requires a steady supply of oxygen-rich blood to function properly (Figure 11-4). If one of the coronary arteries that supplies blood to the heart becomes blocked by a blood clot, a heart attack results. A heart attack caused by a clot is called a coronary thrombosis, a coronary occlusion, or a myocardial infarction. In myocardial infarction, part of the heart muscle (myocardium) may die from lack of oxygen.

Although heart attacks often occur without warning, some people experience pain or an abnormal heartbeat first. Chest pain called **angina pectoris** is a signal that the heart isn't getting enough oxygen to supply its needs. Although not actually a heart attack, angina is a warning that the heart is overloaded. If the electrical impulses that control heartbeat are disrupted, the heart may beat too quickly, too slowly, or in an irregular fashion, a condition known as **arrhythmia**, another sign of impending heart attack.

If symptoms of heart trouble do occur, it is critical to go immediately to the nearest hospital or clinic with a 24-hour emergency cardiac facility (see the box "What to Do in the Event of a Heart Attack"). If a victim gets to the emergency room quickly enough, a clot-dissolving agent can be injected to dissolve a clot in the coronary artery, reducing the amount of damage to the heart muscle.

Physicians have a variety of diagnostic tools and treatments for heart disease. A patient may undergo a stress or

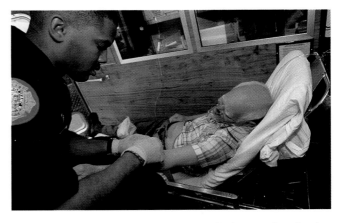

Many heart attack victims aren't sure they've had an attack and wait too long—2 hours or more— before getting help. Prompt attention from a paramedic greatly improves this man's chance of survival.

exercise test, in which he or she runs on a treadmill while being monitored with an electrocardiogram (ECG or EKG). Certain characteristic changes in the heart's electrical activity while under stress can reveal particular heart problems, such as restricted blood flow to the heart muscle. Tools that allow the physician to visualize a patient's heart and arteries include magnetic resonance imaging (MRI) and angiograms.

If tests indicate a problem or if a person has already had a heart attack, several treatments are possible. *Balloon angioplasty* involves threading a catheter with an inflatable balloon tip through a coronary artery until it reaches the area of blockage; the balloon is then inflated, flattening the plaque and widening the arterial opening. In *coronary bypass surgery*, healthy blood vessels are grafted to coronary arteries to bypass blockages. Along with a low-fat diet, regular exercise, and smoking cessation, many patients are also advised to take half an aspirin tablet daily to reduce clotting and inflammation.

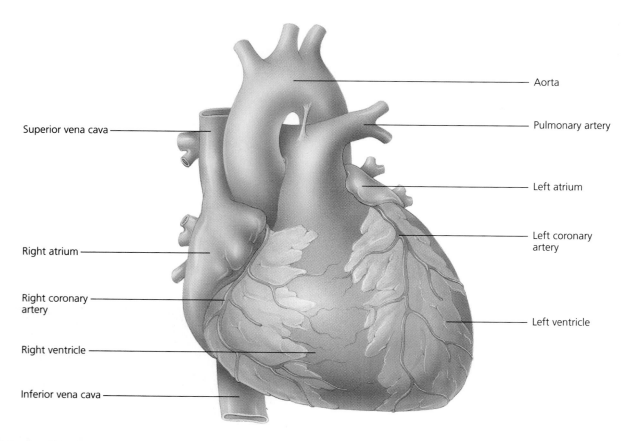

Superior vena cava

Right atrium

Right coronary artery

Right ventricle

Inferior vena cava

Aorta

Pulmonary artery

Left atrium

Left coronary artery

Left ventricle

Figure 11-4 Blood supply to the heart. Blood is supplied to the heart from the right and left coronary arteries, which branch off the aorta. If a coronary artery becomes blocked by plaque buildup and a blood clot, a heart attack occurs; part of the heart muscle may die due to lack of oxygen.

Stroke

For brain cells to function as they should, they must have a continuous and ample supply of oxygen-rich blood. If brain cells are deprived of blood for more than a few minutes, they die. A **stroke,** also called a cerebrovascular accident (CVA), occurs when the blood supply to the brain is cut off. Strokes can be particularly serious because injured brain cells, unlike those of other organs, cannot regenerate.

A stroke may be caused by a blood clot that blocks an artery or by a burst blood vessel (cerebral hemorrhage).

TERMS **stroke** An impeded blood supply to some part of the brain resulting in the destruction of brain cells.

rheumatic fever A disease, mainly of children, characterized by fever, inflammation, and pain in the joints; often damages the heart muscle.

congestive heart failure A condition resulting from the heart's inability to pump out all the blood that returns to it. Blood backs up in the veins leading to the heart, causing an accumulation of fluid in various parts of the body.

High blood pressure and atherosclerosis (especially blockage of the cerebral arteries) greatly increase the risk of stroke. The interruption of the blood supply to any area of the brain prevents the nerve cells there from functioning—in some cases, causing death. Nerve cells control sensation and most body movements; depending on the area of the brain that is affected, a stroke may cause paralysis, walking disability, speech impairment, or memory loss. Of the 500,000 Americans who have strokes each year, approximately one-third die within a year; those who survive usually have some lasting disability.

Effective treatment requires the prompt recognition of symptoms—sudden numbness or weakness of the face, arm, and leg on one side of the body; loss of speech or difficulty speaking or understanding speech; dimming or loss of vision, especially in only one eye; and unexplained dizziness. Depending on the type of stroke, treatment may involve the use of clot-dissolving and antihypertensive drugs. If detection and treatment of stroke come too late, rehabilitation is the only treatment. Although damaged or destroyed brain tissue cannot regenerate, nerve cells in the brain can make new pathways, and some functions can be taken over by other parts of the brain.

TACTICS AND TIPS   *What to Do in the Event of a Heart Attack*

When it comes to a heart attack, delay spells danger. Minutes make a difference, so it's vitally important to know what to do.

Know the Signals of a Heart Attack

- Uncomfortable pressure, fullness, squeezing, or pain in the center of the chest lasting 2 minutes or more.

- Pain may spread to the shoulders, neck, or arms.

- Severe pain, dizziness, fainting, sweating, nausea, or shortness of breath may also occur. Sharp, stabbing twinges of pain are usually not signals of a heart attack.

Know What Emergency Action to Take

- If you are having atypical chest discomfort that lasts for 2 minutes or more, call the local emergency rescue service immediately.

- If you can get to a hospital faster by car, have someone drive you. Find out which hospitals have 24-hour emer-

gency cardiac care, and discuss the choices with your physician. Plan in advance the route that's best from where you live and work.

- Keep a list of emergency rescue service numbers next to your telephone and in a prominent place in your pocket, wallet, or purse.

Know How to Help

- If you are with someone who is having the signals of a heart attack, take action even if the person denies there is something wrong.

- *Call* the emergency rescue service, or

- *Get* to the nearest hospital emergency room that offers 24-hour emergency cardiac care, and

- *Give* mouth-to-mouth breathing and chest compression (CPR) if it is necessary and if you are properly trained.

TACTICS AND TIPS   *A Heart-Healthy Lifestyle*

- Choose a diet that is rich in whole grains, vegetables, and fruits. Limit foods that are high in fat, saturated fat, trans fat, and cholesterol.

- Drink alcohol moderately, if at all.

- Be physically active.

- Don't smoke or use other forms of tobacco; avoid exposure to environmental tobacco smoke.

- Have your blood pressure checked regularly; if it is elevated, take steps to control it.

- Have your blood cholesterol levels measured; if necessary, follow your physician's advice to improve your cholesterol profile.

- Develop effective strategies for handling stress and anger; build up your social support network.

- If you have any medical problems such as diabetes, follow your physician's advice carefully.

Congestive Heart Failure

A number of conditions—high blood pressure, heart attack, atherosclerosis, **rheumatic fever,** birth defects—can damage the heart's pumping mechanism. When the heart cannot maintain its regular pumping rate and force, fluids begin to back up. When extra fluid seeps through capillary walls, edema (swelling) results, usually in the legs and ankles, but sometimes in other parts of the body as well. Fluid can collect in the lungs and interfere with breathing, particularly when a person is lying down. This condition is called *pulmonary edema,* and the entire process is known as **congestive heart failure.**

Congestive heart failure can be controlled. Treatment includes reducing the workload on the heart, modifying salt intake, and using drugs that help the body eliminate excess fluid.

PROTECTING YOURSELF AGAINST CARDIOVASCULAR DISEASE

There are several important steps you can take now to lower your risk of developing CVD in the future (see the box "A Heart-Healthy Lifestyle").

Eat Heart-Healthy

For most Americans, changing to a heart-healthy diet involves cutting total fat intake, substituting unsaturated fats for saturated fats, and increasing fiber. Such changes can lower a person's blood levels of total cholesterol, LDL cholesterol, and triglycerides.

Decreased Fat and Cholesterol Intake   The NCEP recommends that all Americans over the age of 2 adopt a

A diet high in fiber and low in total fat and saturated fat can help lower levels of total cholesterol and LDL. This woman is enjoying a healthy dinner of baked chicken, broccoli, rice, fruit, and juice.

diet in which total fat consumption is no more than 30% of total daily calories. No more than one-third of those fat calories should come from saturated fat, which is found in animal products, palm and coconut oil, and hydrogenated vegetable oils. Most of the fat calories in your diet should come from unsaturated fats, which may raise HDL and lower total cholesterol. By controlling your intake of total fat and saturated fat, you'll also reduce your consumption of cholesterol-raising trans fatty acids (see Chapter 8 for more information on types of dietary fats and strategies for controlling fat intake).

Animal products contain cholesterol as well as saturated fat. The NCEP and AHA recommend that you limit dietary cholesterol intake to 300 mg per day or less.

Increased Fiber Intake   Soluble fiber traps the bile acids the liver needs to manufacture cholesterol and carries them to the large intestine, where they are excreted. It also slows the production of proteins that promote blood clotting. Insoluble fiber may interfere with the absorption of dietary fat and may also help you cut total food intake because foods rich in insoluble fiber tend to be filling. To obtain the recommended 20–35 grams of dietary fiber per day, choose a diet rich in whole grains, fruits, and vegetables. Good sources of fiber include oatmeal, some breakfast cereals, barley, legumes, and most fruits and vegetables.

Alcohol   A large-scale study released in 1997 found that people who average about one drink per day had a 30–40% lower risk of death from cardiovascular disease compared with nondrinkers. However, the mortality rate from breast cancer was 30% higher among women who had at least one drink daily. Other causes of death associated with drinking are alcoholism, cirrhosis of the liver, certain forms of cancer and cardiovascular disease, and injuries; overall death rates rise with the level of alcohol consumption. Because alcohol has both beneficial and adverse effects on health, you should consider your personal risk factors in making decisions about alcohol use. If you do drink, do so moderately (no more than one drink per day for women or two drinks per day for men), with food, and at times when drinking will not put you or others at risk.

DASH   A study released in 1997 called "Dietary Approaches to Stop Hypertension," or DASH, suggests that many Americans can lower their blood pressure by adopting a diet that is low in fat and high in fruits, vegetables, and low-fat dairy products. In the study, the DASH diet caused a significant reduction in blood pressure for people with high and high-normal blood pressure. The DASH diet plan is as follows:

- 7–8 servings per day of grains and grain products
- 4–5 servings per day of vegetables
- 4–5 servings per day of fruits
- 2–3 servings per day of low-fat or nonfat dairy products
- 2 or fewer servings per day of meats, poultry, and fish
- 4–5 servings per *week* of nuts, seeds, and legumes
- 2–3 servings per day of added fats, oils, and salad dressings
- 5 servings per *week* of snacks and sweets

In the future, researchers hope to determine the effects of different levels of sodium intake (salt raises blood pressure in people who are salt-sensitive). The DASH diet also follows the dietary recommendations for lowering one's risk of cancer, osteoporosis, and heart disease.

Exercise Regularly

People who are sedentary develop heart disease an average of 5–6 years earlier than those who are active. You can significantly reduce your risk of CVD with a moderate amount of physical activity. Try to accumulate at least 30 minutes of moderate-intensity physical activity each day through such activities as brisk walking and stair climbing.

Avoid Tobacco

Remember: The number one risk factor for CVD that you can control is smoking. If you smoke, quit. If you don't, don't start. If you live or work with people who smoke, encourage them to quit—for their sake and yours. If you find yourself breathing in smoke, take steps to prevent or stop this exposure.

Know and Manage Your Blood Pressure

Currently, only about 30% of Americans with hypertension have their blood pressure under control. If you have no CVD risk factors, have your blood pressure measured at least once every 2 years; yearly tests are recommended if you have other risk factors. If your blood pressure is high, follow your physician's advice on how to lower it, and have it checked every 6 months.

Know and Manage Your Cholesterol Levels

Have your blood cholesterol levels measured if you've never had it done. When you know your "number," follow these guidelines from the NCEP:

- *Total cholesterol below 200 mg/dl.* If you HDL is 35 mg/dl or higher and you have no other risk factors for CVD, maintain a healthy lifestyle, including eating a low-fat diet, getting regular exercise, maintaining a healthy body weight, and not smoking. Get another test within 5 years. If your HDL level is less than 35 mg/dl, have your LDL level measured and evaluated, and follow your physician's advice.
- *Total cholesterol between 200 and 239 mg/dl.* If your HDL is 35 mg/dl or higher and you have fewer than two other risk factors for CVD, you may or may not be at increased risk. Work with your physician to control other CVD risk factors, and have your cholesterol levels rechecked in 1–2 years. If your HDL level is less than 35 mg/dl or you have two or more other risk factors for CVD, have your LDL level checked and evaluated, and follow your physician's advice.
- *Total cholesterol 240 mg/dl or more.* Your physician should order a more detailed cholesterol analysis and recommend therapy based on the results. Adopt a heart-healthy lifestyle immediately, including a cholesterol-improving diet and regular exercise. Follow your physician's advice for controlling other CVD risk factors, and have your cholesterol levels rechecked as recommended.

Develop Ways to Handle Stress and Anger and Manage Medical Conditions

To reduce the psychological and social risk factors for CVD, develop effective strategies for handling the stress in your life. Shore up your social support network, and try some of the techniques described in Chapter 10 for managing stress. If anger and hostility are problems for you, refer to Part II of Lab 11-1 for tips on diffusing your anger. If you have any medical problems such as diabetes, follow your physician's advice carefully.

COMMON QUESTIONS ANSWERED

Do women have a lower risk for cardiovascular disease than men, and, if so, why?   Until about age 65, women have a significant advantage over men when it comes to CVD. Every year, more than 300,000 people under age 65 have a heart attack; of these, more than 75% are men. Women who develop CVD tend to be about 10 years older than men when they first have symptoms and about 20 years older when they have a heart attack.

What explains this difference? Research thus far has focused on the beneficial effects of estrogen, which, prior to menopause, circulates in high concentrations in a woman's body. Estrogen improves blood cholesterol levels by raising the concentration of HDL and lowering levels of LDL. Women, on average, have much better blood cholesterol profiles than men. Estrogen also seems to prevent blood clots from forming in the body and to dissolve clots that do form. This is significant because clots can lead to heart attacks and strokes. And estrogen may also lower blood concentrations of homocysteine, high levels of which may be linked with heart attacks and strokes.

But women should not be complacent about their risk for cardiovascular disease. CVD is the leading cause of death among women, killing five times as many women as breast cancer and significantly more women than all types of cancers combined. After menopause, estrogen levels fall and LDL levels begin to rise. By age 65, heart attack risk for women is almost equal to that of men. And women are even less likely to survive an attack, in part because they tend to suffer heart attacks at an older age and because CVD is less likely to be diagnosed in women.

As more studies of CVD among women are completed, scientists may learn more about how female biochemistry affects the development of CVD. In the meantime, it's important to note that the major risk factors for CVD are the same for both women and men. The general advice for preventing CVD presented in this chapter—exercising regularly, managing stress, eating a low-fat diet, and so on—is appropriate for everyone.

I know what foods to avoid to prevent CVD, but are there any foods I should eat to protect myself from CVD?   The most important dietary change for CVD prevention is a negative one: cutting back on foods high in fat, particularly saturated and trans fat. However, research indicates that certain foods can be helpful. The positive effects of unsaturated fats, soluble fiber, and alcohol on heart health were discussed earlier in the chapter. Other potentially beneficial foods include those rich in the following:

- *Omega-3 fatty acids.* Found in fish, shellfish, and some nuts and seeds, omega-3 fatty acids may be helpful in lowering cholesterol and triglyceride levels.

(continued)

- *Folic acid, vitamin B-6, and vitamin B-12.* These three vitamins may affect CVD risk by lowering homocysteine levels; see Table 8-3 for a list of food sources.

- *Vitamin E.* Some recent studies indicate that vitamin E—found in nuts, vegetable oils, wheat germ, margarine, and avocados—may have a protective effect against heart disease.

- *Soy protein.* Some studies have shown that replacing some animal protein with soy protein can lower LDL cholesterol. Soy-based foods include tofu, tempeh, and baked goods made with soy flour.

More research is needed to clarify the effects of these compounds on CVD risk. Meanwhile, you can't go wrong by increasing your intake of fruits, grains, and vegetables.

The advice I hear from the news about protecting myself from CVD seems to be changing all the time. What am I supposed to believe? Health-related research is now described in popular newspapers and magazines rather than just medical journals, meaning that more and more people have access to the information. Researchers do not deliberately set out to mislead or confuse people. However, news reports may oversimplify the results of research studies, leaving out some of the qualifications and questions the researchers present with their findings. In addition, news reports may not differentiate between a preliminary finding and a result that has been verified by a large number of long-term studies. And researchers themselves must strike a balance between reporting promising preliminary findings to the public, thereby allowing people to act on them, and waiting 10–20 years until long-term studies confirm (or disprove) a particular theory.

This can leave you in a difficult position. You cannot become an expert on all subjects, able to effectively evaluate all the available health news. However, there are some general strategies you can use to better assess the health advice that appears in the media; see the box "Evaluating Health News."

SUMMARY

- The major controllable risk factors for CVD are smoking, hypertension, unhealthy cholesterol levels, a sedentary lifestyle, and obesity.

- Contributing factors for CVD that can be changed include diabetes, high triglyceride levels, inadequate stress management, a hostile personality, depression, anxiety, lack of social support, and poverty.

- Major risk factors that can't be changed are heredity, aging, being male, and ethnicity.

- Hypertension weakens the heart and scars and hardens arteries, causing resistance to blood flow. It is defined as blood pressure equal to or higher than 140 over 90.

- Atherosclerosis is a progressive hardening and narrowing of arteries that can lead to restricted blood flow and even complete blockage; high blood pressure and high levels of blood cholesterol are contributing factors.

- Heart attacks, strokes, and congestive heart failure are the results of a long-term disease process; hypertension and atherosclerosis are usually involved.

- Reducing heart disease risk involves eating heart-healthy, exercising regularly, avoiding tobacco, managing blood pressure and cholesterol levels, handling stress and anger, and managing medical conditions.

FOR MORE INFORMATION

Books

American Heart Association. 1998. *American Heart Association Guide to Heart Attack Treatment, Recovery, and Prevention.* New York: Times Books. *Provides information on a heart-healthy lifestyle.*

Fortmann, S., and P. Breitrose. 1996. *The Blood Pressure Book: How to Get It Down and Keep It Down.* Palo Alto, Calif.: Bull Publishing. *A step-by-step guide for making lifestyle changes to control blood pressure.*

Notelovitz, M., and D. Tonnessen. 1996. *The Essential Heart Book for Women.* New York: St. Martin's Press. *Explains how women can take action against their number one killer—heart disease—through prevention and treatment.*

Organizations and Web Sites

American Heart Association. Provides information on hundreds of topics relating to the prevention and control of CVD.
    800-242-8721; 214-373-6300
    http://www.americanheart.org

Cardiology Compass. An index and links to cardiovascular information on the Internet.
    http://www.cardiologycompass.com

Dietary Approaches to Stop Hypertension (DASH). Provides information about the design, diets, and results of the DASH study, including tips on how to follow the DASH diet at home.
    http://dash.bwh.harvard.edu

Franklin Institute Science Museum/The Heart: An On-Line Exploration. An online museum exhibit containing information on the structure and function of the heart, how to monitor your heart's health, and how to maintain a healthy heart.
    http://www.fi.edu/biosci/heart.html

Americans face an avalanche of health information from newspapers, magazines, books, and television programs. It's not always easy to decide which news to believe and which news to ignore. The following questions can help you evaluate health news.

1. *Is the report based on research or on an anecdote?* Information or advice based on one or more carefully designed research studies has more validity than one person's experiences.

2. *What is the source of the information?* A study in a respected publication has been reviewed by editors and other researchers in the field—people who are in a position to evaluate the merits of a study and its results. Information put forth by government agencies and national research organizations is also usually considered fairly reliable.

3. *How big was the study?* A study that involves many subjects is more likely to yield reliable results than a study involving only a few people. Another indication that a finding is meaningful is if several different studies yield the same results.

4. *Who were the people involved in the study?* Research findings are more likely to apply to you if you share important characteristics with the subjects of the study. For example, the results of a study on men over age 50 who smoke may not be particularly meaningful for a 30-year-old nonsmoking woman.

5. *What kind of study was it?* Epidemiological studies involve observation or interviews in order to trace the relationships among lifestyle, physical characteristics, and diseases. While epidemiological studies can suggest links, they cannot establish cause-and-effect relationships. Experiments or interventional studies involve testing the effects of different treatments on groups of people who have similar lifestyles and characteristics. They are more likely to provide conclusive evidence of a cause-and-effect relationship. The best interventional studies share the following characteristics:

- *Controlled.* A group of people who receive the treatment is compared with a matched group who do not receive the treatment.

- *Randomized.* The treatment and control groups are selected randomly.

- *Double-blind.* Researchers and participants are unaware of who is receiving the treatment.

- *Multicenter.* The experiment is performed at more than one institution.

6. *What do the statistics really say?* First, are the results described as "statistically significant"? If a study is large and well designed, its results can be deemed statistically significant, meaning there is less than a 5% chance that the findings resulted from chance. Second, are the results stated in terms of relative or absolute risk? Many findings are reported in terms of relative risk—how a particular treatment or condition affects a person's disease risk. Consider the following examples of relative risk.

- According to some estimates, taking estrogen without progesterone can increase a postmenopausal woman's risk of dying from endometrial cancer by 233%.

- Giving AZT to HIV-infected pregnant women reduces prenatal transmission of HIV by 66%.

The first of these two findings seems far more dramatic than the second—until one also considers absolute risk, the actual risk of the illness in the population being considered. The absolute risk of endometrial cancer is 0.3%; a 233% increase based on the effects of estrogen raises it to 1%, a change of 0.7%. Without treatment, about 25% of infants born to HIV-infected women will be infected with HIV; with treatment, the absolute risk drops to about 8%, a change of 17%. Because the absolute risk of an HIV-infected mother passing the virus to her infant is so much greater than a woman's risk of developing endometrial cancer (25% compared with 0.3%), a smaller change in relative risk translates into a much greater change in absolute risk.

7. *Is new health advice being offered?* If the media report new guidelines for health behavior or medical treatment, examine the source. Government agencies and national research foundations usually consider a great deal of evidence before offering health advice. Above all, use common sense, and check with your physician before making a major change in your health habits based on news reports.

SOURCES: Medical news: How to assess the latest breakthrough. 1997. *Consumer Reports,* June. Why do those #&*?@! "experts" keep changing their minds? 1996. *University of California at Berkeley Wellness Letter,* February. Ten tips for judging the medical news. 1993. *Harvard Women's Health Watch,* October. Health headlines. 1994. *Mayo Clinic Health Letter,* December.

HeartInfo—Heart Information Network. Provides information for heart patients and others interested in learning how to identify and reduce their risk factors for heart disease; includes links to many related sites.

http://www.heartinfo.org

National Heart, Lung, and Blood Institute. Provides information on a variety of topics relating to cardiovascular health and disease, including cholesterol, smoking, obesity, and hypertension; Web site has special fact sheets covering women and CVD.

800-575-WELL; 301-251-1222

http://www.nhlbi.nih.gov/nhlbi/nhlbi.htm

National Stroke Association. Provides information and referrals for stroke victims and their families; the Web site has a stroke risk assessment.

800-787-6537

http://www.stroke.org

See also the listings for Chapters 9 and 10.

SELECTED BIBLIOGRAPHY

Alfthan, G. 1997. Plasma homocysteine and cardiovascular disease mortality. *Lancet* 349:397.

American Heart Association. 1998. *Heart and Stroke Statistical Update* (retrieved January 25, 1998; http://www.americanheart.org/Scientific/HSstats98/index.html).

Daviglus, M. L. 1997. Dietary vitamin C, beta-carotene and 30-year risk of stroke: Results from the Western Electric Study. *Neuroepidemiology* 16:69–77.

Daviglus, M. L., et al. 1997. Fish consumption and the 30-year risk of fatal myocardial infarction. *New England Journal of Medicine* 336(15): 1046.

Dietschy, J. M. 1998. Dietary fatty acids and the regulation of plasma low density lipoprotein cholesterol concentrations. *Journal of Nutrition* 128(2): 444S–448S.

Eckel, R. H., and R. M. Krauss. 1998. American Heart Association call to action: Obesity as a major risk factor for coronary heart disease. *Circulation* 97(21): 2099–2101.

Fang, J., S. Madhaven, and M. H. Alderman. 1996. The association between birthplace and mortality from cardiovascular causes among black and white residents of New York City. *New England Journal of Medicine* 335(21): 1545–1551.

Glassman, A. H., and P. A. Shapiro. 1998. Depression and the course of coronary artery disease. *American Journal of Psychiatry* 115(1): 4–11.

Goff, D. C., et al. 1997. Greater incidence of hospitalized myocardial infarction among Mexican Americans than non-Hispanic whites: The Corpus Christi Heart Project, 1988–1992. *Circulation* 95(6): 1433–1440.

Hennekens, C. H. 1997. Antioxidant vitamins and cardiovascular disease: Current perspectives and future directions. *European Heart Journal* 18:177–179.

Howard, G., et al. 1998. Cigarette smoking and progression of atherosclerosis: The Atherosclerosis Risk in Communities (ARIC) study. *Journal of the American Medical Association* 279(2): 119–124.

Hu, F. B., et al. 1997. Dietary fat intake and the risk of coronary heart disease in women. *New England Journal of Medicine* 337: 1491–1499.

Kelley, G. A. 1997. Cardiovascular disease risk factors in black college students. *Journal of American College Health* 45: 165–169.

Kris-Etherton, P. M. 1997. Efficacy of multiple dietary therapies in reducing cardiovascular disease risk factors. *American Journal of Clinical Nutrition* 65:560–561.

Lessmeier, T. J., et al. 1997. Unrecognized paroxysmal supraventricular tachycardia: Potential for misdiagnosis as panic disorder. *Archives of Internal Medicine* 157(5): 537–543.

McCarron, D. A. 1997. Nutritional management of cardiovascular risk factors. A randomized clinical trial. *Archives of Internal Medicine* 157:169–177.

Meade, T. W. 1997. Fibrinogen and cardiovascular disease. *Journal of Clinical Pathology* 50:13–15.

Nagata, C., et al. 1998. Decreased serum total cholesterol concentration is associated with high intake of soy products in Japanese men and women. *Journal of Nutrition* 128(2): 209–213.

Rejeski, W. J., L. R. Brawley, and S. A. Schumaker. 1996. Physical activity and health-related quality of life. *Exercise and Sport Sciences Reviews* 24:71–108.

Ridker, P. M., et al. 1997. Inflammation, aspirin, and the risk of cardiovascular disease in apparently healthy men. *New England Journal of Medicine* 336(14): 973.

Rimm, E. B., et al. 1998. Folate and vitamin B6 from diet and supplements in relation to risk of coronary heart disease among women. *Journal of the American Medical Association* 279(5): 359–364.

Thun, M. J., et al. 1997. Alcohol consumption and mortality among middle-aged and elderly U.S. adults. *New England Journal of Medicine* 337:1705–1714.

Tzonou, A., et al. 1998. Dietary iron and coronary heart disease risk. A study from Greece. *American Journal of Epidemiology* 147(2): 161–166.

U.S. Department of Health and Human Services. 1996. *Physical Activity and Health: A Report of the Surgeon General.* Atlanta, Ga.: U.S. Department of Health and Human Services.

Williams, M. J. 1997. Regional fat distribution in women and risk of cardiovascular disease. *American Journal of Clinical Nutrition* 65:855–860.

LAB 11-1 *Cardiovascular Health*

Part I. CVD Risk Assessment

Your chances of suffering a heart attack or stroke before age 55 depend on a variety of factors, many of which are under your control. To help identify your risk factors, circle the response for each risk category that best describes you.

1. Sex
   - 0 Female
   - 2 Male

2. Heredity
   - 0 Neither parent suffered a heart attack or stroke before age 60.
   - 3 One parent suffered a heart attack or stroke before age 60.
   - 7 Both parents suffered a heart attack or stroke before age 60.

3. Smoking
   - 0 Never smoked
   - 1 Quit more than 2 years ago
   - 2 Quit less than 2 years ago
   - 8 Smoke less than ½ pack per day
   - 13 Smoke more than ½ pack per day
   - 15 Smoke more than 1 pack per day

4. Environmental Tobacco Smoke
   - 0 Do not live or work with smokers
   - 2 Exposed to ETS at work
   - 3 Live with smoker
   - 4 Both live and work with smokers

5. Blood Pressure
   The average of the last three readings:
   - 0 130/80 or below
   - 1 131/81–140/85
   - 5 141/86–150/90
   - 9 151/91–170/100
   - 13 Above 170/100

6. Total Cholesterol
   The average of the last three readings:
   - 0 Lower than 190
   - 1 190–210
   - 2 Don't know
   - 3 211–240
   - 4 241–270
   - 5 271–300
   - 6 Over 300

7. HDL Cholesterol
   The average of the last three readings:
   - 0 Over 65 mg/dl
   - 1 55–65
   - 2 Don't know HDL
   - 3 45–54
   - 5 35–44
   - 7 25–34
   - 12 Lower than 25

8. Exercise
   - 0 Endurance exercise three times a week
   - 1 Endurance exercise once or twice a week
   - 2 Occasional exercise less than once a week
   - 7 Rarely exercise

9. Diabetes
   - 0 No personal or family history
   - 2 One parent with diabetes
   - 6 Two parents with diabetes
   - 9 Type 2 diabetes
   - 13 Type 1 diabetes

10. Weight
    - 0 Near ideal weight
    - 1 6 pounds or less above ideal weight
    - 3 7–19 pounds above ideal weight
    - 5 20–40 pounds above ideal weight
    - 7 More than 40 pounds above ideal weight

11. Stress
    - 0 Relaxed most of the time
    - 1 Occasionally stressed and angry
    - 2 Frequently stressed and angry
    - 3 Usually stressed and angry

Scoring

Total your risk-factor points. Refer to the list below to get an approximate rating of your risk of suffering a heart attack or stroke before age 55.

Score	Estimated Risk
Less than 20	Low risk
20–29	Moderate risk
30–45	High risk
Over 45	Extremely high risk

Part II. Hostility Assessment

Current research indicates that there are three aspects of hostility that are particularly harmful to health: cynicism (a mistrusting attitude regarding other people's motives), anger (an emotional response to other people's "unacceptable" behavior), and aggression (behaviors in response to negative emotions such as anger and irritation). To get an idea of how hostile you are, check any of the following statements that are true for you.

_____ 1. Stuck in a long line at the express checkout in the grocery store, I often count the number of items the people in front of me have to see if anyone is over the limit.

_____ 2. I am often irritated by other people's incompetence.

_____ 3. If a cashier gives me the wrong change, I assume he or she is probably trying to cheat me.

_____ 4. I've been so angry at someone that I've thrown things or slammed a door.

_____ 5. If someone is late, I plan the angry words I'm going to say.

_____ 6. I tend to remember irritating incidents and get mad all over again.

_____ 7. If someone cuts me off in traffic, I honk my horn, flash my lights, pound the steering wheel, or shout.

_____ 8. Little annoyances have a way of adding up during the day, leaving me frustrated and impatient.

_____ 9. If the person who cuts my hair trims off more than I want, I fume about it for days afterward.

_____ 10. When I get into an argument, I feel my jaw clench and my pulse and breathing rate climb.

_____ 11. If someone mistreats me, I look for an opportunity to pay them back, just for the principle of the thing.

_____ 12. I find myself getting annoyed at little things my spouse or significant other does that get under my skin.

Add up the number of items you checked. A score of 3 or less indicates a generally cool head. A score between 4 and 8 indicates that your level of hostility could be raising your risk of heart disease. A score of 9 or more indicates a hot head—a level of cynicism, anger, and aggression high enough to endanger both heart health and interpersonal relationships.

If you are a hot head, try keeping a log of your hostile responses to people and situations. Familiarize yourself with the patterns of thinking that lead to hostile feelings, and try to head them off before they develop into full-blown anger. If you feel your anger starting to build, ask yourself the following questions:

1. *Is this really important enough to get angry about?* For example, is having to wait an extra 5 minutes for a late bus so important that you should stew about it for half an hour?

2. *Am I really justified in getting angry?* Is the person in front of you really driving slowly, or are you trying to speed?

3. *Is getting angry going to make any real difference in this situation?* Will slamming the door really help your friend find the concert tickets he misplaced?

If you answered "yes" to all three questions, then you should calmly but assertively ask for what you want. A "no" to any question means that you should try to diffuse your anger. Reason with yourself, distract your mind with another activity, or try one of the techniques for meditation or deep breathing described in Chapter 10.

To monitor your progress toward your goal, enter the results of this lab in the Preprogram Assessment column of Appendix D. After several weeks of a program to reduce CVD risk, do this lab again and enter the results in the Postprogram Assessment column of Appendix D. How do the results compare?

SOURCE: CVD risk assessment from Insel, P. M., and W. T. Roth. 1998. *Core Concepts in Health.* 8th ed. Mountain View, Calif.: Mayfield. Hostility quiz from Williams, R. B., and V. Williams. 1993. *Anger Kills.* Copyright © 1993 by Redford B. Williams, M.D., and Virginia Williams, Ph.D. Adapted with permission of Times Books, a division of Random House, Inc.

Cancer

12

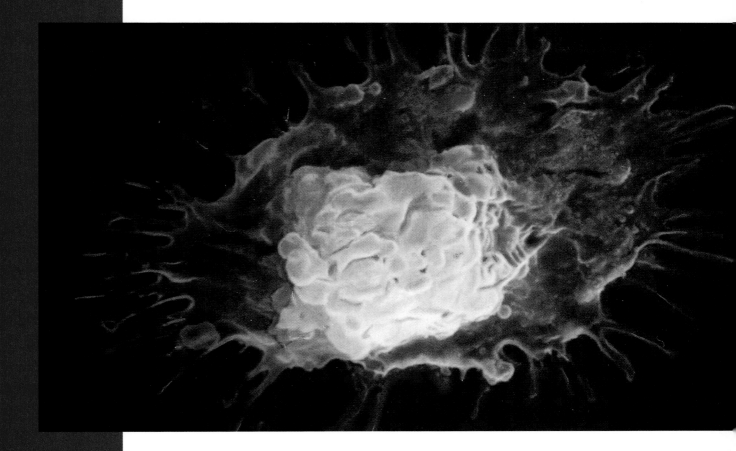

LOOKING AHEAD

After reading this chapter, you should be able to answer these questions about cancer:

- What is cancer? How does it spread?

- What are the most common forms of cancer, and what are the risk factors associated with each form?

- What causes cancer?

- What are the signs and symptoms of cancer in its early stages?

- What can an individual do to lower her or his risk of cancer?

Cancer is probably the most feared illness in the United States, although cardiovascular disease is the leading cause of death. About 85 million Americans, or approximately one in three, will develop cancer. New cancer-causing agents and risks are constantly being identified, and yet to many people the disease continues to seem mysterious and untreatable. In fact, there are many steps most individuals can take to protect themselves from cancer and, if those fail, to detect it in its earliest, most treatable stages.

This chapter provides basic information about common types of cancer, specific guidelines for prevention, and treatment strategies. It describes how to integrate a preventive point of view into your daily life and your general health awareness.

WHAT IS CANCER?

Cancer is the abnormal, uncontrolled growth of cells, which if left untreated, can ultimately cause death.

Benign Versus Malignant Tumors

Most cancers take the form of tumors, although not all tumors are cancerous. A tumor is simply a mass of tissue that serves no physiological purpose. It can be benign, like a wart, or malignant, like most lung cancers. The term **malignant tumor** (or *neoplasm*) is synonymous with cancer.

Benign tumors are made up of cells similar to the surrounding normal cells and are enclosed in a membrane that prevents them from penetrating neighboring tissues. They are dangerous only if their physical presence interferes with body functions. A malignant tumor, or cancer, is capable of invading surrounding structures, including blood vessels, the **lymphatic system,** and nerves. It can also spread to distant sites via the blood and lymphatic circulation. A few cancers, like leukemia, cancer of the blood, do not produce a mass but still have the fundamental property of rapid, uncontrolled growth of cells.

TERMS   **cancer**   Abnormal, uncontrolled cellular growth.

malignant tumor   A tumor that is cancerous and capable of spreading.

benign tumor   A tumor that is not malignant or cancerous.

lymphatic system   A system of vessels that returns proteins, lipids, and other substances from fluid in the tissues to the circulatory system.

metastasis   The spread of cancer cells from one part of the body to another.

carcinogen   Any substance that causes cancer.

Every case of cancer begins as a change in a cell that allows it to grow and divide when it should not. A malignant cell divides without regard for normal control mechanisms and gradually produces a mass of abnormal cells, or a tumor. It takes about a billion cells to make a mass the size of a pea, so a single tumor cell must go through many divisions, often taking years, before the tumor grows to a noticeable size.

Eventually a tumor produces a sign or symptom that is detected. In an accessible location, a tumor may be felt as a lump. In less accessible locations, a tumor may be noticed only after considerable growth has taken place and may then be detected only by an indirect symptom—for instance, a persistent cough, unexplained bleeding or pain, or serious fatigue.

How Cancer Spreads: Metastasis

Metastasis, the spreading of cancer cells, occurs because cancer cells do not stick to each other as strongly as normal cells do and therefore may not remain at the site of the *primary tumor,* the original location. They break away and can pass through the lining of lymph or blood vessels to invade nearby tissue. They can also drift to distant parts of the body, where they establish new colonies of cancer cells. This traveling and seeding process is called metastasizing, and the new tumors are called *secondary tumors,* or *metastases.*

This ability of cancer cells to metastasize makes early cancer detection critical. To control the cancer and prevent death, every cancerous cell must be removed. Once cancer cells enter either the lymphatic system or the bloodstream, it is extremely difficult to stop their spread to other organs of the body.

COMMON CANCERS

Currently, about 1.2 million people are diagnosed with cancer each year, and more than 500,000 die (Figure 12-1). These statistics exclude the more than 1 million cases of the easily curable types of skin cancer. There are currently about 8 million Americans alive today who have a history of cancer.

A discussion of all types of cancer is beyond the scope of this book. In this section we look at some of the most common cancers and their causes, prevention, and treatment.

Lung Cancer

Lung cancer is the most common cause of cancer death in the United States; it is responsible for over 160,000 deaths each year. For over 40 years, breast cancer was the major cause of cancer death in women, but since 1987,

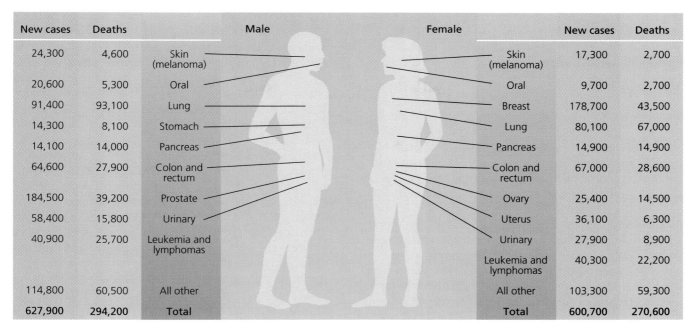

New cases	Deaths	Male	Female	New cases	Deaths
24,300	4,600	Skin (melanoma)	Skin (melanoma)	17,300	2,700
20,600	5,300	Oral	Oral	9,700	2,700
91,400	93,100	Lung	Breast	178,700	43,500
14,300	8,100	Stomach	Lung	80,100	67,000
14,100	14,000	Pancreas	Pancreas	14,900	14,900
64,600	27,900	Colon and rectum	Colon and rectum	67,000	28,600
184,500	39,200	Prostate	Ovary	25,400	14,500
58,400	15,800	Urinary	Uterus	36,100	6,300
40,900	25,700	Leukemia and lymphomas	Urinary	27,900	8,900
			Leukemia and lymphomas	40,300	22,200
114,800	60,500	All other	All other	103,300	59,300
627,900	294,200	Total	Total	600,700	270,600

Figure 12-1   Estimated new cancer cases and deaths by site and sex, United States, 1998.
SOURCE: American Cancer Society, 1998. *Cancer Facts and Figures, 1998.* New York: American Cancer Society.

Smoking is responsible for about 30% of all cancer deaths. The benefits of quitting are substantial: Lung cancer risk decreases significantly after one smoke-free year and approaches that of nonsmokers after 10 smoke-free years.

lung cancer has surpassed breast cancer as a killer of women.

The chief risk factor for lung cancer is tobacco smoke, which accounts for 87% of cancers. When smoking is combined with exposure to other environmental **carcinogens,** such as asbestos particles, the risk of cancer can be multiplied by a factor of 10 or more. But the smoker is not the only one at risk. In 1993 the U.S. Environmental Protection Agency (EPA) classified environmental tobacco smoke (ETS) as a human carcinogen. Long-term exposure

to ETS increases risk for lung cancer, and it's estimated that ETS causes about 3000 lung cancer deaths each year.

Symptoms of lung cancer do not usually appear until the disease has advanced to the invasive stage. Signals such as a persistent cough, chest pain, or recurring bronchitis may be the first indication of a tumor's presence. Lung cancer is most often treated by some combination of surgery, radiation, and chemotherapy; if all the tumor cells can be removed or killed, a cure is possible. Unfortunately, lung cancer is usually detected only after it has begun to spread, and only about 14% of lung cancer patients are alive 5 years after diagnosis.

Colon and Rectal Cancer

Another common cancer in the United States is colon and rectal cancer (also called colorectal cancer). It is clearly linked to both diet and genetic predisposition. In countries where the diet is low in fat and high in fiber, the incidence of this cancer may be only 10–20% of that of the United States. Decreasing the amount of fat and increasing the amount of insoluble fiber (found in fruits, vegetables, and whole grains) in your diet can minimize your risk of colon cancer. A high-fiber diet can slow or even reverse precancerous changes in colon cells. In addition, recent research has shown that regular aspirin use may reduce the risk.

Colon cancer rarely occurs before age 40, but to have the best chance of preventing it, you should begin to make dietary changes now. Most colon cancers arise from preexisting polyps, small growths on the wall of the colon that may gradually develop into malignancies over a period of years. The tendency of an individual to form colon polyps appears to be determined by specific genes, so be particularly vigilant if any close relative has had colon cancer.

Because polyps may bleed as they progress, the standard warning signs of colon cancer are bleeding from the rectum or a change in bowel habits. A stool blood test, performed during a routine physical exam, can detect small amounts of blood in the stool long before obvious bleeding would be noticed. The American Cancer Society (ACS) recommends that this examination be performed annually after age 40. A polyp may be directly detected and even removed with a sigmoidoscope, a flexible fiberoptic device inserted through the rectum. Surgery is the most effective method of treating colon cancer. Colon and rectal cancer is more curable than lung cancer, particularly if caught before it spreads.

Breast Cancer

Breast cancer is the most common cancer in women and causes almost as many deaths in women as lung cancer. In men, breast cancer occurs only rarely. In the United States, about one woman in nine will develop breast cancer during her lifetime. About 79% of patients survive at least 5 years after the diagnosis is made, and most of these achieve a complete cure.

There is a strong genetic factor in breast cancer. A woman who has two close relatives with breast cancer is four to six times more likely to develop the disease than a woman who has no close relatives with breast cancer. However, even though genetic factors do increase the risk of breast cancer, only about 15% of cancers occur in women with a family history of it.

Other risk factors include increasing age, early onset of menstruation, having a first child after age 30, obesity, and alcohol use. The unifying factor for many of these risk factors may be exposure to the female sex hormone estrogen, which circulates in a woman's body in high concentrations between puberty and menopause. Estrogen promotes the growth of cells in a variety of sites, including breast tissue and the uterus. Fat cells also produce estrogen, and alcohol can increase estrogen levels in the blood. Estrogen may promote cancer in sites that are estrogen-responsive.

Breast cancer has been called a "disease of civilization" because incidence is high in industrialized Western countries but remains low in developing non-Western countries. This pattern has led some researchers to point to a link between breast cancer and the Western lifestyle. The links between breast cancer and diet and exercise habits are still being investigated. Research suggests that women may be more likely to get breast cancer if their diet is low in fiber, if they are sedentary, or if they are obese. Maintaining a normal weight by exercising regularly and eating a low-fat, high-fiber diet can minimize the chance of developing breast cancer, even for women at risk from family history or other factors.

The ACS advises a three-part personal program for the early detection of breast cancer:

1. Monthly breast self-examination (BSE) for all women 20 and over (see the box "Breast Self-Examination").

2. A clinical breast exam by a physician every 3 years for women 20 to 40 and every year for women over 40.

3. **Mammography** (low-dose breast X rays) every year for most women 40 and over. (Individual risk factors must be considered in determining the frequency of mammography, and the value of mammography for women in their forties is an area of debate.)

If a lump is detected, it may be scanned by **ultrasonography** and **biopsied** to see if it is cancerous. In 90% of cases, the lump is found to be a cyst or other harmless growth, and no further treatment is needed. If the lump does contain cancer cells, a variety of surgeries may be called for, ranging from a lumpectomy (removal of the lump and surrounding tissue) to a mastectomy (removal of the breast). Chemotherapy or radiation may also be

TERMS **mammography** Low-dose X rays of the breasts used for the early detection of breast cancer.

ultrasonography An imaging method in which inaudible high-pitched sound (ultrasound) is bounced off body structures to create an image on a monitor.

biopsy The removal and examination of a small piece of body tissue for the purpose of diagnosis.

All women age 20 and over should perform a monthly breast self-exam to help in the early detection of breast cancer. When performed regularly, breast self-exam helps you get to know how your breasts normally feel. You will then quickly be able to feel any changes.

The best time to do breast self-exam is right after your period, when your breasts are not tender or swollen. If you do not have regular periods or sometimes skip a month, do breast self-exam on the same day every month. If you discover a lump or detect any changes, seek medical attention. Most breast lumps and changes are not cancerous, but it's best to be sure.

1. Lie down and put a pillow under your right shoulder. Place your right arm behind your head.

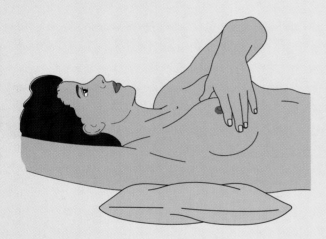

2. Use the finger pads of your three middle fingers on your left hand to feel for lumps or thickening. Your finger pads are the top third of each finger.

3. Press firmly enough to know how your breast feels. If you're not sure how hard to press, ask your health care provider. Or try to copy the way your health care provider uses the finger pads during a breast exam. Learn what your breast feels like most of the time. A firm ridge in the lower curve of each breast is normal.

4. Move around the breast in a set way. You can choose either (a) the circle pattern, (b) the up-and-down pattern, or (c) the wedge pattern. Use the same pattern every time you examine your breasts to help make sure that you've gone over the entire breast area and to remember how your breast feels.

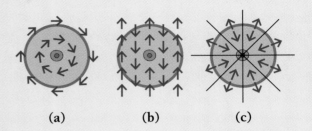

(a)   (b)   (c)

5. Using the same technique, examine your left breast with the finger pads of your right hand.

6. If you find any changes, see your health care provider right away.

For added safety, you should also check your breasts while standing in front of a mirror right after you do your breast self-exam each month. See if there are any changes in the way your breasts look, such as dimpling of the skin, changes in the nipple, or redness or swelling.

You might also want to do a breast self-exam while you're in the shower. Your soapy hands will glide over wet skin, making it easy to check how your breasts feel.

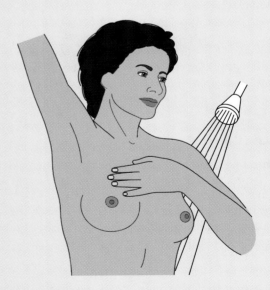

SOURCE: *How to Do Breast Self-Examination.* © 1997, American Cancer Society, Inc. Reprinted by the permission of the American Cancer Society, Inc.

Stanford University psychiatrist Dr. David Spiegel and his colleagues carried out a 3-year study on women with advanced breast cancer to determine how participation in a support group would affect their psychological health. Women in the experimental group not only received standard medical care but also participated in weekly group therapy sessions. In the support group, women shared their fears, planned means of coping with the threat of death, grieved over the loss of group members, learned to control their pain with self-hypnosis, and looked for ways to live more fully in the time they had left.

At the conclusion of the study, researchers found that women in the study had, indeed, been helped by the support group. They were less anxious and depressed and were better able to control their pain than women in the control group, who received only standard medical treatment. The real surprise came several years later when Dr. Spiegel reexamined the data from this study. He found that the women who participated in the support group also lived on average more than twice as long from the start of the study than women in the control group.

How might support groups improve the survival as well as the psychological health of participants? Researchers have hypothesized several ways in which psychosocial support could be translated into changes in physical health.

- Social support may affect behavior, making patients in a support group more likely to engage in healthy behaviors

such as eating well, exercising regularly, and getting plenty of sleep.

- Cancer patients who benefit from group support might interact more effectively with their physicians, eliciting more vigorous medical treatment.

- Support groups may buffer people against stress, cushioning the body from the effects of the stress response.

- In light of the close relationship between the brain and the immune system, feeling understood and supported may affect the functioning of the immune system in some way that enables the body to fight cancer more effectively.

Additional research should help clarify how support groups benefit cancer patients. In the meantime, this study can serve as a reminder of the powerful effects social support has on our physical and emotional well-being, whether we are coping with a life-threatening illness or the challenges of everyday life.

SOURCES: Adapted from Spiegel, D. 1993. *Living Beyond Limits: New Hope and Help for Facing Life-Threatening Illness.* New York: Random House. Spiegel, D., J. R. Bloom, H. C. Kraemer, and E. Gottheil. 1989. Effect of psychosocial treatment on survival of patients with metastatic breast cancer. *Lancet* ii:888–891.

used. In addition, recent studies have shown that social support can have a significant impact on the course of the disease (see the box "Support Groups and Cancer Survival").

The chance of survival in cases of breast cancer varies, depending both on the nature of the tumor and whether it has metastasized. If the tumor is discovered early, before it has spread to the adjacent lymph nodes, the patient has about a 96% chance of surviving more than 5 years.

Prostate Cancer

The prostate gland is situated at the base of the bladder in men. It produces seminal fluid; if enlarged, it can block the flow of urine. Prostate cancer is the most common cancer in men and, after lung and colon cancer, the cause of the most deaths. Some 180,000 new cases of prostate cancer are diagnosed in the United States each year in men over the age of 65.

While age is the strongest predictor of the risk of prostate cancer, diet and lifestyle also influence its occurrence. Dietary fat, in particular, is linked to prostate cancer. For reasons not well understood, African American men are about 30% more likely to develop prostate cancer than white Americans. A family history of prostate cancer is also a risk factor.

The best method of controlling prostate cancer is through early detection. Most cases are first detected by

rectal examination during a routine physical exam. A new blood test that measures the amount of prostate-specific antigen (PSA) in the blood can also be used to help diagnose prostate cancer. The **PSA blood test** is probably most useful if it is repeated over time to chart a rate of change. Ultrasound and biopsy may also be used to detect and diagnose prostate cancer.

If the tumor is malignant, the prostate is usually removed surgically. A newer treatment involves radiation of the tumor by means of radioactive seeds that are surgically placed in the prostate gland. The 5-year survival rate for prostate cancer is currently about 87%.

Cancers of the Female Reproductive Tract

Because the uterus, cervix, and ovaries are subject to similar hormonal influences, the cancers of these organs can be discussed as a group. Uterine cancer is the most common, but ovarian cancer and cervical cancer are more deadly.

Cervical Cancer   Cervical cancer is at least in part a sexually transmitted disease. Probably more than 80% of cervical cancer stems from infection by the human papillomavirus (HPV), which is transmitted during unprotected sex. Screening for the changes in cervical cells that precede cancer is done chiefly by means of the **Pap test.** During a pelvic exam, loose cells are scraped from the cervix, spread on a slide, stained for easier viewing, and examined under a microscope to see whether they are normal in size and shape. If cells are abnormal, a condition commonly referred to as *cervical dysplasia,* the Pap test is repeated at intervals. Sometimes cervical cells spontaneously return to normal, but in about one-third of cases, the cellular changes progress toward malignancy. If this happens, the abnormal cells must be removed.

Uterine or Endometrial Cancer   Cancer of the lining of the uterus, or endometrium, most often occurs after age 55. The risk factors are similar to those for breast cancer: prolonged exposure to estrogen, early onset of menstruation, late menopause, never having been pregnant, and other medical conditions, including obesity. The use of oral contraceptives, which combine estrogen and progestin, appears to provide protection.

Endometrial cancer is usually detectable by pelvic examination. It is treated surgically, commonly by hysterectomy (removal of the uterus). When the tumor is detected at an early stage, about 95% of patients are alive and disease-free 5 years later.

Ovarian Cancer   Although ovarian cancer is rare compared with cervical or uterine cancer, it causes more deaths than the other two combined. It cannot be detected by Pap tests or any other simple screening method, and there are often no warning signs. The risk factors are similar to those for breast and endometrial cancer: increasing age, never having been pregnant, a family history of breast or ovarian cancer, and specific genetic mutations. Anything that lowers a woman's lifetime number of ovulation cycles—pregnancy, breastfeeding, or use of oral contraceptives—appears to reduce risk of ovarian cancer.

Women at high risk should have thorough pelvic exams at regular intervals, perhaps with ultrasound imaging of the ovaries. Ovarian cancer is treated by surgical removal of both ovaries, the fallopian tubes, and the uterus.

Other Female Reproductive Tract Cancers   Daughters born to women who took DES (diethylstilbestrol) to prevent miscarriage have an increased risk, about 1 in 1000, of a vaginal or cervical cancer called clear cell cancer. There is also some risk to DES sons, who may have an increased risk of abnormalities of the reproductive tract, including undescended testicles, a risk factor for testicular cancer. (If you are under age 25, there is little chance that you could have been exposed to DES.) A DES daughter should find a physician who is familiar with the problems of DES exposure; more frequent and more thorough pelvic exams may be recommended.

Skin Cancer

Skin cancer is the most common cancer of all when cases of the highly curable forms are included in the count. (Usually these forms are not included, precisely because

Cumulative exposure to sunlight, beginning in childhood, increases the risk of skin cancer later in life. Blistering sunburns are particularly dangerous, but tanning also poses a hazard. Sunscreens help protect the skin from the sun's radiation.

they are easily treated.) Treatments are usually simple and successful when the cancers are caught early.

Almost all cases of skin cancer can be traced to excessive exposure to the **ultraviolet (UV) radiation** of the sun, especially during childhood. Because of the link between severe sunburns in childhood and greatly increased risk of skin cancer in later life, children in particular should be protected.

People with naturally dark skin pigmentation have a considerable degree of protection against skin cancer. Conversely, people with fair skin have lower natural protection against skin damage from the sun and a higher risk of developing certain skin cancers. Both severe, acute sun reactions (sunburns) and chronic low-level sun reactions (suntans) can lead to skin cancer. Tanning salons do not offer a safe tan.

There are three main types of skin cancer, named for the types of skin cell from which they develop. **Basal cell**

PSA blood test   A diagnostic test for prostate cancer that measures blood levels of prostate-specific antigen (PSA).   **TERMS**

Pap test   A scraping of cells from the cervix for examination under a microscope to detect cancer; also called Pap smear.

ultraviolet (UV) radiation   Light rays of a specific wavelength, emitted by the sun; most UV rays are blocked by the ozone layer in the upper atmosphere. Exposure to ultraviolet A (UVA) and/or ultraviolet B (UVB) rays is linked to the development of skin cancer.

basal cell carcinoma   Cancer of the deepest layers of the skin.

and **squamous cell carcinomas** together account for about 95% of the skin cancers diagnosed each year. They are usually found in chronically sun-exposed areas, such as the face, neck, hands, and arms. They usually appear as pale, waxlike, pearly nodules, or red, scaly, sharply outlined patches. These cancers are often painless, although they may bleed, crust, and form an open sore on the skin.

Melanoma is by far the most dangerous skin cancer because it spreads so rapidly. Since 1973, the incidence of melanoma has increased by about 4% per year. It is the most common cancer among women age 25–29 years. It can occur anywhere on the body, but the most common sites are the back, chest, abdomen, and lower legs. A melanoma usually appears at the site of a preexisting mole. The mole may begin to enlarge, become mottled or varied in color (colors can include blue, pink, and white), or develop an irregular surface or irregular borders. Tissue invaded by melanoma may also itch, burn, or bleed easily.

One of the major steps you can take to protect yourself against all forms of skin cancer is to avoid lifelong overexposure to sunlight. People of every age, including babies and children, need to be protected from the sun with sunscreens and protective clothing (see the box "Protecting Your Skin from the Sun"). You can help with early detection by making it a habit to examine your skin regularly. Most of the spots, freckles, moles, and blemishes on your body are normal. But if you notice an unusual growth, discoloration, or sore that does not heal, see your physician or a dermatologist immediately. The characteristics that may signal that a skin lesion is a melanoma—asymmetry, border irregularity, color change, and a diameter greater than ¼ inch—are illustrated in Figure 12-2.

If you do have an unusual skin lesion, your physician will examine it and possibly perform a biopsy. If the lesion is cancerous, it is usually removed surgically, a procedure that can almost always be performed in the physician's office using a local anesthetic.

Oral Cancer

Oral cancer—cancers of the lip, tongue, mouth, and throat—can be traced principally to cigarette, cigar, or pipe smoking, the use of smokeless (spit) tobacco, and the excess use of alcohol. These risk factors work together to multiply a person's risk of oral cancer. The incidence of oral cancer is twice as great in men as in women and most frequent in men over 40.

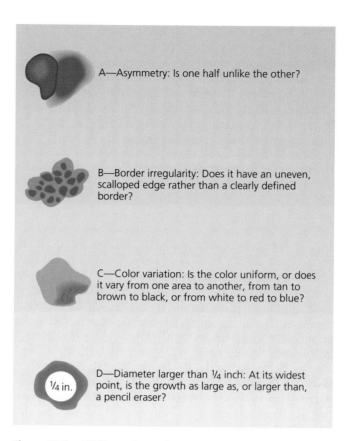

Figure 12-2   ABCD test for melanoma.   SOURCE: American Academy of Dermatology.

Oral cancers do have the virtue of being fairly easy to detect, but they are often hard to cure. The primary methods of treatment are surgery and radiation.

Testicular Cancer

Testicular cancer is relatively rare, accounting for only 1% of cancers in men, but it is the most common cancer in men age 29–35. Self-examination helps in the early detection of testicular cancer (see the box "Testicle Self-Examination"). Testicular cancer is much more common among white Americans than Latinos, Asian Americans, or African Americans. Men with undescended testicles are at increased risk for testicular cancer, and for this reason the condition should be corrected in early childhood. Tumors are treated by surgical removal of the testicle and, if the tumor has spread, by chemotherapy.

Other Cancers

There were about 55,000 cases of bladder cancer in the United States in 1998. Bladder cancer is four times as common in men as in women, and smoking is responsible for about half of all cases in men. People living in urban areas, and workers exposed to dye, rubber, or leather, are at increased risk. The first symptoms are likely to be

TERMS   **squamous cell carcinoma**   Cancer of the surface layers of the skin.

melanoma   A malignant tumor of the skin that arises from pigmented cells, usually a mole.

With proper clothing and the use of sunscreens, you can lead an active outdoor life *and* protect your skin against most sun-induced damage.

Clothing

- Wear long-sleeved shirts made of tightly woven fabric to protect the forearms, chest, and back. Thin, white shirts and wet clothing that clings to the body will not protect you sufficiently.

- Wear a wide-brimmed hat to protect the ears, forehead, and upper cheeks. (Wear UV-blocking sunglasses to protect your eyes.)

Sunscreen

- Use a sunscreen and lip balm with an SPF (sun protection factor) of 15 or higher. (An SPF rating refers to the amount of time you can stay out in the sun before you burn, compared to using no sunscreen; for example, a product with an SPF of 15 would allow you to remain in the sun without burning 15 times longer, on average, than if you didn't apply sunscreen.) If you're fair-skinned or will be outdoors for long hours, use a sunscreen with a high SPF. Look for the seal of approval from the Skin Cancer Foundation, which tests sunscreens with SPF 15 or higher for safety and effectiveness.

- Choose a "broad-spectrum" sunscreen that protects against both types of ultraviolet radiation—UVA and UVB. The SPF rating of a sunscreen currently applies only to UVB rays, which are the primary cause of sunburn; but both UVA and UVB rays play a role in the development of skin cancer. (Many tanning salon devices emit UVA radiation.) Broad-spectrum sunscreens include ingredient combinations that work together to block a broad range of light waves and also wash off less easily.

- Apply sunscreen 30–45 minutes before exposure. This allows time for the sunscreen to penetrate the skin. Shake sunscreen before applying it.

- Reapply sunscreen frequently and generously to all sun-exposed areas. Most people use less than half as much as they would need to attain the full SPF rating. One ounce of sunscreen is about enough to cover an average-size adult in a swimsuit. Use a water-resistant sunscreen if you swim or sweat quite a bit.

- If you're taking medication, ask your physician or pharmacist about possible reactions to sunlight and interactions with sunscreens. If you're using sunscreen and an insect repellent containing DEET, use extra sunscreen (DEET decreases sunscreen effectiveness).

- Don't let sunscreens give you a false sense of security. The effectiveness of sunscreens in preventing skin cancer has not been firmly established, so even if you wear sunscreen and don't burn, sun exposure may increase your cancer risk. For people at greatest risk—those with fair skin and the tendency to develop many moles—avoiding sun exposure may be the safest strategy.

Time of Day and Location

- Try to avoid sun exposure between 10 A.M. and 4 P.M., when the sun's rays are most intense. Clouds allow as much as 80% of UV rays to reach your skin. Stay in the shade when you can, and use an umbrella at the beach.

- Consult the day's UV Index in your local newspaper (or by calling the weather bureau) to get a sense for the amount of sun protection you'll need. The index predicts UV levels on a 0–10 scale; take special care on days with a rating of 5 or above.

- UV rays can penetrate at least 3 feet in water, so swimmers should wear water-resistant sunscreen.

- Locations near the equator have more intense sunlight, so stronger sunscreens should be used and applied often. High elevations also have intense sunlight, because there is less atmosphere to filter the UV rays.

- Snow reflects the sun's rays, so don't forget to apply sunscreen before skiing and other snow activities. Sand and water also reflect the sun's rays, so you still need to apply a sunscreen if you are under a beach umbrella. Concrete and white-painted surfaces are also highly reflective.

SOURCES: American Cancer Society press release. 1998. *American Cancer Society Responds to Report on Sunscreens and Melanoma* (retrieved February 20, 1998; http://www.cancer.org/media/story/021898.html). Potera, C. 1997. Help patients get serious about sunscreens. *The Physician and Sportsmedicine* 25(5). Ten rules to save your skin. *University of California at Berkeley Wellness Letter*, June.

blood in the urine and/or increased frequency of urination. These symptoms should motivate a quick trip to your physician for a thorough exam, because the survival rate for early-stage bladder cancer is 93%.

Pancreatic cancer is the fifth leading cancer killer, with about 29,000 deaths in the United States in 1998. Pancreatic cancer is both hard to detect and almost always fatal. The major environmental risk factor is smoking. In addition, countries where the diet is high in fat have higher rates of pancreatic cancer. The disease often has a "silent" course, and by the time symptoms occur, it is usually far advanced.

Leukemias, cancers of the blood-forming tissues, are characterized by the abnormal production of immature white blood cells. The rapid growth of these cells displaces red blood cell precursors and can lead to anemia. Because malignant white cells no longer fight infection, the immune system also loses its ability to defend against

You can increase your chances of early cancer detection by performing a monthly testicle self-exam. It is important that you know what your own testicles feel like normally so that you will recognize any changes. The best time to perform the examination is after a warm shower or bath, when the scrotum is relaxed.

- First, stand in front of a mirror and look for any swelling on the scrotum.

- Next, examine each testicle. With your thumb on top of the testicle and two fingers underneath, gently roll the testicle to check for lumps or areas of particular firmness. A normal testicle is smooth, oval, and uniformly firm to the touch. Don't be concerned if your testicles are slightly different in size; this is common. Also, don't mistake the epididymis, the tube at the rear of the testicle that carries sperm, for an abnormality.

- If you find any hard lumps or nodules, or if there has been any change in the shape, size, or texture of the testicles since your last self-exam, consult a physician. These signs

may not indicate a malignancy, but only your physician can make a diagnosis.

SOURCES: Testicular Self-Exam (TSE). 1997. *Cancer Smart* 3(3): 11. American Cancer Society. 1990. *For Men Only: Testicular Cancer and How to Do TSE (a Self-Exam)*. New York: American Cancer Society.

VITAL STATISTICS

TABLE 12-1	*Causes of Cancer*

Risk Factor	Percentage of All Cancer Deaths Linked to Risk Factor
Tobacco	30
Diet and obesity	30
Sedentary lifestyle	5
Family history of cancer	5
Occupational factors	5
Viruses and other biological agents	5
Alcohol	3
Environmental pollution	2
Ultraviolet radiation	2

SOURCE: Harvard Center for Cancer Prevention. 1996. *Harvard Report on Cancer Prevention. Vol. 1: Causes of Human Cancer.*

infectious agents. There are about 29,000 new cases of leukemia each year, and about 22,000 deaths. Risk factors for leukemia have not been clearly established, but certain chemicals and viruses may play a role.

Lymphomas, cancers of the lymph system, are closely related to leukemias; they include Hodgkin's disease and lymphosarcoma. Treatments have been greatly improved, and many patients can lead normal lives for many years. The 5-year survival rate for Hodgkin's disease has increased from 40% to 79% over the past 30 years.

THE CAUSES OF CANCER

Although scientists do not know everything about what causes cancer, they have identified genetic, environmental, and lifestyle factors (Table 12-1). Typically, these factors work together (see the box "Can Poverty Cause Cancer?"). There are usually several steps in the transformation of a normal cell into a cancer cell, and in many cases, different factors may work together in the development of cancer.

The Role of DNA

Almost daily, the mass media report on some new link between heredity and cancer. But how exactly do genes influence cancer? And what do these links mean for you and your risk of developing particular cancers?

DNA Basics   The nucleus of each cell in your body contains 23 pairs of **chromosomes**, which are made up of tightly packed coils of **DNA** (deoxyribonucleic acid). Each chromosome contains thousands of **genes**; you have about 100,000 genes in all. Each of your genes controls the production of a particular protein. By making different proteins at different times, genes can act as switches to alter the ways a cell works. Some genes are responsible for controlling the rate of cell division.

DNA Mutations and Cancer   A mutation is any change in the makeup of a gene. Some mutations are inherited; others are caused by environmental agents known as *mutagens*. Mutagens include radiation, certain viruses, and chemical substances in the air we breathe. (When a

Americans with low incomes are more susceptible to cancer and are also more likely to die of it, even if their condition and treatment are similar to those of more affluent cancer victims. Why does cancer afflict the economically disadvantaged so disproportionately? One factor is lifestyle: People with low incomes are more likely to smoke, abuse alcohol, and eat high-fat foods—all of which have been associated with cancer. These unhealthy behaviors usually begin early: A recent study found that 63% of teenagers of parents with low incomes engage in two or more of five cancer-related behaviors: smoking, inactivity, an inadequate intake of fruits and vegetables, excessive fat consumption, and alcohol use. The rates of these behaviors among adolescents of more affluent parents are significantly lower.

Another reason is lack of knowledge and information. People with low incomes are less exposed to information about cancer, less aware of its early warning signs, and less likely to seek medical care when they have such symptoms. A third reason may be an inability to respond to health information and health needs. Many people who have low incomes may know they should eat nutritious foods and get regular checkups, but they still may not be able to afford such foods and may not have transportation or access to health care facilities.

In fact, lifestyle differences account for only about 13% of the gap in death rates between Americans with high and low incomes. Many of the cancer-related threats that people with low incomes face are difficult or impossible to avoid. They may be forced to live and work in unsafe or unhealthy environments. They may have jobs, for example, in which they come into daily contact with carcinogenic chemicals, and they may not have been trained in handling them properly. They face similar risks in their homes and schools, where they may be exposed to asbestos or other carcinogens every day.

Another possible explanation for the association between poverty and cancer is the high levels of stress associated with poverty. Stress can impair the immune system, the body's first line of defense against cancer, and experiments with animals have shown that a stressful environment can enhance the growth of a variety of tumors. The link between poverty, stress, and cancer mortality in humans has not been proven, but studies have shown a link between stress and other illnesses.

What can be done about reducing the rate of cancer and cancer mortality in low-income populations? Educating people about prevention is clearly important, and elementary schools and high schools are places where people can be reached in time to encourage healthy habits and prevent bad habits before they begin. However, people from lower socioeconomic groups tend to have a high rate of school dropout. Furthermore, most people have a difficult time worrying about a disease they might get in 10 or 20 years when their immediate concern is survival.

For these reasons, some medical scientists look to policymakers for solutions. They maintain that living and working conditions in the inner cities must be improved. Then, even without new medical breakthroughs, the United States will see a real decrease in cancer rates in low-income populations.

SOURCES: Lantz, P. M., et al. 1998. Socioeconomic factors, health behaviors, and mortality. *Journal of the American Medical Association* 279: 1703–1708. Lowry, R., et al. 1996. The effect of socioeconomic status on chronic disease risk behaviors among U.S. adolescents. *Journal of the American Medical Association,* 276(10): 792–797. Grabmeier, J. 1992. Poverty can cause cancer. *USA Today,* July.

mutagen also causes cancer, it is called a carcinogen.) Some mutations are the result of copying errors that occur when DNA replicates itself as part of cell division.

A mutated gene no longer contains the proper code for producing its protein. It usually takes several mutational changes before a normal cell takes on the properties of a cancer cell. Genes in which mutations are associated with the conversion of a normal cell into a cancer cell are known as **oncogenes.** In their undamaged form, many oncogenes play a role in controlling or restricting cell growth; they are called suppressor genes. Mutational damage to suppressor genes releases the brake on growth and leads to rapid and uncontrolled cell division—a precondition for the development of cancer.

An example of an inherited mutated oncogene is an alteration in a suppressor gene vital for controlling the growth of colon cells. About 25% of all Americans have this alteration. As these individuals age, they tend to form colon polyps, which can progress to cancer. Another example is BRCA1 (breast cancer gene 1): Women who inherit a damaged copy of this suppressor gene face a significantly increased risk of breast and ovarian cancer.

In most cases, however, mutational damage occurs after birth. For example, only about 5–10% of breast cancer cases can be traced to inherited copies of a damaged BRCA1 gene. In addition, lifestyle factors are important even for those who have inherited a damaged suppressor gene: Consuming a high-fiber diet can help keep colon polyps from becoming cancerous. Testing and identification of hereditary cancer risks can be helpful for some people, especially if it leads to increased attention to controllable risk factors and better medical screening. A down side of genetic testing is that a positive test result may lead to "genetic discrimination" by health insurers and employers.

TERMS

chromosomes The threadlike bodies in a cell nucleus that contain molecules of DNA; most human cells contain 23 pairs of chromosomes.

DNA Deoxyribonucleic acid, a chemical substance that carries genetic information.

gene A section of a chromosome that contains the instructions for making a particular protein; the basic unit of heredity.

oncogene A gene involved in the transformation of a normal cell into a cancer cell.

You don't have to make radical changes in order to increase the amount of phytochemicals in your diet. Begin by monitoring your diet for 1–2 weeks in your health journal. Note both the health-protecting and cancer-promoting foods you eat. Then look for ways to incorporate more plant foods into your diet.

Phase I: Additions

- Add fresh vegetables to omelets, potato dishes, tuna salad, and pasta sauces. Try broccoli or cauliflower florets, mushrooms, sauteed onions and garlic, peas, carrots, or zucchini.

- Use fresh or frozen berries or other fruit as a topping for hot or cold cereal, pancakes, and desserts.

- Get creative with sandwiches; lettuce and tomato are just the beginning. Add slices of cucumber or zucchini, bean sprouts, spinach, carrot slivers, or snow peas.

- Add more veggies at the salad bar. Try fresh spinach, red cabbage, squash, cauliflower, broccoli, peas, mushrooms, onions, or peppers.

Phase II: Substitutions

- Instead of snacking on chips or candy, keep fruits or vegetables on hand. Try apples, oranges, bananas, grapes, peaches, carrot and celery sticks, and cherry tomatoes. You can buy prewashed and cut vegetables in the produce section of many grocery stores.

- Choose fruit-filled cookies, such as fig bars.

- Use salsa or bean dip for chips and veggies, instead of creamy dips.

- Drink fruit or vegetable juices instead of soda.

- Choose whole-grain breakfast cereals, breads, and crackers instead of processed products.

Phase III: New Recipes

- Try one or two vegetarian meals each week. Some good choices are pasta with tomato-vegetable sauce, baked potato topped with sauteed vegetables, and beans and rice.

- Look for quick-fixing grain side dishes at the supermarket. Try something new, like rice pilaf, couscous, or tabbouleh.

- Experiment with soy products like tofu, soy milk, and roasted soybeans.

- Plan meals around grain products, beans, and vegetables. Treat meat and dairy products as side dishes or condiments.

A diet rich in phytochemicals goes beyond cancer prevention; it will help you manage your weight and avoid other chronic diseases like heart disease, stroke, and diabetes. Try making these changes over the course of a few months, to optimize your wellness and improve your chances for a cancer-free future.

Cancer Promoters   Substances known as cancer promoters make up another important piece of the cancer puzzle. They don't directly produce DNA mutations, but they accelerate the growth of cells, which means less time for a cell to repair DNA damage caused by other factors. Estrogen, which stimulates cellular growth in the female reproductive organs, is an example of a cancer promoter.

Although much still needs to be learned about the role of genetics in cancer, it's clear that minimizing mutation damage to our DNA will lower our risk of many cancers. Unfortunately, a great many substances produce cancer-causing mutations, and we can't escape them all. By identifying the important carcinogens and understanding how they produce their effects, we can help keep our DNA intact and avoid activating "sleeping" oncogenes.

Dietary Factors in Cancer

Some foods we eat contain carcinogens; others contain compounds that protect us from cancer.

Fat and Fiber   A diet high in saturated fats, such as those found in red meats, appears to contribute to colon, prostate, and other cancers. Dietary fats stimulate the pro-

duction of bile acids, which are necessary to break down and digest material in the colon. Once produced, these bile acids remove layers of cells from the intestinal lining, which in turn are replaced by the growth of new cells. Newly formed and rapidly growing cells are particularly susceptible to carcinogens.

Colon cancer may also be related to a lack of fiber in the diet. Although fiber does not supply nutrition, it has many other useful properties. It provides bulk, which dilutes any carcinogens that may be present. It reduces the transit time of waste through the intestine so that carcinogens have less time to act on the cells lining the colon. Fiber also binds bile acids and other lipids that promote the development of colon and rectal cancer.

The role of dietary fat in breast cancer risk is also currently being investigated. A 1998 study found that intake of polyunsaturated fat was associated with an increased risk of breast cancer, while intake of monounsaturated fat was associated with a decreased risk of breast cancer.

Alcohol   Alcohol is associated with an increased incidence of several cancers. Although the link between alcohol intake and breast cancer is not well understood, it is dramatic. An average alcohol intake of three drinks per day is associated with a doubling in the risk of breast cancer. As mentioned earlier, alcohol and tobacco (cigarettes or spit tobacco) interact as risk factors for oral cancer. The combination of the two multiplies the carcinogenic effect of each substance. Heavy users of both alcohol and tobacco have a risk for oral cancer up to 15 times greater than that of people who don't drink or use tobacco.

Anticancer Agents in the Diet Some dietary compounds, called anticarcinogens, have the ability to directly act against carcinogens; others prevent the development and spread of cancer in different ways. Preliminary evidence strongly suggests that many vitamins and minerals can help protect against cancer. For example, vitamin C, vitamin E, selenium, and the **carotenoids** (vitamin A precursors) may help block the initiation of cancer by acting as **antioxidants.** Antioxidants prevent **free radicals** from damaging DNA. Vitamin C may also block the conversion of nitrates (food preservatives) into cancer-causing agents and inhibit the growth of a bacterium linked to stomach cancer. Folic acid may inhibit the transformation of normal cells into malignant cells and strengthen immune function. An additional protection against some cancers may be provided by calcium, which inhibits the growth of cells in the large intestine, thereby slowing the spread of potentially cancerous cells.

Many other anticancer agents in the diet fall under the broader heading of **phytochemicals,** substances in plants that help protect against chronic diseases. One of the first to be identified was sulforaphane, a potent anticarcinogen found in broccoli. Sulforaphane induces the cells of the liver and kidney to produce higher levels of protective enzymes, which then neutralize dietary carcinogens. Other examples of phytochemicals include flavonoids, found in citrus fruits; capsaicin, found in chili peppers; and lycopene, found in tomatoes, watermelon, and red peppers.

To increase your intake of potential cancer-fighters, eat a wide variety of fruits, vegetables, legumes, and grains (see the box "Incorporating More Cancer-Fighters into Your Diet"). Don't rely on supplements. Like many vitamins and minerals, isolated phytochemicals may be harmful if taken in high doses. In addition, it is likely that the anticancer effects of many foods are the result of many chemical substances working in combination.

General dietary guidelines for reducing your risk of cancer include the following:

- Eat a varied diet. Choose most of the foods you eat from plant sources (fruits, vegetables, grains) and foods made from them.
- Eat 5 or more servings of fruits and vegetables each day. (Less than one-third of Americans currently meet this recommendation.) Favor foods from the following categories:
  Cruciferous vegetables
  Citrus fruits
  Dark-green leafy vegetables
  Dark-yellow, orange, or red fruits or vegetables

Your food choices significantly affect your risk of cancer. By consuming the recommended 5–9 servings of fruits and vegetables per day, this young woman ensures that her diet is high in fiber and rich in cancer-fighting phytochemicals.

- Eat 6 to 11 servings a day of grains (breads, cereals, grain products, rice, pasta) and foods made from them. Choose whole-grain foods over foods made with processed or refined grains.
- Limit your intake of high-fat foods, particularly those from animal sources. Select small portions of lean cuts of meat. Choose soy products, legumes,

seafood, and poultry as alternatives to beef, pork, and lamb. (See Chapter 8 for information on reducing the fat in your diet.)

- Be moderate in your consumption of salt-cured, smoked, and nitrite-cured foods.
- Limit your consumption of alcoholic beverages, if you drink at all.

Inactivity

Several common types of cancer are associated with an inactive lifestyle, and research has shown a relationship between increased physical activity and a reduction in cancer risk. There is good evidence that exercise reduces the risk of colon cancer, perhaps by speeding the movement of food through the digestive tract, strengthening immune function, and decreasing blood fat levels.

In addition, exercise is important because it helps prevent obesity, an independent risk factor for cancer. A high percentage of body fat appears to increase the risk of prostate cancer, breast cancer, and female reproductive tract cancers.

Carcinogens in the Environment

Some carcinogens occur naturally in the environment, like the sun's UV rays. Others are synthetic substances that show up occasionally in the general environment but more often in the work environments of specific industries.

Ingested Chemicals The food industry uses preservatives and other additives to prevent food from becoming spoiled or stale. Some of these compounds are antioxidants and may actually decrease any cancer-causing properties the food might have. Other compounds, like the nitrates and nitrites found in beer and ale, ham, bacon, hot dogs, and lunch meats, are potentially more dangerous. Although nitrates and nitrites are not themselves carcinogenic, they can combine with dietary substances in the stomach and be converted to nitrosamines, which are highly potent carcinogens. Foods cured with nitrites, as well as those cured by salt or smoke, have been linked to esophageal and stomach cancer, and they should be eaten only in modest amounts.

Environmental and Industrial Pollution The best available data indicate that less than 2% of cancer deaths are caused by general environmental pollution, such as substances in our air and water. Exposure to carcinogenic materials in the workplace is a more serious problem. Occupational exposure to specific carcinogens may account for up to 5% of cancer deaths. With increasing industry and government regulations, we can anticipate that the industrial sources of cancer risk will continue to diminish.

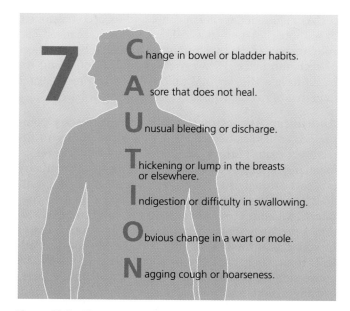

7

Change in bowel or bladder habits.

A sore that does not heal.

Unusual bleeding or discharge.

Thickening or lump in the breasts or elsewhere.

Indigestion or difficulty in swallowing.

Obvious change in a wart or mole.

Nagging cough or hoarseness.

Figure 12-3   The seven major warning signs of cancer.

Radiation All sources of radiation are potentially carcinogenic, including medical X rays, radioactive substances (radioisotopes), and UV rays from the sun. Most physicians and dentists are quite aware of the risk of radiation, and successful efforts have been made to reduce the amount of radiation needed for mammography, dental X rays, and other necessary medical X rays.

Another source of environmental radiation is radon gas. Radon is a radioactive decomposition product of radium, which is found in small quantities in some rocks and soils. Fortunately, in most of our homes and classrooms, radon is rapidly dissipated into the atmosphere, and very low levels of radon do not appear to significantly increase cancer risk. But in certain kinds of enclosed spaces, such as mines, some basements, and airtight houses, it can rise to dangerous levels.

Microorganisms

Investigators estimate that about 15% of the world's cancers are caused by viruses, bacteria, and parasites (although the percentage is lower in developed countries like the United States). The Epstein-Barr virus, which causes mononucleosis, is suspected of contributing to Hodgkin's disease (a lymphoma), cancer of the pharynx, and some stomach cancers. Certain types of human papillomavirus (HPV) may be responsible for 70–80% of cervical cancers worldwide. Hepatitis viruses B and C together cause as many as 80% of the world's liver cancers. HPV and hepatitis are often transmitted sexually. A bacterium, *Helicobacter pylori,* the probable cause of most stomach ulcers, is believed to cause more than half the cases of stomach cancer in the United States.

TABLE 12-2 — Tests Recommended by the American Cancer Society for the Early Detection of Cancer in Asymptomatic People

Test or Procedure	Sex	Age	Frequency
Sigmoidoscopy, preferably flexible	M, F	50 and over	Every 3–5 years
Fecal occult blood test	M, F	50 and over	Every year
Digital rectal exam	M, F	40 and over	Every year
Prostate exam[a]	M	50 and over	Every year
Pap test	F	All women who are, or who have been, sexually active, or have reached age 18, should have an annual Pap test and pelvic examination. After a woman has had three or more consecutive satisfactory normal annual examinations, the Pap test may be performed less frequently at the discretion of her physician.	
Breast self-examination	F	20 and over	Every month
Breast clinical examination	F	20–40; over 40	Every 3 years; every year
Mammography[b]	F	40–49; 50 and over	Every 1–2 years; every year

[a]Annual digital rectal examination and prostate-specific antigen should be performed on men age 50 years and older. If either result is abnormal, further evaluation should be considered.
[b]Screening mammography should begin by age 40.

SOURCE: © 1997, American Cancer Society, Inc. Reprinted by permission of American Cancer Society, Inc.

PREVENTING CANCER

Your lifestyle choices can radically lower your cancer risks, so you *can* take a practical approach to cancer prevention. Here are some guidelines:

- *Avoid tobacco.* Smoking is responsible for 80–90% of all lung cancers and for about 30% of all cancer deaths. People who smoke two or more packs of cigarettes a day have lung cancer mortality rates 15–25 times greater than those of nonsmokers. The carcinogenic chemicals in smoke are transported throughout the body in the bloodstream, making smoking a carcinogen for many forms of cancer other than lung cancer. Environmental tobacco smoke is dangerous to nonsmokers. The use of spit tobacco increases the risk of cancers of the mouth, larynx, throat, and esophagus.

- *Control diet and weight.* Based on hundreds of studies, the National Cancer Institute estimates that about one-third of all cancers are linked to what we eat. Choose a low-fat, high-fiber diet containing a variety of plant foods rich in phytochemicals; avoid salt-cured, smoked, and nitrite-cured foods. Drink alcohol only in moderation, if at all. Maintain a healthy weight to reduce your risk of colon, breast, and uterine cancer.

- *Exercise regularly.* Regular exercise is linked to lower levels of colon and other cancers. It also helps control weight.

- *Protect your skin from the sun.* Almost all skin cancer is considered to be sun-related. Wear protective clothing when you're out in the sun, and use a sunscreen with an SPF rating of 15 or higher. Don't frequent tanning salons.

- *Avoid environmental and occupational carcinogens.* Try to avoid occupational exposure to carcinogens, and don't smoke; the cancer risks of many carcinogens increase greatly when combined with smoking.

- *Follow ACS recommendations for early detection and screening tests.* Your first line of defense against cancer involves the lifestyle changes described in this chapter. Your second line of defense against cancer is early detection. The American Cancer Society recommends that you stay alert for any of the seven major warning signs illustrated in Figure 12-3; you can remember these with the acronym CAUTION. The appearance of any of these warning signs, although not a sure indication of cancer, should send you to your physician. In addition to self-monitoring, the ACS recommends routine tests to screen for common cancers (Table 12-2).

To evaluate your personal risk factors for cancer, complete the self-assessment quizzes in Lab 12-1.

Is it true that a sexually transmitted disease can cause cervical cancer? Yes. Research strongly suggests that the critical event in the development of cervical cancer is infection of the cervical cells by one of the human papillomaviruses (HPV), a large group of viruses that cause common warts as well as genital warts. HPV can cause normally well-behaved cells to divide and grow rapidly. The initial infection begins when the virus is introduced into the cervix by an infected sex partner.

Only a very small fraction of HPV-infected women ever get cervical cancer; other factors work with the HPV infection to produce a cancer. It seems that the two most important other factors are smoking and infection with another common sexually transmitted virus, the genital type of herpesvirus. Both smoking and herpesvirus can speed and intensify the cancerous changes begun by HPV. Nicotine and other mutagenic chemicals in tobacco smoke, carried from the lungs by the blood, can be identified in the cervical secretions of women who smoke.

To protect yourself from cervical cancer, avoid infection with HPV and herpesvirus. This can be done through sexual abstinence, mutually monogamous sex with an uninfected partner, or the regular use of condoms. Women who are infected with one or both viruses may need to have more frequent Pap tests in order to track potentially cancerous changes in cervical cells.

What is a biopsy? A biopsy is the removal and examination of a small piece of body tissue. Biopsies enable cancer specialists to carefully examine cells that are suspected of having turned cancerous. Some biopsies are fairly simple to perform, such as those on tissue from moles or skin sores. Other biopsies may require the use of a needle or probe to remove tissue from inside the body, such as in the breast or stomach. Some biopsies require more extensive surgery.

If a biopsy determines that a sample of tissue is malignant, other tests may be performed to determine the exact location, type, and degree of malignancy. New high-technology diagnostic imaging techniques have replaced exploratory surgery for many patients. In magnetic resonance imaging (MRI), a huge electromagnet is used to detect tumors by mapping, on a computer screen, the vibrations of different atoms in the body. Computed tomography (CT) uses X rays to create cross-sectional images of the brain and other parts of the body. Ultrasonography, or ultrasound, in which sound waves are bounced off body structures to create an image on a monitor, can also be used to visualize tumors.

How is cancer treated? The ideal cancer therapy would kill or remove all cancer cells while leaving normal tissue untouched. Sometimes this is almost possible, as when a surgeon removes a small superficial tumor of the skin. Usually a tumor is less accessible, and some combination of treatments is necessary. Current treatments for cancer are based primarily on the following:

- *Surgery.* Sometimes the organ containing the tumor is not essential for life and can be partially or completely removed. Surgery is less effective when cancer involves widely distributed cells (such as in the case of leukemia) or when the cancer has already metastasized.

- *Chemotherapy.* Cancer cells that can't be surgically removed can be killed by administering drugs that interfere chemically with their growth. Although chemotherapy is targeted at rapidly dividing cancer cells, it can also affect cells in normal tissue, leading to unpleasant side effects.

- *Radiation.* In radiation therapy, a beam of X rays or gamma rays is directed at the tumor, killing the cancer cells. Radiation destroys both normal and cancerous cells but can usually be precisely directed at the tumor.

New and experimental techniques that also show promise for some particular types of cancer include the following:

- *Bone marrow transplants,* in which healthy bone marrow cells from a compatible donor are transplanted following the elimination of the patient's bone marrow by radiation or chemotherapy.

- *Vaccines and genetically modified immune cells,* which enhance the reaction of a patient's own immune system to a tumor.

- *Anti-angiogenesis agents,* which starve tumors by blocking their blood supply.

- *Protease inhibitors,* which interfere with a tumor's ability to invade normal tissue and metastasize.

Are genetic tests for cancer risk beneficial? Recent discoveries of cancer-related genes have opened up a host of issues related to genetic testing and associated legal, financial, and ethical concerns. Tests for hereditary mutations in genes are now available for some types of cancer, including breast cancer. However, such tests are not always beneficial for the individual. Good news from a genetic test is reassuring, but it doesn't guarantee freedom from cancer because most cancers are not due to inherited genetic mutations. For example, only 5–10% of all cases of breast cancer occur among women who inherit the most common genetic mutation associated with the disease. For people who do test positive for a genetic mutation, there aren't many good options beyond increased monitoring. And those who test positive can face problems in addition to an uncertain medical future. Health and life insurers may use results of a genetic test to refuse or cancel coverage; employers may also use the information to screen current or prospective employees.

There is no simple answer to the question of who should undergo genetic testing for disease-related genes. If you think you are at high risk for a genetic abnormality because of your family or ethnic background, consider genetic counseling. A counselor can help you consider all the issues related to testing and can guide you into making the decision that is right for you.

SUMMARY

- Cancer is an abnormal and uncontrollable growth of cells or tissue; cancer cells can metastasize.

- Lung cancer kills more people than any other type of cancer; smoking is the primary cause.

- Colon and rectal cancer is linked to both diet and heredity. A high-fiber diet can prevent and even reverse precancerous changes in colon cells.

- Breast cancer has a genetic component, but lifestyle and hormones are also factors. Prostate cancer is chiefly a disease of aging; diet, heredity, and ethnicity are other risk factors.

- Cancers of the female reproductive tract include cervical, uterine, and ovarian cancer. Cervical cancer is linked to HPV infection; the Pap test is an effective screening test.

- Melanoma is the most serious form of skin cancer; excessive exposure to UV radiation in sunlight is the primary cause.

- Oral cancer is caused primarily by smoking, excess alcohol consumption, and use of spit tobacco.

- Testicular cancer can be detected early through self-examination.

- The genetic basis of some cancers appears to be mutational damage to suppressor genes, which normally limit cell division.

- Cancer-promoting dietary factors include fat and alcohol. Dietary elements that may protect against cancer include fiber, antioxidants, and phytochemicals. An inactive lifestyle is associated with some cancers.

- Some carcinogens occur naturally in the environment; others are manufactured substances. Occupational exposure is a risk for some workers.

- All sources of radiation are potentially carcinogenic, including X rays, UV rays of the sun, and radon gas.

- Strategies for preventing cancer include avoiding tobacco; eating a varied, moderate diet and controlling weight; exercising regularly; protecting skin from the sun; avoiding exposure to environmental and occupational carcinogens; staying alert for cancer warning signs; and getting recommended cancer-screening tests.

FOR MORE INFORMATION

Books

American Cancer Society. 1998. *Cancer Facts and Figures, 1998.* New York: American Cancer Society. *Available in every library and on the Web, a condensed and authoritative summary of current cancer statistics, updated each year.*

Cancer. 1996. *Scientific American* single-topic issue, September. *A broad survey of cancer, from the molecular details of the causes and spread of cancer to new methods of treatment.*

Murphy, G. P., ed. 1997. *Informed Decisions: The Complete Book of Cancer Diagnosis, Treatment, and Recovery.* New York: Viking. *Provides information to help a patient deal with cancer in an informed manner.*

Potter, J. F. 1998. *How to Improve Your Odds Against Cancer,* 2d ed. Hollywood, Fla.: Lifetime Books. *A guide to the prevention and early detection of cancer.*

Schottenfield, D., and J. F. Fraumeni, eds. 1996. *Cancer Epidemiology and Prevention.* New York: Oxford University Press. *A thorough but readable monograph on recent insights into what causes cancer and what we can do about it.*

Organizations, Hotlines, and Web Sites

American Cancer Society. Provides a wide range of free materials on the prevention and treatment of cancer.
> 800-ACS-2345
> http://www.cancer.org

Cancer Guide: Steve Dunn's Cancer Information Page. Links to many good cancer resources on the Internet and advice about how to make best use of information.
> http://www.cancerguide.org

National Cancer Institute. Provides information on treatment options, screening, clinical trials, and newly approved anticancer drugs.
> 800-4-CANCER (Cancer Information Service)
> 800-624-2511 (Cancer Fax)
> http://www.nci.nih.gov
> http://cancernet.nci.nih.gov

New York Online Access to Health (NOAH)/Cancer. Provides information about cancer—causes, symptoms, types, treatments, clinical trials—and links to related sites.
> http://www.noah.cuny.edu/cancer/cancer.html

Oncolink/A University of Pennsylvania Cancer Center Resource. Contains information on different types of cancer—causes, symptoms, screening tests, and prevention—and answers to frequently asked questions.
> http://www.oncolink.upenn.edu

Skin Cancer Foundation. Provides brochures, books, and newsletters relating to skin cancer.
> 800-SKIN-490

SELECTED BIBLIOGRAPHY

American Cancer Society. 1997. *American Cancer Society Workshop on Guidelines for Breast Cancer Detection* (retrieved May 10, 1997; http://www.cancer.org/mammog.html).

American Cancer Society press release. 1998. *American Cancer Society Responds to Report on Sunscreens and Melanoma* (retrieved May 20, 1998; http://www.cancer.org/media/story/021898.html).

Ames, B. N., et al. 1996. The causes and prevention of cancer. *Proceedings of the National Academy of Sciences* 92(12): 5258–5265.

Auvinen, A., et al. 1996. Indoor radon exposure and risk of lung cancer: A nested case-control study in Finland. *Journal of the National Cancer Institute* 88(14): 966–972.

Baron, J. A., et al. 1998. Folate intake, alcohol consumption, cigarette smoking, and risk of colorectal adenomas. *Journal of the National Cancer Institute* 90(1): 57–62.

Bhatia, R., P. Lopipero, and A. H. Smith. 1998. Diesel exhaust exposure and lung cancer. *Epidemiology* 9(1): 84–91.

Clark, K. 1998. Phytochemicals protect against cancer. *ACSM's Health and Fitness Journal* 2(3): 35, 47.

Colls, B. M. 1998. Causes of testicular cancer. *Lancet* 351(9097): 214.

Filella, X., et al. 1996. Usefulness of prostate-specific antigen density as a diagnostic test of prostate cancer. *Tumor Biology* 17(1): 20–26.

Gammon, M. D., E. M. John, and J. A. Britton. 1998. Recreational and occupational physical activities and risk of breast cancer. *Journal of the National Cancer Institute* 90(2): 100–117.

Gotay, C. C., and M. E. Wilson. 1998. Social support and cancer screening in African American, Hispanic, and Native American women. *Cancer Practice* 6(1): 31–37.

Keon, B. 1997. Ashkenazim are not alone: Other ethnic groups have breast cancer gene mutations, too. *Journal of the National Cancer Institute* 89(1): 8–9.

Kleiner, S. M. 1997. Defense plants: Foods that fight disease. *The Physician and Sportsmedicine* (retrieved February 15, 1998; http://www.physsportsmed.com/issues/1997/12dec/defense.htm).

Koibuchi, Y., et al. 1998. The effect of mass screening by physical examination combined with regular breast self-examination on clinical stage and course of Japanese women with breast cancer. *Oncology Reports* 5(1): 151–155.

Lubin, J. H., and J. D. Boice Jr. 1997. Lung cancer risk from residential radon: Meta-analysis of eight epidemiologic studies. *Journal of the National Cancer Institute* 89(1): 49–57.

Melbye, M., et al. 1997. Induced abortion and the risk of breast cancer. *New England Journal of Medicine* 336(2): 81–85.

Morabia, A., et al. 1998. Relation of smoking to breast cancer by estrogen receptor status. *International Journal of Cancer* 75(3): 339–342.

National Cancer Institute. 1997. *Genetic Testing for Breast Cancer Risk: It's Your Choice* (retrieved April 25, 1998; http://cancernet.nci/nih.gov/clinpdq/risk/Genetic_Testing_for_Breast_Cancer_Risk:_It's_y).

Pap smear: An important lifesaver. 1997. *Cancer Smart* 3(3): 10–11.

Parmigiani, G., D. Berry, and O. Aguilar. 1998. Determining carrier probabilities for breast cancer–susceptibility genes BRCA1 and BRCA2. *American Journal of Human Genetics* 62(1): 145–158.

Roth, J. A., and R. J. Cristiano. 1997. Gene therapy for cancer: What have we done and where are we going? *Journal of the National Cancer Institute* 89(1): 21–39.

Thun, M. J., and C. W. Heath Jr. 1995. Aspirin use and reduced risk of gastrointestinal tract cancers in the American Cancer Society prospective studies. *Preventive Medicine* 24(2): 116–118.

Thune, I., et al. 1997. Physical activity and the risk of breast cancer. *New England Journal of Medicine* 336(18): 1269–1275.

Wolk, A., et al. 1998. A prospective study of association of monounsaturated fat and other types of fat with risk of breast cancer. *Archives of Internal Medicine* 158(1): 41–45.

Zaridze, D., et al. 1998. Exposure to environmental tobacco smoke and risk of lung cancer in non-smoking women from Moscow, Russia. *International Journal of Cancer* 75(3): 335–338.

LAB 12-1 *Risk Factors for Cancer*

Part I. Risk Profile

Read the risk factors listed along the top of the chart. For any factor that applies to you, put a check in every unshaded box in its column. For the family history column, note any family member who has had the type of cancer listed at the left—record his or her relationship to you (uncle, brother, etc.) and age at diagnosis.

Risk Factors

Type of Cancer	Smoking	Use of spit tobacco	Diet high in fat	Diet rich in meat	Diet low in fruits and vegetables	Little or no exercise	Obesity	Regular use of alcohol	Family history
Lung		■	■	■		■	■	■	
Colon and rectum	■	■						■	
Breast	■	■		■					
Prostate	■	■					■		
Stomach		■	■	■		■	■		
Esophagus			■	■	■	■	■		
Kidney		■	■	■	■	■		■	
Oral cavity		■	■		■	■	■		
Endometrium	■	■		■		■		■	
Larynx			■	■		■	■	■	

To determine your risk for a particular type of cancer, examine the number of corresponding risk factors you've checked. Strong family history may also increase your risk—the more relatives who have had a particular type of cancer, the closer their relationship to you, and the younger their age at diagnosis, the greater your risk. Use this chart to identify lifestyle behaviors that you can change to lower your risk of cancer.

Part II. Skin Cancer Risk Assessment

Skin cancer is the most common cancer of all when cases of the highly curable forms are included in the count. Your risk of skin cancer from the ultraviolet radiation in sunlight depends on several factors. Take the quiz that follows to see how sensitive you are. The higher your UV-risk score, the greater your risk of skin cancer—and the greater your need to take precautions against too much sun.

Score 1 point for each true statement:

_____ 1. I have blond or red hair.

_____ 2. I have light-colored eyes (blue, gray, green).

_____ 3. I freckle easily.

_____ 4. I have many moles.

_____ 5. I had two or more blistering sunburns as a child.

_____ 6. I spent lots of time in a tropical climate as a child.

_____ 7. I have a family history of skin cancer.

_____ 8. I work outdoors.

_____ 9. I spend a lot of time in outdoor activities.

_____10. I like to spend as much time in the sun as I can.

_____11. I sometimes go to a tanning parlor or use a a sunlamp.

_____**Total score**

Score	Risk of skin cancer from UV radiation
0	Low
1–3	Moderate
4–7	High
8–11	Very high

Part III. Do You Get Enough Phytochemicals?

Fruits and vegetables are rich in compounds believed to protect against cancer, which is why experts urge us to consume at least five servings per day. However, most Americans fail to meet this recommendation. To see whether you're getting all you should, answer whether the following statements are true (T) or false (F) for you.

_____ 1. I always start the day with fruit juice.

_____ 2. I slice fruit onto my cereal or eat a piece of fruit after my toast and jam.

_____ 3. If I have a sandwich for lunch, I have some vegetables or fruit on the side.

_____ 4. When lunch is a salad, it includes tomatoes, peppers, cabbage, and carrots.

_____ 5. My snacks are celery or carrot sticks, apple slices, raisins, and bananas.

_____ 6. There's always something green on my dinner plate.

_____ 7. I never go a day without eating a vegetable.

_____ 8. Whenever I can, I have strawberries, pears, peaches, or fruit pie for dessert.

If you answered true to five or more of these statements, then you're probably getting at least five helpings of fruits and vegetables a day. If you answered true to four or fewer, you're phytochemically deprived. Consult Chapters 8 and 12 in your text for ideas on incorporating more fruits and vegetables into your diet.

SOURCES: Part I risk profile adapted from Beating the odds: Best bets for cancer prevention. 1996. *Tufts University Diet and Nutrition Letter,* December. Reprinted with permission of the publisher, 1-800-274-7581. Part II skin cancer risk assessment adapted from Shear, N. 1996. What's your UV-risk score? *Consumer Reports on Health,* June. Copyright © 1996 by the Consumers Union of the United States, Inc., Yonkers, NY 10703-1057. Reprinted by permission from *Consumer Reports on Health,* June 1996. Part III quiz from Do you get enough phytochemicals? 1997. *Health,* April, p. 113. Used with permission of the publisher.

Substance Use and Abuse

LOOKING AHEAD

After reading this chapter, you should be able to answer these questions about substance use and abuse:

- What are the characteristics of an addictive behavior?

- What are the principal psychoactive drugs used in the United States today, and how can drug abuse be treated and prevented?

- What are the short-term and long-term effects of alcohol use, and how can alcoholism be treated?

- What strategies can help a person drink in moderation?

- What are the health hazards associated with tobacco use and environmental tobacco smoke, and how can people quit smoking?

The use of **drugs** for both medical and social purposes is widespread in American society (Table 13-1). Many people believe that every problem, no matter how large or small, has or should have chemical solutions. Advertisements, social pressures, and the human desire for quick fixes to life's difficult problems all contribute to the prevailing attitude that drugs can ease all pain. Unfortunately, using drugs can—and often does—have serious consequences.

The most serious consequences are abuse and addiction. The drugs most often associated with abuse are **psychoactive drugs**—those designed to alter a person's experiences or consciousness. In the short term, many psychoactive drugs can cause **intoxication,** a state in which sometimes unpredictable physical and emotional changes occur. A person who is intoxicated may experience potentially serious changes in physical functioning; his or her emotions and judgment may be affected in ways that lead to uncharacteristic and unsafe behavior. In the long term, recurrent drug use can have profound physical, emotional, and social effects.

This chapter focuses primarily on psychoactive drugs: their short- and long-term effects, and their potential for abuse and addiction. The information provided is designed to help you make healthy, informed decisions about the role of drugs in your life. Before turning to the specific types of psychoactive drugs, let's take a closer look at addictive behavior in general.

ADDICTIVE BEHAVIOR

Although addiction is most often associated with drug use, many experts now extend the concept of addiction to other areas. **Addictive behaviors** are habits that have gotten out of control, with a resulting negative impact on a person's health. Looking at the nature of addiction and a range of addictive behaviors can help us understand similar behaviors when they involve drugs.

What Is Addiction?

Historically, the term *addiction* was applied only when the habitual use of a drug produced chemical changes in the user's body. One such change is physical tolerance, in which the body adapts to a drug so that the initial dose no longer produces the original emotional or psychological effects. This process, caused by chemical changes, means the user has to take larger and larger doses of the drug to achieve the same "high."

Some scientists think that other behaviors may share some of the chemistry of drug addiction. They suggest that activities like gambling, eating, and exercise trigger the release of brain chemicals that cause a pleasurable "rush" in much the same way that psychoactive drugs do. The brain's own chemicals thus become the "drug" that

TABLE 13-1	*Drug Use Among U.S. College Students*	
	Percentage Using the Substance	
Substance	*In the Past Year*	*In the Past 30 Days*
Alcohol	83	68
Cigarettes	39	27
Marijuana	31	15
Spit tobacco	8	5
LSD	7	3
Stimulants	5	2
Inhalants	4	2
Cocaine	4	<1
Tranquilizers	2	<1
Crack	<1	<1
Heroin	<1	<1

SOURCES: National Institute on Drug Abuse; Harvard School of Public Health College Alcohol Study; U.S. Public Health Service.

causes addiction. However, the view that addiction is based in our own brain chemistry does *not* imply that a person bears no responsibility for his or her addictive behavior. Lifestyle, personality traits, and other factors also play key roles in the development of addictive behavior.

It is sometimes difficult to distinguish between a healthy habit and one that has become an addiction. Experts have identified some general characteristics typically associated with addictive behaviors.

- *Reinforcement.* Some aspect of the behavior produces pleasurable physical and/or emotional states or relieves negative ones.
- *Compulsion or craving.* The individual feels a compelling need to engage in the behavior.
- *Loss of control.* The individual loses control over the behavior and cannot block the impulse to engage in it.
- *Escalation.* More and more of the substance or activity is required to produce its desired effects.
- *Negative consequences.* The behavior has serious negative consequences, such as problems with academic or job performance, difficulties with personal relationships, or health problems.

The Development of Addiction

Many common behaviors are potentially addictive, but most people who engage in them do not develop problems. If a person does something that brings pleasure or dulls pain—drinking a beer or going shopping, for example—he or she is likely to repeat the behavior. When done appropriately and in moderation, most such behaviors can be part of a wellness lifestyle. But if the person becomes increasingly dependent on the behavior and tolerance develops, the behavior is likely to become a central focus in the person's life.

There is no single cause of addiction. Characteristics of an individual person, of the environment in which the person lives, and of the substance or behavior he or she abuses combine in an addictive behavior. Many people with addictions use the substance or activity as a substitute for other, healthier coping strategies. People vary in their ability to manage their lives, and those who have the most trouble dealing with stress and painful emotions may be more susceptible to addiction. Some people may also have a genetic predisposition to addiction to a particular substance.

Examples of Addictive Behaviors

The use and abuse of alcohol, tobacco, and other psychoactive drugs will be explored later in the chapter. In this section, we'll briefly examine some behaviors that are not related to drugs and that can become addictive for some people.

Compulsive or Pathological Gambling   Compulsive gamblers are unable to resist the urge to gamble, even in the face of financial and personal ruin. Most say they are seeking excitement even more than money; they may use gambling to relieve negative feelings or deal with stress. The consequences of compulsive gambling are not just financial: The suicide rate among compulsive gamblers is 20 times higher than that of the general population. Compulsive gambling shares many traits with other addictive behaviors, including preoccupation with gambling, unsuccessful efforts to cut back or quit, and lying to family members to conceal the extent of the involvement with gambling. An estimated 2.5 million Americans may be compulsive gamblers.

Compulsive Spending or Shopping   A compulsive spender repeatedly gives in to the impulse to buy much more than he or she needs or can afford. For the compulsive shopper, spending may serve to relieve painful feelings like depression or anxiety, or it may produce positive emotions like excitement. Compulsive shoppers are usually distressed by their behavior and its social, personal, and financial consequences. Like other addictive behaviors, compulsive shopping is characterized by a loss of control over the behavior and significant negative consequences.

Internet Addiction   Some recent research has indicated that surfing the World Wide Web can also be addictive. In order to spend more time online, Internet addicts skip

Most people who gamble do so casually and occasionally; but for a few, the habit spins out of control and becomes the central focus of their life. A variety of factors appears to influence whether a habit becomes an addiction, including personality, lifestyle, heredity, social environment, and the nature of the activity.

important school, social, or recreational activities. And despite negative financial, social, or academic consequences, they don't feel able to stop. The Internet addicts identified in one study averaged 38 online hours per week.

Other behaviors that can become addictive include exercising, eating, watching TV, and working. Any substance or activity that becomes the focus of a person's life at the expense of other needs and interests can be damaging to health.

We turn now to the substances most commonly associated with addiction: psychoactive drugs.

PSYCHOACTIVE DRUGS

As described earlier, psychoactive drugs are those drugs designed to alter a person's experiences or consciousness. They include legal compounds such as caffeine, tobacco, and alcohol as well as illegal substances such as heroin, cocaine, and LSD (Table 13-2). In this section, we'll examine general issues that apply to the use of any psychoactive drug. Later in the chapter, we'll take a close look at two commonly used and abused psychoactive drugs—alcohol and tobacco.

TERMS

drug   Any chemical other than food intended to affect the structure or function of the body.

psychoactive drug   A drug that can alter a person's consciousness or experiences.

intoxication   The state of being mentally affected by a chemical (literally, a state of being poisoned).

addictive behavior   Any habit that has gotten out of control, resulting in a negative impact on a person's health.

TABLE 13-2 *Effects of Psychoactive Drugs*

Drug Group and Examples	Typical Short-Term Effects	Comments
Opioids (Narcotics): Opium, morphine, heroin, methadone, codeine, meperidine, fentanyl	Pain relief; euphoria; lethargy, apathy, and inability to concentrate; lowered responsiveness to frustration, hunger, and sexual stimulation; nausea and vomiting	• Use of opioids often leads to dependence. • Heroin and other injectable opioids are responsible for much of the spread of HIV infection among injecting drug users. (Injecting drug use often involves the sharing of needles, which may be contaminated with disease organisms from another user's blood.)
Central Nervous System Depressants: Alcohol, barbiturates (Seconal, Nembutal, Amytal, Tuinal), methaqualone (Quaalude), ethchlorvynol (Placidyl), chloral hydrate, benzodiazepines (Xanax, Valium, Librium)	Reduced anxiety; mood changes (obstinacy, irritability, and abusiveness are common); impaired muscular coordination; slurring of speech; drowsiness or sleep; impaired mental functioning	• Some CNS depressants are prescribed for insomnia and anxiety, to control seizures, and to calm patients before operations and other medical or dental procedures. • Use of CNS depressants can lead to dependence even at prescribed dosages. Withdrawal symptoms are severe and can include anxiety, shaking, weakness, convulsions, cardiovascular collapse, and death. • Long-term use can cause brain damage, with impaired ability to reason and make judgments. • Many unintended overdoses result from the use of barbiturates and alcohol together.
Central Nervous System Stimulants: Cocaine, amphetamine, nicotine, caffeine, ephedrine	Accelerated heart rate; increased blood pressure; constriction of blood vessels; dilation of pupils of the eyes and bronchial tubes; increased gastric and adrenal secretions; greater muscular tension; increased motor activity; euphoria; increased alertness; reduced fatigue; disturbed sleep patterns	• Tolerance to cocaine develops rapidly. In large doses, cocaine can cause excessive CNS stimulation and death. Using cocaine in combination with other substances such as alcohol or heroin is particularly dangerous. • Cocaine or amphetamine use during pregnancy is associated with increased risk for miscarriage, premature labor, stillbirth, and some types of birth defects. • The repeated use of moderate doses of amphetamines often leads to tolerance; the result can be severe disturbances in behavior, including hostility, delusions of persecution, and unprovoked violence. • Taking amphetamines to cope with a passing situation, such as cramming for exams or driving long distances, can be dangerous because judgment is impaired and the user may suddenly fall asleep when the effects wear off. • High doses of caffeine can cause nervousness, irritability, headache, disturbed sleep, gastric irritation, and aggravation of the symptoms of premenstrual syndrome. Caffeine is a dependence-producing drug; withdrawal symptoms include headache, irritability, and mild depression.

Drug Use, Abuse, and Dependence

The American Psychiatric Association's *Diagnostic and Statistical Manual of Mental Disorders* is the authoritative reference for defining all sorts of behavioral disorders, including those related to drugs. The APA has chosen not to use the term *addiction,* in part because it is so broad and has so many connotations. Instead, they refer to two forms of substance (drug) disorders: substance abuse and substance dependence. Both are maladaptive patterns of substance use that lead to significant impairment or distress. Although the APA's definitions are more precise and

more directly related to drug use, they clearly encompass the general characteristics of addictive behavior described in the previous section.

Drug Abuse As defined by the APA, **substance abuse** involves one or more of the following:

• Recurrent drug use, resulting in a failure to fulfill major responsibilities at work, school, or home

• Recurrent drug use in situations in which it is physically hazardous, such as before driving a car

• Recurrent drug-related legal problems

TABLE 13-2   *Effects of Psychoactive Drugs (continued)*

Marijuana and Other Cannabis Products	Increased heart rate; dilation of certain blood vessels in the eyes; euphoria, heightened subjective sensory experiences, and sensory distortion; slowing down of time sense; relaxation; impaired memory function; disturbed thought patterns; attention lapses; subjective feelings of depersonalization	• Marijuana is sometimes used to reduce nausea and improve appetite during cancer chemotherapy; it is being studied for possible use in certain forms of glaucoma, an eye disease that causes blindness. • The unpleasant side effects, throat and lung irritation, make the development of tolerance unlikely, but a chronic user of marijuana is more likely to be a heavy user of tobacco, alcohol, and other dangerous drugs. The effects of long-term use of marijuana are largely unknown. • Marijuana use during pregnancy can result in impaired growth and development of the fetus.
Hallucinogens: LSD, mescaline, psilocybin, STP, DMT, MDMA, PCP	Altered states of consciousness (changes in mood, thinking, and perception); dilation of the pupils; dizziness, weakness, nausea, panic; intellectual impairment; psychological disturbances	• Many hallucinogens induce tolerance after one or two doses. • The effects of hallucinogens are unpredictable but are strongly influenced by user expectations and the setting; severe panic reactions sometimes occur. Even after the chemical effects of a hallucinogen have worn off, spontaneous flashbacks and other psychological disturbances can occur.
Inhalants: Volatile solvents (adhesives, aerosols), nitrites, nitrous oxide (laughing gas)	Sedation; loss of inhibitions and sense of control	• High concentrations of inhalants in the blood can cause damage to the central nervous system, liver, kidneys, and bone marrow; hearing loss; loss of consciousness; heart failure; and death. • Inhalant use is difficult to monitor and control because inhalants are found in many inexpensive and legal products.

• Continued drug use despite persistent social or interpersonal problems caused by or exacerbated by the effects of the drug

The pattern of use may be constant or intermittent, and **physical dependence** may or may not be present. For example, a person who smokes marijuana once a week but cuts classes because he or she is high is abusing marijuana, even though he or she is not physically dependent.

Drug Dependence   **Substance dependence** is a more complex disorder and is what many people associate with the idea of addiction. The seven specific criteria the APA uses to diagnose substance dependence are listed below. The first two are associated with physical dependence; the final five are associated with compulsive use. To be considered dependent, an individual must experience a cluster of three or more of these seven symptoms during a 12-month period.

1. *Developing tolerance to the substance.* When a person requires increased amounts of a substance to achieve the desired effect or notices a markedly diminished effect with continued use of the same amount, he or she has developed **tolerance.** For example, heavy heroin users may need to take ten

times the amount they took at the beginning in order to achieve the desired effect.

2. *Experiencing withdrawal.* In an individual who has maintained prolonged, heavy use of a substance, a drop in its concentration within the body can result in unpleasant physical and cognitive **withdrawal** symptoms. For example, nausea, vomiting,

TERMS

substance abuse   A maladaptive pattern of use of any substance that persists despite adverse social, psychological, or medical consequences. The pattern may be intermittent, with or without tolerance and physical dependence.

physical dependence   The result of physiological adaptation that occurs in response to the frequent presence of a drug; typically associated with tolerance and withdrawal.

substance dependence   A cluster of cognitive, behavioral, and physiological symptoms that occur in an individual who continues to use a substance despite suffering significant substance-related problems, leading to significant impairment or distress; also known as *addiction.*

tolerance   Lower sensitivity to a drug so that a given dose no longer exerts the usual effect and larger doses are needed.

withdrawal   Physical and psychological symptoms that follow the interrupted use of a drug on which a user is physically dependent; symptoms may be mild or life-threatening.

and tremors are common withdrawal symptoms for alcohol, opioids, and sedatives.

3. *Taking the substance in larger amounts or over a longer period than was originally intended.*

4. *Expressing a persistent desire to cut down or regulate substance use.* This desire is often accompanied by many unsuccessful efforts to reduce or discontinue use of the substance.

5. *Spending a great deal of time obtaining the substance, using the substance, or recovering from its effects.*

6. *Giving up or reducing important school, work, or recreational activities because of substance use.* A dependent person may withdraw from family activities and hobbies in order to use the substance, or to spend more time with substance-using friends.

7. *Continuing to use the substance in spite of recognizing that it is contributing to a psychological or physical problem.*

If a drug-dependent person experiences either tolerance or withdrawal, he or she is considered physically dependent. However, dependence *can* occur without a physical component, based solely on compulsive use.

Who Uses (and Abuses) Drugs?

The use and abuse of drugs occur at all income and education levels, among all ethnic groups, and at all ages. One reason for our society's concern with the casual or recreational use of illegal drugs is that it is not possible to know when drug use will lead to abuse or dependence. Some casual users develop substance-related problems; others do not. However, some psychoactive drugs are more likely than others to lead to dependence (Figure 13-1).

Some characteristics that place people at higher-than-average risk for trying illegal drugs include being male, being young, having frequent exposure to drugs through family members or peers, being disinterested in school, and having a risk-taking personality. Drug use is less common among young people who attend school regularly, get good grades, have strong personal identities, are religious, have a good relationship with their parents, and are independent thinkers whose actions are not controlled by peer pressure. Coming from a family that has a clear policy on drug use and deals with conflicts constructively is another factor associated with people who don't use drugs.

Why do some people use psychoactive drugs without becoming dependent, while others aren't as lucky? The answer seems to be a combination of physical, psychological, and social factors. Some people may be born with certain characteristics of brain chemistry or metabolism that make them more vulnerable to drug dependence. Psychological risk factors include having difficulty controlling impulses and having a strong need for excitement

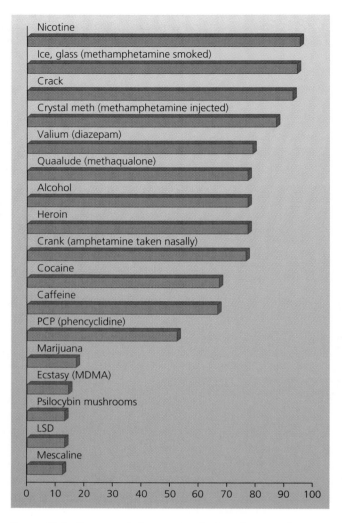

Figure 13-1 How easy is it to get hooked on drugs? The numbers at the bottom of the chart are relative rankings. SOURCE: Hastings, J. 1990. Why do people take drugs? *In Health,* November/December. Used with permission of the publisher.

and immediate gratification. People may turn to drugs to blot out emotional pain or to deal with difficult emotions such as rejection, hostility, or depression. Social factors that may increase the risk for drug dependence include exposure to drug-using family members or peers, poverty, and easy access to drugs.

Treatment for Drug Abuse

Different types of programs are available to help people break their drug habits, but there is no single best method of treatment, and the relapse rate is high for all types of treatment. Nevertheless, numerous studies have shown that being treated is better than not being treated. Professional treatment programs usually take the form of drug substitution programs or treatment centers; nonprofessional self-help groups and peer counseling are also available. To be successful, a treatment program must deal with the reasons behind people's drug abuse and help

- *Bored?* Go for a walk or a run; stimulate your senses at a museum or a movie; challenge your mind with a new game or book; introduce yourself to someone new.
- *Stressed out?* Practice relaxation or visualization, try to slow down and open your senses to the natural world; get some exercise.
- *Shy, lonely?* Talk to a counselor; enroll in a shyness clinic; learn and practice communication techniques.
- *Feeling low self-esteem?* Focus on the areas in which you are competent; give yourself credit for the things you do well.
- *Apathetic, lethargic?* Force yourself to get up and get some exercise to energize yourself; assume responsibility for someone or something outside yourself; volunteer.

- *Depressed, anxious?* Talk to a friend, parent, or counselor.
- *Searching for meaning?* Try yoga or meditation; explore spiritual experiences through religious groups, church, prayer, or reading.
- *Afraid to say no?* Take a course in assertiveness training; get support from others who don't want to use drugs; remind yourself that you have the right and the responsibility to make your own decisions.
- *Still feeling peer pressure?* Begin to look for new friends or roommates. Take a class or join an organization that attracts other health-conscious people.

them develop behaviors, attitudes, and a social support system that will help them remain drug-free.

Young people with drug problems are often unable to seek help on their own. In such a case, friends and family members may need to act on their behalf. The following signals suggest drug dependence:

- Sudden withdrawal or emotional distance
- Rebellious or unusually irritable behavior
- Loss of interest in usual activities or hobbies
- A decline in school performance
- A sudden change in group of friends
- Changes in sleeping or eating habits
- Frequent borrowing of money

Preventing Drug Abuse

Obviously, the best solution to drug abuse is prevention. Government attempts at controlling the drug problem tend to focus on stopping the production, importation, and distribution of illegal drugs. Creative effort also needs to be put into stopping the demand for drugs. Approaches include building young people's self-esteem, improving their academic skills, increasing their recreational opportunities, and providing them with honest information about the effects of drugs. Developing strategies for resisting peer pressure is one of the most effective techniques. In addition, reminding young people that most people, no matter what age, are *not* users of illegal drugs, do *not* smoke cigarettes, and do *not* get drunk frequently is a critical part of preventing substance abuse.

The Role of Drugs in Your Life

Where do you fit into this complex picture of drug use and abuse? Whatever your experience has been up to now, it's likely that you will encounter drugs at some point in your life. To make sure you'll have the inner resources to resist peer pressure and make your own decision, cultivate a variety of activities you enjoy doing, realize that you are entitled to have your own opinion, and don't neglect your self-esteem (see the box "What to Do Instead of Drugs").

Before you try a psychoactive drug, consider the following questions:

- *What are the risks involved?* Many drugs carry an immediate risk of injury or death. Almost all involve the longer-term risk of abuse and dependence.
- *Is using the drug compatible with your goals?* Consider how drug use will affect your education and career objectives, your relationships, your future happiness, and the happiness of those who love you.
- *What are your ethical beliefs about drug use?* Consider whether using a drug would cause you to go against your personal ethics, religious beliefs, social values, or family responsibilities.
- *What are the financial costs?* Many drugs are expensive, especially if you become dependent on them.
- *Are you trying to solve a deeper problem?* Drugs will not make emotional pain go away; in the long run, they will only make it worse. If you are feeling depressed or anxious, seek help from a mental health professional instead of self-medicating with drugs.

ALCOHOL

Two-thirds of Americans over age 15 drink alcohol in some form. Many people think of alcohol the way it's

Ethyl alcohol is the common psychoactive drug in all alcoholic beverages. One drink—a 12-ounce beer, a 1.5-ounce cocktail, or a 5-ounce glass of wine—contains about 0.6 ounce of ethyl alcohol.

portrayed in advertisements, on television, and in movies—as part of a good time, an integral ingredient of celebrations and special events. However, like other drugs, alcohol can impair functioning in the short term and cause devastating damage in the long term. Through automobile crashes and other injuries, alcohol is the leading cause of death among people between ages 15 and 24.

Chemistry and Metabolism

Ethyl alcohol is the common psychoactive ingredient in all alcoholic beverages. The concentration of alcohol varies with the type of beverage; it is indicated by the proof value, which is two times the percentage concentration. For example, if a beverage is 80 proof, it contains 40% alcohol. When alcohol consumption is discussed, "one drink" refers to a 12-ounce bottle of beer, a 5-ounce glass of table wine, or a cocktail with 1.5 ounces of 80-proof liquor. Each of these different drinks contains approximately the same amount of alcohol: 0.6 ounce.

TERMS **ethyl alcohol**   The intoxicating ingredient in fermented liquors; a colorless, pungent liquid.

blood alcohol concentration (BAC)   The amount of alcohol in the blood in terms of weight per unit volume.

cirrhosis of the liver   A disease in which the liver is severely damaged by alcohol, other toxins, or infection.

When consumed, alcohol is absorbed into the bloodstream from the stomach and small intestine. Once in the bloodstream, alcohol is distributed throughout the body's tissues, affecting nearly every body system (Figure 13-2). The main site of alcohol metabolism is the liver, which transforms alcohol into energy and other products.

Immediate Effects of Alcohol

Blood alcohol concentration (BAC) is a primary factor determining the effects of alcohol. BAC is determined by the amount of alcohol consumed and by individual factors such as heredity, body weight, and amount of body fat. Compared to a man who drinks the same amount of alcohol, a woman will typically have a higher BAC because of her smaller size, greater percent of body fat, and less active alcohol-metabolizing stomach enzyme. The body can typically metabolize about half of a drink in an hour. If a person drinks slightly less than that each hour, BAC remains low. People can drink large amounts of alcohol this way over a long period of time without becoming noticeably intoxicated; however, they do run the risk of significant long-term health problems. But if more alcohol is consumed than is metabolized, the BAC will steadily increase, as will the level of intoxication.

Low doses of alcohol induce relaxation and release inhibitions; higher doses lead to less pleasant effects, including flushing and sweating; disturbed sleep; and "hangover," characterized by headache, nausea, and generalized discomfort. The combination of impaired judgment, weakened sensory perception, reduced inhibitions, impaired motor coordination, and, often, increased aggressiveness and hostility that characterize alcohol intoxication can be dangerous or even deadly. Through homicide, suicide, automobile crashes, and other incidents, alcohol kills over 200,000 Americans each year. Alcohol poisoning is also a risk: Drinking large amounts of alcohol over a short period of time can rapidly raise the BAC into the lethal range (Table 13-3).

In addition to an increased risk of injury and death, driving while intoxicated can have serious legal consequences. The legal limit for BAC is 0.08% in some states and 0.10% in others; however, alcohol impairs the user even at much lower BACs (Figure 13-3). States now also have "zero tolerance" laws regarding alcohol use by drivers under age 21. Under these laws, a young driver who has consumed any alcohol can have his or her license suspended. For tips on avoiding alcohol-related automobile crashes, see the box "Protecting Yourself on the Road."

Effects of Chronic Use of Alcohol

The average life span of alcohol abusers is 10–12 years shorter than that of nonabusers. **Cirrhosis of the liver**, a major cause of death in the United States, is one result of continued alcohol use. In this condition, liver cells are

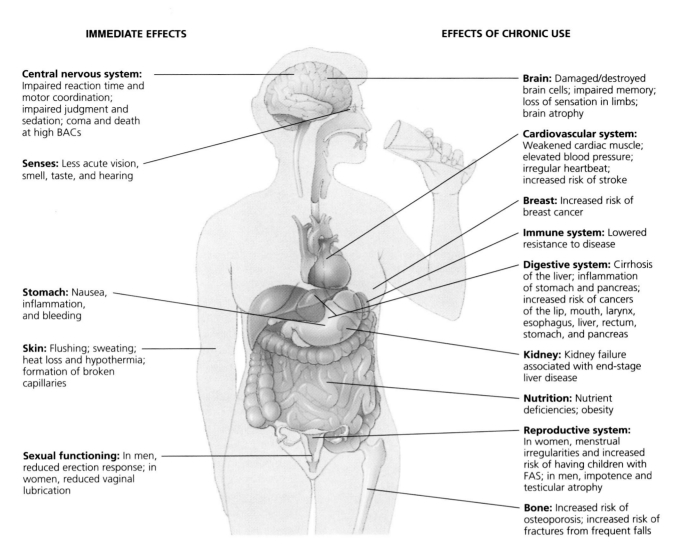

IMMEDIATE EFFECTS

Central nervous system: Impaired reaction time and motor coordination; impaired judgment and sedation; coma and death at high BACs

Senses: Less acute vision, smell, taste, and hearing

Stomach: Nausea, inflammation, and bleeding

Skin: Flushing; sweating; heat loss and hypothermia; formation of broken capillaries

Sexual functioning: In men, reduced erection response; in women, reduced vaginal lubrication

EFFECTS OF CHRONIC USE

Brain: Damaged/destroyed brain cells; impaired memory; loss of sensation in limbs; brain atrophy

Cardiovascular system: Weakened cardiac muscle; elevated blood pressure; irregular heartbeat; increased risk of stroke

Breast: Increased risk of breast cancer

Immune system: Lowered resistance to disease

Digestive system: Cirrhosis of the liver; inflammation of stomach and pancreas; increased risk of cancers of the lip, mouth, larynx, esophagus, liver, rectum, stomach, and pancreas

Kidney: Kidney failure associated with end-stage liver disease

Nutrition: Nutrient deficiencies; obesity

Reproductive system: In women, menstrual irregularities and increased risk of having children with FAS; in men, impotence and testicular atrophy

Bone: Increased risk of osteoporosis; increased risk of fractures from frequent falls

Figure 13-2   The immediate and long-term effects of alcohol use.

TABLE 13-3	*Effects of Alcohol*	
Blood Alcohol Concentration (%)	**Common Behavioral Effects**	**Hours Required to Metabolize Alcohol**
0.00–0.05	Slight change in feelings, usually relaxation and euphoria; decreased alertness.	2–3
0.05–0.10	Emotional instability with exaggerated feelings and behavior; reduced social inhibitions; impairment of reaction time and fine motor coordination; increasingly impaired while driving. Legally drunk at 0.08% in many states and 0.10% in others.	4–6
0.10–0.15	Unsteadiness in standing and walking; loss of peripheral vision. Driving is extremely dangerous.	6–10
0.15–0.30	Staggering gait; slurred speech; impairment of pain perception and other sensory perceptions.	10–24
More than 0.30	Stupor or unconsciousness; anesthesia. Can result from rapid or binge drinking with few earlier effects. Death possible at 0.35% and above.	More than 24

BAC Zones:	90–109 lb	110–129 lb	130–149 lb	150–169 lb	170–189 lb	190–209 lb	210 lb & Over
Time from First Drink	Total Drinks	Total Drinks	Total Drinks	Total Drinks	Total Drinks	Total Drinks	Total Drinks
	1 2 3 4 5 6 7 8	1 2 3 4 5 6 7 8	1 2 3 4 5 6 7 8	1 2 3 4 5 6 7 8	1 2 3 4 5 6 7 8	1 2 3 4 5 6 7 8	1 2 3 4 5 6 7 8
1 hr							
2 hr							
3 hr							
4 hr							

☐ (0.00%) Not impaired   ▨ (0.05–0.07%) Usually impaired
☐ (0.01–0.04%) Sometimes impaired   ☐ (0.08% and up) Always impaired

Figure 13-3 Approximate blood alcohol concentration and body weight. This chart illustrates the BAC an average person of a given weight would reach after drinking the specified number of drinks in the time shown. The legal limit for BAC is 0.08% in some states and 0.10% in most others.

destroyed and replaced with fibrous scar tissue. Alcohol can also inflame the pancreas, causing nausea, vomiting, abnormal digestion, and severe abdominal pain. Though moderate doses of alcohol (one or two drinks a day) may slightly reduce the chances of heart attack in some people, high doses are associated with cardiovascular problems, including high blood pressure and a weakening of the heart muscles. Chronic alcohol abuse has also been linked to certain cancers, asthma, gout, diabetes, recurrent infections, nutritional deficiencies, and nervous system diseases. Psychiatric problems associated with excessive alcohol use include paranoia and memory gaps.

Maternal drinking during pregnancy can result in miscarriage, stillbirth, or **fetal alcohol syndrome (FAS).** Children with this syndrome are small at birth, are likely to have heart defects, and often have abnormal features such as small, wide-set eyes. Many are mentally impaired; others exhibit more subtle problems with learning and fine motor coordination. FAS is the most common preventable cause of mental impairment in the Western world; its incidence in the United States is estimated to be 1 or 2 in every 1000 live births. The effects of alcohol on the fetus are dose-related, and the safest course of action is abstinence from alcohol during pregnancy.

Alcohol Abuse

Alcohol abuse is defined as recurrent alcohol use that has negative consequences, such as drinking in dangerous situations (such as before driving), or drinking patterns that result in academic, professional, interpersonal, or legal difficulties. **Alcohol dependence,** or **alcoholism,** involves more extensive problems with alcohol use, usually involving physical tolerance and withdrawal (see below). Other authorities use different definitions to describe problems associated with drinking. The important point is that one does not have to be an alcoholic to have problems with alcohol. The person who drinks only once a month, perhaps after an exam, but then drives while intoxicated is an alcohol abuser. (Lab 13-1 includes an assessment to help you determine if alcohol is a problem in your life.)

How can you tell if you are beginning to abuse alcohol or if someone you know is doing so? Look for the following warning signs:

- Drinking alone or secretively
- Using alcohol deliberately and repeatedly to perform or get through difficult situations
- Feeling uncomfortable on certain occasions when alcohol is not available
- Escalating alcohol consumption beyond an already established drinking pattern
- Consuming alcohol heavily in risky situations, such as before driving
- Getting drunk regularly or more frequently than in the past
- Drinking in the morning or at other unusual times

Binge Drinking

A common form of alcohol abuse on college campuses is known as **binge drinking.** In a survey of over 17,000 students on 140 college campuses, 44% reported binge drinking, defined as having five drinks in a row for men or four in a row for women on at least one occasion in the 2 weeks prior to the survey. Some 19% of all students were found to be frequent binge drinkers, defined as having at least three binges during the 2-week period. The prevalence of binge drinking was highest among students who lived in fraternity and sorority houses and at residential colleges in the northeastern and north-central states. African American colleges and women's colleges have historically had lower rates of binge drinking.

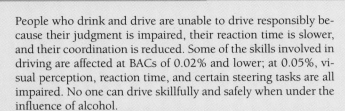
People who drink and drive are unable to drive responsibly because their judgment is impaired, their reaction time is slower, and their coordination is reduced. Some of the skills involved in driving are affected at BACs of 0.02% and lower; at 0.05%, visual perception, reaction time, and certain steering tasks are all impaired. No one can drive skillfully and safely when under the influence of alcohol.

What can you do to protect yourself against alcohol-related automobile crashes? If you are out of your home and drinking, follow the practice of having a *designated driver*, an individual who refrains from drinking in order to provide safe transportation home for others in the group. The responsibility can be rotated for different occasions.

To reduce your chances of being involved in a crash caused by someone else, learn to be alert to the erratic driving that signals an impaired driver. Warnings signs include wide, abrupt, and illegal turns; straddling the center line or lane marker; driving on the shoulder; weaving, swerving, or nearly striking an object or another vehicle; following too closely; erratic speed; driving with headlights off at night; and driving with the window down in very cold weather.

If you see any of these warning signs, what should you do?

- If the driver is ahead of you, maintain a safe following distance. Do not try to pass, because the driver may swerve into your car.
- If the driver is behind you, turn right at the nearest intersection, and let the driver pass.
- If the driver is approaching your car, move to the shoulder and stop. Avoid a head-on collision by sounding your horn or flashing your lights.
- When approaching an intersection, slow down and expect the unexpected.
- Make sure your safety belt is fastened, children are in approved safety seats, and your doors are locked.
- Report suspected impaired drivers to the nearest police station by phone. Give a description of the vehicle, license number, location, and direction the vehicle is headed.

SOURCES: Adapted from National Institute on Alcohol Abuse and Alcoholism. 1996. *Drinking and Driving.* No. 31 PH 362. The designated driver: Being a friend. 1986. *Healthline,* December.

Binge drinking has a profound effect on students' lives. Frequent binge drinkers were found to be 7–10 times more likely than non–binge drinkers to engage in unplanned sex or unprotected sex, to drive after drinking, to get into trouble with campus police, to damage property, and to get hurt or injured. Binge drinkers were also more likely to miss classes, get behind in schoolwork, and argue with their friends. The more frequent the binges, the more problems the students encountered. Despite their experiences, fewer than 1% of the binge drinkers identified themselves as problem drinkers.

Binge drinking also affects non–binge drinkers. At schools with high rates of binge drinking, the non–binge-drinking students were up to three times as likely to report being bothered by the drinking-related behaviors of others than students at schools with lower rates of binge drinking. These problems included being pushed, hit, or assaulted; having property damaged; having sleep or studying disrupted; and experiencing unwanted sexual advances.

Binge drinking is a difficult problem to address because many students arrive at college with drinking patterns already established. And many colleges have drinking "cultures" that may perpetuate the pattern of binge drinking. On many campuses, drinking behavior that would be classified as alcohol abuse in another setting may be viewed as socially acceptable or even socially attractive. This is despite the documented evidence that such behavior leads to automobile crashes, injuries, violence, suicide, high-risk sexual behavior, and death. Reducing binge drinking has become a priority on many college campuses, particularly since the alcohol poisoning deaths of several students in the fall of 1997; however, rates of binge drinking remain high among college students.

Alcoholism

As described earlier, alcoholism is usually characterized by tolerance and withdrawal. Everyone who drinks—even nonalcoholics—develops tolerance to alcohol after

fetal alcohol syndrome (FAS)   A characteristic group of birth defects caused by excessive alcohol consumption by the mother.   **TERMS**

alcohol abuse   The use of alcohol to a degree that causes physical damage, impairs functioning, or results in behavior harmful to others.

alcohol dependence   A pathological use of alcohol, or impairment in functioning due to alcohol; characterized by tolerance and withdrawal symptoms; alcoholism.

alcoholism   A chronic psychological disorder characterized by excessive and compulsive drinking.

binge drinking   Periodically drinking alcohol to the point of severe intoxication.

Whether a woman is a "social drinker," a binge drinker, or a heavy daily user, the impact of alcohol on her will be different, and generally greater, than for comparable use in a man. Women become intoxicated at lower doses of alcohol because of their smaller size, greater proportion of body fat, and less active form of an alcohol-metabolizing stomach enzyme. Hormonal fluctuations may also affect alcohol metabolism, making a woman more susceptible to high BACs at certain times during her menstrual cycle (usually just prior to the onset of menstruation).

Like men, women are more likely to be the perpetrator or victim of a crime when they have been drinking. Sexual assaults of all types, and date rape in particular, are more likely to occur if a woman has been drinking. Alcohol use makes women much less likely to practice safer sex, leaving them especially vulnerable to significant and lasting health problems as a result of sexually transmitted diseases and unintended pregnancy.

Women tend to experience the adverse physical effects of chronic drinking sooner and at lower levels of alcohol consumption than men. Female alcoholics have death rates 50–100% higher than those of male alcoholics. They develop alcohol liver disease after a comparatively shorter period of heavy drinking and at a lower level of daily drinking than men. They have higher death rates from cirrhosis. Other alcohol-related health problems that are unique to women include an increased risk for breast cancer, menstrual disorders, infertility, and, in pregnant women, giving birth to a child suffering from FAS. Because of the social stigma attached to problem drinking, women are also less likely to seek early treatment.

About one-third of all problem drinkers in the United States are women. Women from all walks of life and all ethnic groups can develop alcohol problems, but those who have never married or are divorced are more likely to drink heavily than married or widowed women. Women who have multiple life roles are less vulnerable to alcohol problems than women who have fewer roles.

---

repeated use. When alcoholics stop drinking or cut their intake significantly, they have withdrawal symptoms, which can range from unpleasant to serious and even life-threatening distress. Symptoms of alcohol withdrawal include trembling hands ("shakes" or "jitters"), a rapid pulse and breathing rate, insomnia, nightmares, anxiety, and gastrointestinal upset. Seizures are less common but more serious, and still less common is the severe reaction known as the **DTs (delirium tremens)**, characterized by confusion and vivid, usually unpleasant, hallucinations.

A 1995 survey revealed that 11 million Americans were heavy drinkers and 32 million were binge drinkers. The lifetime risk of alcoholism in the United States is about 10% for men and 3% for women (see the box "Women and Alcohol"). The cost to society and to the personal well-being of its citizens is inestimable. Despite media attention on cocaine, heroin, and marijuana, alcohol causes more problems than illegal drugs.

Some alcoholics recover without professional help, but the majority do not. Treatment is difficult. However, many different kinds of programs exist, including those that emphasize group and "buddy" support, those that stress lifestyle management, and those that use drugs and chemical substitutes as therapy. Although not all alcoholics can be treated successfully, considerable optimism has replaced the older view that nothing can be done.

Drinking and Responsibility

The responsible use of alcohol means drinking in a way that keeps your BAC low and your behavior under control. If you do drink, know your reasons for doing so. Are you being sociable? Giving in to peer pressure? Or are you attempting to satisfy underlying needs that could best be met by other means? Suggestions for keeping your drinking behavior under control are given in the box "Drinking Behavior and Responsibility."

TOBACCO

Smoking is hazardous to everyone's health—smoker and nonsmoker alike. Smoking causes more ill health than any other behavior. According to the U.S. Surgeon General, smoking is the leading preventable cause of illness and death in the United States. Tobacco in any form—cigarettes, cigars, pipes, chewing tobacco, clove cigarettes, or snuff—is unsafe. Despite its well-known hazards, however, tobacco use is still widespread in our society, particularly among certain groups (Table 13-4).

Nicotine Addiction

If smoking is so dangerous, why is it so widespread? Regular tobacco use, and especially cigarette smoking, is not just a habit but a full-blown addiction, involving physical dependence on the psychoactive drug **nicotine**. Addicted tobacco users must keep a steady amount of nicotine circulating in the blood and going to the brain. If that amount falls below a certain level, they experience with-

---

TERMS   **DTs (delirium tremens)**   A state of confusion brought on by the reduction of alcohol intake in an alcohol-dependent person; other symptoms are sweating, trembling, anxiety, hallucinations, and seizures.

nicotine   A poisonous, addictive substance found in tobacco and responsible for many of the effects of tobacco.

Drink Moderately and Responsibly

- *Drink slowly.* Sip your drinks, and don't drink alcoholic beverages to quench your thirst. Avoid drinks made with carbonated mixers.

- *Space your drinks.* Drink nonalcoholic drinks at parties, or alternate them with alcoholic drinks.

- *Eat before and while drinking.* Don't drink on an empty stomach. Food in your stomach will slow the rate at which alcohol is absorbed and thus often lower the peak BAC.

- *Know your limits and your drinks.* Learn how different BACs affect you, and use this knowledge to keep your BAC and your behavior under control.

- *Be aware of the setting.* In dangerous situations, such as driving or operating complicated machinery, abstinence is the only appropriate choice.

- *Use designated drivers.* Arrange carpools to and from parties or events where alcohol will be served. Rotate the responsibility.

- *Learn to enjoy activities without alcohol.* If you can't have fun without drinking, you may have a problem with alcohol.

Promote Responsible Drinking in Others

- *Encourage responsible attitudes.* Learn to express disapproval about someone who has drunk too much. Don't treat the choice to abstain as strange.

- *Be a responsible host.* Serve nonalcoholic beverages as well as alcohol, and serve only enough alcohol for each guest to have a moderate number of drinks. Always serve food along with alcohol, and stop serving alcohol an hour or more before people will leave. Insist that a guest who drank too much take a taxi, ride with someone else, or stay overnight rather than drive.

- *Hold the drinker responsible.* When any alcohol is consumed, the individual must take full responsibility for his or her behavior—and any negative consequences. Pardoning unacceptable behavior fosters the attitude that the behavior is due to the drug rather than the person.

- *Learn about prevention programs.* Find out what programs are available on your campus or in your community.

- *Take community action.* Consider joining an action group such as Students Against Drunk Driving (SADD) or Mothers Against Drunk Driving (MADD).

---

drawal symptoms: muscular pains, headaches, nausea, insomnia, irritability, and other discomforts. Many heavy smokers continue to smoke not for pleasure but in order to avoid the unpleasantness of withdrawal.

Health Hazards of Tobacco

Tobacco has negative effects on nearly every part of the body and increases the risk of many life-threatening diseases. Some of the many damaging chemicals in tobacco are carcinogens and cocarcinogens (agents that can combine with other chemicals to promote cancer). Others irritate the tissues of the respiratory system. Carbon monoxide, the deadly gas in automobile exhaust, is present in cigarette smoke in concentrations 400 times greater than the safety threshold set in workplaces. Table 13-5 lists some of the other hazardous substances in tobacco smoke.

The effects of nicotine on smokers vary, depending on the size of the dose and the smoker's past smoking behavior. Nicotine can either excite or tranquilize the nervous system, generally resulting in stimulation that gives way to tranquility and then depression. Figure 13-4 summarizes the immediate effects of smoking.

In the short term, smoking interferes with the functions of the respiratory system and often leads rapidly to shortness of breath and the conditions known as smoker's throat, smoker's cough, and smoker's bronchitis. Other

VITAL STATISTICS

TABLE 13-4	*Who Smokes?*		
	Percentage of Smokers		
	Men	*Women*	*Total*
Ethnic Group (all ages)			
White	28	24	26
Black	31	23	27
Asian/Pacific Islander	25	6	16
American Indian/ Alaska Native	45	34	39
Latino	23	15	19
Education, in Years (age ≥ 25)			
≤8	28	18	23
9–11	42	34	38
12	34	26	30
13–15	25	23	24
≥16	14	14	14
Total	27	23	25

SOURCES: U.S. Department of Health and Human Services. 1998. *Tobacco Use Among U.S. Racial/Ethnic Groups: A Report of the Surgeon General.* Atlanta: U.S. Department of Health and Human Services. Centers for Disease Control and Prevention. 1997. Cigarette smoking among adults—United States, 1995. *Morbidity and Mortality Weekly Report* 46(51): 1217–1220.

TABLE 13-5	Selected Substances in Cigarette Smoke

Carcinogens

Nitrosamines	Benzo(a)pyrene	Toluidine
Crysenes	Polonium	Urethane
Cadmium	Nickel	

Metals

Aluminum	Mercury	Titanium
Zinc	Gold	Lead
Magnesium	Silver	

Other Substances

Chemical	Typical Use or Source
Acetone	Nail polish remover
Ammonia	Floor or toilet cleaner
Arsenic	Poison
Butane	Cigarette lighter fluid
Carbon monoxide	Car exhaust fumes
DDT/dieldrin	Insecticides
Formaldehyde	Body tissue and fabric preserver
Hydrogen cyanide	Gas chamber poison
Methane	Swamp gas
Methanol	Rocket fuel
Naphthalene	Mothballs
Nicotine	Insecticide, addictive drug
Toluene	Industrial solvent
Vinyl chloride	Makes PVC

SOURCE: Health Partnership Project/California Medical Association Foundation, 1995. Used with permission.

common short-term complaints are loss of appetite, diarrhea, fatigue, hoarseness, weight loss, stomach pains, insomnia, and impaired visual acuity, especially at night.

Long-term effects fall into two general categories. The first is reduced life expectancy: A male who takes up smoking before age 15 and continues to smoke is only half as likely to live to age 75 as one who never smokes. Female smokers, too, experience dramatic losses in life expectancy.

The second category of long-term effects involves quality of life. Both male and female smokes have higher rates of acute and chronic diseases than those who have never

smoked. The more people smoke, and the deeper and more often they inhale, the greater the risk of disease and other complications. Cigarette smoking increases risk for all the following:

- Cardiovascular disease (heart attack, stroke, hypertension, high cholesterol levels), lung disease (emphysema, chronic bronchitis), osteoporosis, diabetes, and many types of cancer (lung, liver, colon, pancreas, kidney, bladder, cervix)
- Tooth decay, gum disease, bad breath, colds, ulcers, hair loss, facial wrinkling, and discolored teeth and fingers
- Menstrual disorders, early menopause, impotence, infertility, stillbirth, and low birth weight
- Motor vehicle crashes and fire-related injuries

In addition, smoking is expensive. A pack-a-day habit costs an average of $1000 per year. Other financial costs include higher health and home insurance premiums; more frequent cleaning of clothes, teeth, home, office, and car; and repair of burnt clothing, upholstery, and carpeting.

People who use other forms of tobacco also face health hazards. Cigar and pipe smokers are at increased risk for many health problems, including cardiovascular and respiratory diseases and many types of cancer. Chewing tobacco and snuff both lead to nicotine addiction. Users of these smokeless tobacco products are at increased risk for cancers of the lip, mouth, larynx, and esophagus; tooth decay; inflammation and recession of the gums; and high blood cholesterol levels.

When smokers quit, many health improvements begin almost immediately. The younger people are when they stop smoking, the more pronounced are these improvements (see the box "The Benefits of Quitting Smoking").

Environmental Tobacco Smoke

Environmental tobacco smoke (ETS), commonly called secondhand smoke, consists of **mainstream smoke**, the smoke exhaled by smokers, and **sidestream smoke**, the smoke that enters the atmosphere from the burning end of the cigarette, cigar, or pipe. Undiluted sidestream smoke is unfiltered by a cigarette filter or a smoker's lungs, so it contains significantly higher concentrations of toxic and carcinogenic compounds than mainstream smoke. Nearly 85% of the smoke in a room where someone is smoking is sidestream smoke. Even though such smoke is diffuse, the concentrations can be considerable. In rooms where people are smoking, levels of carbon monoxide, for instance, can exceed those permitted by Federal Air Quality Standards for outside air.

Effects of ETS Studies show that up to 25% of nonsmokers subjected to ETS develop coughs, 30% develop

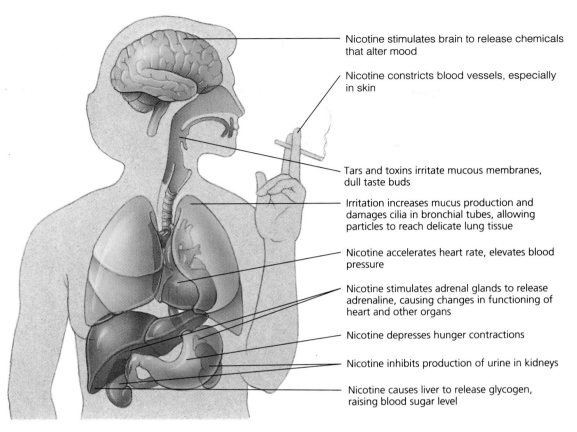

Nicotine stimulates brain to release chemicals that alter mood

Nicotine constricts blood vessels, especially in skin

Tars and toxins irritate mucous membranes, dull taste buds

Irritation increases mucus production and damages cilia in bronchial tubes, allowing particles to reach delicate lung tissue

Nicotine accelerates heart rate, elevates blood pressure

Nicotine stimulates adrenal glands to release adrenaline, causing changes in functioning of heart and other organs

Nicotine depresses hunger contractions

Nicotine inhibits production of urine in kidneys

Nicotine causes liver to release glycogen, raising blood sugar level

Figure 13-4   The short-term effects of smoking a cigarette.

A CLOSER LOOK   *The Benefits of Quitting Smoking*

Within 20 minutes of your last cigarette:
- You stop polluting the air
- Blood pressure drops to normal
- Pulse rate drops to normal
- Temperature of hands and feet increases to normal

8 hours:
- Carbon monoxide level in blood drops to normal
- Oxygen level in blood increases to normal

24 hours:
- Chance of heart attack decreases

48 hours:
- Nerve endings adjust to the absence of nicotine
- Ability to smell and taste things is enhanced

72 hours:
- Bronchial tubes relax, making breathing easier
- Lung capacity increases

2–3 months:
- Circulation improves
- Walking becomes easier
- Lung function increases up to 30%

1–9 months:
- Coughing, sinus congestion, fatigue, and shortness of breath all decrease
- Cilia regrow in lungs, reduce infection
- Body's overall energy level increases

1 year:
- Heart disease death rate is halfway back to that of a nonsmoker

5 years:
- Heart disease risk drops almost to the risk for nonsmokers
- Lung cancer death rate decreases halfway back to that of nonsmokers

10 years:
- Lung cancer death rate drops almost to the rate for nonsmokers
- Precancerous cells are replaced
- The incidence of other cancers (mouth, larynx, esophagus, bladder, kidney, and pancreas) decreases

15 years:
- Risks of heart disease and stroke are about the same as for nonsmokers

SOURCE: Health Partnership Project/California Medical Association, 1995. Used with permission.

The average age of new smokers is 13, and most adult smokers began as teenagers. In polls, about 75% of teen smokers state they wish they had never started.

headaches and nasal discomfort, and 70% suffer eye irritation. Other symptoms range from breathlessness to sinus problems. People with allergies tend to have the worst symptoms. Tobacco odor, which clings to the skin and clothes, is another unpleasant effect of ETS.

But ETS has far more serious effects as well. The EPA estimates that people who live or work among smokers face a 24–50% increase in lung cancer risk and that 3000 Americans die from lung cancer caused by ETS each year. ETS also contributes to heart disease—about 50,000 heart disease deaths are attributed to this cause annually—and aggravates respiratory conditions such as asthma. Scientists have been able to measure changes capable of contributing to lung tissue damage and potential tumor promotion in the bloodstreams of healthy young test subjects who spent just 3 hours in a smoke-filled room.

Children and ETS   Infants and children are particularly vulnerable to the harmful effects of ETS. Because they breathe faster than adults, they inhale more air—and more of the pollutants in the air. And because they weigh less than adults, children inhale proportionately more pollutants per unit of body weight.

The U.S. Environmental Protection Agency (EPA) estimates that secondhand smoke triggers 150,000–300,000 cases of bronchitis, pneumonia, and other respiratory infections in infants and toddlers each year. Older children suffer, too. The EPA has labeled ETS a risk factor for asthma in children who have not previously exhibited symptoms of the disease and has blamed ETS for ag-

gravating the symptoms of the 200,000 to 1 million children who already have asthma. The EPA also links ETS to reduced lung function and identifies it as a cause of fluid buildup in the middle ear, a contributing factor in middle-ear infections. Approximately 9 million American children are regularly exposed to ETS, usually in the home.

As research reveals more about ETS and its effects, nonsmokers are asserting their right to breathe clean air. Many people feel that this right supersedes the right of smokers to smoke when the two conflict (see the box "Avoiding Environmental Tobacco Smoke").

Smoking and Pregnancy

Smoking almost doubles a pregnant woman's chance of suffering a miscarriage, and women who smoke also face an increased risk of **ectopic pregnancy.** Maternal smoking causes an estimated 4600 infant deaths in the United States each year, primarily due to premature delivery and smoking-related problems with the placenta, the organ that delivers blood, oxygen, and nutrients to the fetus. Infants whose mothers smoked during pregnancy are also more likely to die from sudden infant death syndrome (SIDS). Maternal smoking is a major factor in low birth weight, which puts newborns at high risk for infections and other potentially fatal problems. Babies born to mothers who smoke more than two packs per day perform poorly on developmental tests in the first hours after birth when compared with babies of nonsmoking mothers. Later in life, hyperactivity, short attention span, and lower scores on spelling and reading tests all occur more frequently in children whose mothers smoked throughout pregnancy than in those born to nonsmoking mothers. Nevertheless, only about 40% of women who are smokers when they become pregnant quit at any time during their pregnancy.

TERMS   **ectopic pregnancy**   A pregnancy in which the fertilized egg implants itself in an oviduct rather than in the uterus; the embryo must be surgically removed.

As a nonsmoker, you have the right to breathe clean air, free from tobacco smoke. What can you do if you are often, or even occasionally, bothered by ETS? Here are some tips:

- *Speak up tactfully.* Smokers may not be aware of the dangers of secondhand smoke, or they may not know it bothers you.
- *Display reminders.* If you are shy about asking people not to smoke, put up "No Smoking" signs in your home or room, at your work station, and in your car. Get rid of ashtrays so smokers feel less welcome to light up.
- *Don't allow smoking in your home or room.* Help smokers find a place outside where they can smoke.

- *Open a window.* If you cannot avoid being in a room with smokers, at least try to provide some ventilation.
- *Sit in the nonsmoking section in restaurants.* Complain to the manager if none exists.
- *Fight for a smoke-free work environment.* For your sake and that of your coworkers, join with other either to eliminate all smoking indoors or to confine it to certain areas.
- *Discuss quitting strategies.* Many former smokers say social pressure was a big factor in their decision to quit. Demonstrate your concern for the health of the smokers in your life by telling them what you know about strategies for quitting.

Action Against Tobacco

Every hour, 60 Americans die from preventable smoking-related diseases. But in the past several years, individuals and communities have taken action against this major health threat. Thousands of local ordinances have been passed across the country banning or restricting smoking in restaurants, stores, and other public places. Communities are also restricting many forms of tobacco advertising, such as billboards. Many states as well as the federal government have filed lawsuits against the tobacco industry to reclaim money spent on smoking-related health care. And the FDA concluded that tobacco products are delivery devices for an addictive drug, nicotine, and therefore subject to FDA regulation. For these and other reasons, tobacco consumption in the United States is declining. In response, the U.S. tobacco industry has increased its efforts to sell to foreign markets, especially developing nations with few restrictions on tobacco advertising. (For additional information on legal and political activities, contact one of the tobacco-related organizations or Web sites listed in For More Information at the end of the chapter.)

Giving Up Tobacco

Giving up tobacco is a long-term process that involves breaking both the physical and the psychological addiction to nicotine. Although most ex-smokers have stopped using tobacco on their own, some smokers benefit from stop-smoking programs and support groups. Programs that combine several approaches—pharmacological, psychological, behavioral, and so on—tend to work best.

If you use tobacco and decide to quit, use the behavior change plan described in Chapter 1. The quiz in Lab 13-2 can provide clues about your smoking behavior that will be helpful as you plan a strategy for quitting. Begin by completing a personal contract for quitting that specifies the day and time when you will stop using tobacco, as well as some rewards for quitting. You may be unsure whether to quit "cold turkey" or gradually. Research favors the cold turkey approach, but with enough time set aside to learn and practice effective quitting skills. (See the box "Choosing How to Quit" for information on other strategies.)

Your first few days without tobacco will probably be the most difficult. Nicotine is a powerfully addictive drug, and its use quickly becomes a deeply ingrained habit. But remember that 44 million Americans have quit—and you can too. It's important to avoid or control situations that you strongly associate with tobacco use, such as drinking coffee, driving in your car, or socializing with friends. Try strategies such as drinking tea or water instead of coffee, riding your bike instead of driving, and participating in nonsmoking events (movies, shopping, and so on).

Social support can be a big help. Arrange with a friend to encourage you in difficult moments, and call her or him when you feel overwhelmed by a craving for tobacco. Tell people you've just quit. You may discover many former tobacco users who can reassure you that it's possible to quit and lead a healthier life.

Maintaining abstinence from tobacco over time is the ultimate goal of any cessation program. Tracking and controlling any lingering urges make relapses less likely. Keeping track of them in a health journal helps you deal with them. When you have an urge to use tobacco, use a relaxation technique, take a brisk walk, chew gum, or substitute some other activity. Practice time management so you don't get overwhelmed at school or work. Exercise regularly, eat sensibly, and get enough sleep. These habits not only will ensure your success at remaining free from tobacco use but also will serve you well in stressful times throughout your life.

Quitting on Your Own

About 85–95% of smokers who quit do so on their own. Studies of successful ex-smokers have shown that support from others and regular exercise are two factors that improve the chances of success. On the flip side, the more alcohol one drinks, the less successful one will be at quitting smoking. Some people quit "cold turkey," whereas others taper down more slowly.

Help from the Pharmacy

Nicotine replacement therapy involves supplying the tobacco user with nicotine from a source other than standard tobacco products. It allows a tobacco user to overcome the psychological and behavioral aspects of a tobacco habit without having to simultaneously endure the physical symptoms of nicotine withdrawal. Nicotine replacements are available in chewing gum and skin patches; both products are available without a prescription. Each piece of gum delivers about as much nicotine as one cigarette; each patch delivers a timed dose of nicotine equal to as much as three-quarters of a pack of cigarettes over a 24-hour period. After a few weeks or months, the reforming tobacco user begins to gradually taper off use of the replacement, avoiding withdrawal symptoms. Some brands of nicotine patches come in several strengths to make it easier to gradually decrease the dosage.

There are drawbacks to nicotine replacement therapy. Many people find it difficult to manage the dosage of nicotine while using the gum; possible side effects include burning sensations in the mouth and throat, nausea, and vomiting. The patch can cause skin irritation, insomnia, nausea, dry mouth, and nervousness. People who continue to smoke while using a nicotine replacement risk nicotine overdose and possibly heart attack. And some people become hooked on the gum or the patch.

Nicotine replacements can be effective in helping some people quit, especially when used in combination with counseling and behavioral therapy.

Help from Your Physician

Prescription products for smoking cessation include nicotine replacement therapy in the form of an inhaler and the antidepressant drug Zyban. A physician may prescribe additional medications for very heavy smokers or those who have tried unsuccessfully to quit. Some people are helped by clonidine, a drug used to aid heroin addicts during withdrawal. Your physician may have other resources to share with you that are unique to your community, such as cessation programs, support groups, or a hotline number.

Group Programs

Formal programs are particularly recommended for people who have tried repeatedly to quit on their own without success. The American Cancer Society, the American Lung Association, and the Seventh-Day Adventist Church all offer well-respected smoking-cessation programs. Your college health center or community hospital may also do so. Some programs now are geared specifically to spit tobacco users. Although the effectiveness of programs to help adults quit smoking has been mixed, some studies show as many as 30% of the people who enroll in group programs remain tobacco-free a year later. For group programs that also use nicotine replacement therapy, the success rate can climb as high as 47%.

Each individual method of quitting smoking may be successful for some people, but a combined approach usually has the highest success rate. Plan carefully how you will quit, to maximize your chance of conquering this powerful addiction.

SOURCES: Antidepressant drug helps smoking cessation. 1998. *Harvard Heart Letter,* February. The last draw for smokers. 1996. *University of California at Berkeley Wellness Letter,* October. Kolata, G. 1994. Nicotine patch study sees 25% success rate. *New York Times,* 22 July.

COMMON QUESTIONS ANSWERED

Is spit (smokeless) tobacco as dangerous as cigarettes? No, but it carries many of the same health risks. There are two main categories of spit tobacco products: chewing tobacco and snuff. In chewing tobacco, the tobacco leaf may be shredded, pressed into bricks or cakes, or twisted into ropelike strands; it is usually treated with molasses and other flavorings. The user places a wad of tobacco in his or her mouth and then chews or sucks it to release the nicotine. In snuff, the leaf is processed into a coarse, moist powder. The user places a pinch of tobacco between the cheek and gum. All types of spit tobacco cause an increase in saliva production, and the resulting juice is spit out or swallowed. The nicotine in spit tobacco—along with flavorings, additives, and carcinogenic chemicals—is

absorbed through the gums and lining of the mouth. The dose of nicotine the user of spit tobacco products receives is similar to that provided by cigarettes, and spit tobacco is highly addictive. Studies suggest that nearly 40% of professional baseball players in the United States use spit tobacco; most say they have tried to quit but have not yet succeeded in doing so.

After only a few weeks of use, the gums and lips of a spit tobacco user can become dried and irritated and may bleed. Precancerous white or red patches may appear inside the mouth. A 1998 study of major league baseball players sponsored by the National Spit Tobacco Education Program found dangerous mouth lesions in 83 out of the 141 spit tobacco–using players who were examined. Long-term snuff use may increase the risk of cancer of the cheek and gums by as much as 50 times. Spit tobacco use causes bad breath, tooth decay, and gum problems; the senses of taste and smell are usually dulled. It may also have dangerous effects on the cardiovascular system, increasing the risk of heart disease.

The use of spit tobacco products has increased in recent years, especially among young adults. The Centers for Disease Control and Prevention estimates that nearly 16% of male high school students use spit tobacco.

Is there anything I can do for someone I know who has a drug problem? If you believe a family member or friend has a drug problem, obtain information about resources for drug treatment available on your campus or in your community. Communicate your concern, provide information about treatment options, and offer your support during treatment. If the person continues to deny having a problem, you may want to talk with an experienced counselor about setting up an "intervention"—a formal, structured confrontation designed to end denial by having family, friends, and other caring individuals present their concerns to the drug user. Participants in an intervention would indicate the ways in which the abuser is hurting others as well as himself or herself. If your friend or family member agrees to treatment, encourage him or her to attend a support group such as Narcotics Anonymous or Alcoholics Anonymous.

In addition, examine your relationship with the abuser for signs of *codependency*. A codependent is someone whose actions help or enable a person to remain dependent on a drug by removing or softening the effects of the drug use on the user. Common actions by codependents include making excuses or lying for someone to his or her friends, teachers, or employer; loaning money to someone to continue drug use; staying up late waiting for, or going out searching for, someone who uses drugs; and not confronting someone who is obviously intoxicated or high on a drug. People often become enablers spontaneously and naturally because they want to help their friend or loved one. Unfortunately, the habit of enabling can inhibit a drug-dependent person's recovery because the person never has to experience the consequences of her or his behavior. If you see yourself developing a codependent relationship, get help for yourself; friends and family of drug users can often benefit from counseling.

Does drinking benefit health? Studies have shown that moderate drinking—one drink per day for women and two drinks per day for men—is associated with a lower risk of coronary heart disease. The precise mechanism isn't entirely clear, but it appears that moderate drinking raises levels of beneficial HDL cholesterol. Researchers have found that blood levels of HDL are an average of 17% higher in moderate drinkers than in abstainers. Alcohol also appears to make platelets less likely to stick together—an important protection against heart attacks and some types of strokes because platelets that stick together can form dangerous clots.

The bottom line is that limited, regular consumption of alcohol appears to safely reduce the risk of heart disease for some adults. However, it's not for everyone. A major risk of moderate drinking is that it won't stay moderate. People who avoid alcohol because they've had problems with dependence in the past or come from families with a history of alcoholism should not start drinking for their health. In addition, people with medical conditions such as peptic ulcer, diabetes, or depression that are worsened by alcohol use should also probably avoid even moderate drinking. And because some studies have found an association between moderate drinking and an increased risk of breast cancer, women with other breast cancer risk factors should discuss the potential risks and benefits of alcohol with their physician before taking up moderate drinking. Nor should excessive drinkers use this information as an excuse to overindulge. There is a narrow window of benefit, and excessive drinking causes serious health problems.

Does drinking coffee help an intoxicated person sober up more quickly? No. Once alcohol is absorbed into the body, there are no ways of appreciably accelerating its breakdown. The rate of alcohol metabolism varies among individuals, largely as a result of heredity, but it is not affected by caffeine, exercise, fresh air, or other stimulants. It is the same whether a person is asleep or awake. To sober up, you simply have to wait until your body has had sufficient time to metabolize all the alcohol you have consumed.

What should be done for someone who is severely intoxicated or who may be suffering from alcohol poisoning? Acute alcohol poisoning occurs much more frequently than most people realize. Dangerously high blood alcohol levels can result from rapid or binge drinking with few earlier effects. A common scenario for alcohol poisoning occurs when inexperienced drinkers try to outdo each other by consuming glass after glass of alcohol as rapidly as possible. Children are also at high risk for alcohol poisoning: Even a partially empty glass of liquor carelessly left out after a party can result in serious poisoning, or even death, if consumed by a toddler or small child.

The amount of alcohol it takes to make a person unconscious is dangerously close to a fatal dose. Death from acute alcohol poisoning may be caused either by central nervous system and respiratory depression or by inhaling fluid or vomit into the lungs. If you come into contact with a person who has been drinking and becomes unconscious, do not assume he or she is just "sleeping it off." The person should be placed on his or her side (to minimize the possibility of choking if vomiting occurs) and examined carefully. If the person's breathing is slow (less than 8 breaths per minute or lapses of 10 seconds or more between breaths) or if the person looks pale or bluish or the skin feels clammy, call 911 immediately. If you aren't sure, call 911 for help.

- Addictive behaviors are habits that have gotten out of control and have a negative impact on a person's health. Characteristics of addictive behaviors include reinforcement, craving, loss of control, escalation, and negative consequences.

- Drug abuse is a maladaptive pattern of drug use that persists despite adverse social, psychological, or medical consequences. Drug dependence involves taking a drug compulsively; tolerance and withdrawal symptoms are often present. It is not possible to determine when drug use will lead to abuse or dependence.

- Factors to consider when deciding whether to try a psychoactive drug include short- and long-term risks of drug use, one's future goals and ethical beliefs, the financial cost of the drug, and one's reasons for drug use.

- At low doses, alcohol causes relaxation; at higher doses, it interferes with motor and mental functioning and is associated with injuries; at very high doses, alcohol poisoning, coma, and death can occur.

- Continued alcohol use has negative effects on the digestive and cardiovascular systems and increases cancer risk and overall mortality. Women who drink while pregnant risk giving birth to children with fetal alcohol syndrome.

- Binge drinking is a common form of alcohol abuse on college campuses that has negative effects on both drinking and nondrinking students.

- Nicotine is the addictive psychoactive drug in tobacco products.

- In the short term, smoking can either excite or tranquilize the nervous system; it also interferes with the functions of the respiratory system. Long-term effects of smoking include higher rates of acute and chronic diseases and reduced life expectancy.

- Environmental tobacco smoke contains toxic and carcinogenic compounds in high concentrations. It causes health problems, including cancer and heart disease, in nonsmokers exposed to it; infants and children are especially at risk.

- Many approaches and products are available to aid people in quitting smoking.

FOR MORE INFORMATION

Books

Kinney, J., and G. Leaton. 1995. *Loosening the Grip: A Handbook of Alcohol Information*, 5th ed. St. Louis: Mosby. *A fascinating book about alcohol, including information on physical effects, abuse, alcoholism, and cultural aspects of alcohol use.*

Kuhn, C., et al. 1998. *Buzzed: The Straight Facts About the Most Used and Abused Drugs from Alcohol to Ecstasy.* New York: W. W. Norton. *An accurate, straightforward guide to commonly used drugs.*

Pringle, P. 1998. *Cornered: Tobacco Companies at the Bar of Justice.* New York: Henry Holt. *A review of the events leading up to the proposed deal to settle lawsuits against the major tobacco companies in the United States.*

Schuckit, M. A. 1998. *Educating Yourself About Alcohol and Drugs: A People's Primer.* Rev. ed. New York: Plenum Press. *A guide to the physical, emotional, and social effects of drug abuse and to resources that are available to help users stop.*

Stevic-Rust, L., and A. Maximin. 1996. *The Stop-Smoking Workbook.* Oakland, Calif.: New Harbinger. *A self-help book designed to help smokers quit.*

West, J. 1997. *The Betty Ford Center Book of Answers.* New York: Simon and Schuster. *Straightforward answers to commonly asked questions about alcoholism and other addictions.*

Young, K. S. 1998. *Caught in the Net: How to Recognize the Signs of Internet Addiction and a Sure-Fire Strategy for Recovery.* New York: Wiley. *An exploration of the recently identified problem of Internet addiction.*

Organizations, Hotlines, and Web Sites

Action on Smoking and Health (ASH). Provides statistics, news briefs, and other information about the negative effects of smoking.
202-659-4310
http://ash.org

Al-Anon Family Group Headquarters. Provides information and referrals to local Al-Anon and Alateen groups.
800-344-2666; 757-563-1600
http://www.al-anon.alateen.org

Alcoholics Anonymous (AA) World Services. Provides information on AA, literature on alcoholism, and information about AA meetings.
212-870-3400
http://www.alcoholics-anonymous.org

American Lung Association. Provides information on lung diseases, tobacco control, and environmental health.
800-LUNG-USA; 212-315-8700
http://www.lungusa.org

CDC's Tobacco Information and Prevention Source (TIPS). Provides research results, educational materials, and tips on how to quit smoking.
800-CDC-1311; 770-488-5701
http://www.cdc.gov/nccdphp/osh

Habitsmart. Contains information about addictive behavior, including tips for managing problematic habitual behavior, a self-scoring alcohol checkup, and links to related sites.
http://www.cts.com/crash/habtsmrt

Higher Education Center for Alcohol and Other Drug Prevention. Provides information about alcohol and drug abuse on campus and links to related sites; also has an area designed specifically for students.
http://www.edc.org/hec

Mothers Against Drunk Driving (MADD). Supports efforts to develop solutions to the problems of drunk driving and underage drinking; provides brochures about many alcohol-related topics, including a guide for giving a safe party.

http://www.madd.org

National Association for Children of Alcoholics (NACoA). Provides information and support for children of alcoholics.

888-554-COAS; 301-468-0985

http://www.health.org/nacoa

National Clearinghouse for Alcohol and Drug Information. Provides statistics, information, and publications on substance abuse, including resources for people who want to help friends and family members overcome substance-abuse problems.

800-729-6686; 301-468-2600

http://www.health.org

National Institute on Alcohol Abuse and Alcoholism (NIAAA). Provides booklets and other publications on a variety of alcohol-related topics, including fetal alcohol syndrome, alcoholism treatment, and alcohol use and minorities.

301-443-3860

http://www.niaaa.nih.gov

National Spit Tobacco Education Program (NSTEP)/Oral Health America. A national initiative designed to educate Americans about the dangers of spit tobacco.

312-787-6270

Quitnet. Provides interactive tools and questionnaires, support groups, a library, and the latest news on tobacco issues.

http://www.quitnet.org

SmokeScreen Action Network. Sponsored by an advocacy group for tobacco control, a Web site that provides information on your congressional representatives, their voting record on tobacco-related issues, and tobacco PAC money they've accepted.

http://www.Smokescreen.org

Tobacco BBS. A resource center on tobacco and smoking issues that includes news and information, assistance for smokers who want to quit, and links to related sites.

http://www.tobacco.org

Tobacco Control Resource Center and Tobacco Products Liability Project (TPLP). Provides current information about tobacco-related court cases and legislation; based at the Northeastern School of Law.

http://www.tobacco.neu.edu

Web of Addictions. Provides a wealth of information about substance abuse and dependence, including fact sheets, contact information for relevant agencies and organizations, and links to related sites.

http://www.well.com/user/woa

The following hotlines provide support and referrals:

800-662-HELP (National Drug and Alcohol Treatment Referral Routing Service)

800-NCA-CALL (National Council on Alcoholism and Drug Dependence Hopeline)

800-COCAINE (National Cocaine Hotline)

800-ALCOHOL (Alcohol Treatment Referral Hotline)

SELECTED BIBLIOGRAPHY

American Cancer Society. 1998. *Cancer Facts and Figures.* Atlanta, Ga.: American Cancer Society.

American Psychiatric Association. 1994. *Diagnostic and Statistical Manual of Mental Disorders,* 4th ed. *(DSM-IV).* Washington, D.C.: American Psychiatric Association.

Boshuizen, H. C., et al. 1998. Maternal smoking during lactation: Relation to growth during the first year of life in a Dutch birth cohort. *American Journal of Epidemiology* 147(2): 117–126.

Bowdler, M., and S. Mahoney. 1998. Alcohol poisoning on campus. *American Journal of Nursing* 98(1): 65–66.

Centers for Disease Control and Prevention. 1998. Alcohol-related traffic fatalities involving children—United States, 1985–1996. *Journal of the American Medical Association* 279(2): 104–105.

Centers for Disease Control and Prevention. 1998. Selected cigarette smoking initiation and quitting behaviors among high school students—United States, 1997. *Morbidity and Mortality Weekly Report* 47(19): 386–389.

Centers for Disease Control and Prevention. 1998. Tobacco use among high school students—United States, 1997. *Morbidity and Mortality Weekly Report* 47(12): 229–233.

Eyler, F. D., et al. 1998. Birth outcome from a prospective, matched study of prenatal crack/cocaine use: I. Interactive and dose effects on health and growth. *Pediatrics* 101(2): 229–237.

Figueredo, V. M. 1997. The effects of alcohol on the heart: Detrimental or beneficial? *Postgraduate Medicine* 101(2): 165–168, 171–172, 175–176.

Firshein, J. 1998. U.S. public-health groups petition FDA to take tougher action on tobacco. *Lancet* 351(9098): 276.

Gergen, P. J., et al. 1998. The burden of environmental tobacco smoke exposure on the respiratory health of children 2 months through 5 years of age in the United States. *Pediatrics* 101(2): E8.

Howard, G., et al. 1998. Cigarette smoking and progression of atherosclerosis: The Atherosclerosis Risk in Communities (ARIC) Study. *Journal of the American Medical Association* 279(2): 119–124.

Ji, B. T., et al. 1997. Paternal cigarette smoking and the risk of childhood cancer among offspring of nonsmoking mothers. *Journal of the National Cancer Institute* 89(3): 238–244.

Kessler, D. A. 1997. The legal and scientific basis for FDA's assertion of jurisdiction over cigarettes and smokeless tobacco. *Journal of the American Medical Association* 277(5): 405–409.

Kitamura, A., et al. 1998. Alcohol intake and premature coronary heart disease in urban Japanese men. *American Journal of Epidemiology* 147(1): 59–65.

Klerman, G. L., et al. 1996. The role of drug and alcohol abuse in recent increases in depression in the United States. *Psychological Medicine* 26(2): 343–351.

Kodama, M., et al. 1997. Free radical chemistry of cigarette smoke and its implications in human cancer. *Anticancer Research* 17(1A): 433–437.

Koob, G. F. 1998. Drug abuse and alcoholism. Overview. *Advances in Pharmacology* 42: 969–977.

Martin, S. 1996. Zero tolerance laws: Effective public policy? *Alcoholism: Clinical and Experimental Research* 20(8S): 147A–150A.

McLellan, A. T., et al. 1996. Evaluating the effectiveness of addiction treatments: Reasonable expectations, appropriate comparisons. *Milbank Quarterly* 74(1): 51–85.

Nair, J., et al. 1996. Endogenous formation of nitrosamines and oxidative DNA-damaging agents in tobacco users. *Critical*

Reviews in Toxicology 26(2): 149–161.

National Cancer Institute. 1998. *Smoking and Tobacco Control Monograph 9. Cigars: Health Effects and Trends* (retrieved May 10, 1998; http://rex.nci.nih.gov/NCI_MONOGRAPHS/MONO9.HTM).

National Institute on Alcohol Abuse and Alcoholism. 1996. *Drinking and Driving.* NIH Publication No. 31 PH 362. Bethesda, Md.: National Institute on Alcohol Abuse and Alcoholism.

National Institute on Drug Abuse. 1997. *NIDA Capsule: Prevalence for Various Types of Drugs, 1995. Full-Time College Students vs. Others* (retrieved February 28, 1998; http://www.nida.nih.gov/NIDACapsules/NCCollege.html).

Perlman, D. 1998. Ballplayers' 'spit tobacco' penalty. *San Francisco Chronicle,* April 9, A1, A9.

Pich, E. M., et al. 1997. Common neural substrates for the addictive properties of nicotine and cocaine. *Science* 275(5296): 83–86.

Presley, C. A. 1996. *Alcohol and Drugs on American Campuses, Volume III: 1991–1993,* CORE Institute, Southern Illinois University.

Ray, O. S., and C. Ksir. 1996. *Drugs, Society and Human Behavior,* 7th ed. St. Louis: Mosby.

Riley, W. T. 1996. Adults smokeless tobacco use and age of onset. *Addictive Behavior* 21(1): 135–138.

Robinson, T. N., and J. D. Killen. 1997. Do cigarette warning labels reduce smoking? Paradoxical effects among adolescents. *Archives of Pediatrics and Adolescent Medicine* 151(3): 267–272.

Schwartz, R. H., E. A. Voth, and M. J. Sheridan. 1997. Marijuana to prevent nausea and vomiting in cancer patients: A survey of clinical oncologists. *Southern Medical Journal* 90(2): 167–172.

Tashkin, D. D., M. D. Roth, and S. M. Dubinett. 1997. Medical marijuana? *New England Journal of Medicine* 336(16): 1186–1187.

Tobacco Settlement, Proposed Resolution. 1997. Text of preliminary settlement between state attorneys general and tobacco industry, 20 June (retrieved June 22, 1997; http://www.tobacco.neu.edu/smoke01.htm).

U.S. Department of Health and Human Services. 1996. *The Relationship Between Family Structure and Adolescent Substance Use.* U.S. Public Health Service.

U.S. Department of Health and Human Services. 1998. *Tobacco Use Among U.S. Racial/Ethnic Minority Groups: A Report of the Surgeon General.* Atlanta: Office on Smoking and Health, U.S. Department of Health and Human Services.

Wechsler, H. 1995. *Binge Drinking on American College Campuses: A New Look at an Old Problem.* Boston: Harvard University School of Public Health.

Wechsler, H., et al. 1994. Health and behavioral consequences of binge drinking in college. *Journal of the American Medical Association* 272(21): 1672–1677.

World Health Organization. 1997. *World No-Tobacco Day: United for a Tobacco-free World* (retrieved June 3, 1997; http://www.who.ch/programmes/psa/psa3.htm).

Yost, D. 1996. Alcohol withdrawal syndrome. *American Family Physician* 54(2): 657–663.

LAB 13-1   *Is Alcohol a Problem in Your Life?*

Part I. Do You Have a Problem with Alcohol?

For each question, choose the answer that best describes your behavior. Then total your scores.

Questions	Points					Your score
	0	1	2	3	4	
1. How often do you have a drink containing alcohol?	Never	Monthly or less	2 to 4 times a month	2 to 3 times a week	4 or more times a week	___
2. How many drinks containing alcohol do you have on a typical day when you are drinking?	1 or 2	3 or 4	5 or 6	7 to 9	10 or more	___
3. How often do you have six or more drinks on one occasion?		Less than monthly	Monthly	Weekly	Daily or almost daily	___
4. How often during the last year have you found that you were not able to stop drinking once you had started?	Never	Less than monthly	Monthly	Weekly	Daily or almost daily	___
5. How often during the last year have you failed to do what was normally expected from you because of drinking?	Never	Less than monthly	Monthly	Weekly	Daily or almost daily	___
6. How often during the last year have you needed a first drink in the morning to get yourself going after a heavy drinking session?	Never	Less than monthly	Monthly	Weekly	Daily or almost daily	___
7. How often during the last year have you had a feeling of guilt or remorse after drinking?	Never	Less than monthly	Monthly	Weekly	Daily or almost daily	___
8. How often during the last year have you been unable to remember what happened the night before because you had been drinking?	Never	Less than monthly	Monthly	Weekly	Daily or almost daily	___
9. Have you or has someone else been injured as a result of your drinking?	No	Yes, but not in the last year (2 points)		Yes, during the last year (4 points)		___
10. Has a relative or friend or a doctor or other health worker been concerned about your drinking or suggested you cut down?	No	Yes, but not in the last year (2 points)		Yes, during the last year (4 points)		___
					Total	___

A total score of 8 or more indicates a strong likelihood of hazardous or harmful alcohol consumption. Even if your score is below 8, if you are encountering drinking-related problems with your academic performance, job, relationships, or health, or with the law, you should consider seeking help.

Part II. Are You Troubled by Someone Else's Drinking?

Millions of people are affected by the excessive drinking of someone close to them. The following questions are designed to help you decide whether or not you need Al-Anon. If you answer yes to any question, put a check next to it.

_____ 1. Do you worry about how much someone drinks?

_____ 2. Do you have money problems because of someone else's drinking?

_____ 3. Do you tell lies to cover up for someone else's drinking?

_____ 4. Do you feel that if the drinker loved you, he or she would stop drinking to please you?

_____ 5. Do you blame the drinker's behavior on his or her companions?

_____ 6. Are plans frequently upset or canceled or meals delayed because of the drinker?

_____ 7. Do you make threats, such as, "If you don't stop drinking, I'll leave you"?

_____ 8. Do you secretly try to smell the drinker's breath?

_____ 9. Are you afraid to upset someone for fear it will set off a drinking bout?

_____10. Have you been hurt or embarrassed by the drinker's behavior?

_____11. Are holidays and gatherings spoiled because of drinking?

_____12. Have you considered calling the police for help in fear of abuse?

_____13. Do you search for hidden alcohol?

_____14. Do you often ride in a car with a driver who has been drinking?

_____15. Have you refused social invitations out of fear or anxiety?

_____16. Do you sometimes feel like a failure when you think of the lengths you have gone to to control the drinker?

_____17. Do you think that if the drinker stopped drinking, your other problems would be solved?

_____18. Do you ever threaten to hurt yourself to scare the drinker?

_____19. Do you feel angry, confused, or depressed most of the time?

_____20. Do you feel there is no one who understands your problems?

If you answered yes to three or more of these questions, Al-Anon or Alateen may be able to help. You can contact Al-Anon or Alateen by looking in your local telephone directory or by writing to the following address:

Al-Anon Family Group Headquarters, Inc.
1600 Corporate Landing Parkway
Virginia Beach, VA 23454-5617
800-344-2666
http://www.al-anon.alateen.org

SOURCES: Part I from Saunders, J. B., et al. 1993. Development of the Alcohol Use Disorders Identification Test (AUDIT): WHO Collaborative Project on Early Detection of Persons with Harmful Alcohol Consumption—II. _Addiction._ 88:791–804, June. Reprinted with permission from Carfax Publishing Limited, P.O. Box 25, Arbingdon, Oxfordshire OX14 3VE, U.K.

LAB 13-2 *For Smokers Only: Why Do You Smoke?*

Although smoking cigarettes is physiologically addictive, people smoke for reasons other than nicotine craving. What kind of smoker are you? Knowing what your motivations and satisfactions are can ultimately help you quit. This test is designed to provide you with a score on each of six factors that describe many people's smoking. Read the statements and then circle the number that represents how *often* you feel this way when you smoke cigarettes. Be sure to answer each question.

		Always	Frequently	Occasionally	Seldom	Never
A.	I smoke cigarettes in order to keep myself from slowing down.	5	4	3	2	1
B.	Handling a cigarette is part of the enjoyment of smoking it.	5	4	3	2	1
C.	Smoking cigarettes is pleasant and relaxing.	5	4	3	2	1
D.	I light up a cigarette when I feel angry about something.	5	4	3	2	1
E.	When I have run out of cigarettes, I find it almost unbearable until I can get them.	5	4	3	2	1
F.	I smoke cigarettes automatically without even being aware of it.	5	4	3	2	1
G.	I smoke cigarettes to stimulate me, to perk myself up.	5	4	3	2	1
H.	Part of the enjoyment of smoking a cigarette comes from the steps I take to light up.	5	4	3	2	1
I.	I find cigarettes pleasurable.	5	4	3	2	1
J.	When I feel uncomfortable or upset about something, I light up a cigarette.	5	4	3	2	1
K.	I am very much aware of the fact when I am not smoking a cigarette.	5	4	3	2	1
L.	I light up a cigarette without realizing I still have one burning in the ashtray.	5	4	3	2	1
M.	I smoke cigarettes to give me a "lift."	5	4	3	2	1
N.	When I smoke a cigarette, part of the enjoyment is watching the smoke as I exhale it.	5	4	3	2	1
O.	I want a cigarette most when I am comfortable and relaxed.	5	4	3	2	1
P.	When I feel "blue" or want to take my mind off cares and worries, I smoke cigarettes.	5	4	3	2	1
Q.	I get a real gnawing hunger for a cigarette when I haven't smoked for a while.	5	4	3	2	1
R.	I've found a cigarette in my mouth and didn't remember putting it there.	5	4	3	2	1

How to Score

Enter the numbers you have circled in the spaces provided. Total the scores on each line. Total scores can range from 3 to 15. Any score of 11 or above is high; any score of 7 or below is low.

TOTALS

_____ + _____ + _____ = _____
A   G   M   Stimulation

_____ + _____ + _____ = _____
B   H   N   Handling

_____ + _____ + _____ = _____
C   I   O   Pleasurable relaxation

_____ + _____ + _____ = _____
D   J   P   Crutch: tension reduction

_____ + _____ + _____ = _____
E   K   Q   Craving: strong physiological or psychological addiction

_____ + _____ + _____ = _____
F   L   R   Habit

What Your Scores Mean: A Summary

The six factors measured by this test describe ways of experiencing or managing certain kinds of feelings. A high score on any factor indicates that this factor is an important source of satisfaction for you. The higher your score, the more important a particular factor is in your smoking, and the more useful the discussion of that factor can be in your attempt to quit.

Stimulation: If you score high on this factor, it means you are stimulated by a cigarette—you feel that it helps wake you up, organize your energies, and keep you going. If you try to give up smoking, you may want a safe substitute—a brisk walk or moderate exercise, for example—whenever you feel the urge to smoke.

Handling: Handling things can be satisfying, but there are many ways to keep your hands busy without lighting up or playing with a cigarette. Try doodling or toying with a pen, pencil, or other small object.

Pleasurable relaxation: Those who do get real pleasure out of smoking often find that an honest consideration of the harmful effects of their habit is enough to help them quit. They substitute social or physical activities and find they do not seriously miss their cigarettes.

Crutch: Many smokers use cigarettes as a kind of crutch in moments of stress or discomfort, and occasionally it may work; but heavy smokers are apt to discover that cigarettes do not help them deal with their problems effectively. When it comes to quitting, this kind of smoker may find it easy to stop when everything is going well but may be tempted to start again in a time of crisis. Physical exertion or social activity may serve as useful substitutes for cigarettes.

Craving: Quitting smoking is difficult for people who score high on this factor. It may be helpful for them to smoke more than usual for a day or two, so that the taste for cigarettes is spoiled, and then isolate themselves completely from cigarettes until the craving is gone.

Habit: These smokers light up frequently without even realizing it; they no longer get much satisfaction. They may find it easy to quit and stay off if they can break the habit patterns they have built up. The key to success is becoming aware of each cigarette when it's smoked. Ask, "Do I really want this cigarette?"

SOURCE: *Why Do You Smoke?* U.S. Department of Health and Human Services. Public Health Service. National Institutes of Health. NIH Pub. No. 90-1822.

Sexually Transmitted Diseases

14

LOOKING AHEAD

After reading this chapter, you should be able to answer these questions about sexually transmitted diseases (STDs):

- In what ways do STDs pose a threat to wellness?

- What is HIV/AIDS, and how is it transmitted, diagnosed, and treated?

- What are the symptoms, risks, and treatments of the other major STDs?

- How can individuals protect themselves from STDs?

Acquired immunodeficiency syndrome (AIDS) is the number one health priority in the United States. This fatal, incurable disease is the second leading cause of death in America among people age 25–44 (injuries top the list). People between ages 18 and 25 have the highest risk of acquiring HIV infection. One in four new HIV infections occurs in people under age 20.

Although recent public education campaigns have focused primarily on HIV infection, all the **sexually transmitted diseases (STDs)**—gonorrhea, genital warts, chlamydia, herpes, and others—continue to have a high incidence among Americans. The United States has the highest rate of STDs of any developed nation. By age 21, 25% of all people will have had an STD.

In general, seven different STDs pose major health threats: HIV/AIDS, hepatitis, syphilis, chlamydia, gonorrhea, herpes, and genital warts. These diseases are considered major because they are serious in themselves, cause serious complications if left untreated, and/or pose risks to a fetus or newborn. In addition, pelvic inflammatory disease (PID) is a common complication of gonorrhea and chlamydia and merits discussion as a separate disease.

It is important that everyone have a clear understanding of what STDs are, how they are transmitted, and, most important, how they can be prevented. The crucial message is that they *can* be prevented. And many can also be cured if they are treated early and properly. This chapter is designed to provide information about healthy, safe sexual behavior and to help you understand what you can do to reduce the risk of contributing to the further spread of and damage caused by these diseases. Lab 14-1 will help you evaluate your risk of contracting an STD by helping you examine your attitudes and behaviors.

HIV INFECTION AND AIDS

HIV infection is one of the most serious and challenging problems facing the United States and the world today. By the end of 1997, over 640,000 Americans had been diagnosed with AIDS, and nearly 400,000 had died. Nearly 1 million Americans are believed to be infected with HIV, including approximately 1 in 500 college students. Worldwide, over 30 million people are currently living with HIV, and more than 12 million have died. According to the World Health Organization (WHO), close to 16,000 people are infected with HIV every day, or more than 10 every minute. Despite the intense efforts of health professionals all around the world, HIV infection continues to spread, and a cure is yet to be found.

What Is HIV Infection?

HIV infection is a chronic disease that progressively damages the body's immune system, making an otherwise healthy person less able to resist a variety of infections and disorders. Under normal conditions, when a virus or other pathogen enters the body, it is targeted and destroyed by the immune system. But the **human immunodeficiency virus (HIV)** attacks the immune system itself. HIV takes over immune system cells, forcing them to produce new copies of HIV; it also makes them incapable of performing their immune functions.

The destruction of the immune system is signaled by the loss of **CD4 T cells** (Figure 14-1). As the number of CD4 cells declines, an infected person may begin to experience mild to moderately severe symptoms. A person is diagnosed with full-blown AIDS when he or she develops one of the conditions defined as a marker for AIDS or when the number of CD4 cells in the blood drops below a certain level ($200/\mu l$). People with AIDS are vulnerable to a number of serious, often fatal secondary, or opportunistic, infections.

The asymptomatic period of HIV—the time between the initial viral infection and the onset of disease symptoms—may range from 2 to 20 years. In adults, the average is 11 years. More than 50% of infected people experience flulike symptoms shortly after the initial infection, but most remain generally healthy for years. During this time, however, the virus is progressively infecting and destroying the cells of the immune system. People infected with HIV can pass the virus to others—even if they have no symptoms and even if they do not know they have been infected.

Transmitting the Virus

HIV lives only within cells and body fluids, not outside the body. It is transmitted by blood and blood products, semen, vaginal and cervical secretions, and breast milk. It cannot live in air, in water, or on objects or surfaces such as toilet seats, eating utensils, or telephones. The three main routes of HIV transmission are from specific kinds of sexual contact, from direct exposure to infected blood, and from an HIV-infected woman to her fetus during pregnancy or childbirth or to her infant during breastfeeding (Figure 14-2).

TERMS
acquired immunodeficiency syndrome (AIDS) A fatal, incurable, sexually transmitted viral disease.

sexually transmitted disease (STD) A disease that can be transmitted by sexual contact; some STDs can also be transmitted by other means.

HIV infection A chronic, progressive disease that damages the immune system.

human immunodeficiency virus (HIV) The virus that causes HIV infection and AIDS.

CD4 T cell A type of white blood cell that helps coordinate the activity of the immune system; the primary target for HIV infection. A decrease in the number of these cells correlates with the risk and severity of HIV-related illness.

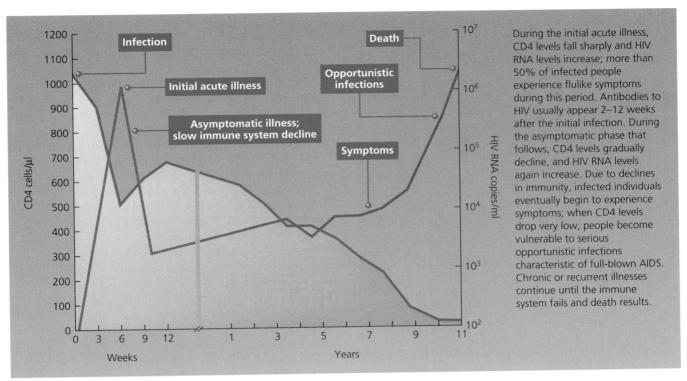

Figure 14-1 The general pattern of HIV infection. The course of HIV infection extends for years. The shaded area under the curve represents the amount of CD4 cells in the blood, a marker for the status of the immune system. The line shows the amount of HIV RNA in the blood.
SOURCE: Adapted from Fauci, A. S., et al. 1996. Immunopathogenic mechanisms of HIV infection. *Annals of Internal Medicine* 124: 654–663. Reprinted with permission of the publisher.

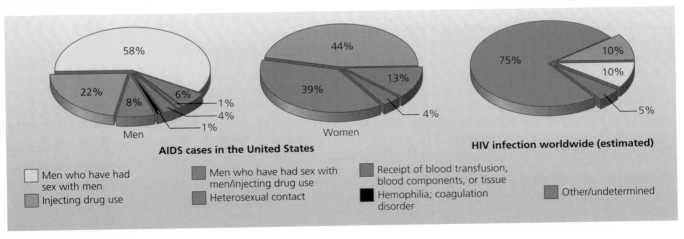

VITAL STATISTICS

Figure 14-2 Routes of HIV transmission among adults. SOURCES: Centers for Disease Control and Prevention. 1997. *HIV/AIDS Surveillance Report* 9(2). Joint United Nations Programme on HIV/AIDS (UNAIDS) (http://www.unaids.org).

Of the different types of sexual contact, HIV is more likely to be transmitted by unprotected anal or vaginal intercourse than by other sexual activities. Oral-genital contact carries some risk of transmission, although less than anal or vaginal intercourse. Any trauma or irritation of tissues, such as might occur from rough or unwanted intercourse or the overuse of spermicides, increases the risk.

The risk of HIV transmission during oral sex increases if a person has poor oral hygiene, has oral sores, or has brushed or flossed just before or after having oral sex. The presence of lesions or blisters from other sexually transmitted diseases also makes it easier for the virus to be passed. During vaginal intercourse, male-to-female transmission is more likely to occur than female-to-male transmission.

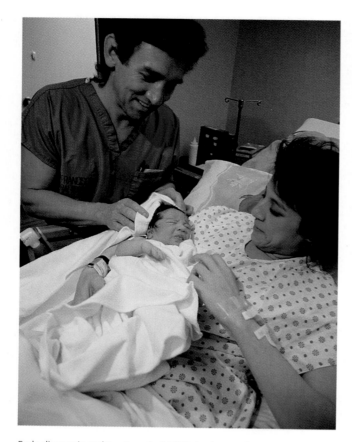

Early diagnosis and treatment of HIV infection are important for everyone, but particularly so for pregnant women. Currently available treatments can significantly increase the chance that this baby, born to an HIV-infected mother, will be free of the virus.

HIV has been found in pre-ejaculatory fluid, so transmission can also occur before ejaculation.

Direct contact with the blood of an infected person is the second major route of HIV transmission. Needles used to inject drugs (including heroin, cocaine, and anabolic steroids) are routinely contaminated by the blood of the user. If needles are shared, small amounts of one person's blood are directly injected into another person's bloodstream. HIV may be transmitted through subcutaneous and intramuscular injection as well, from needles or blades used in acupuncture, tattooing, ritual scarring, and piercing of the earlobes, nose, lip, nipple, navel, or other body part.

HIV has been transmitted in blood and blood products used in the medical treatment of **hemophilia**, injuries, and serious illnesses, resulting in about 12,000 cases of AIDS. The blood supply in all licensed blood banks and

TERMS **hemophilia** A hereditary blood disease in which blood fails to clot and abnormal bleeding occurs, requiring transfusions of blood products to aid coagulation.

HIV-positive A diagnosis resulting from the presence of HIV in the bloodstream; also referred to as *seropositive*.

plasma centers in the United States in now screened for HIV. The odds are less than 1 in 500,000 that a unit of HIV-infected donated blood will fail to be detected with today's testing methods.

The final major route of HIV transmission is mother-to-child, also called *vertical transmission,* which can occur during pregnancy, childbirth, or breastfeeding. Fortunately, the number of new cases of HIV/AIDS among American infants has declined substantially in recent years, due primarily to effective treatment with the antiviral drug Retrovir (AZT). Without treatment, more than 25% of babies born to HIV-infected women are themselves infected with the virus. With treatment during pregnancy, labor, and early infancy, the rate drops to about 8%. However, treatment is expensive, and vertical transmission continues to be a major threat in other parts of the world (see the box "HIV Infection Around the World").

What about contact with other body fluids? Trace amounts of HIV have been found in the saliva and tears of some infected people. However, researchers believe that these fluids do not carry enough of the virus to infect another person. HIV has been found in urine and feces, and contact with the urine or feces of an infected person may carry some risk. Contact with an infected person's sweat is not believed to carry any risk. There is absolutely no evidence that the virus can be spread by insects such as mosquitoes or fleas. HIV is not transmitted through casual contact. A person is not at risk of getting HIV infection by being in the same classroom, dining room, or even household with someone who is infected.

Symptoms and Diagnosis

Signs and symptoms of HIV infection include persistent swollen glands; lumps, rashes, sores, or other growths on or under the skin or on the mucous membranes of the eyes, mouth, anus, or nasal passages; persistent yeast infections; unexplained weight loss; fever and drenching night sweats; dry cough and shortness of breath; persistent diarrhea; easy bruising and unexplained bleeding; profound fatigue; memory loss; the loss of a sense of balance; tremors or seizures; changes in vision, hearing, taste, or smell; difficulty in swallowing; changes in mood and other psychological symptoms; and persistent or recurrent pain. Obviously, many of these symptoms can also occur with a variety of other illnesses.

Because the immune system is weakened, people with HIV infection are highly susceptible to infections, both common and uncommon. The infection most often seen among people with HIV is *Pneumocystis carinii* pneumonia, a protozoal infection. Kaposi's sarcoma, a rare form of cancer, is common in HIV-infected men. Women with HIV infection often have frequent and difficult-to-treat vaginal yeast infections. Cases of tuberculosis are also increasingly being reported in people with HIV.

Early diagnosis of HIV infection is important to mini-

Although first detected among heterosexuals in Africa, AIDS captured world attention in the early 1980s as a disease occurring primarily among homosexual men in the United States and Europe. Since then, AIDS has spread around the world. It's estimated that 30 million people currently carry the virus and that most have no idea they are infected.

The vast majority of cases—90%—have occurred in developing countries, where heterosexual contact is the primary means of transmission, responsible for 75–85% of all adult infections. In the developed world, the pattern of infection is shifting away from homosexual males toward the larger heterosexual population. Women are the fastest-growing group of newly infected people. Worldwide, about 40% of the new cases of HIV infection in 1997 occurred in women, and more than 12 million women carry the virus. In addition, an estimated 1 million children are living with HIV infection and more than 8 million uninfected children are AIDS orphans.

Currently, more than 20 million of those infected with HIV are in Africa, where in some cities, one-third of all adults carry the virus (see the figure). Sub-Saharan Africa remains the hardest hit of all areas of the world. However, experts believe that Asia is now at the same stage of the disease that Africa was 5–10 years ago, and they expect to see an explosion of new cases in Asia.

Efforts to combat AIDS are complicated by political, economic, and cultural barriers in many parts of the world. Education and prevention programs are often hampered by resistance from social and religious institutions and by the taboo on openly discussing sexual issues. Condoms are unfamiliar in many countries, and women in many societies do not have sufficient control over their lives to demand that men use condoms during sex. Prevention approaches that have had success include STD treatment and education, public education campaigns about safer sex, and needle-exchange programs for injecting drug users.

In developed nations such as the United States, new drugs are delaying the onset of symptoms for some patients and reducing the overall death rate from AIDS. But these drugs are almost entirely unavailable in the developing world. Until a vaccine or low-cost cure is developed, efforts must continue to focus on widespread educational campaigns and prevention through behavior change.

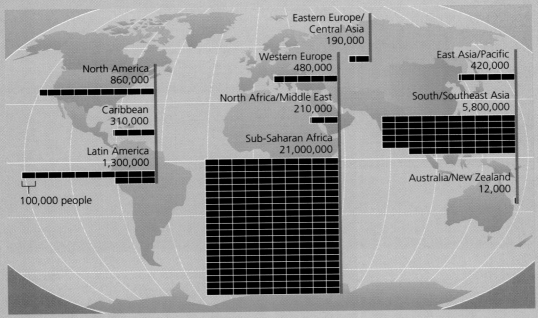

Approximate number of people living with HIV/AIDS at the beginning of 1998.

SOURCE: UNAIDS/WHO. 1997. *Report on the Global HIV/AIDS Epidemic—June 1998* (retrieved July 9, 1998; http://www.unaids.org/highband/document/epidemio/june98/global_report/index.html).

mize the impact of the disease—medically, psychologically, and socially. The most commonly used screening blood test for HIV is the HIV antibody test. This test consists of an initial screening called an ELISA test and a more specific confirmation test called the Western blot. These tests determine whether a person has antibodies to HIV circulating in the bloodstream, a sign that the virus is present in the body (see pp. 351 and 353 for more on HIV testing).

If a person is diagnosed as **HIV-positive,** the next step is to determine the current severity of the disease in order to plan appropriate treatment. The status of the immune

Figure 14-3 What's risky and what's not: The approximate relative risk of HIV transmission of various sexual activities. Safer sex strategies that reduce the risk of HIV infection will also help protect you against other STDs. The main point to remember is that any activity that involves contact with blood, semen, or vaginal fluid can transmit HIV.

High Risk

Unprotected anal sex is the riskiest sexual behavior, especially for the receptive partner.

Unprotected vaginal intercourse is the next riskiest, especially for women, who are much more likely to be infected by an infected male partner than vice versa.

Oral sex is probably considerably less risky than anal and vaginal intercourse.

Sharing of sex toys can be risky because they can carry blood, semen, or vaginal fluid.

Use of a condom reduces risk considerably but not completely for any type of intercourse. Anal sex with a condom is riskier than vaginal sex with a condom; oral sex with a condom is less risky, especially if the man does not ejaculate.

Hand-genital contact and deep kissing are less risky but could still theoretically transmit HIV; the presence of cuts or sores increases risk.

Sex with only one uninfected and monogamous partner is without risk, but effective only if both partners are uninfected and completely monogamous.

Activities that don't involve the exchange of body fluids carry no risk: hugging, massage, closed-mouth kissing, masturbation, phone sex, and fantasy.

Abstinence is completely without risk. For many people, it can be an effective and reasonable method of avoiding HIV infection and other STDs during certain periods of life.

No Risk

system can be gauged by taking CD4 T-cell measurements every few months. The infection itself can be monitored by tracking the amount of virus in the body (the "viral load") through a test that measures the amount of HIV RNA in a blood sample (see Figure 14-1).

The CDC's criteria for a diagnosis of AIDS reflect the stage of HIV infection at which a person's immune system becomes dangerously compromised. Since January 1993, a diagnosis of AIDS has been made if a person is HIV-positive and either has developed an infection or condition defined as an AIDS indicator or has a severely damaged immune system (as measured by CD4 T-cell counts).

Treatment

Although there is no known cure for HIV infection or AIDS, new drugs can significantly alter the course of the disease and extend life. The two main types of antiviral drugs are nucleoside analogs and protease inhibitors, both of which block HIV from replicating itself. Recent research has shown that using combinations of antiviral drugs can sometimes reduce HIV levels in the blood to undetectable levels, and early and aggressive combination drug therapy is now recommended for people with HIV. In addition to antiviral drugs, most patients with low CD4 T-cell counts also take a variety of antibiotics to help prevent opportunistic infections such as pneumonia and tuberculosis.

The cost of treatment for HIV continues to be a major concern. Promising drug combinations can cost $10,000–$25,000 annually; for someone with full-blown AIDS, treatment may cost more than $50,000 per year. These costs place treatment out of reach for many infected people in the United States and for most infected people in the developing world. Even for those who have access to the drugs, treatment is difficult; some people cannot tolerate the side effects of the medications, and the drugs are much more effective for some people than others. In addition, scientists do not know whether long-term drug therapy will eventually eliminate the virus from the body or whether drug therapy for life will be required to keep the virus at bay. It is also unclear to what degree a damaged immune system can rebound from the effects of long-term infection with HIV.

Among people infected with HIV who can afford and tolerate the new treatments, the rate of progression from HIV infection to AIDS and from AIDS to death has declined. However, although the number of new AIDS cases being diagnosed each year in the United States is declining, the number of new cases of HIV infection is not. The best hope for preventing the spread of HIV worldwide rests with the development of a safe and effective vaccine. Many different types of vaccines are currently under investigation, and one has been approved for preliminary human testing. However, none is likely to be ready for widespread use within the next 5–10 years. For more on the development of treatments and vaccines, contact one of the organizations or Web sites listed in the For More Information section at the end of the chapter.

For those who don't have a long-term monogamous relationship with an uninfected partner, abstinence is the only truly safe option. Individuals should remember that it's OK to say no to sex and drugs.

Safer sexual activities that allow close person-to-person contact with almost no risk of contracting STDs or HIV include fantasy, hugging, massage, rubbing clothed bodies together, self-stimulation by both partners, and kissing with lips closed.

If you choose to be sexually active, talk with potential partners about HIV, safer sex, and the use of condoms before you begin a sexual relationship. The following behaviors will help lower your risk of exposure to HIV during sexual activities.

- Limit the number of partners. Avoid sexual contact with people who have HIV or an STD or who have engaged in risky behaviors in the past, including unprotected sex and injecting drug use.

- Use latex condoms during every act of intercourse and oral sex. Even if your partner claims to have been tested for HIV and STDs, there is no guarantee that he or she is uninfected. Many STDs are not easy to diagnose in their asymptomatic stage, which can last for years; and asymptomatic individuals can still infect others. No matter what your partner says, you have no guarantee that you will not contract an STD during any sexual encounter. If you choose to have intercourse, your best protection is to *always* use a condom. They do not provide absolute pro-

tection, but they greatly reduce your risk of contracting an infection.

- Use condoms properly to obtain maximum protection. Use a water-based lubricant; don't use oil-based lubricants such as petroleum jelly or baby oil. Unroll condoms gently to avoid tearing them, and smooth out any air bubbles.

- Avoid sexual contact that could cause cuts or tears in the skin or tissue.

- Get periodic screening tests for STDs and HIV. Women need yearly pelvic exams and Pap tests.

- Get vaccinated for hepatitis B. Take advantage of this safe and effective vaccine.

- Get prompt treatment for any STDs you contract.

- Don't drink or use drugs in sexual situations. Mood-altering drugs can affect your judgment and make you more likely to engage in risky behaviors.

If you inject drugs of any kind, don't share needles, syringes, or anything that might have blood on it. Decontaminate needles and syringes with household bleach and water.

If you are at risk for HIV infection, don't donate blood, sperm, or body organs. Don't have unprotected sex or share needles or syringes. Get tested for HIV soon, and get treated. HIV-infected people who get early treatment generally feel better and live longer than those who delay.

Prevention

Although AIDS is currently fatal and incurable, it is preventable. You can protect yourself by avoiding behaviors that may bring you into contact with HIV. This means making careful choices about sexual activity and not sharing needles if you inject drugs (see Figure 14-3 and the box "Preventing HIV Infection and Other STDs").

Surveys of college students indicate that the majority of students are not engaging in safer sex even though most know that condom use can protect against HIV infection. Many students also report a willingness to lie about past sexual activity in order to obtain sex. Many students believe their risk of contracting HIV depends on "who they are" rather than on their sexual behavior. These attitudes and behaviors place college students at continued high risk for contracting HIV.

CHLAMYDIA

Chlamydia trachomatis causes **chlamydia,** the most prevalent bacterial infection in the United States, with 3–4 million new cases occurring every year. An estimated 10% of all sexually active women in the United States are infected

with chlamydia; rates among men are probably similar. The highest rates of infection occur in single people between ages 18 and 24.

Both men and women are susceptible to chlamydia, but women bear the greater burden because of possible complications and consequences of the disease. If left untreated, chlamydia can lead to pelvic inflammatory disease (PID), a serious infection that can lead to infertility. Chlamydia also greatly increases a woman's risk for ectopic (tubal) pregnancy.

Chlamydia can also lead to infertility in men, although not as often as in women. In men under age 35, chlamydia is the most common cause of *epididymitis,* inflammation of the sperm-carrying ducts (refer to Figures 14-4 and 14-5 for basic information about human sexual anatomy). And up to half of all cases of *urethritis,* inflammation of the urethra, in men are caused by chlamydia.

Symptoms

In men, chlamydia symptoms include painful urination, a slight watery discharge from the penis, and sometimes

chlamydia The most common bacterial infection in the U.S.; an STD transmitted by the bacterium *Chlamydia trachomatis.* **TERMS**

Chlamydia 343

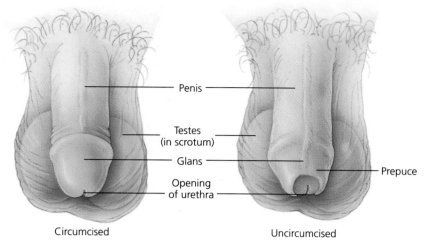

External structures

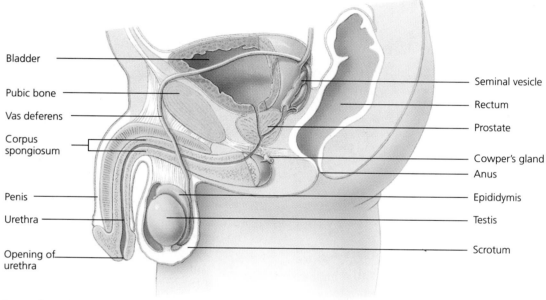

Internal structures (cross section)

Figure 14-4 Male sexual anatomy.

pain around the testicles. Although most women with chlamydia are asymptomatic, some notice increased vaginal discharge, burning with urination, pain or bleeding with intercourse, and lower abdominal pain. Symptoms in both men and women can begin within 5 days of infection. However, most people experience few or no symptoms, increasing the likelihood that they will inadvertently spread the infection to their partners.

Diagnosis and Treatment

Most cases of chlamydia are diagnosed through screening done during a routine Pap test. Testing pregnant women and treating those with chlamydia is a highly effective way to prevent the infection of newborns. Once chlamydia has been diagnosed, the infected person and his or her

partner(s) are given antibiotics, usually tetracycline, doxycycline, or erythromycin. Penicillin is not effective against chlamydia.

GONORRHEA

In the United States, between 400,000 and 500,000 new cases of **gonorrhea** are reported every year. The highest incidence is among 15- to 24-year-olds. Like chlamydia, untreated gonorrhea can cause PID in women and urethritis and epididymitis in men. It can also cause arthritis and rashes, and it occasionally involves internal organs. An infant passing through the birth canal of an infected mother may contract *gonococcal conjunctivitis,* an infection

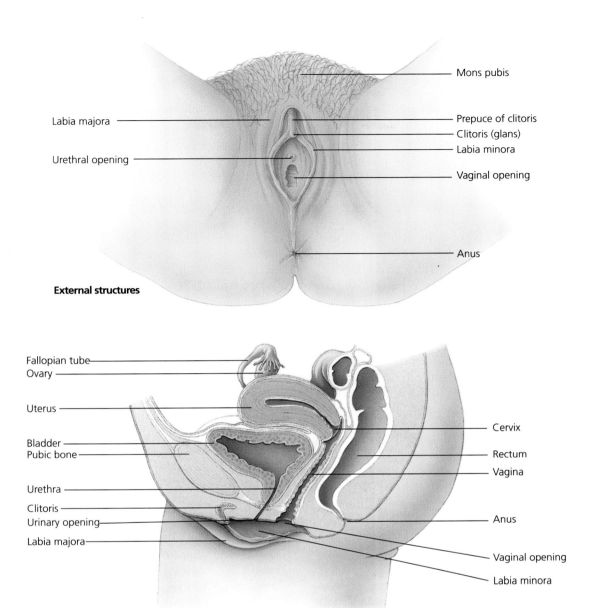

External structures

- Mons pubis
- Labia majora
- Prepuce of clitoris
- Clitoris (glans)
- Labia minora
- Urethral opening
- Vaginal opening
- Anus

Internal structures (cross section)

- Fallopian tube
- Ovary
- Uterus
- Bladder
- Pubic bone
- Urethra
- Clitoris
- Urinary opening
- Labia majora
- Cervix
- Rectum
- Vagina
- Anus
- Vaginal opening
- Labia minora

Figure 14-5   Female sexual anatomy.

in the eyes that can cause blindness if not treated. In most states, all newborn babies are routinely treated with antimicrobial eyedrops to prevent infection.

Gonorrhea is caused by the bacterium *Neisseria gonorrhoeae,* which flourishes in mucous membranes. The microbe cannot thrive outside the warm, moist environment of the human body and dies within moments of exposure to light and air. Consequently, gonorrhea cannot be contracted from toilet seats, towels, or other objects.

Symptoms

In males the incubation period for gonorrhea is brief, generally 2–7 days. The first symptoms are due to urethritis, which causes urinary discomfort and a thick, yellowish-white or yellowish-green discharge from the penis. The

lips of the urethral opening may become inflamed and swollen. In some cases, the lymph glands in the groin become enlarged and swollen. Up to one-third of males have very minor symptoms or none at all.

Most females with gonorrhea are asymptomatic. Those who do have symptoms often experience urinary pain, increased vaginal discharge, and severe menstrual cramps. Up to 40% of women with untreated gonorrhea develop PID. Women may also develop painful abscesses in the Bartholin's glands, a pair of glands located on either side of the opening of the vagina.

gonorrhea   A sexually transmitted bacterial infection that usually affects mucous membranes.   **TERMS**

Gonorrhea can also infect the throat or rectum of people who engage in oral or anal sex. Gonorrhea symptoms in the throat may be a sore throat or pus on the tonsils, and those in the rectum may be pus or blood in the feces, or rectal pain and itching.

Diagnosis and Treatment

Gonorrhea is diagnosed by examining a sample of the discharge. Some new and relatively expensive antibiotics are usually effective in curing gonorrhea. Older, less expensive antibiotics such as penicillin and tetracycline are not currently recommended for treating gonorrhea because many strains of the bacteria are resistant to them. People with gonorrhea very often also have chlamydia, so additional antibiotics are typically given to treat chlamydia.

PELVIC INFLAMMATORY DISEASE

A major complication in up to one-third of women who have been infected with either gonorrhea or chlamydia and have not received treatment is **pelvic inflammatory disease (PID)**. PID occurs when the initial infection travels upward, often along with other bacteria, beyond the cervix into the uterus, oviducts, ovaries, and pelvic cavity. PID is often serious enough to require hospitalization and sometimes surgery. Even if the disease is treated successfully, about 25% of affected women will have long-term problems such as a continuing susceptibility to infection, ectopic pregnancy, infertility, and chronic pelvic pain. PID is the leading cause of infertility in young women.

Symptoms

Symptoms of PID vary greatly. Some women, especially those with PID from chlamydia, may be asymptomatic; others may feel very ill with abdominal pain, fever, chills, nausea, and vomiting. Early symptoms are essentially the same as those described earlier for chlamydia and gonorrhea. Symptoms often begin or worsen during or soon after a woman's menstrual period. Many women have abnormal vaginal bleeding—either bleeding between periods or heavy and painful menstrual bleeding.

Diagnosis and Treatment

Diagnosis of PID is made on the basis of symptoms, physical examination, ultrasound, and laboratory tests. **Laparoscopy** may be used to confirm the diagnosis and obtain material for cultures. Treatment should begin as quickly as possible to minimize damage to the reproductive organs. Antibiotics are usually started immediately; in severe cases, the woman may be hospitalized and antibiotics given intravenously. It is especially important that an infected woman's partners be treated. As many as 60% of the male contacts of women with PID are infected but asymptomatic.

GENITAL WARTS

Genital warts, also known as condyloma, are caused by infection with **human papillomavirus (HPV)**. The CDC estimates that 24 million people in the United States, including up to one-third of all sexually active teenagers, have genital HPV infection. Condyloma is the most common STD for which diagnosis and treatment are sought in student health services. The disease appears to be most prevalent in young people age 16–25.

Symptoms

Genital warts are often dry, painless growths, rough in texture and gray or pink in color. They can be flat or raised, and they vary in size. In males, they appear on the penis and often involve the urethra, appearing first at the opening and then spreading inside. The growths may cause irritation and bleeding, leading to painful urination and a urethral discharge. Warts may also appear around the anus or within the rectum.

In women, warts may appear on the labia or vulva and may spread to the perineum, the area between the vagina and the rectum. They may also appear on the cervix. If warts occur only on the cervix, the woman will generally have no symptoms or awareness that she has HPV.

The incubation period is about 4–6 weeks from the time of contact, but it can be 6 months or longer before any symptoms are identified. People can be infected with the virus and be capable of transmitting it to their sex partners without having any symptoms at all. In addition, newborns can be infected during delivery.

Diagnosis and Treatment

Genital warts are usually diagnosed based on the appearance of the lesions. Sometimes examination with a special

> **TERMS** **pelvic inflammatory disease (PID)** An infection that progresses from the vagina and cervix to the uterus, oviducts, and pelvic cavity.
>
> **laparoscopy** A method of examining the internal organs by inserting a tube containing a small light through an abdominal incision.
>
> **genital warts** A sexually transmitted viral infection characterized by growths on the genitals; also called *genital HPV infection.*
>
> **human papillomavirus (HPV)** The virus that causes human warts, including genital warts.
>
> **genital herpes** A sexually transmitted infection caused by the herpes simplex virus.

Sexual activity has many consequences, including pregnancy, disease, and emotional changes in the relationship. Honest communication is a crucial part of responsible sexual behavior.

magnifying instrument or biopsy is done to evaluate suspicious lesions. Frequently, HPV infection of the cervix is detected on routine Pap tests.

Treatment focuses on individual lesions, but the currently available methods cannot ensure the eradication of HPV. The traditional treatment for genital warts is application of podophyllin, a toxic agent, directly to the lesion. Other treatment options include injections of alpha-interferon or removal of the lesion by electrocautery, cryosurgery (freezing), surgery, or laser. Many of these treatments can be painful and physically destructive. Follow-up care is especially important.

Even after treatment and the disappearance of visible warts, the individual continues to carry HPV in healthy-appearing tissue and can probably still infect others. Anyone who has ever had HPV should inform all partners. Condoms should be used, even though they do not provide total protection (see the box "Male Condoms").

A precancerous condition known as *cervical dysplasia* often occurs among women with genital HPV infection. If untreated, women with this condition sometimes develop cervical cancer. Because of the relationship between HPV and cervical cancer, women who have had genital warts should have Pap tests every 6 months.

GENITAL HERPES

Genital herpes affects over 45 million people in the United States. Two types of herpes simplex viruses, HSV-1 and HSV-2, cause genital herpes and oral-labial herpes (cold sores). Genital herpes is usually caused by HSV-2, and oral-labial herpes is usually caused by HSV-1, although both virus types can cause either genital or oral-labial lesions. HSV can also cause rectal lesions, usually transmitted through anal sex.

HSV-1 infection is so common that over 90% of adults have antibodies to HSV-1 (indicating previous exposure to the virus). Most people are exposed to HSV-1 during childhood. HSV-2 infection usually occurs during adolescence and early adulthood, most commonly between ages 18 and 25. Approximately 22% of adults have antibodies to HSV-2.

HSV-2 is almost always sexually transmitted. It is theoretically possible, but much less common, to become infected through contaminated clothing, towels, or other objects. The infection is more easily transmitted when people have active sores, but HSV-2 can be transmitted to a sex partner even when no lesions are present. If you have ever had an outbreak of genital herpes, you must always consider yourself contagious and inform your partners. Avoid intimate contact when any sores are present, and use condoms during all sexual contact.

Newborns can occasionally be infected with HSV, usually during passage through the birth canal of an infected mother. Without treatment, 65% of newborns with HSV will die, and most who survive will have some degree of brain damage. Pregnant women who have ever been exposed to genital herpes should inform their physician so that appropriate precautions can be taken to protect the baby from infection.

Symptoms

Most people who are infected with HSV have no symptoms. Those who do develop symptoms often first notice them within 2–20 days of having sex with an infected partner. The first episode of genital herpes frequently causes flulike symptoms in addition to genital lesions. The lesions usually heal within 3 weeks, but the virus remains alive in an inactive state within nerve cells. A new outbreak of herpes can occur at any time. On average, newly diagnosed people will experience five to eight outbreaks per year, with a decrease in the frequency of outbreaks over time. Outbreaks can be

Although they're not 100% effective as a contraceptive or as protection from STDs—only abstinence is—condoms improve your chances on both counts. Use them properly by following these guidelines.

- *Buy latex condoms.* If you're allergic to latex, try wearing a lambskin condom under a latex one.

- *Buy and use condoms while they are fresh.* Condom packages have an expiration date or a manufacturing date. Don't use condoms beyond the expiration date or more than 5 years after the manufacturing date.

- *Try different styles and sizes.* Male condoms come in a variety of textures, colors, shapes, lubricants, and sizes. Shop around until you find a brand that's right for you. Condom widths and lengths vary by about 10–20%. A condom that is too tight may be uncomfortable and more likely to break; one that is too loose may slip off.

- *Don't remove the condom from an individual sealed wrapper until you're ready to use it.* Open the packet carefully. Don't use a condom if it's gummy, dried out, or discolored.

- *Store condoms correctly.* Don't leave condoms in extreme heat or cold, and don't carry them in a pocket or wallet.

- *Use only water-based lubricants.* Never use oil-based lubricants like Vaseline or hand lotion, as they may cause the condom to break.

- *Use condoms correctly.* Roll the condom down over the penis as soon as it's erect. Squeeze the air out of the reservoir tip or the top quarter-inch of the condom as you unroll it to leave room for semen. Make sure there are no air bubbles. Remove it after ejaculation before the penis becomes flaccid. Use a new condom every time you have intercourse.

- *Practice.* Condoms aren't hard to use, but practice helps. Take one out of the wrapper; examine it and stretch it to see how strong it is. Practice by yourself and with your partner.

If you feel awkward discussing condoms with your partner, try bringing up the subject when AIDS is in the news. You can talk about its effect on sexual practices and how more and more people are using condoms. Or you can talk about caring for each other. Open the discussion *before* you have sex. If she or he still resists the idea of using condoms, try some of the following approaches.

If your partner says . . .	Try saying . . .
"They're not romantic."	"Worrying about AIDS isn't romantic, and with condoms we won't have to worry." OR "If we put one on together, a condom could be fun."
"You don't trust me."	"I do trust you, but how can I trust your former partners or mine?" OR "It's important to me that we're both protected."
"I don't have any diseases. I've been tested."	"I'm glad you've been tested, but tests aren't foolproof for all diseases. To be safe, I always use condoms."
"I forgot to bring a condom. But it's OK to skip it just this once."	"I'd really like to make love with you, but I never have sex without a condom. Let's go get some."
"I don't like the way they feel."	"They might feel different, but let's try." OR "Sex won't feel good if we're worrying about diseases."
"I don't use condoms."	"I use condoms every time." OR "I don't have sex without condoms."
"But I love you."	"Being in love can't protect us from diseases." OR "I love you, too. We still need to use condoms."
"But we've been having sex without condoms."	"I want to start using condoms now so we won't be at any more risk." OR "We can still prevent infection or reinfection."

SOURCES: Do ask, do tell. 1998. *U.C. Berkeley Wellness Letter*, March. Dialogue from San Francisco AIDS Foundation. 1988. *Condoms for Couples*. (IMPACT AIDS, 3692 18th Street, San Francisco, CA 94110). Copyright © 1998 San Francisco AIDS Foundation. All rights reserved. Used with permission.

triggered by stress, illness, fatigue, sun exposure, sexual intercourse, and menstruation.

Diagnosis and Treatment

Most of the time, genital herpes can be diagnosed on the basis of the person's symptoms and the appearance of the lesions. If doubt exists, a sample of fluid from the lesions can be sent to a laboratory for evaluation.

There is no cure for herpes infections. Once infected, a person carries the virus for life. The drug acyclovir (Zovirax) provides help for many people. Taken continually, it can shorten the severity and duration of herpes outbreaks, although it will not rid the body of the virus. The antiviral drug famciclovir (Famvir) is also sometimes given to speed healing during an outbreak.

People with genital herpes often feel stressed and depressed about their infection. Support groups are available to help individuals learn more about how to cope with herpes.

HEPATITIS B

Hepatitis (inflammation of the liver) has many causes, including infection, drugs, alcohol, and autoimmune diseases. Hepatitis can cause serious and sometimes permanent damage to the liver, which can result in death in severe cases. One of the many types of hepatitis is caused by hepatitis B virus. Hepatitis B virus is somewhat similar to HIV; it is found in most body fluids and can be transmitted sexually, by injecting drug use, and during pregnancy and delivery. However, hepatitis B virus is much more contagious than HIV, and it can also be spread through nonsexual close contact.

The hepatitis B virus is found in all body fluids, including blood and blood products, semen, saliva, urine, and vaginal secretions. It is easily transmitted through any sexual activity that involves the exchange of body fluids, the use of contaminated needles, and any blood-to-blood contact, including the use of contaminated razor blades, toothbrushes, and eating utensils. The primary risk factors for acquiring hepatitis B are sexual exposure and injecting drug use; having multiple partners greatly increases risk.

Symptoms

Many people infected with hepatitis B never develop symptoms; they have what are known as "silent" infections. The normal incubation period is about 30–180 days. Mild cases of hepatitis cause flulike symptoms; as the illness progresses, there may be nausea, vomiting, dark-colored urine, abdominal pain, and **jaundice.** Some people with hepatitis also develop skin rash and joint pain or arthritis.

People with hepatitis B sometimes recover completely, but they can also become chronic carriers of the virus, capable of infecting others for the rest of their lives. Some chronic carriers remain asymptomatic, while others develop chronic liver disease. Chronic hepatitis can cause cirrhosis of the liver, liver failure, and a deadly form of liver cancer. Hepatitis kills some 6000 Americans each year; worldwide, the annual death toll exceeds 1 million.

Diagnosis and Treatment

Blood tests can be used to diagnose hepatitis. There is no cure for hepatitis B, and treatment is primarily aimed at keeping the patient comfortable until the symptoms subside. Rest, adequate nutrition, and plenty of fluids are essential for people with hepatitis.

A safe and highly effective vaccine for hepatitis B is available. All pregnant women should be tested for hep-

atitis B, and infants of infected mothers should be vaccinated immediately after birth. Most physicians recommend routine immunization of all infants and adolescents as part of the normal set of childhood vaccinations. Immunizations are also recommended for adults in high-risk groups, including health care workers, homosexually active men, injecting drug users, and heterosexually active individuals with multiple partners.

SYPHILIS

Although death and disability from **syphilis** declined dramatically after penicillin treatment was introduced in 1943, there are about 7500–10,000 cases of early syphilis reported each year in the United States. Syphilis is caused by a spirochete bacterium called *Treponema pallidum.* It requires warmth and moisture to survive and dies very quickly outside the human body. The disease is usually acquired through sexual contact, although infected pregnant women can transmit it to the fetus. The bacterium passes through any break or opening in the skin or mucous membranes and can be transmitted by kissing, vaginal or anal intercourse, or oral-genital contact.

Symptoms

Syphilis is characterized by sores or lesions known as **chancres** containing large numbers of bacteria; the disease is highly contagious when they are present. Left untreated, a person can remain contagious for as long as 18 months. In later stages, when the lesions have disappeared, the disease can cause devastating damage to almost any system of the body and can still be passed from an infected woman to her unborn child, causing stillbirth, prematurity, or birth defects.

Syphilis progresses through multiple stages that vary in length from one person to the next.

• *First stage: primary syphilis.* Within 10–90 days (usually about 3 weeks) after contact with an infected partner, a single chancre less than the size of a dime

---

hepatitis Inflammation of the liver, which can be caused by infection, drugs, or toxins; some forms of infectious hepatitis can be transmitted sexually.

jaundice Increased bile pigment levels in the blood, characterized by yellowing of the skin and the whites of the eyes.

syphilis A sexually transmitted bacterial infection caused by the spirochete *Treponema pallidum.*

chancre The sore produced by syphilis in its earliest stage.

TERMS

Accurate, confidential answers to personal questions are available from local and national STD hotlines. Separate AIDS hotlines, such as the one shown here, provide referrals, information, and updates on the success of the latest treatments for HIV infection and AIDS.

appears at the site where the organism entered the body, most commonly the genital area. Chancres can also appear in the mouth or armpit or on the tongue, lips, breasts, or fingers. These sores are painless unless they become infected and may not even be noticed. They generally heal within a few weeks.

• *Second stage: secondary syphilis.* Approximately 6 weeks after a chancre first appears, an untreated person begins to have signs and symptoms of secondary syphilis. These include fever, malaise, sore throat, headache, hoarseness, a depressed appetite, swollen lymph glands, and loss of hair. The second stage may also be characterized by a rash that appears anywhere on the body but most typically on the palms of the hands and the soles of the feet. Lesions may also appear in the mouth, genitals, and other warm, moist regions of the body. The skin and mucous membrane lesions of secondary syphilis are highly contagious. With or without antibiotic treatment, skin lesions of secondary syphilis usually heal in 2–10 weeks. However, if the disease remains untreated, relapses can occur.

• *Third stage: latent and late syphilis.* Some people have no symptoms once the lesions of secondary syphilis have disappeared. These people still carry the pathogen and may go on to develop late syphilis at some point in their lives. Late syphilis can affect many organs of the body and can cause central nervous system deterioration (including severe dementia), cardiovascular damage, blindness, and death.

Diagnosis and Treatment

The diagnosis of syphilis is made by microscopic examination of infected tissues and with blood tests. All stages of syphilis can be treated and usually cured with antibiotics.

OTHER STDs

Although they are far less serious than the diseases already described, a few other diseases are transmitted sexually and require responsible sexual behavior. Trichomoniasis, commonly called "trich," is one of the most common protozoal infections in North America. The single-celled organism that causes trich, *Trichomonas vaginalis,* thrives in warm, moist conditions, making women particularly susceptible to these infections in the vagina. This protozoan can remain alive on external objects for as long as 60–90 minutes, in urine for 3 hours, and in seminal fluid for 6 hours. Women who become symptomatic with trich develop a greenish, foul-smelling vaginal discharge and severe itching and pain in the vagina. Trich is treated with metronidazole (Flagyl).

Pubic lice, commonly known as "crabs," and scabies are highly contagious parasitic infections. Treatment is generally easy, although lice infestation can require repeated applications of medications.

WHAT YOU CAN DO

You can take responsibility for your health and contribute to a general reduction in the incidence in STDs in three major areas: education, prevention, and diagnosis and treatment.

Education

Many schools and colleges have peer counseling and education programs about preventing STDs. These programs give you a chance to practice skills in communicating with potential sex partners and negotiating safer sex, to engage in role playing to build self-confidence, and to learn how to use condoms. Studies show that educational programs in which students learn from their peers and then try out what they've learned through role playing are more likely to result in real behavior change.

Free pamphlets and other literature are available from public health departments, health clinics, physicians' offices, student health centers, and Planned Parenthood; easy-to-understand books are available in libraries and bookstores. National hotlines have been set up to provide free, confidential information and referral services to callers anywhere in the country (see the For More Information section at the end of the chapter). It is up to you to assume responsibility for learning about STDs and their potential effects on you, the children you may have, and your sexual partners.

Prevention

The only sure way to avoid exposure to STDs is to abstain from sexual activity. But if you do choose to be sexually active, the key is to think about prevention before you have a sexual encounter or find yourself in the "heat of the moment." Plan ahead for safer sex. Know what sexual behaviors are risky. Find out about your partner's sexual history and practices. Be honest, and ask your partner to do the same; but don't stake your health and life on assumptions about your partner's honesty or awareness. In a 1998 study of HIV-positive people, 40% did not reveal their HIV status to their sexual partners; many did not use condoms consistently.

Next to abstinence, the most effective approach to preventing STDs is having sex with only one mutually monogamous uninfected partner. If you are sexually active, use a condom during every act of intercourse. Although not foolproof, a properly used condom provides an effective barrier against disease-causing organisms. Approaches to STD prevention that are not safe include urinating or douching after intercourse, engaging in oral sex, or genital play without full penetration. Refer to the box on STD prevention on p. 343 for more information.

Diagnosis and Treatment

Early diagnosis and treatment of STDs can help you avoid complications and can also help prevent the spread of STDs. If you are sexually active, be alert for any sign or symptom of disease, such as a rash, a discharge, sores, or unusual pain. If you notice such a symptom, have a professional examination. If you are diagnosed as having an STD, begin treatment as quickly as possible. Inform your partner(s), and avoid any sexual activity until your treatment is complete. Follow instructions for treatment carefully, and complete all the medication as prescribed.

Remember that almost all STDs, including HIV infection, can be completely asymptomatic for long periods of time. Sexually active women should have pelvic exams and Pap tests at least once a year and receive regular STD screening. Sexually active men, especially if they have had more than one partner, should also receive regular STD screening.

Caring about yourself and your partner means asking questions and being aware of signs and symptoms. It may be a bit awkward, but the temporary embarrassment of asking intimate questions is a small price to pay to avoid contracting or spreading disease. Concern about STDs is part of a sexual relationship, not an intrusion into it.

COMMON QUESTIONS ANSWERED

Who should have an HIV test?   Anyone at risk for HIV infection should consider being tested. You are potentially at risk for HIV if you have had unprotected sex (vaginal, anal, or oral) with more than one partner or with a partner who was not in a mutually monogamous relationship with you; if you have used or shared needles, syringes, or other paraphernalia for injecting drugs (including steroids); if you received a transfusion of blood or blood products prior to 1985; or if you have been diagnosed with an STD.

Many people carrying the AIDS virus in the United States don't know they are infected. Early treatment can help keep an infected person free of symptoms for a longer period of time. In addition, if you know you are HIV-positive, you can inform your sex partners and encourage them to consider testing. You can also avoid transmitting HIV to others by abstaining from sex or limiting your sexual activity to safer practices. Testing is particularly important for pregnant women because currently available treatments can significantly lower the risk of vertical transmission. For more on testing options, see the box "Getting an HIV Test."

Does the success of the new AIDS drugs mean that I don't need to worry about HIV infection anymore?   No. The new combination drug therapy has had dramatic effects for some people infected with HIV. In the United States, the number of HIV-infected people who progress to AIDS each year is declining, as is the death rate from AIDS. But the new drugs are expensive, can have serious side effects, and are not effective for everyone. Scientists do not yet know how long the drugs will keep HIV at bay, and no treatment has yet been shown to permanently eradicate HIV from the body. Unfortunately, some people have taken the success of these drugs as an excuse to relax their vigilance against transmission of HIV. AIDS is still

(continued)

an incurable, fatal disease, and everyone needs to take preventive measures.

Which contraceptive methods protect best against STDs?
The only sure way to avoid STDs is to abstain from sexual activity. The next most effective way is to be in a mutually monogamous relationship with an uninfected partner. If you choose to be sexually active, male condoms are the best known protection against HIV and other STDs. Condoms are not foolproof, however, and they do not protect against the transmission of diseases from sores or lesions that aren't covered by condoms.

You can increase their effectiveness by using them properly. Latex condoms are about 88% effective as a contraceptive; researchers estimate that when condoms are used properly, failure rates can be as low as 1–2%. Failure rates vary from brand to brand and batch to batch, as well as according to the user's age, education, and the amount of experience he's had with condoms. Breakage is most often caused by inadequate lubrication, use of an improper (oil-based) lubricant, and failure to smooth out air bubbles, which may pop and break the condom during sexual activity. Condoms slipping off during withdrawal is another common cause of failure. Refer to the box on p. 348 for more information on proper condom use.

Some other contraceptive methods may provide some protection against certain STDs. The diaphragm and cervical cap cover the cervix and may provide some protection against diseases that involve the infection of cervical cells. Spermicides reduce the risk of cervical gonorrhea, chlamydia, and PID; but if vaginal irritation occurs from the use of spermicides, the risk of infection with HIV and other STDs may increase. Hormonal methods such as oral contraceptives do not protect against STDs in the lower reproductive tract but do provide some protection against PID. For sexually active people, the consistent and correct use of latex male condoms provides the best protection against STDs currently available; combining condom use with another method can provide even greater protection.

SUMMARY

- HIV damages the immune system and causes AIDS. People with AIDS are vulnerable to often-fatal opportunistic infections.

- HIV is carried in blood and blood products, semen, vaginal and cervical secretions, and breast milk and is transmitted through the exchange of these fluids.

- Drugs have been developed to slow the course of HIV infection and to prevent or treat certain secondary infections, but there is no cure.

- HIV infection can be prevented by making careful choices about sexual activity, not sharing drug needles, and learning how to protect oneself.

- Chlamydia is a bacterial infection that causes epididymitis and urethritis in men and can lead to PID in women.

- Gonorrhea can cause PID in women and epididymitis in men, leading to infertility. In infants, untreated gonorrhea can cause blindness.

- Pelvic inflammatory disease (PID), a complication of untreated gonorrhea or chlamydia, is an infection of the uterus and oviducts that may extend to the ovaries and pelvic cavity. It can lead to infertility, ectopic pregnancy, and chronic pelvic pain.

- Genital warts, caused by the human papillomavirus (HPV), are associated with cervical cancer. Treatment does not eradicate the virus.

- Genital herpes is a common, incurable viral infection characterized by outbreaks of lesions and periods of latency.

- Hepatitis B is a viral infection of the liver transmitted through sexual and nonsexual contact. Some people become chronic carriers of the virus and may develop serious, potentially fatal complications.

- Syphilis is a highly contagious bacterial infection that can be treated with penicillin. If left untreated, it can lead to deterioration of the central nervous system and death.

- Successful diagnosis and treatment of STDs involves being alert for symptoms, getting tested, informing partners, and following treatment instructions carefully.

- All STDs are preventable; the key is practicing responsible sexual behaviors.

FOR MORE INFORMATION

Books

Ebel, C. 1998. *Managing Herpes: How to Live and Love with a Chronic STD.* 2d ed. Durham, N.C.: American Social Health Association. *Helpful advice and support.*

Institute of Medicine. 1997. *The Hidden Epidemic: Confronting Sexually Transmitted Diseases.* Washington, D.C.: National Academy Press. *An examination of the scope of STDs in the United States and the nation's response to the epidemic.*

Kalichman, S. C. 1996. *Answering Your Questions About AIDS.* Washington, D.C.: American Psychological Association. *Helpful, easy-to-understand information, based on questions addressed to major AIDS hotlines.*

Ward, D. E. 1998. *The AmFAR AIDS Handbook: The Complete Guide to Understanding HIV and AIDS.* New York: W. W. Nor-

Testing Options

If you decide to get an HIV test, you can visit a physician or health clinic, or you can take one of the new home tests. An advantage to having the test performed by a physician or clinician is that you will get one-on-one counseling about the test, your results, and ways to avoid future infection or spreading the disease. Many physicians suggest that if you have good reason to think you may test positive, it is probably best to find a physician or clinic where the test can be done confidentially and where follow-up counseling and medical care will be intensive. The home test is a good alternative for people at low risk who just want to be sure. The advantages of the home test are that it can be done privately and confidentially, and it may be attractive to people who would not otherwise get tested.

Physician or Clinic Testing

Your physician, student health clinic, Planned Parenthood, or local AIDS association can arrange your HIV test. It usually costs $100–$200, but public clinics often charge little or nothing. The test itself is fairly simple. The procedure will be explained to you, and then a sample of blood will be drawn and sent to a laboratory for analysis for the presence of antibodies to HIV. If the first stage of testing, the ELISA test, proves positive, it is followed by a confirmatory test, the Western blot. You'll be asked to phone or come in personally to get your results, which should include appropriate counseling. (Some testing sites also offer "rapid tests" that yield results in about 10 minutes. Rapid tests are more likely to give false-positive results, however, so any positive rapid-test result must be confirmed with the more accurate series of antibody tests.) If you test negative, you need to know how to stay uninfected. If you test positive, you'll need to know what your medical options are; what the psychological, social, and financial repercussions might be; and how to avoid spreading the disease.

A new type of HIV test is the OraSure test, which can detect HIV antibodies in fluid from tissue in the mouth. A treated cotton pad is placed between the gum and cheek for two minutes and then sent to a lab for analysis. This test may be helpful for people who might avoid HIV testing because of a fear of needles.

Before you get an HIV test, be sure you understand whether or not the results will be kept confidential. Unless you are tested anonymously, your results could become part of the medical record available to insurance companies, which could affect future coverage and even employment. Your physician or counselor should be able to tell you how to get a confidential test.

Home Testing

Home test kits for HIV are now available; they cost about $40. To use a home test, you blot a few drops of blood onto blotting paper and mail it to the company's laboratory. There the sample is tested by the same methods used for samples collected by physicians. In about a week, you call a toll-free number to find out your results. Those with a negative result get the news from a recorded message, though they can talk with a counselor if they like. Anyone testing positive is routed to a trained counselor, who can provide emotional and medical support.

The results of home test kits are completely anonymous. Your blood sample is assigned an identification number, and you never give your name or address. Even if you test positive and receive counseling, your conversation will be anonymous.

Understanding the Results

A negative test result means that no antibodies were found in your sample. However, it usually takes at least a month (and possibly as long as 6 months in some people) after exposure to HIV for antibodies to appear, a process called *seroconversion*. Therefore, a person who is HIV-positive may get a false-negative test result. If you think you may have been exposed to HIV recently, get a test now and repeat it in 6 months.

A positive result means that antibodies to HIV were found in your blood and you are HIV-positive. It is important to seek medical care and counseling immediately. Rapid progress is being made in treating HIV, and treatments appear to be most successful when begun early.

---

ton. *A comprehensive guide to HIV infection from the American Foundation for AIDS Research.*

Organizations, Hotlines, and Web Sites

American College Health Association. Offers free brochures on STDs, alcohol use, acquaintance rape, and other college health issues.
    410-859-1500
American Social Health Association. Provides written information and referrals on STDs; sponsors support groups for people with herpes and HPV.
    800-653-HEALTH; 919-361-8400
    http://sunsite.unc.edu/ASHA
CDC National AIDS Clearinghouse. Provides up-to-date statistics, a daily summary of AIDS information, and CDC publications relating to AIDS.
    800-458-5231
    http://www.cdcnac.org

CDC National HIV and AIDS Hotline. Provides confidential information and referrals for testing and treatment.
    800-342-AIDS; 800-344-SIDA (Spanish);
    800-243-7889 (TTY, deaf access)
CDC National STD Hotline. Provides confidential information and referrals.
    800-227-8922
HIV InSite: Gateway to AIDS Knowledge. Provides information about prevention, education, treatment, statistics, clinical trials, and new developments.
    http://hivinsite.ucsf.edu
The Journal of the American Medical Association HIV/AIDS Information Center. Provides a daily news summary, patient information, expert advice, and an extensive glossary.
    http://www.ama-assn.org/special/hiv
Latex Love. Sponsored by the makers of Trojan condoms, this site includes directions for condom use and sample dialogues for overcoming excuses for not using condoms.
    http://www.loveandsex.com/sex/safer/how.html

National Herpes Hotline. Provides counseling to people with herpes.

    919-361-8488

Planned Parenthood Federation of America. Provides information on STDs, family planning, and contraception.

    800-230-PLAN; 202-785-3351

    http://www.plannedparenthood.org

SELECTED BIBLIOGRAPHY

Centers for Disease Control and Prevention. 1997. 1997 USPH/IDSA guidelines for the prevention of opportunistic infections in persons infected with human immunodeficiency virus. *MMWR Recommendations and Reports* 46(RR-12).

Centers for Disease Control and Prevention. 1997. Gonorrhea among men who have sex with men—selected sexually transmitted disease clinics, 1993–1996. *Morbidity and Mortality Weekly Report* 46(38): 889–892.

Centers for Disease Control and Prevention. 1997. Update: Perinatally acquired HIV/AIDS—United States, 1997. *Morbidity and Mortality Weekly Report* 46(46): 1086–1092.

Centers for Disease Control and Prevention. 1998. Primary and secondary syphilis—United States, 1997. *Morbidity and Mortality Weekly Report* 47(24): 493–497.

Centers for Disease Control and Prevention. 1998. Diagnosis and reporting of HIV and AIDS in states with integrated HIV and AIDS surveillance—United States, January 1994–June 1997. *Morbidity and Mortality Weekly Report* 47(15): 309–314.

Centers for Disease Control and Prevention. 1998. *HIV/AIDS Surveillance Report* 9(2).

Centers for Disease Control and Prevention. 1998. 1998 guidelines for treatment of sexually transmitted diseases. *Morbidity and Mortality Weekly Report* 47(RR-1).

Cooper, E., et al. 1996. Impact of ACTG 076: Use of zidovudine during pregnancy and changes in the rate of HIV vertical transmission. Presented at the Third Conference on Retroviruses and Opportunistic Infections. Abstract 26.

Detels, R., et al. 1998. Increased survival time to AIDS and death associated with use of combined therapy in the Multicenter AIDS Cohort Study. Presented at the Fifth Conference on Retroviruses and Opportunistic Infections. Abstract 193/Session 27.

Fisher, J. D., et al. 1996. Changing AIDS risk behavior: Effects of an intervention emphasizing AIDS risk reduction information, motivation, and behavioral skills in a college student population. *Health Psychology* 15(2): 114–123.

Fleming, D. T., et al. 1997. Herpes simplex virus Type 2 in the United States, 1976 to 1994. *New England Journal of Medicine* 337(16): 1105–1111.

Hogg, R. S., et al. 1998. Improved survival among HIV-infected individuals following initiation of antiretroviral therapy. *Journal of the American Medical Association* 279(6): 450–454.

Howell, M. R., T. C. Quinn, and C. A. Gaydos. 1998. Screening for *Chlamydia trachomatis* in asymptomatic women attending family planning clinics. A cost-effectiveness analysis of three strategies. *Annals of Internal Medicine* 128(4): 277–284.

Kilmarx, P. H., F. F. Hamers, and T. A. Peterman. 1998. Living with HIV. Experiences and perspectives of HIV-infected sexually transmitted disease clinic patients after posttest counseling. *Sexually Transmitted Diseases* 25(1): 28–37.

Krieger, L. M. 1998. Human trials OK'd for an AIDS vaccine. *San Jose Mercury News,* 4 June.

Lurie, P., and E. Drucker. 1997. An opportunity lost: HIV infections associated with lack of a national needle-exchange programme in the USA. *Lancet* 349:604–608.

Marwick, C. 1998. HIV/AIDS care calls for reallocation of resources. *Journal of the American Medical Association* 279(7): 491–493.

McNaghten, A. D., et al. 1998. The effects of antiretroviral therapy and opportunistic illness primary chemoprophylaxis on survival after AIDS. Presented at the Fifth Conference on Retroviruses and Opportunistic Infections. Abstract 10/Session 6.

Miller, K. E. 1997. Women's health. Sexually transmitted diseases. *Primary Care* 24(1): 179–193.

Mosure, D. J., et al. 1997. Genital chlamydia infections in sexually active female adolescents: Do we really need to screen everyone? *Journal of Adolescent Health* 20(1): 6–13.

Newkirk, G. 1996. Pelvic inflammatory disease: A contemporary approach. *American Family Physician* 53(4): 1127–1135.

Palella, F. J., et al. 1998. Declining morbidity and mortality among patients with advanced human immunodeficiency virus infection. *New England Journal of Medicine* 338(13): 853–860.

Perlman, D. 1997. HIV can hide in cells despite drug treatment. *San Francisco Chronicle,* September 14, A1, A21.

Ramirez, J. E., et al. 1997. Genital human papillomavirus infections. Knowledge, perception of risk, and actual risk in a nonclinical population of young women. *Journal of Women's Health* 6(1): 113–121.

Rosenberg, P. S., and R. J. Biggar. 1998. Trends in HIV incidence among young adults in the United States. *Journal of the American Medical Association* 279: 1894–1899.

Schacker, T., et al. 1998. Famciclovir for the suppression of symptomatic and asymptomatic herpes simplex virus reactivation in HIV-infected persons. A double-blind, placebo-controlled trial. *Annals of Internal Medicine* 128(1): 21–28.

Stein, M. D., et al. 1998. Sexual ethics: Disclosure of HIV-positive status to partners. *Archives of Internal Medicine* 158(3): 253–257.

Tseng, C. J., et al. 1998. Perinatal transmission of human papillomavirus in infants: Relationship between infection rate and mode of delivery. *Obstetrics and Gynecology* 91(1): 92–96.

UNAIDS and World Health Organization. 1998. *Report on the Global HIV/AIDS Epidemic—June 1998* (retrieved July 9, 1998; http://www.unaids.org/highband/document/epidemio/june98/global_report/index.html).

Volberding, P. A. 1998. An aggressive approach to HIV antiretroviral therapy. *Hospital Practice* 33(1): 81–90.

Wendt, S., and L. Solomon. 1995. Barriers to condom use among heterosexual male and female college students. *Journal of American College Health* 44(6): 105–110.

LAB 14-1 *Behaviors and Attitudes Related to STDs*

Part I. Risk Assessment

All sexually transmitted diseases are preventable. You have control over the behaviors and attitudes that place you at risk for contracting STDs and for increasing their negative effects on your health. To identify your risk factors for STDs, read the following list of statements and identify whether they're true or false for you.

Note: The statements in this assessment assume current sexual activity. If you have never been sexually active, you are not now at risk for STDs. Respond to the statements in the quiz based on how you realistically believe you would act. If you are currently in a mutually monogamous relationship with an uninfected partner or are not currently sexually active (but have been in the past), you are at low risk for STDs at this time. Respond to the statements in the quiz according to your attitudes and past behaviors.

True   False

_____ _____   1. I have only one sexual partner.

_____ _____   2. I always use a latex condom for each act of intercourse, even if I am fairly certain my partner has no infections.

_____ _____   3. I do not use oil-based lubricants with condoms.

_____ _____   4. I discuss STDs and prevention with new partners before having sex.

_____ _____   5. I do not use alcohol or another mood-altering drug in sexual situations.

_____ _____   6. I would tell my partner if I thought I had been exposed to an STD.

_____ _____   7. I am familiar with the signs and symptoms of STDs.

_____ _____   8. I regularly perform genital self-examination to check for signs and symptoms of STDs.

_____ _____   9. When I notice any sign or symptom of any STD, I consult my physician immediately.

_____ _____ 10. I obtain screening for HIV and other STDs regularly. In addition (if female), I obtain yearly pelvic exams and Pap tests.

_____ _____ 11. When diagnosed with an STD, I inform all recent partners.

_____ _____ 12. When I have a sign or symptom of an STD that goes away on its own, I still consult my physician.

_____ _____ 13. I do not use drugs prescribed for friends or partners or left over from other illnesses to treat STDs.

_____ _____ 14. I do not share syringes or needles to inject drugs.

False responses indicate attitudes and behaviors that may put you at risk for contracting STDs or for suffering serious medical consequences from them.

LABORATORY ACTIVITIES

Part II. Communication

1. List three ways to bring up the subject of STDs with a new partner. How would you ask whether or not he or she has been exposed to any STDs or engaged in any risky behaviors? (Remember that since many STDs can be asymptomatic it is important to know about past behaviors even if no STD was diagnosed.)

a. _____

_____

b. _____

_____

c. _____

_____

2. List three ways to bring up the subject of condom use with your partner. How might you convince someone who does not want to use a condom?

a. _____

_____

b. _____

_____

c. _____

_____

3. If you had had an STD in the past that you might possibly still pass on (e.g., herpes, genital warts), how would you tell your partner(s)?

_____

_____

_____

4. If you were diagnosed with an STD that you believe was given to you by your current partner, how would you begin a discussion of STDs with her or him?

_____

_____

_____

Wellness for Life

LOOKING AHEAD

After reading this chapter, you should be able to answer these questions about wellness:

- What characteristics, skills, and behaviors support successful relationships and families?

- What can people do to promote healthy aging?

- What are the components of effective self-care? What skills contribute to effective use of the health care system?

- What role does the environment play in personal health and wellness? What can individuals do to improve the environment?

- What steps are involved in creating and maintaining an effective behavior change program?

357

The goal of this book has been to introduce the concept of wellness and to provide the knowledge and skills you need to live a fit and well lifestyle. Knowing the facts about the effects of your actions on your health enables you to make informed choices. Using behavioral self-management enables you to make important lifestyle changes. This chapter briefly addresses some other skills that are important for a lifetime of wellness: developing and maintaining meaningful interpersonal relationships, meeting the challenges of aging, using the health care system intelligently, and understanding environmental health.

DEVELOPING SUCCESSFUL INTERPERSONAL RELATIONSHIPS

Human beings need social relationships; we cannot thrive as solitary creatures. Nor could the human species survive if adults didn't cherish and support each other, if we didn't form strong mutual attachments with our infants, and if we didn't create families in which to raise children. Simply put, people need people.

Although people are held together in relationships by a variety of factors, the foundation of many relationships is love. Love in its many forms—romantic, passionate, platonic, parental—is the wellspring from which much of life's meaning and delight flows. In our culture, it binds us together as partners, parents, children, and friends. People devote tremendous energy to seeking mates, nurturing intimate relationships, keeping up friendships, maintaining marriages—all for the pleasure of loving and being loved.

Forming Relationships

Intimate relationships satisfy many human needs, including the need for approval and affirmation, for companionship, for a sense of belonging, and for sexual expression. Many of society's needs are also fulfilled by relationships, particularly the need to nurture and socialize children within that society.

Self-Concept and Self-Esteem   Relationships begin with individuals. To have successful relationships, people first have to accept and feel good about themselves. A positive self-concept and healthy level of self-esteem help people love and respect others. The roots of a positive sense of self are found in childhood. People are likely, as adults, to have the sense that they are basically lovable, worthwhile people if, as children, they felt loved, valued, and respected; if their parents or other important adults responded to their needs in appropriate ways; and if they were given the freedom to explore and develop a sense of being separate individuals.

Even if people's earliest experiences and relationships were less than ideal, however, they can still establish satisfying relationships in adulthood. Humans are resilient and flexible; we have the ability to change our ideas and patterns of behavior. We can learn ways to enhance our self-esteem and become more trusting and appreciative of others. We can acquire the communication skills needed to maintain successful relationships.

Friendship   The first relationships we form outside the family are friendships. With members of either the same or the other sex, friendships give people the opportunity to share themselves and discover others. Friendships usually include these characteristics:

- *Companionship*. Friends are relaxed and happy in each other's company. They have common values and interests and spend time together.
- *Respect*. Good friends respect each other's feelings and opinions and work to resolve their differences without demeaning or insulting each other. They also show their respect by being honest with one another (see the box "Being a Good Friend").
- *Acceptance*. Friends feel free to be themselves and express their feelings spontaneously without fear of ridicule or criticism.
- *Help*. Sharing time, energy, and even material goods is important to friendship. Friends know they can rely on each other in times of need.
- *Trust*. Friends are secure in the knowledge that they will not intentionally hurt each other.
- *Loyalty*. Friends can count on each other. They stand up for each other in both word and deed.
- *Reciprocity*. There is give and take between friends, and the feeling that both share joys and burdens more or less equally over time.

Friendships are often more stable and longer lasting than intimate partnerships. Friends are often more accepting and less critical than lovers, probably because their expectations are different. Like love relationships, friendships bind society together, providing people with emotional support and buffering them from stress.

Love and Intimacy   Intimate love relationships are among the most profound human experiences. They may not give people perfect happiness, but they do tend to give life much of its meaning. For most adults, love, sex, and commitment are closely linked ideals in intimate relationships. Love reflects the positive factors that draw people together and sustain them in a relationship—trust, caring, respect, loyalty, interest in the other, and concern for the other's well-being. Sex brings excitement and passion to the relationship, adding fascination and pleasure. Commitment, the determination to continue, reflects the stable factors that help maintain the relationship—responsibil-

How to Make Friends

- Find people with interests similar to your own. Join a club, participate in sports, do volunteer work, or join a discussion group to meet people with common interests.

- Be a good listener. Take a genuine interest in people. Solicit their opinions, and take time to listen to their problems and ideas.

- Take risks. If you meet someone interesting, ask him or her to join you for a meal or an event you would both enjoy.

How to Be a Good Friend

- Be trustworthy. Honor all confidences, and don't talk about your friend behind her or his back.

- Tell your friend about yourself. Self-disclosure—letting your friend know about your real concerns and joys—signals trust.

- Be supportive and kind. Be there when your friend is going through a rough time. Don't criticize your friend or offer unsolicited advice.

- Develop your capacity for intimacy. Intimate relationships are genuine, spontaneous, and caring.

- Don't expect perfection. Like any relationship, your friendship may go through difficult times. Talk through conflicts as they arise.

---

ity, reliability, and faithfulness. Although love, sex, and commitment are related, they are not necessarily connected. One can exist without the others. Despite the various permutations of the three, most people long for a special relationship that contains them all.

When two people fall in love, their relationship at first is likely to be characterized by high levels of passion and rapidly increasing intimacy. In time, passion decreases as the partners become familiar with each other. The disappearance of passionate love is often experienced as a crisis in a relationship. If a quieter, more lasting love fails to emerge, the relationship will likely break up, and each person will search for another who will once again ignite his or her passion.

But love does not necessarily have to be passionate. When intensity diminishes, partners often discover a more enduring love. They can now move from absorption in each other to a relationship that includes external goals and projects, friends, and family. In this kind of more secure love, satisfaction comes not just from the relationship but also from achieving other creative objectives, such as work or child rearing. The key to successful relationships isn't in intensity but in transforming passion into an intimate love, based on closeness, caring, and the promise of a shared future.

Choosing a Partner Although the pool of potential partners for a relationship may appear huge, most people pair with someone who lives in the same geographic area and who is similar in ethnic and socioeconomic background, educational level, lifestyle, physical appearance, and other traits. In simple terms, people select partners like themselves.

When choosing intimate companions, perhaps the most important question two people can ask is "How much do we have in common?" Although differences add interest to a relationship, similarities increase the chances of a relationship's success. If there are major differences, partners should ask, first, "How accepting of differences are we?" and second, "How well do we communicate?" Acceptance and communication skills go a long way toward making a relationship work, no matter how different the partners.

Most Americans find romantic partners through some form of dating. They narrow the field through a process of getting to know each other. Dating often revolves around a mutually enjoyable activity, such as seeing a movie or having dinner. In the traditional male-female dating pattern, the man takes the lead, initiating the date, while the woman waits to be called. In this pattern, casual dating might evolve into steady or exclusive dating, then engagement, and finally marriage.

For many young people today, traditional dating has given way to a more casual form of getting together in groups. Greater equality between the sexes is at the root of this change. Rather than strictly as couples, people go out in groups, and each person pays his or her way. A man and woman may begin to spend more time together, but often in the group context. If sexual involvement develops, it is more likely to be based on friendship, respect, and common interests than on expectations related to gender roles. In this model, mate selection may progress from getting together to living together to marriage.

Communication

The key to developing and maintaining any type of intimate relationship is good communication. Most of the time, we don't actually think about communicating; we simply talk and behave naturally. But when problems arise—when we feel other people don't understand us or

For many college students today, group activities have replaced dating as a way to meet and get to know potential partners.

stand another person's "story" and less time judging, evaluating, blaming, advising, analyzing, or trying to control. Empathy, warmth, respect, and genuineness are qualities of skillful listeners. Attentive listening encourages friends or partners to share more and, in turn, to be attentive listeners. To connect with other people and develop real emotional intimacy, listening is essential.

• *Feedback,* a constructive response to another's self-disclosure, is the third key to good communication. Giving positive feedback means acknowledging that the friend's or partner's feelings are valid—no matter how upsetting or troubling—and offering self-disclosure in response. Self-disclosure and feedback can open the door to change, whereas other responses block communication and change.

For tips on improving your skills, see the box "Guidelines for Effective Communication."

when someone accuses us of not listening—we become aware of our limitations or, more commonly, what we think are other people's limitations. Miscommunication creates frustration and distances us from our friends and partners.

As much as 65% of face-to-face communication is nonverbal. Even when we're silent, we're communicating. We send messages when we look at someone or look away, lean forward or sit back, smile or frown. Especially important forms of nonverbal communication are touch, eye contact, and proximity. If someone we're talking to touches our hand or arm, looks into our eyes, and leans toward us when we talk, we get the message that the person is interested in us and cares about what we're saying. If a person keeps looking around the room while we're talking or takes a step backward, we get the impression the person is uninterested or wants to end the conversation. It's important, when sending messages, to make sure our body language agrees with our words. When our verbal and nonverbal messages don't correspond, we send a mixed message.

Communication Skills
Three keys to good communication in relationships are self-disclosure, listening, and feedback.

• *Self-disclosure* involves revealing personal information that we ordinarily wouldn't reveal because of the risk involved. It usually increases feelings of closeness and moves the relationship to a deeper level of intimacy.

• *Listening,* the second component of good communication, is a rare skill. Good listening skills require that we spend more time and energy trying to fully under-

Conflict and Conflict Resolution
Conflict is natural in intimate relationships. No matter how close two people become, they still remain separate individuals with their own needs, desires, past experiences, and ways of seeing the world. Conflict itself isn't dangerous to a relationship; it may simply indicate that the relationship is growing. But if it isn't handled in a constructive way, it will damage—and ultimately destroy—the relationship.

Conflict is often accompanied by anger—a natural emotion, but one that can be difficult to handle. If we express anger, we run the risk of creating distrust, fear, and distance; if we act it out without thinking things through, we can cause the conflict to escalate; if we suppress it, it turns into resentment and hostility. The best way to handle anger in a relationship is to recognize it as a symptom of something that requires attention and needs to be changed. When angry, partners should back off until they calm down and then come back to the issue later and try to resolve it rationally. Negotiation will help dissipate the anger so the conflict can be resolved. Basic strategies for resolving conflicts include the following:

1. *Clarify the issue.* Take responsibility for thinking through your feelings and discovering what's really bothering you. Agree that one partner will speak first and have the chance to speak fully while the other listens. Then reverse the roles. Try to understand the other partner's position fully by repeating what you've heard and asking questions to clarify or elicit more information.

2. *Find out what each person wants.* Ask your partner to express her or his desires. Don't assume you know what your partner wants and speak for her or him. Clarify and summarize.

3. *Identify various alternatives for getting each person what he or she wants.* Practice brainstorming to generate a variety of options.

Getting Started

- When you want to have a serious discussion with your partner, choose an appropriate time and place. Find time when you will not be interrupted, and a private place.

- Face your partner and maintain eye contact. Use nonverbal feedback to show that you are interested and involved in the communication process.

Being an Effective Speaker

- State your concern or issue as clearly as you can.

- Use "I" statements—statements about how *you* feel—rather than statements beginning with "You," which tell another person how you think he or she feels. When you use "I" statements, you are taking responsibility for your feelings. "You" statements are often blaming or accusatory and will probably get a defensive or resentful response. The statement "I feel unloved," for example, sends a clearer, less blaming message than the statement "You don't love me."

- Focus on a specific behavior rather than on the whole person. Be specific about the behavior you like or don't like. Avoid generalizations beginning with "You always" or "You never." Such statements make people feel defensive.

- Make constructive requests. Opening your request with "I would like" keeps the focus on your needs rather than your partner's supposed deficiencies.

- Avoid blaming, accusing, and belittling. Even if you are right, you have little to gain by putting your partner down. Studies have shown that when people feel criticized or attacked, they are less able to think rationally or solve problems constructively.

- Ask for action ahead of time. Tell your partner what you would like to have happen in the future; don't wait for him or her to blow it and then express anger or disappointment.

Being an Effective Listener

- Provide appropriate nonverbal feedback (nodding, smiling, and so on).

- Don't interrupt.

- Develop the skill of reflective listening. Don't judge, evaluate, analyze, or offer solutions (unless asked to do so). Your partner may just need to have you there in order to sort out feelings. By jumping in right away to "fix" the problem, you may actually be cutting off communication.

- Don't give unsolicited advice. Giving advice implies that you know more about what a person needs to do than he or she does; therefore, it often evokes anger or resentment.

- Clarify your understanding of what your partner is saying by restating it in your own words and asking if your understanding is correct.

- Be sure you are really listening, not off somewhere in your mind rehearsing your reply. Try to tune in to your partner's feelings as well as the words.

- Let your partner know that you value what she or he is saying and want to understand. Respect for the other person is the cornerstone of effective communication.

---

4. *Decide how to negotiate.* Work out some agreements or plans for change: for example, one partner will do one task and the other will do another task, or one partner will do a task in exchange for something she or he wants.

5. *Solidify the agreements.* Go over the plan verbally and write it down, if necessary, to ensure that you both understand and agree to it.

6. *Review and renegotiate.* Decide on a time frame for trying out the new plan, and set a time to discuss how it's working. Make adjustments as needed.

Marriage

Although half of all marriages in our society now end in divorce, the popularity of getting married hasn't diminished. The primary functions and benefits of marriage are those of any intimate adult relationship, including affection, personal affirmation, companionship, sexual fulfillment, and emotional growth. But marriage also provides a setting in which to raise children, and it affords some provision for the future. By committing themselves to their relationship by getting married, people provide themselves with lifelong companions.

Although most people would like to believe otherwise, love is not enough to make a successful marriage. Couples have to have strengths; they have to be successful in their relationship before marriage. The following relationship characteristics appear to be the best predictors of a happy marriage.

- The partners have realistic expectations about their relationship.

- Each feels good about the personality of the other.

- They communicate well.

- They have effective ways of resolving conflicts.

- They agree on religious/ethical values.

- They have an egalitarian role relationship.

- They have a good balance of individual versus joint interests and leisure activities.

Coping with the challenges of marriage requires couples to be committed to remaining married through the inevitable ups and downs of the relationship. They need to be tolerant of each other's imperfections, keep their sense of perspective and their sense of humor, and be willing and able to put energy into providing and sustaining mutually sufficient levels of intimacy, sexual satisfaction, and commitment.

Successful Relationships, Successful Families

Some people view relationships as mysterious connections between people that develop naturally and require no effort to maintain, but this is far from true. Without time spent together and energy invested in maintaining intimacy, people drift apart and relationships die. Because of the importance of healthy, satisfying relationships, people should take the time to develop and nurture this aspect of their lives.

Family relationships are another important part of a healthy life. Researchers have proposed that six major qualities or themes appear in strong families.

1. *Commitment*. The family is very important to its members; sexual fidelity between partners is included in commitment.

2. *Appreciation*. People care about one another and express that caring. The home is a positive place to be.

3. *Communication*. People spend time listening to one another and enjoying one another's company. They talk about disagreements and attempt to solve problems.

4. *Time together*. People do things together, often simple activities that don't cost money.

5. *Spiritual wellness*. The family promotes sharing, love, and compassion for other human beings (see the box "Spiritual Wellness").

6. *Coping with stress and crisis*. When faced with illness, death, marital conflict, or other crises, family members pull together, seek help, and use other coping strategies to meet the challenge.

It may surprise some people that partners in committed relationships and members of strong families often go to counseling centers. They know that the smartest thing to do in some situations is to get help. Many resources are available for individuals and families seeking counseling, including marriage and family counselors, clergy, psychologists, and other trained professionals.

MEETING THE CHALLENGES OF AGING

Aging is a normal process of development that occurs over the entire life span. It happens to everyone, but at different rates for different people. Although youth is not entirely a state of mind, your attitude toward life and your attention to your health significantly influence the satisfaction you

will derive from life, especially when new physical and mental challenges occur in later years. If you take charge of your health during young adulthood, you can exert greater control over the physical and mental aspects of aging, and you can respond better to events that might be out of your control. With foresight and energy, you can shape a creative, graceful, and even triumphant old age (see the box "Multicultural Wisdom About Aging").

What Happens as You Age?

Aging results from biochemical processes that we don't yet fully understand. Physiological changes are caused by a combination of gradual aging and injury from disease. Because most organ systems have an excess capacity for performing their functions, the body's ability to function is not affected until damage is fairly extensive. Studies of healthy people indicate that general functioning remains essentially constant until after age 70.

Some of the physical changes that accompany aging are these:

- Skin becomes looser, drier, and less elastic.

- The ability to hear high-pitched and certain other sounds declines in most people.

- Presbyopia, the inability of the eyes to focus sharply on nearby objects, occurs gradually in most people beginning in their forties. The eyes require more time to adapt to dark conditions, and depth perception may become distorted.

- The sensations of taste and smell diminish somewhat.

- Cells at the base of hair follicles produce progressively less pigment and eventually die. (Hair is thickest at age 20; individual hair shafts shrink after that.)

- Bone mass is lost and muscles become weaker, although both of these changes can be minimized significantly through regular exercise, a proper diet, and other measures.

- The heart pumps less blood with each beat, and maximum heart rate drops. Most of the other changes in the cardiovascular system that are associated with aging can be largely controlled through lifestyle.

- Sexual response slows, but an active and satisfying sex life can continue for both men and women throughout life.

Life-Enhancing Measures

Many of the characteristics associated with aging aren't due to aging at all. They are the result of neglect and abuse of our bodies and minds. These assaults lay the foundation for later mental problems and chronic conditions like arthritis, heart disease, diabetes, hearing loss, and high blood pressure. You can prevent, delay, lessen,

 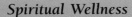
Spiritual wellness means different things to different people. For many, it involves developing a set of guiding beliefs, principles, or values that give meaning and purpose to life. It helps people achieve a sense of wholeness within themselves and in their relationships with others. Spiritual wellness influences people on an individual level, as well as on a community level, where it can bond people together through compassion, love, forgiveness, and self-sacrifice. For some, spirituality includes a belief in a higher power. Regardless of how it is defined, the development of spiritual wellness is critical for overall health and well-being. Its development is closely tied to the other components of wellness, particularly psychological health.

There are many paths of spiritual wellness. One of the most common in our society is organized religion. Some people object to the notion that organized religion can contribute to wellness, asserting that it reinforces people's tendency to deny real difficulties and to accept what can and should be changed. However, many elements of religious belief and practice can promote psychological health.

Organized religion usually involves its members in a community where social and material support is available. Religious organizations offer a social network to those who might otherwise be isolated. The major religions provide paths for transforming the self in ways that can lead to greater happiness and serenity and reduce feelings of anxiety and hopelessness. In Christianity, salvation follows turning away from the selfish ego

to God's sovereignty and grace, where a joy is found that frees the believer from anxious self-concern and despair. Islam is the word for a kind of self-surrender leading to peace with God. Buddhism teaches how to detach oneself from selfish desire, leading to compassion for the suffering of others and freedom from fear-engendering illusions. Judaism emphasizes the social and ethical redemption the Jewish community can experience if it follows the laws of God. Religions teach specific techniques for achieving these transformations of the self: prayer, both in groups and in private; meditation; the performance of rituals and ceremonies symbolizing religious truths; and good works and service to others.

Spiritual wellness does not require participation in organized religion. Many people find meaning and purpose in other ways. By spending time in nature or working on environmental issues, people can experience continuity with the natural world. Spiritual wellness can come through helping others in one's community or by promoting human rights, peace and harmony among people, and opportunities for human development on a global level. Other people develop spiritual wellness through art or through their personal relationships.

Particularly in the second half of life, people seem to have an urge to view their activities and consciousness from a transcendent perspective. At every age, however, people seem to feel better if they have beliefs about the ultimate purpose of life and their own place in the universe.

The following is excerpted from an article written by Dr. Robert Coles, a professor of psychiatry and medical humanities at Harvard Medical School.

Why are so many Americans afraid of growing old? This question occurred to me often during the three years my wife and I lived in New Mexico and Arizona. Not a day went by when we weren't reminded of how much Native American and Hispanic families value old age. These are cultures that grant dignity and authority to their elders.

One young Hispanic woman described to us her relationship with her parents, both in their seventies, in this way: "When I am wondering what to do about a problem, I turn to my mother or my father. Even if they are not here, I still turn to them. I picture them in my mind and I hear them saying words that make good sense." One day, this woman's father made a show of his humorous and practical good sense before his young grandson. "You know what my son said to me that night when he was going to bed?" the woman asked. "He told me he wished he could be old like his grandpapa!"

To be old is to "last" oneself—to go through ups and downs, to survive bad luck and avoid all sorts of hazards. To be old is to

be blessed by fate, by chance and circumstance. Pueblo Indians know that. One Hopi child drew me a picture of an old woman shaking hands with the moon. Then she explained, "When you're old, you're a full moon; you make the night a little less dark." For Hopi children, an older person is a source of encouragement, instruction, inspiration, a part of nature's awesome presence.

For many young people living in other parts of America, old age is regarded not as a major achievement but rather as a last, sad, brief way station. One boy in Boston commented, "It's no fun to be old; it's the worst thing in the world, except to die." To many of us, old age means abandonment, rejection, loneliness, a loss of respect from others, and subsequently a loss of self-respect. This is not the case, though, in Hispanic and Native American cultures. The elders we met in New Mexico and Arizona showed a great deal of self-confidence, and in general they seemed contented with their lives. In their contentment and harmony with nature lies a lesson for all of us.

SOURCE: Adapted from Coles, R. 1989. Full-moon wisdom. *New Choices for the Best Years,* September. Reprinted with permission of Robert Coles, James Agee Professor of Social Ethics, Harvard University.

One of the challenges of aging is finding satisfying activities that provide meaningful connections with others. This retired woman helps out at an after-school activity program by entertaining children.

or even reverse some of the changes associated with aging through good health habits. A few simple things you can do every day will make a vast difference to your health, your appearance, and your energy and vitality. The following suggestions have been mentioned throughout this text, but because they are profoundly related to health in later life, they are highlighted here.

- *Challenge your mind.* Creativity and intelligence remain stable in healthy individuals. Staying involved in learning as a lifelong process can help you stay sharp and retain all your mental abilities.

- *Plan for social changes.* Social roles change over time and require a period of adjustment. Retirement and an "empty nest" confer the advantage of increased leisure time, but many people do not know how to enjoy it. Throughout life, cultivate interests and hobbies you enjoy, both alone and with others, so that you can continue to live an active and rewarding life in your later years. Try new activities, take classes, and meet new people. Volunteering in your community can enhance self-esteem and allow you to be a contributing member of society.

- *Develop physical fitness.* Exercise enhances both psychological and physical health. Enough cannot be said for the positive effects of appropriate exercise throughout your life. Exercise significantly improves

both the quantity and the quality of your life by keeping your body functioning at peak levels and by protecting you from chronic diseases and injuries, even as you age.

- *Eat wisely.* Health at every age is helped by a varied diet with special attention to a lower intake of fat and calories. Eat meals low in fat and high in complex carbohydrates. Concentrate on fresh fruits and vegetables, whole grains, no-fat or low-fat dairy products, and lean portions of fish and poultry.

- *Maintain a healthy body composition.* Sensible eating habits and an active lifestyle can help you maintain a healthy body composition throughout your life.

- *Control drinking and overdependence on medications.* Alcohol abuse ranks with depression as a common hidden mental health problem, affecting 10% of older adults. The problem is often not identified because the effects of alcohol or drug addiction can mimic disease, such as Alzheimer's disease. Don't use alcohol to relieve anxiety or emotional pain; don't take medications when safer forms of treatment are available.

- *Don't smoke.* The average pack-a-day smoker can expect to live about 12 years less than a nonsmoker and to be susceptible to disabilities that affect the quality of life. Premature balding and skin wrinkling are also associated with smoking.

- *Recognize and reduce stress.* Don't wear yourself out through a lack of sleep, the abuse of drugs, or overworking. Practice relaxation and stress management, using the techniques described in Chapter 10.

Other strategies for successful aging include the following:

- Get regular physical examinations to detect treatable diseases.

- Protect your skin and eyes from the sun by using hats, gloves, sunscreen, and sunglasses.

- Avoid extremely loud noises, such as from stereo earphones or loud machines, that can contribute to hearing loss.

The health behaviors you practice now, in your early adulthood, weigh more heavily in determining how long and how well you will live than your behaviors at a later age. By taking care of yourself now, you're buying some insurance for the future.

USING THE HEALTH CARE SYSTEM INTELLIGENTLY

Just as people can prevent many illnesses through healthy lifestyle choices, they can also avoid many visits to the medical clinic by managing their own health care—by gathering information, soliciting advice, making their own decisions, and taking responsibility for following through. People who manage their own health care are informed partners in medical care; they also practice safe, effective self-care.

How can you develop this self-care attitude and take a more active role in your own health care? First, you have to learn to identify and manage medical problems. Second, you have to learn how to make the health care system work for you. This section will help you become more competent in both of these areas.

Managing Medical Problems

The first step in managing medical problems is observing your body and assessing your symptoms. Symptoms—pain, fever, coughing, diarrhea, and so on—are signals that something isn't working right. There are also many self-tests available to help you evaluate medical problems at home: blood pressure monitoring equipment, blood sugar tests for diabetics, pregnancy tests, self-tests for urinary tract infections, and over a dozen other do-it-yourself kits and devices. Careful self-observation and the selective use of self-tests can help provide you with the type of information you need to make informed self-care decisions and participate more actively in your care.

Knowing When to See a Physician   In most cases, and with sufficient time and rest, the body heals itself. The decision to seek professional assistance for a symptom is generally guided by the nature of the symptom and by your own history of medical problems. If you're unsure about a symptom, call your physician. You may be able to obtain medical advice over the telephone. About 15% of all outpatient medical advice and 30% of all pediatric advice is now given by telephone.

Professional assistance is appropriate for any symptom that is severe, unusual, persistent, or recurrent. Medical emergencies requiring a trip to the nearest hospital emergency room include broken bones, severe burns, deep wounds, uncontrollable bleeding, chest pain, loss of consciousness, poisoning or drug overdose, and difficulty breathing.

Self-Treatment: Many Options   In most cases, your body can itself relieve your symptoms and heal a disorder. The prescriptions filled by your body's internal pharmacy are frequently the safest and most effective treatment. So patience and careful self-observation are often the best choices in self-treatment.

Nondrug options are often highly effective. For example, massage, ice packs, and neck exercises may be at times more helpful than drugs in relieving headaches and other pains. Adequate rest, increasing exercise, drinking more water, getting a new chair, and so on are just some of the hundreds of nondrug options for preventing or relieving many common health problems. For a variety of disorders either caused or aggravated by stress, the treatment of choice may be relaxation, time management, realistic self-talk, and other stress-management strategies (see Chapter 10). Before reaching for medications, consider all of your options for self-treatment.

Over-the-counter (nonprescription) drugs do play an important part in our health care system. Many OTC drugs are highly effective in relieving symptoms and sometimes curing illnesses. Common OTC drugs include antihistamines for allergies; expectorants and cough suppressants for coughs; decongestants for nasal congestion; laxatives for constipation; binding agents for diarrhea; aspirin, acetaminophen, ibuprofen, and naproxen sodium for fever or pain; antacids for heartburn and indigestion; hydrocortisone cream for skin rashes; lozenges for sore throats; ice packs, heating pads, and elastic bandages for sprains; and bandages and antibacterial creams for minor wounds.

It's important to remember that any drug, whether bought in the supermarket or prescribed by a physician, may have side effects. Following these simple guidelines will improve your chances of safely and effectively self-medicating:

- Always read drug labels, and follow directions carefully.
- Do not exceed the recommended dosage or length of treatment unless you have discussed this change with your physician.
- Because OTC and prescription drugs can interact, check with your physician or pharmacist before taking both types at the same time.
- Select medications with one active ingredient rather than combination products. Using single-ingredient products allows you to adjust the dosage of each medication separately for optimal symptom relief; you'll also avoid potential side effects from drugs you don't really need.
- Never take or give a drug from an unlabeled container or in the dark when you can't read what the label says.
- If you are pregnant, are nursing, or have a chronic medical condition, consult your physician before self-medicating.
- Store medications in a safe place out of the reach of children; avoid locations where dampness or heat might ruin them. Dispose of all expired medications.
- Use special caution with aspirin. Because of an association with a rare but serious problem known as Reye's syndrome, aspirin should not be used for children or adolescents who may have the flu, chicken pox, or any other viral illness.

Getting the Most Out of Medical Care

Although many health problems can be self-treated, many others require treatment by trained professionals. The key

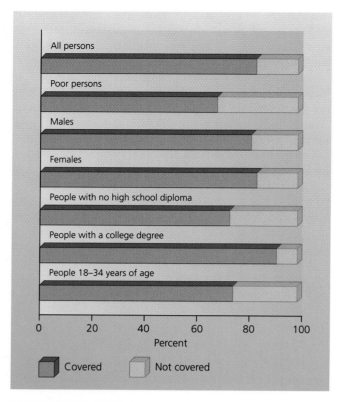

Figure 15-1 Health insurance coverage among Americans.
More than 15% of Americans, some 40 million people, have no
health insurance. Young adults and people who are poor and/or have
low educational attainment are most likely to be uninsured. SOURCE:
Data from U.S. Bureau of the Census, *Current Population Survey* (retrieved
March 9, 1998; http://www.bls.census.gov/cps/ads/sdata.htm).

to using the health care system effectively is good communication with your physician and other members of
the health care team.

Communicating with Your Physician   When interacting with health care providers, you should be assertive in
a firm but not aggressive manner. Feel free to ask questions, express your concerns, and be persistent. Strategies
for good communication include the following:

- *Before the visit.* Make a written list of your questions
  and concerns; include notes about your symptoms.
  Bring a list of all medications (prescription and nonprescription) you are taking, or bring them with you
  to the office.

- *During the visit.* Present your major concerns at the
  beginning of the visit. Be specific and concise. Try to
  be as open and honest as you can in sharing your
  thoughts, feelings, and fears. If you're not sure about
  something your physician has said, ask to go over it
  again. If appropriate, ask your physician to write

down her or his instructions or to recommend reading material for more information.

- *At the end of the visit.* In your own words, briefly
  state what you understood the physician to say
  about your problem and what you're supposed to
  do. Make sure you understand what the next steps
  are—return for another visit, phone for test results,
  obtain a prescription drug, and so on.

Obtaining Appropriate Screening Tests   Another important part of preventive health care is regular screening for various conditions and diseases. The guidelines
shown in the box "Preventive Medicine for Healthy
Adults" represent the minimum testing recommended for
people without symptoms. People who have symptoms
or who are at risk for a particular disease should discuss
their individual needs with their physician.

Paying for Health Care   Health care in the United
States is currently financed by a combination of patient
out-of-pocket payments, private and public insurance
plans, and government assistance. However, this system
of financing does not cover everyone, and people without
insurance are more likely to receive care that is inadequate (Figure 15-1). Health insurance enables people to
budget in advance for health care costs that may otherwise be unpredictable and ruinously high. Most people
are insured through a group policy obtained through
their place of employment or through their parents' or
spouse's employer. Others are covered by government
programs such as Medicare and Medicaid.

If you work for a large company, you may be given a
choice of several types of plans, some with a traditional
framework and some offering managed care. In a traditional plan, you pay a premium up front, a fixed de-
ductible, and a percentage of expenses thereafter. In a
managed-care plan, you (or your employer) pay just the
premium and usually a small per-visit fee. When services
are used, the fixed fees remain the same, regardless of the
amount or level of services that are provided. Managed-
care plans tend to cost consumers less money, but they
have restrictions governing which physicians, facilities,
tests, and treatments are available to patients (see the box
"Managing with Managed Care").

When you are choosing between several health insurance plans, obtain a copy of each policy that sounds suitable and read it carefully. Ask the following questions
about each plan:

- What services are covered? Are all the services that
  I am likely to need covered?

- Are there exclusions for any preexisting conditions
  or chronic problems?

- What preventive health services are covered?

- What premiums, deductibles, and copayments will
  I need to pay?

While many people associate medical care solely with an illness or injury, preventive medicine can help healthy people stay healthy. Good preventive care includes:

1. Counseling and support to develop healthy habits and reduce health risks.

2. Selective screening tests based on your age, gender, and medical or family history (see the chart below).

3. Appropriate immunizations and use of medications to prevent disease.

The prevention recommendations below are based on scientific research. They apply to generally healthy adults. If you have ongoing health problems, if certain diseases run in your family, or if you have other special health needs or risks, your prevention plan may be somewhat different. Your health care providers can help you design a personalized plan for staying healthy based on your individual needs. And remember, don't rely just on medical exams, tests, and treatments to protect your health. Developing and maintaining a wellness lifestyle is the cornerstone of disease prevention and health promotion.

SOURCES: U.S. Preventive Services Task Force. 1996. *Guide to Clinical Preventive Services: Report of the U.S. Preventive Services Task Force,* 2d ed. Baltimore: Williams & Wilkins.

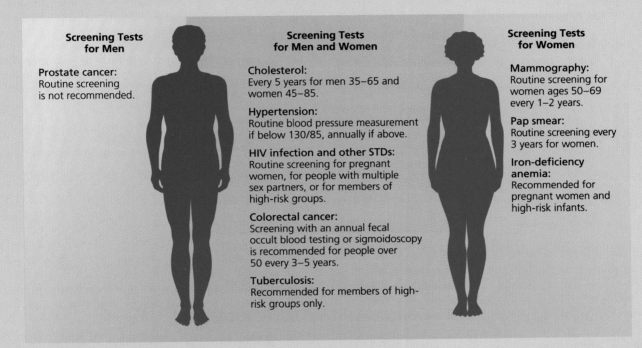

Screening Tests for Men

Prostate cancer: Routine screening is not recommended.

Screening Tests for Men and Women

Cholesterol: Every 5 years for men 35–65 and women 45–85.

Hypertension: Routine blood pressure measurement if below 130/85, annually if above.

HIV infection and other STDs: Routine screening for pregnant women, for people with multiple sex partners, or for members of high-risk groups.

Colorectal cancer: Screening with an annual fecal occult blood testing or sigmoidoscopy is recommended for people over 50 every 3–5 years.

Tuberculosis: Recommended for members of high-risk groups only.

Screening Tests for Women

Mammography: Routine screening for women ages 50–69 every 1–2 years.

Pap smear: Routine screening every 3 years for women.

Iron-deficiency anemia: Recommended for pregnant women and high-risk infants.

The recommendations of the U.S. Preventive Services Task Force differ from those of the American Heart Association, American Cancer Society, and other organizations. See Chapters 11 and 12 for other sets of testing guidelines, and check with your physician about which tests are best for you.

- Is there a maximum limit on services? If so, is it high enough?

- Will I be able to see the physicians I prefer? Does my current physician participate in the plan?

Most of the time, you can take care of yourself without personally consulting an expert. When you do need professional care, you can continue to take responsibility for yourself by making reasoned decisions about the care and health insurance you obtain.

ENVIRONMENTAL HEALTH

Because of the close relationship between human beings and the environment, even the healthiest lifestyle can't protect a person from the effects of polluted air, contaminated water, or a nuclear power plant mishap. Environmental health encompasses all the interactions between humans and the environment and the health consequences of these interactions (see the box "Nature and the Human Spirit").

Managed-care plans can save insurers and patients money, but they can also be costly for those who don't follow the plan's rules. The key to getting the most from managed care is knowing how your plan works. The following guidelines can help you work successfully within a managed-care plan.

• *Consider your options.* If you have the option of choosing among several managed-care plans, read through the materials for each. Look especially at the cost of the plan and the types of services covered. What is the copayment for physician visits? How much do prescriptions cost?

• *Investigate.* Talk with a physician who works with each of the plans you're considering. Ask the physician how happy she or he is with the plan. Are there bureaucratic hassles or delays? Find out how approval for treatments and specialist referrals are handled.

• *Know how each plan will affect your current health care situation.* Is your current physician a participant? Will the plan approve the continuation of any current treatments you are receiving, such as a drug regimen for allergies or asthma?

• *Learn the rules of the plan you choose.* Know what payments are required and what the process is for making an appointment or obtaining a referral. Find out what facilities in your area are covered by your plan and what restrictions apply. Know how to obtain care when you're away from home.

• *Choose a physician carefully.* If you will be choosing a new physician when you join a plan, the health plan's office can provide you with information about participating physicians; in addition, ask your friends, family, and colleagues for recommendations. Schedule an initial examination; don't wait until you're ill to see your physician for the first time.

• *Take advantage of wellness programs.* Find out what types of lifestyle management and wellness programs your managed-care plan offers. In addition to programs for losing weight, quitting smoking, and reducing stress, your plan may offer discounts on health club memberships, eyeglass frames, and other such items. Take full advantage of opportunities to make positive changes in your lifestyle.

• *Speak up if you're not happy.* If you're not satisfied with the care you receive, or if you don't get an appointment or a referral when you think you need one, complain to the plan's administrative office. Also, discuss your problem with your company's benefits manager. Unless your employer hears about problems with a particular plan, the health insurance options you are offered won't change.

SOURCES: How good is your health plan? 1996. *Consumer Reports,* August. Managing your care. 1994. *Harvard Women's Health Watch,* September.

Although environmental health still focuses on such longstanding concerns as clean air and water, food inspection, and waste disposal, in recent years its focus has expanded and become more complex. Many of the health challenges of the twenty-first century will involve protecting the environment from the by-products of human activity. Technological advances and rapid population growth have increased the ability of humans to affect and damage the environment. Water supplies are being depleted; landfills are filling up with paper trash, disposable diapers, and plastic packaging; toxic wastes threaten to contaminate both soil and water; and air pollution may be altering the Earth's atmosphere and climate. Today there is a growing recognition that we hold the world in trust for future generations and for other forms of life. Our responsibility is to pass on an environment no worse—and preferably better—than the one we enjoy today.

Population Growth

The rapid expansion of the human population, particularly during the past 50 years, is generally believed to be responsible for most of the stress humans put on the environment. At the beginning of the first century A.D., there were about 200 million people alive. By the seventeenth century, world population had gradually increased to 500 million. But then it started to rise exponentially, increasing to 1 billion by about 1830, to 2 billion by 1930, to 4 billion by 1975, to 5 billion by 1987, and to 6 billion by 1999. The United Nations now projects that world population will grow to 9.4 billion in 2050 and 10.4 billion in 2100 and will stabilize at slightly under 11 billion in about 2200. Most of this growth will take place in the developing world, where population growth rates remain high. With so many people consuming and competing for the Earth's resources, it is difficult for societies to provide such basics as clean air and water and to work toward a better environment.

Although population trends are difficult to influence, many countries recognize the importance of population management. A key goal of population management is to improve the conditions of people's lives so they feel less pressure to have large families. Research indicates that improved health, better education, and increased opportunities for women work together with family planning to cut fertility rates and uncontrolled population growth.

Pollution

Many modern environmental problems are problems of pollution—contaminants in the environment that may pose a health risk. Air pollution is not a human invention—it can be caused by a forest fire, a dust storm, a pollen bloom, or the eruption of a volcano—but it is magnified by human activities, particularly the burning of fossil fuels like coal and gasoline. Air pollution can cause illness and death if pollutants become concentrated for a period of several days or weeks. Increased amounts of carbon monoxide and other pollutants and decreased amounts of oxygen in the air put extra strain on people suffering from heart or respiratory illnesses.

Three atmospheric problems have surfaced in recent years that may have long-range effects on human health.

The Greenhouse Effect, or Global Warming
This is a gradual raising of the temperature of the lower atmosphere of the Earth. Warming occurs as a result of the burning of fossil fuels, which releases "greenhouse gases." Experts predict that temperatures on Earth will increase by 1–7°F over the next 75 years, a change that could melt polar ice caps, raise the level of the sea, and change weather patterns. The health implications of such an increase are unknown.

Thinning of the Ozone Layer
Ozone depletion in the Earth's atmosphere is occurring primarily as a result of the release of chlorofluorocarbons (CFCs), industrial chemicals used in coolants, propellants, solvents, and foaming agents. The ozone layer absorbs ultraviolet (UV) radiation from the sun. If this layer becomes too thin or disappears in spots, increased exposure to UV light may cause more cases of skin cancer, increase the incidence of cataracts and blindness, and impair immune system functioning. It

Recycling paper, cans, bottles, and plastics conserves resources, saves energy, and keeps large amounts of solid wastes out of landfills. Some communities have curbside pickup recycling, while others have drop-off sites.

may also interfere with photosynthesis and cause lower crop yields.

Acid Precipitation
When atmospheric pollutants, most of which are produced by coal-burning electric power plants, combine with moisture in the air, they fall to Earth as highly acidic rain or snow. Acid precipitation has damaged trees and aquatic life in many parts of the world, including the northeastern United States, Canada, and northern Europe.

Other forms of pollution pose problems as well. Chemical substances, including lead, asbestos, pesticides, and hundreds of other products, can cause illness and death. Radiation, whether from the sun, X rays, nuclear power plants, or other sources, can cause cancer, chromosome damage, sterility, and other health problems.

- Ride your bike, walk, use public transportation, or carpool in a fuel-efficient vehicle instead of driving.

- Keep your car tuned up and well maintained.

- Make sure your residence is well insulated.

- Use compact fluorescent light bulbs instead of incandescent bulbs to save energy.

- Buy energy-efficient appliances, and use them only when necessary.

- Run the washing machine or dishwasher only when they have full loads.

- Buy products with the least amount of packaging you can, or buy products in bulk. Avoid disposable products. Buy recycled or recyclable products.

- Recycle newspapers, glass, cans, paper, and other recyclable items.

- Store food in glass jars and reusable plastic containers rather than plastic wrap.

- Take your own bag along when you go shopping.

- Dispose of household hazardous wastes according to instructions.

- Take showers rather than baths to save water.

- Install sink faucet aerators, water-efficient showerheads, and water-displacement devices in toilets.

- Don't let the water run when you're brushing your teeth, shaving, or hand-washing clothes.

- Buy products and services from environmentally responsible corporations. Don't buy products made from endangered species.

- Join or support organizations working on environmental causes.

- Vote for political candidates who support environmentally sound practices. Communicate with your elected representatives about environmental issues.

Even noise pollution—loud or persistent noise in the environment—can cause hearing loss and stress.

What Can You Do?

Faced with an array of complex and confusing environmental issues, you may feel overwhelmed and conclude that there isn't anything you can do. This isn't true. People can take many actions to limit their negative impact on the environment and to promote environmentally sound practices in the social and political arenas. If everyone made individual changes in his or her life, the impact would be tremendous. Refer to the box "What You Can Do for the Environment" for actions you can take.

Assuming responsibility for your actions in relation to the environment isn't very different from assuming responsibility for your own health behaviors. It involves knowledge, awareness, insight, motivation, and commitment. The same strategies that work to change personal health behaviors can be used to change environment-related behaviors.

FIT AND WELL FOR LIFE

Adopting a wellness lifestyle is the most important thing you can do to ensure a high quality of life for yourself, now and in the future. The first chapter of this book described a behavior change program that can be used to change problem behaviors and move toward wellness. Subsequent chapters have provided information on im-

portant areas of wellness—physical fitness, nutrition, weight management, stress management, cardiovascular health, cancer, substance use and abuse, and sexually transmitted diseases. As you learned about these aspects of wellness and assessed your own status in relation to each of them, you probably identified personal behaviors that fell short of the ideal. Take the opportunity now (if you haven't already) to consider which of these behaviors you can begin to change. As you do so, let's review the basics of behavior change.

- Choose one behavior to change at a time. Begin with something simple.

- Make sure your motivation and commitment are sufficient to carry you through to success. If they're not, review the health consequences of *not* changing this behavior.

- Follow the five-step program outlined in Chapter 1: (1) monitor your behavior and gather data; (2) analyze the data and identify patterns; (3) set specific goals; (4) devise a strategy and put it into action; (5) make a personal contract. The Behavior Change Workbook at the end of the text contains a blank contract and program plan, which you can adapt to fit most behavior change programs.

- Build rewards into the plan.

- Make sure the new behavior is enjoyable and fits into your routine.

- Get support from family and friends.

- Forgive yourself when you slip. Don't blame yourself or others or undermine yourself by feeling guilty.

- Expect to succeed. Use positive self-talk to create a new self-image—one that includes your new behavior.

You live in a world in which your own choices and actions have a tremendous impact on your health. Don't let the broad scope of wellness be an excuse for apathy; instead, let it be a call to action. The time to start making changes in *your* lifestyle—to start becoming fit and well—is right now!

SUMMARY

- A wellness lifestyle includes healthy interpersonal relationships, an ability to meet the challenges of aging, knowledge of the health care system, and an understanding of environmental issues.

- Individual and social needs are fulfilled by interpersonal relationships. Self-esteem, trust, and communication skills are the essential elements for building and maintaining good relationships.

- Friendships are characterized by companionship, respect, acceptance, help, trust, loyalty, and reciprocity.

- Intimate love relationships encompass love, sex, and long-term commitment. Passion normally decreases with time and is replaced by closeness, caring, shared goals, and family activities.

- Communication skills and conflict resolution are especially important to successful relationships.

- Strong families are characterized by commitment, appreciation, communication, time spent together, spiritual wellness, and the ability to cope with stress and crisis.

- Many of the changes associated with aging are the result of an unhealthy lifestyle. There are many things that people can do to prevent, delay, lessen, or reverse these changes.

- Managing one's own health care involves identifying and managing medical problems and making the best use of the existing health care system.

- Self-care means knowing which symptoms need professional attention and understanding how to self-treat responsibly, with or without over-the-counter and prescription drugs.

- The best use of the health care system requires good communication with physicians and getting regular medical screenings.

- Today's environmental health challenges include protecting the environment from the by-products of human activity. Overpopulation contributes to environmental problems, as do the greenhouse effect, depletion of the ozone layer, and acid precipitation—all results of human activities. Individual actions to minimize negative environmental effects can have a tremendous impact.

FOR MORE INFORMATION

Books

Columbia University Health Education Program. 1998. *The "Go Ask Alice" Book of Answers: A Guide to Good Physical, Sexual, and Emotional Health.* New York: Owl. *Provides information in a question-and-answer format as well as lists of additional resources; based on the "Go Ask Alice" Web site.*

Consumer Guide, ed. 1998. *Family Health and Medical Guide.* New York: Signet. *Provides information to help consumers take an active part in their own health care.*

Kausler, D. H., and B. C. Kausler. 1996. *The Graying of America: An Encyclopedia of Aging, Health, Mind and Behavior.* Urbana-Champaign, Ill.: University of Illinois Press. *Provides a variety of information about the mental, physical, behavioral, and social aspects of aging.*

Lerner, H. 1997. *Life Preservers: Staying Afloat in Love and Life.* New York: Harper Collins. *Sound advice from a well-known psychologist.*

McKay, M., M. Davis, and P. Fanning. 1997. *How to Communicate: The Ultimate Guide to Improving Your Personal and Professional Relationships.* New York: Fine Communications. *Practical suggestions for improving communication.*

Moeller, D. W. 1997. *Environmental Health.* Rev. ed. Cambridge, Mass.: Harvard University Press. *A survey text by a Harvard professor who has taught environmental health for 25 years.*

Rowe, J., and R. Kahn. 1998. *Successful Aging.* New York: Pantheon Books. *Describes a lifestyle for successful aging.*

Schwartzberg, J. E., and S. Margen. 1998. *The U.C. Berkeley Wellness Self-Care Handbook: The Everyday Guide to Home Remedies.* New York: Rebus. *A helpful guide to self-care.*

Strong, B., C. DeVault, and B. Sayad. 1999. *Human Sexuality*, 3d ed. Mountain View, Calif.: Mayfield. *A comprehensive, up-to-date textbook covering all aspects of love, intimacy, and sexuality.*

World Health Organization. 1997. *Health and Environment in Sustainable Development: Five Years After the Earth Summit.* Geneva: World Health Organization. *Provides a current assessment of the state of environmental degradation, its root causes, and the specific consequences for human health.*

Organizations, Hotlines, and Web Sites

American Association of Retired Persons (AARP). Provides information on all aspects of aging, including health promotion, health care, and retirement planning.
   800-424-2277
   http://www.aarp.org

American Medical Association (AMA). Provides information about physicians, including their training, licensure, and board certification; the Web site provides recent medical news, advice for consumers, and links to related sites.
   312-464-5000
   http://www.ama-assn.org

The Earth Times. An international online newspaper devoted to global environmental issues.
   http://www.earthtimes.org

Electronic Policy Network Idea Central/Health Policy Page. A "virtual" magazine with articles on managed care, the uninsured, the future of Medicare, and other issues.

    http://www.epn.org/idea/health.html

Go Ask Alice. Professional and peer educators provide answers to questions on many topics relating to interpersonal relationships and communication.

    http://www.goaskalice.columbia.edu

National Safety Council Environmental Health Center. Provides information on lead, radon, indoor air quality, hazardous chemicals, and other environmental issues.

    800-55-RADON (Radon Hotline)

    http://www.nsc.org/ehc.htm

Student Environmental Action Coalition (SEAC). A coalition of student and youth environmental groups; Web site has contact information for local groups.

    215-222-4711

    http://www.seac.org

U.S. Administration on Aging. Provides fact sheets, statistical information, and Internet links to other resources on aging.

    202-619-7501

    http://www.aoa.dhhs.gov

U.S. Food and Drug Administration. Provides information on FDA activities and publishes *FDA Consumer magazine,* which frequently includes helpful strategies for evaluating health products and services.

    800-532-4440

    http://www.fda.gov

There are many national and international organizations working on environmental health problems. A few of the largest and best known are listed below.

Greenpeace

    202-462-1177

    http://www.greenpeace.org

National Wildlife Federation

    800-822-9919

    http://www.nwf.org

Nature Conservancy

    703-841-5300

    http://www.tnc.org

Sierra Club

    415-977-5500

    http://www.sierraclub.org

SELECTED BIBLIOGRAPHY

Agency for Health Care and Policy Research. 1997. *Choosing and Using A Health Plan* (retrieved June 27, 1997; http://www.ahcpr.gov:80/consumer/hlthpln1.htm).

Brown, S., and A. Booth. 1996. Cohabitation versus marriage: A comparison of relationship quality. *Journal of Marriage and the Family* 58:668–678.

Burnett, R. T., et al. 1997. Association between ozone and hospitalization for respiratory diseases in 16 Canadian cities. *Environmental Research* 72:24–31.

Constanza, R., et al. 1997. The value of the world's ecosystem services and natural capital. *Nature* 387(6230): 253–260.

Gordon, G. H., L. Baker, and W. Levinson. 1995. Physician-patient communication in managed care. *Western Journal of Medicine* 163(6): 527–531.

Hartup, W. 1995. The three faces of friendship. *Journal of Social and Personal Relationships* 12(4): 569–574.

Klein, R., B. E. Klein, and S. E. Moss. 1998. Relation of smoking to the incidence of age-related maculopathy. *American Journal of Epidemiology* 147(2): 103–110.

Lydon, J. E., D. W. Jamieson, and J. G. Holmes. 1997. The meaning of social interactions in the transition from acquaintanceship to friendship. *Journal of Personality and Social Psychology* 73(3): 536–548.

Morrison, T. L., B. L. Goodlin-Jones, and A. J. Urquiza. 1997. Attachment and the representation of intimate relationships in adulthood. *Journal of Psychology* 131(1): 57–71.

Olson, D., and J. DeFrain. 1997. *Marriage and the Family,* 2d ed. Mountain View, Calif.: Mayfield.

Rice, F. P. 1999. *Intimate Relationships, Marriages, and Families,* 4th ed. Mountain View, Calif.: Mayfield.

Roter, D. L., et al. 1997. Communication patterns of primary care physicians. *Journal of the American Medical Association* 277:350–356.

Russell, J., et al. 1996. Satellite confirmation of the dominance of chlorofluorocarbons in the global stratospheric chlorine budget. *Nature,* 8 February.

Shephard, R. J. 1995. Physical activity, health, and well-being at different life stages. *Research Quarterly for Exercise and Sport* 66:298–302.

Swan, G. E., and D. Carmelli. 1996. Curiosity and mortality in aging adults: A 5-year follow-up of the Western Collaborative Group Study. *Psychology and Aging* 11(3): 449–453.

Tanaka, H., C. A. DeSouza, and D. R. Seals. 1998. Absence of age-related increase in central arterial stiffness in physically active women. *Arteriosclerosis, Thrombosis and Vascular Biology* 18(1): 127–132.

Thoms, D. H., and B. Campbell. 1997. Patient-physician trust: An exploratory study. *Journal of Family Practice* 44:169–176.

Tseng, B. S., et al. 1995. Strength and aerobic training attenuate muscle wasting and improve resistance to the development of disability with aging. *Journal of Gerontology. Series A: Biological Sciences and Medical Sciences* 50:113–119.

United Nations. Population Division of the Department of Economic and Social Affairs. 1998. *World Population Projections to 2150* (retrieved March 6, 1998; http://www.undp.org/popin/wdtrends/execsum.htm).

Wallerstein, J. S. 1996. The psychological tasks of marriage. *American Journal of Orthopsychiatry* 66(2): 217–227.

LAB 15-1 *Wellness Profile*

Now that you've had an opportunity to examine your wellness-related behaviors in detail, consider how your lifestyle, attitudes, and characteristics relate to each of the six dimensions of wellness. Fill in your strengths for each dimension (examples of strengths are listed with each dimension).

Physical wellness: To maintain overall physical health and engage in appropriate physical activity (e.g., stamina, strength, flexibility, healthy body composition).

_____

_____

_____

Emotional wellness: To have a positive self-concept, deal constructively with your feelings, and develop positive qualities (e.g., optimism, trust, self-confidence, determination, persistence, dedication).

_____

_____

_____

Intellectual wellness: To pursue and retain knowledge, think critically about issues, make sound decisions, identify problems, and find solutions (e.g., common sense, creativity, curiosity).

_____

_____

_____

Spiritual wellness: To develop a set of beliefs, principles, or values that give meaning or purpose to one's life; to develop faith in something beyond oneself (e.g., religious faith, service to others).

_____

_____

_____

Interpersonal/social wellness: To develop and maintain meaningful relationships with a network of friends and family members, and to contribute to the community (e.g., friendly, good-natured, compassionate, supportive, good listener).

_____

_____

_____

Environmental wellness: To protect yourself from environmental hazards, and to minimize the negative impact of your behavior on the environment (e.g., carpooling, recycling).

_____

_____

_____

Next, choose what you believe are your five most important strengths, and record them below.

Core Wellness Strengths

1. _____

2. _____

3. _____

4. _____

5. _____

Finally, mark on the continuums where you think you fall for each dimension.

Low Level of Wellness	Physical, Psychological, Emotional Symptoms	Change and Growth	High Level of Wellness

← ─── →

Physical wellness

← ─── →

Emotional wellness

← ─── →

Intellectual wellness

← ─── →

Spiritual wellness

← ─── →

Interpersonal/social wellness

← ─── →

Environmental wellness

SOURCE: Insel, P. M., and W. T. Roth. 1998. Wellness Worksheet 4. *Core Concepts in Health,* 8th ed. Mountain View, Calif.: Mayfield.

Injury Prevention and Personal Safety

Injuries are the fifth leading cause of death among Americans overall and the leading killer of young people. Injuries affect all segments of the population, but they are particularly common among minorities and people with low income, primarily due to social, environmental, and economic factors. The economic cost of injuries in the United States last year alone was over $400 billion.

Injuries are generally classified into four categories, based on where they occur: motor vehicle injuries, home injuries, work injuries, and leisure injuries. The greatest number of deaths occur in motor vehicle crashes, but the greatest number of disabling injuries occur in the home.

MOTOR VEHICLE INJURIES

Incidents involving motor vehicles are the most common cause of death for people under age 45, the most common cause of paralysis due to spinal injury, and the leading cause of severe brain injury.

Nearly two-thirds of all motor vehicle injuries are caused by bad driving, especially speeding. As speed increases, momentum and force of impact increase and the time allowed for the driver to react (reaction time) decreases. Speed limits are posted to establish the safest *maximum* speed limit for a given area under *ideal* conditions. Anything that distracts a driver—sleepiness, bad mood, children or pets in the car, use of a cellular phone—can increase the risk of having a collision.

A second factor contributing to injury and death in motor vehicle collisions is failure to wear a safety belt. A person who doesn't wear a safety belt is twice as likely to be injured in a crash as a person who does wear a safety belt. Safety belts not only prevent the individual from being thrown from the car at the time of the crash but also provide protection from the "second collision," which occurs when the occupant of the car hits something inside the car, such as the steering column, dashboard, or windshield. The safety belt also spreads the stopping force of the collision over the body.

Since 1998, all new cars have been equipped with dual air bags—one for the driver and one for the front passenger seat. Although air bags provide some supplemental protection in the event of a collision, most are useful only in head-on collisions. They also deflate immediately after inflating and therefore do not provide protection in collisions involving multiple impacts. To ensure that air bags work as intended, always follow these basic guidelines: place infants in rear-facing infant seats in the back seat; transport children age 12 and under in the back seat; always use safety belts or appropriate safety seats; and keep 10 inches between the air bag cover and the breastbone of the driver or passenger. In the rare event that a person cannot comply with these guidelines, permission to install an on-off switch that temporarily disables the air bag can be applied for from the National Highway Traffic Safety Administration.

A third common factor in motor vehicle injuries is alcohol; it is involved in about half of all fatal crashes. Alcohol-impaired driving, defined by blood alcohol concentration (BAC), is illegal. The legal BAC limit varies from 0.08% to 0.10%, but driving ability is impaired at much lower BACs. All psychoactive drugs have the potential to impair driving ability.

About 75% of all motor vehicle collisions occur within 25 miles of home and at speeds lower than 40 mph. These crashes often occur because the driver believes safety measures are not necessary for short trips. Clearly, the statistics prove otherwise.

To prevent motor vehicle injuries:

- Obey the speed limit. If you have to speed to get to your destination on time, you're not allowing enough time. Try leaving 10–15 minutes earlier.

- Always wear a safety belt. Strap infants and toddlers into government-approved car seats in the back seat of the vehicle. Never hold a child in your lap while a car is moving.

- Never drive under the influence of alcohol or other drugs. Never ride with a driver who has been drinking or using drugs.

- Keep your car in good working order. Regularly inspect tires, oil and fluid levels, windshield wipers, spare tire, and so on.

- Always allow enough following distance. Follow the "3-second rule": When the vehicle ahead passes a reference point, count out 3 seconds. If you pass the reference point before you finish counting, drop back and allow more following distance.

- Always increase following distance and slow down if weather or road conditions are poor.
- Choose interstate highways rather than rural roads. Highways are much safer because of better visibility, wider lanes, fewer surprises, and other factors.
- Always signal when turning or changing lanes.
- Stop completely at stop signs. Follow all traffic laws.
- Take special care at intersections. Always look left, right, and then left again. Make sure you have plenty of time to complete your maneuver in the intersection.
- Don't pass on two-lane roads unless you're in a designated passing area and have a clear view ahead.

Motorcycle and Moped Injuries

About one out of every ten traffic fatalities among people age 15–34 involves someone riding a motorcycle. Injuries from motorcycle collisions are generally more severe than those involving automobiles because motorcycles provide little, if any, protection. Moped riders face additional challenges. Mopeds usually have a maximum speed of 30–35 mph and have less power for maneuverability.

To prevent motorcycle and moped injuries:

- Always wear a helmet.
- Wear eye protection in the form of goggles, a face shield, or a windshield.
- Maximize your visibility by wearing light-colored clothing, driving with your headlights on, and correctly positioning yourself in traffic.
- Develop the skills necessary to operate the vehicle; operator error is a contributing factor in 75% of fatal crashes involving motorcycles. Skidding from improper braking is the most common cause of loss of control.
- Drive defensively, and never assume that you've been seen by other drivers.

Pedestrian and Bicycle Injuries

Injuries to pedestrians and bicyclists are considered motor vehicle–related because they are usually caused by motor vehicles. About one-seventh of all motor vehicle deaths each year involve pedestrians; almost 90,000 pedestrians are injured each year. In most injuries, poor decision making is the crucial factor, not the traffic situation itself.

To prevent injuries when walking or jogging:

- Walk or jog in daylight.
- Maximize your visibility by wearing light-colored, reflective clothing.
- Face traffic when walking or jogging along a roadway, and follow traffic laws.

- Avoid busy roads or roads with poor visibility.
- Cross only at marked crosswalks and intersections.
- Don't listen to a radio or tape on headphones while walking.
- Don't hitchhike; it places you in a potentially dangerous situation.

Bicycle injuries result primarily from not knowing or understanding the rules of the road, failing to follow traffic laws, and not having sufficient skill or experience to handle traffic conditions. *Bicycles are considered vehicles; bicycle riders must obey all traffic laws that apply to automobile drivers, including stopping at traffic lights and stop signs.*

To prevent injuries when riding a bike:

- Wear a helmet. Three out of four cyclists killed in crashes die as a result of head injuries. The brain is very sensitive to any impact, even at low speeds. Since 1999, all bike helmets sold in the United States have met federal safety standards established by the U.S. Consumer Product Safety Commission. These standards ensure that helmets adequately protect the head and that chin straps are strong enough to prevent the helmet from coming off during a fall or crash.
- Wear other safety equipment, including eye protection, proper footwear, and gloves. Secure your pants with clips, and secure your shoelaces so they don't get tangled in the chain.
- Maximize your visibility by wearing light-colored, reflective clothing. Make sure your bicycle is equipped with reflectors. Use lights, especially at night or when riding in wooded or other dark areas.
- Ride with the flow of traffic, not against it, and follow traffic laws. Use bike paths when they are available.
- Ride defensively; never assume that drivers have seen you. Be especially careful when turning or crossing at corners and intersections. Watch for cars turning right.
- Know and use hand signals. Look around and signal before turning.
- Stop at all traffic lights and stop signs.
- Continue pedaling at all times to help keep the bike stable and to maintain your balance.
- Properly maintain the working condition of your bike.

HOME INJURIES

Contrary to popular belief, home is one of the most dangerous places to be. The most common fatal home injuries are caused by falls, fires, poisoning, and incidents involving firearms.

Falls

Falls are second only to motor vehicle injuries in terms of causing deaths. They are the fifth leading cause of unintentional death for people under age 25. Nearly two-thirds of the deaths occurring from falls are from falls at floor level (tripping, slipping, and so on) rather than from a height. Alcohol is a contributing factor in many falls.

To prevent injuries from falls:

- Place skidproof backing on rugs and carpets.
- Install handrails and nonslip applications in the shower and bathtub.
- Keep floors clear of objects or conditions that could cause slipping or tripping, such as heavy wax coating, electrical cords, and toys.
- Put a light switch by the door of every room so that no one has to walk across a room to turn on a light. Use night lights in bedrooms, halls, and bathrooms.
- Outside the house, clear dangerous surfaces created by ice, snow, fallen leaves, or rough ground.
- Install handrails on stairs. Keep stairs well lit and clear of objects.
- When climbing a ladder, use both hands. Never stand higher than the third step from the top. When using a stepladder, make sure the spreader brace is in the locked position.
- If there are small children in the home, place gates at the top and bottom of stairs. Never leave a baby unattended on a bed or table.

Fires

Each year about 80% of fire deaths and 65% of fire injuries occur in the home. Most home fires begin in the kitchen, living room, or bedroom. Many are caused by careless actions such as smoking in bed or leaving a cigarette burning in an ashtray.

To prevent fires:

- Dispose of all cigarettes in ashtrays. Never smoke in bed.
- Do not overload electrical outlets.
- Do not place extension cords under rugs or where people walk. Replace worn or frayed extension cords.
- Place a wire screen in front of fireplaces and wood stoves. Remove ashes carefully and store them in airtight metal containers, not paper bags.
- Properly maintain electrical appliances, kerosene heaters, and furnaces, and clean flues and chimneys annually.
- Keep portable heaters at least 3 feet away from curtains, bedding, towels, or anything that might catch fire. Never leave heaters on when you're out of the room or sleeping.

To be prepared for a fire:

- Plan at least two escape routes out of each room. Designate a location outside the home as a meeting place.
- Install a smoke-detection device on every level of your home. Clean the detectors and test batteries once a month, and replace the batteries at least once a year.
- Keep a fire extinguisher in your home, and know how to use it. Most fire extinguishers are operated by breaking the seal and pulling the pin on the handle, aiming the discharge at the base of the flames, and using a sweeping motion to cover the burning area.

To prevent injuries from fire:

- Get out as quickly as possible and go to the designated meeting place. Don't stop for a keepsake or a pet. Never hide in a closet or under a bed. Once outside, count heads to see if everyone is out. If you think someone is still inside the burning building, tell the firefighters. Never go back inside a burning building.
- If you're trapped in a room, feel the door. If it is hot, or if smoke is coming in through the cracks, don't open it; use the alternative escape route. If you can't get out of a room, go to the window and shout or wave for help.
- Smoke inhalation is the largest cause of death and injury in fires. To avoid inhaling smoke, crawl along the floor away from the heat and smoke. Cover your mouth and nose, ideally with a wet cloth, and take short, shallow breaths.
- If your clothes catch fire, don't run. Drop to the ground, cover your face, and roll back and forth to smother the flames. Remember: stop-drop-roll.

Poisoning

Over 2 million poisonings occur every year, a majority of them among children under age 5.

To prevent poisoning:

- Store all medicines out of the reach of children. Use medicines only as directed on the label or by a physician.
- Use cleaners, pesticides, and other dangerous substances only in areas with proper ventilation. Store them out of the reach of children.
- Never operate a vehicle in an enclosed space, have your furnace inspected yearly, and use caution with any substance that produces potentially toxic fumes, such as kerosene. If appropriate, install carbon monoxide detectors.
- Many common house and garden plants are poisonous if ingested, including azalea, oleander,

rhododendron, wild mushrooms, daffodil and hyacinth bulbs, mistletoe berries, apple seeds, morning glory seeds, wisteria seeds, and the leaves and stems of potato, rhubarb, and tomato plants. Keep these plants out of the reach of young children.

To be prepared in case of poisoning:

- Keep the number of the nearest Poison Control Center (or emergency room) in an accessible location.
- Keep a bottle of syrup of ipecac (this induces vomiting) on hand.

Emergency first aid for poisonings:

1. Remove the poison from contact with eyes, skin, or mouth, or remove the victim from contact with poisonous fumes or gases.

2. Do not follow emergency instructions on labels. Some may be out of date and carry incorrect treatment information.

3. Call the Poison Control Center immediately for instructions. You may be asked the name of the substance and its ingredients; the amount of substance involved; when exposure occurred and how long it lasted; whether any symptoms are present; and characteristics of the person exposed, including name, age, weight, and general health history.

4. If you are instructed to go to an emergency room, take the poisonous substance or container with you.

5. Administer syrup of ipecac to induce vomiting— *but only if advised by the Poison Control Center or a physician.*

Guidelines for specific types of poisonings:

- *Swallowed poisons:* If the person is awake and able to swallow, give water only; then call the Poison Control Center or a physician for advice.
- *Poisons on the skin:* Remove any affected clothing. Flood affected parts of the skin with warm water, wash with soap and water, and rinse. Then call for advice.
- *Poisons in the eye:* For children, flood the eye with lukewarm water poured from a pitcher held 3–4 inches above the eye for 15 minutes; alternatively, irrigate the eye under a faucet. For adults, get in the shower and flood the eye with a gentle stream of lukewarm water for 15 minutes. Then call for advice.
- *Inhaled poisons:* Immediately carry or drag the person to fresh air and, if necessary, give mouth-to-mouth resuscitation. If the victim is not breathing easily, call 9-1-1 for help. Ventilate the area. Then call for advice.

Unintentional Injury from Firearms

Firearms pose a significant threat, especially to people between ages 15 and 24, with most fatalities involving males who are cleaning or handling guns they thought were unloaded.

To prevent firearm injuries:

- Never point a loaded gun at something you do not intend to shoot.
- Store unloaded firearms under lock and key and separately from ammunition.
- Inspect firearms carefully before handling them.
- Follow the safety procedures advocated in firearms safety courses.

Other Home Injuries

Burns, choking, suffocation, and electrocution are other dangers in the home, particularly for small children. Burns are the third leading cause of death in young children (following motor vehicle collisions and drowning). House fires cause the most deaths, but hot water causes the most nonfatal burns. When a burn occurs, cold water should be poured on it immediately to cool the tissue and prevent the burn from going deeper.

To prevent burns in children:

- Place barriers around stoves and radiators, and keep children out of the kitchen where they might be burned by spills.
- Set your hot water heater no higher than 120°F.
- Always test the contents of a baby bottle on the wrist before feeding the baby. When bottles are heated in microwave ovens, the liquid can become scalding before the outside of the bottle gets very hot.
- Unplug and store extension cords when not in use.
- Apply sunscreen to children's skin when they are out in the sun.

To prevent other home injuries:

- Keep small objects out of the reach of children under age 3, and don't give them raw carrots, nuts, popcorn, or hard candy. Inspect toys for small parts that could be put in the mouth. Balloons also pose a serious choking hazard for young children.
- Keep infants away from plastic bags, which can suffocate them, and don't put infants to bed wearing jackets with drawstring hoods, which can strangle them.
- Keep electrical appliances away from a filled tub or sink. Use plastic covers over electrical outlets.

Leisure injuries are defined as those that occur in public places but do not involve a motor vehicle. Most leisure injuries involve recreational activities, such as swimming and boating, playground activities, and sports.

Drowning

Drowning is a special danger for children and for adolescents and adults who are using alcohol. Children under age 5 and people between ages 15 and 24 have the highest rates of death from drowning. Many drownings of children occur in residential pools, often when there is inadequate supervision. Many drownings also occur when people on boats fall overboard. Between one-third and two-thirds of these drownings involve alcohol.

To prevent drowning:

- Develop adequate swimming skills, and make sure children learn to swim.
- Make sure residential pools are fenced and adequately supervised.
- Use caution when swimming in unfamiliar surroundings (such as the ocean) or for an unusual length of time.
- Avoid being chilled by water colder than 70°F.
- Don't swim or boat under the influence of alcohol or other drugs.
- Don't swim alone.
- Check the depth of water before diving.
- When on a boat, use a personal flotation device. The U.S. Coast Guard recommends six different types, keyed to particular water conditions.

Playground Injuries

Over 200,000 injuries occur on school, park, and residential playground equipment every year. Most injuries are the result of falls from equipment to the ground; deaths are usually the result of head injuries.

To prevent playground injuries:

- Make sure equipment and surfaces under equipment comply with safety standards.
- Teach children to use equipment properly.

In-Line Skating Injuries

In-line skating has become a very popular recreational activity among people of all ages. Most injuries occur because users are not familiar with the equipment and do not wear appropriate safety gear. Injuries to the wrist and head are the most common. To reduce your risk of being injured while skating, wear a helmet, elbow and knee pads, wrist guards, a long-sleeved shirt, and long pants.

Sports Injuries

An increase in the number of people exercising to improve their health has brought with it an increase in sports-related injuries.

To prevent sports injuries:

- Develop the skills required for the activity.
- Recognize and guard against the hazards associated with the activity.
- Include appropriate exercises for warming up and cooling down.
- Make sure facilities are safe.
- Follow the rules, and practice good sportsmanship.
- Use proper safety equipment, including, where appropriate, helmets, eye protection, knee and elbow pads and wrist guards, and correct footwear.
- When it is excessively hot and humid, avoid heat stress by following the guidelines given in the box "Exercising in Hot Weather" in Chapter 3.

Many aspects of workplace safety are monitored by the Occupational Safety and Health Administration (OSHA), a federal agency. The highest rate of work-related injuries occurs among laborers, whose jobs usually involve extensive manual labor and lifting—two areas not addressed by OSHA safety standards. Back injuries are the most common work injury.

To protect your back when lifting:

- Don't try to lift beyond your strength. If you need it, get help.
- Get a firm footing, with your feet shoulder-width apart. Get a firm grip on the object.
- Keep your torso in a relatively upright position and crouch down, bending at the knees and hips. Avoid bending at the waist. To lift, stand up or push up with your leg muscles. Lift gradually, keeping your arms straight. Keep the object close to your body.
- Don't twist. If you have to turn with an object, change the position of your feet.
- Plan ahead. Make sure your pathway is clear before you pick up the object.

- Put the object down gently, reversing the rules for lifting.

A new type of work-related injury involves damage to the musculoskeletal system caused by repeated strain on the hand, arm, wrist, or other part of the body. Such injuries and disorders are referred to as repetitive-strain injuries. Carpal tunnel syndrome is one type. It is characterized by pain and swelling in the tendons of the wrists and sometimes numbness and weakness. Its growing incidence is associated with the use of computers.

To prevent carpal tunnel syndrome:

- Maintain good posture at the computer. Use a chair that provides back support, and place the feet flat on the floor or on a foot rest.
- Position the screen at eye level and the keyboard so the hands and wrists are straight.
- Take breaks periodically to lessen the cumulative effects of stress.

VIOLENCE AND INTENTIONAL INJURIES

Violence is emerging as a major public health concern. The United States ranks first among developed nations in the rate of violent death; the number of deaths caused by firearms (intentionally and unintentionally) exceeds the combined total of such deaths in the next 17 nations. Violence includes assault, homicide (murder), sexual assault, domestic violence, suicide, and various forms of abuse. About 2.2 million Americans are victims of violent injury every year.

Assault

Assault is the use of physical force to inflict injury or death on another person. Most assaults occur during arguments or in connection with another crime, such as robbery. Poverty, urban settings, and the use of alcohol and drugs are associated with higher rates of assault.

Homicide is the twelfth leading cause of death in the United States. Homicide victims are most likely to be male, between ages 19 and 24, and members of minority groups. Most homicides are committed with a firearm; the murderer and the victim usually know each other.

To protect yourself at home:

- Secure your home with good lighting and effective locks, preferably deadbolts.
- Make sure that all doors and windows are securely locked. Always lock windows and doors, including sliding glass doors, whenever you go out.
- Get a dog, or post "Beware of Dog" signs.
- Ensure that the landscaping around your home doesn't provide opportunities for concealment.
- Don't hide keys in obvious places. Don't give anyone the chance to duplicate your keys; for example, give only the car key, not your entire set of keys, to a parking attendant.
- Install a peephole in your front door. Don't open your door to people you don't know.
- Don't let strangers into your home or yard. When repair or delivery people or utility workers come to the door, ask to see identification, or call the company to verify that they've sent someone out.
- If you or a family member owns a weapon, store it securely. Store guns and ammunition in separate locations.
- If you are a woman living alone, use your initials rather than your full name in the phone directory. Don't use a greeting on your answering machine that implies you live alone or are not home.
- Teach everyone in the household how to obtain emergency assistance.
- Know your neighbors. Work out a system for alerting each other in case of an emergency.
- Establish a neighborhood watch program.

To protect yourself on the street:

- Avoid walking alone, especially at night. Stay where people can see and hear you.
- Dress sensibly, in clothing that allows you freedom of movement.
- Walk purposefully. Act alert and confident.
- Walk on the outside of the sidewalk, facing traffic.
- Know where you are going. Appearing to be lost increases your vulnerability.
- Don't hitchhike.
- Carry valuables in a fanny pack, pants pocket, or shoulder bag strapped diagonally across the chest. Conceal small purses inside a tote or shopping bag. Keep at least one hand free.
- Always have your keys ready as you approach your vehicle or home.
- Carry enough change so that you can make a telephone call or take public transportation. Carry a whistle to blow if you are attacked or harassed.
- Be aware of suspicious behavior. Listen to your own inner warning signals.
- If possible, allow at least two arm lengths between yourself and a stranger.
- If you feel threatened, run and/or yell. Go into a store or knock on the door of a home. If someone grabs you, yell "Help!" or "Fire!"

To protect yourself in your car:

- Keep your car in good working condition, carry emergency supplies, and keep the gas tank at least half full.
- When driving, keep doors locked and windows rolled up at least three-quarters of the way.
- Park your car in well-lighted areas or parking garages, preferably those with an attendant or a security guard.
- Lock your car when you leave it, and check the interior before opening the door when you return.
- Don't pick up strangers. Don't stop for vehicles in distress; drive on and call for help.
- Note the location of emergency call boxes along highways and in public facilities. If you travel alone frequently, consider investing in a cellular phone.
- If your car breaks down, raise the hood and tie a white cloth to the antenna or door handle. Wait in the car with the doors locked and windows rolled up. If someone approaches to offer help, open a window only a crack and ask the person to call the police or a towing service.
- When you stop at a light or stop sign, leave enough room to maneuver out if you need an escape route.
- If you are involved in a minor automobile crash and you think you have been bumped intentionally, don't leave your car. Motion to the other driver to follow you to the nearest police station. If confronted by a person with a weapon, give up your car.
- Don't get into disputes or arguments with drivers of other vehicles.

To protect yourself on public transportation:

- While waiting, stand in a populated, well-lighted area.
- Sit near the driver or conductor in a single seat or an outside seat.
- If traveling to an unfamiliar location, call the transit agency for the correct route and time. Make sure that the bus, subway, or train is bound for your destination before you board it.
- If you flag down a taxi, ensure that it's from a legitimate service. When you reach your destination, ask the driver to wait until you are safely inside the building.

To protect yourself on campus:

- Ensure that door and window locks are secure and that halls and stairwells have adequate lighting.
- Don't give dorm or residence keys to anybody.
- Don't leave your door unlocked or allow strangers into your room.

- Avoid solitary late-night trips to the library or laundry room. Take advantage of on-campus escort services.
- Don't jog or exercise outside alone at night. Don't take shortcuts across campus that are unfamiliar or seem unsafe.
- If security guards patrol the campus, know the areas they cover, and stay where they can see or hear you.

Sexual Assault, or Rape

Sexual assault, or rape, is sexual coercion that relies on the threat and use of physical force or takes advantage of circumstances that render a person incapable of giving consent (such as when drunk). If the victim is younger than the legally defined age of consent, the act constitutes statutory rape, regardless of whether consent is given. Coerced sexual activity in which the victim knows the rapist is often referred to as date rape or acquaintance rape. At least 3.5 million females are raped annually in the United States, and perhaps 10,000 males are raped each year by other males.

Rape victims suffer both physical and psychological injury. For most, the physical wounds are not severe, but the psychological pain can be substantial and long-lasting. Many victims experience shock, anxiety, depression, shame, and psychosomatic symptoms. These psychological reactions are called rape trauma syndrome; other symptoms include fear, nightmares, fatigue, crying spells, and digestive upset. Self-blame is common, a reaction reinforced by our society's tendency to blame the victim. Fortunately, this tendency is giving way to a more realistic view of the violent nature of rape.

To protect yourself against rape:

- Follow the guidelines listed earlier for protecting yourself against assault.
- Think out in advance what you would do if you were threatened with rape. However, no one knows what he or she will do when scared to death. Trust that you will make the best decision at the time— whether to scream, run, fight, or give in to avoid being injured or killed.

If you are raped:

- Tell what happened to the first friendly person you meet.
- Call the police. Tell them you were raped, and give your location.
- Try to remember everything you can about your attacker, and write it down.
- Don't wash or douche before the medical exam. Don't change your clothes, but bring a new set with you if you can.
- At the hospital you will have a complete exam. Show the physician any bruises or scratches.

- Tell the police exactly what happened. Be honest, and stick to your story.
- If you do not want to report the rape to the police, see a physician as soon as possible. Be sure you are checked for pregnancy and STDs.
- Contact an organization with skilled counselors so you can talk about the experience. Look in the telephone directory under "Rape" or "Rape Crisis Center" for a hotline number.

Date Rape

Most women are in much less danger of being raped by a stranger than of being sexually assaulted by a man they know or date. Surveys suggest that as many as one woman in four has had sex forced on her by a man she knew or was dating. Victims of date rape tend to shoulder much of the responsibility for the incident, questioning their own judgment rather than blaming the aggressor.

One factor in date rape appears to be the double standard about appropriate sexual behavior for men and women. It is still a cultural belief in our society that "nice" women don't say yes to sex, even when they want to, and that "real" men don't take no for an answer. There are also widespread differences between men and women in how romantic signals are perceived. Researchers in one study found that men tend to interpret women's actions on dates, such as smiling or talking in a low voice, as indicating an interest in having sex, while the women interpret the same actions as being "friendly." Men who rape their dates also tend to have certain characteristics, including hostility toward women and an acceptance of sexual violence. Both men and women must take responsibility for reducing the incidence of rape.

To protect yourself from date rape:

- Believe in your right to control what you do. Set limits and communicate them clearly, firmly, and early. Be assertive; men often interpret passivity as permission.
- Remember that some men think flirtatious behavior or sexy clothing indicates an interest in having sex.
- If you are unsure of a new acquaintance, go on a group date or double date. If possible, provide your own transportation.
- Remember that alcohol and drugs interfere with judgment, perception, and communication about sex.
- Use the statement that has proven most effective in stopping date rape: "This is rape and I'm calling the cops!"

Guidelines for men:

- Be aware of social pressure. It's OK not to "score."
- Understand that "No" means "No." Stop making advances when your date says to stop. Remember that she has the right to refuse sex.

- Don't assume that flirtatious behavior or sexy clothing means a woman is interested in having sex, that previous permission for sex applies to the current situation, or that your date's relationships with other men constitute sexual permission for you.
- Remember that alcohol and drugs interfere with judgment, perception, and communication about sex.

PROVIDING EMERGENCY CARE

You can improve someone else's chances of surviving if you are prepared to provide emergency help. A course in first aid, offered by the American Red Cross and on many college campuses, can teach you to respond appropriately when someone needs help.

Emergency rescue techniques can save the lives of people who have stopped breathing, who are choking, or whose hearts have stopped beating. Pulmonary resuscitation (also known as rescue breathing, artificial respiration, or mouth-to-mouth resuscitation) is used when a person is not breathing (Figure A-1). Cardiopulmonary resuscitation (CPR) is used when a pulse can't be found. Training is required before a person can perform CPR. Courses are offered by the American Red Cross and the American Heart Association.

Many choking victims can be saved with the Heimlich maneuver (also called abdominal thrusts). For instructions on performing this maneuver, see Figure A-1. Blows to the upper back in conjunction with chest thrusts are an acceptable way to dislodge an object from an infant's throat.

When you have to provide emergency care:

- Remain calm, and act sensibly. The basic pattern for providing emergency care is check-call-care.
- *Check the situation:* Make sure the scene is safe for both you and the injured person. Don't put yourself in danger; if you get hurt too, you will be of little help to the injured person.
- *Check the victim:* Conduct a quick head-to-toe examination. Assess the victim's signs and symptoms, such as level of responsiveness, pulse, and breathing rate. Look for bleeding and any indications of broken bones or paralysis.
- *Call for help:* Call 9-1-1 or a local emergency number. Identify yourself and give as much information as you can about the condition of the victim and what happened.
- *Care for the victim:* If the situation requires immediate action (no pulse, shock, etc.), provide first aid if you are trained to do so. Figure A-1 illustrates basic first aid for several types of emergency situations.

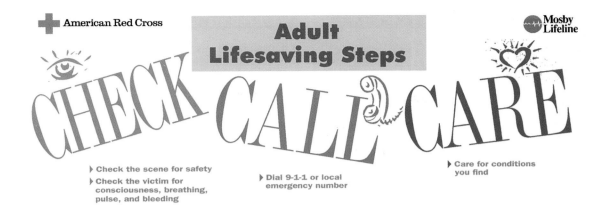

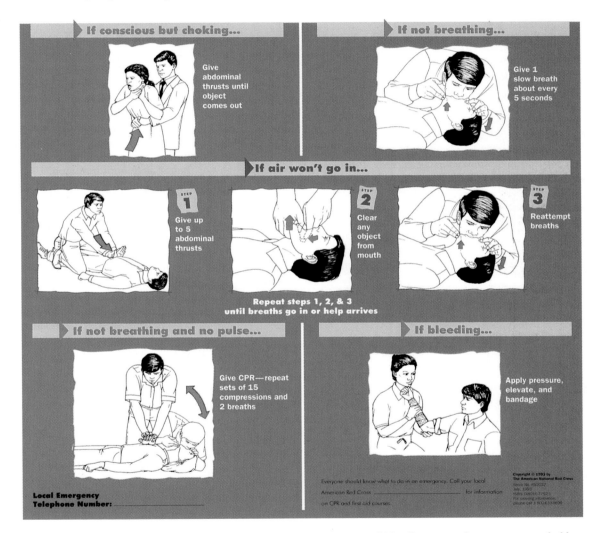

Figure A-1 Rescue breathing, first aid for choking, and ways to control bleeding; procedures recommended by the American Red Cross.

FOR MORE INFORMATION

Books

American Red Cross. 1996. *First Aid: Responding to Emergencies,* 2nd ed. St. Louis, Mo.: Year Book Medical. *Provides current, straightforward information.*

Bever, D. L. 1996. *Safety: A Personal Focus,* 4th ed. New York: McGraw-Hill. *An overview of injury prevention, including automobile, fire, and recreational safety.*

Lipman, I. A. 1997. *How to Protect Yourself from Crime.* Pleasantville, N.Y.: Reader's Digest. *Provides advice to help you be safer at home, on the road, at work, and on vacation.*

Mufson, S., and R. Kranz. 1997. *Straight Talk About Date Rape.* New York: Facts on File. *Provides information about date rape, including strategies for prevention and suggestions for how victims can get help.*

Organizations, Hotlines, and Web Sites

American Automobile Association Foundation for Traffic Safety. Promotes research and provides consumer information, including brochures and videos about all aspects of traffic safety; Web site has links to many related sites.
> 800-305-SAFE
> http://www.aaafts.org

CDC National Center for Injury Prevention and Control. Provides consumer-oriented information about preventing unintentional injuries and violence.
> 770-488-1506 (automated information line)
> http://www.cdc.gov/ncipc/ncipchm.htm

National Highway Traffic Safety Administration. Supplies materials about reducing death, injuries, and economic losses from motor vehicle crashes, including safety test and recall information.
> 800-424-9393
> http://www.nhtsa.dot.gov

National Safety Council. Provides information and statistics about preventing unintentional injuries.
> 630-285-1121
> http://www.nsc.org

National Violence Hotlines. Provide information, referral services, and crisis intervention.
> 800-222-2000 (family violence); 800-799-SAFE (domestic violence); 800-422-4453 (child abuse)

SELECTED BIBLIOGRAPHY

American Red Cross Staff. 1996. *Community First Aid and Safety.* St. Louis, Mo.: Mosby-Year Book.

Bayne, C. G. 1997. Falling: Why and what to do about it. *Nursing Management* 28:22–23.

Bicycle Helmet Safety Institute. 1998. *Bicycle Helmet Pamphlet* (retrieved March 10, 1998; http://www.helmets.org/webdocs/guide.htm).

Centers for Disease Control and Prevention. 1997. Rates of homicide, suicide, and firearm-related death among children—26 industrialized countries. *Morbidity and Mortality Weekly Report* 46:101–105.

Dobrin, A., et al., eds. 1996. *Statistical Handbook on Violence in America.* Phoenix, Ariz.: Oryx Press.

Jaffe, M. S., M. P. Dijkers, and M. Zametis. 1997. A population-based survey of in-line skaters' injuries and skating practices. *Archives of Physical Medicine and Rehabilitation* 78:1352–1357.

Mallonee, S., et al. 1996. Surveillance and prevention of residential-fire injuries. *New England Journal of Medicine* 335: 27–31.

National Center for Injury Prevention and Control. 1998. *Fact Sheet: Pedestrian Deaths and Injuries* (retrieved March 10, 1998; http://www.cdc.gov/ncipc/duip/pedes.htm).

National Highway Traffic Safety Administration. 1997. *Air Bags and On-Off Switches: Information for an Informed Decision* (retrieved March 10, 1998; http://www.nhtsa.dot.gov/airbags/brochure).

National Safety Council. 1997. *Accident Facts, 1997 Edition.* Itasca, Ill.: National Safety Council.

Redelmeier, D. A., and R. J. Tibshirani. 1997. Association between cellular telephone calls and motor vehicle collisions. *New England Journal of Medicine* 336(7): 453–458.

Sinaver, N., J. L. Annest, and J. A. Mercy. 1996. Unintentional, nonfatal firearm-related injuries: A preventable public health burden. *Journal of the American Medical Association* 277(22): 1740–1743.

U.S. Consumer Product Safety Commission (CPSC). 1998. *Press Release: CPSC Issues New Safety Standards for Bike Helmets* (retrieved April 13, 1998; http://www.cpsc.gov/gophroot/pre%5Frel/pre%5Frel/98%5Fpre/98062.txt).

Nutritional Content of Common Foods

This food composition table has been prepared for Mayfield Publishing Company and is copyrighted by DINE Systems, Inc., the developer and publisher of the DINE System family of nutrition software for personal computers. The values in this food composition table were derived from the USDA Nutrient Data Base for Standard Reference Release 10 and nutrient composition information from over 300 food companies. Nutrient values used for each food were determined by collapsing similar foods into one food, using the median nutrient values. In the food composition table, foods are listed within the following eight groups: fruits, vegetables, beverages, alcoholic beverages, grains, dairy, fats/sweets/other, and protein foods. Further information can be obtained from DINE Systems, Inc., 586 N. French Road, Amherst, NY 14228, 716-688-2492, 716-688-2505 fax. SOURCE: © 1994 Dine Systems, Inc.

Order of fields: Name, Amount/Unit, Calories, Protein, Total Fat, Saturated Fat, Carbohydrates (minus added sugar), Added Sugar, Fiber, Cholesterol, Sodium, Calcium, Iron.

FRUITS

Name	Amount/Unit	Cal.	Pro. g	TFat g	SFat g	Carb. g	Sug. g	Fbr. g	Chol. mg	Sod. mg	Calc. mg	Iron mg
Apples, sweetened	½ cup	68	0	0.11	0	12.5	3.25	2	0	334	334	0.3
Apples, unsweetened	½ frt, ½ cup	41	0.25	0	0	9.5	0	2.1	0	0	4	0.2
Applesauce, sweetened	½ cup	97	0.25	0	0	12	11	1.8	0	4	4	0.4
Applesauce, unsweetened	½ cup	53	0.25	0	0	12.5	0	2.5	0	2	4	0.2
Apricots, sweetened	3 hlv, ¼ cup	65	0.5	0	0	3.75	10.75	1.1	0	3	8	0.4
Apricots, unsweetened	3 halves	27	0.5	0	0	5.5	0	1.1	0	3	8	0.3
Banana	1 fruit	105	1	0.33	0.22	24	0	2.3	0	1	7	0.4
Blueberries, sweetened	½ cup	103	0.5	0.11	0	8.5	16.25	2.3	0	3	7	0.4
Blueberries, unsweetened	½ cup	41	0.5	0.22	0	9	0	1.7	0	2	5	0.2
Cherries, sweetened	½ cup	106	0.75	0	0	12.25	13	0.9	0	4	13	0.4
Cherries, unsweetened	10 frt, ½ cup	44	0.75	0	0	10	0	0.9	0	2	12	0.4
Dates	5 frt, ¼ cup	118	0.75	0.22	0.11	28.5	0	3.7	0	1	14	0.5
Dried fruit	¼ cup	92	1	0	0	21.75	0	2.4	0	9	11	0.7
Figs, sweetened	2 fruit	45	0.25	0	0	7	3.75	1.3	0	1	15	0.2
Figs, unsweetened	2 frt, ¼ cup	74	0.75	0.33	0.11	17.5	0	4.2	0	3	39	0.6
Fruit cocktail, sweetened	½ cup	83	0.5	0	0	8.75	11	1.4	0	8	8	0.3
Fruit cocktail, unsweetened	½ cup	50	0.5	0	0	11.5	0	1.4	0	4	6	0.3
Grapefruit, sweetened	½ cup	76	0.5	0	0	10	8	0.5	0	2	18	0.5
Grapefruit, unsweetened	½ frt, ½ cup	39	0.5	0	0	9	0	0.7	0	0	14	0.2
Grapes, sweetened	½ cup	94	0.5	0	0	10.5	12	0.5	0	7	12	1.2
Grapes, unsweetened	20 frt, ½ cup	48	0.5	0	0	11.5	0	0.5	0	2	8	0.2
Guava	1 fruit	45	0.5	0.33	0.11	9.5	0	5	0	2	18	0.3
Juice, unsweetened	¾ cup	90	0.5	0	0	22.5	0	0.2	0	8	16	0.5
Kiwi fruit	1 fruit	46	0.75	0.33	0.11	10	0	2.1	0	4	20	0.3
Mango	½ frt, ½ cup	61	0.5	0.11	0	14.25	0	1.8	0	2	9	0.2
Melon	½ cup	30	0.5	0	0	7	0	0.7	0	9	8	0.2
Nectarines	1 fruit	68	1	0.56	0	14.5	0	3.3	0	0	6	0.2
Orange	1 frt, ¾ cup	63	1	0	0	14	0	3.9	0	1	53	0.2
Papaya	½ frt, ½ cup	56	0.75	0	0	12.75	0	1.8	0	4	35	0.2

continued

Name	Amount/Unit	Cal.	Pro. g	TFat g	SFat g	Carb. g	Sug. g	Fbr. g	Chol. mg	Sod. mg	Calc. mg	Iron mg
Peaches, sweetened	½ cup	94	0.5	0	0	5.25	17	1.2	0	8	3	0.4
Peaches, unsweetened	1 frt, ½ cup	44	0.5	0	0	10.75	0	1.3	0	3	5	0.1
Pears, sweetened	2 halves	103	0.5	0	0	6	18.5	3.2	0	8	8	0.4
Pears, unsweetened	2 hlv, ½ cup	60	0.5	0	0	15	0	3	0	4	10	0.2
Pineapple, sweetened	2 slices, ½ cup	93	0.5	0	0	7.5	15	0.9	0	2	15	0.4
Pineapple, unsweetened	2 slices, ½ cup	70	0.25	0	0	17.5	0	0.9	0	2	6	0.4
Plums, sweetened	2 fruit	67	0.5	0.11	0	8	7.75	0.7	0	17	9	0.7
Plums, unsweetened	1 raw, 2 canned	37	0.5	0	0	8.25	0	0.9	0	1	5	0.2
Prunes, cooked	½ cup	136	1.25	0.33	0	32	0	4.9	0	3	29	1.4
Prunes, dried	½ cup	209	2	0.44	0	49.25	0	6.8	0	4	45	2.1
Pumpkin, canned	½ cup	41	0.75	0.11	0.11	8.75	0	3.5	0	6	32	1.7
Raisins	¼ cup	109	1	0	0	26	0	2.5	0	5	19	0.8
Raspberries, sweetened	½ cup	117	0.75	0.11	0	12	18.25	4.2	0	0	19	0.5
Raspberries, unsweetened	½ cup	30	0.5	0.22	0	6.5	0	3	0	0	14	0.3
Strawberries, sweetened	½ cup	100	0.5	0.11	0	9	15	2	0	4	14	0.6
Strawberries, unsweetened	½ cup	24	0.5	0.22	0	5.5	0	1.6	0	2	11	0.5
Tangerines, sweetened	½ cup	76	0.5	0	0	10	8.5	0.9	0	8	9	0.4
Tangerines, unsweetened	1 frt, ½ cup	43	0.5	0	0	9.75	0	0.9	0	2	14	0.1
Watermelon	½ cup	25	0.5	0.22	0.22	5	0	0.3	0	2	6	0.2

VEGETABLES

Name	Amount/Unit	Cal.	Pro. g	TFat g	SFat g	Carb. g	Sug. g	Fbr. g	Chol. mg	Sod. mg	Calc. mg	Iron mg
Asparagus	6 spears, ½ cup	24	1.75	0.33	0.11	3.75	0	1.5	0	4	22	0.6
Asparagus, canned	½ cup	21	1.5	0.33	0.11	2.75	0	1.9	0	425	17	1.5
Avocados	½ frt, ½ cup	166	2	14.22	2.56	7.25	0	2.7	0	10	12	1
Bamboo shoots	¼ cup	4	0.25	0	0	0.5	0	0.3	0	1	4	0.1
Bamboo shoots, canned	¼ cup	6	0.5	0.11	0	1	0	0.6	0	2	1	0.1
Bean sprouts	½ cup	16	1.25	0	0	2.75	0	2.2	0	3	7	0.5
Bean sprouts, canned	½ cup	8	0.75	0	0	1.25	0	2.3	0	149	9	0.3
Beets, canned	½ cup	36	0.75	0	0	8	0	2.9	0	324	17	0.8
Beets, pickled	½ cup	82	0.75	0	0	8.5	11.25	2.8	0	250	13	0.5
Beets, raw, cooked	½ cup	31	0.75	0	0	6.75	0	2.5	0	49	11	0.6
Bok choy, chinese cabbage	½ cup	5	0.25	0	0	0.75	0	0.6	0	23	37	0.3
Broccoli, cooked	½ cup	24	1.75	0.11	0	4.25	0	2.5	0	15	68	0.8
Broccoli, raw	½ cup	12	0.75	0.11	0	2	0	1.5	0	12	21	0.4
Brussels sprouts	½ cup	32	1.5	0.33	0.11	5.75	0	2.4	0	18	24	0.8
Cabbage, raw or cooked	½ c rw, ¼ c ckd	9	0.25	0	0	1.75	0	1	0	7	13	0.2
Carrots, canned	½ cup	17	0.25	0.11	0	3.75	0	2.7	0	176	19	0.5
Carrots, raw or cooked	½ cup	26	0.5	0	0	5.75	0	2.2	0	43	21	0.4
Cauliflower, raw or cooked	½ cup	15	0.75	0.11	0	2.5	0	1.3	0	7	15	0.3
Celery, raw or cooked	½ cup	10	0.25	0	0	2.25	0	1.4	0	51	25	0.2
Coleslaw	½ cup	154	0.5	14.44	2.67	4.25	1	1.5	7	287	32	0.4
Corn	½ cup	80	1.75	0.33	0	17.5	0	4.6	0	4	2	0.5
Corn, canned	½ cup	83	1.5	0.44	0.11	13	5.5	4.7	0	324	5	0.4
Cucumber	½ cup	7	0.25	0	0	1.5	0	0.7	0	1	7	0.1
Eggplant	½ cup	13	0.25	0	0	3	0	1	0	2	3	0.2
French fries	½ cup	174	1.75	7.33	3.22	19	0	2.6	0	37	6	0.6
Fried vegetables/onions	½ cup, 6 rings	180	2	10.78	2.67	15.5	0	1	0	150	12	0.7
Green beans, canned	½ cup	13	0.75	0	0	2.5	0	1.5	0	170	18	0.6
Green beans, raw or cooked	½ cup	20	1	0	0	4	0	1.8	0	3	30	0.7

continued

Vegetables, continued

Name	Amount/Unit	Cal.	Pro. g	TFat g	SFat g	Carb. g	Sug. g	Fbr. g	Chol. mg	Sod. mg	Calc. mg	Iron mg
Greens, mustard, turnip, ckd	½ cup	15	1	0.11	0	2.5	0	1.4	0	16	87	0.7
Greens, mustard, turnip, raw	½ cup	7	0.5	0	0	1.5	0	0.9	0	9	41	0.4
Greens, turnip, canned	½ cup	17	1	0.22	0.11	2.5	0	2.2	0	325	138	1.8
Kale, raw or cooked	½ cup	20	0.75	0.11	0	3	0	1.7	0	15	47	0.6
Lettuce, endive	½ cup	4	0.25	0	0	0.75	0	0.7	0	6	13	0.2
Lettuce, iceberg	1 leaf	3	0	0	0	0.5	0	0.3	0	2	4	0.1
Miso	½ cup	284	14.25	7.33	1.11	39.25	0	7.4	0	5032	92	3.8
Mixed vegetables, canned	½ cup	39	1.25	0.11	0	8	0	3.5	0	122	22	0.9
Mixed vegetables, frozen	½ cup	22	0.75	0	0	4.5	0	2	0	22	27	0.6
Mushrooms, canned	½ cup	19	1	0.11	0	3.25	0	1.1	0	178	1	0.6
Mushrooms, fresh, cooked	½ cup	25	1.75	0.11	0	4.25	0	1.5	0	1	7	1.7
Mushrooms, raw	½ cup	9	0.5	0	0	1.5	0	0.6	0	1	2	0.4
Okra	½ cup	26	1	0.11	0	5.5	0	2.1	0	5	55	0.5
Onions	½ cup	29	0.5	0.11	0	6.25	0	1.4	0	8	20	0.3
Parsnips	½ cup	64	0.75	0.11	0	14.75	0	3.2	0	8	30	0.5
Peas, green	½ cup	63	3.75	0.11	0	11.5	0	3.5	0	70	19	1.2
Peas, green, canned	½ cup	59	3.25	0.11	0	8	2.75	5.3	0	186	17	0.8
Peas, snowpeas	½ cup	35	2.25	0.11	0	5.75	0	3.4	0	4	37	1.6
Peppers, hot	2 tablespoons	8	0.25	0	0	1.5	0	0.2	0	1	3	0.2
Peppers, sweet, green	½ cup	12	0.25	0.11	0	2.25	0	0.6	0	2	3	0.6
Peppers, sweet, red	½ cup	12	0.25	0.11	0	2.25	0	0.8	0	2	3	0.6
Potato, baked/boiled	½ bkd/1 bld	113	1.5	0	0	26.5	0	2.6	0	7	9	0.4
Potatoes, mashed	½ cup	118	1.5	4.56	1.44	17	0	1.8	4	340	40	0.3
Potato skins, cheese, bacon	2 halves	302	11	15.89	7.44	27.5	0	1.4	34	267	225	4.5
Rutabaga	½ cup	35	0.75	0.11	0	7.5	0	2.1	0	19	43	0.5
Salad, potato	½ cup	153	3	7.78	1.89	15	1.5	1.9	47	512	19	0.5
Salad, three bean	½ cup	80	2	0	0	16.25	1.75	5	0	540	20	3.6
Sauerkraut	½ cup	22	0.75	0.11	0	4.5	0	4.1	0	780	36	1.7
Soup, vegetable	1 cup	81	2	1.56	0.44	11.25	2.25	0.5	2	892	16	1
Spaghetti sauce	½ cup	118	2	5	0.89	12.75	1.5	3.3	0	589	20	1.1
Spaghetti sauce with meat	½ cup	80	2	3.11	0.67	12.5	2	3.3	2	630	20	1.1
Spinach, canned	½ cup	25	1.75	0.33	0.11	3.25	0	3.9	0	29	135	2.5
Spinach, fresh, cooked	½ cup	24	1.75	0.11	0	3.75	0	3	0	73	131	1.7
Spinach, raw	½ cup	6	0.5	0	0	0.75	0	1.1	0	22	28	0.8
Squash, summer	½ cup	18	0.5	0.11	0	3.75	0	1.5	0	3	22	0.4
Squash, winter	½ cup	41	0.75	0.11	0	9.5	0	3	0	4	23	0.6
Squash, zucchini, fresh, ckd	1 c rw, ½ c ckd	18	0.75	0	0	3.5	0	1.4	0	2	19	0.5
Sweet potato	½ cup	98	1.25	0	0	23	0	4	0	11	30	0.5
Sweet potato, candied	½ cup	190	1	0	0	26.5	20	4.4	0	60	20	0.7
Tomatoes, canned or stewed	½ cup	34	0.75	0.11	0	6.5	0.25	2.4	0	305	33	0.7
Tomatoes, raw	½ cup	17	0.5	0.11	0	3.5	0	1.3	0	8	6	0.5
Waterchestnuts, canned	½ cup	34	0.25	0	0	8.25	0	1.5	0	3	3	0.3
Waterchestnuts, raw	½ cup	66	0.75	0	0	15.75	0	1.4	0	9	7	0.4
Watercress, raw	½ cup	2	0.25	0	0	0.25	0	0.2	0	7	20	0

BEVERAGES

Name	Amount/Unit	Cal.	Pro. g	TFat g	SFat g	Carb. g	Sug. g	Fbr. g	Chol. mg	Sod. mg	Calc. mg	Iron mg
Beer, nonalcoholic	12 fluid ounces	55	0.75	0	0	11	0	0	0	19	25	0.1
Wine, nonalcoholic	5 fluid ounces	42	0.5	0	0	9.75	0	0	0	7	12	0.6
Cola	12 fluid ounces	150	0	0	0	0	37	0	0	70	0	0

continued

Beverages, continued

Name	Amount/Unit	Cal.	Pro. g	TFat g	SFat g	Carb. g	Sug. g	Fbr. g	Chol. mg	Sod. mg	Calc. mg	Iron mg
Cola, diet	12 fluid ounces	2	0.25	0	0	0.25	0	0	0	70	0	0
Cola, diet, no caffeine	12 fluid ounces	2	0	0	0	0	0	0	0	70	0	0
Cola, no caffeine	12 fluid ounces	155	0	0	0	0	38.75	0	0	73	0	0
Mellow Yellow, Mountain Dew	12 fluid ounces	177	0	0	0	0	44	0	0	30	0	0
Noncola, diet, no caffeine	12 fluid ounces	4	0	0	0	0.5	0	0	0	42	0	0
Noncola, no caffeine	12 fluid ounces	157	0	0	0	0	37.75	0	0	46	2	0.1
Juice drink	¾ cup/1 box	106	0	0	0	6.5	19.5	0	0	7	1	1
Coffee	1 cup	5	0.25	0	0	1	0	0	0	7	6	0.6
Coffee, decaffeinated	1 cup	3	0.25	0	0	0.75	0	0	0	8	8	0.1
Postum	1 teaspoon	12	0	0	0	3	0	1.3	0	0	0	0
Tea, herbal, no caffeine	1 cup	4	0	0	0	0.75	0	0	0	3	5	0.2
Tea, plain	1 cup	3	0	0	0	0.5	0	0	0	0	0	0

ALCOHOLIC BEVERAGES

Name	Amount/Unit	Cal.	Pro. g	TFat g	SFat g	Carb. g	Sug. g	Fbr. g	Chol. mg	Sod. mg	Calc. mg	Iron mg
Beer	12 fluid ounces	145	1	0	0	13.25	0	0	0	8	12	0
Beer, light	12 fluid ounces	110	1	0	0	7	0	0	0	8	15	0
Chianti	5 fluid ounces	106	0.25	0	0	2.5	0	0	0	8	12	0.6
Cocktail, mixed drink	1 cocktail	139	0	0	0	1	1.5	0	0	6	4	0.1
Liqueur	1 glass, 1½ oz	167	0	0.11	0	8.5	9.5	0	0	4	1	0
Liquor	1 jigger	110	0	0	0	0	0	0	0	0	0	0
Vermouth	5 fluid ounces	100	0.25	0	0	1	0	0	0	8	12	0.4
Wine	5 fluid ounces	104	0.25	0	0	2.5	0	0	0	12	12	0.4
Wine, light	5 fluid ounces	73	0.5	0	0	1	0	0	0	10	13	0.6
Wine cooler	12 fluid ounces	173	0.75	0	0	7.75	9.75	0	0	25	32	1.4

GRAINS

Name	Amount/Unit	Cal.	Pro. g	TFat g	SFat g	Carb. g	Sug. g	Fbr. g	Chol. mg	Sod. mg	Calc. mg	Iron mg
Cereal, bran, fiber	⅓ cup	62	2	0.78	0.22	7.75	2.75	3.8	0	113	13	3
Cereal, frosted	1 cup	147	1.75	0.11	0	18.75	14.75	0.5	0	93	4	2.4
Cereal, fruit-flavored	1 cup	110	1.75	0.22	0.11	12	13	0.5	0	168	5	4.5
Cereal, granola	¼ cup	130	3	4.89	0.89	13.5	4.5	1.7	0	55	19	0.9
Cereal, oat flakes	1 cup	182	5	1.78	0.44	24.75	4.5	3.2	0	115	32	5.8
Cereal, other, cold	1 cup	110	2	0.22	0.11	19.5	3	0.6	0	226	4	1.8
Cereal, other, hot	⅔ cup	100	3	0	0	22	0	0.7	0	54	18	1.1
Cereal, whole-grain	¾ cup	105	3	0.78	0.22	19	0	2.3	0	160	8	1.4
Granola, fat-free	¼ cup	90	2	0	0	21	0.25	2.5	0	20	0	0.4
Oatmeal, flavored	1 packet	140	4	2.22	0.44	18	8.25	2.4	0	181	100	4.5
Oatmeal, plain	⅔ cup cooked	109	4	1.78	0.33	18.25	0	3.3	0	1	15	1.9
Pancakes, waffles	2 pnck/2 wfl	173	4.75	4	1.11	26	3.5	1	44	503	100	1.5
Bagel	1 bagel	175	7	1.22	0.22	32.5	2.25	1.5	0	325	20	1.8
Biscuit	1 biscuit	100	2	3.78	1.22	13.5	0	0.5	2	262	47	0.7
Bread or roll, wheat	1 slice, 1 roll	65	2	0.89	0.22	10	2	1.4	0	106	20	0.7
Bread or roll, white	1 slice, 1 roll	70	2.75	1.11	0.33	11	2	0.5	0	132	20	0.7
Bread, mixed-grain	1 slice	65	2	0.89	0.22	9.75	2.25	1.4	0	106	27	0.8
Bread, oatmeal	1 slice	90	4	1.78	0.33	10.5	4	1.5	0	140	40	1.1
Bread, pita, wheat	1 pita (6″ diam)	145	5.5	0.89	0.22	28.5	0.5	4.1	0	360	50	1.4

continued

Grains, continued

Name	Amount/Unit	Cal.	Pro. g	TFat g	SFat g	Carb. g	Sug. g	Fbr. g	Chol. mg	Sod. mg	Calc. mg	Iron mg
Bread, pita, white	1 pita (6″ diam)	160	6	1	0.22	30	1	1.1	0	300	80	0.7
Bread, raisin	1 slice	70	2	1	0.33	8.25	3	0.9	0	85	20	0.7
Bread, rye, pumpernickel	1 slice	80	2.75	0.89	0.11	13	1	1.1	0	185	22	1.1
Bread, wheat, diet	1 slice	40	2.5	0.56	0.11	4.25	2	2	0	120	40	0.7
Bread, white, diet	1 slice	40	3	0	0	6	1	2	0	110	40	0.7
Bread, whole wheat	1 slice, 1 roll	70	2.75	1.11	0.22	10	1.25	1.9	0	160	20	1
Breadsticks	⅓ lrg/2 sm	36	1.25	0.78	0.22	6	0.5	0.6	0	72	0	0.2
Cornbread, hushpuppies	2.5″ sq/3 hpup	166	3	5.33	1.78	25.75	0	1.6	42	421	87	0.8
Croissants	1 croissant	310	7	19	11.22	27	6	2	0	240	38	1.8
Danish, nonfat	1 piece	90	2	0	0	20	9.75	0.2	0	85	20	0
English muffin	1 muffin	130	5	0.89	0.33	25	1.5	1.6	0	280	96	1.7
Muffin	1 muffin	140	3	4.67	1.56	11.75	8	1.2	21	198	42	1.1
Muffins, fat free	1 muffin	155	3	0.11	0	35	11.5	0.9	0	140	50	0.5
Roll, hmbrgr, hot dog, wheat	1 roll	114	4	1.11	0.22	21.25	0.75	2.5	0	242	46	1
Roll, hmbrgr, hot dog, white	1 roll	138	3.25	2.44	0.67	22.5	2	1.4	0	271	67	1.3
Roll, hoagie, sub	½ roll	200	5.5	3.56	0.89	34.25	2	0.9	0	342	50	1.9
Stuffing	½ cup	210	4.5	12.67	3	17.5	2.5	0.5	22	578	40	1.1
Cake, nonfat	1 piece/slice	70	1.5	0	0	16	7.75	0.6	0	85	0	0
Cookies, nonfat	2 cookies	75	1	0	0	17.5	6.5	0.6	0	115	0	0.2
Cracker sandwiches	2 lrg, 5 sm	70	1.75	3.11	1.11	7.75	0.75	0.2	1	135	20	0.4
Crackers, butter type	5 lrg, 10 sm	70	1	3.56	1.11	8	0.25	0.2	1	193	4	0.4
Crackers, crispbread	1 lrg, 2 sm	40	1	0.89	0.33	8.5	0	1.6	0	112	0	0.5
Crackers, low-fat	2 lrg, 5 sm	60	2.25	2.33	0.33	10	0	0.6	0	100	0	0.4
Crackers, wheat	4 crackers	70	1	2.22	0.44	8	0.5	1.5	0	75	0	0.4
Matzo or melba toast	½ matzo, 5 melba	72	2.75	0.67	0.22	14	1.5	0.6	0	189	2	1
Barley, cooked	½ cup	84	2.25	0.11	0	18.5	0	2.5	0	3	11	0.5
Bulgur	½ cup	113	4.25	0.22	0	23.5	0	3	0	3	13	3.7
Couscous	⅔ cup	120	4	0	0	26	0	4.3	0	5	0	0.7
Grits	½ cup	73	1.5	0.11	0	16	0	0.3	0	136	0	0.8
Lasagna, meat	1 serving	350	27.5	23.11	6	31	1.5	2.6	73	1040	275	2.1
Lasagna, vegetable	1 serving	315	22	12	5.89	27	0.5	4.6	40	970	350	2.3
Macaroni and cheese	½ cup	191	6	8.56	2.67	22.75	0	1.4	18	434	71	1.2
Macaroni, whole-wheat	1 cup	202	8	1.11	0.22	39	0	7.4	0	10	20	4.5
Noodles, chow mein	½ cup	130	3	6.44	1.11	14.5	0	0.5	2	228	4	0.8
Noodles, egg, macaroni	1 cup	190	7	0.56	0.11	37	0	1.1	0	30	14	2.1
Pasta w/parmesan cheese	½ cup	252	6.5	14.67	6.33	22.5	0	1.1	38	479	78	1.5
Salad, pasta	½ cup	250	4	16	3.33	20.75	0	0.7	28	410	40	0.7
Spaghetti	1 cup	200	7.5	1	0.22	40.5	0	1.1	0	19	14	2
Spaghetti w/meatballs	1 cup	307	12	10.56	3.89	37	0	2.7	34	1220	53	3.3
Spaghetti, whole-wheat	1 cup	200	9	1.11	0.22	39.5	0	5.8	0	10	20	2.7
Rice cake	1 large cake	35	0.75	0	0	7.5	0	0.3	0	13	0	0
Rice, brown	½ cup	115	2.5	0.67	0.22	25	0	1.8	0	2	12	0.5
Rice, long-grain/wild, mix	½ cup	137	3	2	0.56	23	2	0.9	0	579	11	1.1
Rice, seasoned	½ cup	150	3.5	3.78	1.67	23	1	1	5	700	13	1.2
Rice, white	½ cup	92	2	0	0	20.5	0	0.5	0	225	10	0.7
Tabouli	½ cup	170	3	8.67	1.33	20	0	1.6	0	290	0	0.7
Taco shell	1 shell	50	0	2	1.11	8	0	0.2	0	5	0	0
Tortilla	1 tortilla	65	2	1	0.11	12	0	0.9	0	1	42	0.6

Name	Amount/Unit	Cal.	Pro. g	TFat g	SFat g	Carb. g	Sug. g	Fbr. g	Chol. mg	Sod. mg	Calc. mg	Iron mg
Buttermilk	1 cup	99	8.75	2	1.33	11.25	0	0	9	257	285	0.1
Hot cocoa prepared w/milk	1 cup	218	8	9	5.67	13.5	11.25	3	33	123	298	0.8
Meal replacement drinks	1 cup	200	14	1	0.44	36	17	4	5	230	500	6.3
Milk, chocolate	1 cup	179	8.5	4.67	3	10.5	14.5	1.1	17	150	284	0.6
Milk, low-fat	1 cup	112	8.75	3.56	2.22	11.25	0	0	14	123	299	0.1
Milk, skim	1 cup	86	9	0.44	0.33	11.5	0	0	4	126	302	0.1
Milk, whole	1 cup	150	8.5	7.67	5	11	0	0	33	120	291	0.1
Cheese spread	2 tablespoons	81	3.5	6.56	4.33	2	0	1	89	293	95	1
Cheese, American	1 ounce, 1 slice	106	6.75	8.22	5.44	0.5	0	0	27	406	174	0.1
Cheese, cheddar	1 ounce, 1 slice	113	7.5	8.67	5.89	0.5	0	0	30	177	203	0.2
Cheese, cottage	½ cup	113	14.5	4.78	3.11	3	0	0	17	440	65	0.2
Cheese, cottage, nonfat	½ cup	90	14	0	0	7	0	0	10	400	60	0
Cheese, cottage, low-fat	½ cup	96	15	1.22	0.78	4	0	0	5	440	74	0.2
Cheese, mozzarella	1 ounce, 1 slice	80	6	5.67	3.67	0.5	0	0	22	106	147	0.1
Cheese, mozzarella, light	1 ounce	72	7.25	4.11	2.78	0.75	0	0	16	150	183	0.1
Cheese, parmesan	1 tablespoon	23	2.25	1.44	0.89	0.25	0	0	4	93	69	0.1
Cheese, provolone	1 ounce, 1 slice	100	7.75	7	4.78	0.5	0	0	20	248	214	0.2
Cheese, reduced-fat	1 ounce	80	8	5	3	1	0	0	20	220	350	0
Cheese, ricotta	½ cup	216	15	14.89	10	3.75	0	0	63	104	257	0.5
Cheese, ricotta, part-skim	½ cup	166	14.5	8.67	5.67	6.25	0	0	37	143	369	0.3
Cheese, Swiss	1 ounce	101	8	6.89	4.67	0.75	0	0	25	231	246	0.1
Ice cream	½ cup	148	2.5	7.44	4.67	4.5	11.75	0.2	30	58	88	0.3
Ice milk	½ cup	110	3	2.78	1.89	10	8	0.3	8	75	100	1
Tofutti	½ cup	150	2.5	6.67	1.11	9	11	1.5	0	105	1	0.6
Yogurt, frozen	½ cup	100	3	1.78	1.11	8	10.25	0.1	7	59	100	1
Yogurt, low-fat w/fruit	1 container	240	9	3	2	27	16	0.3	10	120	330	1
Yogurt, nonfat w/fruit	1 container	95	3.5	0	0	8	12	0	0	70	150	1
Yogurt, plain, low-fat	1 container	142	11.25	3.67	2.44	15.75	0	0	15	160	422	0.6
Yogurt, plain, nonfat	1 container	110	11	0.22	0.22	16	0	0	4	160	430	1
Yogurt, plain, whole-milk	1 container	145	8.75	6.89	4.56	11.5	0	0	32	123	312	0.6
Yogurt, w/frt, art. swtner	1 container	90	7	0.67	0.44	14	0	0.5	5	110	250	1

FATS/SWEETS/OTHER

Name	Amount/Unit	Cal.	Pro. g	TFat g	SFat g	Carb. g	Sug. g	Fbr. g	Chol. mg	Sod. mg	Calc. mg	Iron mg
Bacon	1 slice	36	5.25	1.78	0.67	0	0	0	12	360	2	0.2
Bacon bits	1 tablespoon	21	2.5	1.11	0.33	0	0	0	6	181	1	0.1
Butter	1 tablespoon	104	0	11.44	7.22	0	0	0	32	119	2	1
Gravy	¼ cup	30	1	1.44	0.56	2.25	0.5	0.1	1	260	3	0.4
Lard	1 tablespoon	115	0	12.22	5	0	0	0	12	0	0	0
Margarine, stick	1 tablespoon	101	0	10.56	2	0	0	0	0	133	4	0
Margarine, stick, light	1 tablespoon	60	0	6.67	1	0	0	0	0	110	1	1
Margarine, tub	1 tablespoon	101	0	8.89	2	0	0	0	0	152	4	0
Margarine, tub, light	1 tablespoon	50	0	5.89	1	0	0	0	0	110	1	1
Mayonnaise	1 tablespoon	100	0.25	11	1.89	0.25	0.25	0	8	74	1	1
Mayonnaise, light	1 tablespoon	48	0.25	4.56	1	0.75	1	0	5	95	1	1
Mayonnaise, nonfat	1 tablespoon	12	0	0	0	3	3	0	0	190	0	0
Miracle Whip	1 tablespoon	64	0	5.89	0.89	2.5	0.5	0	5	95	2	1
Miracle Whip, nonfat	1 tablespoon	20	0	0	0	5	5	0	0	210	0	0
Oil	1 tablespoon	120	0	12.78	1.89	0	0	0	0	0	0	0.1

continued

Fats, Sweets, Other, continued

Name	Amount/Unit	Cal.	Pro. g	TFat g	SFat g	Carb. g	Sug. g	Fbr. g	Chol. mg	Sod. mg	Calc. mg	Iron mg
Salad dressing	1 tablespoon	80	0	8.22	1.33	0.25	0.25	1	0	146	2	1
Salad dressing, light	1 tablespoon	16	0.25	0.33	0.11	0.75	0.5	0.3	0	137	1	1
Salad dressing, no oil	1 tablespoon	12	0	0	0	2.5	0	0.7	0	0	1	1
Salad dressing, nonfat	1 tablespoon	16	0	0	0	3	3	0	0	143	0	0
Brownie	1¾″ square	150	2	6.22	1.67	6.5	15	0.9	10	105	1	0.7
Cake	1 piece/slice	280	4	11.33	3	15.25	22.25	0.5	56	285	57	1
Candy, choc/peanut butter	1 pkg, 1½ oz	237	6	13.78	5.89	4	22	2.5	3	90	34	0.7
Candy, chocolate	1-ounce piece	150	2	8.22	4.78	2.25	15	0.8	6	24	50	0.3
Candy, chocolate-covered	1 ounce	132	1.25	5.56	2.11	3	13.25	1.5	3	43	33	0.4
Candy, fudge	1″ cube	88	0.75	3	0.78	1.25	13.25	0.3	2	40	20	0.2
Candy, hard	5 pieces	110	0	0	0	0	27.5	0	0	7	1	0.1
Cookies, fig bars	2 fig bars	100	1	1.78	0.44	10.5	10.5	1.2	1	90	20	0.7
Cookies, oatmeal raisin	3 cookies	195	2.25	8.11	1.89	13.5	13.5	1.4	1	150	0	0.8
Cookies, other	3 cookies	180	1.5	8.11	2.89	10	15	0.3	3	131	1	0.7
Danish	1 roll	252	4.5	11.67	3.67	10.25	19	0.7	14	249	36	1.1
Diet bar	1 bar	120	2	4	1.44	19	9.5	3	1	30	150	2.7
Doughnut or sweet roll	1 serving	201	3	8.11	2.89	12.5	13.25	0.6	19	145	21	0.8
Frozen desserts, nonfat	½ cup	100	2	0.22	0.11	23.5	9.5	0.4	1	48	100	0
Frzn yogurt cone, low-fat	1 serving	105	4	1	0.56	22	13	0.1	3	80	112	0.2
Frzn yogurt sundae, low-fat	1 serving	240	6	3	2.33	50.5	43	0.8	6	170	190	0.1
Gelatin	½ cup	105	2	1	1	23	22	0	0	57	0	0
Gelatin, sugar-free	½ cup	8	1.5	0	0	0	0	0	0	31	0	0
Granola bars	1 bar	133	2	6	2	18.25	13	0.6	0	70	20	0.5
Pie, custard or cream	⅙ of 9″ pie	346	6.75	13.11	6.22	20.75	25.75	1	125	375	122	0.8
Pie, fruit	⅙ of 9″ pie	405	4	16.22	5.33	34.75	25.25	4	6	423	17	1.6
Pie, pecan	⅙ of 9″ pie	575	7	29.67	5.67	33	37.25	2.2	100	305	65	4.6
Pudding	½ cup	150	4.5	2.22	1.44	10	18	0	9	443	152	0
Pudding, diet	½ cup	90	4	2.44	1.56	13	0	0.4	9	423	152	0.1
Cream, whipped	1 tablespoon	15	0.25	1.33	1.11	0.25	0.25	0	2	4	3	1
Dessert topping, no sugar	1 tablespoon	5	0	0.56	0.44	0	0	1	4	5	2	1
Jam or jelly	2 teaspoons	35	0	0	0	1	7.5	0.1	0	1	1	1
Cream, coffee, half & half	1 tablespoon	25	0.5	2.22	1.44	0.5	0	0	8	6	15	0
Nutrasweet, Equal	1 packet	4	0.5	0	0	0	0.5	0	0	0	0	0
Saccharin	1 packet	2	0	0	0	0	0	0	0	2	0	0
Salt	4 shakes	0	0	0	0	0	0	0	0	64	0	0
Sugar	1 teaspoon	15	0	0	0	0	3.75	0	0	0	0	0
Syrup, pancake, table	2 tablespoons	110	0	0	0	0	27.5	0	0	21	1	1
Coffee whitener	1 tablespoon	22	0	2.11	1.33	0	1	0	0	12	1	1
Cream cheese	2 tablespoons	106	2.5	10.22	6.67	1	0	0	34	90	24	0.4
Cream cheese, light	2 tablespoons	80	3	7	4	1	0	0	25	115	20	1
Sour cream	1 tablespoon	26	0.25	2.56	1.56	0.5	0	0	5	17	14	0
Sour cream, imitation	1 tablespoon	25	0.75	2.33	2	0.75	0	0	1	10	7	0
Sour cream, nonfat	1 tablespoon	8	1	0	0	1	0	0	0	10	20	0
Catsup	1 tablespoon	17	0	0	0	2.75	1.5	0.2	0	168	3	0.1
Cheese sauce	¼ cup	71	3.5	3.56	1.89	6.5	0	0	10	412	139	0.1
Chili sauce	1 tablespoon	17	0.25	0	0	2.75	1.25	0.9	0	196	2	0.1
Hollandaise sauce	¼ cup	230	2.25	23.22	8.44	2.5	0	0	140	316	50	1
Mustard	1 teaspoon	6	0.25	0.33	0	0.25	0	0	0	60	0	0
Olives	3 olives	15	0.25	1.56	0.22	0.25	0	0.3	0	234	8	0.2
Pickles, dill	2 spears	7	0	0.11	0	1	0.75	0.9	0	584	9	0.4
Pickles, sweet	1 pickle, 3 sl.	18	0	0	0	0.5	4	0.3	0	107	2	0.2
Soy sauce	1 tablespoon	10	1.25	0	0	1.25	0	0	0	1015	3	0.4

continued

Name	Amount/Unit	Cal.	Pro. g	TFat g	SFat g	Carb. g	Sug. g	Fbr. g	Chol. mg	Sod. mg	Calc. mg	Iron mg
Steak, Worcestershire sauce	1 tablespoon	11	0	0	0	1	1.75	0	0	143	0	0
White sauce	¼ cup	99	2.5	5.67	2.22	6	0	0.1	8	222	73	0.2
Soup, beef or chicken	1 cup	74	4.25	2.22	0.67	8.5	0	1	7	910	17	0.9
Soup, bouillon, broth	1 cube/packet	9	0.75	0.22	0.11	0.25	1	0	1	965	1	0.1
Soup, broth-based, no-salt	1 cup	135	5.75	3.89	0.78	16.5	0	2.8	0	115	47	1.8
Soup, cream, chowder	1 cup	140	5.5	6.11	2.89	14	0	0.9	22	1010	150	0.6
Soup, low-salt	1 cup	110	4	3	1	12	0	0.5	2	100	17	1.3
Soup, miso	1 cup	152	4.5	6.44	0.89	19	0	3	0	490	20	1.3
Breakfast milk powder	1 packet	130	6	0	0	0	26.25	0.4	0	185	80	4.5
Hot chocolate mix	1 envelope	110	1.5	2.78	1.56	3.5	16	1.1	2	165	40	0.7
Meal replacement bar	1 serving	270	11	14	5	24	22.5	0	0	330	250	4.5
Milkshake	10 oz, 1¼ cup	368	10	12.78	8.22	26.5	19.25	0.5	54	243	375	0.5
Milkshake, low-fat	1 serving	320	10.75	1.33	0.56	66	44.75	0	10	170	327	0.1
Popcorn	1 cup	32	0.75	1.44	0.44	5.5	0	0.8	0	68	0	0.2
Potato chips, corn chips	1 cup	152	2	9.44	1.78	15	0	1.4	0	229	15	0.4
Pretzels	⅔ cup	110	2.75	0.89	0.22	21.75	1	0.9	0	610	9	1.4
Tortilla chips	1 cup	95	1.25	4.67	1.33	12	0	0.9	0	123	23	0.3

PROTEIN FOODS

Name	Amount/Unit	Cal.	Pro. g	TFat g	SFat g	Carb. g	Sug. g	Fbr. g	Chol. mg	Sod. mg	Calc. mg	Iron mg
Biscuit w/egg, meat, cheese	1 biscuit	489	18.75	31.22	9.67	29	4	0.8	347	1240	151	2.9
Egg salad	½ cup	267	11	22.89	5.78	1	3	0.3	418	513	43	1.8
Egg, boiled, poached	1 egg	79	6.5	5.56	2.11	0.5	0	0	274	69	28	1
Egg, fried, scrambled	1 egg	89	6.25	6.78	3	1	0	0	281	150	37	0.9
Egg, omelet	1 omelet	342	23.25	25.44	12.56	4	0	0	861	553	243	2.8
Egg, substitute	¼ cup	43	5.5	1.56	0.22	1.5	0	0	0	115	30	0.8
Chicken breast sandwich	1 sandwich	509	26	26.89	4.78	34.75	1.75	1.2	83	1082	80	2.7
Chicken salad	½ cup	179	14.75	12.22	2.89	0.75	0.75	0.3	118	329	21	0.9
Chicken wings	10 wings	1282	90	91.11	35.78	11.5	5	0.2	326	1750	62	4
Chicken, turkey, no skin	4 ounces	137	27.25	3.33	1.11	0	0	0	77	58	12	1.3
Chicken, turkey, w/skin	4 ounces	145	19.75	7.22	2.44	0	0	0	57	49	10	0.9
Chicken, fried, no skin	4 ounces	107	19.25	4.22	1.33	0.25	0	0	50	46	9	0.8
Chicken, fried, w/skin	4 ounces	206	21	11.22	3.22	6.25	0	0.2	69	199	14	1.1
Chicken, mixed dish	1 cup	365	15.25	17.78	5.56	13.5	0	1	103	600	30	2.2
Beef stew	1 cup	207	15.25	9	4.22	16.5	0.5	2.5	53	616	29	2.6
Beef, corned	4 ounces	242	24.25	16.11	7	0	0.25	0	87	1024	15	2
Beef, grnd, hmbrgr, not fried	4 ounces	200	21.25	13.67	6.11	0	0	0	70	60	8	1.9
Beef, grnd, hmbrgr, fried	4 ounces	207	21.25	13.56	5.89	0	0	0	68	62	8	1.9
Beef, mixed dish	1 cup	310	19.25	13.56	5.89	23.5	1.25	2.1	68	840	52	3.5
Beef, roast beef	4 ounces	198	21.25	11.11	4.89	0	0	0	59	47	6	2.1
Cheeseburger (large) w/roll	1 sandwich	711	32	43.33	16.78	33	4	1	113	1164	295	5
Cheeseburger (low-fat) w/roll	1 sandwich	370	24	14	5	35	3.5	1.6	75	890	200	3.6
Cheeseburger (small) w/roll	1 sandwich	461	29	27.56	13.67	25.25	3	0.8	95	906	245	3.3
Hamburger (large) w/roll	1 sandwich	594	27.5	33	12.67	33.25	2	0.9	101	688	87	4.8
Hamburger (low-fat) w/roll	1 sandwich	320	22	10	4	35	3.5	1.6	60	670	150	3.6
Hamburger (small) w/roll	1 sandwich	355	22	19.33	8.22	22.25	3	1.7	95	556	71	3.2
Liver	4 ounces	169	23.5	6	2.67	3.25	0	0	344	69	10	7.7
Pate	1 tablespoon	41	2	3.67	1.44	0	0	0	51	91	9	0.7
Roast beef sandwich	1 sandwich	353	27.25	14.89	7.33	30.25	2.25	0.7	49	766	87	4.1

continued

Protein Foods, continued

Name	Amount/Unit	Cal.	Pro. g	TFat g	SFat g	Carb. g	Sug. g	Fbr. g	Chol. mg	Sod. mg	Calc. mg	Iron mg
Tripe	4 ounces	61	12.5	1.11	0.67	0	0	0	58	44	77	0.3
Veal	4 ounces	177	21.75	9.78	4.78	0	0	0	78	52	9	2.7
Veal, mixed dish	1 serving	327	28.25	17.78	9.78	9.5	0.75	1.7	137	634	138	3.7
Bacon substitute	1 strip	52	3	4.11	1.56	0	0	0	13	207	1	0.2
Ham	4 ounces	165	21	8.67	3.11	0	0	0	54	1419	8	1
Hot dog	1 hot dog	144	5.75	12.89	5.22	0.25	1.25	0	30	547	20	0.7
Hot dog and roll	1 sandwich	298	9.25	17.56	6.67	20	2.5	0.7	29	880	60	2.2
Pork feet	8 ounces	138	14.5	8.78	3.22	0	0	0	71	597	32	1.1
Pork rinds	4 ounces	610	69	34.67	13.33	0	0	0	106	3033	25	0.7
Pork spareribs	4 ounces	176	13.75	13.11	5.22	0	0	0	54	41	21	0.8
Pork, fresh, fried	4 ounces	192	14.5	14.89	5.67	0	0	0	55	33	5	0.5
Pork, fresh, roasted	4 ounces	164	15.75	10.22	3.89	0	0	0	54	37	4	0.6
Sausage	1 ounce	88	4	7.44	2.89	0	0.5	0	14	258	4	0.4
Lamb	4 ounces	225	26.25	14.78	7.11	0	0	0	91	65	10	2
Caviar	1 tablespoon	40	4.25	2.11	0.78	0.5	0	0	94	240	44	1.8
Clams, oysters, shrimp, fried	4 pieces	103	5.25	6.11	1.11	6	0	0.1	23	183	20	0.6
Clams, oysters, shrimp	½ cup	71	12.25	1.22	0.33	2.5	0	0	62	108	41	6
Crabmeat	3 ounces	86	12.5	1	0.22	4.5	0	0	26	713	25	0.4
Fish casserole	1 cup	407	18.5	23.78	7.56	26.25	0.75	1.8	70	1314	182	2.3
Fish sandwich	1 sandwich	488	19	26.56	5.89	39.25	3.75	1.5	70	928	46	2
Fish, fried	4 ounces	279	11.5	15.33	3.56	21.5	1.5	0.9	52	467	0	0.7
Fish, not fried	4 ounces	108	22.75	1.33	0.44	10	0	0	60	76	17	0.5
Fish, smoked, pickled	1 ounce	56	6.25	2.33	0.67	0	0	0	14	235	5	0.3
Seafood or fish salad	½ cup	160	13.5	9.78	2.33	1.75	0.25	0.4	142	250	31	0.9
Tuna in oil	½ cup	142	22	5.44	1.11	0	0	0	18	275	7	0.8
Tuna in water	½ cup	90	19.25	1.44	0.44	0	0	0	28	400	0	0.7
Chili con carne	1 cup	286	15.75	12.44	5.78	28.5	0	6.5	43	964	86	3
Chili, vegetarian	1 cup	240	18	12	1.78	13	2	16.4	0	860	6	3.2
Luncheon meat, beef, pork	1 ounce slice	76	4.25	6.11	2.56	0	0.5	0	18	348	3	0.4
Luncheon meat, chkn, trky	1 ounce slice	32	5.75	0.67	0.22	0	0	0	12	358	3	0.3
Pepperoni	1 slice	27	1.25	2.33	0.89	0.25	0	0	5	112	1	0.1
Pizza, cheese topping	2 slices	352	21.75	13.44	7.33	36.25	0.75	3	33	890	474	2.3
Pizza, French bread	1 slice	410	17.5	19.22	8	39	2	2	35	1030	200	2.7
Pizza, meat topping	2 slices	445	25	17	8	50	0.5	4.3	31	906	263	3
Pizza, vegetable topping	2 slices	419	24.75	10.33	5.56	64.25	1	10	19	685	285	5
Chop suey	1 cup	300	26	16	4.33	13	0	1.5	68	1053	60	4.8
Chow mein, beef or chicken	¾ cup	65	6.5	1.44	0.56	5.25	0.75	1.4	26	845	80	1.3
Eggroll	1 eggroll	173	6.75	4.56	0.89	25	3	0.8	7	471	20	1.1
Sweet & sour chicken, pork	1 cup	426	17.5	13.89	3.33	23.5	31.75	1.3	83	1209	27	1.9
Burrito	2 burritos	426	16	14.33	7.11	57.75	0	6.4	65	1116	105	4.5
Chimichanga	1 chimichanga	425	18.5	17.11	8.33	41.25	0	5.2	30	933	145	4
Enchilada	1 enchilada	322	10.5	16.89	9.67	30	0	5.8	42	1052	276	2.2
Taco	1 small	370	21	18.44	11.11	26.5	0	3.4	57	802	221	2.4
Taco salad	1½ cups	279	13.5	13.33	6.67	24	0	4.3	44	763	192	2.3
Tostada	1 tostada	325	13.75	13.89	9.67	28	0	7.5	40	834	214	2.2
Beans, baked	½ cup	140	6	1.67	0.67	15	7.5	6	8	423	60	2.1
Beans, black	½ cup	113	6.5	0.33	0.11	20.75	0	4.4	0	1	24	1.8
Beans, kidney, pinto	½ cup	115	6.5	0.33	0.11	22.25	0	4.5	0	2	33	2.4
Beans, kidney, pinto, canned	½ cup	104	5.75	0.22	0	19.5	0	6.1	0	445	35	1.6
Beans, lima	½ cup	94	5.5	0.22	0.11	17.5	0	4.6	0	26	25	1.8
Beans, lima, canned	½ cup	93	4.75	0.22	0.11	17.5	0	5.8	0	309	35	2

continued

Protein Foods, continued

Name	Amount/Unit	Cal.	Pro. g	TFat g	SFat g	Carb. g	Sug. g	Fbr. g	Chol. mg	Sod. mg	Calc. mg	Iron mg
Beans, navy, chickpeas	½ cup	132	6.75	1	0.22	23.75	0	4.8	0	4	52	2.4
Beans, navy, chickpeas, cnd	½ cup	146	7	0.78	0.11	27.5	0	5	0	473	51	2
Beans, white, canned	½ cup	153	8.25	0.22	0.11	29.25	0	5	0	7	96	3.9
Beans, white, split peas	½ cup	125	7	0.22	0.11	23	0	5.3	0	2	66	2.6
Broadbeans, fava	½ cup	93	5.5	0.22	0	17	0	4.4	0	4	31	1.3
Broadbeans, fava, canned	½ cup	91	6	0.11	0	16.25	0	4.5	0	580	34	1.3
Chickpeas	½ cup	138	6.5	1.67	0.11	24.75	0	4.8	0	183	39	2
Lentils	½ cup	115	7.75	0.22	0	20.25	0	2.8	0	2	19	3.3
Peas, black-eyed	½ cup	100	5.75	0.33	0.11	18.25	0	8.3	0	3	21	2.2
Peas, black-eyed, canned	½ cup	92	5	0.33	0.11	16.5	0	8.2	0	359	24	1.2
Soybeans, roasted	¼ cup	205	14.25	10.22	1.56	13.5	0	1.9	0	1	89	2
Tahini	1 tablespoon	92	2.5	7.33	1.11	3.75	0	1.5	0	10	109	2.2
Nuts, mixed	3 tablespoons	170	4.25	13.56	2.22	6.25	0	1.6	0	170	20	1.1
Peanut butter	2 tablespoons	190	9	14.56	2.78	4.5	2	2.4	0	150	11	0.6
Peanuts	3 tablespoons	164	6.25	12.33	1.78	5.25	0	2.5	0	110	7	0.5

Nutritional Content of Popular Items from Fast-Food Restaurants

Arby's

	Serving size (g)	Calories	Protein (g)	Total fat (g)	Saturated fat (g)	Total carbohydrate (g)	Sugars (g)	Fiber (g)	Cholesterol (mg)	Sodium (mg)	Vitamin A	Vitamin C	Calcium	Iron	% calories from fat
											% Daily Value				
Regular roast beef	154	388	23	19	7	33	N/A	3	43	1009	N/A	N/A	N/A	N/A	44
Super roast beef	247	523	25	27	9	50	N/A	5	43	1189	N/A	N/A	N/A	N/A	46
Light roast beef deluxe	182	296	18	10	3	33	N/A	6	42	826	N/A	N/A	N/A	N/A	30
Roast chicken deluxe	216	433	24	22	5	36	N/A	2	34	763	N/A	N/A	N/A	N/A	46
French dip	195	475	30	22	8	40	N/A	3	55	1411	N/A	N/A	N/A	N/A	41
Turkey sub	277	550	31	27	7	47	N/A	2	65	2084	N/A	N/A	N/A	N/A	44
Light roast turkey deluxe	195	260	20	7	2	33	N/A	4	33	1262	N/A	N/A	N/A	N/A	21
Grilled chicken BBQ	201	388	23	13	3	47	N/A	2	43	1002	N/A	N/A	N/A	N/A	30
Cheddar curly fries	120	333	5	18	4	40	N/A	0	3	1016	N/A	N/A	N/A	N/A	49
Potato cakes	85	204	2	12	2	20	N/A	0	0	397	N/A	N/A	N/A	N/A	53
Red ranch dressing	14	75	0	6	1	5	N/A	0	0	115	N/A	N/A	N/A	N/A	72
French-toastix	124	430	10	21	5	52	N/A	3	0	550	N/A	N/A	N/A	N/A	44
Jamocha shake	340	384	15	10	3	62	N/A	0	36	262	N/A	N/A	N/A	N/A	23

N/A: not available.

Burger King

	Serving size (g)	Calories	Protein (g)	Total fat (g)	Saturated fat (g)	Total carbohydrate (g)	Sugars (g)	Fiber (g)	Cholesterol (mg)	Sodium (mg)	Vitamin A	Vitamin C	Calcium	Iron	% calories from fat
											% Daily Value				
Whopper®	270	640	27	39	11	45	8	3	90	870	N/A	N/A	N/A	N/A	55
Whopper Jr.®	164	420	21	24	8	29	5	2	60	530	N/A	N/A	N/A	N/A	51
Double Whopper® with cheese	375	960	52	63	24	46	8	3	195	1420	N/A	N/A	N/A	N/A	59
BK Big Fish™ sandwich	252	720	23	43	9	59	4	3	80	1180	N/A	N/A	N/A	N/A	54
BK Broiler® chicken sandwich	247	530	29	26	5	5	4	2	105	1060	N/A	N/A	N/A	N/A	44
Chicken Tenders® (8 pieces)	123	350	22	22	7	17	0	1	65	940	N/A	N/A	N/A	N/A	57
Ranch dipping sauce	28	170	0	17	3	2	1	0	0	200	N/A	N/A	N/A	N/A	90
Barbeque dipping sauce	28	35	0	0	0	9	7	0	0	400	N/A	N/A	N/A	N/A	0
Broiled chicken salad (no dressing)	302	190	20	8	4	9	5	3	75	500	N/A	N/A	N/A	N/A	38
Garden salad (no dressing)	215	100	6	5	3	8	4	4	15	115	N/A	N/A	N/A	N/A	45
Bleu cheese salad dressing	30	160	2	16	4	1	0	<1	30	260	N/A	N/A	N/A	N/A	90
French fries (medium, salted)	116	400	3	21	8	50	0	4	0	820	N/A	N/A	N/A	N/A	47
Onion rings	124	310	4	14	2	41	6	6	0	810	N/A	N/A	N/A	N/A	41
Chocolate shake (medium)	284	320	9	7	4	54	48	3	20	230	N/A	N/A	N/A	N/A	20
Croissan'wich® w/sausage, egg, and cheese	176	600	22	46	16	25	3	1	260	1140	N/A	N/A	N/A	N/A	69
French toast sticks	141	500	4	27	7	60	11	1	0	490	N/A	N/A	N/A	N/A	49
Dutch apple pie	113	300	3	15	3	39	22	2	0	230	N/A	N/A	N/A	N/A	45

N/A: not available.

Domino's Pizza

(1 serving = 2 of 12 slices or ⅙ of 14-inch pizza; 2 of 8 slices or ¼ of 12-inch pizza; 1 6-inch pizza)

	Serving size	Calories	Protein	Total fat	Saturated fat	Total carbohydrate	Sugars	Fiber	Cholesterol	Sodium	Vitamin A	Vitamin C	Calcium	Iron	% calories from fat
	g		g	g	g	g	g	g	mg	mg	% Daily Value				
14-inch lg. hand-tossed cheese	137	317	13	10	5	45	3	3	14	669	10	9	17	18	28
14-inch lg. thin crust cheese	99	253	11	11	5	29	2	2	14	757	9	4	20	5	39
14-inch lg. deep dish cheese	173	455	18	20	8	54	5	3	18	1029	11	5	22	21	39
12-inch med. hand-tossed cheese	149	347	14	11	5	50	3	3	15	723	11	8	18	20	29
12-inch med. thin crust cheese	106	271	12	12	5	31	3	2	15	509	10	4	22	5	40
12-inch med. deep dish cheese	180	477	18	22	8	55	5	3	19	1085	12	5	23	21	42
6-inch deep dish cheese	215	595	23	27	11	68	6	4	24	1300	13	5	28	26	41
Toppings: pepperoni	*	66	3	6	2	<1	<1	<1	14	212	†	†	†	†	82
ham	*	17	2	1	<1	<1	<1	0	7	156	†	†	†	†	53
Italian sausage	*	44	2	3	1	1	<1	<1	9	137	†	†	†	†	61
bacon	*	75	4	6	2	<1	<1	0	11	207	†	7	†	†	72
beef	*	44	2	4	2	<1	<1	<1	8	123	†	†	†	†	82
anchovies	*	23	3	1	<1	0	0	0	9	395	†	†	3	3	39
extra cheese	*	45	3	4	2	<1	<1	<1	7	140	3	†	12	†	80
cheddar cheese	*	48	3	4	2	<1	<1	0	12	73	3	†	9	†	75
Barbeque wings	25	50	6	2	1	2	1	<1	26	175	†	†	†	†	38
Hot wings	25	45	6	2	1	<1	<1	<1	26	354	3	†	†	†	40
Breadsticks (1 piece)	22	78	2	3	1	11	<1	<1	0	158	†	†	†	3	35
Cheesy bread (1 piece)	28	103	3	5	2	11	<1	<1	6	187	†	26	†	4	44

* Topping information is based on minimal portioning requirements for one serving of a 14-inch large pizza; add the values for toppings to the values for a cheese pizza. The following toppings supply fewer than 15 calories per serving: green and yellow peppers, onion, olives, mushrooms, pineapple.

† Contains less than 2% of the Daily Value of these nutrients.

Jack in the Box

	Serving size	Calories	Protein	Total fat	Saturated fat	Total carbohydrate	Sugars	Fiber	Cholesterol	Sodium	Vitamin A	Vitamin C	Calcium	Iron	% calories from fat
	g		g	g	g	g	g	g	mg	mg	% Daily Value				
Breakfast Jack®	126	280	17	12	5	30	3	1	195	920	8	4	15	20	39
Supreme croissant	163	520	21	32	13	39	6	2	245	1240	15	20	10	20	57
Hamburger	97	280	13	11	4	31	5	1	45	560	2	2	10	20	39
Jumbo Jack®	263	590	25	36	11	42	6	4	80	720	8	20	15	35	55
Sourdough Jack	229	690	31	46	15	38	3	3	110	1180	10	15	30	20	60
Chicken fajita pita	187	280	24	9	4	25	5	3	75	840	25	0	15	15	29
Grilled chicken fillet	231	520	27	26	6	42	9	4	140	1240	8	15	20	25	45
Chicken supreme	235	680	23	45	11	46	8	4	85	1500	10	15	20	15	60
Chicken Caesar sandwich	232	490	24	26	6	41	6	3	55	1050	15	15	20	20	48
Garden chicken salad	253	200	23	9	4	8	4	3	65	420	70	20	20	4	41
Blue cheese dressing	57	210	1	15	2.5	11	4	0	25	750	0	0	2	0	64
Chicken teriyaki bowl	502	670	26	4	1	128	27	3	15	1730	130	40	10	25	5
Monster taco	125	270	12	17	6	19	2	4	30	678	8	2	20	8	57
Egg rolls (3 pieces)	170	440	15	24	6	40	5	4	35	1020	15	20	8	25	49
Chicken breast pieces (5)	150	360	27	17	3	24	0	1	80	970	4	2	2	10	39
Stuffed jalapeños (10 pieces)	240	750	20	44	17	65	7	5	80	2470	30	50	45	10	53
Barbeque dipping sauce	28	45	1	0	0	11	7	0	0	310	0	0	0	0	0
Seasoned curly fries	125	410	6	23	5	45	0	4	0	1010	6	0	4	10	50
Onion rings	120	460	7	25	5	50	3	3	0	780	4	30	4	15	49
Cappuccino ice cream shake	16*	630	11	29	17	80	58	0	90	320	15	0	35	0	41

*Fluid ounces

KFC

	Serving size g	Calories	Protein g	Total fat g	Saturated fat g	Total carbohydrate g	Sugars g	Fiber g	Cholesterol mg	Sodium mg	Vitamin A	Vitamin C	Calcium	Iron	% calories from fat
											\% Daily Value				
Original Recipe®: breast	153	400	29	24	6	16	0	1	135	1116	*	*	4	6	54
thigh	91	250	16	18	4.5	6	0	1	95	747	*	*	2	4	65
Extra Tasty Crispy™: breast	168	470	31	28	7	25	0	1	80	930	*	*	4	6	54
thigh	118	370	19	25	6	18	0	2	70	540	*	*	2	4	61
Hot & Spicy: breast	180	530	32	35	8	23	0	2	110	1110	*	*	4	6	59
thigh	107	370	18	27	7	13	0	1	90	570	*	*	*	4	66
Tender Roast™: breast (as served)	139	251	37	11	3	1	<1	0	151	830	*	*	*	*	39
breast (skin removed)	118	169	31	4	1	1	0	0	112	797	*	*	*	*	21
thigh (as served)	90	207	18	12	4	<2	<1	0	120	504	*	*	*	*	52
thigh (skin removed)	59	106	13	6	2	<1	<1	0	84	312	*	*	*	*	51
Hot Wings™ Pieces	135	471	27	33	8	18	0	2	150	1230	*	*	4	8	63
Colonel's Crispy Strips™ (3)	92	261	20	16	4	10	0	3	40	658	*	*	*	3	55
Chunky chicken pot pie	368	770	29	42	13	69	8	5	70	2160	80	2	10	10	49
Corn on the cob	162	150	5	2	0	35	8	2	0	20	2	6	*	*	12
Mashed potatoes w/gravy	136	120	1	6	1	17	0	2	<1	440	*	*	*	2	45
Mean Greens™	152	70	4	3	1	11	1	5	10	650	60	10	20	10	39
BBQ baked beans	156	190	6	3	1	33	13	6	5	760	8	*	8	10	14
Potato salad	160	230	4	14	2	23	9	23	15	540	10	*	2	15	55
Cole slaw	142	180	2	9	1.5	21	20	3	5	280	*	60	4	4	45
Biscuit (1)	56	180	4	10	2.5	20	2	<1	0	560	*	*	2	6	50

*Contains less than 2% of the Daily Value of these nutrients.

McDonald's

	Serving size g	Calories	Protein g	Total fat g	Saturated fat g	Total carbohydrate g	Sugars g	Fiber g	Cholesterol mg	Sodium mg	Vitamin A	Vitamin C	Calcium	Iron	% calories from fat
											\% Daily Value				
Hamburger	107	260	13	9	3.5	34	7	2	30	580	*	4	15	15	31
Cheeseburger	121	320	15	13	6	35	7	2	40	820	6	4	20	15	37
Quarter-Pounder®	172	420	23	21	8	37	8	2	70	820	2	4	30	25	45
Quarter-Pounder® w/cheese	200	530	28	30	13	38	9	2	95	1290	10	4	15	25	51
Big Mac®	216	560	26	31	10	45	8	3	85	1070	6	4	25	25	50
Arch Deluxe™	239	550	29	31	11	39	8	4	90	1010	10	10	15	25	51
Fish Filet Deluxe™	228	560	23	28	6	54	5	4	60	1060	6	4	8	15	45
Grilled Chicken Deluxe™	223	440	27	20	3	38	6	4	60	1040	6	8	6	15	41
French fries (large)	147	450	6	22	4	57	0	5	0	290	*	30	2	6	44
Chicken McNuggets® (6 pieces)	106	290	18	17	3.5	15	0	0	60	510	*	*	2	6	53
Barbeque sauce	28	45	0	0	0	10	10	0	0	250	*	6	*	*	0
Garden salad (no dressing)	177	35	2	0	0	7	3	3	0	20	120	40	4	6	0
Grilled chicken salad (no dressing)	257	120	21	1.5	0	7	3	3	45	240	120	25	4	8	1
Ranch dressing (1 pkg.)	N/A	230	1	21	3	10	6	0	20	550	*	2	4	*	82
Fat-free herb vinaigrette (1 pkg.)	N/A	50	0	0	0	11	9	0	0	330	*	2	*	2	0
Egg McMuffin®	136	290	17	12	4.5	27	3	1	235	790	10	2	20	15	37
Hash browns	53	130	1	8	1.5	14	0	1	0	330	*	4	*	2	55
Hotcakes w/margarine & syrup	222	570	9	16	3	100	42	2	15	750	8	*	10	15	25
Chocolate shake, small	N/A	360	11	9	6	60	54	1	40	250	6	2	35	4	23
Baked apple pie	77	260	3	13	3.5	34	13	<1	0	200	*	40	2	6	45

*Contains less than 2% of the Daily Value of these nutrients.

Taco Bell

	Serving size (oz)	Calories	Protein (g)	Total fat (g)	Saturated fat (g)	Total carbohydrate (g)	Sugars (g)	Fiber (g)	Cholesterol (mg)	Sodium (mg)	Vitamin A	Vitamin C	Calcium	Iron	% calories from fat
											% Daily Value				
Taco	2.75	180	9	10	4	12	1	3	25	330	10	0	8	6	50
Taco Supreme®	4	220	10	14	6	14	2	3	35	350	15	6	10	6	57
Double Decker Taco Supreme®	7	390	15	19	8	40	3	9	35	760	15	6	15	10	44
BLT soft taco	4.5	340	11	23	8	22	3	2	40	610	4	6	10	4	61
Burrito Supreme®	9	440	17	19	8	51	4	10	35	1230	50	8	15	15	39
Big Beef Burrito Supreme®	10.5	520	17	23	10	54	4	11	55	1520	60	8	15	15	40
Chili cheese burrito	5	330	10	13	6	37	2	5	35	870	60	0	20	8	35
Beef Gorditas Supreme®	5	300	21	13	6	31	3	3	35	390	10	4	8	15	39
Chicken Gorditas Supreme®	5	290	14	12	5	30	4	2	55	420	10	4	8	10	37
Big Beef MexiMelt®	4.75	290	21	15	7	23	0	4	45	850	25	6	20	6	47
Taco salad	19	850	9	52	15	65	1	16	60	1780	160	40	30	35	55
Taco salad w/o shell	16.5	420	5	21	11	32	1	15	60	1520	160	35	25	25	47
Chicken Fajita Wrap™	8	470	9	21	6	51		4	60	1290	35	6	15	8	42
Veggie Fajita Wrap™	8	420		19	5	53		3	20	980	35	6	15	8	41
Steak Fajita Wrap™ Supreme	9	510		25	8	52		3	50	1200	30	10	15	10	44
Big Beef Nachos Supreme	7	450		24	8	45		9	30	810	10	6	15	15	48
Nachos BellGrande®	11	720		39	11	84		17	35	1310	15	6	20	20	46
Pintos 'n cheese	4.5	190		9	4	18		10	15	650	50	0	15	10	43
Mexican rice	4.75	190		9	3.5	23		1	15	760	100	2	15	8	43
Fiesta breakfast burrito	3.5	280		16	6	25		2	25	580	15	0	8	4	51

Wendy's

	Serving size (g)	Calories	Protein (g)	Total fat (g)	Saturated fat (g)	Total carbohydrate (g)	Sugars (g)	Fiber (g)	Cholesterol (mg)	Sodium (mg)	Vitamin A	Vitamin C	Calcium	Iron	% calories from fat
											% Daily Value				
Single w/everything	219	420	25	20	7	37	9	3	70	920	6	10	13	26	43
Big Bacon Classic	282	580	34	30	12	46	11	3	100	1460	15	25	25	30	47
Jr. hamburger	118	270	15	10	3.5	34	7	2	30	610	2	2	11	17	33
Jr. bacon cheeseburger	166	380	20	19	7	34	7	2	60	850	8	10	17	19	45
Grilled chicken sandwich	189	310	27	8	1.5	35	8	2	65	790	4	10	10	15	23
Caesar side salad (no dressing)	92	110	10	5	2.5	7	1	1	15	650	35	25	15	6	41
Grilled chicken salad (no dressing)	338	200	25	8	1.5	9	6	3	50	720	120	60	19	11	36
Taco salad (no dressing)	468	380	26	19	10	28	9	7	65	1040	45	45	37	23	45
Blue cheese dressing (2T)	28	180	1	19	3	0	0	0	15	180	2	0	2	0	95
Ranch dressing, reduced fat (2T)	28	60	1	5	1	2	1	0	10	240	0	0	1	0	75
Soft breadstick	44	130	4	3	0.5	23	N/A	1	5	250	0	0	4	9	21
French fries, medium	130	390	5	19	3	50	0	5	0	120	0	10	2	6	44
Baked potato w/broccoli & cheese	411	470	9	14	2.5	80	6	9	5	470	35	120	21	25	27
Baked potato w/chili & cheese	439	630	20	24	9	83	7	9	40	770	20	60	35	28	34
Chili, small, plain	227	210	15	7	2.5	21	5	5	30	800	8	6	8	16	30
Chili, large w/cheese & crackers	363	405	28	16.5	7	37	8	7	60	1380	14	10	25	26	37
Chicken nuggets (5)	75	230	11	16	3	11	0	0	30	470	0	2	2	2	63
Barbeque sauce	28	45	1	0	0	10	7	0	0	160	0	0	1	3	0
Frosty dairy dessert, medium	298	440	11	11	7	73	56	0	50	260	20	0	41	8	23
Chicken club sandwich	216	470	31	20	4	44	6	2	70	970	4	10	11	17	38

N/A: not available.

Monitoring Your Progress

Name _____ **Section** _____ **Date** _____

As you completed the 11 labs listed below, you entered the results in the Preprogram Assessment column of this lab. Now that you have been involved in a fitness and wellness program for some time, do the labs again and enter your new results in the Postprogram Assessment column. You will probably notice improvement in several areas. Congratulations! If you are not satisfied with your progress thus far, refer to the tips for successful behavior change in Chapter 1 and throughout this book. Remember—fitness and wellness are forever. The time you invest now in developing a comprehensive, individualized program will pay off in a richer, more vital life in the years to come.

	Preprogram Assessment	**Postprogram Assessment**
LAB 2-1 Activity Index	Activity index: _____ Classification: _____	Activity index: _____ Classification: _____
LAB 3-1 Cardiorespiratory Endurance 1-mile walk test 3-minute step test 1.5-mile run-walk test Åstrand-Rhyming test	$\dot{V}O_{2max}$: _____ Rating: _____ $\dot{V}O_{2max}$: _____ Rating: _____ $\dot{V}O_{2max}$: _____ Rating: _____ $\dot{V}O_{2max}$: _____ Rating: _____	$\dot{V}O_{2max}$: _____ Rating: _____ $\dot{V}O_{2max}$: _____ Rating: _____ $\dot{V}O_{2max}$: _____ Rating: _____ $\dot{V}O_{2max}$: _____ Rating: _____
LAB 4-1 Muscular Strength Maximum bench press test Maximum leg press test Hand grip strength test	Weight: _____ lb Rating: _____ Weight: _____ lb Rating: _____ Weight: _____ kg Rating: _____	Weight: _____ lb Rating: _____ Weight: _____ lb Rating: _____ Weight: _____ kg Rating: _____
LAB 4-2 Muscular Endurance 60-second sit-up test Curl-up test Push-up test	Number: _____ Rating: _____ Number: _____ Rating: _____ Number: _____ Rating: _____	Number: _____ Rating: _____ Number: _____ Rating: _____ Number: _____ Rating: _____
LAB 5-1 Flexibility Sit-and-reach test	Score: _____ in. Rating: _____	Score: _____ in. Rating: _____

	Preprogram Assessment	Postprogram Assessment
LAB 6-1 Body Composition		
Body mass index	BMI: _____ kg/m² Rating: _____	BMI: _____ kg/m² Rating: _____
Skinfold measurements (or other method for determining percent body fat)	Sum of 3 skinfolds: _____ mm Percent body fat: _____% Rating: _____	Sum of 3 skinfolds: _____ mm Percent body fat: _____% Rating: _____
Waist circumference	Circumference: _____ Rating (√ high risk): _____	Circumference: _____ Rating (√ high risk): _____
Waist-to-hip-circumference ratio	Ratio: _____ Rating (√ high risk): _____	Ratio: _____ Rating (√ high risk): _____
LAB 8-1 Daily Diet		
Number of servings	Milk, cheese, etc.: ____	Milk, cheese, etc.: ____
Number of servings	Meat, poultry, fish, etc.: ____	Meat, poultry, fish, etc.: ____
Number of servings	Fruits: ____	Fruits: ____
Number of servings	Vegetables: ____	Vegetables: ____
Number of servings	Breads, cereals, rice, etc.: ____	Breads, cereals, rice, etc.: ____
LAB 8-2 Dietary Analysis		
Percentage of calories	From protein: _____%	From protein: _____%
Percentage of calories	From fat: _____%	From fat: _____%
Percentage of calories	From saturated fat: _____%	From saturated fat: _____%
Percentage of calories	From carbohydrate: _____%	From carbohydrate: _____%
LAB **9-1** Daily Energy Balance	Approximate daily energy expenditure: ____ cal/day	Approximate daily energy expenditure: ____ cal/day
LAB **10-1** Identifying Stressors	Average weekly stress score: ___	Average weekly stress score: ___
LAB **11-1** Cardiovascular Health CVD risk assessment Hostility assessment	Score: ____ Estimated risk: ____ Score: _____ Rating: _____	Score: ____ Estimated risk: ____ Score: _____ Rating: _____

Behavior Change Workbook

This workbook is designed to take you step by step through the process of behavior change. The first eight activities in the workbook will help you develop a successful plan—beginning with choosing a target behavior and moving through the program planning steps described in Chapter 1, including the completion and signing of a behavior change contract. The final seven activities will help you work through common obstacles to behavior change and maximize your program's chances of success.

Part 1   Developing a Plan for Behavior Change and Completing a Contract

1. Choosing a Target Behavior
2. Gathering Information About Your Target Behavior
3. Monitoring Your Current Patterns of Behavior
4. Setting Goals
5. Examining Your Attitudes About Your Target Behavior
6. Choosing Rewards
7. Breaking Behavior Chains
8. Completing a Contract for Behavior Change

Part 2   Overcoming Obstacles to Behavior Change

9. Building Motivation and Commitment
10. Managing Your Time Successfully
11. Developing Realistic Self-Talk
12. Involving the People Around You
13. Dealing with Feelings
14. Overcoming Peer Pressure: Communicating Assertively
15. Maintaining Your Program over Time

ACTIVITY 1   CHOOSING A TARGET BEHAVIOR

Use your knowledge of yourself and the results of Lab 1-1 (Lifestyle Evaluation) to identify five behaviors that you could change to improve your level of wellness. Examples of target behaviors include smoking cigarettes, not exercising regularly, eating candy bars every night, not getting enough sleep, getting drunk frequently on weekends, and not wearing a safety belt when driving or riding in a car. List your five behaviors below.

1. _____
2. _____
3. _____
4. _____
5. _____

For successful behavior change, it's best to focus on one behavior at a time. Review your list of behaviors and select one to start with. Choose a behavior that is important to you and that you are strongly motivated to change. If this will be your first attempt at behavior change, start with a simple change, such as wearing your bicycle helmet regularly, before tackling a more difficult change, such as quitting smoking. Circle the behavior on your list that you've chosen to start with; this will be your target behavior throughout this workbook.

ACTIVITY 2   GATHERING INFORMATION ABOUT YOUR TARGET BEHAVIOR

Take a close look at what your target behavior means to your health, now and in the future. How is it affecting your level of wellness? What diseases or conditions does this behavior place you at risk for? What will changing this behavior mean to you? To evaluate your behavior, use information from this text, from the resources listed in the For More Information section at the end of each chapter, and from other reliable sources.

Health behaviors have short-term and long-term benefits and costs associated with them. For example, in the short term, an inactive lifestyle allows for more time to watch TV and hang out with friends but leaves a person less able to participate in recreational activities. In the long term, it increases risk for cardiovascular disease, cancer, and premature death. Fill in the blanks below with the benefits and costs of continuing your current behavior and of changing to a new, healthier behavior. Pay close attention to the short-term benefits of the new behavior—these are an important motivating force behind successful behavior change programs.

Target (current) behavior _____

| Benefits | *Short-Term* | *Long-Term* |

| Costs | *Short-Term* | *Long-Term* |

New behavior _____

| Benefits | *Short-Term* | *Long-Term* |

| Costs | *Short-Term* | *Long-Term* |

ACTIVITY 3   MONITORING YOUR CURRENT PATTERNS OF BEHAVIOR

To develop a successful behavior change program, you need detailed information about your own behavior patterns. You can obtain this information by developing a system of record keeping, geared toward your target behavior. Depending on your target behavior, you may want to monitor a single behavior, such as your diet, or you may want to keep daily activity records to determine how you could make time for exercise or another new behavior. Consider tracking factors such as the following:

- The behavior
- When and for how long it occurs
- Where it occurs
- What else you were doing at the time
- What other people you were with and how they influenced you
- Your thoughts and feelings
- How strong your urge for the behavior was (for example, how hungry you were or how much you wanted to watch TV)

continued

Figure 1-4 (p. 11) shows a sample log for tracking daily diet. Below, create a format for a sample daily log for monitoring the behavior patterns relating to your target behavior. Then use this sample log to monitor your behavior for a day. Evaluate the log you've created as you use it. Ask yourself if you are tracking all the key factors that influence your behavior; make any necessary adjustments to the format of your log. Once you've developed an appropriate format for your log, use a separate notebook (your health journal) to keep records of your behavior for a week or two. These records will provide solid information about your behavior that will help you develop a successful behavior change program. Later activities in this workbook will ask you to analyze your records.

ACTIVITY 4 SETTING GOALS

For your behavior change program to succeed, you must set meaningful, realistic goals. In addition to an ultimate goal, set some intermediate goals—milestones that you can strive for on the way to your final objective. For example, if your overall goal is to run a 5K road race, an intermediate goal might be to successfully complete 2 weeks of your fitness program. If you set a final goal of eating five servings of fruits and vegetables every day, an intermediate goal would be to increase your daily intake from two to three servings. List your intermediate and final goals below. Don't strive for immediate perfection. Allow an adequate amount of time to reach each of your goals.

Intermediate Goals   **Target Date**

_____   _____

_____   _____

_____   _____

_____   _____

_____   _____

Final Goal

_____   _____

ACTIVITY 5 EXAMINING YOUR ATTITUDES ABOUT YOUR TARGET BEHAVIOR

Your attitudes toward your target behavior can determine whether or not your behavior change program will be successful. Consider your attitudes carefully by completing the following statements about how you think and feel about your current behavior and your goal:

1. I like _____ because _____
           (current behavior)

_____

2. I don't like _____ because _____
                (current behavior)

_____

3. I like _____ because _____
           (behavior goal)

_____

4. I don't like _____ because _____
                (behavior goal)

_____

5. I don't _____ now because _____
           (behavior goal)

_____

6. I would be more likely to _____ if _____
                              (behavior goal)

_____

continued

If your statements indicate that you have major reservations about changing your behavior, work to build your motivation and commitment before you begin your program. Look carefully at your objections to changing your behavior. How valid and important are they? What can you do to overcome them? Can you adopt any of the strategies you listed under statement 6? Review the facts about your current behavior and your goals.

ACTIVITY 6   CHOOSING REWARDS

Make a list of objects, activities, and events you can use as rewards for achieving the goals of your behavior change program. Rewards should be special, relatively inexpensive, and preferably unrelated to food or alcohol: for example, tickets to a ball game, a CD, or a long-distance phone call to a family member or friend—whatever is meaningful for you. Write down a variety of rewards you can use when you reach milestones in your program and your final goal.

_____   _____

_____   _____

_____   _____

_____   _____

Many people also find it helpful to give themselves small rewards daily or weekly for sticking with their behavior change program. These could be things like a study break, a movie, or a Saturday morning bike ride. Make a list of rewards for maintaining your program in the short term.

_____   _____

_____   _____

_____   _____

And don't forget to congratulate yourself regularly during your behavior change program. Notice how much better you feel, and savor how far you've come and how you've gained control of your behavior.

ACTIVITY 7   BREAKING BEHAVIOR CHAINS

Use the records you collected about your target behavior in Activity 3 and in your health journal to identify what leads up to your target behavior and what follows it. By tracing these chains of events, you'll be able to identify points in the chain where you can make a change that will lead to your new behavior. The sample behavior chain on the next page shows a sequence of events for a person who wants to add exercise to her daily routine—but who winds up snacking and watching TV instead. By examining the chain carefully, one can identify ways to break it at every step. After you review the sample, go through the same process for a typical chain of events involving your target behavior. Use the blank behavior chain on the following page.

Some general strategies for breaking behavior chains include the following:

- *Control or eliminate environmental cues that provoke the behavior.* Stay out of the room where your television is located. Go out for an ice cream cone instead of buying a half gallon for your freezer.
- *Change behaviors or habits that are linked to your target behavior.* If you always smoke in your car when you drive to school, try taking public transportation instead.
- *Add new cues to your environment to trigger your new behavior.* Prepare easy-to-grab healthy snacks and carry them with you to class or work. Keep your exercise clothes and equipment in a visible location.

See also the suggestions in Chapter 1 and in the box "Maximizing Your Chances of Success" on p. 14.

continued

A Sample Behavior Chain and Strategies for Breaking It

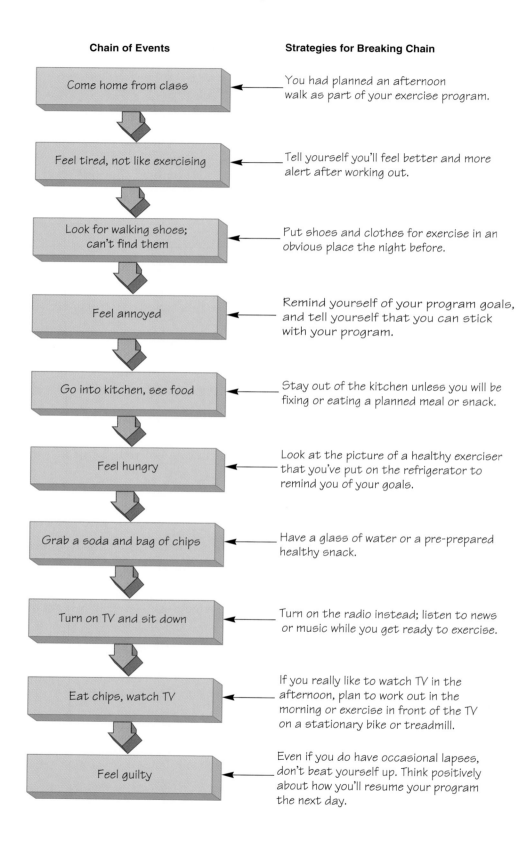

Chain of Events

Come home from class

Feel tired, not like exercising

Look for walking shoes; can't find them

Feel annoyed

Go into kitchen, see food

Feel hungry

Grab a soda and bag of chips

Turn on TV and sit down

Eat chips, watch TV

Feel guilty

Strategies for Breaking Chain

You had planned an afternoon walk as part of your exercise program.

Tell yourself you'll feel better and more alert after working out.

Put shoes and clothes for exercise in an obvious place the night before.

Remind yourself of your program goals, and tell yourself that you can stick with your program.

Stay out of the kitchen unless you will be fixing or eating a planned meal or snack.

Look at the picture of a healthy exerciser that you've put on the refrigerator to remind you of your goals.

Have a glass of water or a pre-prepared healthy snack.

Turn on the radio instead; listen to news or music while you get ready to exercise.

If you really like to watch TV in the afternoon, plan to work out in the morning or exercise in front of the TV on a stationary bike or treadmill.

Even if you do have occasional lapses, don't beat yourself up. Think positively about how you'll resume your program the next day.

continued

A Behavior Chain for Your Target Behavior

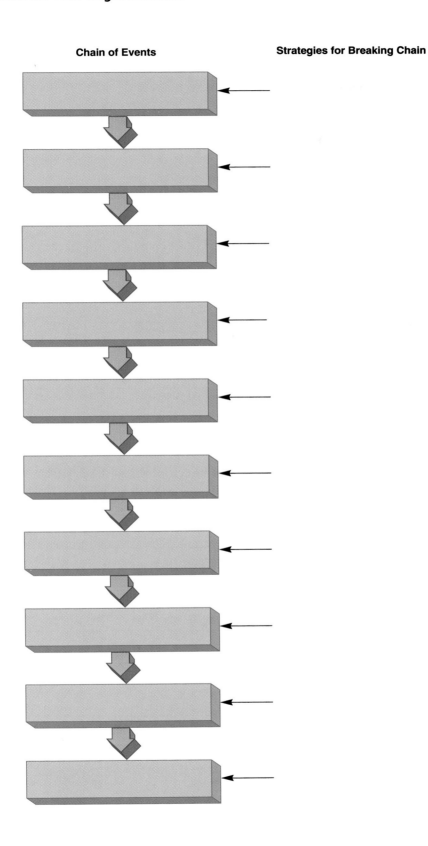

Chain of Events

Strategies for Breaking Chain

ACTIVITY 8 COMPLETING A CONTRACT FOR BEHAVIOR CHANGE

Your next step in creating a successful behavior change program is to complete and sign a behavior change contract. Your contract should include details of your program and indicate your commitment to changing your behavior. Use the information from previous activities in this workbook to complete the following contract. (If your target behavior relates to exercise, you may want to use the program plan and contract for a fitness program in Lab 7-1.)

1. I _____ agree to _____
   _____(name)_____   (specify behavior you want to change)

   _____

2. I will begin on _____ and plan to reach my goal of _____
                (start date)   (specify final goal)

   _____ by _____
                                                                       (final target date)

3. In order to reach my final goal, I have devised the following schedule of mini-goals. For each step in my program, I will give myself the reward listed.

(mini-goal 1)	(target date)	(reward)
(mini-goal 2)	(target date)	(reward)
(mini-goal 3)	(target date)	(reward)
(mini-goal 4)	(target date)	(reward)
(mini-goal 5)	(target date)	(reward)

   My overall reward for reaching my final goal will be _____

4. I have gathered and analyzed data on my target behavior and have identified the following strategies for changing my behavior: _____

   _____

   _____

5. I will use the following tools to monitor my progress toward reaching my final goal:

   _____
                               (list any charts, graphs, or journals you plan to use)

   I sign this contract as an indication of my personal commitment to reach my goal.

   _____   _____
                  (your signature)   (date)

   I have recruited a helper who will witness my contract and _____

   _____
                   (list any way in which your helper will participate in your program)

   _____   _____
                (witness's signature)   (date)

continued

Describe in detail any special strategies you will use to help change your behavior (refer to Activity 7).

Create a plan below for any charts, graphs, or journals you will use to monitor your progress. The log format you developed in Activity 3 may be appropriate, or you may need to develop a more detailed or specific record-keeping system. Examples of journal formats are included in Labs 3-2, 4-3, 5-2, 7-2, 8-1, and 10-1. You might also want to develop a graph to show your progress; posting such a graph in a prominent location can help keep your motivation strong and your program on track. Depending on your target behavior, you could graph the number of push-ups you can do, the number of servings of vegetables you eat each day, or your average daily stress level.

BEHAVIOR CHANGE WORKBOOK

Complete the following checklist to determine whether you are motivated and committed to changing your behavior. Check the statements that are true for you.

_____ I feel responsible for my own behavior and capable of managing it.

_____ I am not easily discouraged.

_____ I enjoy setting goals and then working to achieve them.

_____ I am good at keeping promises to myself.

_____ I like having a structure and schedule for my activities.

_____ I view my new behavior as a necessity, not an optional activity.

_____ Compared with previous attempts to change my behavior, I am more motivated now.

_____ My goals are realistic.

_____ I have a positive mental picture of the new behavior.

_____ Considering the stresses in my life, I feel confident that I can stick to my program.

_____ I feel prepared for lapses and ups-and-downs in my behavior change program.

_____ I feel that my plan for behavior change is enjoyable.

_____ I feel comfortable telling other people about the change I am making in my behavior.

Did you check most of these statements? If not, you need to boost your motivation and commitment. Consider these strategies:

- Review the potential benefits of changing your behavior and the costs of not changing it (see Activity 2). Pay special attention to the short-term benefits of changing your behavior, including feelings of accomplishment and self-confidence. Post a list of these benefits in a prominent location.

- Visualize yourself achieving your goal and enjoying its benefits. For example, if you want to manage time more effectively, picture yourself as a confident, organized person who systematically tackles important tasks and sets aside time each day for relaxation, exercise, and friends. Practice this type of visualization regularly.

- Put aside obstacles and objections to change. Counter thoughts such as "I'll never have time to exercise" with thoughts like "Lots of other people do it and so can I."

- Bombard yourself with propaganda. Take a class dealing with the change you want to make. Read books and watch television shows on the subject. Post motivational phrases or pictures on your refrigerator or over your desk. Talk to people who have already made the change.

- Build up your confidence. Remind yourself of other goals you've achieved. At the end of each day, mentally review your good decisions and actions. See yourself as a capable person, one who is in charge of her or his behavior.

List two strategies for boosting your motivation and commitment; choose from the list above or develop your own. Try each strategy, and then describe how well it worked for you.

Strategy 1: _____

How well it worked: _____

_____

Strategy 2: _____

How well it worked: _____

_____

"Too little time" is a common excuse for not exercising or engaging in other healthy behaviors. Learning to manage your time successfully is crucial if you are to maintain a wellness lifestyle. The first step is to examine how you are currently spending your time; use the following grid broken into blocks to track your activities.

Time	Activity	Time	Activity
6:00 A.M.		6:00 P.M.	
6:30 A.M.		6:30 P.M.	
7:00 A.M.		7:00 P.M.	
8:00 A.M.		8:00 P.M.	
9:00 A.M.		9:00 P.M.	
10:00 A.M.		10:00 P.M.	
11:00 A.M.		11:00 P.M.	
12:00 P.M.		12:00 A.M.	
1:00 P.M.		1:00 A.M.	
2:00 P.M.		2:00 A.M.	
3:00 P.M.		3:00 A.M.	
4:00 P.M.		4:00 A.M.	
5:00 P.M.		5:00 A.M.	

continued

BEHAVIOR CHANGE WORKBOOK

Next, list each type of activity and the total time you engaged in it on a given day in the chart below (for example, sleeping, 7 hours; eating, 1.5 hours; studying, 3 hours; working, 3 hours; and so on). Take a close look at your list of activities. Successful time management is based on prioritization. Assign a priority to each of your activities according to how important it is to you: essential (A), somewhat important (B), or not important (C). Based on these priority rankings, make changes in your schedule by adding and subtracting hours from different categories of activities; enter a duration goal for each activity. Add your new activities to the list, and assign a priority and duration goal to each.

Activity	Current Total Duration	Priority (A, B, or C)	Goal Total Duration

Prioritizing in this manner will involve tradeoffs. For example, you may choose to reduce the amount of time you spend watching television, listening to music, and chatting on the telephone while you increase the amount of time spent sleeping, studying, and exercising. Don't feel that you have to miss out on anything you enjoy. You can get more from less time by focusing on what you are doing. Strategies for managing time more productively and creatively are described in Chapter 10.

ACTIVITY 11   DEVELOPING REALISTIC SELF-TALK

Self-talk is the ongoing internal dialogue we have with ourselves throughout much of the day. Our thoughts can be accurate, positive, and supportive, or they can be exaggerated and negative. Self-talk is closely related to self-esteem and self-concept. Realistic self-talk can help maintain positive self-esteem, the belief that one is a good and competent person, worthy of friendship and love. A negative internal dialogue can reinforce negative self-esteem and can make behavior change very difficult. Substituting realistic self-talk for negative self-talk can help you build and maintain self-esteem and cope better with the challenges in your life.

First, take a closer look at your current pattern of self-talk. Use your health journal to track self-talk, especially as it relates to your target behavior. Does any of your self-talk fall into the common patterns of distorted negative self-talk shown in Chapter 10 (p. 263)? If so, use the examples of realistic self-talk from Chapter 10 to develop more accurate and rational responses. Write your current negative thoughts in the left-hand column, and then record more realistic responses in the right-hand column.

Current Self-Talk About Target Behavior

More Realistic Self-Talk

Your behavior change program will be more successful if the people around you are supportive and involved—or at least are not sabotaging your efforts. Use your health journal to track how other people influence your target behavior and your efforts to change it. For example, do you always skip exercising when you're with certain people? Do you always drink or eat too much when you socialize with certain friends? Are friends and family members offering you enthusiastic support for your efforts to change your behavior, or do they make jokes about your program? Have they even noticed your efforts? Summarize the reactions of those around you in the chart below.

Target behavior: _____

Person	Typical Effect on Target Behavior	Involvement in/Reaction to Program

It may be difficult to change the actions and reactions of the people who are close to you. For them to be involved in your program, you may need to develop new ways of interacting with them (for example, taking a walk rather than going out to dinner as a means of socializing). Most of your friends and family members will want to help you—if they know how. Ask for exactly the type of help or involvement you want. Do you want feedback, praise, or just cooperation? Would you like someone to witness your contract or to be involved more directly in your program? Do you want someone to stop sabotaging your efforts by inviting you to watch TV, eat rich desserts, and so on? Look for ways that the people who are close to you can share in your behavior change program. They can help to motivate you and to maintain your commitment to your program. Develop a way that each individual you listed above can become involved in your program in a positive way.

Person	Target Involvement in Behavior Change Program

Choose one person on your list to tackle first. Talk to that person about her or his current behavior and how you would like her or him to be involved in your behavior change program. Below, describe this person's reaction to your talk and her or his subsequent behavior. Did this individual become a positive participant in your behavior change program?

_____

_____

_____

_____

BEHAVIOR CHANGE WORKBOOK

Longstanding habits are difficult to change in part because many represent ways people have developed to cope with certain feelings. For example, people may overeat when bored, skip their exercise sessions when frustrated, or drink alcoholic beverages when anxious. Developing new ways to deal with feelings can help improve the chance that a behavior change program will succeed.

Review the records on your target behavior that you kept in your health journal. Identify the feelings that are interfering with the success of your program, and develop new strategies for coping with them. Some common problematic feelings are listed below, along with one possible coping strategy for each. Put a check mark next to those that are influencing your target behavior, and fill in additional strategies. Add the other feelings that are significant roadblocks in your program to the bottom of the chart, along with coping strategies for each.

✔	Feeling	Coping Strategies
	Stressed out	Go for a 10-minute walk.
	Anxious	Do one of the relaxation exercises described in Chapter 10.
	Bored	Call a friend for a chat.
	Tired	Take a 20-minute nap.
	Frustrated	Identify the source of the feeling, and deal with it constructively.

- Julia is trying to give up smoking; her friend Marie continues to offer her cigarettes whenever they are together.

- Emilio is planning to exercise in the morning; his roommates tell him he's being antisocial by not having brunch with them.

- Tracy's boyfriend told her that in high school he once experimented with drugs and shared needles; she wants him to have an HIV test, but he says he's sure the people he shared needles with were not infected.

Peer pressure is the common ingredient in these situations. To successfully maintain your behavior change program, you must develop effective strategies for resisting peer pressure. Assertive communication is one such strategy. By communicating assertively—firmly, but not aggressively—you can stick with your program even in the face of pressure from others. Review your health journal to determine how other people affect your target behavior. If you find that you often do give in to peer pressure, try the following strategies for communicating more assertively.

- Collect your thoughts, and plan in advance what you will say. You might try out your response on a friend to get some feedback.

- State your case—how you feel and what you want—as clearly as you can.

- Use "I" messages—statements about how you feel—rather than statements beginning with "You."

- Focus on the behavior rather than the person. Suggest a solution, such as asking the other person to change his or her behavior toward you. Avoid generalizations. Be specific about what you want.

- Make clear, constructive requests. Focus on your needs ("I would like . . .") rather than the mistakes of others ("You always . . .").

- Avoid blaming, accusing, and belittling. Treat others with the same respect you'd like to receive yourself.

- Ask for action ahead of time. Tell others what you would like to happen; don't wait for them to do the wrong thing and then get angry at them.

- Ask for a response to what you have proposed. Wait for an answer, and listen carefully to it. Try to understand other people's points of view, just as you would hope that others would understand yours.

With these strategies in mind, review your health journal and identify three instances in which peer pressure interfered with your behavior change program. For each of these instances, write out what you might have said to deal with the situation more assertively. (If you can't find three situations from your own experiences, choose one or more of the three scenarios described at the beginning of this activity.)

1. _____

_____

_____

2. _____

_____

_____

3. _____

_____

_____

Assertive communication can help you achieve your behavior change goals in a direct way by helping you keep your program on track. It can also provide a boost for your self-image and increase your confidence in your ability to successfully manage your own behavior.

If you maintain your new behavior for at least 6 months, your chances of lifetime success are greatly increased. However, you may find yourself sliding back into old habits at some point. If this happens, there are some things you can do to help maintain your new behavior.

• Remind yourself of the goals of your program (list them here).

_____

_____

_____

_____

_____

• Pay attention to how your new pattern of behavior has improved your wellness status. List the major benefits of changing your behavior, both now and in the future.

_____

_____

_____

_____

_____

• Consider the things you enjoy most about your new pattern of behavior. List your favorite aspects.

_____

_____

_____

_____

_____

• Think of yourself as a problem solver. If something begins to interfere with your program, devise strategies for dealing with it. Take time out now to list things that have the potential to derail your program, and develop possible coping mechanisms.

Problem	**Solution**
_____	_____
	_____
_____	_____
	_____
_____	_____
	_____

• Remember the basics of behavior change. If your program runs into trouble, go back to keeping records of your behavior to pinpoint problem areas. Make adjustments in your program to deal with new disruptions. And don't feel defeated if you lapse. The best thing you can do is to renew your commitment and continue with your program.

Index

Boldface numbers indicate pages on which glossary definitions appear. "*t*" indicates that the information is in a table.

accidents. *See* injuries
acid precipitation, 369–370
acquired immunodeficiency syndrome (AIDS), **338**–343, 351–352
   See also HIV infection
ACSM. *See* American College of Sports Medicine
active stretching, **113**–114
activities. *See* physical activity
activity index, 35–36
addictive behaviors, 312–**313**
adenosine triphosphate (ATP), **42**
adipose tissue, 138, **139**
   See also body fat
aerobic, **42**, 43
aerobic exercise. *See* cardiorespiratory endurance exercise
aerobic (oxidative) energy system, **42**, 43–44, 43*t*, 44
African Americans
   body image ideal of, 238
   cancer among, 296, 298
   cardiovascular disease (CVD) among, 278, 279
   diabetes among, 140
   exercise among, 20*t*
   hypertension among, 7, 278, 279
   obesity among, 228*t*
   smoking among, 323*t*
aging, 362–364
   attitude toward, 363
   body composition and, 364
   cardiovascular disease (CVD) and, 277–278
   flexibility and, 24, 110
   free radicals and, 45
   life-enhancing measures for, 362–364
   muscular strength and, 24, 70–71
   nutrition and, 209
   physical activity and, 5
   physical changes with, 362
agonists, **74**, 75–76
AIDS (acquired immunodeficiency syndrome), **338**–343, 351–352
   See also HIV infection
air bags, A-1
air quality, exercise and, 58
   See also pollution
alcohol, 4*t*, 17, 317–322
   assessment of problem with, 333–334
   binge drinking, 320–**321**
   blood alcohol concentration (BAC), **318**, 320
   calories from, 184, B-4
   cardiovascular disease and, 277, 284, 320, 329
   cancer and, 294, 298, 302, 329
   coffee and, 329
   deaths and, 4*t*, 318
   driving and, 321, 323, A-1
   effects of, 318–320, 319*t*
   ethyl, **318**
   fetal alcohol syndrome (FAS), 320, **321**
   insomnia and, 259
   moderate consumption of, 206, 284, 322, 323
   osteoporosis and, 196
   responsible use of, 322, 323
   wellness and, 5
   women and, 322, 329
   See also psychoactive drugs
alcohol abuse, 320, **321**–322, 364

alcohol dependence, 320, **321**
Alcoholics Anonymous, 14, 334
alcoholism, 320, **321**
alcohol poisoning, 318, 329
alveoli, **42**
amenorrhea, **141**, 209, 239
American Cancer Society (ACS), 294, 305
American College of Sports Medicine (ACSM), 28, 29*t*, 51–52, 77, 114, 236
American Dietetic Association, 209, 236
American Heart Association (AHA), 274, 284
American Indians. *See* Native Americans
American Psychiatric Association, 314
amino acids, 96*t*, **184**–186
anabolic steroids, **95**, 96*t*
anaerobic, **42**, 43
anaerobic (nonoxidative) energy system, **42**, 43, 43*t*, 44
anatomy
   cardiorespiratory system, 40–42
   digestive system, 185
   heart blood supply, 282
   muscular system, 80, 81
   nervous system, 254, 256
   respiratory system, **42**
   sexual, 344, 345
   spine, 119–121
androgens, 71
androstenedione, 96*t*
anemia, **194**, **195**
anger, 277, 285, 290
angina pectoris, **280**, 281
anorexia nervosa, **196**, 238–**239**
antagonists, **74**, 75–76
antioxidants, 45, **192**, 197, **303**
anxiety, 277
aorta, 40, **41**
apples vs. pears, in body shape, 139, 141
arrhythmia, **280**, 281
arteries, **41**–42, 280–282
   See also cardiovascular disease
arthritis, 110, 167
Asian Americans
   cardiovascular disease (CVD) among, 278
   diet of, 211
   osteoporosis among, 196
   smoking among, 323*t*
aspirin, 281, 294, 365
assessment
   alcohol problem, 333–334
   body composition, 142–144, 149–154
   cancer risk factors, 309–310
   cardiorespiratory fitness, 47–50, 49*t*, 50*t*, 61–66
   cardiovascular health, 289–290
   diet/nutrition, 17, 217–224
   eating disorders, 251–252
   energy balance, 245–248
   flexibility, 112, 129–134
   hostility, 290
   lifestyle, 17–18
   maximal oxygen consumption, 47–50, 49*t*, 50*t*, 61–66
   muscular endurance, 71, 103–106
   muscular strength, 71, 99–102
   physical activity level, 35–36
   physical activity readiness (PAR-Q), 37–38
   physical fitness, 27
   smoking habits, 335–336
   STD-related behaviors and attitudes, 355–356
   stress, 269–270
   wellness dimensions, 373–374
asthma, 167
Åstrand-Rhyming cycle ergometer test, 49, 63–66

atherosclerosis, **274**, 280–281
   See also coronary heart disease; stroke
athletes, nutritional guidelines for, 209–210
ATP (adenosine triphosphate), **42**
   See also energy systems
atria, 40, **41**
attitude
   toward aging, 363
   about locus of control, 9–10
   sexually transmitted diseases (STDs) and, 355–356
auricles. *See* atria
autonomic nervous system, **254**
AZT, 340

back
   low-back pain, 70, 110–111, 121–126
   spinal anatomy, 119–121
back, exercises for, 123–126
ballistic stretching, **113**
balloon angioplasty, 281
basal cell carcinoma, 297–298
behavior
   addictive, 312–**313**
   changing, 9–13, W-1–W-16
   STDs and, 355–356
   target, **10**
   for wellness, 4–7
behavioral self-management. *See* lifestyle management
behavior chains, 10, W-5–W-7
behavior change plans, 10–13, W-1–W-16
   contracts for, 11–12, 13, 159, 179–180, W-8–W-9
   goals in, 10, 11–12, W-4
   health journals for, 10, 11, 12, W-2–W-3
   rewards in, 11, 13, W-4
   sample, 12
   workbook for, W-1–W-16
   See also lifestyle; personal fitness program; stress management; weight management
benign tumors, **292**
Benson, Herbert, 263
bicycling
   calorie costs for, 175*t*
   equipment for, 173
   safety when, 169, 174, A-2
   sample program for, 173–174
binge drinking, 320–**321**
binge eating, **230**
binge eating disorder, **239**
bioelectrical impedance analysis (BIA), 144, 153
biopsy, **294**, 306
blacks. *See* African Americans
bladder cancer, 298–299
blister, 55*t*
blood alcohol concentration (BAC), **318**, 320, A-1
blood lipids. *See* cholesterol
blood pressure, **44**, 45, 279–280, 285, 289
   See also hypertension (high blood pressure)
blood vessels, 41–42
BMI. *See* body mass index (BMI)
body composition, 24–**25**, 138–156
   aging and, 364
   assessment of, 142–144, 149–154
   cardiorespiratory endurance and, 51, 145
   coronary heart disease and, 139, 228, 276
   developing healthy, 29, 29*t*, 160–161*t*
   frequently asked questions about, 145–146
   gender differences in, 138, 153
   genetics and, 144, 145–146
   and health, 139–141
   physical fitness and, 146
   self-image and, 141–142
   spot reducing, 145

body composition (*continued*)
  weight training and, 70, 95, 145
  wellness and, 142
  See also weight management
body fat, 42
  assessment of, 142, 144–145, 149–154
  cardiorespiratory endurance exercise and, 46
  cellulite, 146
  distribution of, 139, 141, 144, 153–154, 276
  essential vs. nonessential, 138, 139
  liposuction of, 146
  low, 141
  muscle vs., 95
  percent, **138–139**, 139*t*, 144, 150–153, 155
  physical activity and, 138–139
  See also obesity; overweight
body image, **237–239**
  exercise and, 141
  "perfect," 141–142, 237–238, 242
  See also self-image
body mass index (BMI), **142**–143, 143*t*, 144, 155,
  228, 237
body weight. *See* weight
bone density. *See* osteoporosis
botulism, 213
bread, cereals, rice, and pasta food group, 202, 204*t*
  See also carbohydrates; grains
breast cancer, 294–296
  behavior/heredity role in, 7, 9–10
  detecting, 294, 295, 305*t*, 367
  genetic testing for, 306
  incidence of, 293
  risk factors for, 46, 302–303, 304, 309, 329
breast self-examination, 294, 295, 305*t*
breathing, for relaxation, 264–265, 266
bruises, 55*t*
buddy system
  for changing behavior, 14
  for exercising, 165
  for weight training, 95
bulimia nervosa, **239**
burnout, 166, **258**, 259–260
butter, vs. margarine, 212, B-6

caffeine, 196, 259, 314*t*, 329
  See also psychoactive drugs
calcium, 194, 195*t*, 196, 200*t*, 201*t*, 203, 208
calipers, **142**, 143
calorie costs, 160–161*t*, 162, **163**, 234*t*
  for bicycling, 175*t*
  for in-line skating, 178
  for physical activities, 22, 160–161*t*, 234*t*,
  246–248
  for sports, 160–161*t*
  for swimming, 176*t*
  for walking/jogging/running, 171*t*
calories, **184**
  from alcohol, 184, 231
  avoiding hidden, 231
  from carbohydrates, 184, 232
  in common foods, B-1–B-10
  in fast food, C-1–C-4
  from fats, 184, 188, 189, 231–232
  from proteins, 184, 232–233
  See also diet; food; nutrition
cancer, **292–310**
  alcohol and, 294, 298, 302, 329
  bladder, 298–299
  breast, 7, 9–10, 46, 293, 294–296, 302–303,
  304, 309, 329
  causes of, 300–304
  cervical, 296–297, 304, 306, 347
  colon, 46, 189, 191, 293, 294, 302, 304,309
  deaths caused by, 3, 4*t*, 292, 293

defined, **292**
  diet and, 189, 191, 197, 206, 294, 296, 302–304,
  305, 310
  exercise and, 46, 294, 304, 305
  frequently asked questions about, 306
  genetics and, 300–301, 306
  leukemia, 292, 293, 299–300
  lung, 5, 292–294, 309, 324, 326
  lymphomas, 293, 300, 304
  oral, 293, 298, 303, 309, 328–329
  ovarian, 293, 297
  pancreatic, 293, 298
  physical activity and, 46, 294, 304, 305
  preventing, 305
  prostate, 293, 296, 302, 304, 309
  rectal, 293, 294, 309
  risk factors for, 306, 309–310
  screening tests for, 294, 295, 296, 300, 305,
  305*t*, 367
  skin, 293, 296–298, 305, 310, 369
  smoking and, 293, 303, 305, 324, 326
  socioeconomic status and, 301
  spit tobacco and, 298, 328–329
  support groups and, 296
  testicular, 297, 298
  treatment of, 306
  uterine (endometrial), 293, 296, 297, 309
  warning signs of, 304, 305
capillaries, **41**–42
carbohydrates, 42, 190–192
  calories from, 184, 232
  in diet of athletes, 209
  as essential nutrient, 185*t*, 190–192
  fiber in, 191–192, 192*t*
  goals for intake of, 189
  refined vs. unrefined, 140, 190–191, 303
  simple vs. complex, 190–191, 202–204, 205
  See also dietary fiber
carcinogens, **292**, 293, 304, 305
cardiorespiratory endurance, **23–24**, 40–68
  activities/sports for, 28–29, 29*t*, 51, 52, 158,
  160–161*t*
  assessing level of, 61–66
  body composition and, 51, 145
  gender differences in, 51
  physiology of, 40–44
cardiorespiratory endurance exercise
  benefits of, 44–47, 48, 51
  cool down/warm up for, 53, 170
  creating program for, 50–53, 67–68, 162–163
  duration of, 26, 28, 53, 54, 162, 170
  frequency of, 25, 28, 51, 163, 168, 170
  frequently asked questions about, 57–58
  intensity of, 51–52, 54, 162–163, 170
  sample programs for, 170–173, 174, 175–176,
  177–178
  with special health concerns, 57–58, 167–168
cardiorespiratory fitness, **23–24**
  assessment of, 47–50, 49*t*, 50*t*, 61–66
  maintaining, 53
cardiorespiratory system, **40**–42, 44–45, 48
cardiovascular disease (CVD), **46, 274**
  alcohol and, 284, 320, 329
  body fat distribution and, 276
  cardiorespiratory endurance exercise and, 46
  deaths caused by, 3, 4*t*
  diet and, 188–189, 190, 191, 283–284,
  285–286
  frequently asked questions about, 285–286
  gender differences in, 277, 278, 285
  major forms of, 279–283
  preventing, 46, 283–286
  risk assessment for, 289–290
  risk factors for, 46, 274–279

smoking and, 274, 279, 284, 289, 324
  stress and, 258, 277, 285, 289
  See also specific forms of cardiovascular disease
carotenoids, **303**
CD4 T cells, **338**, 339
cellulite, 146
Centers for Disease Control and Prevention (CDC),
  139, 231, 329
cervical cancer, 296–297, 304, 306, 347
chancres, **349**–350
change. *See* behavior change plans
chemicals
  in environment, 304, 369
  in foods, 304
  phytochemical, **197, 303**, 310
chemotherapy, 306
children
  environmental tobacco smoke and, 326
  fetal alcohol syndrome (FAS) in, 320
  genital herpes and, 347
Chinese food, guidelines for choosing, 211
chlamydia, 279, **343**–344, 346
cholesterol, **188**
  blood levels of, 46, 188, 189, 274–276, 276*t*,
  285, 367
  cardiovascular disease (CVD) and, 274–276, 289
  reducing intake of, 283–284
  See also lipoproteins
chromosomes, 300, **301**
chronic diseases, **2**, 3
  cardiorespiratory endurance exercise and, 45–46
  diet and, 4–5
  free radicals and, 45, 197
  See also specific diseases
circulation, pulmonary/systemic, 40, **41**
cirrhosis of the liver, 4*t*, **318**
clothing
  exercise, 57, 169
  shoes, 164–165
cocaine, 312*t*, 314*t*, 316
codependency, **329**
cold weather, and exercise, 58
collagen, **110**, 111
collars, in weight training, 79
college students
  binge drinking among, 320–321
  drug use among, 312*t*
  eating strategies for, 210
  nutritional guidelines for, 209
  sexually transmitted diseases among, 338, 343
  stressors for, 259, 260
colon cancer, 46, 293, 294, 302, 304, 309
commitment
  in behavior change programs, 13, 164, 240, W-10
  in interpersonal relationships, 361–362
communication
  in interpersonal relationships, 359–361
  with physicians, 366
  about STDs, 348, 356
  stress management and, 263
complex carbohydrates, 190–191, 202–204, 205
compulsive gambling, 313
compulsive shopping/spending, 313
computed tomography, 306
concentric muscle contractions, **72**, 73, 74
condoms, 347, 348, 351, 352, 356
conflict resolution, 360–361
congestive heart failure, **282**, 283
connective tissues, 111–112, 113
consumer guidelines
  evaluating health news, 287
  exercise equipment, 57, 59
  exercise footwear, 164–165
  fitness centers, 33

food labels, 207
HIV tests, 353
managed care, 368
quitting smoking, 328
weight-loss programs, 236, 237
contraceptives
and sexually transmitted diseases, 352
and smoking, 274
See also condoms
contracts
for behavior change, 11–12, 13, 159, 179–180,
W-8–W-9
for personal fitness programs, 159, 179–180
control, locus of, **9**–10
cool down, 30, 166
in cardiorespiratory endurance exercise, 53, 170
in weight training, 77
Cooper Institute for Aerobics Research, 236
coping strategies
for family crises, 362
weight management and, 235
coronary arteries, 42, 46, **280**
coronary bypass surgery, 281
coronary heart disease (CHD), **46, 280**
body composition and, 139, 228
deaths caused by, 3, 4*t*
exercise and, 168
weight training and, 81
cortisol, **254**, 255
counseling
for changing behavior, 14
for stress management, 265
See also psychotherapy
cramps, muscle, 55*t*
creatine monohydrate, 96*t*
cross-training, 57, 160, **161**, 166
cruciferous vegetables, **202, 303**
Cuban Americans. *See* Hispanic Americans
CVD. *See* cardiovascular disease (CVD)

Daily Values, 200–**201**
dairy products, 203, 204*t*, 208, B-6
date rape, A-8
death, causes of, 3, 4*t*, 5, 6, 292, 293
delayed-onset muscle soreness, **110**, 111
delirium tremens (DTs), **322**
dependence. *See* psychoactive drugs
depression
cardiovascular disease (CVD) and, 277
in older adults, 364
osteoporosis and, 196
stress and, 267
suicide and, 267
DES (diethylstilbestrol), 297
dexfenfluramine, 236–237
diabetes, 4*t*, 7, 140
and body mass index (BMI), 143
cardiovascular disease (CVD) and, 46, 277, 289
diet and, 140
ethnic background and, 7, 140
exercise and, 46, 140, 167–168
gestational, 140
obesity and, 139, 140
Type 1 and Type 2, 140
warning signs of, 140
Diagnostic and Statistical Manual of Mental Disorders
(American Psychiatric Association), 314
diastole, 40, **41**
diet
aging and, 209, 364
assessment of, 17, 217–224
cancer and, 189, 197, 206, 294, 296, 302–304,
305, 310
for cardiorespiratory exercise, 57, 209

cardiovascular disease (CVD) and, 188–189,
197, 283–284, 285–286
diabetes and, 140, 190, 191
ethnic, 211
healthy, 184–197, 212
meat in, 213, 214
osteoporosis and, 194, 196
record of, 11, 217–220, 241
serving sizes and, 231
vegetarian, 206–208
for weight management, 231–233, 235–236, 241
weight training and, 95, 96*t*
for wellness, 5
See also nutrients, essential; nutrition
diet aids, 236
"Dietary Approaches to Stop Hypertension"
(DASH), 284
dietary fiber, 140, **190**, 191–192, 192*t*, 236, 284,
294, 302
Dietary Guidelines for Americans, **197**–198,
205–206
Dietary Reference Intakes (DRIs), **197**, 198, 200–201*t*
dietary supplements, 57, 95, 96*t*, 198–200, 209
diet books, 236
dieting, 230, 231, 235–237
See also weight management
digestion, **184**
digestive system, 185
disabilities, physical fitness and, 26
disaccharides, **190**
diseases
chronic, **2**, 3, 4–5, 45–46, 197
infectious, **2**, 3
preventing, 18, 45–46
stress and, 257–258
See also sexually transmitted diseases (STDs);
specific diseases
distress, **256**, 257
diversity
attitudes toward aging, 363
cardiorespiratory endurance, 51
cardiovascular disease and, 278, 279, 285
ethnic foods, 211
HIV infection worldwide, 341
muscular strength and, 71
physical fitness and disabilities, 26
poverty and cancer, 301
wellness and, 7
women and alcohol, 322
See also educational attainment; ethnic groups;
gender differences; socioeconomic status
DNA (deoxyribonucleic acid), 300, **301**
drinking
aging and, 364
binge, 320–**321**
and driving, 4*t*, 321, 323, A-1
health and, 4*t*, 329
responsibility and, 322, 323
See also alcohol
driving, alcohol and, 4*t*, 321, 323, A-1
drug abuse, 312*t*, 314–317, 329, 349
drugs, 17, 312, **313**
See also medications; psychoactive drugs
DTs (delirium tremens), **322**
duration of exercise, 26, 28, 29*t*, 30, 35, 53,
162–163, 164–165
for cardiorespiratory endurance, 26, 28, 29*t*, 53,
54, 162, 170
for flexibility, 29*t*, 114, 163
in weight training, 29*t*, 76–77, 163
dynamic flexibility, 110

eating disorders, 230, 237, **238**–240
assessment of, 251–252

helping someone with, 240
treatment of, 239
types of, 238–239
See also body image
eating habits
for college students, 210
weight management and, 232, 233, 241
See also diet; nutrition
eccentric loading, **74**
eccentric muscle contractions, **72**, 73, 74
ectopic pregnancy, **326**, 343
educational attainment, 7, 20*t*, 277, 301, 316,
323*t*, 366
elastin, **110**, 111
emergency care, A-8–A-9
emotional wellness, 2, 3
assessment of, 373, 374
cardiorespiratory endurance exercise and, 47
See also mind-body connection; stress
emotions
behavior change and, 12–13, W-14
stress and, 256
weight management and, 234–235
endocrine system, **254**–255
endometrial (uterine) cancer, 293, 297, 309
endorphins, **46**, 47, **254**, 255
endurance. *See* cardiorespiratory endurance;
muscular endurance
energy balance, 229–230
assessment of, 245–248
exercise and, 145
to gain weight, 230, 242
to lose weight, 230, 240
energy expenditures. *See* calorie costs
energy systems, 42, 43–44, 43*t*
environment
carcinogens in, 304, 305
for changing behavior, 10–11, W-5–W-7
protecting, 370
stressors in, 260
wellness and, 7
environmental health, 367–370
environmental tobacco smoke (ETS), **274**, 289,
293, 305, **324**–326, 327
environmental wellness, 2–3, 373, 374
ephedrine, 96*t*, 236, 314*t*
epinephrine, **46**, 47, **254**, 255
equipment. *See* exercise equipment
essential fat, 138, **139**
essential nutrients. *See* nutrients, essential
Estimated Minimum Requirements, 198, 199*t*
Estimated Safe and Adequate Daily Dietary Intakes
(ESADDIs), 198, 199*t*
estrogen, 196, 278, 285, 294
ethnic groups
cancer among, 296, 298
cardiovascular disease (CVD) among, 278,
279
diabetes among, 7, 140
diet of, 211
eating disorders among, 238
exercise among, 20*t*
overweight/obesity among, 228*t*
smoking among, 323*t*
testicular cancer among, 298
wellness and, 7
See also specific groups
ethyl alcohol, **318**
eustress, **256**, 257
exercise
advice on, 32
benefits of, 21
body composition and, 145, 146
body image and, 141

exercise (*continued*)
  cancer and, 46, 294, 304, 305
  cardiovascular disease (CVD) and, 46, 276, 284, 289
  clothing for, 57, 164–165, 169
  cool down after, 30, 53, 77, 166
  defined, 20–**21**
  designing program for, 27–31
  diabetes and, 46, 140, 167–168
  duration of, 26, 28, 29*t*, 30, 35, 53, 162–163, 164–165
  energy systems and, 43–44
  fluids and, 57, 58, 209
  frequency of, 25, 28, 29*t*, 30, 35, 51, 77, 114, 162–163, 165, 168
  frequently asked questions about, 32, 57–58, 95, 126, 146, 168–169
  intensity of, 26, 28, 29*t*, 30, 35, 51–53, 76, 114, 162–163, 164–165
  isokinetic, **74**
  isometric, **72**, 73, 75, 88
  isotonic, **72**, 73–74, 75
  metabolism and, 45, 70, 145, 230
  osteoporosis and, 46, 168, 196
  for physical fitness, 22, 27
  recommended amount of, 27, 29*t*
  safety of, 32, 37, 57–58, 78–80, 168–169
  scheduling, 32
  with special health concerns, 32, 57–58, 167–168
  stress management and, 260–261, 262, 271
  warm up before, 30, 53, 77, 166
  weather and, 58, 166
  weight management and, 45, 70, 95, 138–139, 233–234
  See also cardiorespiratory endurance exercise; personal fitness programs; physical training; stretching; weight training
exercise equipment
  bicycling, 169, 173
  consumer guidelines on, 57, 59
  in-line skating, 169, 177
  safety and, 169, A-5
  swimming, 175
  weight training, 74, 75, 81–83, 82*t*, 84–94, 99–101
exercise injuries. *See* injuries
exercise machines
  Nautilus weight machines, 74, 81, 82*t*, 83, 89–94
  safety with, 79–80
  Universal weight machines, 82*t*, 83, 99–101
  in weight training, 74, 75, 79–80, 81–83, 82*t*, 99–101
exercise stress test, **32**, 281

family relationships, 362
fast food, 212, 225–226
  guidelines for choosing, 210
  nutritional content of, C-1–C-4
fast-twitch fibers, **72**
fat-free foods. *See* reduced-fat foods
fat-free mass, 24, **25**
  See also body composition
fats, 42, 186–190
  in butter vs. margarine, 212
  calories from, 184, 188, 189, 231–232
  cancer and, 189, 294, 296, 302
  cardiovascular disease and, 188–189, 276, 283–284
  as essential nutrient, 185*t*, 186–190
  goals for intake of, 189
  in meat, 213, 214
  reducing intake of, 203–204, 205, 206, 231, 242, 283–284

types of, 186–188
  See also body fat; cholesterol
fats, oils, and sweets food group, 203–204
fatty acids
  monounsaturated, 186, **187**, 283, 302
  omega-3, **188**–189, 285
  polyunsaturated, 186, **187**, 188–189, 283, 302
  saturated, 186, **187**, 188, 212, 276, 283, 302
  trans, **187**, 188, 212, 276, 284
feelings. *See* emotions
females. *See* women
fenfluramine, 236–237
fen-phen, herbal, 236
fetal alcohol syndrome (FAS), 320, **321**
fiber, dietary, **190**, 191–192, 192*t*
  cancer and, 191, 294, 302
  cardiovascular disease and, 190, 191, 284
  diabetes and, 140, 191
  in diet aids, 236
  in foods, 192*t*, B-1–B-10, C-1–C-4
  increased intake of, 191–192, 284
  insoluble vs. soluble, **190**, 191
fibers, muscle, 72
fight-or-flight reaction, **254**, 255, 256
fitness. *See* cardiorespiratory fitness; physical fitness
fitness centers, 32, 33
fitness programs. *See* personal fitness programs
flexibility, 24, **25**, 110–136
  activities for developing, 28, 29, 160–161*t*
  aging and, 24, 110
  assessment of, 112, 129–134
  benefits of, 110–111
  creating program for, 112–119, 135–136, 163
  dynamic, 110
  exercises for, 115–127
  frequency of exercise for, 25, 28, 29*t*, 114
  frequently asked questions about, 126
  injuries and, 110–111
  intensity of exercise for, 114, 163
  jogging and, 126
  joint structure and, 111
  low-back pain and, 110–111, 119–126
  physiological determinants of, 111–112
  safe stretching for, 114, 126, 127
  sample programs for, 115–127, 173, 174, 177, 178
  static, 110
  stretching techniques for, 112–113
  types of, 110
  weight training and, 126
  See also stretching
fluids, exercise and, 57, 58, 209
folate, 192, 193*t*, 194, 198, 201*t*
food
  chemicals in, 304
  fast, 210, 212, 225–226, C-1–C-4
  nutritional content of, B-1–B-10, C-1–C-4
  reduced-fat, 204, 242
  reducing calorie intake from, 231
  serving sizes of, 203, 212, 213, 231
  See also diet; nutrition
Food Guide Pyramid, **197**, 201–205, 208
  vs. actual diet, 204*t*, 217–220
  food groups in, 202–204
  food labels and, 206
  servings in, 202, 212–213
food journals, 11, 217–224, 241
food labels, 206, 207, 225
food poisoning, 213
footwear, 164–165
fractures, 55*t*
free radicals, **44**, 45, **197**, 303
free weights, in weight training, 74, 75, 79, 81, 82, 83, 84–88

frequency of exercise, 25, 28, 29*t*, 30, 35, 51, 77, 114, 162–163, 165, 168
  for cardiorespiratory endurance, 25, 28, 51, 163, 168, 170
  for flexibility, 25, 28, 29*t*, 114
  in stretching, 114, 163
  in weight training, 28, 77, 95, 163, 168
frequently asked questions
  about body composition, 145–146
  about cancer, 306
  about cardiorespiratory endurance exercise, 57–58
  about cardiovascular disease (CVD), 285–286
  about nutrition, 212–213
  about personal fitness programs, 168–169
  about physical fitness, 32
  about sexually transmitted diseases, 351–352
  about stress, 267
  about stretching and flexibility, 126
  about substance abuse, 328–329
  about weight management, 242
  about weight training, 95
friendships, 260, 261, 358, 359
fruits
  fiber in, 192*t*
  food group, 202–203, 204*t*
  increasing intake of, 302
  nutritional content of, B-1–B-2

gambling, compulsive, 313
GAS (general adaptation syndrome), **256**, 257
gender differences
  in body composition, 138, 153
  in cancer incidence, 293
  in cardiorespiratory endurance, 51
  in cardiovascular disease (CVD), 277, 278, 285
  in effects of STDs, 343, 345, 346, 350
  in muscular strength, 71
  in rates of exercise, 20*t*
  in smoking hazards, 324
  weight training and, 70, 71, 95
  wellness and, 7
  See also men; women
general adaptation syndrome (GAS), **256**, 257
genes, 300, **301**
genetics
  body composition and, 144, 145–146
  cancer and, 300–301, 306
  cardiovascular disease (CVD) and, 277, 279, 289
  obesity/overweight and, 228–229, 232
  physical training and, 26–27
  wellness and, 7
genital herpes, **346**, 347–349
genital warts, **346**–347
global warming, 369
glucose, **42**, 43*t*, **190**
glycogen, **42**, 43*t*, **190**
goals
  for behavior change, 10, 11–12, W-4
  for cardiorespiratory endurance programs, 50
  for fat, protein, and carbohydrate intake, 189
  of Healthy People initiative, 8*t*
  for personal fitness programs, 27, 158, 163
  time management and, 261–262
  for weight loss, 238, 249–250
  in weight management, 144–145, 240
gonorrhea, 344–346, **345**
grains
  fiber in, 192*t*
  increasing intake of, 302
  nutritional content of, B-4–B-5
  whole, 191, 192
  See also bread, cereals, rice, and pasta food group; carbohydrates; phytochemicals
greenhouse effect, 369

hatha yoga, 265
HDLs (high-density lipoproteins), 46, **188**, 189, **274**, 275, 276, 285, 289
health
    body composition and, 139–141
    drinking and, 329
    environmental, 367–370
    obesity and, 139, 141
    See also wellness
health care, 7, 301, 364–367, 368
health clubs, 32, 33
health information, evaluating, 286, 287
health insurance, 366–367
health journals, 10, 12, W-2–W-3
    food journals, 11, 217–224, 241
    for quitting smoking, 327
Healthy People initiative, 8, 8t
heart
    blood supply to, 282
    cardiorespiratory endurance exercise and, 44–45
    circulation in, 40–41
    See also cardiorespiratory system
heart attacks, 274, 278, **280**, 281–282, 283, 285
heart disease. *See* coronary heart disease (CHD)
heart rate
    monitoring, 49, 50
    physical fitness and, 45
    target heart rate zone, **51**–52
heat disorders, 58
hemophilia, **340**
hepatitis, 304, **349**
herbal fen-phen, 236
heredity. *See* genetics
heroin, 312t, 314t, 316
herpes, genital, **346**, 347–349
high blood pressure. *See* hypertension (high blood pressure)
high-density lipoproteins (HDLs), 46, **188**, 189, **274**, 275, 276, 285, 289
Hispanic Americans
    attitude toward aging, 363
    cardiovascular disease (CVD) among, 278
    diabetes among, 7, 140
    diet of, 211
    exercise among, 20t
    obesity among, 228t
    smoking among, 323t
HIV antibody test, 341, 351, 353
HIV infection, 4t, **338**–343, 351–352, 353
    information on, 350–351
    prevalence of, 338, 341
    preventing, 341, 343, 348, 351
    symptoms of, 340–342
    transmission of, 338–340
    treatment for, 342
HIV-positive, **340**, 341–342
homeostasis, **254**, 255–256
homocysteine, 278–279, 286
hormone replacement therapy (HRT), 196
hormones
    androgens, 71
    estrogen, 196, 278, 285, 294
    stress and, **254**, 255
    testosterone, **70**
hostility, 277, 285, 290
hot weather, and exercise, 58, 166
human immunodeficiency virus (HIV), **338**
human papillomavirus (HPV), **346**–347
    cancer caused by, 296, 304, 306, 347
hydrogenation, 186–**187**
    See also trans fatty acids
hydrostatic (underwater) weighing, 143–144, 145, 153

hypertension (high blood pressure), 46, **274**, 279–280, 367
    body composition and, 139, 143
    diet and, 210, 284
    exercise and, 168
    among ethnic groups, 7, 278, 279
    weight training and, 81
hypertrophy, **72**

illness, exercise and, 32
imagery, 264
immediate energy system, **42**, 43, 43t, 44
immune system
    cardiorespiratory endurance exercise and, 47
    stress and, 258, 261
inactivity. *See* physical inactivity
income. *See* socioeconomic status
Indian food, guidelines for choosing, 211
Indians. *See* Native Americans
infectious diseases, **2**, 3
    See also sexually transmitted diseases (STDs)
infertility, 343, 346
injuries, 4t, 53–56, 70, A-1–A-10
    alcohol and, 4t, 318, 320, 321, A-1, A-2, A-5, A-8
    exercise and, 53–56, 70, 81, A-5
    flexibility and, 110–111
    intentional, A-6–A-10
    medical attention for, 54, A-8
    motor vehicle–related, 4t, 318, 320, 321, A-1, A-2
    preventing, 54, 56, 70, A-1–A-10
    rehabilitation after, 55
    R-I-C-E treatment for, 55, 81
    sports and, A-5
    treatment for minor, 54, 55, 55t
    unintentional, 4t, **5**, 7, A-1–A-6
    violence and, A-6–A-10
    in weight training, 81
    See also low-back pain
in-line skating
    calorie costs for, 178
    equipment for, 177
    injury prevention for, 177, A-5
    sample program for, 177–178
insoluble fiber, **190**, 191, 294
insomnia, 259
intellectual wellness, 2, 3, 373, 374
intensity of exercise, 26, 28, 29t, 30, 35, 51–53, 76, 114, 162–163, 164–165
    for cardiorespiratory endurance, 51–52, 54, 162–163, 170
    for flexibility, 114, 163
    in weight training, 76, 163
Internet addiction, 313
interpersonal relationships, 358–362
    commitment in, 361–362
    communication in, 359–361
    conflict resolution in, 360–361
    in families, 362
    forming, 358–359
    in friendships, 358, 359
    intimacy and, 358–359
    marriage, 361–362
    as stressors, 260
    See also social support
interpersonal wellness, 2, 3, 373, 374
interval training, **167**, 170
intervertebral disks, **119**–121
intimacy, 358–359
intoxication, 312, **313**
Ionamin, 236
iron, 194, 195t, 199t, 205, 208
isokinetic exercise, **74**
isometric exercise, **72**, 73, 75, 88

isotonic exercise, **72**, 73–74, 75
Italian food, guidelines for choosing, 211

Japanese food, guidelines for choosing, 211
jaundice, **349**
jobs, stress related to, 259–260
jogging
    calorie costs for, 171t
    flexibility and, 126
    progression in, 25, 172t
    safety when, 168–169
    sample program for, 168–173
    shoes for, 164–165
    See also running
joint capsules, **110**, 111
joints, 110, 111
journals. *See* health journals

Kaposi's sarcoma, 340
kilocalories (kcalories), **184**

lactic acid, **42**, 43
lacto-ovo-vegetarians, **208**
lacto-vegetarians, **208**
laparoscopy, **346**
Latinos. *See* Hispanic Americans
LDLs (low-density lipoproteins), 46, **188**, 275, **276**, 279, 285
legumes, **190**, 191, 192t, 202, B-9–B-10
leukemia, 292, 293, 299–300
lice, pubic ("crabs"), 350
life events
    changing behavior and, 9
    stressful, 258–259, 269
life expectancy, 3, 5, 324
lifestyle
    assessment of, 17–18
    breast cancer and, 294
    for cancer prevention, 305
    for cardiovascular disease (CVD) prevention, 283–285
    daily physical activity in, 21–22, 163
    for healthy aging, 364
    inactive, 4, 6, 20, 276, 284, 300t, 304
    stress management and, 258–260, 271
    weight management and, 230–235
    for wellness, 4–7
lifestyle management, 8–15, 370–371, W-1–W-16
    behavior change plan for, 10–13
    locus of control and, 9–10
    motivation for, 9, 13
    persistence with, 13–14
    physical training and, 30–31
    stress and, 13–14
    support for, 13, 14
    target behavior in, 10
    workbook for, W-1–W-16
ligaments, 70
lipids. *See* cholesterol; fats
lipoproteins, 46, **274**, 275–276
    high-density (HDLs), 46, **188**, 189, **274**, 275, 276, 285, 289
    lipoprotein(a) [Lp(a)], 279
    low-density (LDLs), 46, **188**, 275, **276**, 279, 285
liposuction, 146
liver, cirrhosis of, 4t, **318**
locus of control, **9**–10
love relationships, 358–359, 361–362
low-back pain
    exercises for, 123–126
    flexibility and, 110–111, 119–126
    posture and, 121–122

low-back pain (continued)
  preventing, 70, 121–122
  risk factors for, 121
low-density lipoproteins (LDLs), 46, **188**, 275, **276**, 279, 285
lung cancer, 292–294, 309, 324, 325, 326
lymphatic system, **292**
lymphomas, 293, 300, 304

magnesium, 194, 195t, 200t, 201t
magnetic resonance imaging (MRI), 281, 306
mainstream smoke, **324**
males. See men
malignant tumors, **292**
  See also cancer
mammography, **294**, 305t, 367
managed care, 366, 368
margarine, vs. butter, 212, B-6
marijuana, 312t, 315t, 316
marriage, 361–362
Matthews, Dale, 278
maximal oxygen consumption, **44**, 46–50, 49t, 50t, 61–66
meat
  guidelines for choosing, 213, 214
  nutritional content of, B-8–B-9
  serving sizes of, 203
meat, poultry, fish, dry beans, eggs, and nuts food group, 203, 204t
medical care, 364–367, 368
medications, 17
  aging and, 364
  AIDS, 342, 351–352
  to enhance weight training, 96t
  for quitting smoking, 328
  self-treatment with, 365
  for weight loss, 236–237
meditation, 264
melanoma, **298**
men
  body composition of, 138, 151
  cardiorespiratory endurance of, 51
  cardiovascular disease in, 278
  condoms for, 347, 348, 351, 352, 356
  muscular strength of, 71
  nutritional guidelines for, 208
  prostate cancer in, 293, 296, 302, 304, 309
  screening tests for, 367
  sexual anatomy of, 344
  smoking by, 323t, 324
  testicle self-examination by, 300
  testicular cancer in, 297, 298
  See also gender differences
menopause, 196
menstruation, 57, 199, 239
mental health, 47
  See also emotional wellness
Meridia, 236
metabolic rate
  physical activity and, 42, 230
  physical fitness and, 44
metabolism, 24, **25**, 42, 229–230
  of alcohol, 318
  exercise and, 45, 145, 230
  overweight/obesity and, 229–230
  resting metabolic rate (RMR), **228**, 229–230, 245–246
metastasis, **292**
Mexican Americans. See Hispanic Americans
Mexican food, guidelines for choosing, 211
microorganisms, and cancer, 304
milk, yogurt, and cheese food group, 203, 204t
  See also dairy products

mind-body connection
  emotions and cardiovascular disease, 277, 285, 290
  exercise and body image, 141
  exercise and emotional wellness, 21, 47
  exercise and total wellness, 4–6, 21, 47, 111
  natural world and wellness, 369
  psychoneuroimmunology, **258**
  religion, 278, 363
  self-talk, 234–**235**, 262–263, 271, W-12
  stress and immunity, 258
  in weight management, 234–235
  See also social support; spiritual wellness; stress
minerals
  as essential nutrients, 185t, 194, **195**, 195t
  supplements of, 198–200, 209
mitochondria, **44**
moderate physical activity, 21–22
monosaccharides, **190**
monounsaturated fatty acids, 186, **187**, 283, 302
mood and exercise, 21, 47
motivation
  for changing behavior, 9, 13, W-10
  for weight management, 240
motor units, **72**–73
motor vehicle–related injuries, 4t, 318, 320, 321, A-1, A-2
MRI, 281, 306
muscle dysmorphia, 239
muscle fibers, **72**
muscles
  agonists vs. antagonists, **74**, 75–76
  cardiorespiratory endurance exercise and, 48
  contractions of, **72**, 73, 74
  vs. fat, 95
  flexibility and, 111–112
  names of, 80–81
  soreness of, 55t, 95, **110**, 111
  weight training and. See weight training
muscular endurance, 24, **25**, 76
  activities for, 29, 160–161t
  assessment of, 71, 103–106
  benefits of, 70–71
  sample programs for, 81–94, 173, 174, 176–177, 178
  See also weight training
muscular strength, 24, **25**, 76
  activities for, 29, 160–161t
  aging and, 70–71
  assessment of, 71, 99–102
  benefits of, 70–71
  gender differences in, 71
  sample programs for, 81–94, 173, 174, 176–177, 178
  See also weight training
muscular system, 80–81
myofibrils, **72**

National Cholesterol Education Program (NCEP), 276t, 283–284, 285
National Heart, Lung, and Blood Institute, 143, 237
National Spit Tobacco Education Program, 328
National Weight Control Registry (NWCR), 233
Native Americans
  attitude toward aging, 363
  diabetes among, 7, 140
nature, 369
  See also environment
Nautilus weight machines, 74, 81, 82t, 83, 89–94
nerve roots, **119**, 120
nervous system
  autonomic, **254**
  flexibility and, 112

muscular strength and, 72–73, 75
  somatic, **256**
  stress and, 254
neurotransmitters, **46**, 47
nicotine, 316, **322**–323
  See also smoking; spit tobacco
nicotine replacement therapy, 328
nonessential (storage) fat, 138, **139**
nonoxidative (anaerobic) energy system, **42**, 43, 43t, 44
norepinephrine, **46**, 47, **254**, 255
nucleoside analogs, 342
nutrients, essential, 184–197, 185t
  calories from, 184
  carbohydrates, 42, 185t, 189, 190–192, 232
  fats, 42, 185t, 186–190, 231–232
  minerals, 185t, 194, **195**, 195t
  proteins, 42, 184–186, 185t, 189
  vitamins, 185t, 192–194, 193t
  water, 57, 58, 185t, 194–197, 209
nutrition, 184–225
  assessment of, 17, 217–224
  eating strategies for, 210
  food labels and, 206, 225
  food poisoning and, 213
  frequently asked questions about, 212–213
  personal plan for, 210–212
  in restaurants, 212, 225–226
  serving sizes and, 203, 212, 213
  stress management and, 261, 271
  weight management and, 231–233, 241
  See also diet
nutritional content of foods, B-1–B-10, C-1–C-4
nutritional guidelines, 197–210
  for athletes, 57, 95, 209–210
  for college students, 210
  Daily Values, 200–**201**
  Dietary Guidelines for Americans, **197**–198, 205–206
  Dietary Reference Intakes (DRIs), **197**, 198, 200–201t
  Food Guide Pyramid, **197**, 201–205, 204t, 206, 212–213, 217–220
  Recommended Dietary Allowances (RDAs), **197**, 198–201, 199t
  for special population groups, 208–210
  for vegetarians, 206–208

obesity, 138–**139**
  classification of, 138–139, 143
  factors contributing to, 228–230
  genetics and, 228–229, 232
  health implications of, 46, 139, 141, 228, 276, 304
  metabolism and, 229–230
  physical activity and, 138–139, 168
  prevalence of, 228t
  See also body composition; overweight; weight management
Olean, 242
olestra, 242
omega-3 fatty acids, **188**–189, 285
oncogenes, **301**
oral cancer, 293, 298, 303, 309, 328
osteoporosis, 46, 71, 168, 194, **195**, 196
ovarian cancer, 293, 297
overfat, 138
  See also body fat
overload. See progressive overload
overtraining, 30, **31**, 261
overweight, 138, **139**, 142
  cardiovascular disease and, 276–277, 289
  classification of, 143

I-6   Index

factors contributing to, 228–230
genetics and, 228–229, 232
health implications of, 140, 228
metabolism and, 229–230
prevalence of, 228t
See also body composition; obesity; weight
management
oxidative (aerobic) energy system, **42**, 43–44,
43t, 44
oxygen, maximal consumption of, **44**, 47–50, 49t,
50t, 61–66
ozone layer, 369

pain
flexibility and, 111
low-back, 70, 110–111, 121–126
pancreatic cancer, 293, 298
Pap tests, 296–**297**, 305t, 344, 347, 351, 367
Paralympics, 26
parasympathetic division of autonomic nervous
system, **254**
partial vegetarians, **208**
partners
for changing behavior, 14
exercise, 165
sexual, 359
weight training, 95
passive stretching, **113**, 114
pears vs. apples, in body shape, 139, 141
peer counseling, 265
peer pressure, W-15
pelvic inflammatory disease (PID), 343, 345, **346**
perceived exertion, ratings of (RPE), 52–**53**, 168
percent body fat, 138–**139**, 139t, 144, 150–153,
155
personal contracts. *See* contracts
personal fitness programs, 158–182
activities for, 28–29, 158–162
assessment for, 27
beginning and maintaining, 164–166, 168
contract for, 159, 179–180
designing, 27–31, 158–164
examples of, 29–30, 159, 170–178
frequently asked questions about, 168–169
goals of, 27, 158, 163
interval training in, **167**, 170
program log in, 163, 181–182
sample programs for, 170–178
with special health concerns, 167–168
warm up and cool down in, 166
See also cardiorespiratory endurance exercise;
stretching; weight training
personality traits
cardiovascular disease (CVD) and, 276
stress and, 256
personal trainers, 32
pesco-vegetarians, **208**
phentermine, 236
phenylpropanolamine hydrochloride (PPA), 236
physical activity, 20, **21**–23
adults regularly engaging in, 20t, 139
assessment of level of, 35–36
benefits of, 4–5, 6, 20–23
calories burned in, 22, 160–161t, 234t,
246–248
cancer and, 4, 294, 304, 305
for cardiorespiratory endurance, 28–29, 29t, 51,
52, 158, 160–161t
continuum of, 20–23, 28
defined, 20–**21**
exercise and, 20–21, 22–23
for flexibility, 28, 29, 160–161t
metabolic rate and, 42, 230
moderate, 21–22

for muscular strength/endurance, 19, 70, 160–161t
obesity and, 138–139
for personal fitness programs, 28–30, 158,
160–162
for physical fitness, 21–23, 160–161t, 162
Surgeon General on, 20, 21–23, 139, 234
tips for increasing, 23
weight management and, 138–139, 233–234, 240
weight training and, 83t
See also exercise; sports
physical activity pyramid, 28
Physical Activity Readiness Questionnaire (PAR-Q),
32, 37–38
physical dependence, **315**
physical fitness, 4–**5**, 6, 20–38
activities/sports for, 28–29, 160–161t
aging and, 24, 364
assessment of, 27
benefits of, 4–5, 6, 23–25
body composition and, 146
components of, 23–25
disability and, 26
exercise for, 22–23, 27
metabolic rate and, 44
reversibility of, 26
See also body composition; cardiorespiratory
endurance; flexibility; muscular endurance;
muscular strength; personal fitness programs
physical inactivity, 4, 6, 20, 139
cancer and, 294, 300t, 304
cardiovascular disease (CVD) and, 276, 284
physical training, **25**
cross-training, 57, 160, **161**, 166
designing program for, 27–31, 158–164
guidelines for, 30–31
heredity and, 26–27
interval training, **167**, 170
mental aspects of, 30–31
overtraining, 30, **31**, 261
partners for, 30
principles of, 25–27
progressive overload in, 25–26, 30, 31
recommended amounts of, 29t
resistance training, 26, 29t, 74, 233
reversibility and, 26
specificity of, 25
strength training, 24, 28, 46
See also exercise; weight training
physical wellness, 2, 3, 373, 374
physicians, 365, 366
phytochemicals, **197**, 285–286, 302, **303**, 310
PID. *See* pelvic inflammatory disease
planetary wellness, 2–3, 373, 374
See also environmental health
plaque, **280**, 281
platelets, **274**, 281
plyometrics, **74**
PNF. *See* proprioceptive neuromuscular facilitation
(PNF)
pollution, 304, 369–370
See also environmental tobacco smoke (ETS)
polysaccharides, **190**
polyunsaturated fatty acids, 186, **187**, 188–189,
283, 302
Pondimin, 236–237
population growth, 368
posture
flexibility and, 111
low-back pain and, 121–122
poverty
cancer and, 301
cardiovascular disease (CVD) and, 277, 279
and health insurance coverage, 366
See also socioeconomic status

power, muscular, **72**
pregnancy
alcohol use during, 320
diabetes during, 140
ectopic, **326**, 343, 346
exercise and, 57–58
nutrition during, 198, 199t, 200–201t
sexually transmitted diseases and, 340, 343, 344,
346, 347, 349
smoking during, 326
progressive overload, **25**–26, 30, 31, 165
progressive relaxation, 264
proprioceptive neuromuscular facilitation (PNF),
112, **113**
prostate cancer, 293, 296, 302, 304, 309
protease inhibitors, 306, 342
proteases, **95**
proteins, 42, 184–186
calories from, 184, 232, B-8–B-10
as essential nutrient, 184–186, 185t
exercise and, 42, 95, 96t, 209
goals for intake of, 189
in weight-loss diets, 236
PSA blood test, 296, **297**
psychoactive drugs, 5, 312, **313**–317
abuse of, 314–315
considerations before trying, 317
dependence on, 315–316
effects and uses of, 314–315t
preventing abuse of, 317, 329
substitutes for, 317
treatment for abuse of, 316–317
types of, 314–315t
users (abusers) of, 312t, 316
withdrawal from, 315–316
See also alcohol; smoking
psychoneuroimmunology (PNI), **258**
See also mind-body connection
psychotherapy
for stress management, 265
for weight management, 237
See also counseling
pubic lice ("crabs"), 350
Puerto Rican Americans. *See* Hispanic
Americans
pulmonary circulation, 40, **41**
pulse, 49, 50, 51–52
See also target heart rate zone
purging, **239**
pyramid
Food Guide, **197**, 201–205
physical activity, 28

race. *See* ethnic groups
radiation
as cancer treatment, 306
as carcinogen, 304, 369
ultraviolet (UV), **297**, 369
range of motion, 24, 73, **110**, 130–134
rape, A-7–A-8
ratings of perceived exertion (RPE), 52–**53**,
168
Recommended Dietary Allowances (RDAs), **197**,
198–201, 199t
record keeping
food journals, 11, 217–220, 241
health journals, 10, 12, 327, W-2–W-3
program logs, 68, 108, 136, 163, 181–182,
D-1–D-2
stress logs, 270
rectal cancer, 293, 294, 309
reduced-fat foods, 204, 242
Redux, 236–237
relationships. *See* interpersonal relationships

relaxation
  flexibility exercises for, 111
  techniques for, 263–265, 266–267, 271–272
relaxation response, **263**
religion, 278, 363
  See also spiritual wellness
repetitions, 29*t*, **70**, 71, 76–77, 95, 114
repetitions maximum (RM), **70**, 71
resistance, in weight training, 76, 77, 95
resistance training, 26, 29*t*, 74, 233
  See also weight training
respiratory system, **42**
restaurants, healthy diet in, 210, 212, 225–226
resting metabolic rate (RMR), **228**, 229–230, 245–246
restrained eating theory, 230
reversibility, 26, **27**
rewards
  for behavior change, 11, 13, W-5
  in personal fitness program, 163
rheumatic fever, **282**, 283
R-I-C-E treatment, 55, 81
RM (repetitions maximum), **70**, 71, 76–77, 95
RPE (ratings of perceived exertion), 52–**53**, 168
running, 26, 44
  benefits of, 21
  calorie costs for, 171*t*
  flexibility and, 126
  progression in, 25
  safety when, 168–169
  sample program for, 170–173
  shoes for, 164–165

safety, 18, A-1–A-10
  when bicycling, 174, A-2
  for cardiorespiratory endurance assessment tests, 49
  when driving, 321, 323, A-1–A-2
  of exercise, 32, 37–38, 57–58, 168–169
  when jogging or walking, 168–169, A-2
  during pregnancy, 57–58
  in stretching, 114, 126, 127
  when swimming, 175, A-5
  weather and, 58
  in weight training, 78–79
  See also injuries
salt (sodium), 195*t*, 199*t*, 205–206, 280, 284, 304
sample exercises,
  low back, 123–126
  stretching, 115–119
  weight training/free weights, 84–88
  weight training/weight machines, 89–94
sample fitness programs, 170–178
  advanced walking, 170, 171, 173
  beginning jogging, 170, 171–172, 173
  beginning walking, 170, 171, 173
  bicycling, 173–175
  in-line skating, 177–178
  jogging/running, 170–171, 173
  swimming, 175–177
saturated fatty acids, 186, **187**, 188, 212, 276, 283, 302
screening tests, 367
  cancer, 294, 295, 296, 300, 305, 305*t*, 367
sedentary lifestyle. *See* physical inactivity
self-esteem, 358
self-examination
  breast, 294, 295, 305*t*
  testicle, 300
self-help groups. *See* support groups
self-image
  body composition and, 141–142
  interpersonal relationships and, 358
  stress management and, 267

weight training and, 70
  See also body image
self-talk, 263, W-12
  stress management and, 262–263, 271
  weight management and, 234–**235**
self-treatment, 54, 55, 365
Selye, Hans, 257
semivegetarians, **208**
serving sizes, 202–203, 212–213
sets, in weight training, 29*t*, 76–77, 95
sexual anatomy, 344, 345
sexual assault, A-7–A-8
sexually transmitted diseases (STDs), **338**–356
  AIDS, **338**–343, 351–352
  behaviors and attitudes related to, 355–356
  cervical cancer and, 296, 304, 306, 347
  chlamydia, **343**–344, 346
  communication about, 356
  frequently asked questions about, 351–352
  genital warts, **346**–347
  gonorrhea, 344–346, **345**
  hepatitis, **349**
  herpes, **346**, 347–349
  HIV infection, **338**–343, 351–352, 353
  infertility and, 343, 346
  information about, 350–351
  pelvic inflammatory disease (PID), 343, 345, **346**
  preventing, 5, 7, 343, 348, 351, 352
  pubic lice ("crabs"), 350
  syphilis, **349**–350
  treatment of, 351
  trichomoniasis ("trich"), 350
shin splints, 55*t*
shoes, 164–165
sibutramine, 236
side stitch, 55*t*
sidestream smoke, **324**
simple carbohydrates (sugars), 140, 190–191, 202–204, 205, 232
skin, protection of, 297, 298, 299, 305, 364
skin cancer, 293, 296–298, 305, 310, 369
skinfold measurements, 143, 144, 149–152
sleep, 259, 271
slow-twitch fibers, **72**
smog, exercise and, 58
smokeless (spit) tobacco, 298, 312*t*, 328–329
smoking, 4*t*, 5, 17, 322–328
  aging and, 364
  cancer and, 293, 303, 305, 328
  cardiovascular disease (CVD) and, 274, 279, 284, 289, 324
  environmental tobacco smoke (ETS), 293, 305, 324–326, 327
  health effects of, 4*t*, 5, 323–324, 325
  incidence of, 323*t*
  osteoporosis and, 196
  pregnancy and, 326
  public action against, 327
  quitting, 325, 327–328
  reasons for, 335–336
  substances in cigarette smoke, 324*t*
  wellness and, 5
  women and, 323*t*, 324, 326
  See also spit tobacco
social support
  for behavior change, 11, 13, W-13
  cardiovascular disease (CVD) and, 277
  for quitting smoking, 327
  stress management and, 260, 261, 271
  See also interpersonal relationships; support groups
social wellness, 2, 3, 47, 373, 374
socioeconomic status
  cancer and, 301

cardiovascular disease (CVD) and, 277, 279
  exercise and, 20*t*
  health insurance coverage and, 366
  obesity and, 230
  wellness and, 7
sodium (salt), 195*t*, 199*t*, 205–206, 280, 284, 304
soft tissue, **110**, 111
soluble fiber, **190**, 191
somatic nervous system, **256**
soy foods, 197, 203, 208, 286
specificity, **25**
speed loading, **74**
Spiegel, David, 296
spine, function and structure of, 119–121
spiritual wellness, 2, 3, 362, 363
  in family relationships, 362
  nature and, 369
  personal profile of, 373, 374
  religion and, 278, 363
  See also mind-body connection
spit tobacco, 298, 312*t*, 328–329
sports
  calorie costs of, 160–161*t*
  for cardiorespiratory endurance, 28–29, 29*t*, 51, 52, 158, 160–161*t*
  energy systems and, 44
  flexibility and, 111
  for physical fitness, 160–161*t*
  safety for, A-5
  weight training for, 83*t*, 95
  See also exercise; physical activity
spot reducing, 145
spotters, **74**, 75, 79, 84, 86
sprains, 55*t*
squamous cell carcinoma, **298**
static flexibility, 110
static stretching, 112–**113**
STDs. *See* sexually transmitted diseases (STDs)
steroids, anabolic, **95**, 96*t*
strength, muscular. *See* muscular strength
strength training, 24, 28, 46
  See also weight training
stress, 254–272, **254**
  aging and, 364
  assessment of, 269–270
  cardiorespiratory endurance exercise and, 47
  cardiovascular disease (CVD) and, 258, 277, 285, 289
  depression and, 267
  disease and, 257–258
  experience of, 254–256, 269
  frequently asked questions about, 267
  immune system and, 258, 261
  lifestyle management and, 13–14, 265
  poverty and, 301
  signals of, 269
  sleep and, 259, 271
  sources of, 258–260, 269, 270
  and wellness, 5
stress management, 18, 260–265, 271–272
  communication and, 263
  counseling for, 265
  exercise and, 47, 111, 260–261, 262, 271
  nutrition and, 261, 271
  psychotherapy for, 265
  relaxation techniques for, 263–265, 266–267, 271–272
  self-talk and, 262–263, 271, W-12
  social support and, 260, 261, 271
  support groups for, 265
  time management and, 261–262, 271, W-11–W-12
  weight management and, 235
  for wellness, 5

stressors, **254**, 269–270
  common, 258–260
  general adaptation syndrome (GAS) and, 257
  responses to, 254–256, 269
stress response, **254**
stress test, exercise, **32**
stretching
  active, **113**–114
  ballistic, **113**
  benefits of, 110–111
  duration of, 114, 163
  to end exercise session, 166
  exercises for, 115–127
  frequency of, 25, 28, 29t, 114, 163
  frequently asked questions about, 126
  intensity of, 114, 163
  passive, **113**
  safe, 114, 126, 127
  static, 112–**113**
  types of techniques for, 112–113
  vs. warm up, 114, 126
  See also flexibility
stretch receptors, 112, **113**
stroke, **282**
  body fat distribution and, 139
  deaths caused by, 3, 4t
  exercise and, 46
  high blood pressure and, 46, 282
  smoking and, 274
  See also cardiovascular disease
substance abuse, 312–336, **315**
  addictive behavior and, 312–313
  frequently asked questions about, 328–329
  See also alcohol; psychoactive drugs; smoking
substance dependence, **315**–316
  See also alcoholism; psychoactive drugs
sugar
  in blood, 140, 190
  in food, 140, 190–191, 204t, 232, B-1–B-10
  reducing intake of, 203–204, 205, 232
  See also carbohydrates
suicide, 4t, 267, 313
sunlight, and cancer, 297–298, 299
sunscreen, 299, 305
supplements, dietary, 96t, 198–200, 207, 209
support groups
  cancer, 296
  for changing behavior, 14
  genital herpes, 348–349
  for quitting smoking, 327, 328
  stress management, 265
  See also social support
Surgeon General, U.S., 6, 20, 21–23, 139, 234
surgery
  for cancer treatment, 306
  for weight loss, 146, 237
swimming
  asthma and, 167
  calorie costs for, 176t
  equipment for, 175
  safety in, 175, A-5
  sample program for, 175–177
sympathetic division of autonomic nervous system, **254**
synovial fluid, **53**
syphilis, **349**–350
systemic circulation, 40, **41**
systole, 40–**41**

t'ai chi ch'uan, 265
tanning salons, 297, 299, 305
target behavior, **10**, W-1
  See also behavior change
target heart rate zone, **51**–52

tendinitis, 55t
tendons, **70**, 111
testicle self-examination, 300
testicular cancer, 297, 298
testosterone, **70**
Thai food, guidelines for choosing, 211
thought patterns. *See* self-talk
time management
  exercise and, 32, 162
  stress management and, 261–262, 271, W-11–W-12
tissues
  adipose, 138, **139**
  connective, 111–112, 113
  muscle, 72, 111–112
  soft, **110**, 111
  See also body fat
titin, **110**, 111
tobacco use. *See* smoking; spit tobacco
tofu, 192t, 203, 208, 286
tolerance, drug, **315**, 320
training. *See* physical training
trans fatty acids, **187**, 188, 212, 276, 284
trichomoniasis ("trich"), 350
triglycerides, 186, **187**, 275, 277
tumors, benign/malignant, **292**

ultrasonography, **294**, 306
ultraviolet (UV) radiation, **297**, 369
underwater (hydrostatic) weighing, 143–144, 145, 153
unintentional injuries, 4t, **5**, 7, A-1–A-6
Universal weight machines, 82t, 83, 99–101
unsaturated fatty acids
  monounsaturated, 186, **187**, 283, 302
  polyunsaturated, 186, **187**, 188–189, 283, 302
U.S. Department of Health and Human Services, 142
U.S. Environmental Protection Agency (EPA), 326
U.S. Food and Drug Administration (FDA), 142
U.S. Surgeon General, 6, 20, 21–23, 139, 234
uterine (endometrial), cancer, 293, 296, 297, 309

vegans, **208**
vegetables
  cruciferous, **202**, **303**
  fiber in, 192t
  food group, 202, 204t
  increasing intake of, 302
  nutritional content of, B-2–B-3
  See also carbohydrates; dietary fiber
vegetarians, 199, 206–208
veins, **41**
venae cavae, 40, **41**
ventricles, 40, **41**
vertebrae, **119**, 120
violence, and injuries, 318, 321, A-6–A-8
visualization, 264
vitamins
  as essential nutrients, 185t, **192**–194, 193t
  supplements of, 198–200, 209, 261
  See also antioxidants

waist circumference, 141, 143, 145, 153–154
waist-to-hip circumference ratio, 141, 145, 153–154
walking, 31, 170–173
  to begin fitness program, 168
  calorie costs for, 171t
  progression in, 172t
  safety when, 168–169
  sample programs for, 170–173
  shoes for, 164–165
warm up, 30, 166
  for cardiorespiratory endurance exercise, 53, 170

  vs. stretching, 114, 126
  for weight training, 77
warts, genital, **346**–347
water
  as essential nutrient, 185t, **194**–197
  exercise and, 57, 58, 209
weather, exercise and, 58, 166
weighing
  assessing body composition with, 142
  underwater (hydrostatic), 143–144, 145, 153
weight
  blood alcohol level and, 320
  gaining, 145, 242
  losing, 145, 231, 233, 235–238, 242, 249–250
  realistic, 142, 144
  target, 144–145, 155–156
  for wellness, 5
  See also body composition; obesity; overweight
weight cycling, 230
weight gain, strategies for, 145, 242
weight loss
  aids for, 236
  books for, 236
  commercial programs for, 236, 237
  personal plan for, 235–236, 240–242, 249–250
  prescription drugs for, 236–237
  psychotherapy for, 237
  surgery for, 146, 237
weight management, 228–252
  coping strategies and, 235
  creating plan for, 240–242, 245–250
  diet for, 231–233, 241
  eating habits and, 232, 233, 241
  exercise and, 45, 70, 95, 233–234, 249–250
  frequently asked questions about, 242
  lifestyle and, 230–235
  nutrition and, 231–233, 241
  physical activities and, 233–234, 240
  strategies for successful, 233, 241
  thoughts and emotions and, 234–235
weight training, 30, 71–96, 158
  anabolic steroids and, 95, 96t
  benefits of, 70–71, 72–73
  body composition and, 70, 95, 145
  cool down in, 77
  creating program for, 75–83, 107–108, 163
  diet and, 95, 96t
  duration of exercise in, 76–77, 163
  exercise machines in, 74, 75, 79–80, 81–83, 82t, 89–94, 99–101
  exercises for, 75–76, 81–94, 82t, 83t
  flexibility and, 126
  free weights in, 74, 75, 79, 81, 82, 83, 84–88
  frequency of exercise in, 28, 29t, 77, 95, 163, 168
  frequently asked questions about, 95
  gender and, 70, 71, 95
  injuries in, 81
  intensity of exercise in, 29t, 76, 163
  isokinetic exercise in, **74**
  isometric exercise in, **72**, 73, 75, 88
  isotonic exercise in, **72**, 73–74, 75
  with partner, 95
  physiological effects of, 72–73, 73t
  progress in, 77–78
  repetitions in, 29t, 76–77, 95, 163
  resistance in, 76, 77, 95
  safety in, 78–81
  self-image and, 70
  sets in, 29t, 76–77, 95, 163
  with special health concerns, 167–168
  for sports and activities, 83t, 95
  warm up in, 77
Weight Watchers, 14

wellness, **2**–15
    behavior change for, 8–15, W-1–W-16
    behaviors for, 4–7
    body composition and, 142
    chronic disease prevention and, 3–4
    dimensions of, 2–3, 363, 373–374
    diversity and, 7
    exercise and, 4–6, 21, 47, 111
    flexibility and, 111
    genetics and, 7
wellness (*continued*)
    lifestyle management and, 8–15, 370–371, W-1–W-16
    national goals for, 7–8
    personal profile of, 373–374
    signs of, 15
    See also specific dimensions of wellness
withdrawal, **315**

alcohol, 322
    drug, **315**–316
    nicotine, 322–323
women
    alcohol and, 318, 322
    body composition of, 138, 152
    breast cancer in, 293, 294–296, 302–303, 304, 309
    breast self-examination by, 294, 295, 305t
    cardiorespiratory endurance in, 51
    cardiovascular disease and, 278, 285
    eating disorders in, 238–240
    HIV infection among, 341
    lung cancer in, 292–293
    menopause, 196
    menstruation, 57, 199, 239
    muscular strength and, 71
    nutritional guidelines for, 198–199, 200–201t, 208

    obesity in, 228t
    osteoporosis in, 71, 194, 195, 196
    "perfect" body image and, 237–238
    reproductive tract cancers in, 293, 296–297
    screening tests for, 367
    sexual anatomy of, 345
    smoking by, 274, 323t, 324, 326
    weight training by, 70, 71, 95
    See also gender differences; pregnancy
Women's Sports Foundation, 236
World Health Organization (WHO), on AIDS, 338

yoga, 265
yo-yo dieting. *See* weight cycling

zinc, 194, 195t, 199t
Zyban, 328